To Wake the Nations

To Wake the Nations
Race in the Making of American Literature

Eric J. Sundquist

The Belknap Press of
Harvard University Press
Cambridge, Massachusetts
London, England
1993

Page 694 constitutes an extension of the copyright page.

This book is printed on acid-free paper, and its binding materials
have been chosen for strength and durability.

Library of Congress Cataloging-in-Publication Data

Sundquist, Eric J.
To wake the nations : race in the making of American literature / Eric J. Sundquist.
p.   cm.
Includes bibliographical references and index.
ISBN 0-674-89330-1
1. American literature—Afro-American authors—History and criticism.
2. Afro-Americans—Intellectual life.   3. Afro-Americans in literature.
4. Race relations in literature.   5. Segregation in literature.   I. Title.
PS153.N5S9   1993
810.9′896073—dc20   92-34164
CIP

For Tania

Contents

Part II. The Color Line

Part III. W. E. B. Du Bois:
African America and the Kingdom of Culture

Our song, our toil, our cheer, and warning have been given to this nation in blood-brotherhood. Are not these gifts worth the giving? Is not this work and striving? Would America have been America without her Negro people?

W. E. B. Du Bois, *The Souls of Black Folk*

Introduction

My title is borrowed from the African American spiritual "My Lord, What a Mourning," which includes this first verse and chorus:

> You'll hear the trumpet sound,
> To wake the nations underground,
> Lookin' to my God's right hand,
> When the stars begin to fall.
> My Lord, what a mournin',
> My Lord, what a mournin',
> My Lord, what a mournin',
> When the stars begin to fall.

Readers familiar with the spiritual will know that the song's title is variously printed as "mourning" and "morning," an ambiguity that is not insignificant insofar as the message of many spirituals—like the promise of delivery through Christ's death and resurrection alluded to here—is double, if not paradoxical. When W. E. B. Du Bois identified this spiritual as the source of his musical epigraph to the chapter "Of the Dawn of Freedom" in *The Souls of Black Folk,* he chose the spelling "mourning," perhaps to emphasize its resonance as one of the "sorrow songs," as he termed the spirituals, or perhaps simply because he followed *The Story of the Jubilee Singers,* from whose collection of spirituals he took many of his examples. (The music he reprinted, however, came from the other contemporary collection he consulted, *Hampton and Its Students,* which opts for "morning.") Whatever Du Bois's intention, the elision of meanings is purposeful. The promised advance of African American rights following the Civil War, as the chapter describes it, has turned out to be a false dawn. In the post-Reconstruction years the "morning" song of joy and resurrection has been converted again into a song of "mourning" and despair, as a new slavery of racism and economic oppression once more subverts true freedom for black Americans. As the phrase must initially be construed in the spiritual, the "nations underground" are the dead, raised up at Judgment Day. But in the referential context constructed over the course of *The Souls of Black Folk*, the "nations" to be awakened by the trumpet's call are at once the spirits (the souls) of the ancestors, on American soil and in the homeland of Africa; the many nations of Africa historically represented in the diaspora; and those present generations who still lead an underground existence, subjugated by the neo-slavery of segregation but nevertheless drawing sustaining spiritual power from the heritage of slave culture.

The sounding trumpet, the falling stars, the further significance of "morning" and "mourning," and the spiritual's role in Du Bois's critique of postbellum race relations are taken up in more detail in my analysis of Du Bois's masterwork in chapter 5. I have appropriated the phrase "to wake the nations" as a title for this book because of its rich constellation of meanings within the African American tradition represented by Du Bois and because it suggests something of the complex dialectic between "white" and "black" cultures that has given rise to some of our most important national literature. To begin with, the phrase is an implicit call to consciousness and action. As in many of the spirituals employed by Du Bois, "My Lord, What a Mourning" has militant overtones that are evocative of his own sometimes strident rhetoric and polemical use of literature, and it therefore offers a succinct instance of his constant fusion of aesthetics and politics into one voice of cultural advocacy. At the same time that it prophesies striving in the secular world to come, however, the spiritual also looks backward, announcing the (re)awakening of present generations of black Americans to their own hidden history in slavery and beyond—a history frequently denigrated by whites and sometimes unacknowledged or scorned by nineteenth-century African Americans as well. To wake the nations—both the nation of black Americans and the nation of the United States—to the survival and prospering of African culture and slave culture alike in the modern world was among Du Bois's foremost goals in *The Souls of Black Folk*. Like "folk," "souls," and "race," and indeed like the concept of nationalism itself, "nation" is a term with multiple connotations in Du Bois's work. It takes different shapes and absorbs his own easy crossing of both geographic borders and chronological divisions in characterizing the cultural heritage of Africans in America and the disapora. Especially in the aftermath of emancipation the civic and cultural identity of African Americans was particularly complex, and the debate over slavery's legacy was frequently productive of volatile disagreements. Du Bois's variegated usage lends the idea of nation a flexibility that is reflected in much of the best writing, folklore, popular performance, and music of African Americans from slave culture through the high noon of segregation. What is more, the plural, "nations," encompasses the double cultural worlds of "American" and "Negro" which Du Bois made the foundation of his famous theory of double consciousness. Du Bois's theory, I will argue, is more complicated than any simple division between racial or national groups can indicate; but such an application of it provides a suitable starting point for a study that seeks to reconstruct the history of American literary culture in its formative period, spanning the decades before the Civil War until the early twentieth century.

Some thirty years ago, in the course of a corrective review of Leroi Jones's (Amiri Baraka's) *Blues People,* Ralph Ellison observed that "any viable theory of Negro American culture obligates us to fashion a more adequate theory of American culture as a whole." If we "attempt to discuss jazz as a hermetic expression of Negro sensibility," he remarked, "immediately we must consider what the 'mainstream' of American music really is." Much the same might be said of the history of American literary culture—hardly less so today than when Ellison wrote in the midst of the civil rights movement. Although he admonished those who would interpret black American culture as a racially or ethnocentrically closed field, the contrary danger that the "mainstream" might be forever defined with no reference at all to black culture (or other minority cultures) was, of course, far greater. And the burden of Ellison's argument in this essay, as elsewhere, was to suggest that the mainstream of American culture, whether the fact was widely recognized or not, had always been significantly black and southern, bearing the clear inflections of African American language and creativity in popular as well as high culture. More recently, in an essay that cannily (and justly) puts her own work in a multiracial American mainstream alongside that of Herman Melville, Toni Morrison likewise directs readers and critics to become aware of the informing African American presence in traditional American literature.[1] Much has changed in the last generation, to be sure—witness Morrison's own wide recognition—but her essay reminds us as well that much has not.

The case of African American music, Ellison's subject in a number of his best essays in cultural criticism, is distinctive in that spirituals, the blues, and jazz have been recognized throughout much of the twentieth century as central to the mainstream of American music, even to constitute the nation's true "classical" tradition. Still, the argument (which has its detractors yet) had to be made, and it was part of Du Bois's avowed purpose in *The Souls of Black Folk,* for example, to demonstrate that the black spirituals *were* integral to American culture, as much as slavery and the explosive issue of race itself. The case for African American music did not become self-evident for several more generations. But think, then, of the case for African American literature: perhaps no other book of such stature, such beautiful accomplishment and influence, is so little appreciated even today by a general scholarly audience, let alone a literate public, as *The Souls of Black Folk.* Among other peculiarities of this heterogeneous, brilliant work is the fact that some of the very elements that give the book its unique force—Du Bois's featuring of the music and the message of the spirituals; his relative foregrounding of the question of African retentions in slave culture and the effusive poetry of his plea for African American rights in the new century; his penchant for mystical tropes and messianic self-conception—have also rendered it opaque or bewildering to many readers. Despite the book's exceptional interpretive demands, however, nothing can cloud Du Bois's cogent arguments that white American culture simply cannot be imagined apart from black American culture. An American of both African and European ancestry, Du Bois wrote toward the close of the volume:

> Your country? How came it yours? Before the Pilgrims landed we were here. Here we have brought our three gifts and mingled them with yours: a gift of story and song—soft, stirring melody in an ill-harmonized and unmelodious land; the gift of sweat and brawn to beat back the wilderness, conquer the soil, and lay the foundations of this vast economic empire two hundred years earlier than your weak hands could have done it; the third, a gift of the Spirit. Around us the history of the land has centered for three hundred years; out of the nation's heart we have called all that was best to throttle and subdue all that was worst; fire and blood, prayer and sacrifice, have billowed over this people, and they have found peace only in the altars of the God of Right. Nor has our gift of the Spirit been merely passive. Actively we have woven ourselves with the very warp and woof of this nation,—we have fought their battles, shared their sor-

row, mingled our blood with theirs, and generation after generation have pleaded with a headstrong, careless people to despise not Justice, Mercy, and Truth, lest the nation be smitten with a curse. Our song, our toil, our cheer, and warning have been given to this nation in blood-brotherhood. Are not these gifts worth the giving? Is not this work and striving? Would America have been America without her Negro people?[2]

Du Bois's sometimes ornate diction should not obscure the continuing power of his claim, which exemplified the multiculturalism of the United States, its several nations within one, long before such a notion became orthodox—if it is now orthodox. I have dwelt briefly on *The Souls of Black Folk* in part because of its commanding presence in turn-of-the-century intellectual and literary history. But I have also singled out the book because it provides a kind of case study for interpretations that must account for the effect, and finally the value, of contending cultural languages and figurative systems—in this case the vernacular "language" of the black spirituals and the host of implied questions about cultural origins, historical memory, and racial assimilation that go together to make up African America's contested relation to the prevailing intellectual traditions and literary canon of European American culture. As Du Bois understood, a reconstruction of the "work and striving" of American culture was a matter not merely of adding a few new novels and poems to the traditional list of cultural documents but rather of recognizing the degree to which American culture, properly read, was already saturated with the black gifts of story, song, and spirit. It was a matter, that is to say, of responding to linguistic structures and modes of expression that had long been woven into the fundamental fabric of American culture but that few had the ears to hear.

At one time I had thought to derive a title for this book from a brief but compelling essay by Franz Boas, "On Alternating Sounds," which first appeared in the *American Anthropologist* in 1889, about the time Charles Chesnutt began publishing short fiction about the American color line and the tragic perplexities of cultural miscommunication. My reason is still relevant. Although from a theoretical point of view (for both anthropologists and literary critics) Boas's argument is today more or less a commonplace, his formulation is worth reiterating for the particular bearing that it has on several of the chapters in this book and for the general significance it holds for the practice of cultural criticism. Setting forth the fundamental premises on which his major findings about cultural perception and epistemology were to be based in coming years, Boas's essay in relativism challenged the prevailing opinion that languages are evolutionary (hence hierarchical or progressive) and the scientific theory that held so-called alternating sounds—apparently inexplicable or random variations—in an observed subject's dialect or phonetic schema to be the sign of primitive development. After a careful review of his own methodology, Boas concluded that there were no such phenomena as alternating sounds. What the anthropologist interpreted as variations in articulation were, in fact, examples of his own "sound-blindness," his inability to perceive the subtleties and actual semantics of the speech, the cultural sounds, he was hearing. For this reason it was likely that anthropologists of different nationalities, or the very same anthropologist over a period of time, would produce transcriptions of the same sounds that were at great variance with one another (for example, rendering the same Eskimo word by notably distinct phonetic spellings). Because the hearer perceives "unknown sounds by the means of the sounds of his own language," imposing his own culturally conditioned patterns upon ones unfamiliar to him, Boas concluded, "alternating sounds are in reality alternating apperceptions of one and the same sound."[3]

In the chapters that follow one could take Boas's argument as a general paradigm for the relationship of two conflicting yet coalescing cultural traditions—"American" and "African," to use for the moment an inadequate shorthand—that together have produced a sustained tradition of the most significant literature of race in America. The applicability of Boas's essay is obvious. Just as anthropologists are likely to misperceive the "sounds" of another culture they attempt to record or analyze, so readers and literary critics (or historians, sociologists, jurists, and so on) are likely to misperceive and misunderstand the signs generated by another cultural tradition when they force unfamiliar signs into familiar and hence potentially inappropriate paradigms drawn from their own experience; or when they ignore features that seem inconsequential, perhaps even antagonistic or nonsensical, to them. In some cases the misperceptions generated by the confrontation of cultural traditions (or disparate social conditions) are very much the subject of an author's work. For example, in Chesnutt's adaptation of African American folklore in his short fiction or in Du Bois's incorporation of the black spirituals into *The Souls of Black Folk*, the phenomenon of alternating sounds, in a nearly literal way, forms part of the text's own cultural strategy. In these two instances the extraordinary importance of sound, of the aural dimension, to black vernacular language is made especially pointed by the roles that dialect and vocal music, respectively, play in grounding African American culture for Chesnutt and Du Bois.

More broadly, the concept of alternating sounds provides an apt way to characterize the shortcomings in our understanding of what constitutes American literature. No matter the breadth or diversity of new formulations of the canonical tradition: as the arguments by Ellison, Morrison, and Du Bois to which I have already referred make evident, it remains difficult for many readers to overcome their fundamental conception of "American" literature as solely Anglo-European in inspiration and authorship, to which may then be added an appropriate number of valuable "ethnic" or "minority" texts, those that closely correspond to familiar critical and semantic paradigms. Instead, a redefinition of the premises and inherent significance of the central literary documents of American culture is in order. My intention is certainly not to depose canonical figures but to see their less often celebrated works—Herman Melville's *Benito Cereno,* Frederick Douglass's *My Bondage and My Freedom,* and Mark Twain's *Pudd'nhead Wilson*—from the new point of view provided by the introduction of comparatively ancillary but nonetheless important works such as Nat Turner's "Confessions" and Martin Delany's *Blake; or the Huts of America,* and the more extended serious treatment of major authors such as Chesnutt and Du Bois, who are the equals of most any writers in the history of American literature.

Although the weight of *To Wake the Nations* falls on African American texts, my argument moves back and forth—alternates, so to speak—between black and white texts in order to suggest that neither perspective is by itself adequate to account for the ongoing crisis over race in American cultural and political life, just as neither black nor white authorship guarantees any sort of univocal vision or moral advantage. Certain themes and tropes recur throughout the book, but there is not a single running argument. Rather, I have been interested in a group of issues—revolutionary ideology, folklore and vernacular culture, the debate over African retentions (and what is now sometimes called Afrocentrism), the role of music in black culture, the superimposition of antebellum and post-Reconstruction historical time frames, prophetic leadership, and others—that seem to accompany one another harmonically through the defining period of American race literature. The book is a study of traditions but not necessarily of literal origins, of epochal movements but not of linear progression. Thus, very different phenomena such as African cultural retentions and racist minstrelsy occupy more or less equal analytic positions in this book; and although I concentrate on a limited number of authors and texts, the larger historical moments I isolate are assumed to be interwoven with the cross-currents of two traditions that are always dynamically defining each other. I would be willing to take an observation by Zora Neale Hurston as an epigrammatic gloss on my general method: "What we really mean by originality is the modification of ideas. . . . While [the African American] lives and moves in the midst of a white civilization, everything that he touches is reinterpreted for his own use. . . . Thus has arisen a new art in the civilised world, and thus has our so-called civilisation come. The exchange and re-exchange of ideas between groups."[4]

The studies in this book are not exhaustive of the authors and texts in question, let alone the sweep of American literature over a hundred-year period, though given the number of pages devoted to a relative handful of authors, the consequences of any extension of such a method would be forbidding. Moreover, because my definition of race is deliberately limited to the relationship between black and white cultures, I cannot claim that my study tells anything like the whole story or that it necessarily provides a model for the study of other questions of race and ethnicity in American culture. Leaving aside the very different set of questions raised by American Indian literature and oral tradition, however, the presence of black literature and culture in America, throughout the nineteenth and on into the early twentieth centuries, is far more pronounced than that of other ethnic minorities. If this book is neither a complete history nor an inclusive multicultural account of American literature in its first major phase, I do mean each section and the chapters comprised therein to represent the major issues that have framed the problem of race as it may be seen from the perspective of African American slavery and its aftermath, notably in the post-Reconstruction decades.

To speak of the "problem of race" is, of course, to speak too narrowly. Such a formulation more often than not betrays a white perspective and therefore a white problem, as in the standard turn-of-the-century formulation "the Negro problem." But to speak only of the obverse, of racism per se, is equally limiting. Despite the obvious fact that racism, the cruelties of bondage, economic deprivation, and the humiliations of segregation belong directly to the experiences that have been hammered into life stories, fiction, and poetry by the authors studied here, I do not consider this a book about racism in literature. A valuable term that has proliferated to the point of being meaningless in some contemporary critical thought and one that seems frequently to lock readers into rigid, unimaginative structures of analysis, racism is secondary to my concern to trace the expressive heritage of a biracial culture. Degree is all, and the constant appeal to categorical or institutional modes of racism is less likely to make an argument wrong than to render it mundane. In the case of both white and black authors, the key is to understand the authorial context, the historical moment and reigning cultural pressures, even the deliberate strategies employed for producing signs of both racial consciousness and racial antagonism. In a cultural tradition often formed under the pressures of hatred and violence, I have nevertheless been more interested in the processes of preservation and nation building, in the several senses that idea implies. Although both strands make up the marrow of American tradition, the accumulated suffering and rank prejudice in the nation's history and cultural work is here overshadowed by the equal accumulation of power devoted, as Du Bois might have said, to cultural "striving," to the work of discovering and creating the nation's—or the *nations'*—cultural memory. Like "race" itself, the dilemma of racism is one whose parameters are difficult to pin down, and I would rather maximize the ground of study shared by blacks and whites without pretending that both cultures perceive the "problem of race," defined either as race or as racism, in the same way more than a fraction of the time.

Under the rubric of race in American literature and culture seen from a dialectical African American and European American perspective, this remains quite a selective study, and one whose balance may seem strange when the lengths of various chapters are compared. The logic of my choices is not unassailable. But let me sketch briefly a rationale for the organization and emphases of the three parts of this book: slavery and revolution, the color line, and W. E. B. Du Bois.

I take the question of revolution—and hence the right of slaves to claim the same moral authority for their own freedom that had served as the foundation of the United States itself, what was sometimes labeled the "right of revolution"—to encompass and to highlight all important issues in the debate over slavery; and I take it to offer a profoundly new way to appreciate the illuminating power of two texts, Nat Turner's "Confessions" and Martin Delany's *Blake,* which have seldom even been considered (though for different reasons) to belong to the canon of American literature. It would be presumptuous to characterize the chapter as an argument for a complete revisionary understanding of the American Renaissance, the great flowering of mid-nineteenth-century literature which has rightly been considered without parallel in the nation's cultural history. To include new names in the canon of the renaissance—Frederick Douglass, Harriet Beecher Stowe, and Harriet Jacobs have seemed obvious to the majority of recent readers—would be one means of making it more democratically inclusive and reflective of the era's critical events and ideas. My aim, however, is to focus attention on the very premise of democracy as it was articulated and challenged in the crisis over slavery, and therefore to modify the underlying notion of a "renaissance" to include the most daring rebirth of all—the rebirth of African American resistance to slavery, and the rebirth of unbiased principles of liberty that had been wrenchingly betrayed in the flawed revolution of the founders. From this particularized perspective Nat Turner, Frederick Douglass, Herman Melville, and Martin Delany are the leading authors of the American Renaissance. (Such figures as Stowe, Jacobs, and Abraham Lincoln might also be included—and I do devote some attention to them—but the political and aesthetic issue of slave revolution is less central in their works than in the other cases.) Ignoring for the moment the unorthodox formal properties of Turner's "Confessions," one can designate it a remarkable combination of autobiography, religious reflection, and political oratory—and therefore a key document in a proper reconceptualization of the renaissance. Indeed, given its formative role in the course of African American cultural history and both anti- and proslavery argument, it is hard to imagine why Turner's "Confessions" should not be accorded the same attention granted, say, Emerson's "Self-Reliance" or Thoreau's "Civil Disobedience."

To put this point differently, and in a manner that bears on the whole of *To Wake the Nations:* this is an American Renaissance seen largely from an African American perspective, even including what could be styled the idiosyncratic "black" point of view of Melville as it appears in *Benito Cereno,* a matter to which I will return. And yet my argument is not that either Part I or this book as a whole is primarily an interpretation of African American literature, even though this is technically true. Rather, it treats American literature defined to include—even to feature—the literary struggle to redeem the national promise of equality and freedom. In the case of Frederick Douglass's lengthened and revised second autobiography, *My Bondage and My Freedom,* his embrace of the democratic ideology of the American Revolution, which some readers have dismissed as an unseemly capitulation to "white" ideology, is integral to Du Bois's self-dramatizing revision both of his text and of his very identity as an African American wrapped in a tormenting struggle with the paradox of slavery in America. Yet, as Douglass's fine short story "The Heroic Slave" demonstrated, the boundaries of America and of United States slavery were open to question. A novel such as Delany's *Blake* therefore acquires new importance less for its stylistic innovation, which is negligible, than for its startling panorama of African Americans in slavery, both in the American South and in the Caribbean, and its consequent capacity to reflect upon the entire history of enslavement, middle passage, plantation life, and the growth of an ethos of slave resistance. Delany's conceptualization of resistance to slavery as pervasive, operating across the spectrum of black politics, religion, and cultural expression, is unique in antebellum literary history and nearly so in antislavery argument and subsequent historiography. *Blake* is thus a perfect companion to *Benito Cereno,* for Delany alters our understanding of Melville's achievement (as well as the limitations of Melville's vision) even as he too extends the boundaries of America, underlining its New World foundations and the long-standing contention over the role of slavery in nationalist expansion.

"Slavery, Revolution, Renaissance" is therefore a set of terms that are not quite in apposition but are interlocked by their necessary pressure upon one another. To the extent that this is a study of the origins of postcolonial American literature, the opening chapters assume that slavery—especially as it is understood as the governing aspect of a revolutionary ideology articulated by both whites *and* blacks, often, but not always, in radically different ways—is the overarching American issue, and that it remains so, as memory and as unresolved social crisis, into the modern period. The antebellum literature of slavery constitutes a rebirth with echoes and refractions in the age of Jim Crow and beyond—in the late twentieth-century renaissance of African American literature, for example, much of which casts back to the history of slave culture for inspiration. The preeminent works that join revolution to the culture of slavery arise from creative energies that are at once painful and hopeful, frightening and vibrant with promise, more so perhaps than some of the heretofore celebrated works of the American Renaissance.

Part II, "The Color Line," rests on the assumption that the problem of segregation—the theory, the fact, and the living reality of segregation— was the defining legal and social experience of the late nineteenth century for many Americans, not least for what it implied in retrospect about the meaning of the Civil War and what it may be said to have implied in prospect about the history of race relations for the next century in the United States. Therefore, Twain's *Pudd'nhead Wilson,* the novel of segregation par excellence, and the fiction of Charles Chesnutt, our most incisive and inventive analyst of the many ways in which the color line could be drawn in American society, are central to my evaluation of literature in the post-Reconstruction years. In the case of Twain, my claim is not that *Pudd'nhead Wilson* is a greater novel than *Adventures of Huckleberry Finn,* which I treat only briefly, but rather that it takes the famous crisis of conscience over race that Twain resolved at best provisionally in Huck Finn's narrative to a new and tormenting level of awareness that is analogous to the escalating destruction of African American civil and political rights with the rise of Jim Crow. Continuing to dwell in the carnivalesque world of racial parody and epistemological nightmare that marks the concluding chapters of *Adventures of Huckleberry Finn* (which some critics have wrongly considered the novel's downfall), Twain unleashed in a kind of offhand, nearly unconscious frenzy a masterpiece of self-examination and cultural reflection. What else might one expect, or ask for, at a moment when the Supreme Court's landmark ruling in favor of segregation, *Plessy* v. *Ferguson,* turned on the case of a plaintiff who was legally black but visibly white? Pervaded by paralyzing bifurcations and doublings, *Pudd'nhead Wilson* and "Those Extraordinary Twins" reach out to encompass not just the extensive late nineteenth-century literature of miscegenation but more tellingly the range of theoretical and legal arguments about racial identity and segregation, which were themselves as rife with paradox as Twain's novel and its Siamese twin of a short story.

If I devote nearly a third of this book to Chesnutt alone, it is because his career was one of extraordinary richness and (more to the point) because he, unlike Twain, has scarcely been read with anything approaching the seriousness he deserves. In fact, I would argue that Chesnutt is among the major American fiction writers of the nineteenth century. If it is objected that, after all, he wrote "only" about race, one would have to bear in mind that, as James Weldon Johnson would later contend in his provocative essay "The Dilemma of the Negro Author," it was nearly impossible for the minority writer to do otherwise. One would have to note also that canonical authors have not always been known for their social and thematic range; and that, again, race might arguably be considered the defining issue of an era that saw the escalation of virulent segregation and race violence, the decimation of American Indian tribes, and widespread conflict over non–Anglo-Saxon immigration and its challenge to the prevailing racial identity of America.

What is more, Chesnutt wrote successfully in a number of forms, including occasional essays, short stories, and novels. *The Marrow of Tradition* is probably the most astute political-historical novel of its day, both for its recapitulation of the 1898 "race riot"—more accurately the white political coup—in Wilmington, North Carolina, and for its cunning extrapolation from the causal issues of the riot to a complex meditation on post-Reconstruction reunion politics, genealogy and the New South, Jim Crow cultural forms, intraracial "racism," and the rise of a black middle class. Chesnutt's short stories, for their part, offer an unparalleled bridge between the art of black folk vernacular and published literature, and in their diversity, historical scope, and incisive commentary on a wide array of racial topics, they are one of the most impressive achievements in all of nineteenth-century American fiction. The complex aesthetic and professional negotiation between "folklore" and "literature" is one of their persistent topics, just as they frequently derive some of their greatest power from a conscious interplay with, and critique of, African American stage minstrelsy and the popularized black storytelling of Joel Chandler Harris's Uncle Remus stories. Like Du Bois, Chesnutt worked within the confines of literate high culture but did so by locating the premises of modern black literature in the historical memory and vernacular practice of slave culture and its implied African resources. Conversely, I argue, Harris must also be seen both to have made a significant, if frequently flawed and vexing, contribution to the African American presence in literature in his own right and, in particular instances, to have provided the ground on which Chesnutt constructed his own vernacular account of the aftermath of African American slavery.

Chapter 4, "Charles Chesnutt's Cakewalk," includes a good deal of commentary on popular and folk culture in the age of Jim Crow. This long chapter examines the ethnological debate over African American folktales and songs; the transition from blackface minstrelsy to the black musical stage, and thus those symbolic links between slave culture (and its African retentions) and modern black culture represented, for example, in the phenomenon of the cakewalk; and the centrality of a vernacular aesthetic, governed by considerations of orality, tonality, and dialect, to any comprehensive definition of African American literature. Such discussions could, of course, be pursued in relation to other authors besides Chesnutt, but my aim has been to accord his work the attention it deserves while at the same time laying out a theoretical and historical account of the process by which elements of antebellum folk consciousness have been transfigured into the public forms of American literature, at once preserving the world of black culture while challenging the ascendancy of white. In this respect my book joins a number of recent scholarly studies that have built on an earlier generation of work in black language, folklore, and song, and have begun to investigate the formative dynamic relationship betweeen vernacular culture and the evolution of modern black literature and culture in the decades surrounding the turn of the century.[5] Because these issues are so fully engaged by Chesnutt throughout his work, and because they constitute a field of literary study that has barely been opened to view, I have risked analyzing them at some length—virtually writing a book within a book—in order to redefine, once more largely from the point of view of African American culture, both the potential reach of literary criticism and the groundwork of responses to the history of segregation.

Last, the same might be said of my interpretations of Du Bois, whose career was so extensive (he wrote virtually until his death in 1963) and whose importance was so marked in many different arenas of political, educational, and cultural life that the negligible attention he has received in intellectual history and literary study alike is all the more astounding. (In the preface to a reissue of his book on Du Bois, Arnold Rampersad rightly laments the "void of commentary on Du Bois," the "stillness that has surrounded his name in the scholarly world.")[6] My two chapters devoted to Du Bois are an attempt in part to redress this surprising lack of attention. But as in the case of Chesnutt they are also, I suggest, an attempt to redefine the basic questions we ask about American literature and the strategies we employ to teach and write about that literature. Approaching Du Bois's central literary works from two distinct but related angles—*The Souls of Black Folk* in its relation to the black spirituals and the foundations of African American culture, and *Darkwater* as a prism through which to read his developing views of Africa as a force in world and American culture—I attempt to evaluate the meaning, as the subtitle of Part III suggests, and as this introduction has already argued, of writing about *African America* as integral to American literary culture. Thus, like Chesnutt, Du Bois gets the space he does not so much because he is more important than, say, Melville or Twain, but because he is *as* important, a fact that is still very far from received wisdom. The problem lies in part in our inability to account for works whose generic boundaries are so unusual, in part in our simple blindness to cultural work rooted in the originating resources of African American life. Although I do not think of my chapters on Du Bois, especially chapter 6, as a brief for Afrocentrism, there is little question that Du Bois, skeptical though he was of most nationalist arguments or essentialist notions of race, exploited a special vein of romantic racialism and wrote with a stronger interest in diaspora cultural paradigms than many readers have been ready to admit. His theory of double consciousness, I argue, referred less to American and Afro-American than to American and African—or Negro, to use his own historically limiting but suitably amorphous term—a distinction of appreciable power.

Du Bois's importance lies both in the influence of *The Souls of Black Folk*—the founding text of modern African American thought, as numerous black writers and intellectuals have testified—and in the fact that he made the twentieth-century "problem of the color line," to cite his other famous aphorism, the point of departure for a diaspora aesthetic whose ramifications would be realized only over the course of the century in the growth of postcolonial and minority literatures. For this reason, and also because his various early Pan-African writings are best understood as fragments that make up a whole, I have found it profitable to include peripheral examinations of Ethiopianism, other nationalist movements and leaders, and African anticolonialism. Like better-known literary expatriates of the First World War generation, Du Bois was transnational in his intellectual scope, and he must be so studied. Encompassing the broadest definitions of race and nation, he sought to "wake the nations." My reading of Du Bois stops before the depression, with a brief look at *Dark Princess,* a political novel of 1928, and thus before his turn toward a more trenchant Marxism; yet his long writing life easily obscures the fact that *Darkwater* was published in 1920, when he was already fifty-one years old, and constitutes the premature culmination, as it were, of an already varied and distinguished intellectual career as teacher, editor, race leader, and writer.

To contextualize Du Bois's central works, then, I venture a considerable amount of analysis on the role of the spirituals in nineteenth-century American culture and on the rise of Pan-Africanism. As in the case of Chesnutt, I do so in order to provide a cultural context that is not yet widely familiar but also to reorganize the methodology of literary study. A good deal of Du Bois's creative writing, strictly defined, is more powerful in conception than in execution, and *Darkwater* and especially *Dark Princess* have their decidedly weak moments. But added to *The Souls of*

Black Folk, one of the few indispensable works of American culture, they provide a remarkably commanding definition of African American culture in its transition from the era of slavery to the era of Jim Crow and modernism. Du Bois thus stands at the end of a historical trajectory beginning with Nat Turner and Frederick Douglass, among others. On the one hand, *The Souls of Black Folk* recapitulates the genre of black autobiography (and slave narrative) raised to such a height first in Douglass's *My Bondage and My Freedom,* and it saves the memory of slave culture from the kind of oblivion to which Douglass's "Americanism" (even more pronounced in the *Life and Times of Frederick Douglass,* the third version of his life story) or the calculated accommodationism of Booker T. Washington might have appeared to consign it. On the other hand, Du Bois's own Pan-African messianism, summed up with passionate compression in *Darkwater,* is a fitting counterpoint to the messianic vision of freedom articulated in Turner's "Confessions." Symbolically, and perhaps consciously, Du Bois's anticolonialism rewrites Turner's millenarian vision in twentieth-century terms and puts it directly in the service of a new racial aesthetic. Few American writers, certainly none whose writing was such a small portion of their activities, saw as clearly as Du Bois the ideological structures that both supported and became codified within dominant modes of national literature from the middle passage (a major history of the slave trade was his first book) through bondage, freedom, and the simultaneous advent of Jim Crow and the New Negro.

Needless to say, even this brief summary of my book indicates that any proposal to "wake the nations" also embraces contemporary debates over canonicity, whether or not one takes account of the antagonistic voices that often seem to speak past one another, announcing either the demise of Western intellectual and aesthetic traditions or, on the contrary, the imperialist destruction of minority cultures by white hegemony. Such stark claims threaten to become alternating sounds of the worst, and most misrepresentative, kind. Du Bois was not right about everything, of course; but one must admire his righteous, realistic sense of shared endeavor and his understanding of the necessary dialectic between separatism and pluralism that makes for effective cultural advocacy. Other ethnic or racial groups could, of course, be included in his democratic claim that the African American had every right to be recognized as a "co-worker in the kingdom of culture."[7] Perhaps we are finally approaching a point of departure for the embracing dialogue Du Bois envisioned a century ago. Even though I do not directly take up current debates over the literary canon, this book is a contribution, I hope, to understanding such debates as well as the grounds on which they should be judged. More precisely, I would assert again that it is a statement that the canon of American literature in the period I cover, seen from one important angle, might look quite different. Given the long failure of American legislation, jurisprudence, social theory, and artistic endeavor truly to erase color from our consciousness of opportunity and right, it is hard not to hold that race remains very much at the center of the American experience. Many other texts and authors could be adduced in such an argument, but I take those that I discuss to be central and my interpretations to be representative.

Insofar as it is an exposition of the criteria, categories, and languages according to which distinctions such as that between "American" and "African American" are made to begin with, this is also a study in literary values and their just estimation, for I believe that one should not (and does not) have to make a special plea for Chesnutt and Du Bois, for instance, in order to place them at the center of American literature and cultural thought. (Frederick Douglass, because he was wise enough to write a conveniently short volume that could be entered onto a syllabus without greatly disrupting the recognized tradition, has been canonical for some time now, though his *Narrative* is a lesser work than *My Bondage and My Freedom,* according to my arguments.) Nevertheless, one does have to shift paradigms, see with new eyes, hear with new ears. Value, after all, is not solely an aesthetic criterion. To put it another way, value cannot be severed from justice and, therefore, from politics, no matter what anxiety now exists in certain quarters about the "politicization" of literary study. This is not to say that literature and politics are the same thing. All modes of discourse, no matter how they interpenetrate, borrow from, and influence one another, operate under differing restrictions and enjoy differing privileges in their exercise of authority, and I have tried to be alert to such distinctions throughout my readings and analysis. By the same token, it is not my main concern either to foster or to allay anyone's anxiety about the politics of literary criticism. The studies herein will have to speak for themselves: either they are convincing in their demonstration that ideology embraces both aesthetics and political or legal currents or they are not. I would add only that the role of value, or justice, which I see to operate in the literary domain corresponds to a large degree to a definition of justice advanced by Patricia Williams in an essay on social policy: "Justice is a continual balancing of competing visions, plural viewpoints, shifting histories, interests, and allegiances. To acknowlege that level of complexity is to require, to seek, and to value a multiplicity of knowledge systems, in pursuit of a more complete sense of the world in which we all live."[8] Multiplicity need not imply randomness or the splintering of a society or a culture into so many discrete and uncommunicating pieces defined along essentialist lines of race (or gender, class, sexuality, and so on). Nevertheless, multiplicity does imply some level of contention and dissonance. It also implies the necessity of living with the paradox that "American" literature is both a single tradition of many parts *and* a series of winding, sometimes parallel traditions that have perforce been built in good part from their inherent conflicts. Williams's statement exists as part of an argument in support of affirmative action, which she goes on to denote "an act of verification and vision, an act of social as well as professional responsibility." This could serve equally well as a statement in support of canon and pedagogical reform, and in both cases the heart of the matter is how best to implement a theory of inclusion, where to strike the balance between pluralism and separatism. I do not propose here a blueprint for the reconstruction of literary studies, nor is my scope wide enough to offer in detail a new genealogy of American authorship. I find the avowal of a comprehensive theory to be less important than the pursuit of such verification, a term that admirably sums up the acts of location, identification, evaluation, and endowing with value or truth that any act of criticism should include as its principal goals.

What makes a piece of literature worthy of sustained attention is not simple to imagine, let alone describe. It is not complexity, irony, or ingenuity alone, but those qualities can hardly be missing; nor is it only the commitment to some fine political ideal or social theory. Service to ideology has produced some pathetically dull and trivial literature on both sides of the color line. At the least, however, the value of a work of literature—what defines it as literature, for that matter—derives from its contribution to articulating and sustaining the values of a given culture, whether or not that culture is national or "racial" in scope. Justice and value therefore must be recognized to be aesthetic as well as philosophical terms, to have literary as well as legal application. This does not mean that all "resistance" literature is automatically valuable or that any text with a minority perspective is inherently worth studying. (Nor does it mean, in addition, that overtly racist texts are not worthy of study, if only for the very reason that they are deeply informative of the values of an influential segment of American society at a particular historical moment.

I also leave aside here the more radical inclination, unfortunately common in some criticism today, to seize upon *any* sign of racism as a reason to expunge canonical texts.) In the chapters that follow I have attempted to delineate both the strengths and weaknesses of some works previously defined as marginal (when they were defined at all). Any argument for the value of Delany's *Blake* or Du Bois's *Darkwater,* for example, requires an admission that they depend less on verbal intricacy and narrative sub-tlety than do Chesnutt's stories or Melville's *Benito Cereno.* The power of these works, like that of *Pudd'nhead Wilson,* a "marginal" work by a "major" author, must be measured instead within the new conception of American culture that they are able to bring forth. The challenge of revising the contours of literary tradition need not produce thoughtless leveling or uninformed displacements. But it does require rethinking the definitions whose patterns of "sound-blindness" (to recall Boas's term) have served to continue the segregation of American literature through most of the twentieth century.

A similar argument might apply as well to questions of gender and sexuality, especially when they intersect with race, as they inevitably do in the case of the authors studied here. Neither gender nor sexuality is often foregrounded in this book; and the fact that I do not treat women authors in detail (Harriet Jacobs, Harriet Beecher Stowe, Pauline Hopkins, and Zora Neale Hurston in particular provide significant points of reference throughout) would be a decided shortcoming if my intention had been to write a comprehensive study. At the same time, however, masculinity and its implied relation to the feminine and thus to racial domination and violence are constant themes for these male writers, and all of them— most notably Du Bois, as it happens—wrote with some interest and passion about the position of women, black women in particular, under slavery or in a racist society. The current outpouring of excellent critical study of women writers and feminist interpretations of race leaves it unlikely that other authors or issues will want for analysis or that my own readings will remain unchallenged on this score. In any case, the problems of black "manhood," miscegenation, and racial paternalism, as well as the representation of women's roles, keep sexuality and gender in view throughout the book. As the chapters that follow demonstrate repeatedly, neither slavery nor segregation in America has ever been conceptualized or practiced apart from sexual subjugation, and my contention is that the intersection of gender and race can also be pursued quite fruitfully in

Chesnutt's or Twain's writings on genealogy and racial mixture, for example, or in Du Bois's rather visionary writings on the gender exploitation of colonial systems generally, whether in Africa or America.

Within the past several years the study of racial and ethnic diversity in American literature has undergone a remarkable renaissance. Even so, multicultural study of American literature often seems richer in position papers than in practical criticism, a distinction in method that is difficult but worthwhile to make. In the case of African American literature the recent movement in favor of developing the tools of vernacular interpretation, to which I have already alluded, has helped emphatically to confirm the value of primary research and reading. Along with the simultaneous inventiveness and historical awareness that make possible the very recognition of new knowledge, only rigor and scope combined can bring about a meaningful realignment of the standards of verification for literary study in America.

To Wake the Nations is meant to be a contribution to this process. Breaking down the race barrier in American literary history, as I see it, entails referring not solely to a culture of the arts and creative endeavor narrowly defined, but rather to a larger culture of intellectual argument, political and legal theorizing, and the social production of racial archetypes. Any reconstruction of American literature depends not just on acknowledging the importance and place of neglected authors but on reconceptualizing the extent of textuality, the cultural and historical integuments that bind any work irrevocably to a time, a geography, and an array of social and aesthetic practices. Thus, *The Souls of Black Folk* must be seen to include the history of African American spirituals and their accompanying musicology as an unmistakable component of the text that has had little voice in the years since Du Bois first wrote. *Pudd'nhead Wilson* includes the manifold theories of segregation, and the political reunion of North and South, legally codified in *Plessy* v. *Ferguson,* as an inseparable part of Twain's text. Similarly, Delany's *Blake* and Melville's *Benito Cereno,* because they include the explosive international contentions over Caribbean slavery that were of such urgency in the 1850s, help us to see the boundaries of America and of black culture, both past and present, in a different way, despite their having become lost to view among later generations. And in a more encompassing sense, Chesnutt can be studied only as part of the tradition of African American (and African) folk performance, and consequently as part of the turn-of-the-century rush to "preserve" the remnants of slave culture, which in turn entailed an acrimonious debate about African retentions lasting on through the twentieth century.

More unusually, I have placed Nat Turner's "Confessions" in a central position among antebellum texts about race and slavery, not because its nominal authorship by the white attorney Thomas Gray is irrelevant (indeed, it is a signal instance of "alternating sounds" deployed for conscientious purpose), but because mistaken assumptions about the meaning of that authorship have entirely obscured the possibility that Nat Turner's voice—and hence his thought, his vision, and his leadership—remains strongly present in the historic "text" that may be reconstructed from the accounts of his revolt and his published document. Turner, that is to say, can be identified as an author, and his "Confessions" may be read as a strategic extension of his resistance to slavery. But just as important, the interpretable meaning of his text, including its resonant invocation of the "right of revolution" anchored in a messianic tradition of prophecy, is contained in the surrounding apparatus of legal and political suppression, journalistic commentary, and mythic reconstruction that shape the "Confessions" as a coherent cultural text despite its divergence from standard preconceptions of the literary work. In fact, the nearly scriptural quality of the Turner text—its arcane and fragmentary account of the foundations of the revolt, its symbology and mysticism, its pseudo-apostolic framing narrative by Thomas Gray—makes it an appropriate pathway from the world of the colonial jeremiad to that of secular revolution as it is defined by Douglass, Melville, and Delany. With Du Bois's comparably difficult *Darkwater* at the other end, Turner's "Confessions" frames this study by challenging our assumptions about what constitutes the limits of a text, the power of its message and its ability to act in the arena of culture, and ultimately its value as part of a "national" literature.

My argument in the case of Turner specifically is that too narrow an understanding of the literary text, not to mention the conflicting traditions of which it may be a part, blinds us to the possibility that the problematic text, the fragment, the document in another genre (not just the conventionally composed and marketed fiction or narrative) may cast a powerful light on the flaws in our assumptions about literature and our critical methods for disclosing the terrain where text gives way to context. Thus, I would also argue that *To Wake the Nations,* although it does not overtly address contentions over historicist methodology, is also a contribution to that discussion. I might prefer to call it a demonstration of historicist theory rather than an articulation of it. What will be perfectly obvious, however, is that I do not claim that a single unifying thesis or particular theoretical model holds these studies together. Instead, I believe that each author or text—or each group of texts contained within the three broad categories into which the book is divided—produces to some degree its own context and defining languages. Other critical languages could be found, to be sure, but these are central. That is to say, I have tried to identify the key generative issues through which each text is framed as a historical artifact and without which, to be strict, the text does not exist with anything like clarity, and I have felt free to go outside the domains of textual history, biography, and formal analysis to find support for my reading strategies. Persuasive historicist criticism consists in choosing what is indispensable. But it also depends on construing value and justice in a different way. Although the weight in this book turns out to be on African American writers for reasons I have indicated, this is not a study of them alone, nor is it a study, to repeat, of contrasting "black" and "white" approaches to the problem of race. Rather, I would like to keep alive the necessary contradiction that the two traditions can be seen as both one and separate. I entertain the assertion of "separate but (and) equal" European American and African American literary-critical traditions—though one might ask, if it never worked in law, why should it work in literary criticism?—in order to promote the strength and integrity of the latter tradition as well as the former. Still, I would also assert that, finally, they form a single tradition—and that therefore Chesnutt, for instance, is an "American" writer, while Melville is a writer whose contribution to African American culture is worth careful attention.

Not many will quarrel with the first part of that formulation, but the second may seem open to question. I do not mean, obviously, that Melville wrote in the same way as either Delany or Douglass about slavery in the Americas. The three are much in accord, however, and I would contend that Melville, along with Douglass, is probably the foremost analyst of American slavery in the nineteenth century—and not simply from a "white" perspective. That is not necessarily the burden of my Melville chapter, and this is certainly not the place to pursue the argument in detail. To be brief: the fact that Melville does not write *Benito Cereno* from Babo's point of view—indeed, he calculatedly eschews that point of view—does not prohibit him from giving Babo centrality and heroic meaning, or prevent him from displaying a stringent understanding of key elements of African culture in New World slavery. This point is worth making because it defines my sense that, as readers, teachers, or critics, we make a serious

error if we imagine that race alone determines an author's capacity to cross
cultural boundaries with something approaching understanding of the
other race's imaginative matrix or its necessarily different legacy and perspective. This does not mean that one cannot, for instance, detect degrees
of racism in Melville or in Twain or, differently, in Du Bois; far from it.
The last thing I would claim is that such critiques of a writer's work have
no merit or that they cannot be cogently put or productive of vital
knowledge. Criticism and intellectual history cannot afford to ignore the
imputation of racism or the advocacy of critical essentialism, yet neither
should those pressures rule the act of interpretation.

Issues such as those I have outlined here lie at the heart of America's
national literature as much as they lie at the heart of the nation's very
complex and fragile conception of its ideology and mission. For this reason
they are also crucial to the story that the nation tells about itself in public
proclamations and educational policies as they come to be applied in
scholarship and classroom pedagogy. An observation by Arna Bontemps
in his 1965 essay on his lifelong journey back to the South, "Why I
Returned," is therefore worth notice here. Recalling the opposing attitudes
toward African American folklore and folk wisdom taken by his father, a
modern skeptic, and his great-uncle Buddy, a believer, Bontemps put the
issue in the larger context of his own education at an all-white boarding
school near Los Angeles, where he had been raised after his birth in
Louisiana, and later at Pacific Union College:

> In their opposing attitudes toward roots my father and my great-
> uncle made me aware of a conflict in which every educated American
> Negro, and some who are not educated, must somehow take sides.
> By implication at least, one group advocates embracing the riches of
> the folk heritage; their opposites demand a clean break with the past
> and all it represents. Had I not gone home summers and hob-nobbed
> with folk-type Negroes, I would have finished college without know-
> ing that any Negro other than Paul Laurence Dunbar ever wrote a
> poem. I would have come out imagining that the story of the Negro
> could be told in two short paragraphs: a statement about jungle
> people in Africa and an equally brief account of the slavery issue in
> American history. The reserves of human vitality that enabled the
> race to survive the worst of both these experiences while at the same
> time making contributions to western culture remained a dark secret
> with my teachers, if they had considered the matter at all. I was given

no inkling by them, and my white classmates who needed to know such things as much as I did if we were to maintain a healthy regard for each other in the future, were similarly denied.[9]

Bontemps's language is specific to a historical moment, no doubt, and yet there is little one can add to his concise, eloquent statement, which argues both for a multiracial perspective on American life and for serious attention to the creative knowledge preserved and passed down in folk culture. Echoing the words of Du Bois and others before him, he asks that justice and value be held in balance with power in our construction of American literary culture. Nothing seems simpler, and nothing has proven more difficult, than to recognize and understand all the reserves of human vitality.

I

Slavery, Revolution, Renaissance

· 1 ·

Signs of Power: Nat Turner and Frederick Douglass

We stole words from the grudging lips of the Lords of the Land, who did not want us to know too many of them or their meaning. And we charged this meager horde of stolen sounds with all the emotions and longings we had; we proceeded to build our language in inflections of voice, through tonal variety, by hurried speech, in honeyed drawls, by rolling our eyes, by flourishing our hands, by assigning to common, simple words new meanings, meanings which enabled us to speak of revolt in the actual presence of the Lords of the Land without their being aware! Our secret language extended our understanding of what slavery meant and gave us the freedom to speak to our brothers in captivity; we polished our new words, caressed them, gave them new shape and color, a new order and tempo, until, although they were the words of the Lords of the Land, they became *our* words, *our* language.

Richard Wright, *12 Million Black Voices*

One day the South will know that when these disinherited children of God sat down at lunch counters they were in reality standing up for the best in the American dream and the most sacred values of our Judeo-Christian heritage, and thusly, carrying our whole nation back to those great wells of democracy which were dug deep by the Founding Fathers in the formulation of the Constitution and the Declaration of Independence.

Martin Luther King, Jr., "Letter from Birmingham City Jail"

In the climactic scene of Herman Melville's *Benito Cereno*, after the terrified Spanish captain has flung himself threateningly into Captain Delano's

27

boat, followed by the rebel slave Babo, dagger in hand, Melville writes: "All this, with what preceded, and what followed, occurred with such involutions of rapidity, that past, present, and future seemed one." The revelation of Babo's true design, as his disguise of dutiful servant falls away to reveal a "countenance lividly vindictive, expressing the centered purpose of his soul," is mirrored in the countenance of Delano himself, who, as if "scales dropped from his eyes," sees the whole host of slaves "with mask[s] torn away, flourishing hatchets, and knives, in ferocious piratical revolt." The masquerade staged by Babo and his enslaved master to beguile the benevolent Delano probes the limits of the American's contrived innocence at the same time that it eloquently enacts the haltingly realized potential for slave revolution in the New World. The American, the European, and the African, yoked together in the last crisis as they are throughout the pantomime of interrupted revolution that constitutes Melville's story, play parts defined by the ultimate phase slavery in the Americas had entered when Melville composed his politically volatile tale. "In 1860 pressures, past, present, and future, blasted the Union apart," writes Frederick Merk in his study of manifest destiny.[1]

With expansion at a fever pitch, Melville's tale, superimposing past, present, and future upon one another, brought into view the convulsive history of the entire region and epoch—from the Columbian arrival in the Americas, through the democratic revolutions in the United States, Haiti, and Latin America, to the contemporary crisis over the expansion of the "Slave Power" in the United States. He demonstrated, as did Nat Turner, David Walker, Frederick Douglass, and Martin Delany, among others, that the history of American resistance to slavery was a history of superimposed moments in which the destiny of the new republic, what some considered its providential design, was still very much at issue. Both in Europe and in the New World—a problematic term that I will retain since for Europeans and Africans alike the Americas *were* the New World— the Age of Revolution lasted well into the nineteenth century. The great power of *Benito Cereno,* as I argue in chapter 2, lay in Melville's apprehension of the scope and intricacy of slavery's contending forces, which were entangled in the ethos of revolution that defined America from its beginning and remained ironically bound up with African American slavery in its rise, its maturity, its dismantling, and indeed its long aftermath. More specifically, Melville saw the centrality of slavery and revolution in antebellum American political and cultural life—not least in the corresponding "shadow" of blackness that San Domingo's successful slave revolution cast over the failed design for a democratic social world in the United States—and, by implication, the general failure of American writers to confront the nation's most pressing moral challenge.

Or, one should say, the failure of white writers, not of black: African American writers such as Douglass, Delany, Walker, William Wells Brown, and Harriet Jacobs had been quick to link slavery to its complex revolutionary heritage, and they joined Melville, Harriet Beecher Stowe, and a few others in forging a strong tradition of political, and often polemical, literature that has not yet been adequately understood in its broad New World context. I begin this book—one about *American* literature yet seen from a particular angle—with less than orthodox texts: Nat Turner's "Confessions," which defies our normal conceptions of authorship and narrative; and Frederick Douglass's autobiographical writings, principally *My Bondage and My Freedom,* which have a secure place in the African American canon and now appear on many general college reading lists, but which would not, even so, often be put at the very center of the American Renaissance. My concern is less to demonstrate that *My Bondage and My Freedom* is as indisputably "classic" as *Moby-Dick* or *Walden* than to demonstrate that our terminology, our methods of analysis and judgment, and our very capacity to formulate the notion of the literary classic can be productively reconstructed.

"While [the African American] lives and moves in the midst of a white civilisation, everything that he touches is re-interpreted for his own use," wrote Zora Neale Hurston in an essay on black language which I cited in my introduction.[2] Her observation, intended primarily to indicate how African American culture has of necessity absorbed and reconfigured white culture, could as well be read as a commentary on the criteria of classic American literature. Were we similarly to reconfigure the American Renaissance from an African American perspective—reading the texts made of words stolen from the "Lords of the Land," as this chapter's epigraph from Richard Wright might likewise suggest—Douglass, Jacobs, Harriet Wilson, William Wells Brown, Solomon Northup, and others would no doubt undergo a sudden shift in value and position. And yet it could not be a tradition of black writers alone, for Stowe, Melville, and Abraham Lincoln, for instance, would also prove crucial to such a reformulation. That is a corollary of my argument: in an account of antebellum literature defined along the axis of revolution and slavery, the African American perspective may be dominant but cannot be exclusive. A further corollary is that slavery be defined in hemispheric terms, as it most often was in the

early nineteenth century by black and white writers alike; and therefore
that black slave revolution be a primary point of historical reference and
the African American literature of resistance the primary point of departure.

Beginning with that foundation, the very idea of antebellum classic
literature, and the entire array of cultural implications that flow from it,
will perforce be seen anew. And yet such a shift in perspective should
hardly require a wrenching adjustment. The renaissance of American literature occurred in an era in which the authority of the Revolution had
become the subject of anxious meditation and in which the national crisis
over slavery's limits everywhere compelled a return to the fraternally divisive energies of the revolutionary generation. That cultural rebirth of
many kinds should issue from a historical moment as rife with ideological
tensions as with democratic opportunities, as much with violence as with
concord, is no surprise. What has not been realized, however, is the degree
to which writing about the problem of slavery—in particular, writing
about slavery by African Americans—can be seen to have animated that
rebirth, not because it was central to every major literary text of the period
but because it defined the overarching ideology of liberty which left the
nation in a state of unresolved crisis while at the same time authorizing
its cultural independence, territorial expansion, and rise to world power.
When the major issues are reoriented only this slightly, not New England
and New York but rather the South and the Caribbean become the
significant geography, the social and political soil on which a cultural
renaissance could occur.

"A man, without force, is without the essential dignity of humanity,"
wrote Douglass in the revised account of his celebrated victory over the
slavebreaker Edward Covey. "Human nature is so constituted, that it
cannot *honor* a helpless man, although it can *pity* him; and even this it
cannot do long, if the signs of power do not arise."[3] Along with those of
other former slave narrators, Douglass's autobiographical writings, especially *My Bondage and My Freedom* and its allied short work of fiction "The
Heroic Slave," participate in the most radical aspects of the liberation and
self-reconstruction that have often been said to constitute the renaissance
of our national literature. In revising his life story while immersing it
rhetorically in the ideology of the Revolution, Douglass at once engaged
the ancestral masters in struggle and made their language and principles
his weapons of resistance. Likewise, Nat Turner, although the authority
of his "Confessions" must be deduced from a complex network of cultural-

political forces at work in and around his revolt and the written records of it, entered directly into the nation's revolutionary paradigm by yoking Christian messianism to the language of the founding fathers. The struggle against slavery was fundamentally physical, as Douglass's fight with Covey and Turner's crusade to the death make obvious; but it was also linguistic, and their written acts of resistance have meant far more to readers of the day and generations to follow. In the texts of Douglass and Turner, as well as those of Melville and Delany treated in the next chapter, the "signs of power" arise with dramatic intensity. The abolitionist Theodore Parker once asserted that "the relation of master and slave begins in violence" and must be "sustained by violence, the systematic violence of general laws, or the irregular violence of individual caprice."[4] Both Turner and Douglass, in their markedly different ways, made the truth of Parker's observation the means of their redemption. Far from capitulating to a corrupt ideology, Douglass and Turner found the "signs of power" both to spring from and to redeem the vision of liberty. Like Martin Delany after them (and like Melville's Babo), they appealed not just to the white but also to the *black* fathers of the Age of Revolution, and they wove elements of African belief and African culture into their seizure of American rights in redesigning the geographic scope and racial ideology of the nation.

San Domingo and Its Patriots

San Domingo's slave revolution offered to both American slaves and American writers a distilled symbolic representation of the doubleness of the democratic ideal born in the Revolutions of 1776 and 1789, matured in continuing European revolutions, but still awaiting fulfillment in the colonial holdings of Latin America as well as in the southern United States. Replete with ironies, as W. E. B. Du Bois was to argue in his landmark study of the slave trade, San Domingo caught the fire of the French Revolution. It ended Napoleon's vision of American empire; it bolstered the antislavery movement in England and accelerated the suppression of the slave trade; and it became a primary point of reference for both proslavery and antislavery forces in the United States. Abolitionists claimed that Haitian slaves, exploiting the upheaval of the French Revolution, had successfully seized the same Rights of Man as had Americans two decades earlier; proslavery forces, to the contrary, claimed that the black revolution led to wholesale carnage, moral and economic degradation, and a political system that was (in the words of the British minister to Haiti in the 1860s) "but a series of plots and revolutions, followed by barbarous military executions." The immediate effect of San Domingo was paradoxical: it strengthened resistance to the slave trade but also provided a major setback for abolitionist sentiment. The outbreak of revolution in 1791 brought a flood of white planter refugees to the United States, some ten thousand in 1793 alone, most of them carrying both slaves and tales of terror to South and North alike. Thereafter, especially in the wake of Nat Turner's uprising in 1831 and the emancipation of slaves in British Jamaica in the same year, Haiti came to seem the fearful precursor of black rebellion throughout the New World, becoming an entrenched part of master-class ideology in both Latin America and the United States.[5]

Like a prism, the trope of San Domingo reflected all conflicting sides of the tangled question of bondage and became a prophetic simulacrum of events feared to lie on the horizon of American slavery. On the first anniversary of the *Liberator* in 1832, for example, the radical abolitionist William Lloyd Garrison invoked the "Spirit of Liberty" that was "thundering at castle-gates and prison-doors" throughout the world. Rather than celebrate the spreading fires of democratic revolution, however, Garrison dwelled on the threat of coming bloody revenge at the hands of African American slaves. When liberty "gets the mastery over its enemy," Garrison asked rhetorically, "will not its retaliation be terrible?" Because "timely repentance" on a national scale did not appear likely, Garrison introduced a paradoxical possibility: in order to avoid having to join in defending the South against slave insurrection, the North ought to dissolve the Union. Were this threat to "break the chain which binds [the South] to the Union" carried out, however, Garrison predicted that "the scenes of St. Domingo would be witnessed throughout her borders." Arguing from another perspective, the southern abolitionist Angelina Grimké asserted that the worst bloodshed in San Domingo took place not because of black revolution and emancipation but because of France's partially successful attempt to reimpose slavery in 1802. In reply to this a northern moderate, Catharine Beecher, contended in 1837 that radical abolitionism, by evoking such examples and making slavery more severe in reaction, was itself raising "the paean song of liberty and human rights" among slaves and preparing the way for the "terrors of insurrection" and catastrophic civil war.[6] San Domingo, like the ideology of revolution when applied to slavery, in political argument as in literature, cut not just both ways but all ways.

For those whose power rested on slavery or who feared the effects of emancipation, not to mention racial equality, San Domingo wrote large the kind of bloody revolt brought to pass by Nat Turner, and well into the 1850s most Americans agreed with Beecher. What Bryan Edwards had asserted of the British West Indies in 1801 remained persuasive in much of the United States, certainly the South, for decades: if encouragement is given to those "hot-brained fanaticks and detestable incendiaries, who, under the vile pretense of philanthropy and zeal for the interests of suffering humanity, preach up rebellion and murder to the contented and orderly negroes," the same "carnage and destruction" now found in San Domingo will be renewed throughout the colonial world and the United States. Implicit in the assumption of abolitionist conspiracy was a doubt of the slaves' own ability to organize and carry out a successful large-scale revolt, a doubt reflected also in the writings of some antebellum black intellectuals, who, despite the hope aroused by the example of San Domingo, could not always be confident about the spread of revolutionary power. Although he avowed that Haiti offered a model for black rule and black freedom because despotism there had been overcome by the "keen avenging axe of liberty," the black emigrationist James Holly doubted that the "bastard democracy" of the United States could be touched by black resistance, so ingrained was "republican despotism" in its political system. The slave conspiracies of both Gabriel Prosser and Denmark Vesey, in 1800 and 1822, respectively, were clearly marked by the influence of the Haitian Revolution but remained just that: conspiracies. If they proved Holly correct, however, each contributed to the *fear* of slave revolt, which was itself enough to hold the avenging axe of liberty over the heads of southern slaveholders and their northern sympathizers. In the wake of Vesey's near revolt, Charleston editor Edwin C. Holland called for vigorous suppression and warned his readers not to forget that "our Negroes are truely [sic] the *Jacobins* of the country; that they are the *anarchists* and the *domestic enemy; the common enemy of civilized society,* and the barbarians who would, if they could, become the destroyers *of our race.*" Another southerner likewise spoke for many in 1825 when he warned: "God will raise up a Toussaint or a Spartacus against us. . . . Our history has verified the melancholy truth, that one educated slave or colored freeman, with an insinuating address, is capable of infusing the poison of insubordination into a whole body of the black population."[7]

This indeed was the lesson of every significant slave conspiracy or slave revolt in the United States. But there was another lesson as well, one frequently inscribed in representations of the leader of San Domingo's black revolution, Toussaint L'Ouverture (though less often attributed to the leaders of domestic slave revolts), namely, that he belonged to the great age of the founding fathers and should rightly have stood beside them as an ancestral hero.* Widely acclaimed by abolitionists, white and black alike—but also, in the first decades of the century, by some southern supporters of slavery as well, who rightly considered him dignified, compassionate, and economically conservative—Toussaint was the subject of numerous essays, biographies, and poems (Wordsworth's famous sonnet was probably the most significant). *The Freedman's Book* by Lydia Maria Child (1865) traced Toussaint's lineage to an African chief and portrayed him as a Christlike healing figure, and James Redpath's 1863 biography was widely read by black soldiers in the Civil War. Throughout African American writings of the antebellum years and well beyond—for example, *Black Thunder* (1938), Arna Bontemps's novel about Gabriel Prosser's 1800 uprising in Richmond—Toussaint was counted a key mythic figure in the war on slavery. To invoke Toussaint was to lay bare the paradoxical way in which slavery and revolution were linked throughout antebellum history, dark twins of a national ideology riddled with ambiguities and tension. When he compared Toussaint in an 1854 lecture not only to Nat Turner ("the Spartacus of the Southampton revolt") but also, as had Garrison and others, to Napoleon and Washington, William Wells Brown underscored the withering irony that whereas Washington's government "enacted laws by which chains were fastened upon the limbs of millions of people," Toussaint's "made liberty its watchword, incorporated it in its constitution, abolished the slave trade, and made freedom universal amongst the people."[8]

Brown's lecture on San Domingo, subtitled *Its Revolutions and Its Patriots,* adopted the increasingly familiar antislavery strategy of declaring the San Domingo uprising the model for an American slave rebellion that would bring to completion the stymied Revolution of 1776, and he challenged his audience to see clearly the irony of slaveholding within Amer-

---

* In addition to being invoked constantly by antislavery polemicists for comparison to the heroes of the American Revolution, Toussaint matched figures such as Washington, Jefferson, and Adams, as they came to be portrayed, in considering himself the "father" of his new country's "children." In warning the Directory in 1797 of a reactionary move in the legislature to restore slavery, he cautioned that the slaveholding interests were "unable to conceive how many sacrifices a true love of country can support in a better father than they." See Toussaint L'Ouverture, letter of 5 November 1797, quoted in C. L. R. James, *The Black Jacobins: Toussaint L'Ouverture and the San Domingo Revolution,* rev. ed. (New York: Vintage Books, 1963), p. 196.

ica's revolutionary tradition. But irony, a form of masquerade and rhetorical inversion, is a matter of perspective and power. The most famous document produced by the 1832 Virginia debates over emancipation and colonization that took place in the wake of Nat Turner's revolt, Thomas Dew's "Abolition of Negro Slavery" (expanded as *Review of the Debate in the Virginia Legislature of 1831–2*), characteristically called the Haitian Revolution a failure, productive only of disorder and poverty; predicted that emancipation would lead to the South's "relapse into darkness, thick and full of horrors"; and asserted that black rebels, unlike contemporary revolutionaries in Poland and France, were "unfit for freedom." Dew thought that slave rebels, inspired to tear apart the extended family of the plantation system and its structure of paternalism, would have to be classed as *"parricides* instead of *patriots."* Frederick Douglass said they could be both. Whether kind or cruel, Douglass wrote in his revised autobiography, *My Bondage and My Freedom* (1855), the slaveholder is a slaveholder still: "He never lisps a syllable in commendation of the fathers of this republic, nor denounces any attempted oppression of himself, without inviting the knife [of vengeance] to his own throat, and asserting the rights of rebellion for his own slaves."[9]

Although he did not say so explicitly, Dew appeared to grasp as well as Douglass that the "parricide" of slave rebellion conflated two acts: it destroyed the cherished southern fiction of the tranquil plantation "family," exposing it as a romantic charade; and at the same time it revealed that parricide and patriotism were genealogically intertwined in both the psychology and political philosophy of the postrevolutionary generations. Even though Garrison spoke radically when he advocated the dissolution of the Union, his nonviolent passion summarized the extreme ambivalence that pre–Civil War generations felt and expressed toward the legacy of the founding fathers. As the values and intent of the Revolution became less and less vivid as doctrine, yet more and more compelling as a set of symbols to be seized with equal insistence by North and South alike in their battle for the "house divided," in Lincoln's famous New Testament image, a chronological division between the revolutionary past and the nationalistic present was superimposed upon a geographic one, driving both toward crisis. The anxiety of the "post-heroic generations" in the face of the inimitable achievements of the Revolution left them at once unable to act with originality and unwilling obediently to follow the example set by the fathers. They were rebellious and conservative at the same time, on no issue more so than slavery. The failure to abolish slavery in the late eighteenth and early nineteenth centuries, which was the result of racism and economic self-interest as much in the North as in the South, left succeeding generations balked, imprisoned by the Constitution's apparent protection of slavery, yet conscious of the implicit attack on it in the Declaration of Independence.[10] By the time of the war, Lincoln and others would have no trouble appropriating the fiery vision of the revolutionary fathers to their own regenerative purposes; but Lincoln's apparent desire to punish the South and redeem the fathers *without* abolishing slavery betrays a problem that the national (northern) consensus could not in retrospect conceal, that it was not he but Frederick Douglass—or William Wells Brown, or Henry Highland Garnet, or Harriet Jacobs—who may best have embodied the clarified will of the founders.

In his 1861 essay in praise of Nat Turner, Thomas Wentworth Higginson recalled the remarks of James McDowell, a member of the Virginia House of Delegates, who observed during the historic 1832 debates that southern paranoia was prompted by the "suspicion that a Nat Turner might be in every family; that the same bloody deed might be acted over at any time and in any place; that the materials for it were spread through the land, and were always ready for a like explosion."[11] Just so: the slave rebel was par excellence a son of the Revolution; he belonged to the perverse family of the southern plantation but also, and more important, to the flawed family of liberty. In his rhetorical crusade against slavery (as in the case of Frederick Douglass) or even in his millenarian uprising against it (as in the case of Nat Turner), the slave rebel, one could say, became most American. To watch the spread of black rebellion in the New World, or to observe its potential in the United States, was to witness not necessarily the erosion of the ideology of the American Revolution,[12] but rather its transfer across the color line. To embrace the ideals of the Revolution was not to capitulate to an evil order but instead to seek to purify and redeem it.

Nat Turner, Thomas Gray, and the Phenomenology of Slavery

To claim that Nat Turner's purported "Confessions," a text composed by a white man and permeated by problems of authenticity and narrative bias, is a crucial document in the development of African American literature and political consciousness may seem not just implausible but perverse. Modern cultural readings of Turner's confessions (most of which appeared in the wake of the great controversy aroused by William Styron's 1967 fictionalization of Turner's narrative, *The Confessions of Nat Turner*) have typically placed the greatest emphasis on the unreliability of Thomas R. Gray's narrative and its manifest representation of Turner's revolt as an aberration inspired by religious madness.[13] Such an emphasis serves persuasively to bring the "Confessions," a text ripe for exposing the discourses of power, into the general domain of literary interpretation. But there is little else from which to construct his thought or his biographical identity, and one should be careful not to obscure his accomplishment in new modes of mystification. No doubt the confessions recorded and published by Gray, an attorney appointed by the court to defend four of the rebels (but not Turner himself), constitute a most important commentary on the *suppression* of rebellion and are first of all a preeminent example of disciplinary discourse, of the countersubversive containment of revolutionary energy. Too concentrated a focus on the repressive mechanisms of Gray's text, however, can blind us to the unique revelatory powers of Nat's own story, and I therefore want to concentrate on the intersection of these vectors, the statement and counterstatement of revolutionary principles that are critical for estimating the significance of much African American literature in the antebellum period.

The bifurcating movements of Turner's "Confessions" are precisely what make up its instrumental power by opening to view the remnants of Turner's own voice and his prophecy, as well as the mechanisms of control and definition that the ideology of slavery brought to bear on the revolt and its leader. Its very peculiarity when taken as a literary text subject to an analysis of authorial "intention," semiotic structure, or generic conventions makes the "Confessions" worthy of attention. Like the central text with which I conclude this study, Du Bois's *Darkwater,* which also combines literary and ideological issues in a highly unorthodox formal structure, Turner's "Confessions" abruptly redirects the main lines of the American literary tradition in both historical and theoretical ways. The document created by Turner and Gray casts into sharp relief our assumptions about the ideological capacities (or constraints) of literature, even as it redefines, in a more specific way, the originating antebellum features of African American cultural expression.

On the one hand, the slave's "confession," like the larger genre of the slave narrative to which it has an ancillary relation, is a document guaranteed to meld revelation and deception. Not least because it mimics legal testimony, which slaves were in most instances not allowed to provide in courts of law, the confession sets the asserted reproduction of truth against a likely masking or manipulation of motives. On the other hand, the recording of the confession by a white amanuensis places it within the disciplinary bondage of the ruling order. However accurate Gray's representation of Turner's spoken words might be in this case, the apparatus of domination inevitably changes their effect, whether or not one assumes that such change entails a diminution of political resistance. William Andrews suggests that the resulting text issues from the "diametric collaboration" of Turner and Gray in a contest of opposing wills, and Thomas Parramore has gone so far, on the basis of his accurate biographical identification of Gray, as to argue that Turner and Gray together "conspired to create the most compelling document in the history of black resistance to slavery."[14] The conceptualization of the Turner-Gray relationship as one of "collaboration" is probably closer to the mark, as long as "diametric" is never allowed to crystallize into a connotation of "equal"— not simply because slaves were by definition not equal to their masters, but rather for the counterintuitive reason that it is Turner, not Gray, who should be seen to be in control of his text. Parramore's detective work allows us to see Gray more clearly and to speculate more soundly about his personal motives in publishing Turner's narrative.* But Parramore's

---

* Previous scholars had identified Thomas R. Gray as Captain Thomas Gray, an elderly planter and horse breeder near Jerusalem. Thomas Parramore determined that the Gray who worked in the Turner trials and authored the "Confessions" was, in fact, Thomas Ruffin Gray, Captain Gray's son, an attorney who had been born in 1800, the same year as Nat Turner. For reasons that are not clear, the young Gray's own personal fortunes declined radically beginning in the late 1820s apparently with the death of his wife, the dwindling of his own substantial property, and his disinheritance by his father, who died in the midst of the Turner trials and specifically excluded his son from the estate. Parramore therefore concludes that the younger Gray's large debts were a significant factor in his publication of the "Confessions" and moreover that he was likely, because of his ambivalence about the social station and wealth represented by his father, to have found in Turner's defiance "the mirror image of his own ravaged soul" and seen him as a kindred spirit: "The same blind destiny that cast Nat into a life of slavery had robbed Gray of his patrimony, his wife, the affection of his father, his standing in the community. As with the narrator, so with the recorder, might the pattern of regulatory beliefs and devices of white dominion have appeared more as an enemy than an ally. Unwilling to acknowledge his affinity with the rebel, yet unable to escape it, the young attorney seems to have found in the recesses of his own heart a chord that responded vibrantly and in unison with the savage confessions of the slave." Be that as it may, the document composed by Turner and Gray, which could be construed as the record of "savage" confessions only in a highly qualified sense, makes evident a more complicated interplay, both historical and literary, between the forces of rebellion and bondage. See Thomas C. Parramore, *Southhampton County, Virginia* (Charlottesville: University Press of Virginia, 1978), pp. 105–21; quote at p. 113. Cf. Peter H. Wood, "Nat Turner: The

provocative characterization of the relationship as one of "conspiracy" also inadvertently obscures the intricate antagonism between slave's voice and master's voice that the language and formal structure of the "Confessions" makes evident, and it has the further ironic effect of weakening Nat Turner's command of his narrative, which will be the focus of my attention.

Whereas slave narratives were written primarily by freed or escaped slaves (or by their white sympathizers), Turner's text at first glance remains locked within the prisonhouse of slavery. His spiritual autobiography is fraught with interpretive difficulties resulting from the condition of chattel slavery, where legal identity and the public articulation of selfhood, or subjectivity, were particularly problematic and writing itself was often proscribed. Still, the prisonhouse of slavery was not by any means the prisonhouse of thought. Turner was far more than Gray's *equal*, as a man certainly and also as an "author." The collaboration of Turner and Gray embraces both the subversive liminality of minority literature against the dominant tradition and the constantly effaced historical figure of "Nat Turner," who is a clear signification of neither Turner's nor Gray's intentions alone but instead a joint semiotic construction that has acquired in the last century and a half all manner of mythographic significance. Because their collaboration also resembles the collaboration of master and slave, the "Confessions" recapitulates the dynamics of bondage. That in turn, however, entails our reading Turner's text—like the "text" of slavery itself—from more than the master's perspective and therefore with an eye to the slave's own intellectual and cultural power. In addition, it entails that we take seriously the pervasive ambiguity of slave writings—not just the slave's reluctance to reveal incriminating details, for example, or the issue of their being ghostwritten by abolitionists, but instead the semiotically marked ambiguities of language, belief, and cultural identity that replicate the conditions of slavery and the sustenance of an African world in America.

It is in the nature of the act itself, as well as the documentary evidence that remains to corroborate it, that slave rebellion exists in a fluid, ambiguous field of definition. To begin with, it is a fine point to decide exactly what constitutes "rebellion": work stoppage, sabotage, permanent or short-term escape, marronage, physical resistance, lying and stealing, clan-

Unknown Slave as Visionary Leader," in Leon Litwack and August Meier, eds., *Black Leaders of the Nineteenth Century* (Urbana: University of Illinois Press, 1988), pp. 21–40.

destine prayer meetings, drumming and singing, learning to read and write—all manner of slave behavior that went against the wishes of the master and the plantation regime has rightly been counted by commentators as manifestations of resistance, if not rebellion. In the case of an actual uprising, the problem of definition is even more acute. Turner's rising has been variously called a revolt, a rebellion, and an insurrection. I will use all these terms on occasion but generally follow the lead of Henry Tragle, who chooses *revolt* over *rebellion* because of the limited scale of the Turner event (although a full-scale, successful political revolution, as in Haiti, might suggest the opposite usage), and over *insurrection,* which was typically directed against particular laws (not a whole regime) and technically applied to instances of treason, with which slaves, as chattel, could not legally be charged.[15] Both rebellion and insurrection nevertheless have connotations that are of particular value—the former because it points to the fluid state of resistance in which many slaves could be said to live; the latter because it highlights the fact that the ideology of Turner's revolt, like that expressed in David Walker's or Frederick Douglass's writings, was grounded in a belief that what was to be overthrown was not the entirety of democratic government but the immoral institution of slavery. Moreover, revolt has the added significance of referring implicitly to the Haitian Revolution, with its extension of French principles, and explicitly to the American revolutionary tradition, with which Turner would align himself.

Perhaps, therefore, it would be more appropriate to think of the relationship between Turner and Gray not simply as one of literary or textual significance but rather as a manifestation of the entire phenomenology of slavery in which the dialectic of opposing wills was subject to continual borrowings and absorptions of power, alterations of ascendancy, and recognitions that the ontological planes of bondage and mastery could from time to time—in sudden flarings of resistance, escape, or deceit—become inverted. One could mark analogies for the relationship between Turner and Gray in several realms of cultural history. David Brion Davis ingeniously argues that the relationship between Napoleon and Toussaint mirrored on a grand scale the classic Hegelian definition of the entanglement between mastery and slavery. For Hegel, the master's power is hedged by his discovery that his very identity *as a master* is bound to, and mediated through, another consciousness, that of the slave. The slave in turn, although he is in thrall to the master and lives to a degree for his enhancement, nonetheless wields power over the master by refusing to grant him autonomy and forcing him into a psychological posture of dependence. The condition of slavery, says Hegel, is inverted in the fact that, while the master is conscious only of control, of mastery, it is the slave, in fact, who is conscious of freedom: "The truth of the independent consciousness is accordingly the consciousness of the bondsman. . . . Just as lordship showed its essential nature to be the reverse of what it wants to be, so, too, bondage will, when completed, pass into the opposite of what it immediately is: being a consciousness repressed within itself, it will enter into itself, and change round into real and true independence." Once he had achieved a nationalist freedom through revolutionary force but had been returned to Europe in political bondage, as Davis suggests, Toussaint appealed to Napoleon for leniency as a "servant of the Republic in San Domingo." In remaining in bondage to his master's ideology, however, Toussaint set in motion the dialectic of autonomy, like the dialectic of revolution itself, on a different, more complex plane where his achievement and his vision as a slave constituted consciousness of true independence.[16]

Although hardly as grand as that between Toussaint and Napoleon, the Hegelian relationship between Turner and Gray, along with what it implies about the relationship between masters and slaves generally in New World slavery, might be pursued along similar lines. The paradoxical nature of their relationship mimics the tensions of slavery and the ideological dilemma of Virginia itself, in which the rise of liberty and the rise of slavery had occurred simultaneously, inviting the sarcasm of Theodore Parker once its economy had become saturated in domestic slave trading: "The most valuable export of Virginia, is her Slaves, enriched by the 'best blood of the old dominion;' the 'Mother of Presidents' is also the great Slave Breeder of America." Casting back to the foundations of America, the text of the "Confessions" also resonates with, and within, the charged double context of radical Christianity and New World revolution. Nat Turner, as Eugene Genovese remarks, was "a messianic exhorter," a black slave who nonetheless spoke "in the accents of the Declaration of Independence and the Rights of Man."[17] Contrary to expectation, the paradox of that fact is underlined rather than effaced by Gray's published document, which is nothing less than Turner's consciousness of freedom made public. Unlike Toussaint in his relationship to Napoleon, Turner did not submit to Gray or plead for sympathy. And yet, in phrases that came to seem blasphemously tautological to his listeners and readers, he appealed overtly to the founding religious and political ideologies of America for his justification and hence for his subjectivity.

Like Toussaint, however, Turner did not simply reiterate the ideology of the Age of Revolution: his blackness and his condition as a slave made a difference. For this reason one does better to look past Hegel's rather arcane terminology to the greater flexibility found in Orlando Patterson's reconceptualization of the master-slave relation as one of "parasitism," a relation in which the master, by various paternalistic strategies that amounted to self-deceptions rather than statements of natural relations, camouflaged his own parasitic dependence on the slave with the pretense that slaves were parasites upon their masters. For their part, slaves in turn camouflaged, or masked, their resistance to slavery—and hence the nature of their freedom through consciousness—only on occasion removing the mask and exposing the parasitic relationship of slavery as an "ideological inversion of reality."* Patterson's more fluid trope suggests rather precisely the unmasking performed by Turner's "Confessions," which, although it was inevitably contained in the framework of the slaveholder's dominating ideology, revealed that ideology as a deception. But Turner's brilliance— if we may provisionally ascribe authorial intention to his text, a point to which I will return—lay moreover in the fact that he, like Douglass after him, derived the authority for his revolt from the equivocations of democracy and Christianity, revealing slavery to be a parasitic inversion of American ideology. The slave, not the master, was the truer American.

---

* Because of its bearing on the relationship between Turner and Gray, Patterson's theory is worth quoting at length: "The slaveholder camouflaged his dependence, his parasitism, by various ideological strategies. Paradoxically, he defined the slave as a dependent. This is consistent with the distinctly human technique of camouflaging a relation by defining it as the opposite of what it really is. The slave resisted his desocialization and forced service in countless ways, only one of which, rebellion, was not subtle. Against all odds he strove for some measure of regularity and predictability in his social life. Because his kin relations were illegitimate, they were all the more cherished. Because he was considered degraded, he was all the more infused with the yearning for dignity. Because of his formal isolation and liminality, he was acutely sensitive to the realities of community. . . . The slave retaliated not only existentially, by refusing to be among his fellow slaves the degraded creature he was made out to be, but also directly on the battlefront of the political psychology of his relation with the slaveholder. He fed the parasite's [the slave-holder's] timocratic character with the pretense that he *was* what he was supposed to be. Still, in his very pretense there was a kind of victory. . . . All slaves, like oppressed peoples everywhere, wore masks in their relations with those who had parasitized them. It is in their statements to one another, whether via folk sayings or—infrequently—in folk literature, that they revealed what they knew and what they were. Occasionally a slave, feeling he had nothing to lose, would remove the mask and make it clear to the slaveholder that he understood perfectly the parasitic nature of their interaction." See Orlando Patterson, *Slavery and Social Death: A Comparative Study* (Cambridge, Mass.: Harvard University Press, 1982), pp. 334–42; quote at pp. 337–38.

We may read Turner's "Confessions" as if it were Gray's text, then, yet it is never possible *not* to read it also as Turner's. Like Melville's refashioning of Delano's historical narrative, the "Confessions" contains a slave revolt within a masquerade; but although Gray's text serves to contain and suppress Turner's revolt by situating it within a description of fanaticism, it does not obliterate the meaning of the revolt as an event or as a textual reflection on religious and political principles of liberation. As though Babo had spoken in Delano's and subsequently in Melville's account, Turner's difficult heroism remains intact as a historical moment and in his confessional words, a surplus of revolutionary energy that Gray did not efface but rather unwittingly—perhaps deliberately—augmented. The obvious critique of Gray's text—that he fabricated elements of the tale or, at the least, prejudiced it by his own dramatizations and editorial commentary—touches only the most superficial question about the text's manifold discursive junctures. The deeper implications lie in the fact that Turner, as much as Gray, wore the mask, that he too manipulated the rhetorics available to him and sought to shape the public performative function of his tale of rebellion. The intense wave of panic and paranoia among slaveholders set off by Turner's uprising was motivated in largest part, of course, by the shocking bloodshed of the event.[18] But the immediate availability of Gray's pamphlet gave Turner's own words a role in continuing his insurrection in the arena of propaganda, with a vocal force that could scarcely be contained by the controlling mechanisms of Gray's editorial apparatus, which on the face of it appeared calculated to quiet the public's grave apprehensions about further slave violence.

Whether on a small or a large scale, revolt or rebellion need not be actualized in order to exist in a state of intention or desire (on the part of slaves) or manifest itself as a threat (on the part of slaveholders). That is to say, revolt must be understood to have a phenomenology comprising several states of "action." Two of the most menacing slave uprisings in the early nineteenth century, those of Gabriel Prosser and Denmark Vesey, were stopped short of actualization. Yet as conspiracies that were very mature and likely to have produced much violence and measurable victories if carried out, they achieved in the arena of terror and propaganda many of the effects of successful revolts. Bringing San Domingo home to the United States, the nightmare threat of Turner's own revolt galvanized the potential forestalled in the cases of Gabriel and Vesey, and it left much of the South in a state of apprehension that was periodically revived by newly discovered threats or minor risings. In the Charleston of 1838, Fanny

Kemble was greeted by the ominous tolling of bells and beating of drums at sunset, which announced the slave curfew and warned not of alien invasion, as in feudal Europe, but of possible "domestic insurrection." (Such precautions were no doubt "trifling drawbacks upon the manifold blessings of slavery," Kemble dryly remarked; "still I should prefer going to sleep without the apprehension of my servants' cutting my throat in my bed.") In fact, the lesson internalized by planters, however they might mystify it by a philosophy of paternalism, was finally not so different from the liberating promise of Turner that was to survive in African American folk life:

> Well you can be milk-white and just as rich as cream
> And buy a solid gold carriage with a four-horse team
> But you caint keep the world from movering round
> Or stop old Nat Turner from gaining ground.[19]

"Gaining ground" could run all the way from outright revolt to a refusal to recognize the legitimacy of the slave regime. Included here would be the widespread instances of feigned docility or subservience that throw into doubt virtually any recorded instance of planter faith in the loyalty and good will of slaves. The meaning of Turner's revolt—both in the text that he left behind and in the chain reaction of slaveholder alarm that he set in motion—must thus be understood within the spectrum of intentional acts of resistance open to him. The archeology of his story, however, requires that we first examine the framing apparatus in which his life is contained.

Thomas Gray's text, it should be said at the outset, resembles the depository documents attached to *Benito Cereno* in that it operates simultaneously in the narrative and legal registers. Despite the vengeful campaign against blacks that followed Turner's revolt and the summary justice dealt the rebels themselves, it is evident that, in comparative terms, the Southampton court was careful to avoid any appearance of vigilantism and hoped instead to make the trials a test of the ideological underpinnings of the slave system.[20] The "Confessions" itself participates in this process. Gray's legalism and his account of the execution orders mirror not a miscarriage of justice but rather a careful application of it within the bounds of the slave codes. The text does not just supplement the court records, newspaper accounts, and gubernatorial or legislative documents that make up the otherwise available evidence about Turner's life and his

rebellion. It recapitulates or mimics those materials through the intervention of Gray's own voice into the confession—most notably through his
narrative interpolations or, at times, his eliding representation of Turner
through indirect speech—and by the addition of a dramatized version of
the court's sentence, supplemented by lists of the whites killed by Turner's
men and the blacks tried and sentenced for their part in the rebellion. In
this respect the legal materials that run through the text paradoxically
undermine the bold assertion that this is Turner's "confession" of guilt—
a confession that by itself shows little remorse and no signs of expiation,
and thus wears a transparent mask. More strikingly, however, Turner's
confessions are submerged beneath an opening welter of discursive agenda,
beginning with the copyright issued to Gray, as the "proprietor" of Turner's story, by the District Court of the District of Columbia. The copyright
immediately reminds us that we are reading a text placed before the public
as a commercial venture (Gray hoped for a first printing of fifty thousand
copies; according to Higginson, some forty thousand were sold over the
next thirty years) and casts an especially bright light on the slave's status
as property and commodity. Next comes Gray's narrative introduction—
the primary evidence adduced by most readers to reveal Gray's manipulation of Turner's story—and this is followed by the seals and signatures
of the court's six justices certifying that Turner's confessions were "read
to him in our presence, and that Nat acknowleged the same to be full,
free, and voluntary." Although none of the justices had been present
during the confession, and no effort, it seems, was made to determine its
precision or Nat's understanding of what was read back to him during his
trial, the attestations of the justices are further reinforced by the signature
and seal of the clerk of the County Court of Southampton, who attests
that these justices sat on the bench of the Jerusalem court on November
5, 1831, and "that full faith and credit are due, and ought to be given to
their acts as Justices of the peace aforesaid."[21]

Leaving aside for the moment the issue of Gray's own revision of
Turner's language, then, the legal apparatus alone requires the reader to
pass through three screens of authority before reaching the confession:
the copyright, the statement by the justices, and the attestation of the
court clerk. All of these documents have as their purpose the clarification
and authentication of the revolt and of Turner's confessions, and in this
respect they function in much the same way as similar authenticating
frame materials attached to slave narratives in order to guarantee their
accuracy.[22] Their effect, however, is more accurately the reverse: the le-

galistic materials further the imprisonment of Turner and, although they finally do not undermine his account, at first glance lend greater weight to Gray's judgmental language and to the economic relation he now bears to Turner as the legal "proprietor" of his text. As in many newspaper accounts, Turner throughout the "Confessions" is stripped of his master's name and designated by the generic "Nat," and the legal documents, no matter that they make him masterless in name for the first time in his life, thus put a fine point on this ironic emasculation of his identity. They assist in the execution of Nat Turner by corroborating the evidence brought against him, and they also assist in the transfiguration of "Nat *alias* Nat Turner, a negro slave, late the property of Putnam Moore, deceased," into property now divided between Thomas Gray and the estate of the twelve-year-old boy who had become Nat's legal master in 1828.* The "faith" in the acts of the justices elicited by the county clerk's attestation is of a piece with the "faithful record of [Nat's] confessions" that Gray offers to the public; likewise, the set opening of the copyright notice, *"Be it remembered,"* is congruent with the deep stamp upon public memory, white and black, that Gray and most government officials wished the trials and executions to make.²³ Just as Melville ironically represents his depositions as a "key" to unlock the mystery of the revolt aboard the *San Dominick,* all the while demonstrating that they serve to bind the chains of slavery and the sentence of death more securely about Babo, so Gray's legal documents reinforce the essential doubleness and ambiguity of his enterprise. Nevertheless, the full ramifications of the legal framework, as well as the complicated relationship between Gray and Turner, can be seen only when Gray's language, Turner's act, and the suppressive response to his revolt have been taken in full measure.

Gray composed Turner's "Confessions" on November 1–3; Turner's trial took place on November 5; Gray secured copyright on November 10; Turner was executed on November 11; and the "Confessions" were published on November 22. There is little question that Gray, deeply in debt

---

* A document that does not appear as part of Gray's narrative but that bears an even more profound relation to Turner's legal status is the certificate signed by the sheriff of Southampton County signifying that "the within named slave Nat" has been officially executed. Because the estate of Putnam Moore was entitled to reimbursement by the Commonwealth of Virginia for the destruction of its "property," a slave who had been valued by the court at $375, the sheriff's certification of the execution was required for such reimbursement to be made. See Henry Irving Tragle, *The Southampton Slave Revolt of 1831: A Compilation of Source Material* (Amherst: University of Massachusetts Press, 1971), p. 427.

and perhaps humiliated by his late father's disinheritance of him, had an economic stake in his publication of the pamphlet and might therefore be considered a new "master" among the sequence of masters who had profited from the lifelong labors of Nat Turner and, now, even from his uttermost rejection of the condition of slavery. Nevertheless, the greater interest of Gray's motives, not least if he secretly identified with Turner's violent defiance, lies in the apparent public service he performed in explaining Turner and accounting for his rebellion. Because it embodied the central paradox of southern representations of slaveholding—that the peculiar institution was one of affectionate paternalism but that bloody insurrection could break forth at the least relaxation of vigilance—the "Confessions" served to sound an alarm but also to suppress the significance of Turner's revolt by disguising its motives. Accordingly, Gray's rhetoric moves in rapid fluctuation across a variety of conceptions of the revolt and its lingering meaning for the Virginia public.

Even though Turner, as I have suggested, embodied the spirit of the Age of Revolution, the ideas of rebellion and freedom are at first glance carefully masked in the text. Instead, the emphasis falls on his messianic visions and, in Gray's editorial commentary, on the derangement of Turner and his "dreadful conspiracy" of "diabolical actors." By characterizing Turner as a "gloomy fanatic" lost "in the recesses of his own dark, bewildered, and overwrought mind" as he plotted his apocalyptic drama and carried it out in methodical, cold-blooded fashion, Gray attempted to reduce this "first instance in our history of an open rebellion of the slaves," as he deceptively termed it, to a unique example of deviation from the normally safe, paternalistic relationship of master and slave. The motives for freedom, which in Turner's case reside principally but not exclusively within the millenarian symbolism of his visions, are placed behind a secondary screen in Gray's focus on his "fanaticism" and "enthusiasm," and the whole subsequent confessional statement appears to be drained of ideological meaning by Gray's assertion that the confession "reads an awful, and it is hoped, a useful lesson, as to the operations of a mind like his, endeavoring to grapple with things beyond its reach. How it first became bewildered and confounded, and finally corrupted and led to the conception and perpetration of the most atrocious and heart-rending deeds."[24]

But a useful lesson to whom? Nat's mask of contented slave, which was torn off in the fury of his violent rising, is deployed once again, with more complication, in the account of his rebellion which Gray offers to the public. Those things that are said to be "beyond his reach" can hardly be restricted to biblical teaching but must include that which cannot be forthrightly named: the desire for liberty and the rejection of bondage. Implicit in Gray's account is the charge, one frequently made in the aftermath of the revolt, that abolitionist propaganda or insurrectionist black texts such as David Walker's *Appeal to the Coloured People of the World* (1829) were responsible. This, in any event, appears to be the burden of Gray's rather confusing claim that the insurrection was the "offspring of gloomy fanaticism, acting upon materials but too well prepared for such impressions." The widespread calls for the suppression of religious instruction and abolitionist propaganda that followed the revolt would undercut any belief that Turner was entirely unique in his so-called fanaticism, and Gray's attempt to place the contemplation of freedom beyond the mental reach of a Nat Turner (in "natural intelligence and quickness of apprehension," Gray admits, he "is surpassed by few men I have ever seen") is patently absurd. Absurd, but absolutely necessary: with a "mind capable of attaining any thing," Turner, it must have been obvious to Gray, was dangerous not alone because he was "warped and perverted by the influence of early impressions" concerning his spiritual destiny, but because in deed and thought he stood so far outside the stereotype of slave behavior, revealing it to be a charade. "He is a complete fanatic," Gray admonished, drawing in his own careful assessment a stark line between intention and mask that runs like a chasm through the history of African American slavery, "or plays his part most admirably."[25]

This is the crisis point in Gray's text, and it is also the point at which Gray and Turner merge in their parasitic rhetorical relationship, bondage sliding over into mastery, and the ideology of paternalism becoming inverted. What is revealed in the interstices of Gray's text—a momentary lapse in the countersubversive regulation of his own language—is the possibility that Turner has played the trickster, perhaps even with Gray's conscious recognition. But the linguistic sign of that duplicity is to be located not in Gray's falsification of Turner's voice but rather in his virtual reproduction of it. The *Richmond Enquirer* was probably not alone in complaining that Gray's text gave Turner an eloquence that he did not deserve and therefore undermined its claim to authenticity. Yet such a charge covers several possibilities: that Gray for any of a number of reasons had recomposed Turner's language (at the least eschewing any markings of dialect, making it "white"); that southern racism could not allow itself to conceive of such eloquence in a slave; or that Turner himself had staged a performance for Gray and his audience, adopting the guise of religious madness in order to protect other slaves or potential plots, or simply to exercise his intelligence and imagination. The tricksterism of African American folk life and slave resistance to the brutalization of the plantation regime were two sides of the same coin, and Turner may well have set out to beguile a credulous Gray, though it seems unlikely that Gray was a man to be easily taken in. But the slave's mask could also mediate intentions or emotions that hid in plain sight, as it were, and were constituted less by concealment than by the master's misunderstanding. Turner's text, that is simply to say, may be his own, whatever degree of Gray's "conspiracy" in the authorship may be hypothesized. Its authenticity may rest, too, not just in its factualism or its correspondence to other available testimony about his preaching or his visions. (Because Turner initially set out to act in the political world rather than the literary world, however, such evidence cannot be discounted.)[26] More important, its authenticity may appear most poignantly in its manifold invention: its enunciation of a speaking subject whose messianic and ideological messages are one, in which mania and performance coexist in the desire for liberty.

The "confidence" of other slaves in his superior judgment, Turner tells us (tells Gray), was "perfected by Divine inspiration," corroborated by the legends of his infant powers, and "ever afterwards zealously inculcated by the austerity of my life and manners." "Having soon discovered to be great," he adds, "I must appear so, and therefore studiously avoided mixing in society, and wrapped myself in mystery, devoting my time to fasting and prayer." Gray's text also shows Turner "wrapped in mystery," and the subtlety of each voice's complicity in what "appears so" is remarkable. My suggestion is not that Turner the preacher was a fraud or a confidence man (I will argue that such a notion, even if it were true, is finally irrelevant) but rather that the "appearance" of authenticity in Turner's text, as in Gray's surrounding language, is crucial. Without questioning the legitimacy of his religious inspiration, one can entertain the possibility that Turner consciously played the trickster and that the language of irony and double vision that is often associated with African American rhetorical forms and the liminality of slavery was his vehicle of revelation.[27] The ambivalence of the "Confessions" arises less in Gray's manipulation of Turner's story than in Turner's own manipulation of his story and in his shocking embrace of millenarian revolutionary violence. In offering his mystique of fanaticism to the public, Turner appears to have submitted to Gray's objectification while at the same time donning it as a mask, achieving by contrast his own dynamic and articulate subjectivity. There is, indeed, no reason to doubt that Nat's language and self-portrait are substantially his own, that he created himself as a subject, and that in so doing, as Gray recognized, he offered the utmost danger to Virginia slaveholders.

Gray's rhetoric, that is to say, is in contest with, and parasitically bound to, Nat's, as masters and slaves were bound in a game of cunning. In a manner reminiscent of the Master-John folktales, in which power and the capacity to deceive frequently flow on a continuum between the master and slave, the Gray-Turner tale shows us the master working not against the brute object, the chattel, Turner, but against a speaking and conspiring subject—a fact that is not overborne by Gray's abstract references to slaves as "this population" or "this class of persons," or by his more callous statement that the insurgents have all been "destroyed" (like animals) or brought to trial and execution "without revealing any thing at all satisfactory, as to the motives which governed them." The "Confessions," of course, tells us nothing of the motives of the other slaves who joined Turner and his initial band of six men, upwards of seventy men and women who in some way participated in the rising, not to mention others who may have lent it their support. Their motives are all distilled into Turner's fanaticism, much as Melville would reduce the revolt aboard the *San Dominick* to the inspiration fermented in Babo's lone "hive of subtlety," in the process constructing a complex and enigmatic hero but nonetheless evacuating the communal significance of slave resistance in a manner comparable to Gray's. Consequently, Gray's account must be perceived, and must surely have been perceived even in its own day, not to exhaust the causes of the revolt but to obscure them by the singular focus on Turner. Subsequent panics about slave rebellion proved that few Virginians, or southerners generally, thought Turner unique. In bringing forth a text meant to answer the "thousand idle, exaggerated and mischievous reports" caused by the revolt, and acting for "the gratification of public curiosity," Gray thus produced one as likely to cause alarm as to allay fears.[28]

It is not difficult to see that the legal paradox embodied in the slave rebel or in any slave resisting his bondage—namely, that he was at once property and yet capable of volitional acts—was the central cause of Gray's excessive ambivalence. In recognizing the free will of the slave, so as to be able to hold him accountable for violations of the law, southern courts worked through a thicket of legal fictions designed to keep the perilous balance between property and volition in taut suspension.* Gray's narrative bridges the philosophical gap between property and volition—a gap that held within it nothing less than the recognition of natural rights, including the right to rebel against tyrannical authority—by feebly asserting that Turner was acted upon by ideas beyond his comprehension. As the object of ideas rather than their instigator, Turner superficially disappears as subject, or rather appears as subject only under the guise of madness and demonic possession. At the same time, however, Gray cannot entirely repress Turner's volition: "I shall not attempt to describe the effect of his narrative, as told and commented upon by himself, in the condemned hole of the prison. The calm, deliberate composure with which he spoke of his late deeds and intentions, the expression of his fiend-like face when excited by enthusiasm, still bearing the stains of the blood of helpless innocence about him; clothed with rags and covered with chains; yet daring to raise his manacled hands to heaven, with a spirit soaring above the attributes of man; I looked upon him and my blood curdled in my veins." Although Gray next asserts that he will "not shock the feelings of humanity" by detailing the "fiend-like barbarity" of the rebels, he immediately proceeds to add further details to the grisly account he has already recorded from Turner. If the effect is not quite to place Gray in the devil's own party, as Parramore would contend, we are nonetheless

---

* As Eugene Genovese points out, this is one element that William Styron's novel effectively exploits. In conversation about his trial for insurrection and murder, Styron's fictional Thomas Gray explains to Turner: "The point is that *you* are *animate* chattel and animate chattel is capable of craft and connivery and wily stealth. You ain't a wagon, Reverend, but chattel that possesses moral choice and spiritual volition. Remember that well. Because that's how come the law provides that animate chattel like you can be tried for a felony." See William Styron, *The Confessions of Nat Turner* (New York: Random House, 1967), pp. 21–22; Eugene D. Genovese, *Roll, Jordan, Roll: The World the Slaves Made* (New York: Random House, 1974), pp. 28–30. As I have noted, however, Turner and his band could not be tried for treason, a fact that changes the legal complexion of his revolt and makes it technically not an "insurrection." The fictional Gray's speech notwithstanding, Styron seems to have taken the real Gray's assessments of the real Turner's "fanaticism" at face value: "I took the perfectly legitimate liberty of humanizing this man, or monster, by giving him a rational revolutionary plan . . . I gave this man a dimension of rational intelligence which he most likely did not really possess, and as a result smoothed down that stark fanaticism I think was deeply buried in the man's nature." See Ben Forkner and Gilbert Schricke, "An Interview with William Styron," in *Conversations with William Styron*, ed. James L. West III (Jackson: University of Mississippi Press, 1985), p. 193. Styron's novel has at times been unfairly maligned, but it is safe to say, on the basis of this statement, that he assumed that "fanaticism" precluded "rational" political intelligence. I take this to be a fundamental misunderstanding of Nat Turner.

invited to witness the momentary identification with Turner, the identification of master with slave, that Gray's text first requires and then abruptly renounces. The gothic touches (conventions, one might say) would have made Turner only marginally alien to white readers of the 1830s. Specifically, the heroic posture enacts a philosophy of volition that completely supersedes any suggestion that Turner is mere chattel, and it also allows him momentarily to escape from the pervasive ascription of his motives to religious fanaticism. Turner's own characterization of his intelligence, in fact, breaks away from a philosophy of chattelism in a most profound way: "I had too much sense to be raised [that is, cultivated in the slave regime], and if I was, I would never be of any service to any one as a slave."[29]

The greater source of alarm aroused by Gray's text, then, may reside less in the sheer surprise and brutality of Turner's revolt than in Gray's inability, or unwillingness, to sever Turner from the world of volition and natural rights. Speaking in chains from the "condemned hole of the prison" (in this he anticipates the trope of underground existence, deriving from the entombment of the middle passage, that appears throughout African American literature from the slave narratives through the fiction of Jean Toomer, Richard Wright, Ann Petry, Ralph Ellison, and others), Turner is to some degree an archetypal romantic figure; and his confession, represented in his own voice, constructs an autobiographical identity with all the attributes of free choice and self-possession available under slavery. Because Nat Turner exists in the liminal space between chattel ("late the property of Putnam Moore") and actor ("for natural intelligence . . . surpassed by few men I have ever seen"), he occupies the psychic territory, where slavery gives way to freedom, that slaveholders could not afford to recognize without jeopardizing more than their lives, but whose compelling logic they were nonetheless unable to deny.

The mainstream antislavery movement would not begin to endorse violent slave resistance for another two decades. Strikingly, but therefore not surprisingly, northern and southern responses to Turner were on the whole not very different. The foremost analyst of the viability of slavery in the wake of the revolt, Thomas Dew, employed by Governor John Floyd to study the legislative debates about emancipation, concluded in his "Abolition of Negro Slavery" that Nat's violence was a manic deviation from the principled structure of slaveholding paternalism:

But one limited massacre is recorded in Virginia history; let her liberate her slaves, and every year you would hear of insurrections and plots, and every day would perhaps record a murder; the melancholy tale of Southampton would not alone blacken the page of our history, and make the tender mother shed the tear of horror over her babe as she clasped it to her bosom . . . The slave, as we have already said, generally loves the master and his family; and few indeed there are, who can coldly plot the murder of men, women, and children; and if they do, there are fewer still who can have the villany [*sic*] to execute. We can sit down and imagine that all the negroes in the south have conspired to rise on a certain night, and murder all the whites in their respective families; we may suppose the secret to be kept, and that they have the physical power to exterminate; and yet, we say the whole is *morally impossible*. No insurrection of this kind can ever occur where the blacks are as much civilized as they are in the United States. . . . Nothing, then, but the most subtle and poisonous principles, sedulously infused into [the slave's] mind, can break his allegiance, and transform him into the midnight murderer.

For Dew, only the "poisonous principles" of antislavery propaganda could be the source of Nat's religious dementia, which put him "under the impression that heaven had enjoined him to liberate the blacks."[30] White antislavery polemicists, however, took a view not so different from Dew's. As though in a mirror image of the proslavery argument, the pacifist Garrison imagined a race war if slaves were *not* emancipated, and contended in the *Liberator* that the revolt showed only "the first drops of blood, which are but the prelude to a deluge from the gathering clouds." Benjamin Lundy, echoing much southern journalistic opinion, dismissed Turner as a "bandit," while a poem about Turner's revolt appearing in the *Liberator* in March 1832 epitomized antislavery's stated abhorrence of (perhaps also its leering fascination with) slave violence:

> A shriek was heard by night!
> The startled eye but saw
> The gleaming axe, and the ear just caught
> The sable fiend's hurra!
> Out of the polished floor
> Ran the ensanguined flood;
> The babe slept on its mother's breast,
> And its bruised lips dashed with blood.
> Upon the cold hearth stone
> The unripened virgin lay,

Crushed in her budding loveliness,
And dawn of her opening day.[31]

The gothic rhetoric of radical abolition was a fair echo of reaction in Virginia. Like Dew, the Garrisonians appealed to the image of a marauding attack upon domesticity to figure the horror of slave violence. The leading ideologues of proslavery and white antislavery, divided by principle, were united in their unwillingness to concede the justness of any form of slave terror. In both cases the charge of fanaticism against Turner masked the violence and meaning of his revolt by channeling it into conventional gothic structures. More important, though, it masked the fear that, to repeat James McDowell's apt warning, "a Nat Turner might be in every family," a view frequently attested to in the aftermath of the revolt by slaveholding families who said they could never again trust their slaves—and one reflected in much northern commentary as well. Turner's subversion of that trust demonstrated that the familial, domestic rhetoric of slaveholding, its appeal to paternalism, was coded with a gothic structure that concealed—in psychological terms, barely repressed—the ideological underpinnings of black slave revolution and its potential for bloodshed.

With no doubt some isolated exceptions of complete subservience to the rule of slavery, Nat Turner *was* in every family, whether he acted out his violent impulses or not. Still, resistance need not be considered constant or unalloyed. As George Rawick has remarked: "Unless the slave has had a tendency to be Sambo he can never become Nat Turner. One who has never feared becoming Sambo, never need rebel to maintain his humanity." Neither pure Sambos nor pure rebels, Rawick argues, can be said to exist; and only the "contradictory nature of the rebel personality" can illuminate the ambivalent reality of the slave's world.[32] The recent generation of historiography, much of it undertaken in response to Stanley Elkins's *Slavery,* which argued the case for a widespread dehumanization of African American slaves comparable to the effects of incarceration within other total institutions such as prisons and concentration camps, has demolished the notion that "Sambo" subservience, except in minor instances, was anything but a complicated act, whether deployed for gain or for simple survival. What is more, the myth of slave docility was created by a mutual effort—by a masquerade on the part of slaves combined with a pathological need to justify their regime by slaveholders or, for that matter, by antislavery advocates unwilling to grant slaves the capacity or the right to resist. "With Nat perennially in the wings," John Blassingame points out, "the creation of Sambo was almost mandatory for the Southerner's emotional security. . . . The more fear whites had of Nat, the more firmly they tried to believe in Sambo in order to escape paranoia."[33] The contradictions of the rebel personality, in which slave "behavior" was constantly being constructed by a shifting combination of racism and deceit, and in which the slaves' everyday actions were not just liable to deception but likely to be composed of it, help to explain the utter ambivalence one finds in the portrait of Turner, both in the "Confessions" and in surrounding accounts.

Gray's judgment that Turner's rising came as a complete surprise, "whilst every thing upon the surface of society wore a calm and peaceful aspect," also extrapolates from the claim that Turner considered Joseph Travis, his most recent master, a kind man who had placed much confidence in him, indeed, that Travis might be considered "too indulgent." (Because there is some evidence that Turner had been physically disciplined by Travis, his generous assessment of his master—if he did in fact make the statement—may also have been a calculated part of his dissimulation.) What Turner's revolt brought to the fore, however, was that accommodation and assimilation (or appearances to that effect) were no guard whatsoever against rebellion. Most shocking in the conspiracies planned by Gabriel Prosser in 1800 and Denmark Vesey in 1822 was the fact that those most intimately involved were among the most trusted slaves. In the case of Gabriel's conspirators, the liberalization of slavery in postwar Virginia had helped to create a class of highly assimilated, well-traveled, and skilled slaves who, not remarkably, first imbibed and then came to articulate the belief that the rights of the revolutionary era belonged to them as well. Likewise, Vesey's South Carolina conspiracy, although it seems to have had a stronger basis in the shared African values of slaves more recently imported to the United States, was also dominated by assimilated, skilled, and highly trusted slaves, some of whom, strikingly enough, had resisted simple opportunities for escape but were ready to hazard all for the extremely ambiguous rewards of insurrection.[34]

Except for the centrality of millenarian ideas to his rebellion, Turner would not stand out from this pattern of revolt arising within centers of assimilation. Gray's hiding of revolutionary justice behind the cloak of fanaticism does not mitigate the fact that Turner's threat came from within the circle of slaveholding trust. The deceptive tranquillity disrupted by Turner's rebellion cannot be fully restored by the explanatory language of

Gray's pamphlet; the most he can claim is that his text will give "general satisfaction" and remove "doubts and conjectures from the public mind which otherwise must have remained."[35] If read with any care, however, the "Confessions" could no more restore trust and remove doubt than could the execution of Nat Turner.

Ibo Warriors

Among the incidents recounted by Harriet Jacobs in her 1861 narrative of slave life in early nineteenth-century North Carolina, *Incidents in the Life of a Slave Girl,* is the alarm that spread in the aftermath of Turner's rising, one result of which was the suppression of slave worship: "The slaves begged the privilege of again meeting at their little church in the woods, with their burying ground around it. It was built by the colored people, and they had no higher happiness than to meet there and sing hymns together, and pour out their hearts in spontaneous prayer. Their request was denied, and the church was demolished." Instead, they were permitted into the gallery of the white church, the slaveholders having concluded that "it would be well to give the slaves enough of religious instruction to keep them from murdering their masters."[36] Jacobs's account is one of many that chart the reactionary effects rippling through the South, and the mid-Atlantic in particular, in the wake of Turner's capture and execution, in almost all cases including attempts to control or abolish slave worship. The strictures against slave preaching and religious assembly passed by the Virginia legislature in the wake of Turner's rebellion (though they were never closely enforced) demonstrated that Gray's focus on fanaticism and insanity, which echoed numerous descriptions in the wider press, was not mistaken but was nonetheless too narrow. Gray's dominant trope could not account for the revolt; it did not touch the true danger of slave religion; and it did not begin to grasp how for Turner worship and freedom both fell under the concealing name of fanaticism.

Preaching, it was clearly understood by those who moved to suppress slave worship, could become the vehicle of an ideology more subversive than faith in the Bible; or rather the Bible itself, as the language of the spirituals demonstrated with great eloquence, could become the vehicle of a liberation theology (as it might be called today) capable of tying together San Domingo and Jerusalem, Virginia. Samuel Warner, whose pamphlet on the rebellion, "Authentic and Impartial Narrative of the

Tragical Scene Which Was Witnessed in Southampton County," preceded Gray's by about a month, understood this clearly enough. Placing Turner's rising against a detailed backdrop of San Domingo's bloody achievement of independence, Warner asserted that Turner assumed the guise of preacher so as to further his "nefarious designs," appearing to teach the slaves faith and obedience to their masters while actually preparing them "in the most sly and artful manner to become the instruments of their slaughter." In this penetrating but also misleading account, Turner's appropriation of the principles of the Age of Revolution is hidden behind his sense of messianic calling, yet it is by no means erased by it. (Nor is it credible that Turner's preaching, although it was surely part of his charisma, was simply a means to fool his fellow slaves into following him.) There is no doubt that slave religion, certainly when directed by white ministers but also at times when practiced within the protected confines of black, sometimes secret worship, acted partially to control rebelliousness and at times to instill docile passivity in the face of hopeless odds. Stowe's fictional Uncle Tom had counterparts of a kind on the plantation, and numerous slaves, as well as slaveholders, found the Bible an instrument of comfort or salvation rather than oppression. But a contrary view, succinctly contained in the words of an antebellum blues, was equally prevalent:

> White man use whip
> White man use trigger,
> But the Bible and Jesus
> Made a slave of the nigger.[37]

Instruction and subjugation were never mutually exclusive intentions, however, and no univocal interpretation of the potential for, or the lack of, resistance nurtured by slave religion is possible. Orlando Patterson's view that the paradoxical nature of Pauline Christianity could comfort both slaves and slaveholders, and that therefore the radicalizing tendencies of slave worship were minimal, is worth consideration but seems fundamentally flawed. Patterson to the contrary, there is no question, for example, that the black spirituals were often laden with messages of resistance (even if combined with accommodation) and that Christ appeared in them less as a forgiving, benevolent savior than as a warrior-leader in the Old Testament style. The further incorporation of the spirituals into a tradition of African American literary and intellectual argument—in Du Bois's *Souls of Black Folk,* for example, or novels such as John Killens's *Youngblood* or

Margaret Walker's *Jubilee*—confirms that spiritual uplift was almost always accompanied by varying degrees of militancy. (Miles Mark Fisher has even argued, with more conviction than plausibility, that Turner was the actual author of "Steal Away," whose lyrics—"My Lord, He calls me, He calls me by the thunder, / The trumpet sounds within my soul, / I ain't got long to stay here"—he contends, correspond to the circumstances of Turner's call to prophecy in 1825.) Also, any preponderance in slave worship of New Testament Scripture—rather than Exodus, the prophets, or Revelation, which other scholars have found to characterize slave exegesis—could easily be misleading in an atmosphere in which simple things such as prayer and faith, particularly in view of the harsh restrictions placed on them in the aftermath of slave revolts, might themselves be construed as acts of rebelliousness.[38]

As Turner's case makes perfectly clear, the centrality of Christ to slave worship would not guarantee pacifistic subservience, and in any event his primary inspiration lay elsewhere. More prominent in his confession than the presence of Christ, the "Spirit" for Turner was one ordained by Revelation and one, he says, "that spoke to the prophets in former days." Turner would invoke Christ in his mission—indeed, he would identify with Christ as the final revolutionary prophet—but as with many slaves, even the majority according to some observers, his own inspiration bypassed the New Testament teaching that slaveholders preferred and came instead from the Scriptures of prophecy and apocalypse: Revelation is the text from which Turner is reputed to have preached in his last sermon before the rising. The overpowering presence of Moses and the story of the Israelite delivery from bondage, the fiery accounts of the Old Testament prophets, and the prediction of the New Jerusalem—these were a strong counterpoint to Jesus' redemption and often constituted the heart of slave religion, particularly when, as in the cases of Vesey and Turner, it became interwoven with the language of revolution. It is likely that Gayraud Wilmore overestimates the number of black preachers willing to foment rebellion and surely exaggerates in saying that "one careless word or gesture [by the preacher] could transform a religious meeting into a boiling cauldron of emotion that would send the hearers pouring out of the brush-arbor church and into the homes of the slavemasters to kill and burn," but his sense that black evangelism was poised on the brink of resistance, if not outright revolution, is very much to the point. The counsel of patience and Christian submission could not block entirely the revolutionary message of prophetic Scripture. In fact, the one could simply be inverted into the other.[39]

Both Gabriel and Vesey exploited prayer meetings and biblical prophecy in organizing their conspiracies (the latter in particular by reading passages from the Bible, one conspirator testified, *"where God commanded, that all should be cut off, both men, women, and children"*), and the community hysteria that followed each exposed conspiracy frequently focused on the purported blasphemy and profanity of the slaves' misinterpretation of Scripture. Although the court that sentenced Vesey and ten of his conspirators to death pointedly quoted the Pauline Scripture most often cited by slaveholders (*"Servants, obey in all things your masters"*) and counseled them to repent and confess at their hour of death, the leading figures of the conspiracy appear to have been more moved by the command of their comrade Peter Poyas, who said: *"Do not open your lips! Die silent, as you shall see me do."*[40] The revelation of conspiracies and the occurrence of actual risings show that the attempt on the part of slaveholders to control their slave population by means of preaching and catechism always ran the risk that such instruction would be ignored as rank hypocrisy or taken over and made an instrument of resistance by slaves in their own secret services. Witness Turner's citation of Luke 12:47: "For he who knoweth his Master's will, and doeth it not, shall be beaten with many stripes, and thus have I chastened you." Here Turner appropriates and overturns one of proslavery's favorite passages, transfiguring a text of racist subjugation into his own prophetic call to revolt. For many slaveholders Scripture was a tool of suppression; for Turner it became a weapon of God's own violent chastening of the masters. When the editors of the *Norfolk Herald* remonstrated that Turner's "profanity in comparing his pretended prophecies with passages in the Holy Scriptures should not be mentioned, if it did not afford proof of his insanity," they put tautology in the place of logic. The true profanity, Turner revealed, lay in the long-standing proslavery appeal to Scripture.[41]

It was not just Turner's teaching or charisma as such (the evidence would suggest that Vesey had more magnetic intellectual power) but his messianic character—his precocity as a child, his claimed parapsychological power, his visions—along with the success of his rising that made him an object of fascination. The authenticity of Turner's visions (his own belief in them) does not, finally, seem open to question. Any objection that Gray invented or made melodramatic Nat's prophetism would have to account for the fact that Nat himself told substantially the same story in the days immediately following his capture and that no countervailing testimony was forthcoming.[42] In any event, the real tension lies in the degree to which Turner himself wore the mask and in what he himself made of his visions. What is most striking about Gray's text is that the very elements that are seemingly meant to discredit Turner as a subject and a heroic leader are what constitutes his vital presence. The characteristic that Gray writes off as "enthusiasm," a term that by the 1830s would have connoted an excessive emotionalism, also harks back to instances of "enthusias" (a belief in special revelations and dispensations) associated, for example, with revolutionary sects of English Protestantism, and it indicates a soaring of spirit common in accounts of the prophet-martyr. Although Gray tries to suggest that Turner must "atone at the gallows" for his sins (this seems a clear interpolation by Gray), the rebel will not plead guilty, "saying to his counsel, that he did not feel so," and his "enthusiasm," despite Gray's misconstruction of it, is at once the cause and the result of his liberating act of revolt.[43] Thus, while it is no doubt valuable to gauge the suppressive action of Gray's text by its insistence that Turner be treated as a bewildered fanatic, his role *as* a prophetic figure can also tell us something valuable about slave religion, about his deployment of prophetism as an instrument of revolution, and about the intersection of his millenarian pronouncements with the principles of democratic revolution.

Secret religious meetings in the slave community offered more than simply an opportunity to interpret the Bible free from the hypocritical instruction of the institutional church or missionaries, or to escape from the dehumanizing routine of oppression. If it strains the evidence to designate all such services as "African cult" meetings (as have a few recent historians), slave worship without question forged communal bonds that were largely invisible to planters—and when they were visible were often enough the object of surveillance and suppression because of their association, especially in the wake of San Domingo, with conspiracy and insurrection. Taking place in a cabin or in an outdoor "hush harbor" (brush arbor, arbor church) sometimes considered to have sacred or magical properties, the prayer meeting brought together Christian and African forms of worship and connected American slaves to an ancestral past through syncretic performance of song and dance. Christianity itself could provide a mechanism for the continuation of African practices such as the ring shout and the communal antiphony (call and response) of the spirituals. African retentions could appear in particular methods of promoting secrecy such as the widespread practice of turning upside down an iron pot or kettle to "catch the sound" of the secret service, a practice that has been interpreted variously as an inversion of the all-important drums of African culture and as a reflection of the West African god Eshu Elegba, one of whose emblems is an earthen pot turned upside down.[44] Slaves also recalled lowering their heads, lying in holes in order to muffle the sounds of worship, or speaking low to the ground to conceal their conversations, a practice that Arna Bontemps was to depict with magnificent power in a scene in *Black Thunder* where the slave conspirators, lying together on the ground, join their own songlike voices to the echoing natural language of the earth itself in plotting Gabriel's rebellion.

The issue of such retentions in African American culture, although it has been the subject of long-standing debate among scholars and has had a strong influence on present-day Afrocentric arguments about black American culture and theories of vernacular, is still little appreciated in literary studies. In chapters 4 and 5 I will look in more detail at the nineteenth-century debate about African retentions and the formative role they play in Chesnutt's conjure stories and *The Souls of Black Folk;* but their significance is marked, if less obvious, in numerous antebellum texts as well, including many slave narratives (Douglass's among them), Jacobs's *Incidents in the Life of a Slave Girl,* Delany's *Blake,* and spiritual polemics such as those of Garnet and Turner. To reconstruct the fullest cultural context in which Turner's messianic leadership occurred casts a different light on his text by casting a different light on the function of the slave preacher, particularly the lay minister such as Turner, who was nominally a Baptist but functioned outside of any formal church structure. To be more precise, it is possible to say that Turner's messianic role, most likely a syncretic blend of Christian and African beliefs, operates in Gray's text as it did in historical reality. Infused with elements of African belief and communal leadership, Turner's preaching was an act that combined spirituality and ideology. Looking ahead to the anticolonial prophet figures of twentieth-century Africa as well as to black ministers in the American political tradition, Turner made the languages of Christianity and democracy into a cultural instrument that both preserved Africanisms and reconfigured Americanisms. Occupying a secret place of communion, a hush harbor within the disciplinary regime of Gray's legalistic, incarcerating analysis, Turner's "fanaticism," which Gray apparently employs to condemn the errant rebel mind, is precisely the sign of his heroic leadership and perhaps of his distinct African American prophetic role.

That Turner belittled conjure ("I always spoke of such things with contempt," he says in Gray's text) does not for a moment undercut the possibility that he took part of his power from the exercise of the eminently more political authority of the African priest, a power that Du Bois and other commentators saw to have been readily transferred to the role of the preacher in the antebellum African American community, and that he exercised a messianic influence that included survivals of African practices. As Du Bois later put it, the black preacher acted as "bard, physician, judge, and priest," and carried forward into an American setting some of his African communal functions as "the interpreter of the Unknown, the comforter of the sorrowing, [and] the supernatural avenger of wrong." Likewise, Melville Herskovits's assertion that magic is "the natural prop of revolt" need not be taken in a literal sense (as it might in the case of Vesey, who employed a known conjure man, Gullah Jack, to incite his followers and in whose conspiracy Africanisms were more evident) in order to elucidate Turner's power.[45] By the same token, there is every reason to believe that African spiritualism, something in the eyes of slaveholders akin to magic but operating behind the cloak of Christian teleology, helped to catalyze the rebellion—not because Turner was duplicitous toward his fellow slaves but because his acculturation to Protestantism was no more likely to be pure than that of any other slave, and because Gray's interview, inevitably cast in the language known to his readers, may have erased not just Turner's style (if he spoke in a slave dialect at all) but also remnants of African belief unfamiliar to Gray.

Turner's mother, apparently a northern African captured in her teens and taken to the western coast for sale, had been in America only five years before she married and gave birth to Nat. The legend that she tried to kill her son rather than see him raised a slave does not appear in the "Confessions." (Turner's father, who escaped from slavery when his son was very young, was not an African native, but in his case a more unusual legend was to spring up. In a 1920 account of Turner's revolt, John W. Cromwell maintained that Turner's father escaped to Liberia, "where it is said that his grave is quite as well known as . . . Franklin's, Jefferson's or Adams's is to the patriotic American.") But Turner's account of his mother and his paternal grandmother marveling over his prophetic vision of things that had happened before his birth, and their interpretation of "certain marks on my head and breast" as the signs of "some great purpose," both suggest that his spirituality was nurtured in a neo-African environment before being molded to any Christian pattern. Moreover, his references to the "spirit" that called him to service can be interpreted as at least partly African in character.[46] Robert Hayden captured well this confluence of forces in Turner in his haunting poem "The Ballad of Nat Turner," several stanzas of which run:

> In scary night I wandered, praying,
>   Lord God my harshener,
> speak to me now or let me die;
>   speak, Lord, to this mourner.
>
> And came at length to livid trees
>   where Ibo warriors
> hung shadowless, turning in wind
>   that moaned like Africa,
>
> Their belltongue bodies dead, their eyes
>   alive with the angry deep
> in my own heart. Is this the sign,
>   the sign forepromised me? . . .
>
> Sudden brightness clove the preying
>   darkness, brightness that was
> itself a golden darkness, brightness
>   so bright that it was darkness.
>
> And there were angels, their faces hidden
>   from me, angels at war
> with one another, angels in dazzling
>   combat. And oh the splendor,
>
> The fearful splendor of that warring.[47]

Hayden reclaims Turner's prophetism from the overtly Christian context in which the "Confessions" confines it, exposing an ambiguity in Christian instruction and a syncretism to which the text itself barely alludes. At the same time, however, one must recognize the scope of Turner's uniqueness when he is measured against slave revolutionaries or colonial rebels elsewhere. The conditions of American slavery, including curbs on the wider development of an African slave culture that might compete successfully with the dominant culture or occupy a comparable space, prohibited the sustained appearance of millenarian revolutionary leaders of the kind that appeared more frequently under Latin American slavery or colonialism in Africa. In addition, to the extent that traditional African religions were based on cyclical rather than teleological conceptions of time, they did not so readily lend themselves to appropriation by millenarian revolutionists, even if they did lend resistance a spiritual dimension.[48] (Were more evidence available, however, it seems likely that the same sort of syncretism of African and Christian elements that was to underlie the messianic revolts of Simon Kimbangu and John Chilembwe in early twentieth-century colonial Africa, discussed in chapter 6, might also be found in Turner's worship.) In this respect, Turner's ideology, though it seems to have worked within the construct of African notions of prophetic leadership, became decidedly Christian and therefore engaged most directly the eschatology of the American Revolution.

It would be another two decades before white antislavery would begin significantly to veer away from Thomas Dew's opinion, quoted near the outset of this chapter, that freedom or its prospect would make African Americans "*parricides* rather than *patriots.*" The millenarian tradition that Turner invoked in 1831, intentionally or not, shared with radical abolitionism a theoretical belief in the power of Christianity as an agent of sudden, revolutionary change. Yet in his willingness to accept the practical consequences of violent revolt, Turner descended not from the largely nonviolent tradition of white antislavery, with its strong Quaker influence, but from the secular example of David Walker or the more overt call for a revolutionary messiah in Robert Alexander Young's "Ethiopian Manifesto" of 1829, which predicted the coming signs of a mulatto savior who would seize for blacks the "rights of man," which were also the "Ethiopian's rights." By breaking dramatically with both the nonviolence of abolitionism and the self-perpetuating national consensus of America's dominant political ideology, Turner brought forth the radical possibility, latent in perfectionist traditions of sectarian reform, that God could enter history in the person of a revolutionary messiah.[49] Christian piety was one means of ideological control that he shattered in his rising; another was the dominant paradigm of America's progressive revolutionary fulfillment as the coming of the New Jerusalem. Turner did not so much dissent from that paradigm, one might say, as Africanize it, much as Du Bois, at least in his creative writing, was to Africanize liberalism on his way to a more radical politics.

The panic about further uprisings and the strengthening of suppressive measures against slave and free black preaching, assembly, and literacy which occurred in the wake of Turner's revolt were fueled by claims of abolitionist subversion that have not been convincingly substantiated in particulars but probably played some part. This is hardly to say that Turner could not have acted on his own, but rather to indicate that the atmosphere of debate about slavery *before* the revolt, by which Turner can be assumed to have been affected and to have exploited, is just as pertinent as the rearing of a suppressive machinery afterward. Connected to the 1829–30 legislative debate about the possibility that emancipation might bolster Virginia's declining economy and also to such incidents as the July 4, 1829, killing of one white and the wounding of another by eight slaves in Hanover County, fears of slave uprising and race war were already significant in the year preceding Turner's revolt. The militia had been strengthened in many parts of the state, and one legislator, anticipating the charge made during the debates the following year that debate *itself* was incendiary, warned that if the Bill of Rights were given "all the force which the words literally import," it would amount to "a declaration of universal emancipation" for all slaves in Virginia. Whether or not Turner was influenced by any single text such as David Walker's *Appeal* is less important than the fact that his revolt took place in a context already charged with tension over black liberty.[50]

That Turner originally planned his revolt to occur on the Fourth of July (because of his illness it was postponed until August) is therefore of the utmost significance. On the one hand, it could be that the initial choice of dates was pragmatic rather than philosophical, or perhaps that it was intended at most to evidence a kind of symbolic irony; on the other hand, these subsidiary possibilities may also be embraced in Turner's sense that a Fourth of July revolt would strike at the slaveholding regime on several levels at once. Such a precise intention is not easy to pin down in the "Confessions." But the chosen date would appear to indicate Turner's comprehension, as I will argue, that the effects of his revolt were to be felt well beyond the brief outbreak of bloodletting, and also to show that his prophetism included a recognizable secular dimension.

What is more, Turner's choice of the Fourth of July alerts us to the intricate tension between ritual tributes to the revolutionary ethos and the paralyzing problem of African American slavery. Frederick Douglass rightly perceived that slave holidays could function countersubversively against "the spirit of insurrection among the slaves," working as "safety valves to carry off the explosive elements" of discontent. At the same time, Douglass, recognizing that the Fourth of July performed much the same ritual function for white Americans, preserving allegiance to a flawed, incomplete democracy under the name of consensus in a progressive, postrevolutionary tradition, made much of the holiday in his development of a strident antislavery discourse. Slaveholders who attempted, without much success, to keep their slaves from witnessing Fourth of July orations found themselves hung on just the dilemma that Turner and Douglass would exploit. The holiday of American independence might, like any holiday, burn off slave dissension through calculated leisure, but it might also expose what Douglass called "the gross fraud, wrongs and inhumanity of slavery" and thus offer itself, as it did on more than one occasion, as the ideal date for black uprising.[51]

Neither the tradition of the revolutionary fathers, paralyzed by the problem of slavery, nor the antislavery movement, which often styled itself the true moral inheritor of the Revolution, ran in a single stream. Black antislavery, some time before the advent of Douglass, did not hesitate to invoke violent resistance, and Henry Highland Garnet provided one of the most striking articulations of a countertradition of black American patriotism in his 1843 "Address to the Slaves of the United States of America." Berating slaves for their timidity, challenging their manhood for submitting to the sexual abuse of their wives and daughters, Garnet asked: "Where is the blood of your fathers? Has it all run out of your veins? Awake, awake; millions of voices are calling you! Your dead fathers speak to you from their graves." Those fathers, of course, were not primarily the white fathers of the Revolution but a group in which Garnet placed Toussaint, Vesey, Turner, Joseph Cinque, and Madison Washington (the last two the respective leaders of the slave revolts aboard the *Amistad* and the *Creole*) side by side with Washington and Lafayette.[52]

The fathers, that is to say, were both European American and African American; and if one takes seriously the possibility of the strong infusion of Africanity in Turner's messianism, the fathers were not just rebel heroes but also the immediate slave fathers and their African ancestors before them (Hayden's "Ibo warriors / hung shadowless, turning in wind / that moaned like Africa"). However Turner might have conceived his relationship to a tradition of fathers or ancestors, it is difficult to believe that, anticipating Garnet and echoing David Walker, he did not conceive of his rising, targeted for the Fourth of July, as an embodiment of revolutionary sentiment, yet one that radically redirected the paradigm of ritual veneration. Although no evidence survives that Turner was directly inspired by Walker's fiery *Appeal* (as Virginia authorities would later charge), his revolt and his text are securely within the tradition of revolutionary Christianity advocated by Walker. Blacks, Walker said, needed only to be awakened to the potential for revolution within their hearts:

> I do declare it, that one good black man can put to death six white men; and I give it as a fact, let twelve black men get well armed for battle, and they will kill and put to flight fifty whites.—The reason is, the blacks, once you get them started, they glory in death. . . . I advance it therefore to you, not as a *problematical,* but as an unshaken and for ever immoveable *fact,* that your full glory and happiness, as well as [that of] all other coloured people under Heaven, shall never be fully consummated, but with the *entire emancipation of your enslaved brethren all over the world.* You may therefore, go to work and do what you can to rescue, or join in with the tyrants to oppress them and yourselves, until the Lord shall come upon you all like a thief in the night. . . . O my brethren! I say unto you again, you must go to work and prepare the way of the Lord.

The manifest threat of Walker's *Appeal,* which joined the Bible and the Declaration of Independence as documents authorizing black freedom, stimulated the enactment of antiliteracy laws in Virginia (in April 1831) and North Carolina which preceded Turner's own rising.[53] The exact influence of Walker on Turner is immaterial; what is evident is that together their texts constitute the most dramatic seizure of natural democratic rights as they were defined in the Age of Revolution. In his early apprenticeship to prophecy, Nat recalls, he spent his time in prayer and experiments with the manufacture of gunpowder and paper. Between the two he had the tools of physical revolt and literate propaganda, insurrection and subversion, that working together would constitute the meaning of his revolt and allow him to "slay my enemies with their own weapons."[54]

Blackhead Signpost: Prophecy and Terror

> Multiple set, the skeleton of which, in the first two acts, is the Negro church, and, in the third act, the courthouse. The church and the courthouse are on opposite sides of a southern street; the audience should always be aware, during the first two acts, of the dome of the courthouse and the American flag. During the final act, the audience should always be aware of the steeple of the church, and the cross.
> The church is divided by an aisle. The street door upstage faces the

audience. The pulpit is downstage, at an angle, so that the minister is simultaneously addressing the congregation and the audience. In the third act, the pulpit is replaced by a witness stand.

James Baldwin, stage directions, *Blues for Mister Charlie*

So a military force has no constant formation, [as] water has no constant shape: the ability to gain victory by changing and adapting according to the opponent is called genius.

Sun Tzu, *The Art of War*

Without question one of the most difficult misconceptions to overcome about Turner's revolt is its purported lack of a goal and, in the end, its lack of success. Of course, it did not bring about the overthrow of Virginia slavery; on the contrary, it helped harden resistance to proposals for gradual emancipation that were gaining support at the time, and it certainly brought forth a harsh white backlash that resulted in the murder of many slaves and free blacks. One of the most perplexing questions for observers, moreover, was what, if anything, Turner had hoped to achieve. Whereas Gabriel had plausibly intended to seize Richmond as the spark to the larger insurrection he hoped would follow, and Vesey had intended to take Charleston (and, failing in greater success, to escape to the Caribbean or to Africa), there is no evidence that Turner had any clear purpose beyond the destruction of slaveholders and an assault on Jerusalem itself. Conceivably Turner may have intended to establish a maroon stronghold in the Dismal Swamp, there to raise a colony of rebels large enough to lead a significant war against Virginia slavery, but apparently no such plan was ever outlined either to his followers (unless they all preserved the secret) or to his captors. Connections to smaller contemporary uprisings or revealed conspiracies in Virginia, Maryland, and North Carolina, which flourished in the month following, were denied by Turner, and no direct links have been shown to exist. But the panics in Raleigh and Wilmington in particular point to the ease with which the slaves could, in fact, exercise their own limited tyranny over the masters.[55]

Turner was routinely described as the "great bandit," despite the fact that theft and property destruction during the revolt were minimal and sexual assault nowhere in evidence. When Gray reproduces the phrase in the "Confessions," he encloses it in quotation marks, as if to admit its ironic inadequacy. Theories of fanaticism and simple revenge against particular masters belong to Gray and to the court, not to Turner; and the more gothic indications of bloodlust attributed to Turner and his comrades are most likely editorial insertions by Gray. On the face of it, Gray echoed prevailing sentiment and was not necessarily coy when he said that the whole event was "wrapt in mystery."[56] The editor of the *Richmond Constitutional Whig*, John Pleasants, was typical in his assessment: "If there was any ulterior purpose, [Turner] alone probably knows it. For our own part, we still believe there was none . . . [and] that he acted upon no higher principle than the impulse of revenge against the whites, as the enslavers of himself and his race; that, being a fanatic, he possibly persuaded himself that Heaven would interfere." The motive of revenge, which Gray subordinated to fanaticism, eventually came to define the prevailing countermyth of Turner, as Higginson, William Wells Brown, and others stripped Turner of his aura of religious calling and created a rebel driven by entirely rational motives of retribution. Although the countermyth was almost certainly as much a distortion as the appeal to religious dementia, it served to reveal elements that contemporaries observed but were loath to dwell upon. An anonymous letter appearing in the *Whig* later in the month of September (which, for reasons to be mentioned, may have been written by Gray) came closer to admitting the rudimentary truth of Turner's "plot": "His object was freedom and indiscriminate carnage his watchword. The seizure of Jerusalem, and the massacre of its inhabitants, was with him, a chief purpose, & seemed to be his ultimatum."[57]

"Massacre" and "carnage": another word, bearing in the modern era a wider array of political connotations appropriate to Turner's guerilla war than in his own day, may be more appropriate—namely, *terror*, which has seldom been absent from successful (or unsuccessful) rebellions by any servile population. The white paranoia that followed the revolt bred distortions that in turn heightened apprehension—accounts suggesting that the rebels wore outfits ceremoniously dyed red in their victims' blood or, more strikingly, that they drank the blood of the slaveholders. The most inflammatory journalistic account of rebel terror was reiterated in an 1891 article by Stephen Weeks, which played to the contemporary rise of radical segregationist thought. Recounting the apocryphal fate of children at a log schoolhouse, Weeks reports: "Their heads were chopped off and the bodies piled up. The blood was caught in the water bucket. The negroes got in a circle and one of them, perhaps Nat himself, sprinkled them with blood, repeating, 'Such is the will of your Father in heaven.'"[58]

It has been argued that the portion of Gray's text devoted to Turner's confession splits into discrete halves: the rhetorically charged and passionate account of Nat's divine inspiration, and the factual, cold-blooded recital of the killings. To consider the relationship between these elements of the story one of intentionally "grotesque" contrast, however, misses the point. Gray himself may have considered the relationship terrifying and hence inserted his periodic editorial comments about "barbarous villains" and their "thirst for blood"; and it was no doubt part of his rhetorical strategy to make the account of destruction, already widely covered in the press, as methodical as possible. But there is no reason to believe that Nat Turner—if his messianic inspiration was real, or if his revolutionary fervor was full enough, or if, as is most likely, the two states of passion were one—saw inspiration and slaughter to be separable. Despite his notorious inability to carry out some of the deeds himself (whether through clumsiness or hesitation, the only person he actually killed was Margaret Whitehead, a fact that became the linchpin of Styron's speculative construction of Nat's psychosexual personality), Turner's interpretation of the revolt is admirably summed up in one statement: "I sometimes got in sight in time to see the work of death completed, viewed the mangled bodies as they lay, in silent satisfaction, and immediately started in quest of other victims."[59]

Turner's "silence" itself has wider implications to which I would like to return; but the methodicalness of the killings—including infanticide, decapitations by axe, and repetitious bludgeonings (such as Turner's own killing of Margaret Whitehead) in which slow, crude killing provides a more terrifying effect than swift annihilation—is essential to any understanding of the revolutionary import of Turner's rising and his own personality as a leader. Emerging from behind the mask of paternalistic acceptance, even intimacy, which slaveholders treasured, the ability of slaves simply to kill their masters with indiscriminate abandon was a truth of slavery that demanded recognition. In addition to being a simple result of the methods of killing, the *mangling* of the bodies—not least because reports were bound to be exaggerated as the myth of Turner grew—and Turner's own *witness* of the events is crucial. The "body" of slaveholding had to be smashed and eviscerated, just as slaves' bodies had been smashed and mangled for generations. But the emphasis he placed on his own observation and witness of the carnage with satisfaction is perhaps the most telling feature of Turner's testimony. Whereas his own ability to do the violent deeds may have been circumscribed, Turner became the audience—the African American audience, not the white—for those deeds. In this respect he further accentuated his usurpation of the master's own power and augmented his display of subjectivity. Turner first witnessed in justice the execution of slaveholders for their crimes; then in his "Confessions" he witnessed once more in the court of public opinion, which was sure to vilify him, and in the court of history, which might one day exonerate him.

Accounts such as that of Weeks, though they might be considered an extended part of the suppressive mechanism that unleashed a counterterror against the black community, therefore served less to controvert Turner's justifications than to magnify the dimension of propaganda in which they most effectively operate. One of the most often cited symbolic events in the suppression of Turner's rising provides an important clue here. As in numerous other instances of slave revolt in the New World, retribution mirrored or outstripped the violence of rebellion. Inverting the decapitations so grimly featured among the rebels' carnage, vigilante whites decapitated a black man and fixed his head on a pole at a crossroads near Jerusalem. The figure of warning, repeated often enough in the history of slave revolt and other warfare to become commonplace (as Melville had realized when he appropriated the gesture in Babo's execution in *Benito Cereno*), became designated in this instance "Blackhead Signpost," the spot living on in memory long after the head itself was gone.[60] The meaning of the black head, however, lies not solely in its power of retributive terror on the part of whites. However much it was meant to frighten and subjugate the slave community, the display of "blackhead signpost" may also be taken as a manifestation of white revulsion at Turner's power as well as a mesmerizing fascination with his own "hive of subtlety," to repeat Melville's phrase—with the glaring subjectivity that his rising announced and that he then recapitulated in perhaps more unnerving form in his reputed "Confessions." The severed black head was not Turner's; but in standing for Turner and the defeat of his revolt, it also perforce stood for the "silent satisfaction" with which he (and presumably many other slaves) had witnessed the like dismemberment of the masters. Blackhead signpost was an instance of suppressive terror, but it was also an instance of admission that such terror was inadequate—that it was always, and in this case belatedly, *counter*terror.

A written simulacrum of Turner's violent rising and a jeremiad of the most extreme kind, the text of the "Confessions" itself depended upon terror. Although it would not be prudent to push the analogy far, Turner's war was a form of guerrilla assault and his text an extension of it. His war clearly did not mount a sustained effort (this constitutes one of its most peculiar aspects) and cannot be called a guerrilla war with any precision—except in the fact that it can be said to have sharpened into sudden destructiveness the ongoing warfare that slavery itself was. More to the point, however, Turner's revolt and his whole representation of himself can be seen to operate according to the necessary secrecy, local knowledge or intelligence, fluidity of force, and intangibility that mark guerrilla warfare against an occupying force.[61] If one conceives of Turner's war as operating beyond the limits of its hours of slaughter—that is, of being extended into the domain of propaganda and thus producing, as it did, disruptive terror for years to come—its strategies of dynamism, deceit, and near invisibility may be seen to transfigure the language of the jeremiad into a weapon of political resistance that would outlast the defeat and execution of the rebels. Turner's exercise of power by means of terror depended not just on the overt brutality of the revolt but, more important, on his calculated intervention, by means of his "Confessions," into the historical memory of Southampton, and on his wrapping himself in the mantle of divine prophecy. Blasphemy operated on all levels at once, yoking horrible acts that had now transpired to ones yet to come.

The nature of Turner's scriptural invocations is therefore particularly revealing. Rather than obscurely predicting the destruction of the sinful community of southern slaveholders, the "Confessions" described the accomplishment as one that had already, as it were, come to fruition. True, Turner fell short of the annihilation of Jerusalem, Virginia, but his rising recapitulated God's promise to Jeremiah (Jeremiah 4–6) and especially Ezekiel that the sinning city of Jerusalem would fall under the sword of righteousness:

> He cried also in mine ears with a loud voice, saying, Cause them that have charge over the city to draw near, even every man with his destroying weapon in his hand. . . . Go through the midst of the city, through the midst of Jerusalem . . . and smite: let not your eye spare, neither have ye pity: slay utterly old and young, both maids, and little children, and women: but come not near any man upon whom is the mark; and begin at my sanctuary. . . . Defile the house, and fill the courts with the slain: go ye forth. And they went forth, and slew in the city. And it came to pass, while they were slaying them, and I was left, that I fell upon my face, and cried, and said, Ah Lord God!

Wilt thou destroy all the residue of Israel in thy pouring out of thy fury upon Jerusalem? (Ezekiel, 9:1–8)[62]

Whatever implications in the name of Jerusalem were recognized by Virginia authorities, it is beyond question that Turner himself understood the symbolic significance of his attempted destruction of the city of "abominations" and "perverseness," and the land "full of blood." As we have already seen in the case of his cunning play upon Luke 12:47, Turner's biblical exegesis was far from simplistic or haphazard. The typology of his reading, moreover, supported his own messianism. He tells Gray that the Spirit spoke to him one day while he was "praying at my plough," addressing him in Scripture: "'Seek ye the kingdom of Heaven and all things shall be added unto you'" (Matthew 6:33, Luke 12:31). In answer to Gray's query about the identity of the Spirit, Turner converts Christ's own words into "the Spirit that spoke to the prophets in former days."[63] The effect of Turner's typological reading, which brackets the uniqueness of Christ's message and draws it back toward the realm of Old Testament prophecy, is to enforce his own identification with Christ while at the same time collapsing all temporal frames into a single epoch of revelation.

The February 1831 eclipse that provided the spark for the revolt (confirmed, for Turner, by unusual sunspots in August) might have coincided in Turner's interpretation of his calling with any of a number of scriptural passages that forecast Christ's millennial reign: Joel 2:31, Matthew 24:29, Acts 2:20, Revelation 7:12. Because it incorporates and interprets the prophetic Scripture of Joel, however, Acts 2:17–21 seems most likely to have been in Turner's mind. Explaining the Pentecostal visitation, when the many nations under Jerusalem heard the disciples speaking in tongues, Peter reminds them of the prophecy of Joel:

But this is that which was spoken by the prophet Joel; And it shall come to pass in the last days, saith God, I will pour out of my Spirit upon your flesh: and your sons and your daughters shall prophesy, and your young men shall see visions, and your old men shall dream dreams: and on my servants and on my handmaidens I will pour out in those days of my Spirit; and they shall prophesy: and I will show wonders in heaven above, and signs in the earth beneath; blood, and fire, and vapor of smoke: the sun shall be turned into darkness, and the moon into blood, before that great and notable day of the Lord come: and it shall come to pass, that whosoever shall call upon the name of the Lord shall be saved.

Along with Turner's own reference to the signs of blood in the earth ("drops of blood on the corn as though it were dew from heaven," and the hieroglyphs in blood "found on the leaves in the woods"), which may echo "Stars in the Elements" ("The stars in the elements are falling / And the moon drips away into blood"), the eclipse suggests that Turner saw his revolt ordained by Peter's Scripture.[64] Although the various signs Turner invokes obviously point also to the apocalyptic symbology of Revelation, Peter's words are important in that they conflate the dimensions of prophecy, Crucifixion, and Second Coming into one time. More than that, they suggest that Turner may have seen himself not just as Christ (both crucified and come again) but also as Peter, the rock on whom Christ founded his church. Turner's church, of course, was one of resistance, a church of slave terror against the masters. His fanaticism was profane; but its true danger lay in the clarity of his witness, which held forth the possibility that a holy community outlasting his brief leadership would survive to break forth again.

Because he probably profited from the role played by terror in the great revolutions of the late eighteenth century and was surely cognizant of widespread indulgence in sheer violence, as a politics of vengeful recrimination, on both sides during the Haitian Revolution, it may be said of Turner that his lack of purpose—or rather his casting of that purpose in the direction of millenarian prophecy—at first obscures but ultimately reveals the meaning of his leadership. In his maturity, he tells us, "I began to direct my attention to this great object, to fulfil [sic] the purpose for which, by this time, I felt assured I was intended."[65] His successive visions represent the "great object" in special symbolic terms that are more critical to his self-conception than to the effects or even to the ideology of his revolt. Turner's rising might therefore be classed among those primitive social movements that Eric Hobsbawm locates midway between pure millenarianism (which expects revolution to be made by divine revelation, by a miracle) and pure revolutionism (which undertakes by itself the entire overthrow of an existing social order). Marked by Christian messianism but at the same time by a fundamental vagueness and lack of clear purpose, such movements, in their want of effective strategy, "push the logic of the revolutionary position to the point of absurdity or paradox," becoming visionary, apocalyptic, and utopian.* In such a context, carnage, the de-

---

* E. J. Hobsbawm, *Primitive Rebels: Studies of Archaic Forms of Social Movements in the Nineteenth and Twentieth Centuries* (1959; rpt. New York: Norton, 1965), pp. 57–60. This distinction

struction of slaveholders present and to come (thus, Turner's legal owner, the twelve-year-old Putnam Moore, was among the children killed), could become the single measure of success and be enough to constitute freedom.

Perhaps no one, aside from Turner, understood this better than the anonymous author of a little-known text certain to have influenced Governor Floyd in his December 1831 message to the legislature, in which he precipitately omitted a planned, guarded suggestion in favor of gradual emancipation. The text, an anonymous letter from a northerner claiming to be the mulatto son of a Virginia slave, corroborated not the *facts* of slave subversion so much as southern *fears* of such subversion, marking psychological terror as the primary goal of revolutionary thought. Signed simply "Nero," the letter recalled the similar travels through southern states by David Walker and looked forward to the plot of Martin Delany's *Blake* by suggesting that the mysterious leader of a vast slave conspiracy in the South, a former slave of great scholarly and intellectual gifts, had for three years been traveling throughout the South and "has visited almost every Negro hut and quarters in the South States." "Nero" invoked the example of San Domingo; but he wisely insisted that assimilation and seeming intimacy between slaves and masters was itself the deceptive harbinger of violence: "Revenge possesses some properties in common with love. We cannot enjoy either in full fruition unless the object of affection, or vengeance be conscious of being loved, or punished." No torture of a captured conspirator could bring confession, he warned, because the band of rebels had pledged themselves "in a goblet made of the skull of a slaveholder" and signed their names "to articles of confederation with our own life blood." Taunting both slaveholders and weak-willed slaves, and outlining intricate plots of "sweet," premeditated revenge against slaveholders (rather than an implausible conquest of the South), the letter hardly shrank from the advocacy of violence. More unnervingly it claimed

---

is comparable to the one between millenarianism and millennialism outlined by Ernest Tuveson, upon which I have been drawing in my characterization of Turner. In this usage "millenarian" refers to an expectation that the millennium of Christ's reign will begin with his actual physical return, whereas "millennial" refers to the belief that historical progress, under divine guidance, will bring about the holy utopia. The latter is progressivist in nature, the former antiprogressivist. See Ernest Lee Tuveson, *Redeemer Nation: The Idea of America's Millennial Role* (1968; rpt. Chicago: University of Chicago Press, 1980), p. 34. Rhetoric about the destruction of slavery both before and during the Civil War would be saturated with the language of apocalypse, but the vision was almost exclusively millennial rather than millenarian. Closer to the latter in his representation of the cataclysmic insertion of the messianic into historical time, Turner still stood between the two, as he did between revolutionism and millenarianism as defined by Hobsbawm.

that Nat Turner was but an automaton being moved by the web of conspiracy, and that other such revolts, more in the nature of jihads, were being fomented by secret agents: "Our plan is to . . . arrouse [*sic*] in [the slaves'] feelings a religious frenzy which is always effectual; only make them think that their leaders are inspired, or that they are doing God's service, and that will be enough to answer our purpose. We must make them believe that if they are killed in this crusade that heaven will be their reward, and that every person they kill, who countenances slavery, shall procure for them an additional jewel in their heavenly crown."[66]

Whoever "Nero" was, he seems to have apprehended the dictum of twentieth-century revolutionary movements and jihads that terror and propaganda are elaborations of each other. His overweening rhetoric of holy war uncannily points to its own character of self-fulfillment in the further suggestion that the suppression of religious meetings among blacks "is exactly what we want," and it therefore alerts us to the possibility latent in Turner's own text that his "fanaticism," if it was not exactly the act that Gray feared it might be, could nevertheless have the strongest political dimension—that religion and politics might be entirely blurred together. There is no guarantee that "Nero" was black (although his radicalism makes it likely that he was, and that he was acquainted with Walker, or at least with Walker's philosophy), and it is even conceivable that the text is an arch example of countersubversion, either an outright hoax (as the postal officials who forwarded the letter to Governor Floyd believed) or a disguised proslavery document intended to frighten Floyd or the legislature into suppressive measures. The effect, in any event, was the same, for Floyd filed the letter in his scrapbook of insurrectionary literature (along with other threatening letters, copies of the *Liberator,* and the like) and alluded to it in his message to the legislature as among those "incendiary pamphlets and papers with which we are . . . inundated."[67]

In the apocrypha of African American legend, Turner's final words to his band of rebels were: "Remember, we do not go forth for the sake of blood and carnage. . . . Remember that ours is not a war for robbery, nor to satisfy our passions; it is a *struggle for freedom*." With the exception of the pointed remark attributed by Turner to Will in Gray's text—that "his life was worth no more than others, and his liberty as dear to him"—such an overt exclamation of the principles of freedom is muted in the text and, if it had ever been clearly articulated, was deleted from contemporary accounts and court records. But as "Nero's" letter implies, the version of Turner's logic surviving in legend, which foresaw a "Christian basis" (that is, a less terroristic, more conventional strategy) for his war against slavery once a large enough army had been raised, may be just as misleading as Gray's pacifying focus on fanaticism.[68] It is more likely that blood and freedom were as closely linked in Turner's intentions as they were in his published "Confessions." Caught between the revolutionary and the millenarian positions, Turner's revolt could not "succeed" on either front (general revolution would not occur, and God would not intervene to destroy slavery). Instead, its success must be counted simply in the fact of its occurrence: the frenzy of destruction, Turner's witness, and his prophecy of greater destruction to come.

A true revolutionary millenarianism can arise only where religion so dominates a society as to leave its religious and political life undifferentiated. By the time of Turner's rising, the secularization of the revolutionary tradition in the United States was virtually complete. As part of a larger process of democratization of revolutionary ideology which replaced ideas of supernatural deliverance and dependence upon messianic leaders with rationalism and allegiance to popular movements, it was the very ascent of secularism itself that allowed Turner to be cast in the role of fanatic. But Turner's leadership, harking back to a presecular moment, depended upon the chiliastic prophetism that could catalyze popular will by an appeal to inspiration and salvationist vision. Like other such figures whose revolutions were grounded in millenarian promise, Turner, we must surmise, depended upon the charismatic creation of an ideology that linked the sacred and the secular, just as the charismatic leader himself is seen to link God and man.[69]

His jeremiad is thus not coincident with, but is attached at a critical angle to, the evolving postrevolutionary tradition outlined by Sacvan Bercovitch, whereby the secular and sacred traditions of revolution were merged in a national ideology of the Revolution as a vehicle of Providence, "a mighty, spontaneous turning forward, both regenerative and organic, confirming the prophecies of Scripture as well as the laws of nature and history." *Rebellion*, in this tradition, was antithetical to *revolution;* the latter led to progress and fulfillment, whereas the former led to discord and destruction.[70] Turner, of course, was classed a rebel from the vantage point not just of the slaveholding South but of most abolitionists as well. What his presecular revolt exposed, however, was the inadequacy, even the fraudulence of the revolutionary paradigm as it was characteristically interpreted. A time of new revolutions in Europe, the moment of Turner's rising was one during which the national memory of the Revolution took on an increasingly fragile cast as the forces of social and sexual reform, the accelerating mobility and class fluidity produced by the market, and the crisis over territorial acquisition and the extension of slavery, all of which would create the major issues of the antebellum literary renaissance, first became tangible. Turner echoed David Walker's prophecy, but by realizing the wrathful judgment contained in the tradition of the black jeremiad, by making regeneration dependent upon discord and destruction, he broke with the consensus affirmation of continuing revolutionary time in much the same way that Christ broke into temporality itself. So long as slavery existed, the redemptive time of the Revolution and the redemptive time of Christ remained at odds. By recontaining the sacred moment within secular history, Turner, both in his act and in his narrative, offered the possibility, like an African hush harbor within the regime of slavery, that the present moment of American history could be reanimated with transcendent purpose. The significance of Turner's revolt, that is to say, lay outside the proscriptions of Gray's analysis not because Gray was wrong but because his interpretation, virtually a mirror of Turner's prophetism, was destined to be misread. The prophetism that Gray attempted to present as madness—its core being the judgment that the prevailing regimes of religion and politics, as defined by slaveholders, were fundamentally illegitimate—was contrary to neither Christianity nor the revolutionary tradition but rather offered a purification, a sacralization, of each.

The overt statement of Turner's judgment appears in his conversion of "Spirit"—whether it had biblical significance alone or included a corresponding African dimension—into the visions of Christ that drive him to revolution: "And from the first steps of righteousness until the last, was I made perfect; and the Holy Ghost was with me, and said, 'Behold me as I stand in the Heavens'—and I looked and saw the forms of men in different attitudes—and there were lights in the sky to which the children of darkness gave other names than what they really were—for they were the lights of the Savior's hands, stretched forth from east to west, even as they were extended on the cross of Calvary for the redemption of sinners." Upon the appearance of drops of blood on the corn and leaves in the woods inscribed with hieroglyphic characters of blood, the Holy Ghost reveals to Turner the significance of these miracles: "For as the blood of Christ had been shed on this earth, and had ascended to heaven for the salvation of sinners, and was now returning to earth again in the form of dew—and as the leaves in the trees bore the impression of the figures I had seen in the heavens, it was plain to me that the Savior was about to lay down the yoke he had borne for the sins of men, and the great day of judgment was at hand." Following his further act of radical dissent in the baptism of the white man Brantley, with his purported stigmata of blood oozing from his pores, the final manifestation of Spirit is made, instructing Turner to take up the yoke of Christ himself and fight against the Serpent that had been loosened, "for the time was fast approaching when the first should be last and the last should be first." To Gray's interjected question, "Do you not find yourself mistaken now?" Turner replies with the final evidence of his identification with Christ: "Was not Christ crucified?" Turner's rhetorical question at once subverts the Christological significance of slave religion as taught by the masters; makes Christ a typological prefiguring of himself, the slave rebel; and effectively turns his confession into a revelation of Scripture and final judgment.[71] In Turner's prophecy slavery is the Antichrist, Revelation is equivalent to revolution, and he is the Redeemer whose acts of chastening, completed by martyrdom, will inaugurate the holy utopia.

Nat Turner looked forward by several decades to the millennial resolutions of the problem of slavery latent, for example, in the conclusion of *Uncle Tom's Cabin,* where Stowe admonishes her readers to beware the coming day of God's wrathful vengeance, or in Lincoln's Second Inaugural: "If God wills that [slavery] continue until all the wealth piled by the bondsmen's two hundred and fifty years of unrequited toil shall be sunk, and until every drop of blood drawn with the lash shall be paid by another drawn by the sword, as was said three thousand years ago, so still it must be said, 'The judgments of the Lord are true and righteous altogether.'" Neither Stowe nor Lincoln, however, would have acted violently against black slavery; and Turner's explicitly millenarian prophetism was at once more overtly sacred and more overtly political in its significance than the quasi-millennial interpretations that accompanied the onset of the Civil War.[72] Whatever the psychological complexities of Lincoln's own martyrdom to the conjoined causes of union and emancipation, he was a political pragmatist; Stowe, for her part, was a racialist for whom considerations of black resistance could be imagined only as heroic pacifism (as in the case of Uncle Tom), or as the upshot of white blood (as in the case of George Harris), or as a species of insanity (as in the case of her maroon rebel Dred, who is killed before his Turner-like revolt can be launched). Turner's prophetism, however, exists as the pure expression of millenarian belief that the rising of American slaves would be the mechanism of God's judgment. It converts "theological terror," to which James Baldwin ascribed Stowe's inability to conceive of antislavery as anything but a mode of exorcism, into a vehicle of burning redemption.[73]

That Turner's text is riddled with difficult problems of authenticity and intentionality, that corroborating evidence must be pieced together and even then remains highly speculative, only accentuates the scriptural quality of the "Confessions" itself. The text must be pondered like the hieroglyphic manifestations of the Spirit in nature, which are themselves matched by the hieroglyphic texts and map left behind by Turner and confiscated from his wife before his capture. Both the perspective and the knowledge about Turner evident in his account suggest that, as I noted earlier, Gray may have been the author of the anonymous letter appearing in the *Constitutional Whig* that contained the description of Turner's hieroglyphic texts. Like Gray, the writer of the anonymous letter attributes the revolt to Turner's fanaticism and warns against the danger of allowing missionary proselytizing among the slaves. At the same time, however, he denies that Nat was a preacher, representing him instead as an "exhorter" and a confidence man who "had acquired the character of a prophet" but whose visions would have to be treated with contempt by any rational public. Tracing his divinations in blood on leaves, the writer asserts, Nat would arrange them in a conspicuous place in the woods, pretend to have a dream, and send some ignorant slave to retrieve them for his interpretation. The anonymous letter indicates too that among the papers "given up by [Turner's] wife, under the lash," are ones "filled with hieroglyphical characters, having no definite meaning. The characters on the oldest paper, apparently appear to have been traced with blood; and on each paper, a crucifix and the sun, is distinctly visible; with the figures, 6,000, 30,000, 80,000, &e."[74] Also found was a list of fewer than twenty conspirators.*

---

* The letter is important, too, for its indication that Turner, in fact, had a wife (a probability Styron simply dismisses). Samuel Warner's "Authentic Narrative" of the Southampton insurrection, apparently the source of Higginson's similar information, indicates that Nat's wife was tortured to produce the information in his hieroglyphic documents and confirms that she was a slave belonging to Giles Reese, whose home was deliberately bypassed by the rebels. Turner's wife, a woman named Cherry, was also put up for sale at the time of Samuel Turner's death. Nat was purchased by Thomas Moore and upon his death six years later became the property of his nine-year-old son Putnam Moore; Cherry was purchased by Reese, a small farmer living close by. Despite their separation, Cherry apparently bore a daughter and one or perhaps two sons by Nat. Tragle persuasively speculates that it was because of her that Reese's family was spared in the bloodshed. See Warner, "Narrative," quoted in Tragle, *The Southampton Slave Revolt*, p. 296; Thomas Wentworth Higginson, "Nat Turner's Insurrection," in *Travellers and Outlaws: Episodes*

It is always possible that the writer's attempt to undermine the legitimacy of Turner's prophetic acts may be warranted and based on reliable information that Turner was a fraud (although Gray himself would add no such extreme skepticism to his own narrative); or it may be a calculated attempt, like that of Gray in his published account, to counteract the impact of the revolt with ridicule. In the second case it can be absorbed, along with Gray's editorial judgments, into the discourse of countersubversion; in the first case, far from discrediting Turner's charisma, it may simply raise it to a higher pitch of effectiveness, endowing him with an even more skillful ability to manipulate a cohort of slaves. Nevertheless, there remains the alternative view, less palatable to 1830s Virginia but more plausible, that the writer was correct to see Nat as an exhorter, but one whose identification with Christ was a sign neither of madness nor of guile. Rather, his identification with Christ, like his preaching out of Protestant biblical tradition itself, was an appropriation of the symbolic language of the white man—the "signs of power"—to his own purposes, in both his preparations for the revolt and his later account of it. The language of prophecy was the medium in which Turner worked, joining it to the language of revolutionary democracy because these were the principal semiotic systems in which the African slave found himself placed. They were not his ancestral systems and did not entirely displace them, but they could be made to express his needs and, in the case of the slave preacher, his political leadership. There is no reason to doubt that the hieroglyphic texts left behind (or even those that Turner purported to discover written in blood in the woods) were legitimate manifestations of his inspiration; if they are to be doubted, then the whole of his "Confessions" must be doubted as well. By the same token, these enigmatic signs of prophecy—are the numbers allusions to millennial time, to population to be killed or freed in the course of revolt, or to some secret code of communication?—traced in blood remain a ghostly array of signs that self-reflexively fall in upon one another. They command assent even as they bewilder, promote fearful apprehension even as they force Turner to the margins of credibility. They tell us only that in the moment of the eclipse, Turner became the black Christ of the South.

It is in the very nature of religion, as Guenter Lewy has argued, that it

in American History (Boston: Lee and Shepard, 1889), pp. 280–81; Tragle, *The Southhampton Slave Revolt,* pp. 11–12, 408, 327n.2; and Stephen B. Oates, *The Fires of Jubliee: Nat Turner's Fierce Rebellion* (New York: Harper, 1975), pp. 29–30, 163n.

may both integrate and disrupt society, at once legitimating an existing order and offering a means to transform that same order, perhaps violently, through the articulation of a revolutionary theology. The double-edged charisma of the messianic leader also contains this ambiguity, allowing him "to sanctify the existing political and social order . . . [or] use his exceptional powers to convince his followers of the truth of his chiliastic prophecy."[75] The same doubleness would pertain, of course, to secular prophecy as well. Fusing the secular and the sacred elements of prophecy, Turner acted against slavery with both of its primary ideological weapons. Moreover, that doubleness of purpose offers a key to the ideological construct of Gray's text, for what Turner's confessions indicate in their focus on prophetism is how inadequate a screen for his revolutionary import was the description of him as a visionary fanatic. In the disjunction between Gray's seeming intention to reassure his audience and the widespread panic about the effects of black preaching that followed the revolt lies the striking power that cannot be suppressed in Turner's text. What Gray apparently offered as a form of countersubversion was, in fact, the very truth of Turner's prophecy.

In his rhetorical question to Gray ("Was not Christ crucified?"), Nat's reanimation of the secular with chiliastic prophecy was complete. The question has no reply but tautology; like the hieroglyphs of Turner's apocalyptic semiosis, it is absorbed into a kind of textual silence. It is unclear whether the assertion that he is to "atone at the gallows" for that "enthusiasm, which has terminated so fatally to many," belongs to Nat or to Gray (the choice of language no doubt belongs to Gray), yet the question is immaterial in light of the fact that Turner refuses to plead guilty.[76] If he does "atone," the implication is of course that he, like Christ, atones for the sins of the slaveholders, not for his own.

Later accounts of Turner's execution claimed variously that his body was skinned and tanned, with one piece of it reportedly handed down as an heirloom, or that the body was boiled into oil and sold as a panacea known as "Nat's Grease." If these bits of folklore belong to the grisly apocrypha of legend, there is also a variation, apparently first printed in the *Anglo-African Magazine* of 1859, that adds to Turner's last moments a resolute composure in the face of death and a physical description of the execution that bears notice: "Not a limb or muscle was observed to move. His body, after death, was given over to the surgeons for dissection."[77] Whether or not the lack of muscular spasms in Turner's case, as in that of Melville's Billy Budd, is meant to reinforce his Christology (other reports said the body bore Christlike stigmata after the hanging), the fascination with his serenity is a further mark of his sacralization by a black audience. Like Gabriel in his refusal to confess or Peter Poyas in his command to the Vesey conspirators to "die silent," and like Melville's Babo, silent before the tribunal that orders his decapitation and the official display of his head, Nat Turner, having spent his energy in a wild revolutionary outbreak against the enslavement of African Americans, appears nonetheless to draw power back into himself in his execution. In his refusal to plead guilty, in his sacrifice itself, and most of all in the enigmatic scripture he left in the wake of his uprising, Turner continued his confession in a dimension certain to outlast the historical moment of his death.

Frederick Douglass's Revisions

> When a man starts out with nothing,
> When a man starts out with his hands
> Empty, but clean,
> When a man starts out to build a world,
> He starts first with himself.
>
> Langston Hughes, "Freedom's Plow"

When Frederick Douglass drew together his band of "revolutionary conspirators" to plot an escape from slavery on the Eastern Shore of Maryland, his plans were matured under the cover of his Sabbath school—not an authorized school, of course, but a hush harbor of secrecy in which Scripture, literacy, and notions of revolution made common cause in the quest for freedom. Meeting with his fellow slaves "in the woods, behind the barn, and in the shade of trees," before eventually securing a room in the house of a free black man, Douglass, as he described the events in his revised autobiography, *My Bondage and My Freedom* (1855), stood before them in the role of a Nat Turner without his dimension of millenarian prophecy. Two earlier revisions in the text also point specifically in this direction. Turner's name first appears in the wake of Douglass's description of his acquisition of literacy. He was drawn immediately to the abolitionist movement, Douglass tells us, because he saw that it alarmed slaveholders: "The insurrection of Nathaniel Turner had been quelled, but the alarm and terror had not subsided." Douglass's literacy led him to seek his first religious instruction—and his first *black* "spiritual father"—in Uncle, or Father, Lawson, whose pacifism Douglass would later conclude made him a perfect replica of Stowe's Uncle Tom but whose instruction of Douglass in the reading of Scripture forged the first link in a chain leading to freedom. Although Uncle Lawson counsels that faith itself will lead to deliverance from bondage, Douglass's deliberate insertion of the example of Nat Turner into the revised account suggests otherwise, as does the next added allusion to Turner, in Douglass's account of the destruction of his Sabbath school at St. Michaels by the white community's leading religious hypocrites. His Sunday school (which in its initial manifestation *was* little more than a Bible class) is rushed by a white mob, and Douglass is told that "if I wanted to be another Nat Turner . . . I should get as many balls into me, as Nat did into him." (Turner, of course, was hanged, not shot.) By chapter 18, in his mature role as rebel leader on the plantation of Mr. Freeland, Douglass unites the accumulating force of these earlier allusions, redirects his vociferous condemnation of slaveholding religious practice, and aligns himself as closely as possible with Turner the political theorist rather than Turner the "fanatic." Describing the "double meaning" of the spirituals and the coded language used by slaves, and identifying himself both with Moses (planning an escape "out of our Egypt") and with Christ ("if any one is to blame for disturbing the quiet of the slaves and slave-masters . . . *I am the man*"), Douglass creates a virtual compendium of slave subterfuge in his account of the "run-away plot."[78] Among the more noteworthy revisions that Douglass engaged in when transfiguring his first autobiography, *Narrative of the Life of Frederick Douglass, An American Slave* (1845), into *My Bondage and My Freedom* are the scattered but substantial details of slave resistance to, and cultural reactions against, bondage that are woven into Douglass's variegated account of his own embrace of the ideals of liberty.

Whether or not Douglass considered Turner's "Confessions" legitimate testimony, he certainly apprehended the ideological significance of Turner's actions and the rhetorical value of invoking his example in a secular context, mentioning him quite often in speeches before and during the Civil War. In his stated philosophy, however, Douglass was closer to the views of Gabriel Prosser, whose thwarted 1800 conspiracy in Richmond, Virginia—far larger than Turner's and more likely to have had a profound impact on the course of slaveholding had it succeeded—was animated by astute, cogent political ideas congruent with the Age of Revolution in which Gabriel's cohort saw themselves to be acting. Likewise, Douglass over the course of the 1840s and 1850s returned to the American Revolution for his political principles, and his revised life story links him alternately with the white founding fathers and those black men—Toussaint L'Ouverture, Gabriel Prosser, Denmark Vesey, Nat Turner, and Madison Washington, among others—who also belong to the era of revolutionary greatness and its aftermath. In the new account of his plotted rebellion in *My Bondage and My Freedom,* Douglass refers his readers simultaneously to Nat Turner and to Patrick Henry, whose sentiments are said to be "incomparably more sublime" when "asserted by men accustomed to the lash and chain," and Douglass's philosophy, as this chapter presents it in an extensive amendment to the original *Narrative,* is derived quite explicitly from the rhetoric of the founding fathers: "We were generally a unit, and moved together. Thoughts and sentiments were exchanged between us, which might well be called incendiary, by oppressors and tyrants; and perhaps the time has not even now come, when it is safe to unfold all the flying suggestions which arise in the minds of intelligent slaves."[79]

The account of Douglass's plot of rebellion and its remembered basis in the ideology of the founding fathers is worth careful consideration, not least because it affords one of the best examples of his extensive revision in the second autobiography and therefore clarifies his complex process of self-definition as an *American* who happens to have been a slave of African descent. "It is an American book, for Americans, in the fullest sense of the idea," wrote the black abolitionist James McCune Smith in his preface to *My Bondage and My Freedom.* The revised version of Douglass's life story, with its forceful invocation of republican principles and the rights of revolution, is heavily marked by the versatile rhetoric of the escaped slave turned public orator, and modern readers have been quick to regret the ornate, even theatrical language of the narrative. Whereas the power of the *Narrative of the Life of Frederick Douglass* lay in part in its spare style and candid dramatization of the main facts of Douglass's life as a slave, *My Bondage and My Freedom* pointed ahead to the iconographic black American success story Douglass would tell of himself in the third version of his autobiography, the *Life and Times of Frederick Douglass* (1881; revised in 1892). In the more self-congratulatory prose of the *Life and Times,* Douglass's story would appear to be a classic account of the model African American life, one that, in the words of Rayford Logan's 1962 introduction to the volume, "has inspired Negroes and other disadvantaged Americans to believe that, despite the imperfections of American democracy, a self-made man may aspire to greatness."[80] No black American before Martin Luther King, Jr., more fully articulated the dream of self-determination through political action and self-education than Douglass; if the *Life and Times* begins to appear tarnished by repetition and a mild smugness, and most of all by the stark irony that Douglass's high principles grated against the steep decline of black civil rights in the post-Reconstruction years, *My Bondage and My Freedom* remains vividly, energetically alive with a sense of struggle and hope that contains nothing false, nothing futile.

The doubleness of Frederick Douglass's constructed persona and his narrative, his uneasy reconciliation of American and African American traditions, came from several sources: his preservation of the materials and memories of slave life within a narrative devoted to public action in predominantly white intellectual and political circles; his own notable ambivalence about his unknown but almost certainly white father and his subsequent fascination with the theme of genealogy; and his acute understanding that, whether in the South or the North, he was still a black man in nineteenth-century America and liable everywhere to discrimination and violent treatment. Douglass belonged to an age in which economic mobility and increasing confusion over the fluidity of social roles gave rise in both literature and political culture to a self-consciousness about roles and fragmented or doubled identities. Perhaps no one better exemplified this mobility and fragmentation than the escaped slave, who inevitably brought out of slavery a complicated social persona that derived from the adoption of those subtle strategies of masquerade necessary to combat the daily pain and indecency of slavery.[81] The slave narrator (or the slave orator) bore evidence of that behavior and often illustrated the complex construction of a newly figured self in a contradictory world of freedom and racism. If he or she usually stood on the furthest margin of realized social aspirations in Jacksonian America, the ex-slave nonetheless exemplified the nation's liberation from genealogical contraints and its penchant for the creation of a persona capable of defining its own origins and station in the world. Such freedom often remained a cruel illusion for free blacks, as much in the North as in the South. By the same token, however, the revolutionary impulse—or general rebellion against hierarchy and domination—could more intimately merge the personal and the public for black abolitionists and slave narrators. Because the very idea of "freedom" thus afforded an arena in which the constructed subject of the autobiographies was given the greatest latitude, the slave narrator who composed his own story was among the most "American" of antebellum writers.

Still, in crucial respects Douglass's embrace of an American identity hindered as much as helped him in his initial quest for self-determination. One must understand his revolt against constraining authority—and consequently his comprehensive rewriting of himself in *My Bondage and My Freedom*—to reach beyond resistance to slaveholding and beyond the attempt to redeem the flawed revolutionary ideals of the founding fathers, to a further rebellion against the new bondage imposed upon him by white antislavery liberalism and, as it happens, modern critical liberalism. Ironically enough, resistance to Douglass's creation of a public persona in keeping with the political principles of liberal democracy subsided over the course of his career as an abolitionist only to reappear in twentieth-century estimations of his written work. But in both instances Douglass's power as a narrator may be seen to arise from his capacity to break through and critique the discourses of subordination that are imposed upon him, whether by northern abolitionists or later readers. Having begun his career as an abolitionist speaker within two years of his escape in 1838, Douglass found his rise to prominence marred by continual reminders that, as a black man, he was subject to northern segregation laws, to mob violence, and to insulting condescension at the hands of his white co-workers.[82] The *Narrative* was set down primarily so that Douglass might guarantee its authenticity (although it too was considered to be fraudulent by some readers), but also that he might take personal possession of it, declare it his own property, thereby capping the quest for literacy that had been so crucial to his resistance to and escape from slavery. When he transfigured the text of his scarred slave's body into the *Narrative,* Douglass changed "property in man" into property in himself and took the first step in a lifelong series of reinterpretations of his life. By offering a virtually mythic embodiment of the acts of speech and self-making denied to most slaves, the *Narrative* summed up the purpose of testimony by former slaves— namely, to illustrate the spiritual survival of the black family and community within the cauldron of plantation life, and to explore the means by which dehumanization could be overcome and power gained through political actions and cultural achievements that would be both black and American.

But in making himself an orator capable of combating slavery in the South and racism in the North, Douglass faced a considerable paradox:

the less like a slave he acted or sounded, the less likely audiences were to believe his spoken story. And this reaction has been repeated in critical response to *My Bondage and My Freedom*. The chronological point at which the second autobiography surpasses the *Narrative* offers an instructive scene in this regard. The *Narrative* concludes with a brief description of Douglass's first significant public speech, in Nantucket on August 11, 1841. "I spoke but a few moments," Douglass writes, "when I felt a degree of freedom, and said what I desired with considerable ease. From that time until now, I have been engaged in pleading the cause of my brethren— with what success, and with what devotion, I leave those acquainted with my labors to decide." In *My Bondage and My Freedom*, by contrast, Douglass reports: "It was with the utmost difficulty that I could stand erect, or that I could command and articulate two words without hesitating or stammering. I trembled in every limb." The latter version heightens rhetorically the crisis of articulation in order to galvanize our attention to the account of the career to follow—Douglass's success as an orator, his founding of the *North Star,* his battle against northern discrimination, and his break with radical abolitionism, particularly with William Lloyd Garrison. "But excited and convulsed as I was," Douglass continues in the second version of his Nantucket initiation, "the audience, though remarkably quiet before, became as much excited as myself. Mr. Garrison followed me, taking me as his text; and now, whether I had made an eloquent speech or not, his was one never to be forgotten by those who heard it." To be taken as another speaker's "text" was Douglass's primary role in his early career: "I was generally introduced as a *'chattel'*—a *'thing'*—a piece of southern *'property'*—the chairman assuring the audience that *it* could speak." Or, "I was a 'graduate from the peculiar institution . . . *with my diploma on my back!'*" The condescending instructions Douglass received from Garrison and other abolitionists required that he stick to the "facts," keep "a *little* of the plantation manner" in his speech, and leave the "philosophy" to others. As Douglass noted, however, he was by then "reading and thinking," and it "did not entirely satisfy me to *narrate* wrongs; I felt like denouncing them."[83]

The differences between the life stories recorded in the *Narrative* and *My Bondage and My Freedom* must be judged in the context of these remarks. The *Narrative* is the most widely read of Douglass's writings; but as Douglass's own reflections on his early career suggest, there are definite limitations to it as a revelation of his identity and his thought. The preference that a number of readers have shown for the 1845 *Narrative* over *My Bondage and My Freedom* and especially the more self-indulgent *Life and Times* indicates not just a distrust of the patriotic rhetoric, the gothic and sentimental literary conventions, and the myth of self-made success that are more characteristic of the later volumes. It also suggests a problematic historiographic choice to be made between the Douglass closest to, and thus presumably best able to articulate, the experience of slavery and the Douglass who purposely constructed for himself a linguistically more sophisticated "American" identity with figures such as the framers of the Constitution, Daniel Webster, and John Quincy Adams, as well as black leaders such as Madison Washington, as his models. No doubt the *Narrative* made a more decided contribution to rallying public support for black abolition, and it more resembles the spontaneous diary or memoir of a man suddenly asked to account for his life. The argument that the *Narrative* is more "authentic," however, is without merit. (Another version of this response, William McFeely's assessment that Douglass never significantly altered the character or the plot of his story, that "the Frederick Douglass of the *Narrative* remains inviolate," is much more plausible but still, I think, misleading.)[84] In its brevity and skeletal structure the *Narrative* may create the greater illusion of immediacy, for Douglass's speaking career had already made him a master of rhetorical effect. Nonetheless, any careful comparison of the texts quickly reveals that *My Bondage and My Freedom* tells us far more about Douglass as a slave, and about slave culture generally, than does the *Narrative,* whose main virtue now, as in Douglass's own day, is pedagogical: it is easily absorbed and taught. The *Narrative* is, in fact, something of a memorized lecture performance transferred to paper, and Douglass's language already, and unavoidably, therefore corresponds to the oratorical codes and literary conventions, the audience expectations of white America, which was increasingly Douglass's America.[85] Even though it is unquestionably a key work in any estimation of Douglass's life, just as it is central to the history of slave narratives, the *Narrative* is not Frederick Douglass's "masterpiece."

Precisely because the second autobiography is even more overtly composed of recollections interwoven with the record of Douglass's speeches, essays, and editorials, his blending of a campaign for black freedom and black rights with a telling of his own representative story in *My Bondage and My Freedom* is the key to interpreting his rise to self-possession and to historical greatness. Douglass's very revision of his own life is the central element of his entry into America's revolutionary tradition of liberal individualism and the sign of his embrace of the principles of autonomy, property, and equal rights. Besides giving a much more valuable portrait of slave life and customs, *My Bondage and My Freedom* continually expands key passages about the politics of race and freedom in order to demonstrate that Douglass was, in fact, qualified to interpret the meaning of his own life. The second autobiography is therefore a book not just about what it means to be a slave in the South but rather what it means to be a slave in America. Although it could be and has been argued that Douglass thus remained enslaved to the hypocritical political discourse of American equality, which had been proven by the survival of slavery to be one more instrument of repression—that is to say, that his appropriation by, not of, liberalism was simply a new kind of incarceration—the paranoid reading of Douglass belittles both his intelligence and his craft. Such forces of constraint cannot be discounted, of course, but one must look instead to the manner in which Douglass himself fashioned a position of power that mediated between the ruthless deprivations of slave culture on the one hand and the failings of liberal democracy on the other.

Questions of slavery are never far from questions of authority, and by extension questions of authorship, for Douglass. Authority is in turn never far from mastery; and mastery, not least in its broadest cultural implications, is barbed with difficult choices for a black American set to narrate his own "escape" from the world of slavery while at the same time identifying with it in complex and powerful ways. The revisions of *My Bondage and My Freedom* accentuate the fact that creating his own subjectivity entailed constructing his past self as a chattel object that underwent a traceable metamorphosis, taking on new, more contradictory roles, as though in successively expanding circles, as his career developed. Douglass now stands outside his former self as it appeared in the first narration so as to reflect on the process of construction. This is dramatized in the very titles of *My Bondage and My Freedom*'s opening chapters—"The Author's Childhood," "The Author Removed from His First Home," and "The Author's Parentage"—which demonstrate Douglass's simultaneous figuring of himself as author (as subject) and as slave (as object). Because the rhetorical force of the opening chapters is directed toward Douglass's critique of slavery's destruction of the family, which he says left him "without an intelligible beginning in the world," they function in one sense as an anti-beginning, a countertype to the standard autobiography.[86] But in his capacity to objectify his own achievement of free consciousness, Douglass reconfigures that beginning as an act of willed subjectivity, of authority over the self concretized in his public recognition as an "author."

Adopting a national ideology of revolution as a personal strategy of self-creation, Douglass makes authorial revision a mode of revolutionary action—revolt against the dehumanizing law of chattel slavery but revolt, too, against any form of mastery that he has not forged for himself.

The double bind in which Douglass's revisions—in his public role as well as in his published narratives—place him is pronounced: to revolt against slaveholding seems to entail a rejection of both his paternity and slave culture itself; any preservation or redemption of slave culture, anti-slavery in principle though it may be, threatens at once to undermine his advocacy of political liberalism and to leave him in the demeaning role of platform slave specimen defined for him by Garrisonian abolitionism. A brief but telling example of this paradox appears in the well-known passage on slave songs that *My Bondage* quotes from the *Narrative*, beginning: "'I did not, when a slave, understand the deep meaning of those rude, and apparently incoherent songs. I myself was within the circle, so that I neither saw nor heard as those without might see and hear.'" This pregnant passage, which resembles other instances in which Douglass quotes verbatim from the *Narrative*, raises a number of critical issues that pertain to his newly fashioned subjectivity. As it appears in the *Narrative*, the passage finds in slave songs the message of humanity and resistance, of ironic concealment and subversion, that Douglass, Du Bois, and others have invited us to see in them: "They were tones, loud, long and deep, breathing the prayer and complaint of souls boiling over with the bitterest anguish. Every tone was a testimony against slavery, and a prayer to God for deliverance from chains." Even here, however, there is a peculiar dissonance, for Douglass represents himself as one unable to comprehend the spiritual or—what he will later state more clearly—the subversive character of the songs while he was a slave. What appears as "incoherence" and "jargon" to outsiders (to those planters who heard neither pain nor longing nor threat in slave music) is likewise beyond the young Douglass's "feeble comprehension," as he depicts it. This peculiar doubleness, which posits deep moral value in slave culture while at the same time detaching Douglass from sympathetic immersion in it, is echoed, it might be added, in an 1855 speech he appended to *My Bondage and My Freedom*. When he defined "our national music," seeming to anticipate turn-of-the-century arguments over the role of the black spirituals in forging an American classical music, he spoke not of the original slave music but of the "Ethiopian songs" into which they had been transformed by Stephen Foster and others.[87]

Douglass's complicated detachment from, and re-creation of, slave culture, to which I will return, is one of the more notable ways in which his self-critical doubleness is thematized in his second autobiography. The quotation of the *Narrative* is not simply a convenience but a secondary commentary on the "feeble comprehension" of his life as a "free" man Douglass was able to express in the first *Narrative*. The original passage defines the unformed Douglass—implausibly, it must be said—as both oblivious to the songs' double meaning and yet aware that in them lies some dim message of freedom. Except by virtue of his being a child, the likelihood that the black spirituals and work songs Douglass heard at Tuckahoe or on Lloyd's plantation were "incoherent" to him is slight; rather, we must assume that this claim, as it is first made in the *Narrative*, is a rhetorical gesture intended to draw readers (like their predecessors, Douglass's platform audience) into a sympathetic understanding of the double meaning of slave music. But what might be styled the meta-rhetorical gesture of Douglass's revisionary "quotation" is more important here. As it is quoted and elaborated in *My Bondage and My Freedom*, the passage on the slave songs insists that we read the new autobiography in a similar way, as a sign of Douglass's recognition that in the *Narrative* he stood "within the circle"—not of the total institution of slavery, as in the first instance, but of Garrison's radical antislavery and the defined self of the platform storyteller it provided. Quotation itself, in this passage and others like it, is a mode of artifice and reflection, a textual objectification of the *Narrative*'s Douglass as property once owned by white abolitionists but now owned freely by Douglass himself. (That Douglass's freedom had by this point been legally purchased must also have contributed to his phenomenology of self-possession.) The process of revision, of detaching himself in successive "quotations" from the objectified selves of the past, itself became an act of revision—more specifically an act of revolt against the constraining authority of slavery, the radical wing of abolitionism, and the racism that Douglass fervently believed could be separated from the idea of democratic equality.

The doctrine of self-reliance that would become conspicuous in Douglass's later speeches and the *Life and Times* partakes of an impulse to liberate the ego from inherited constraints, to seize and aggrandize the power of domineering ancestors or their surrogates in order to fashion one's own ancestry. For Douglass, a slave without an "intelligible beginning," the archetypal American gesture became an archetypal *black* American gesture, and revision a means to take mastery unto himself. Although there are many reasons why Douglass's life, and his conception of his slave past, might be considered uncharacteristic, he sought to make his story representative of African Americans' complex, unending passage from bondage to freedom. Standing, by the mid-1850s, within the wider circle of literacy provided by the abolitionist movement, his public success as a "slave" orator, and his flourishing career as an editor and writer, Douglass gathered a number of the dominant tropes in the argument over slavery—paternalism, revolution, and literacy the foremost among them—into a single "American" matrix from which he might create an ideological alternative set against both the peculiar institution and the limited "text" of his early career. If he remained enslaved by principles that might in the end betray him as a black man, he did so freely.

Iron Sentences: Paternity, Literacy, Liberty

Throughout the late 1840s and the 1850s Douglass continually chastised free African Americans for their comparative lack of interest in abolitionism, and antislavery newspapers in particular (some 80 percent of his subscribers were white). If blacks were more active in the Underground Railroad or the freeing of fugitive slaves, they were, Douglass argued, unsupportive of freedom's most crucial instrument. "They reason thus: Our fathers got along pretty well through the world without learning and without meddling with abolitionism, and we can do the same." But their fathers were not Douglass's father. Peter Walker and Allison Davis are surely right in their arguments that Douglass's "lost patrimony," his fascination with the recovery of a nurturing tie to the white father who never recognized him in youth, is the deep theme of all his autobiographies.[88] But from the perspective of his published work it is less evident that the lost father is the individual father, for whom Douglass may have searched in vain, than the function of paternal legitimation itself—a function with social and political, as well as personal, value.

Antislavery polemics conspicuously portrayed slavery's fracturing of traditional family bonds, both those of African American slaves themselves, frequently subject to separation, punishment, and death, and those of the slaveholding family, often caricatured as an arena of corrupted affections and sexual dissipation. Although slavery hardly annihilated the African American family—indeed, some kinship ties, however distended, may have been made stronger because of the pressure they had to endure—virtually every slave narrator and antislavery author found that sentimental family relations presented a particularly acute stage of dramatic action and public protest. Douglass put this argument in a compelling form when he wrote that slavery "made my brothers and sisters strangers to me; it converted the mother that bore me, into a myth; it shrouded my father in mystery, and left me without an intelligible beginning in the world."[89] If it obsessed him, however, Douglass's own lost patrimony also became his most stringent means of attacking slavery, for it allowed him the freedom to identify with other "fathers" and to manipulate the ideology of the Revolution in compelling ways.

Douglass could not escape the conclusion that he was born of an act that may not have been rape but in any event had no legal sanction, gave him no name or inheritance, and stripped him of the genealogical property of manhood. He spoke from the conviction of personal experience when he repeatedly denounced every slaveholder as the "keeper of a house of ill-fame" and "every kitchen [as] a brothel," or when he ridiculed John Calhoun's benign characterization of slavery as a "domestic institution." Like other abolitionists, he focused attention on the degradation and loss of moral restraint that could be shown to be the dark undercurrent of proslavery protestations, by George Fitzhugh and others, that the slave economy afforded more nearly perfect familial relations among masters and slaves than did northern free market labor. Fitzhugh was only one of the more articulate defenders of slavery to contend that "human law cannot beget benevolence, affection, maternal and paternal love . . . it may abolish slavery; but it can never create between the capitalist and the laborer, between the employer and the employed, the kind and affectionate relations that usually exist between master and slave." Within the "family circle" of slavery, he said, "the law of love prevails."[90]

The countervailing representations of family destruction in the discourse of antislavery, brought to a magnificent climax in *Uncle Tom's Cabin,* had become something of a cliché by the time Douglass's second autobiography appeared. What he added to the attack on proslavery appeals to domestic sentiment and paternal protection was a meditation upon the patriarchy in its most profoundly American form: the revolutionary principles of equal rights. The contradictory laws of the southern slaveholding fathers and the northern democratic fathers—agonizingly fused in the Fugitive Slave Law—required of Douglass a complex psychological response. To fight the political fathers, however, Douglass first had to confront the trauma of his own loss of an "intelligible beginning." Even when he returned to the post–Civil War South for an emotional reunion with surviving members of his white "family," Douglass had not overcome the pain of his missing patrimony, but by that time he had discovered— or better, reconstructed—his own fathers.

Key facts about Douglass's early life and family are likely to remain forever uncertain, but substantial evidence about his parentage and his masters exists and is worth brief reiteration.[91] Douglass would have been able to trace his African American roots on Maryland's Eastern Shore back five generations, to at least 1701. His grandmother, Betsy Bailey, born in 1772, was a strong, self-reliant woman who, although a slave, lived a comparatively independent life and was considered a community leader; and his mother, Harriet Bailey, was one of twelve children born to Betsy and Isaac Bailey (Douglass's apparent grandfather, a slave manumitted in the late eighteenth century). Most of them, like Harriet, were raised to be field hands on the extensive plantation of Colonel Edward Lloyd V, Maryland's three-time governor and two-time senator, whose holdings comprised numerous farms and used the labor of more than five hundred slaves. Harriet bore six children besides Frederick, but little else is known of her apart from the fragmentary memories recorded in Douglass's autobiographies, the most striking, perhaps, being the fact that she had apparently learned to read. Most of what Douglass himself says of his life on the Eastern Shore and in Baltimore, as a young slave in the households of Hugh and Thomas Auld, seems to be accurate. The evidence suggests, however, that Douglass was not so physically deprived in childhood as his narratives would indicate; and when his gifted intelligence was recognized, Douglass was afforded opportunities not given other slaves, including being sent at age eight to the Baltimore home of Hugh Auld, where he acquired his literacy and had his first glimpse of the conjoined worlds of intellectual achievement and freedom. Douglass's probable father, his first master, Aaron Anthony, was employed by Colonel Lloyd and was known to be a harsh and capricious man who raised himself from poverty to middling success as the owner of Holme Hill Farm on Tuckahoe Creek before declining into ill health and mental instability. He died in 1826, within a year of Harriet Bailey; the two of them are buried in unmarked graves near each other on Anthony's land.

In his early writings Douglass offered contradictory opinions about whether or not Anthony actually was his father, and in the *Life and Times,* in fact, Anthony is not mentioned at all as his possible father. What is most at issue here, however, is what Douglass claimed to know and what rhetorical use he made of his information and his speculations, particularly in the revised accounts of his life that form the core of his antislavery writing in the decade after the *Narrative*. The portrait of Anthony is complicated by the superimposition of Douglass's fundamental uncertainty about Anthony's status upon his literary representations of him as an archetypal master. Anthony's own behavior, in any case, seems to have been ambivalent, and in this too he may have been typical of the slaveholder in whom were united the roles of master and father to his own slave children. In addition to the physical cruelties Douglass himself recorded, such as the dramatic whipping of his Aunt Esther when she preferred the affections of a black man over those of Anthony, he once sold the two children of Douglass's Aunt Jenny and Uncle Noah, prompting them to escape (events Douglass would later set down only in his *Life and Times,* when it was safer to do so). At the same time, Anthony appears to have treated Douglass fairly well and to have been indirectly responsible (perhaps because he *was* Douglass's father) for setting him on the path to escape and success. Douglass's narratives also mention the kindness of his first mistress, Lucretia Auld, Anthony's daughter (and thus probably Douglass's half-sister) and of Sophia Auld, her Baltimore sister-in-law. It did not, however, serve his rhetorical purposes to reveal that he had ever received special treatment. Later in his career Douglass would take note of such facts; but the life as he records it in the 1840s and 1850s partakes instead of the strategy he admitted in a well-known public letter to his one-time owner, Thomas Auld (Lucretia's husband).* Published in Gar-

---

* William McFeely suggests that, among other possibilities (and even fantasies on Douglass's part), Thomas Auld may indeed have been Douglass's father, but this speculation is based on ambiguities in the available details about both Auld's life and that of Harriet Bailey. Douglass was born in 1818 on Aaron Anthony's property at Tuckahoe Creek and lived there in his grandmother's cabin until he came to Anthony's house at the Lloyd plantation in 1824. Although Douglass recalls several of his mother's visits at a time when, he said, she had to walk twelve miles from the Lloyd plantation, where she was then working, surviving records show that Harriet Bailey had worked on, or been hired out near, Anthony's Tuckahoe Creek farms until 1816, after that staying at the main farm, Holme Hill, where she worked, until her death, for Anthony's tenant, a Mr. Stewart (who may also have been Douglass's father). According to Dickson Preston, Thomas Auld came to Lloyd's (as sailing master of his sloop, *Sally Lloyd*) in 1819, marrying Lucretia Anthony in 1823. It seems, on the one hand, therefore, that Thomas Auld first came to Lloyd's plantation, Wye House, after Douglass was born, while, on the other, it is not at all clear that Harriet Bailey spent considerable time at Anthony's house on the Lloyd plantation. To be sure, there is a certain duplicity in Douglass's use of the title "old master," which usually refers to Anthony in the autobiographies but is also applicable to Auld, as in the public letter; and it is possible that Douglass thought Auld might be his father. My argument, however, is that Douglass represented Thomas Auld as a "father"—as indeed he did the uncer-

rison's antislavery newspaper the *Liberator* in 1848 and later appended to *My Bondage and My Freedom,* the "Letter to My Old Master" makes charges of brutality against Thomas Auld that were grossly inaccurate, an act for which Douglass later apologized. But he revealed his hand in saying that, while "I entertain no malice towards you personally," "I intend to make use of you as a weapon with which to assail the system of slavery—as a means of concentrating public attention on the system, and deepening their horror of trafficking in the souls and bodies of men." Thomas Auld became the symbol of the peculiar institution, just as Frederick Douglass, author and orator, was its refutation.[92]

The "Letter to My Old Master" can stand as an emblem of Douglass's intention to use both his life and those who figured in it as "weapons" in his fight for freedom and equality. Even so, the weapons were wrenchingly personal. Surely rhetoric and emotional pain exist in equal measure in Douglass's further claim in the public letter to Auld that he spoke for the desire of many escaped and freed slaves one day to return home to the South: "It is not that I love Maryland less, but freedom more. You will be surprised to learn that people at the north labor under the strange delusion that if slaves were emancipated at the south, they would flock to the north. So far from this being the case, in that event, you would see many old and familiar faces back again in the south. The fact is, there are few here who would not return to the south in the event of emancipation. We want to live in the land of our birth, and to lay our bones by the side of our fathers; and nothing short of an intense love of personal freedom keeps us from the south." Increasingly throughout the 1850s and beyond, Douglass depicted slaveholders to be just as much the victims of slavery as their slaves. Indeed, when he met the eighty-year-old Thomas Auld in 1877, they both shed tears, and Douglass remarked, "I did not run away from *you,* but from *slavery.*" Moreover, in an 1859 letter to Hugh Auld (whom he had also abused publicly), Douglass had written, "I love you, but hate slavery"—this to the man whose suppression of his wife's reading instruction of the young slave, says Douglass, led her to become even more of a tyrant than he.[93] Although they cannot be ignored and no doubt contained well-founded elements of mutual affection and respect, such episodes also have the character of wish fulfillment, of emotions strained

tainty of his paternity itself—for strategic purposes. See William S. McFeeley, *Frederick Douglass* (New York: Norton, 1991), p. 13, and Dickson J. Preston, *Young Frederick Douglass: The Maryland Years* (Baltimore: Johns Hopkins University Press, 1980), pp. 27, 34–35, 62, 219n.7.

through the hard press of political devastations on both sides of the color line. Whereas most other slaves and ex-slaves wanted to be buried beside their *black* ancestors in the South, Douglass was hardly alone in having to dream of laying his bones beside those of a *white* man whose love, if it existed at all, was almost certain to have been shot through with disregard and casual brutality. Leaving aside the exact character of Douglass's psychological reconciliation with his white masters, "our fathers" exist in his writings in a state of purposeful ambiguity.

The letter to Auld is especially instructive insofar as it reveals that Thomas Auld the person was less important than Thomas Auld the weapon of humiliation. In an extraordinary instance Douglass had already straightforwardly identified him, in his powerful and widely cited "Farewell Speech to the British People" (1847), as the "father" who had given Douglass to his "uncle" Hugh Auld, thus making possible his controversial purchase by British abolitionists, which allowed him to return safely to the United States.[94] This elision between father and master, though it is conceivable that it came from Douglass's belief that Thomas Auld was his true father, was more likely a trope for the conjunction of sexual exploitation and ownership which lay at the corrupt heart of proslavery paternalism. McFeely may well be correct to say that Douglass "loved" Auld, covering the pain of his necessary break with the master-"father" by draining Auld of any sympathetic personality. Yet Douglass's willingness to flay before all America the man to whom he probably most owed his comparatively good treatment—the man twice responsible for sending him to Baltimore, which allowed him to acquire literacy, a craft, and, finally, the means to escape slavery, and possibly for saving him from lynching after his aborted escape plot at Freeland's farm—suggests how inconsequential was Auld the person next to Auld the sign of slavery.[95]

In case there is any doubt on this score, one need only consider the most sensational thrust of Douglass's persecution of Auld in the public letter:

> How, let me ask, would you look upon me, were I, some dark night, in company with a band of hardened villains, to enter the precincts of your elegant dwelling, and seize the person of your own lovely daughter, Amanda, and carry her off from your family, friends, and all the loved ones of her youth—make her my slave—compel her to work, and I take her wages—place her name on my ledger as property—disregard her personal rights—fetter the powers of her immor-

tal soul by denying her the right and privilege of learning to read and write—feed her coarsely—clothe her scantily, and whip her on the naked back occasionally; more, and still more horrible, leave her unprotected—a degraded victim to the brutal lust of fiendish over-seers, who would pollute, blight, and blast her fair soul—rob her of all dignity—destroy her virtue, and annihilate in her person all the graces that adorn the character of virtuous womanhood?

Such a treatment of Amanda Auld (his onetime childhood companion, with whom he would again form a friendship in the late 1850s) would be no more, Douglass contended, than one might expect of Auld's treatment of Douglass's three "beloved sisters," who were still Auld's property. That there was no evidence to support the charges that Douglass conjures up (nor to support his accusation, later retracted, that Auld had turned out his grandmother, Betsy Bailey, "like an old horse to die in the woods") is not very important.[96] Brutality and sexual exploitation were common enough in southern slaveholding, and it was the institution, not Auld himself, that was Douglass's target—the more so, not less, because his invective conjured up a terrifying spectacle of incestuous violence.

Even without Douglass's identification of Auld as his "father" in the speech of 1847, the "Letter to My Old Master" invited readers to see master and father blend into a single figure and therefore to see staged a challenging psychodrama of slaveholding sexual antagonism. It was one thing for abolitionists leeringly to catalogue the erotic dissipation of the southern plantation;[97] it was quite another for the black man Douglass to issue a hypothetical threat to degrade a young white woman who could be represented symbolically, if not actually, as his half-sister. Douglass may in the public letter have deflected the threat of rape onto vague overseers, but the ambiguity of his own patrimony and his excoriation of Auld suggest that this was but an indirect way to specify the master's own licentiousness. The strength of Douglass's attack rested not just on its calculated sensationalism but also on its intentional, cruel disordering of the idealized "family circle" of slaveholding. No matter that there were instances of affection between masters and slaves, the *institution* of slavery thrived not on the "law of love," as Fitzhugh claimed, but on tearing apart family bonds on the one hand and on discounting white acts of rape and incest on the other. His hypothetical threat to punish and rape Amanda may thus have been a conscious inversion of the notorious scene of the whipping of his Aunt Esther by Aaron Anthony (a primal scene appearing in both the *Narrative* and *My Bondage and My Freedom*), which makes eroticized violence not so much a substitute for as an extension of sexual mastery which acts out the utmost domination of plantation patriarchy.[98] Yet such a displacement on Douglass's part reversed only race, not gender, and his identification with the father, whether Auld or Anthony, was troublingly defined by the very sexual violence it set out to protest. As it risked playing a part that was to become in the wake of Reconstruction the archetypal projection of white racism—the black man as savage rapist—Douglass's polemical fantasy economically represented the sexual dynamics of nineteenth-century racism. In its oedipal replacement of the slaveholding father, its usurpation of his rights, Douglass's scenario was a chilling bifurcation of his own double racial identity, a refashioning of both the slave family and his own family that joined his rights as a "white" son to his revenge as a "black" son. Elsewhere that bifurcation would be more successfully sublimated, but the "Letter to My Old Master" demonstrates that Douglass's most effective political rhetoric sprang from stilled sources of pain that would never find full resolution, even when Douglass masked his search for patrimony and mastery in an identification with the fathers of the Revolution.

"Genealogical trees do not flourish among slaves," Douglass writes in *My Bondage and My Freedom*. "A person of some consequence here in the north, sometimes designated *father,* is literally abolished in slave law and practice." The whimsy and punning is less overt in a later passage: "I say nothing of *father,* for he is shrouded in a mystery I have never been able to penetrate. Slavery does away with fathers as it does away with families. . . . When they *do* exist, they are not the outgrowths of slavery but are antagonistic to that system." By the mid-1850s Douglass had to some degree transcended his desire for revenge against the southern fathers on the one hand and his need to identify with them on the other. The ease, the expansiveness, and even the comic spirit with which he rewrote his life in *My Bondage and My Freedom*—the formal developments that William Andrews has rightly spoken of as Douglass's "novelization" of key elements of his life—were a sign that the manifold activities of his authorship had given him a self-fathering authority that was in its own right a signal of patrimony and freedom.[99] As it became entangled with revolution, the act of literary revision at once rendered Douglass's narration more fraught with ideological and psychological contradictions and liberated him to stage those same contradictions to the fullest purpose. The condition of slavery was one in which the function of the father had been deliberately destabilized, obscured, or altogether emptied out; the condition of American individualism was also one in which the genealogical imperative of the father function had been elided in favor of self-determination. Yet whereas slavery's elision of the father led to an erasure of the self, a total stricture on freedom to act, democracy's elision led to a plenitude of the self, a totalizing capacity to act. In this ironic discrepancy, along this razor's edge, lay the key to Douglass's literary formulation of African American identity, as the discourse of political democracy and the discourse of sentimental domesticity were likewise pried open to include slave culture and black America.

The sacred image of the family, claimed by North and South alike in the debates over slavery, had become part of an ideological conflict that Douglass the public figure could by 1855 more accurately judge and use to advantage as fact, memory, and rhetorical strategy merged into the multi-dimensional phenomenon that Douglass made his life story. Accordingly, his account of his relations with his mother and grandmother—those elements of his life presumably closest to the authenticity of the African American slave experience—are augmented in the changes from the *Narrative* to *My Bondage and My Freedom,* not just in order to tell us more about Douglass's childhood, but also to accentuate Douglass's overarching examination of slaveholding paternalism and its consequent corruption of the family. In the *Narrative,* for example, he writes of the separation of children and mothers: "For what [reason] this separation is done, I do not know, unless it be to hinder the development of the child's affection toward its mother, and to blunt and destroy the natural affection of the mother for the child." The account of Douglass's life with his grandmother, her symbolic carrying of him into slavery at Aaron Anthony's farm at age six, and the scant recollections he has of his mother's visits are all fleshed out and given new emphasis in *My Bondage and My Freedom* in order to underline Douglass's argument that a central purpose of slavery is to obliterate "from the mind and heart of the slave, all just ideas of the sacredness of *the family,* as an institution." Likewise, the extended description of his mother's death in *My Bondage and My Freedom,* about which he had a slight recollection, must be seen to reflect Douglass's own intervening reading of *Uncle Tom's Cabin,* whose popular melodrama now provided an ironic counterpoint to his own vague memories: "Scenes of sacred tenderness, around the deathbed, never forgotten, and which often arrest the vicious and confirm the virtuous during life, must be looked for among the free, though they may sometimes occur among the slaves."

Having "no striking words of hers treasured up," Douglass has to "learn the value of my mother long after her death, and by witnessing the devotion of other mothers to their children."[100]

Because he later discovers that his mother could read, Douglass attributes his "love of letters" to her "native genius," and this mythic ascription further validates the fact that Douglass's maternity, especially as it is portrayed in *My Bondage and My Freedom*, participates as much in the literary construction of an ideological family as does the portrait he draws of his shadowy, anonymous father. The appeal to "scenes of sacred tenderness" that were denied the slave was fictive, of course, in the sense that slave family ties could be as sacred and tender as those of any white family, but moreover in the sense that Douglass's saccharine passage amounted to a virtual quotation from *Uncle Tom's Cabin*, less overtly a subversion of Stowe's ideology of black pacifism than some of Douglass's other allusions but perhaps nonetheless ironic in its pointed circumscription of Stowe's vision. Douglass's rewriting of *Uncle Tom's Cabin* into the fabric of his own narrative traded on its power while at the same time reducing it to a set of impotent racialist conventions. Like his direct quotations from the *Narrative*, however, it was also a thematization not of literacy alone but of public authorship.* Douglass's tracing of the source of his

---

* It seems more than a little paradoxical that Douglass magnifies the largely speculative family of his childhood with rhetorical detail while telling us almost nothing about his own wife and children. For Douglass, however, narrative constructions of the family, like his speculations about his paternity, were part of his rhetorical arsenal, and it may be that far from demeaning his own family by leaving them out of account, Douglass was holding them close to his heart, protected from the kind of abuse that he was ready to heap upon Thomas Auld. Even so, one of the disappointments of the autobiographies is their virtual deletion of his relation with his wife, Anna Murray. The daughter of Bambarra and Mary Murray, Anna was a free black woman who was working as a housekeeper when Douglass met her at a meeting of the East Baltimore Mental Improvement Society after he had been returned to the city a second time, at age eighteen, to live with the Aulds while laboring in a shipyard. Immediately after his escape from slavery in 1838, Anna followed him north to become his wife and eventually the mother of his five children. The relatively greater prominence accorded white women in Douglass's story—beginning with Lucretia and Sophia Auld, but including the British abolitionist Julia Griffiths (reputed by Douglass's detractors to have become his lover for a time), and his second wife, Helen Pitts, a white former secretary whom he married in 1884, two years after the death of Anna—painfully obscures the important personal role played by Anna. The subordination of his own wife and children, and the relatively minor role played by women, especially black women, in Douglass's autobiographies, cannot be overlooked. But such facts are evidence as well that Douglass's narratives corresponded to the male model of most nineteenth-century autobiography and were public political acts with a single goal foremost in view: the establishment of (male) racial equality by the swiftest means. Douglass was, in fact, a constant supporter of women's rights and other

own literacy to his mother may or may not have been justified. Nonetheless, it establishes a motive in his self-creation that is not coincidental in his autobiographical portrait. As a slave, Douglass received his legal identity from his mother, despite the fact that he could barely recall her, and mothers throughout his autobiographies are portrayed as his best teachers. Whereas the southern (white) fathers denied him the weapon of language, mothers were ready to supply it. From them comes not just his legal being but the authority for his true "beginning in the world," which crystallizes in the moment he discovers the means to gain mastery of himself and seize control of his most powerful weapon of liberation—language, or more precisely writing.

Although his autobiographies had a significant readership throughout his lifetime, Douglass's newspaper career was arguably more instrumental in shaping and disseminating his views. Launched in Rochester in 1847 over the objections of Garrison and others, the *North Star* (its name was later changed to *Frederick Douglass' Paper*) made Douglass more independent of white abolitionists and quickly became the most influential black abolitionist newspaper in the country. Despite the fact that it exacerbated his differences with Garrison, Douglass's editorial role gained him a wider audience and augmented his personal campaign to make literacy the most potent weapon in the battle against slavery. "But for the responsibility of conducting a public journal, and the necessity of meeting opposite views from abolitionists in this state," Douglass wrote of his break with Garrison, "I should in all probability have remained as firm in my disunion views as any other disciple of William Lloyd Garrison." Douglass's treatment of the break—which dated to his founding of the *North Star,* perhaps even to the writing of the *Narrative,* but which increased to the point of no return with Douglass's adherence to the Liberty party, his endorsement of the Constitution, and his critique of the limits of pacifistic Christian radicalism—is very brief and restrained. It is absurdly out of proportion

---

reform causes. He attended the Seneca Falls conference in 1848 as an advocate of women's suffrage and frequently spoke in favor of women's political rights both within and beyond the antislavery movement. By the same token, however, he did not hesitate before the war and more openly after, during debate over the Fifteenth Amendment, to argue that suffrage for black men was more important than—and separable from—suffrage for white (and black) women. On Douglass and women's rights, see Waldo E. Martin, Jr., *The Mind of Frederick Douglass* (Chapel Hill: University of North Carolina Press, 1984), pp. 136–64, and Paula Giddings, *When and Where I Enter: The Impact of Black Women on Race and Sex in America* (New York: Bantam, 1984), pp. 57–74.

to Garrison's own vindictive attacks on Douglass, which at their peak led him to print Douglass's articles in the "Refuge of Oppression" column of the *Liberator,* a space normally devoted to proslavery opinion. Yet Douglass's linking of the break to the founding of the *North Star* and his writing and publishing career substantiates the editorial opinion of a contemporary black journal, *The Rising Sun:* "Frederick Douglass' ability as an editor and publisher has done more for the freedom and elevation of his race than all his platform appearances." In the retrospective view of the *Life and Times,* Douglass's longer account of his newspaper career demonstrates that he conceived of it as a signal instance of American self-reliance. "I have come to think," he would write in 1881, "that, under the circumstances, it was the best school possible for me," making it "necessary for me to lean upon myself, and not upon the heads of our antislavery church. . . . There is nothing like the lash and sting of necessity to make a man work, and my paper furnished the motive power." This striking conversion of slavery's whip into the self-wielded work ethic of American success is emblematic of Douglass's postwar role as a black leader, but it also underlines the function of the weekly newspaper in the construction of Douglass the public *author.* "Shut up in the prison-house of bondage," said Douglass in his highly influential 1848 "Address to the Colored People of the United States" at the National Negro Convention in Cleveland, "we are blotted from the page of human existence, and placed beyond the limits of human regard."[101] Not simply the voice but the pen was the key to liberty, no less for black Americans than it had been for the pamphleteers of the revolutionary period. By itself the lecture platform, one might guess, was too much like the auction block; the newspaper, like the autobiography or his one short story, "The Heroic Slave," offered Douglass the opportunity to revise the previous account of his life and publish a new "edition" of himself.

When Douglass issued *My Bondage and My Freedom* in 1855, the revised persona had been shaped by his intervening activities and therefore recast in terms that emphasized the links between literacy, freedom, and revolution. It is not incidental, for instance, that one of the passages in which *My Bondage and My Freedom* expands the *Narrative* is in its account of the contents of *The Columbian Orator,* the text of liberty speeches by which Douglass secretly increased his literacy. In this regard the "dialogue between a master and his slave" that Douglass found there takes on special resonance in the new version. Captured in his attempt to flee, the slave makes an argument for his freedom that vanquishes his master, who immediately emancipates him. "I could not help feeling," writes Douglass, "that the day might come, when the well-directed answers made by the slave to the master, in this instance, would find their counterpart in myself."[102] The inclusion of this new detail in *My Bondage and My Freedom* points severally to Douglass's greater audacity toward the slaveholding audience, to the strategy of conversion dramatized in "The Heroic Slave," and to his access of power distinct from that associated with the Garrisonians. Douglass's revision of the passage about *The Columbian Orator* underscores the act of literacy in every way in order to show—Frantz Fanon to the contrary—that the acquisition of the "colonizer's" language need not be simply a new form of enslavement.[103] Douglass was far from contemptuous of slave culture and slave language, and *My Bondage and My Freedom,* it should be said again, is notable for its increased atttention to the details of African American folk life on the plantation. Nevertheless, Douglass was realistic about the need to appropriate the tools of the master. He could do so, according to his calculation, only by standing outside the broken language of the surrounding slaves—"I could not have been dropped anywhere on the globe, where I could reap less, in the way of knowledge, from my immediate associates, than on this plantation," he writes in a blunt, dismaying passage—which he considered a mark of the ignorance intentionally stamped on slaves by the southern regime, and by embracing the colonizer's own political language. It is likely that Douglass would have taken a somewhat ironic view of Alexander Crummell's contemporary claim that, as a language of force, power, and freedom, English was indisputably an "enshrinement of those great charters of liberty which are essential elements of free governments, and the main guarantees of personal liberty."[104] But his willingness not simply to make it his own language but indeed to claim that the high political ideals enshrined in it belonged rightfully to African Americans was the strongest sign that the achievement of freedom superseded all else. Such a choice meant that the elements of slave culture to which Chesnutt, Du Bois, Hurston, and others would return as a fundamental source of African American consciousness and cultural power, and on which Delany and Jacobs drew more forthrightly in the antislavery cause, were strictly subordinated in Douglass's revisions of the archetypal slave narrative.

The power of literacy, of course, stood in contrast to the folk culture of slavery in Douglass's view less for any inherent reason than because literacy was a weapon of resistance frequently forbidden to slaves. Anti-literacy laws, made more restrictive in the wake of Turner's 1831 uprising, were often justified philosophically on the grounds that slaves, because they were not fit for the exercise of democratic rights, would misunderstand the power given them by literacy or be misled by abolitionist propaganda. In his proslavery tract *Liberty and Slavery: Or, Slavery in the Light of Moral and Political Philosophy* (1860), for example, the Virginian Albert Taylor Bledsoe argued that laws directed against slave learning and abolitionist writings were based on the fact that African Americans could "neither comprehend the nature, nor enjoy the blessings, of the freedom which is officially thrust upon them. [For] if the Negro race should be moved by their appeals, it would only be to rend and tear in pieces the fair fabric of American liberty . . . by far the most beautiful ever yet conceived or constructed by the genius of man." When he tied his lessons in reading and writing to an initial attempt to learn the meaning of the talismanic word "abolition," which he had heard in connection with acts of slave resistance, Douglass overturned the central tenet of proslavery ideology. Slavery had the power, Douglass knew, "to write *indelible* sorrow, at a single dash, over the heart of a child"; his writing, in reply, must have the power to undo the text of slavery.[105] Crummell's accommodation to the language of the oppressors was preferable to Bledsoe's racist argument that black America could not be trusted with either the political power it guaranteed or the liberty it promised.

Throughout *My Bondage and My Freedom* Douglass drills into his reader the fact that literacy is linked to the power to enslave and, alternatively, the power to create one's own subjectivity and redeem one's community. In the well-known passage about Hugh Auld's forbidding his reading instruction, which concludes "from that moment I understood the direct pathway from slavery to freedom," Douglass begins in the *Narrative:* "These words sank deep into my heart, stirred up sentiments within that lay slumbering, and called into existence an entirely new train of thought." In *My Bondage and My Freedom,* however, the passage begins: "His iron sentences—cold and harsh—sunk deep into my heart, and stirred up not only my feelings into a sort of rebellion, but awakened within me a slumbering train of vital thought." The essential lesson, that language is the key to "the *white* man's power to perpetuate the enslavement of the *black* man," is the same in both texts. But against those who argue that the second version of Douglass's life is verbose or loosely structured, this passage, among others, displays not just a greater philosophical depth and clarity on Douglass's part but also a firmer command of irony, one that informs both the verbal surface of the texts and the drama of masking and double personality which he has discovered his own life to be. His characterization of himself as an object to be stolen, what he alludes to as his "mastery" of the alphabet, and Auld's "iron sentences," which here take their place alongside passages devoted to the "cold, cruel iron" power of Aaron Anthony, the "iron cage" at Easton into which the plotting Douglass is thrown, the "iron grating of my house of bondage," and the "iron-like" institution of Lloyd's enormous plantation which echo throughout *My Bondage and My Freedom*—all these revisions suggest that the "opposition of my master" to which Douglass attributes his literacy, as much as to Sophia Auld's initial kindness, contains now a more vivid struggle which unfolds along paternal, or more accurately paternalistic, lines. The language of the fathers offers two choices: capitulation and ignorance, or resistance and knowledge. Literacy is linked to the power to enslave and, alternatively, the power to liberate and father oneself. Hugh Auld stands now more emphatically in the book's sequence of fathers that leads toward the revolutionary fathers themselves, against whom Douglass in the 1850s was working to define himself yet again as though in "opposition to my master."[106]

The speeches Douglass reads in *The Columbian Orator* add to his "limited stock of language" and allow him "to give tongue to many interesting thoughts, which had frequently flashed through my soul, and died away for want of utterance." In *My Bondage and My Freedom,* however, this literacy takes on a special tone. Sheridan's "bold denunciation of slavery, and . . . vindication of human rights" becomes his "powerful denunciation of oppression, and . . . most brilliant vindication of the rights of man." Not the "silver trump of freedom" but "Liberty! the inestimable birthright of every man" now rouses Douglass; and the much extended passage becomes a virtual oration itself, yoking together spoken and written powers, attacking religion as the opiate of the slaves, and indulging in rhetoric at once revolutionary and sentimentally gothic: "Knowledge had come; light had penetrated the moral dungeon where I dwelt; and, behold! there lay the bloody whip, for my back, and here was the iron chain; and my good, *kind master,* he was the author of my situation."[107] It is exactly such language that some modern readers have found most regrettable in *My Bondage and My Freedom*. Yet the text reminds us often that the language of revolutionary liberation and the rising language of sentiment, with its cultivation of the virtues of compassion and sympathetic identification with an inferior class or the oppressed, are virtually synonymous, not just in the best antislavery writing but in the whole era's grappling with the problem of bondage. The literature of American slavery transplants the language of oppression and liberation from the continental Romantic tradition, where it had been a particular spur to Britain's successful antislavery movement, into a new national setting where it is bound together with the language of sentiment derived from the Revolution.

Douglass's lectures frequently burlesqued the purported paternalism of slavery and held up the slave codes themselves, along with abundant fugitive testimony to the institution's brutality, in counterpoint. Just as he tired of showing the scars on his own back, however, Douglass tended not to focus on instances of brutality but rather, as his own rhetoric become more engaged in the moral justification of violent slave resistance, increased his concentration on the *ideology* of brutality. He could do so all the more effectively because he saw, as he argued in a speech of 1846, that "the whip, the chain, the gag, the thumb-screw, the bloodhound, the stocks, and all the other bloody paraphernalia of the slave system are indispensably necessary to the relation of master and slave. The slave must be subjected to these, or he ceases to be a slave."[108] In *My Bondage and My Freedom* the greater detail in Douglass's descriptions of incidents of whipping is thus not simply a function of the book's rhetorical ornamentation. Rather, the gothic, as Douglass learned from Stowe and others, had become a powerful instrument of social reform. Gothic was the psychic nightmare of sentimentality, whose central novelistic strategy was the elicitation of compassion for the marginalized—women, the lower classes, prisoners, the insane, children, and, most of all in America, slaves. Nonetheless, if the primary vector of sentimentality pointed in the direction of increased democracy, a broader extension of rights to the marginalized and oppressed,[109] the rhetoric of sentimentality could also be appropriated by proslavery paternalism. Again, George Fitzhugh is exemplary: "Besides wife and children, brothers and sister[s], dogs, horses, birds and flowers—slaves, also, belong to the family circle."[110] Protection and incarceration were one in the logic of proslavery, whereas protection and liberation were one in antislavery's version of compassion. Like the language of liberty, the language of sentiment offered parallel but distinct courses. Following the example of Stowe, Douglass exploited the fact that slavery contradicted sentimentality's extension of rights. In his case, however, the primary tropes of family and home became archetypes of the nation-state not by virtue of a visionary feminism, a new rule of domesticity, but by their identification with the "manly" principles of revolutionary politics.

Stowe was willing to grant African Americans the language of sentiment, but she withheld the language of liberty.

Scenes of punishment for Douglass therefore operate on a different plane and with different consequences than in *Uncle Tom's Cabin*. In both instances the depiction of gothic punishment extracts benevolence from the sublime; sadistic terror is made to yield pity and compassion alongside arousal and fear (although in the case of Anthony's whipping of Esther, as I have suggested, Douglass's potential identification with the master-father makes male voyeurism an even more pronounced element of benevolence). But for Stowe the whipping death of Uncle Tom, the novel's extreme instance of paternal corruption, leads to a martyrdom in which nonresistance is a special source of feminized, spiritual power; revolt is for men like George Harris who have the "Anglo Saxon blood" of the revolutionary fathers coursing through their veins and are thus, ironically, the only blacks capable of leading the revolt if ever the "San Domingo hour comes" in the United States. Tom's crucifixion by Legree has powerful emotive consequences but, in the novel, lacks an applicable political meaning; the final deliverance from slavery, as the novel portrays it with no little ironic tension, will come from the paternalistic white God in his good time. For Douglass, on the contrary, punishment is the source of both particularized physical resistance and a principled revolutionary ideology. He borrows various scenes from the stock vocabulary of antislavery (his sketch of Mr. Sevier, who dies "uttering horrid oaths and flourishing the cowskin, as though he was tearing the flesh off some helpless slave" is akin to Simon Legree's descent into insanity), yet for the Douglass of *My Bondage and My Freedom,* the gothic was not a trap of sentimentality, of issueless compassion. Rather, it was a means of exposing the ideology of enslavement: to be punished was to be a slave; to resist punishment was to be free.[111] Both Nat Turner's millenarian climax and Uncle Tom's liberation through prayer and suffering are thus secularized, as we will see, in Douglass's "resurrection" through acts of resistance and revolution.

No longer are the stripes of suffering, the slave's physical body as an object of horror and compassion, at the center of Douglass's argument in *My Bondage and My Freedom*. Instead, the whip itself displays the semiotics of power. The added peroration to the overseer's cowskin ("it condenses the whole strength of the arm to a single point, and comes with a spring that makes the air whistle"); the new (and perhaps apocryphal) anecdote about Colonel Lloyd's "white" slave son, William Wilkes, whom he tries pathetically to whip before selling; the greater detail in Captain Anthony's erotically charged whipping of Esther; the expanded accounts of the whipping of other slaves such as Douglass's cousin Henny, whose Christian master indulged in the greatest cruelties while quoting with "blood-chilling blasphemy" the passage from Luke that Nat Turner had put to such ironic use ("'That servant which knew his lord's will, and prepared not himself, neither did according to his will, shall be beaten with many stripes'"); the ambiguous suggestion that his regular whipping by Anthony was "such as any heedless and mischievous boy might get from his father"; and the new story of Doctor (Uncle) Isaac Copper, the old slave who teaches slave children the "Our Father" of the Lord's Prayer with whip in hand—the cumulative purpose of such passages is to demonstrate the infectious power of power itself, the fact that "everybody, in the south, wants the privilege of whipping somebody else."[112] The whip permeates and defines slaveholding paternalism, breaking across the white-black boundary to contaminate and enslave all. In Charles Chesnutt's "The Web of Circumstance" the purported theft of a white planter's whip by a black man symbolically challenges the hierarchy of racial superiority that remains in place after emancipation; in *My Bondage and My Freedom* the whip is likewise the icon of white masculinity coveted even by those who most often feel its punishing power. Without question the whip, as Stowe and Jacobs certainly recognized, was as much a sign of sexual as of racial power. It is crucial, however, to keep in view the fact that Douglass entered the antislavery argument from a vantage point that demanded that his acquisition of power, his capacity to act, be defined in specifically masculine terms. Tom was a "thing"; Douglass would be a "man."

The whip is therefore the primary metonym of Douglass's more precisely characterized total institution of slavery and as such puts his dramatization of the climactic resistance to Covey in the position of moral exemplum, with Douglass standing spiritually, if not yet physically, outside the confinement of slavery. In complete opposition to Stowe's popular hero, he stands also outside the confining circle of antislavery paternalism which had marked his career through the *Narrative,* "roused to an attitude of manly independence." As Douglass concludes after his struggle with Covey: "When a slave cannot be flogged he is more than half free. He has a domain as broad as his own manly heart to defend, and he is really '*a power on earth.*'"[113]

One need not consent to the much-debated thesis originated by Stanley Elkins that, in its brutal dehumanization of slaves and inducement in them of an imitative pattern of behavioral bondage, the plantation resembles the concentration camp, the prison, or other total institutions, in order to be struck by this aspect of Douglass's revision of his life portrait in *My Bondage and My Freedom*.[114] Douglass's interest in the comprehensive ideology of power is evident to begin with in his new account of Lloyd's immense plantation. Not only does he give a fuller picture of slave life, but the greater detail and the gothic emphasis on the plantation's self-sufficient, dark seclusion, maintained by diverse labor and transbay trade on Lloyd's own vessels, create out of this deceptively abundant "Eden-like" garden world a veritable heart of darkness. Both the size of Lloyd's estate and his prominent public role as governor and senator allow Douglass to expand his own unusual experience into a national emblem of institutional slavery. In this era of reform movements and utopian communal projects, the plantation posed as a pastoral asylum in which state control and paternal coercion alike imprisoned the slave in a corrupt "family"—one he might belong to by blood but not by law—and fused the theory of property in man with the sexuality of power. Like Lloyd's estate, it functioned with the near impunity of a "pirate ship" while presenting to the world, at least in proslavery argument, an idyllic facade of paternalism. The apotheosis of the total institution of slavery lay for Douglass in its own contradictory appeal to the trope of domesticity and the masculine ruling ideal, both likewise descended from the revolutionary era—to this "double relation of master and father" as he called it in the *Narrative* before making it the defining figure of *My Bondage and My Freedom*.[115]

At the same time, Douglass's comparative advantages left him in a unique position to see the slaveholding regime's pervasive power without being crushed by it. Douglass was hardly alone in his refusal to capitulate to the coercion of proslavery thought. For one thing, total power was an illusion (for slaveholders and theoreticians such as Elkins alike), as virtually the entire record of slave culture—that is, the writing, oral narrative, music, religious practice, and so on—would indicate. In addition, any recognition of reciprocal powers and dependencies on the plantation revealed that paternalism was but the rhetorical shadow of rule by force, and in this respect Douglass was among countless slaves who made the master's appeal to discipline their own weapon of resistance. Both the surrender of the slave's will and the slaveholder's recourse to unlimited force in order to command such a surrender, as Eugene Genovese has suggested, were contradicted by the least recognition of reciprocity and resistance.[116]

Douglass was that contradiction writ large. In rhetorically heightening the "total institution" of proslavery ideology, he recognized neither its abstract truth nor its power over slaves, but only its discursive posture, its corrosive use of the languages of benevolent care and liberty for purposes that mocked both. In doing so, he represented a choice between the contrasting "iron sentences" of two paternalistic ideals, between doubled ineluctable forces in the language of American liberty that claimed common ancestors. The total institution of slavery, that is to say, became ranged against its antagonist, the total institution of revolutionary democracy. However complete their entanglement up through the 1850s, Douglass insisted that they be torn apart.

Broken Fetters: The Right of Revolution

> We few, we happy few, we band of brothers.
> For he today that sheds his blood with me
> Shall be my brother.
>
> Shakespeare, *Henry V*

Douglass entered the postrevolutionary era's debate about the authority of the founding fathers—in particular its paralysis on the problem of slavery—from a compelling angle, a fact that is seen in his 1854 response to the murder of James Batchelder, one of Anthony Burns's "kidnappers" (Batchelder was in fact serving as a temporary United States marshal). Burns, a fugitive eventually returned to slavery in Virginia after President Pierce ordered out federal troops to quell the disturbance surrounding his trial in Boston, became one of antislavery's central martyrs, and Douglass's view of the attempt to free him reveals from the field, as it were, the meaning of the patriotic and sentimental rhetoric that would so mark his second autobiography a year later. Invoking the bloodstained streets of Boston within sight of the Bunker Hill Monument, Douglass compares Batchelder's murder to the "slaughter of a ravenous wolf in the act of throttling an infant." This, Douglass says, is the real character of the South's benevolent paternalism. We hardly need weep for Batchelder's "*widow and fatherless*" children, when the Fugitive Slave Law "had *no tears* for the *widows and orphans* of poor innocent fugitives," least of all in this revolutionary city "where the blood of the oppressor was poured out in torrents making thousands of *widows and orphans*."[117]

Douglass's invocation of the Bunker Hill Monument inevitably brought to mind Webster's famous speeches on the monument's iconic meaning. In 1825 Webster had chosen a popular rhetorical figure (later echoed to different effect by Emerson in the opening of *Nature*) in order to celebrate the laying of the cornerstone of the monument. As a race of "children" standing "among the sepulchres of the fathers," Webster counseled, Americans should be thankful that the "great wheel of political revolution," which started turning in America but soon spread "conflagration and terror" around the world, issued here in tranquillity and prosperity. In the spirit of nationalism with which we are blessed, the American children should accept as their great duty the "defense and preservation" of the fathers' creation, the cultivation of "a true spirit of union and harmony." When the monument was completed in 1843, its "foundations in soil which drank deep of early Revolutionary blood," Webster again commemorated the fathers, especially Washington, but spoke ominously against the day when the American Union "should be broken up and destroyed" and "faction and dismemberment obliterate for ever all the hopes of the founders of our republic and the great inheritance of our children." Contemptuously alluding to Webster's "noble words" at Bunker Hill, "the spot so reddened with the blood of our fathers," Theodore Parker replied to Webster that "the question is, not if slavery is to cease, and soon to cease, but shall it end as it ended in Massachusetts, in New Hampshire, in Pennsylvania, in New York, or shall it end as in St. Domingo? Follow the counsel of Mr. Webster—it will end in fire and blood." In courting the attacks of Emerson (who would caricature Webster, following his support for the Compromise of 1850, as "the head of the slavery party" in the United States), Parker, and others, Webster illustrated the crisis that convulsed the Union and made appeals to the spirit of the Revolution ironic, if not, as Emerson said of the Fugitive Slave Law, "suicidal." Perhaps, however, the vision of the fathers and the suicide of the sons were entangled. As early as his 1838 Lyceum address, a speech that stigmatized mob violence against abolitionists and the lynching of blacks "suspected of conspiring to raise an insurrection," Lincoln had warned that "as a nation of freemen we must live through all time, or die by suicide."[118]

To maintain the Union in the face of the contradiction between liberty and slavery was to court suicide. The entrapments of perpetual union and perpetual youth inflicted upon the postrevolutionary generations a paralysis on the issue of slavery that was not broken until Lincoln, a figure equal to the founding fathers' heroic stature, embraced and overcame them at the same time, saving the union *and*—expediently or not—abolishing slavery.[119] During the 1850s Douglass's oratory, which was said by some observers to rival that of both Webster and Lincoln, was frequently built upon precisely these themes, as was his most important writing. Webster, until his death, remained locked in the revolutionary fathers' paralyzing grip; Lincoln appropriated the fathers' power in order to return it to the true course of democratic liberty. When Douglass invoked the Bunker Hill Monument to lacerate the captors of Anthony Burns, however, Webster was dead and Lincoln was still following the moderate proslavery course that would rule American politics until the cataclysm of war finally forced him to act against the peculiar institution. In the decade preceding the Civil War, Frederick Douglass was the truer "son," the truer inheritor of the flawed yet redeemable ideals of the Revolution. In his speech on Burns, the sacrifice of the revolutionary fathers links the murdered proslavery father to the enslaved black father. The appeal to revolutionary sentiment that characterizes the most eloquent defenses of Union throughout the 1850s is thus used by Douglass not just to capitalize on the commonplace antislavery defense of domestic virtues but also to probe his own double identity. Douglass's gradual conversion from Garrisonian pacifism to an acceptance of violent slave resistance entailed, in essence, killing the white fathers of proslavery and antislavery alike in order to save the widows and orphans of black America.

The new invocations of Nat Turner in *My Bondage and My Freedom* suggest, as do a number of Douglass's speeches, that his heroes would be not white patriots alone but black patriots such as Joseph Cinque and Madison Washington as well. Throughout the late 1840s and early 1850s Douglass condemned American aggrandizement in Mexico and the Caribbean, and invoked the 1848 European revolutions as models of action, calling in the most notorious speech, an 1849 attack on the American Colonization Society, for a slave uprising in which "sable arms which had been engaged in beautifying and adorning the South [would be] engaged in spreading death and devastation there." The revolutionary fathers, like Thomas Auld, had become weapons in the battle against slavery, but the blockage in their own power could be broken only by placing *black* fathers among their ranks. In "Men of Color," his famous 1863 call to arms of black troops, Douglass would invoke the black followers of John Brown, Denmark Vesey, and Nat Turner. Like Henry Highland Garnet in his "Address to the Slaves of the United States," that is to say, he made black fathers part of the pantheon and spoke with the fierce irony echoed by

William Wells Brown in his 1854 lecture and book, *St. Domingo: Its Revolution and Its Patriots,* in which Washington the slaveholder is ridiculed as the despotic father of a slave nation and Toussaint L'Ouverture celebrated as the patriot leader of a people. Whereas proslavery ideologues such as Thomas Dew warned that abolitionist propaganda would tear down the slave "family" and its white paternal structure of protection, making slaves *"parricides* instead of *patriots,"* Douglass said that parricide was a necessary consequence of patriotism.[120] If the white postrevolutionary generations remained paralyzed in the face of the fathers' ambiguous authority on the law of slavery, the black generations were, in fact, not yet *post*revolutionary at all. For them in particular, the Age of Revolution—not just in the United States but throughout the slaveholding New World—was far from over.

One of the most significant indexes of Douglass's changed conception of himself as a black leader during the early 1850s may be found in his only work of fiction, "The Heroic Slave." Appearing in an 1853 gift book entitled *Autographs for Freedom* (a collection of antislavery statements edited by Julia Griffiths to raise money for the financially troubled *North Star*), the story is a compelling reconstruction of the events leading up to the 1841 slave revolt aboard the *Creole,* an American slave ship, led by Madison Washington. But it also has resonant autobiographical overtones and may be read as Douglass's own "autograph for freedom," the signature of his declaration of liberty through escalating acts of literacy and rebellion that extend the fictive dimension of his self-authorization. Madison Washington appeared in Douglass's speeches as early as the 1847 lectures in Britain, and he is featured in a resounding 1849 address at a New York Anti-Colonization Society meeting as a model of African American achievement. As Douglass announced in his tirade against the official posture of the government, which sought the return of the escaped rebels after they had landed in the Bahamas and been granted freedom by British authorities, it was "a black man, with wholly head [*sic*], high cheek bones, protruding lip, distended nostril, and retreating forehead, [who] had mastery of that ship." And in his 1857 address "West India Emancipation," one of Douglass's most radical orations, he cited the examples of Joseph Cinque, Nat Turner, and Madison Washington in arguing that violent slave insurrectionary movements could act as a catalyst to abolition in the United States as they had in the British West Indies.[121]

Madison Washington was, however, more than a justification of slave violence for Douglass; he was also a figure around which to gather Douglass's most characteristic arguments about liberty. In the final segment of the short story, Douglass has his interlocutors—the *Creole*'s first mate, Tom Grant, and Jack Williams, an "old salt" who is denigrating the crew's handling of the revolt—place the central legal question of the incident, the "right of revolution," within the context of the story's appeal to a Romantic natural rights philosophy. Defending the crew's failure to put down the black rebels, Grant contends: "It is one thing to manage a company of slaves on a Virginia plantation, and quite another thing to quell an insurrection on the lonely billows of the Atlantic, where every breeze speaks of courage and liberty. For the negro to act cowardly on shore, may be to act wisely. . . . During all the storm [which swept over the ship soon after the revolt], Madison stood firmly at the helm,—his keen eye fixed upon the binnacle. . . . The first words he uttered after the storm had slightly subsided, were characteristic of the man. 'Mr. mate, you cannot write the bloody laws of slavery on those restless billows. The ocean, if not the land, is free.'" To the surprise of his audience, the first mate confesses that the color bar alone is all that would prevent him from following the superior Madison Washington, whose motivation is nothing less than the "principles of 1776."[122]

It is the distinction drawn between land and sea—by implication a distinction between state law by force and natural law by right—that bears most closely on the actual case of the *Creole* revolt. The United States government, led by Secretary of State Daniel Webster and acting on behalf of proslavery interests, argued for the return of the slaves as legal Virginia "property" by referring to the previous revolt aboard the slave ship *Amistad* in 1839. In that case African slaves aboard a Spanish ship bound for a Cuban port seized the ship and sailed up the North American coast, where they were taken into custody off Long Island. After lengthy negotiations and trials, the United States Supreme Court ruled that the slaves must be freed because the ship that carried them was doing so *illegally*, Spain having outlawed the slave trade in 1820. The *Amistad* case, which bears also upon *Benito Cereno* and *Blake*, therefore offered a converse precedent for the *Creole*, which had been engaged in a domestic, coastal transport of slaves that was legal according to United States law. Arguments made on behalf of the *Creole*'s rebel slaves rested on appeals to the distinction between land and sea of just the kind that Douglass repeats in the first mate's tale. In the most notorious instance, Ohio congressman Joshua Giddings introduced House resolutions arguing that the *Creole*, having left the territorial waters of Virginia, was no longer subject to its state laws but rather to the federal jurisdiction of commerce on the high seas. The Constitution, he said, did not authorize the government to seek either the return of the slaves or redress, for slaves on the high seas were subject only to the "law of nature," which compelled them to seek their freedom. Likewise, a pamphlet by the antislavery theorist William Jay argued, as had John Quincy Adams in his famous *Amistad* brief, that the *Creole* rebels were governed only by the "universal law of nature." In language that Douglass seems deliberately to have echoed in this particular and others, Jay contended that "the case is stronger for Liberty on the ocean than on the land—for the Earth may be, has been, subjugated by the iron hand of Power; but the free, the untamed Sea, disdains the puny grasp of the mightiest of earthly despots." For that reason, the slaves' resistance was consistent with the right of revolution; it could not be "called mutiny or murder—because they [were] violating no law by such resistance, but on the contrary vindicating their natural freedom—the gift of God alike to all."[123]

Neither Giddings nor Jay intended the logic of his arguments to respect the strict difference between sea and land; like Douglass, each meant to provide a legal theory for the *natural* right of revolution belonging to slaves generally. As the proslavery *Baltimore Sun* warned, if Giddings's resolution had passed, it would have been tantamount to placing a knife in the hands of every slave and encouraging him to kill his masters.[124] (The House agreed, voting overwhelmingly to censure Giddings.) Legal contention over the *Creole* was from the outset intertwined with diplomatic tensions with Britain. Once the slaves had been freed in Nassau, moreover, the only question left was redress, which would not be decided until 1855— the year *My Bondage and My Freedom* was published—when it was determined by a claims commission that the slaves had been "property" aboard a ship on a lawful voyage and that they therefore remained subject to the laws of Virginia. Although Douglass was not much concerned with the technicalities of international law that came into play in the diplomatic debate about the *Creole,* the central issues of the illegality of the slave trade (more specifically the glaring contradiction latent in the fact that the United States had outlawed international slave trade but not domestic trade), the right of revolution, and the appeal to the law of nature are everywhere evident in "The Heroic Slave."

Whereas Douglass's speeches place some emphasis on Madison Washington's African features, his blackness, and on his relationship to other black rebels such as Turner and Cinque, "The Heroic Slave" is carefully modulated to appeal to a white antislavery audience and dwells more on the principles of revolution than on the actual revolt aboard the *Creole*. The story as presented by Douglass contains both a standard slave narrative (Madison's escape and his return to rescue his wife) and a discourse on the right of revolution within several layers of white narrative frame. The tales told by Listwell, the converted abolitionist who aids Washington (a figure probably modeled on the abolitionist James Gurney), and by the first mate, who says he would follow Madison Washington but for his color, are transparent attempts by Douglass to gain white recognition of African American heroism and revolutionary rights. Madison Washington is portrayed as a conventional Byronic hero, a figure of "mesmeric power which is the invariable accompaniment of genius," whose leadership is as much philosophical as physical. In "The Heroic Slave" Douglass downplays his hero's African features and diminishes Madison Washington's role in the violence, although in this respect he may simply have followed the congressional testimony, which showed that Washington and another rebel restrained their comrades from killing the whites. (In his sketch of Washington in *The Black Man, His Antecedents, His Genius, and His Achievements* [1863], in contrast, William Wells Brown made his hero more central to the violence of the revolt.) Extrapolating—indeed, inventing—on the basis of very little information about Washington's life (what Douglass refers to as mere "marks, traces, possibles, and probabilities"), he also accentuates Washington's strength, courage, and masculinity in such a way as to make him a model classical hero with Old Testament and Greek analogues. His account therefore strips Washington of his own personalized black voice at the same time that it distances him from the claims to liberty belonging to every common slave. As Richard Yarborough has argued, however, Douglass's stylized construction of an overtly "masculine" black hero derives both from his need to create an ideal palatable to white readers and from the well-established tradition of appeal for black political rights as the just desert of democratic "manhood," which paradoxically had to be made exceptional in order to be made visible at all to white America.[125]

Because revolution is both a psychological and a political act in Douglass's short story, his focus on Washington's solitude and his power to persuade others through the medium of his voice suggests that his hero is located at once in the private, Romantic discourse of revolution as an act of imagination and cognition, and in the pragmatic public discourse of Douglass's own antislavery career. Madison Washington's liberation is not a physical act alone but also one of liberating consciousness. Hence Douglass's invocation of the panoply of natural life—birds and reptiles that are more free than Washington—and his portrait of the Romantic mind infused with Enlightenment language which pervades Washington's plaintive soliloquy in the woods:

> A giant's strength, but not a giant's heart was in him. His broad mouth and nose spoke only of good nature and kindness. But his voice, that unfailing index of his soul, though full and melodious, had that in it which could terrify as well as charm. . . . There came another gush from the same full fountain; now bitter, and now sweet. Scathing denunciations of the cruelty and injustice of slavery; heart-touching narrations of his own personal suffering, intermingled with prayers to the God of the oppressed for help and deliverance, were followed by presentations of the dangers and difficulties of escape, and formed the burden of his eloquent utterances; but his high resolution clung to him,—for he ended each speech by an emphatic declaration of his purpose to be free.

The court cases concerning the revolts aboard the *Amistad* and the *Creole* had failed to establish a legal right to revolution, declaring only that existing law did not allow the rebels to be reenslaved, not that natural law transcended the rule of slavery. Douglass's story was one means of altering the philosophical basis of legalism. Through the heroic figure of Madison Washington, who speaks to an audience open to the double rhetoric of benevolence and liberty, he sought to bridge the distance between the law of the land (state law) and the law of the sea (natural law). His mythic portrait of the revolutionary cannily exploits the domestic cult of George Washington as a hybrid paternal and maternal figure but subverts its inherent conservatism by making Madison Washington, the *African American* Virginian rebel, an archetypal slave patriot, able to articulate his ideal of liberty: "We have done that which you applaud your fathers for doing, and if we are murderers, so were they."[126] Or, as William Jay had argued, the revolt did not involve an act of "murder" at all.

The loosely parallel facts of Washington's and Douglass's lives, Robert Stepto has suggested, support the implication that "The Heroic Slave" belongs to the series of "acts of literacy" through which Douglass defined his increasing independence and augmented his public stature. As a further means of staging himself as both subject and object of his autobiographical act—of constructing a public persona that extended the facts of his slave life into a national archetype—Douglass's fictive story can therefore be seen as part of the bridge of activities linking the two autobiographies. Its primary rhetorical form, in which a fugitive slave, by the power of his character and his eloquent story, converts a white man to antislavery, echoes the unlikely role in which Douglass, punning on the chattelism of his former identity, placed himself as a young editor: "A slave, brought up in the very depths of ignorance, assuming to instruct highly civilized people of the north in the principles of liberty, justice, and humanity! The thing looked absurd." Even more so, the representation of Washington was an idealized figuring of Douglass the orator—but perhaps not too idealized, as a contemporary judgment about one of Douglass's speeches would suggest: "It was the volcanic outbreak of human nature, long pent up in slavery and at last bursting its imprisonment. It was a storm of insurrection . . . [that] reminded me of Toussaint among the plantations of Haiti. There was great oratory in his speech, but more of dignity and earnestness than what we call eloquence. He was not up as a speaker, performing. He was an insurgent slave, taking hold on the right of speech, and charging on his tyrants the bondage of his race."[127] Like his invention of the story of Washington, Douglass's invention of himself created subjectivity by internalizing mastery, standing outside of chattelism as a "thing" that had been escaped and transcended, and putting himself on the same stage with both the white and the black heroes of the Age of Revolution.

In defining for himself a role of public leadership analogous to that of Madison Washington, Douglass deepened and complicated the intricate symbolism of fathers that preoccupied him in so much of his autobiographical work. The coincidence of his two names—"it seemed as if the souls of both the great dead (whose names he bore) had entered him" in the very act of revolt, says the first mate—underscores Madison Washington's role as a founding father in both personal and national terms. The black father Madison Washington performs two functions, filling the gap left by the real father, or the desired black father, in Douglass's own life (thus repairing the slave family) and filling the gap left by slavery in the revolutionary paradigm of the founding fathers (thus repairing the democratic family). In his identification with Washington, Douglass composes for himself a mask or fictive self made up of the absent father who so absorbs his attention in the opening chapters of *My Bondage and My Freedom*, the black rebel slave who leads others to freedom *and* converts a white audience to antislavery, and the founding fathers whose rhetoric of democratic liberty punctuates his writing after 1848 and begins fully to flower in the break with Garrison. Madison Washington gains his freedom with Listwell's aid and, one might say, by means of his problematic "white" ideology. But the fact that many of the national fathers were slaveholders themselves and that Douglass must therefore employ as his central weapon a discourse and a mythology shot through with irony does not, as some readers have contended, invalidate his struggle in the least. Rather, it illustrates the crucial symbolic truth that Douglass builds into "The Heroic Slave." Once the *Creole* has been taken, Madison Washington announces his new command: "All resistance to my authority will be in vain. My men have won their liberty, with no other weapons but their own BROKEN FETTERS."[128]

"Broken fetters" are the very weapons Douglass used throughout his career. The trope encompasses his resistance to and escape from slavery itself using the tools of the master—his language, his learned craft, his guarded benevolence. And it encompasses the master himself, that is, the patrimony that begins as an imprisoning nightmare of ambiguous origins for Douglass but is fashioned into his ideology and his discourse of resistance. Most of all, "broken fetters," as the *Creole* case underlying "The Heroic Slave" helps us to see, refers to the "right of revolution" drawn from the "law of nature"—a right that, whatever its betrayal by the continuing sin of slavery, was a liberating ideology (as it would remain for numerous revolutions on through the twentieth century). For Douglass, as for any slave or, indeed, any African American, the ideology of the founding fathers unavoidably presented an ironic enigma that is summed up well in the words of the title of Douglass's revised life story, "my bondage and my freedom." The account of life in the North demonstrates, of course, that freedom is partial at best; there is no stark line drawn between bondage and freedom except in pure legal or physical terms, and the whole of Douglass's revised book goes to suggest that the apparently polar terms have fluid significations. Nonetheless, the notion that the language of the Revolution was but a new form of totalizing imprisonment, a thorough mockery of freedom, is a view that would have been anathema to Douglass. To be sure, the national promise of freedom and equal rights had not been kept; the promise remained in fetters. But, Douglass said, the fetters had been broken and turned into weapons of resistance, and it was African American men and women most of all who had done this already and who were willing to continue the struggle, by violence if necessary. To borrow Nat Turner's words, Douglass was prepared to "slay my enemies with their own weapons."[129]

Readers unwilling to recognize this strategy in Douglass's development as a thinker and a writer will be hard pressed to appreciate the power of *My Bondage and My Freedom,* which is stylized, even melodramatic, in its exclamations of the right of revolution. The tendency for *My Bondage and My Freedom* to become an oration, however, is hardly a mark of its failure of coherence, for oratory was the crux of Douglass's identity and his primary vehicle for the construction of himself as an actor in the rowdy theater of antislavery politics. The revisions of *My Bondage and My Freedom* in this vein include the many significant reformulations of his origins and literacy, noted earlier, and major statements of Douglass's mature political philosophy which drew on his wider experience as a speaker and a writer. Both the self-consciousness and the subtle sense of a predominantly sentimental audience evident in "The Heroic Slave" are played upon throughout *My Bondage and My Freedom,* where Douglass's representation of himself as a Romantic hero in the revolutionary tradition is even more elaborate. The passage on the ethics of stealing, for example, is revised in his second autobiography by the assertion that, if the slave steals, "he takes his own; if he kills his master, he imitates only the heroes of the revolution." Perhaps nowhere are Douglass's revisions of this kind more in evidence than in the most remarkable event of Douglass's life story, the fight with the slavebreaker Edward Covey. As Andrews has demonstrated in convincing detail, the revised account finely displays Douglass's novelization of his life—his arch reconstruction of dialogue, his comic familiarization of crucial scenes, his complex awareness of dramatic irony—and moves the episode toward a form of literary realism. The revisions also move in another direction as well, however, for the expanded text alters the *Narrative*'s succinct description of freedom into an oratorical declaration of liberty, adding layers of ideological resistance to the physical resistance recorded in the initial passage:

> I was a changed being after that fight. I was *nothing* before; I WAS A MAN NOW. It recalled to life my crushed self-respect and my self-confidence, and inspired me with a renewed determination to be a FREEMAN. A man, without force, is without the essential dignity of humanity. Human nature is so constituted, that it cannot *honor* a helpless man, although it can *pity* him; and even this it cannot do long, if the signs of power do not arise.

He only can understand the effect of this combat on my spirit, who has himself incurred something, hazarded something, in repelling the unjust and cruel aggressions of a tyrant. Covey was a tyrant, and a cowardly one, withal. After resisting him, I felt as I had never felt before. It was a resurrection from the dark and pestiferous tomb of slavery, to the heaven of comparative freedom. I was no longer a servile coward, trembling under the frown of a brother worm of the dust, but, my long-cowed spirit was roused to an attitude of manly independence. I had reached the point, at which I was *not afraid to die*. This spirit made me a freeman in *fact*, while I remained a slave in *form*. When a slave cannot be flogged he is more than half free. He has a domain as broad as his own manly heart to defend, and he is really *"a power on earth."* While slaves prefer their lives, with flogging, to instant death, they will always find christians enough, like unto Covey, to accommodate that preference. From this time, until that of my escape from slavery, I was never fairly whipped. Several attempts were made to whip me, but they were always unsuccessful. Bruises I did get . . . but the case I have been describing, was the end of the brutification to which slavery had subjected me.[130]

Like the representation of Madison Washington in "The Heroic Slave," Douglass's new appeal to international democratic ideals and especially to a more pronounced philosophy of "manly" resistance highlights the passage's alternative to the then widely popular capitulation of Uncle Tom to the murderous whip of Simon Legree. The conjunction of revolutionary and Christian rhetorics ironizes both: Douglass is "resurrected" from the tomb of slavery, but it is the Christian slaveholders who have martyred and hence spiritually freed him; likewise, though he is still in the physical chains of slavery, he stands now arrayed in masculine liberty, endowed with the "signs of power" that separate him from the pitiable slave who submits to punishment and tyranny. In this celebrated scene, perhaps more than anywhere else in his revised text, Douglass accentuates his own conversion to mastery—mastery of Covey, in a reversal of the relationship of power, and mastery of himself, in a release from the condition of chattelism. A "boy of sixteen," Douglass has vanquished his master, assumed his place psychologically, and fathered himself in the dramatic act of resistance.

In doing so, he has nearly made literal the Hegelian dialectic of master and slave. Covey in his humiliation by Douglass realizes that his identity is bound by his constrained dependence on his slave; and Douglass becomes aware that his liberation rests in his acute consciousness of both life and freedom. More specifically, Douglass's passage is an excellent illustration of Orlando Patterson's rewriting of Hegel: "Freedom can mean nothing positive to the master, only control is meaningful. For the slave, freedom begins with the consciousness that real life comes with the negation of his social death." Douglass's mastery of Covey now echoes the portrayal of Madison Washington and even, to a degree, the "Letter to My Old Master," in which Douglass had threatened to stand in the master's place and brutalize his white daughter. Douglass's negation of the condition of slavery, this passage tells us, is first of all an act of consciousness, a refutation of the social death imposed upon him as a slave. Yet it is also necessary—Hegel notwithstanding—to move that consciousness toward *action*, toward physical *resistance*. "I had drawn blood from him," Douglass writes, "and even without this satisfaction, I should have been victorious, because my aim had not been to injure him, but to prevent his injuring me."[131] It is appropriate that the revised chapter concludes with the well-known lines from Byron's *Childe Harold's Pilgrimage*—"Hereditary bondmen, know ye not / Who would be free, themselves must strike the blow?" The Byron passage, which Douglass had already used in "The Heroic Slave," had also appeared in Henry Highland Garnet's famous 1843 "Address to the Slaves of the United States," and it would later be quoted by Delany in *Blake* and Du Bois in *The Souls of Black Folk*. In addition to promoting physical resistance by slaves, what Douglass demonstrates through his revisions in *My Bondage and My Freedom* is the necessity of extending individual courage into the domain of cultural politics, mastering a tradition of literature and political philosophy as well as the dogma of revolutionary opposition.

Transfiguring his slave narrative into a text of revolution became an act in which Douglass's literacy, the ability to command through manipulating the "signs of power" in a public arena, *was* resurrection, a secularization of Turner's example that cannily brought Turner into the mainstream of American political ideology while at the same time endowing Douglass's own revolt with a slight sacred or mystic dimension it otherwise lacked. The *Narrative* had included as an appendix a blistering attack on the hypocrisy of organized churches and Christians generally in their acquiescence to slavery. *My Bondage and My Freedom* provides one instance after another of masters who profess Christianity but practice terror. Of Covey, for example, Douglass writes: "His religion hindered him from breaking the Sabbath, but not from breaking my skin," and Douglass's resistance, in turn, depends on breaking the fetters of religion: "My hands were no longer tied by religion," he says. In contrast, of course, Nat Turner's liberation of consciousness occurred in the discourse of revelation: "And by signs in the heavens that it would make known to me when I should commence the great work." His time of apocalypse collapses narrative into a singularity, the moment of Christ's life that intervenes in history so as to reorder it into a messianic, eternal present. Although Turner grafted millennial time onto the time of revolution by planning his revolt for the Fourth of July, his vision, like his revolt itself, contained no secular teleology and nowhere forecast the purification of the democratic state through the unfolding of progressive time. As an element of prophecy, "the great work laid out for me to do," as Turner calls it, exists in and of itself, essentially outside of time.[132]

Unlike Turner's, Douglass's acts of revolt, as he describes them in *My Bondage and My Freedom,* are bound very closely to the paradigm of progress implicit in the revolutionary tradition. His Sabbath school, unlike Turner's, is specifically a means to spread literacy and quicken the desire for freedom. As Douglass reenvisions it from the perspective of a political activist caught up in the great work of antislavery, the plans of escape and rebellion are infused with a very specific teleology that is present in virtually every slave narrative but noticeably suppressed in Turner's. The reawakening of his desire for freedom, which had become partially numbed under the "brutalizing dominion of Covey" and postponed during his first year at Freeland's, plunges Douglass back into history: "The thought of only being a creature of the present and the past, troubled me, and I longed to have a future—a future with hope in it. To be shut up entirely to the past and present, is abhorrent to the human mind; it is to the soul—whose life and happiness is unceasing progress—what the prison is to the body; a blight and mildew, a hell of horror."[133] To be without a future, the condition of slavery, is to be in hell—a social death, in Patterson's term, of the most extreme kind. To have a future, as Douglass figures it, is to be free; it is thus, according to his reconstruction of the trope of patrimony, to be able to enter into the self-making process of being an American. The several invocations of Nat Turner suggest, as well they might in 1855, that the attainment of African American liberty may still come in acts that will seem a violent intervention by God, a divine judgment of slaveholders, and to this extent Douglass's manipulation of scriptural teaching as a source of slave resistance (rather than subjugation) has millenarian elements. But by placing him back into the flow of history, Douglass's "resurrection," in contrast to that of Turner, projects a secular teleology very much bound to, and yet drawing its instrumental power from, the authorizing myths of the Revolution.

The way in which the promise of resurrection by means of the right of revolution functions in *My Bondage and My Freedom* is clarified by Douglass's famous "Fifth of July" address of 1852. David Walker's *Appeal to the Colored Citizens of the World* had already provided the model for Douglass's main line of argument. After attacking corrupt American institutions, Walker quoted the Declaration of Independence and asked his audience, presumably mostly white, to "hear your language" and compare it "with your cruelties and murders inflicted by your cruel and unmerciful fathers and on our fathers and on us." In Douglass's address on the meaning of the Fourth of July to the Negro, which was also appended to *My Bondage and My Freedom* along with the "Letter to My Old Master," as though in further commentary on the autobiography, Douglass placed himself outside the American teleology but within the circle of the postrevolutionary generation's principal rhetoric and its ritual repetition of the promised covenant:

> It is the birthday of your National Independence, and of your political freedom. This, to you, is what the Passover was to the emancipated people of God. . . . Your fathers have lived, died, and have done their work, and have done much of it well. You live and must die, and you must do your work. You have no right to enjoy a child's share in the labor of your fathers, unless your children are to be blessed by your labors. . . . [George] Washington could not die until he had broken the chains of his slaves. Yet his monument is built up by the price of human blood, and the traders in the bodies and souls of men shout— "We have Washington [as] *our father.*"[134]

Any interpretation of Douglass's fifth of July address, and of his ironic deployment of its protestations of democratic ideals, depends on the manner in which he treats slave holidays in one of the most penetrating passages of *My Bondage and My Freedom,* his account of the Christmas–to–New Year's slave holidays. The whole of chapter 18, which begins with Douglass's remarks on the holidays and ends with his most explicit invocation of revolutionary violence, could be said to enfold the critical elements of Douglass's philosophy. Even more overtly than Delany in his portrait of the Cuban "King's Day" in *Blake,* Douglass puts our focus on the countersubversive implications of holidays in general and slave holidays in particular, in this case especially those between Christmas and New Year's but including the others frequently granted by slaveholders, Easter and the Fourth of July. Nat Turner was not alone in recognizing that the leisure and free movement of the latter holiday could conceal a profound opportunity for slaves to learn too well the lessons of liberty, and slaveholders themselves periodically took counsel against allowing slaves to witness or participate closely in Fourth of July celebrations.[135] But the mechanism of the holiday also had a regulating function within the slave regime that joins it to the similar ideological regulating function of national political observance. As Douglass remarks in *My Bondage and My Freedom,* the holidays function primarily as "safety valves," a calculated means of "keeping down the spirit of insurrection among the slaves" by diverting their energies, at the breaking point of rebellion after a year's work, into modes of pleasure and physical relief. The free exercise of religion, family visitations and courtship, dissipation in drink, athletic contests, even labor for hire—all forms of license, Douglass writes—mimic freedom without granting anything resembling liberty. Holidays are the most effective manifestation of such controlling events, burning off the danger of "earthquakes" and "insurrectionary fires" by allowing slaves to stand momentarily outside the "narrow circle" of slavery's compulsory regulation. The holidays are therefore the deeply ironic counterpart to the principles celebrated on the Fourth of July: they are "part and parcel of the gross fraud, wrongs and inhumanity of slavery. Ostensibly, they are institutions of benevolence designed to mitigate the rigors of slave life, but, practically, they are a fraud, instituted by human selfishness, the better to secure the ends of injustice and oppression."[136]

Douglass here reconfigures the circle of slavery, whose confining boundaries he earlier located in the round of labor associated with slave songs. Standing outside the "narrow circle" allows him to recognize the countersubversive tendency (the controlled rebellion, as it were) of the slave holidays, which in turn imitated more transparently the controlled rebellion, in festive repetition, of America's founding revolutionary ethos. One's first impression, then, might be that the invocation of revolutionary principles with which the chapter concludes, and indeed with which *My Bondage and My Freedom* becomes preoccupied, registers the most grotesque dissonance, that Douglass's standing within the circle of postrevolutionary rhetoric leaves him blind to the fact that the Fourth of July itself may have a similar ritual function of mystification, affirming America's revolutionary progress while masking its fundamental flaws. There is no question that such a dissonance is present, but its meaning lies less in Douglass's equivocal embrace of the principles of the American Revolution than in his equally equivocal detachment from the power of slave culture, which here reaches a simultaneous crisis and resolution, one that illuminates Douglass's ambivalence about African American vernacular language and culture and his innermost, unanswerable questions about his very identity.

His notation of "jubilee beating," or "juba" clapping, as it is more widely known, captures this ambivalence well. In his remarks on the circle of slave songs, Douglass had advanced the probably specious claim that the double meanings of slave spirituals and work songs had not been evident to him while a slave. It is most likely, I suggested earlier, that this was a covert means for him to measure the progress of his political literacy, as he stood in consecutively wider and wider circles of comprehension and power. Here his recording of the work song "We Raise de Wheat," a folk song deeply inscribed with political resistance, is itself contained within such a circle by Douglass. "Among a mass of nonsense and wild frolic," he says in speaking of the musical indulgences made possible by the holidays, once in a while a "sharp hit" is given the slaveholders:

> We raise de wheat,
> Dey gib us de corn;
> We bake de bread,
> Dey gib us de cruss;
> We sif de meal,
> Dey gib us de huss;
> We peal de meat,
> Dey gib us de skin,
> And dat's de way
> Dey takes us in.
> We skim de pot,
> Dey gib us the liquor,
> And say dat's good enough for nigger.

The song is one of the few remaining signs in *My Bondage and My Freedom* of the slave's linguistic power underlying Douglass's own oratory, "not a bad summary of the palpable injustice and fraud of slavery." As such, it is an index of the tenacity of oral culture, of African survivals in labor patterns, folk art, and music that are scattered throughout Douglass's work.[137] Nevertheless, Douglass's comments also move in the other direction as well, underlining his likely agreement with a later ethnographer who argued that the songs were also a "safety valve," without which "the slaves might well have either sunk into degradation or broken out into rebellion again and again, and there would have been ghastly bloodshed and ruin."[138] It is certain that planters could make both holidays and songs part of the regime intended to defuse rebellion and control slave behavior ("dats de way dey takes us in"), and Douglass portrays the signifying spirit of resistance in "We Raise de Wheat" as something of an accident, at the least as an isolated instance among the "mass of nonsense and wild frolic." But slave culture, as Douglass recognized, was always necessarily double and deceptive. Like his general account of slave singing, his introduction of juba beating (a combination of hand-clapping, thigh-slapping, and foot-tapping that took the place of, or accompanied, other percussion or instrumental music, usually as a vehicle for dance) might have allowed Douglass, writing from a different perspective, the opportunity to catalogue a complex transformation of African rhythmic traditions into the work system and cultural expression of African American life.[139] Instead, juba bifurcates in his presentation. He does not strip it of those elements of resistance and political consciousness that mark one end of the spectrum of slave cultural nationalism (its preservation or cultivation of distinct folk art forms of the kind that Delany would weave effectively into the plot of *Blake*), but he himself demonstrates its limitations as an instrument of rebellion by embedding it within the countersubversive practice of the holidays, whose purpose is to extend the discipline of slavery.

"We Raise de Wheat" is a thus a commentary on the palpable injustice of slavery, but its very expression is folded into "de way dey takes us in." Moreover, Douglass's representation of it amounts to a quotation of the kind that seems to place the song within the register of "objects" from his past slave life that he has now mastered and transcended. Douglass's devaluing of slave culture and slave language was not, however, the product of disinterest or disrespect; rather, it was an honest attempt to measure the limits placed on resistance by the regime of slavery and the very culture it produced and in which it had to operate. Work songs, as he points out, could just as easily function as safety valves forestalling dissent—even if they also expressed that dissent—as could religion and slave holidays. The key for Douglass, writing at a time when neither massive slave rebellion nor southern emancipation seemed possible, was to counsel individual resistance and champion the education and skills that had allowed him to acquire what political power he had. In this passage, as in most others devoted to slave folk culture in *My Bondage and My Freedom* (his dismissal of the traitor Sandy's belief in the power of the root is the notorious example), Douglass stands outside the circle of slavery and at the same time magnifies, in retrospect, his capacity to utilize slave culture as a bridge to the independence that he now associates with the principles of the Revolution. Chapter 18 concludes with his account of the formation of his revolutionary "band of brothers," the group of "revolutionary conspirators" whose incendiary plot will be foiled by betrayal but whose "manly, generous, and brave" circle constitutes an elite cell within the general slave populace. Revolution, that is to say, is recognized by Douglass to grow out of slave culture but hardly to be synonymous with it.[140] And yet the question remains whether Douglass himself, in representing his act of rebellion and now making it into a national paradigm, can break free of the containing force of the revolutionary ethos, its countersubversive capacity—comparable to that of the Fourth of July and the work songs alike—to release dissent and resistance through the safety valve of philosophically just but necessarily unfulfilled claims to the right of revolution.

It is obvious that Douglass's "run-away plot," in order to be a conspiracy at all, required a communal participation and the trust of a "band of brothers." The last chapters of *My Bondage and My Freedom,* devoted to rewriting Douglass's life as a slave, certainly place somewhat more emphasis on the fraternal bonds that are necessary to Douglass's theory of resistance, and it may be that this aspect of the revision was a reflection of Douglass's increasing need to work as an abolitionist within *black* circles, to stimulate political activity on behalf of and among "my sable brothers," as he writes in the closing pages of the revised autobiography.[141] The revolutionary cohort described by Douglass in the prolegomena to the "insurrection" itself is the most succinct statement of Douglass's 1855 political philosophy:

> They were as true as steel, and no band of brothers could have been more loving. . . . We were generally a unit, and moved together. Thoughts and sentiments were exchanged between us, which might well be called incendiary, by oppressors and tyrants; and perhaps the time has not even now come, when it is safe to unfold all the flying suggestions which arise in the minds of intelligent slaves. . . . The

slaveholder, kind or cruel, is a slaveholder still—the every hour violator of the just and inalienable rights of man; and he is, therefore, every hour silently whetting the knife of vengeance for his own throat. He never lisps a syllable in commendation of the fathers of this republic, nor denounces any attempted oppression of himself, without inviting the knife to his own throat, and asserting the rights of rebellion for his own slaves.

The sentiments are fraternal, but Douglass himself remains paternally linked to the rhetoric and philosophy of the fathers, having identified himself as the single leader capable of espousing the right of revolution and planning the revolt. Despite his casting himself in the role of a Madison Washington or a Toussaint, the Easter conspiracy of Douglass's band of conspirators, armed with his forged passes for holiday travel, would fail. Betrayed by an unidentified Judas figure—presumably by Sandy, whose folk superstitions are but one sign for Douglass that he is not free from "slaveholding priestcraft"—Douglass would be momentarily cast into prison. He describes himself now as the "yellow devil" who his captors said ought to be hanged or burned rather than a martyred Christ, as had Turner, though elements of his Christology remain.[142] His "resurrection" in the contest with Covey had already indicated that Douglass's messianism was secular; likewise, his choice of Easter as the moment of rebellion was pragmatic. As it is represented in *My Bondage and My Freedom,* however, the holiday revolt is contained within Douglass's own admonition about holidays as instruments of countersubversion, while at the same time it demonstrates that the "broken fetters" of ritual veneration could be made redemptive.

Easter, of course, was symbolically a double holiday in the sense that, for Douglass's purposes, it fused the ideologies of the Revolution and Christianity, whose seemingly paradoxical teachings in the regime of slavery Turner had already proved could be yoked into a single axe of liberty. Because he robed himself in the apocalyptic message of Revelation, Turner is less likely than, say, David Walker or Madison Washington to be seen as Douglass's forefather. Nonetheless, when Douglass added Turner to his pantheon of African American fathers and invoked his name in describing the origins of his conspiracy in the Sabbath school, he suggested that the typological figuring of his life might serve not just as a message of messianism but also as a vehicle to engage the more profound truths of Enlightenment thought. At once alluding to the potential for unrecognized insurrectionary plots within black slave culture but placing his focus on the circle of a revolutionary elite that aspired to clarify and redeem the vision of the fathers, Douglass's philosophy thus ranged itself against two countersubversive tendencies in America's own national culture of slavery. If the capacity for resistance within the generality of the slave community was circumscribed by brutal regulation and channeled into comparatively diffuse cultural expressions, as Douglass saw it, he nonetheless cunningly anchored his rebellion within one of its principal institutions, the black church. Likewise, if the postrevolutionary generation was paralyzed by the apparently immutable will of the founding fathers or by simple self-interest, Douglass proclaimed that black men could nonetheless seize the weapons of revolution as their own. They could have the "Fifth of July."

Frederick Douglass continually declared himself a man, not a thing, a man, not a child. Freedom and the new powers of literacy it offered him countered the fear he had experienced on his second arrival at Hugh Auld's in Baltimore, when he saw how little Tommy Auld had grown toward the pattern of adult slaveholding, aware of his place and power: "He could grow, and become a MAN; I could grow, though I could *not* become a man, but must remain, all my life, a minor—a mere boy."[143] It is not surprising that this passage should have been added to *My Bondage and My Freedom,* since Douglass's own growth between 1845 and 1855 must have seemed to him a new maturation that left behind the boy orator of Nantucket, as well as the chattel object of slavery. Even so, Dougiass's life would entail a continued fight for the "manhood" of his race against the paternalism that prevailed in American law and custom regardless of emancipation, a fight his revised life story would reflect to the end.

Because large-scale slave revolution never became a significant threat in the United States, at least in the late antebellum years, and was obviously not the means by which slavery was finally destroyed, Douglass's appeal to the right of revolution was left hanging in the balance, neither affirmed nor denied. When war came on, African American soldiers joined their cause to the preservation of the Union, which, having long authorized slavery, at last prevailed to end it—an irony with which Douglass was surely content to live, for it allowed him to join the cause of the founding fathers on new ground. The "parricidal rebellion" of the slaveholders against "the Constitution, the Union, and the Flag," as Lincoln described secession, was a necessary vehicle for Douglass to close fast his distance from the fathers and embrace the legacy of the Revolution as truly his own. In a speech devoted to the "Slaveholders' Rebellion" delivered on the Fourth of July 1862 (not the fifth of July this time), Douglass spoke of the struggle for democratic freedoms begun eighty-six years earlier by both "your fathers and my fathers," a struggle now subverted by the "grim and hideous" monster of the South's "perfidious revolt."[144]

Having left behind entirely the circle of slavery, however, Douglass, as a black man in America, would never in his lifetime stand entirely within the circle of freedom. Throughout the nineteenth and early twentieth centuries it was the ironic fate of Douglass and other black leaders to remain in Lincoln's shadow. Although he had come to be an active supporter of the new Republican party by 1860 (first switching for pragmatic reasons from the abolitionist Liberty party to the Free Soil party), Douglass, like other black and white abolitionists, was disappointed by Lincoln's hesitancy about immediate emancipation, his apparent endorsement of colonization, and his reluctance to act more quickly on issues of interest to African Americans. What Douglass recognized was that the cause of the Union and the cause of black freedom remained far from synonymous. In the wake of the 1859 rejection by New York voters of a state amendment granting blacks nondiscriminatory voting rights even as they cast ballots in favor of Lincoln's presidency, Douglass wrote: "We were overshadowed and smothered by the presidential struggle. . . . The black baby of Negro Suffrage was thought too ugly to exhibit on so grand an occasion. The Negro was stowed away like some people put out of sight their deformed children when company comes." Douglass's own ambivalence about Lincoln and what he represented can be judged best by the terms he employed to celebrate Lincoln on the public occasion of the dedication in Washington of the Freedman's Lincoln Monument in 1876. Douglass no doubt identified with Lincoln the self-made man, who studied his "English Grammar by the uncertain flare and glare of the light made by a pine-knot," the "son of toil himself [who] was linked in brotherly sympathy with the sons of toil in every part of the Republic." But he stood apart from Lincoln just the same: "It must be admitted, truth compels me to admit, even here in the presence of the monument we have erected to his memory, Abraham Lincoln was not, in the fullest sense of the word, either our man or our model. In his interests, in his associations, in his habits of thought, and in his prejudices, he was a white man." "You," Douglass spoke, returning to the divisive rhetoric he had employed in such powerful forms as the fifth of July address, "you are the children of Abraham Lincoln. We are at best only his step-children; children by adoption, children by forces of circumstance and necessity."[145]

Douglass later confessed that he did not like Thomas Ball's design for the monument, which may itself have inspired his metaphor of the step-child. The statue, in Benjamin Quarles's words, "revealed Lincoln in a standing position, holding in his right hand the Emancipation Proclamation, while his left hand was poised above a slave whom he gazed upon. The slave was represented in a rising position with one knee still on the ground. The shackles on his wrists were broken. At the base of the monument the word 'EMANCIPATION' was carved."[146] It is especially significant, then, that Douglass appended his speech to his third autobiography, the *Life and Times,* for in comparison to the appendixes to his earlier narratives it reveals an interesting pattern. In his apprentice mode of platform oratory, the famous appendix to the *Narrative* attacks the relation of American churches and American slavery with vicious irony; the appendixes of *My Bondage and My Freedom* consist of extracts from Douglass's public letter to Thomas Auld, the fifth of July address, and other documents whose message and tone belong to the phase of revolutionary fervor that informs his thought from 1848 through the Civil War; and the Lincoln Monument speech shows Douglass at his most formal and public, ambiguously embracing America's martyred hero while struggling with him at the same time, just as Lincoln himself had embraced and overthrown the founding fathers.

During Douglass's life African Americans would not fully escape the legal status of "step-children"; indeed, over the course of his lifetime the gains of the immediate postwar years in the Reconstruction amendments would be slowly diluted or destroyed by legislative and judicial action. If the ideology of revolution had produced a freedom still deeply flawed, however, it was not for want of commanding intellectual leadership of a kind that should have placed Frederick Douglass beside, even above, Abraham Lincoln as one of the national fathers. The broken fetters were fetters still. But Douglass had already taken from them a dignity that embraced race while transcending it; an identity forged in an act of revolutionary revision; and a narrative that was nothing less than the story of liberty. In his strong, incomplete passage from bondage to freedom, Douglass fully took on the "signs of power."

· 2 ·

Melville, Delany, and New World Slavery

> Bones. I saw bones. They were stacked all the way to the top of the ship. I looked around. The underside of the whole ark was nothin but a great bonehouse. I looked and saw crews of black men handlin in them bones. There was a crew of two or three under every cabin around that ark. Why, there must have been a million cabins. They were doing it very carefully, like they were holdin onto babies or something precious. Standin like a captain was the old man we had seen top deck. . . .
>
> I comest to think about a sermon I heard about Ezekiel in the valley of dry bones. The old man was lookin at me now. He look like he was sizin me up. . . .
>
> "Son, you are in the house of generations. Every African who lives in America has a part of his soul in this ark."
>
> Henry Dumas, "Ark of Bones"

When the sixty-three slaves aboard Benito Cereno's ship revolted, killing twenty-five men, some in the course of struggle, some out of simple vengeance, they especially determined to slay their master, Don Alexandro Aranda, "because they said they could not otherwise obtain their liberty." To Amasa Delano's original account of the revolt, Melville's fictionalized version of the slave revolt aboard the *San Dominick* adds that the death would serve as a warning to the other seamen: not only that, but a warning that takes the form of deliberate terror. Aranda's body, instead of being thrown overboard, as in reality it was, is seemingly cannibalized or otherwise stripped of its flesh and the skeleton then "*substituted for the ship's proper figure-head—the image of Cristobal Colon, the discoverer of the New World,*" from whose first contact with the New World in Hispaniola— that is, San Domingo, or Haiti—flowed both untold prosperity and human slavery on an extraordinary scale.[1] (Again, I have retained the problematic designation New World because for both the Europeans and the Africans, whose perspective is most the concern of Melville and Delany, the Americas were the "New World.") The thirty-nine men from the *Santa Maria* whom Columbus left on the north coast of Navidad on Hispaniola in 1492 were killed by the native people after quarreling over gold and Indian women; on his second voyage in 1494 Columbus himself took command, suppressed an Indian uprising, and authorized an enslavement of Indians to work in the gold fields, which was destined to destroy close to 1 million natives, by some estimates, within fifteen years. Responding to pleas of the Dominican priests, led by Bartholomew de Las Casas, that the Indian population would not survive slavery, Charles V, Holy Roman Emperor, in 1517 authorized the first official transport of African slaves to San Domingo: the New World slave trade, destined to carry some 15 million slaves across the Atlantic by 1865, had begun.[2]

The substitution of Africans for New World Indians was justified by Las Casas on the supposedly humanitarian grounds that the blacks, unlike the Indians, were hardy and suited to such labors in a tropical climate. "Like oranges," wrote Antonio de Herrera in 1601, "they found their proper soil in Hispaniola, and it seemed even more natural than Guinea." Just so, added the American author who quoted Herrera in 1836: "The one race was annihilated by slavery, while the other has ever since continued to thrive and fatten upon it." Only the master class or their sympathizers could make such an argument. Their antagonists, such as the black abolitionists David Walker and Henry Highland Garnett, especially stigmatized Charles V and his "evil genius" Las Casas: "Clouds of infamy will thicken around them as the world moves on toward God."[3]

Like Melville, and like Martin Delany in his neglected novel *Blake; or the Huts of America,* Garnett took a perspective on African American slavery that is of marked importance but has played a comparatively small role in literary and cultural studies—namely, the recognition that slavery was hemispheric and that its fullest literary representation as well as its fullest political critique required a view that embraced several cultures, several nations, much as Du Bois was later to recognize that the attack on American racial injustice and the reconstruction of African American cultural history had to be pursued in a diasporic Pan-African framework. In each case the contemporary racial crisis could be shown to derive from historical forces of great complexity and sweep: in Du Bois's case the intertwined histories of slavery in the Americas and colonial rule in Africa (and the Third World generally); in that of Melville and Delany the contest of European and American political and religious power played out in the rise of the slave economies of the southern United States and Latin America, principally the Caribbean.

Alongside the embracing paradoxical outcome of prosperity and destruction brought on by the Columbian encroachment and settlements, the compressed structure of monastic symbolism in Melville's tale is meant to evoke the role of the Catholic church, the Dominicans in particular, in the initiation of New World slavery at the same time that it anticipates resonant elements of the crisis over slavery in the antebellum period. The comparison of Benito Cereno to Charles V, who had become a virtual tool of the Dominicans by the end of his reign, and Delano's momentary vision of the *San Dominick* as a "whitewashed monastery" or a shipload of Dominican "Black Friars pacing the cloisters" are only a few of the ecclesiastical scenes and metaphors that animate the tale. The aura of ruin and decay that links Benito Cereno and his ship to Charles V and his empire points forward as well to the contemporary demise of Spanish power in the New World and the role of slave unrest in its revolutionary decline. George Bancroft in particular remarked the racist hypocrisy implicit in the coincidence of Charles's military liberation of white Christian slaves in Tunis and his enslavement of Africans bound for the Americas, and emphasized the further coincidence, virtually commonplace by Melville's day, that "Hayti, the first spot in America that received African slaves, was the first to set the example of African liberty." It is this coincidence and its ironic origins that are illuminated by Babo's symbolic display of the skeleton of a modern slaveholder in place of the image of Columbus. Along with the chalked admonition *"Follow your leader,"* the skeleton too appears to Delano at the climactic moment when the frightened Benito Cereno and the former slave Babo, his "countenance lividly vindictive," plunge into his boat and the "piratical revolt" is unveiled: "All this, with what preceded, and what followed, occurred with such involutions of rapidity, that past, present, and future seemed one."[4]

For Delano, however, the mask is torn away only from the story's action and from the ship's figurehead, not from the allegory of Melville's tale. The benevolent American, self-satisfied and of good conscience, appears oblivious to the end to the meaning of Babo's terror and to the murderous satire contained in Melville's symbolic gesture. The masquerade performed by Babo and Benito Cereno to beguile Delano tests both the American captain's posture of innocence and that of Melville's audience.

All three of the tale's actors play parts defined by the climactic phase slavery in the Americas had entered when Melville composed his simultaneously explosive and paralytic tale during the winter and spring of 1854–55. Their stylized enactment of a rebellion contained within the illusion of mastery, as though in ritual pantomime, finely depicts the haltingly realized potential for slave revolution in the New World, then entering its last phase in the mid-nineteenth century. Through the display of Aranda's skeleton, the sacred bones of Columbus, rumored still in 1830 to have been lodged in the cathedral of Santo Domingo before being transferred to Havana upon the Treaty of Basle in 1795, were joined to those of the millions of slaves who had sailed to their deaths in dark cargo holds or, if they survived the middle passage, under a brutal regime of field labor in the New World. Of them is built Benito Cereno's decaying ship the *San Dominick* as it drifts into the harbor of the Chilean island of Santa Maria: "Her keel seemed laid, her ribs put together, and she launched, from Ezekiel's Valley of Dry Bones."[5]

The American Civil War reduced New World slavery to Cuba and Brazil; it brought to an end the threatened extension of slavery throughout new territories of the United States as well as Caribbean and Latin American countries coveted by the South. *Benito Cereno*'s general significance in the debates over slavery in the 1850s is readily apparent; in addition, Melville's exploitation of the theme of balked revolution through an elaborate pattern of suppressed mystery and ironic revelation has helped draw attention to the wealth of symbolic meanings the slave revolt in San Domingo in the 1790s would have had for an alert audience in the immediate antebellum years. Even so, it has been easy for readers since then to miss the full implications of Melville's invocation of Caribbean revolution or to misconstrue the historical dimensions of his masquerade of rebellion. Abraham Lincoln's diplomatic recognition of Haiti in 1862 ensured the island's harassment of Confederate privateers, and black rule was hardly an issue between the two governments once the South seceded. Moreover, the Caribbean and Latin America ceased for the moment to be of pressing national interest once the issue of slavery was resolved and a transcontinental railroad completed later in the decade. The disappearance from view of the region until conflicts fifty and a hundred years later brought it back into the public mind—first in the Spanish-American War and subsequent military actions, and later through Cuba's critical role in the cold war—has contributed to the general disregard of its centrality in *Benito Cereno, Blake,* and other works of the period. As the possibilities for renewed Caribbean revolution linked to civil conflict in the United States unfolded in the 1850s, however, they brought into special tropological focus the historical and contemporary role of both San Domingo and, in the case of Delany, Cuba in the struggle over American slavery.

Although he plausibly argues that Babo is the most heroic character in Melville's fiction and declares the tale a masterpiece, C. L. R. James nonetheless laments that *Benito Cereno* is in essence propaganda posing as literature, a sign that Melville had "lost his vision of the future," which would allow him to see "what will endure and what will pass." James's judgment on this score is incorrect, and his casting of his critique in terms of Melville's historical vision seems obtuse in the case of *Benito Cereno,* a work preoccupied with, and guided by, the superimposition of critical historical moments. Still, James offers an important clue to the tale's strategy of claustrophobic repression and its narrative entanglement in the ritual staging of authority. By reconfiguring the machinery of slavery as a masquerade, exposing its appeal to natural law as the utmost artifice, Melville suggested that there was *no future,* as it were, for the experiment of American democracy so long as the paralysis of inequality continued. What is more, he wrote in a culture in which every gesture toward slave subversion was itself open to countersubversion—if not by proslavery polemicists then by the forces of northern political and popular culture. Many years in advance of the similar fate of *Uncle Tom's Cabin,* for example, the *Amistad* mutiny and Nat Turner's revolt had been appropriated by stage minstrelsy and drained of their import in productions that obscured the deaths of whites while focusing on the comic punishment of the rebels. (In one case Turner's revolt was merged with Gabriel's conspiracy under a title that turned both in the direction of Stowe's melodrama: "Uncle Gabriel the Negro General.")[6] Minstrelsy also lay to some degree behind Melville's imaginative recapitulation of New World slave history, but to altogether different purpose, for it offered to him, as it would to Twain, a means to see history itself dress in costume. If Melville's tale presents no clear solution to the problems of racism and bondage, it nevertheless stands forth like Aranda's skeleton, a figurehead of revolution and slavery in stunning crisis.

Memory, Authority, and the Shadowy Tableau

. . . a little island set in a smiling and fury-lurked and incredible indigo sea, which was the halfway point between what we call the jungle and what we call civilization, halfway between the dark, inscrutable continent from which the black blood, the black bones and flesh and thinking and remembering and hopes and desires, was ravished by violence, and the cold known land to which it was doomed, the civilized land and people which had expelled some of its own blood and thinking and desires that had become too crass to be faced and borne longer, and set it homeless and desperate on the lonely ocean . . .

William Faulkner, *Absalom, Absalom!*

In changing the name of Benito Cereno's ship from the *Tryal* to the *San Dominick*, Melville gave to Babo's slave revolt a specific character that has often been identified. Haiti, known as San Domingo (Saint-Domingue) before declaring its final independence from France in 1804 and adopting a native name,* remained a strategic point of reference in debates over slavery in the United States. In altering the date of Amasa Delano's encounter with Benito Cereno from 1805 to 1799, moreover, Melville accentuated the fact that his tale belonged to the Age of Revolution, in particular the period of violent struggle leading to Haitian independence presided over by the heroic black general Toussaint L'Ouverture, which prompted Jefferson to remark in 1797 that "the revolutionary storm, now sweeping the globe," shall, if nothing prevents it, make us "the murderers of our own children." As I have already noted in connection with Nat Turner's revolt, the example of Haiti was appropriated by proslavery and antislavery forces alike. Although it strengthened resistance to the slave trade, San Domingo's revolution also provided a setback to abolitionists who seized upon its extension of the principles of the Age of Revolution. The large number of refugee planters from the island who came to the South in the wake of the revolution spread tales of terror that were reawakened with each newly discovered conspiracy or revolt—most notably, of course, those of Gabriel Prosser, Denmark Vesey, and Turner—and the history of Haiti and its revolution became deeply ingrained in southern history. As the epigraph just quoted suggests, Faulkner, a century later, would provide an impressive representation of the interlocked des-

---

* In English and American usage of the nineteenth century, the entire island at times, and even after the revolution the western half (a French possession since the seventeenth century), was often designated San Domingo or St. Domingo. The Spanish, eastern half (the Dominican Republic after 1844) was usually designated Santo Domingo, as was the principal city founded by the Columbian expeditions and named in memory of Columbus's father, Dominick.

tinies of revolutionized Haiti and the slaveholding South when he derived Thomas Sutpen's destiny from the historical convulsions of the island, "a theater for violence and injustice and bloodshed and all the satanic lusts of human greed and cruelty . . . a soil manured with black blood from two hundred years of oppression and exploitation." San Domingo thus offered both a distilled symbolic representation of the legacy of the American and French Revolutions, a realization of the Rights of Man, and a fearful prophecy of black rebellion throughout the New World.[7]

After Napoleon's plans to retake San Domingo (in order to retrieve in the Gulf of Mexico glory he had lost in the Mediterranean) were undercut by the demise of General Charles Leclerc's army in 1802, he lost the main reason to retain and occupy Louisiana. "Without that island," Henry Adams wrote, the colonial system "had hands, feet, and even a head, but no body. Of what use was Louisiana, when France had clearly lost the main colony which Louisiana was meant to feed and fortify?" The economic ruin and seeming barbarism of the island, and the excessive expense and loss of lives it would require to retrieve and rebuild, made San Domingo a lost cause of large dimensions to France and at the same time the key to an extraordinary territorial expansion of the United States—an expansion that would soon make the Caribbean appear as vital to American slave interests as it had been to France and prepare the way for the crisis question of slavery's expansion into new territories. In making their country "the graveyard of Napoleon's magnificent army as well as his imperial ambitions in the New World," Eugene Genovese has written, the slaves of San Domingo thus cleared the way for a different expression of New World colonial power destined to have more decisive and lasting effect on the stage of world history.[8]

Even though contention over the Gulf of Mexico did not ultimately play a large role in the Civil War, it seemed a vital issue throughout the 1850s—all the more so because, like Melville's tale, it represented the shadow play, one might say, of America's own incomplete Revolution and its ensuing domestic turmoil. It is, indeed, the spectral presence of San Domingo within Melville's story that constitutes the most somber, suffusing "shadow of the Negro" that falls on Benito Cereno (and Melville's reader) at the story's end. The threat of black rebellion is historically latent in all contemporary allusions to San Domingo—and always barely repressed, by extension, in the slaveholding South's psyche—but it also provides a continual analogue and point of reference for antebellum debates about the expansion of slavery. From Melville's perspective in the early 1850s, the nature and extent of future American power inevitably remained a function of the unfolding pattern of anticolonial and slave revolutions in the Americas. Although slaves fought at different times on opposing sides, the national revolutions of South and Central America in the early part of the century helped undermine slavery throughout the region (in most cases slaves were not freed immediately upon independence, but legislation abolishing slavery was at least initiated—in Mexico, Uruguay, Chile, Argentina, and Bolivia in the 1820s; in Venezuela and Peru in the 1850s). The end of slavery in the British West Indies in 1833 and in the Dutch and French islands in 1848 left the United States more and more an anomaly, its own revolutionary drama absurdly immobilized. Expansion and revolution were often linked, but not so expansion and antislavery. Thus, when extremists of southern slavery in the 1850s sought to increase their hegemony by encompassing slaveholding interests in Cuba and by extending the peculiar institution through new revolutions in Latin America, they ignored the degeneration of colonial rule on the one hand and on the other the trepidations expressed by one of the best known of South American revolutionaries, Francisco Miranda, who wrote as early as 1798: "As much as I desire the liberty and independence of the New World, I fear the anarchy of a revolutionary system. God forbid that these beautiful countries become, as St. Domingue, a theatre of blood and of crime under the pretext of establishing liberty. Let them rather remain if necessary one century more under the barbarous and imbecile oppression of Spain." Miranda's plea expresses well the paradox of New World liberation and of the United States' continued, expanding enslavement of Africans and their American-born children between 1776 and 1860. Drawn by the territorial dreams opened by Louisiana, the postrevolutionary generations advocated expansion through a conscious policy of America's manifest destiny to revolutionize the continent—eventually the entire hemisphere—spreading Anglo-Saxon free institutions, as one writer put it, from the Atlantic to the Pacific and "from the icy wilderness of the North to . . . the smiling and prolific South."[9]

That dreams of a global millennium always exceeded reality is less relevant than the fact that the harsh conflict between dream and reality was anchored in the wrenching paradox that had come to define New World revolution itself: would it advance freedom or increase slavery? The question could better be put differently: would it advance the cause of *slave* revolution? Although the North resisted the expansion of the Union for fear of advancing the power of slavery, not because it hoped to promote slave insurrection, expansion appears to have had the effect of dissipating the demographic cohesion and concentration that might have made American slave revolts more numerous or threatening in scope.[10] It was hardly clear in the 1850s that the expansion of slavery was, paradoxically, a means of containing slave rebellion in the South. At the time of *Benito Cereno*'s publication, the elimination of slavery was frequently *not* an adjunct to "revolutionizing" the hemisphere—or if not the hemisphere, then the Caribbean, where the energy of manifest destiny had been redirected after its initial efforts had failed to bring "All Mexico," as a popular slogan had it, into the United States orbit. The region offered in miniature an emblem of the Americas in their historical revolutionary moment, with the remnants of Spain's great empire (Benito Cereno), free blacks who had revolutionized their own nation (Babo), and American expansionist interests (Delano) all in contention.

Benito Cereno does not prophesy a civil war but rather anticipates, just as plausibly, an explosive heightening of the conflict between American democracy, Old World despotism, and Caribbean New World revolution. Its pervasive aura of paralysis, its revolutionary gestures held in perilous suspension, replicates in narrative form a crisis in temporality in which past, present, and future, as in Delano's moment of lucid perception, seem one. It is a universe, in Richard Chase's words, "poised upon a present that continually merges with the opulent debris of a dying past and reaches into a vacant and terrifying future." Melville's ship is a perfect chronotrope (in Bakhtin's phrase) of his story's engagement in the historical moment.* Operating simultaneously within the historical and the narratological registers, Melville maintains his text, like the progress of New World slavery, poised in a barely suppressed revolutionary gesture, one that seems to duplicate the prior navigation, the prior history, of the doomed *San Dominick*, which, "like a man lost in the woods, more than once . . . had doubled upon her own track." In addition to its formal and temporal significance, the double course of Melville's story suggests the essential doubleness of the American ship of state: at once the ark of the covenant that authorized both liberty and slavery, leaving the national mission adrift,

---

* "In the literary artistic chronotrope, spatial and temporal indicators are fused into one carefully thought-out, concrete whole. Time, as it were, thickens, takes on flesh, becomes artistically visible; likewise, space becomes charged and responsive to the movements of time, plot, and history. This intersection of axes and fusion of indicators characterizes the artistic chronotrope." See M. M. Bakhtin, *The Dialogic Imagination*, trans. Caryl Emerson and Michael Holquist (Austin: University of Texas Press, 1981), p. 84.

becalmed amidst incalculable danger; and therefore the "ark of bones," the charnel house of slavery whose long, haunted middle passage is evoked in the superb story by Henry Dumas, written more than a century after *Benito Cereno,* from which this chapter's epigraph is drawn. Incorporating the tension between liberty and slavery into its formal structure and its cunning manipulation of authority, Melville's narrative voice expresses, by both suggesting and containing, the rebellion that cannot be completed, implicating at once the potential spread of black revolution to the United States and the paralyzed realization of America's own revolutionary inheritance. Melville's containment of Delano's own consciousness at the point of explosive possibility brings the narrative by analogous form into closer and closer coincidence with the rebellion on board the ship and the imminent spread of New World revolt, creating in the reader, as in Delano, "a fatality not to be withstood." Like the dramatic presentations of the chained Atufal, the striking at intervals of the ship's flawed bell, and the seemingly "coincidental" activities of the oakum pickers, the singing women, and the hatchet polishers, the narrative voice performs an act of ritual control, regulating and containing acts of near revolt in which the ceremonial may at any moment give way to the actual, in which roles threaten to be reversed, and the figurative revolt contained in the liminal realm of Delano's consciousness threatens to be forced into the realm of the literal.[11]

To enter the realm of the literal, for Delano as well as for most of Melville's contemporary audience, was to enter a catalogue of nightmares and racial chaos. Readers of *Benito Cereno* who take account at all of Melville's use of the San Domingo Revolution focus for the most part on its extension of the French Revolution and the heroism of Toussaint. Yet the island's continuing turmoil in subsequent years not only kept it alive in the southern imagination of racial violence, as we have seen, but also made it of strategic significance in counterarguments to Caribbean filibustering, thus accentuating the standoff between imperial powers. For example, an 1850 pamphlet by Benjamin C. Clark, though sympathetic to Haitian freedom, condemned the "condition worse than that of slavery" into which he thought the island had been plunged by Great Britain's political maneuvering in the Caribbean; Haiti's failure to develop its resources and its continued threat of revolution to Cuba and the Dominican Republic thus made it a barrier both to United States interests in the region and to the emancipation of American slaves. On a different note, an essay entitled "About Niggers," appearing in one of the same 1855 issues of *Putnam's Monthly* that carried the serialization of *Benito Cereno*, argued that Haiti, unlike the United States, demonstrated that liberty and slavery cannot coexist and that the "terrible capacity for revenge" unleashed in the San Domingo Revolution proves that the "nigger" is "a man, not a baboon." The sarcastic article, in line with the general antislavery tone of *Putnam's*, anticipated black colonizationists in voicing the novel hope that the black West Indies would one day develop "a rich sensuous civilization which will bring a new force into thin-blooded intellectualism, and save our noble animal nature from extreme emasculation and contempt."[12] Melville's tale, antislavery though it may be, contains no invocation of noble savagery and no such hope about the fruitful merging of cultures.

Were the noble and humane Toussaint the only representative figure of the Haitain revolution, fears of slave insurrection in the United States might not have taken on such a vicious coloring. But when white Americans contemplated what would happen if the black revolt in San Domingo were "reenacted in South Carolina and Louisiana" and African American slaves wiped out "their wrongs in the blood of their oppressors," as William Wells Brown wrote in *St. Domingo: Its Revolutions and Its Patriots* (1855), not Toussaint but his successor as general in chief, Jean-Jacques Dessalines, sprang to mind. Whatever ambivalent gratitude might have existed toward Haiti for its mediating role in the United States' acquistion of Louisiana was diluted by the final achievement of independence under Dessalines in 1804. His tactics of deceitful assurance of safety to white landowners, followed by outright butchery, were almost certainly justified as a response to the equal terror waged against blacks in the French attempt to restore slavery, but they nevertheless enhanced his own claim that his rule would be initiated by vengeance against the French "cannibals" who have "taken pleasure in bathing their hands in blood of the sons of Haiti."[13] A sympathetic writer could claim in 1869 that the independence of Haiti constituted "the first great shock to this gigantic evil [slavery] in modern times," but what southerners in particular remembered were accounts of drownings, burnings, rapes, limbs chopped off, eyes gouged out, disembowelments—the sort of gothic violence typified by an episode in Mary Hassal's so-called *Secret History; or, The Horrors of St. Domingo* (1808), in which a young white woman refuses the proposal of one of Dessalines's chiefs: "The monster gave her to his guard, who hung her by the throat on an iron hook in the market place, where the lovely, innocent, unfortunate victim slowly expired."[14] Although Hassal's "history" in both form and substance resembles epistolary novels such as *Wieland*, its account of the Haitian trauma is hardly more sensational than the standard histories and polemics of the day. Antislavery forces for good reason hesitated to invoke Haiti as a model of black rule; even those sympathetic to its revolution considered its subsequent history violent and ruinous. Melville therefore took an extraordinary risk in his characterization of Babo and his revolt, pushing to the limit his readers' capacity to discriminate between just political resistance and macabre terror—or rather, to see their necessary fusion.

Contemporary representations of Haiti's revolution and subsequent history provided Melville not just the central trope of slavery and its subversion but also a set of discourses interweaving Jacobinism and the Inquisition, the terror of liberation and the terror of repression. *De Bow's Review,* the influential organ of southern interests, carried an essay in 1854 typical in its critique of Haitian commerce and government that displays such arguments in miniature. For over thirty years, the essay claims, the "march of civilization" has been dead in Haiti, its social condition one of sustained indolence and immorality: "From its discovery by Columbus to the present reign of Solouque [*sic*], the olive branch has withered under its pestilential breath; and when the atheistical philosophy of revolutionary France added fuel to the volcano of hellish passions which raged in its bosom, the horrors of the island became a narrative which frightened our childhood, and still curdles our blood to read. The triumphant negroes refined upon the tortures of the Inquisition in their treatment of prisoners taken in battle. They tore them with red-hot pincers—sawed them asunder between planks—roasted them by a slow fire—or tore out their eyes with red-hot corkscrews." Here, then, are the central ingredients that Melville's tale adds to Delano's own *Narrative*. The conflation of Spanish and French rule, coupled with the allusion to the Inquisition, yokes anti-Catholic and anti-Jacobin sentiment. Fear of spreading (black) revolution and fear of Inquisitorial violence were one. Indeed, the rhetoric of manifest destiny in the Caribbean was often a mix of the two, though with the submerged irony—one Melville treats with complex care—that northern critics of slavery's expansion liked as well to employ the analogies of European despotism and Catholic subversion in attacking the South. For the North, national expansion would morally entail the eradication of slavery, not its extension. It would illuminate the world in such a way, Lyman Beecher had already argued in *A Plea for the West* (1835), that "nation after nation, cheered by our example, will follow in our footsteps till the whole earth is free . . . delivered from feudal ignorance and servitude." The only danger, according to Beecher's anti-Catholic tract, lay in the Roman church's attempt to salvage its dying power by subversion of liberty in the New World, notably in South America, Canada, and San Domingo, which were "destined to feel the quickening powers of Europe, as the only means remaining to them of combating the march of liberal institutions . . . and perpetuating for a season her political and ecclesiastical dominion." The slave power of the South, said the generation of Beecher's children, would behave precisely the same way in order to rescue and extend their dying institution.[15]

As Melville was quick to comprehend, however, antislavery sentiment was frequently bound to a different but not entirely oppositional imperial agenda, and the antislavery imagination, no less than the proslavery, tended to collapse history into timeless images of terror and damnation. Theodore Parker, for instance, comparing the strength of Anglo-Saxon free institutions to the decay of Spain and her colonies in "The Nebraska Question" (1854), had no trouble linking together the early butchery and plunder of Indians in Hispaniola and greater Latin America in the name of the Virgin Mary, and the contemporary confluence of slaveholding power and Catholicism. Spain "rolled the Inquisition as a sweet morsel under her tongue . . . butchered the Moors and banished the plundered Jews," Parker wrote. In San Domingo she "reinvented negro Slavery" six thousand years after it had vanished in Egypt and "therewith stained the soil of America." With what legacy? Spain's two resulting American empires, Haiti and Brazil, so Parker saw it, were "despotism throned on bayonets"; over Cuba, France and England "still hold up the feeble hands of Spain"; most of South and Central America takes the form of a republic "whose only permanent constitution is a Cartridge-box"; and Mexico goes swiftly back to despotism, a rotting carcass about which "every raven in the hungry flock of American politicians . . . wipes his greedy beak, prunes his wings, and screams 'Manifest Destiny.'" Parker attacked the North for conciliating slave interests time after time (most recently in the Compromise of 1850) and predicted the slaveholders' attempted acquisition of Cuba, the Mesilla Valley, Nebraska, Mexico, Puerto Rico, Haiti, Jamaica and other Caribbean islands, the Sandwich Islands, and so on. In his view despotic, Catholic tyranny was at work, which so far the Puritan, Anglo-Saxon spirit of liberty and religious freedom had been unable to contain. "I never knew a Catholic Priest who favored freedom in America," Parker admonished. "A Slave himself, the medieval theocracy eats the heart out from the celibate Monk."[16]

Benito Cereno, as he delivers his halting, incoherent narrative to Delano, seems to be "eating his own words, even as he ever seemed eating his own heart." This coincidence in phrasing need do no more than remind us that Don Benito, who resembles a monk or a "hypochondriac abbott" and in the end retires to a monastery to die, is made by Melville a symbol of American paranoia about Spanish, Catholic, slaveholding despotism. To the extent that he also represents the southern planter, the dissipated cavalier spiritually wasted by his own terrifying enslavement, Benito Cereno requires the reader to see the tale in Parker's imperial terms, ones that most later readers of Melville's tale have lost sight of but that is crucial to the paralyzing crisis over slavery in the 1850s: North and South, like Delano and Cereno as they are mediated by Babo, play the parts of Anglo-Saxon and Roman-European currently working out the destiny of colonial territories enriched by African slavery in the New World. Benito Cereno, at once a genteel courtier ("a sort of Castilian Rothschild") and an impotent master painfully supported by the constant "half embrace of his servant," virtually *is* the Spanish New World, undermined by slave and nationalist revolutions and adrift aboard a deteriorated ghost ship on the revolutionary waters of history, which are now "like waved lead that has cooled and set in the smelter's mold." For his part, Delano, like the nation he represents, vacillates between dark suspicion and paternalistic disdain of the Spaniard. The tale cannily keeps hidden what Benito Cereno, the enfeebled master, knows well: that it is Babo who stages the events Delano witnesses aboard the *San Dominick,* artistically fashioning his former master like "a Nubian sculptor finishing off a white statue-head."[17] Melville's scenario—driving between the example of *De Bow's Review,* which saw Haiti as a volcano of Jacobin horrors, and that of Theodore Parker, who saw New World slaveholding itself as a manifestation of Old World despotism and popish insurgency—makes the African slave the true subversive, the exponent of revolutionary vengeance and the mock inquisitor of his now debilitated master.

Delano, as Jean Fagan Yellin suggests, may portray the stock Yankee traveler in plantation fiction, delighted by the warm patriarchal bond between the loyal, minstrel-like slave and his languid master. He may even, like Thomas Gray in his relationship to Nat Turner, penetrate the violent center of that relationship and yet prefer to ignore or mystify its meaning in a narrative dedicated to regulating and containing the threat of black revolution. Delano constantly enacts the mechanics of repression, not simply in the sense that he puts down the revolt aboard the *San Dominick* and thereby restores the authority that has been overturned, but also in the sense that his refusal to understand the "shadow" that has descended upon Benito Cereno is itself a psychologically and politically repressive act that replicates the ideology of America's crisis over slavery.[18] The repressing "bright sun" and "blue sky" that have "forgotten it all," which Delano invokes at the tale's conclusion, echo Daniel Webster's praise of the Union and the founding fathers in the wake of the nearly insurrectionary struggle over the Compromise of 1850: "A long and violent convulsion of the elements has just passed away," Webster remarked, "and the heavens, the skies, smile upon us." Benito Cereno's reply? "Because they have no memory . . . because they are not human."[19]

Memory and consciousness, past and present, are the twin planes on which the *San Domingo*'s revolt occurs. That is, since the actual revolt has already transpired but has been forced back behind the curtain of Babo's machinations, we see only its array of frequently erupting shadows, the set of clues presented to Delano. The theater of the ship is replicated in the theater of Delano's mind, each a stage on which revolt and repression play out the parasitic dialectic of slavery. The atmosphere of ambiguity and mystery with which the tale of the *San Dominick* is saturated connects the space of the ship and the space of Delano's perception, both of them regulated, finally, by Melville's cunning narrative, which replicates in historical form the fluidity of revolt and containment by which Delano's countersubversive consciousness operates. Continually Delano tries "to break one charm" only to be "becharmed anew," as he gets progressively enveloped in a vapor of "currents [that] spin one's head around almost as much as they do the ship."[20] The effect of enchantment by a nearly suffocating mystery brings Delano closer and closer to the melancholy depression of Benito Cereno, utterly immobilized in the artificial posture of his former authority. The incipient merger of the two characters, progressively suggested but never allowed to take place—and in the end radically denied by their completely divergent views of the significance of the slave revolt—is a measure of the operative irony in the tale, which finally goes beyond the revelation of apparent deception to verge more closely upon outright tautology, suspending meaning between possibilities that are not simply exclusive and opposite but rather, like the vectors of proslavery and antislavery, dangerously equal. Suspense pervades the ghostly and dreamlike setting of the slave ship stranded in symbolic significance between Europe, America, and Africa, and enveloped in a mysterious gray calm, a conspiracy of nature that seems to mock the paralysis

of morality and law. Likewise, it defines the crisis aboard the ship in which
the authority of each of three leaders, three possible "captains," is asserted
and restrained in frozen confrontation—Delano's because he is a guest
aboard the San Dominick and must defer to Benito Cereno's ostensible
command; Cereno's because his authority has been usurped by Babo; and
Babo because he must continue to play the part of the slave while maturing
his plot against Delano's ship. Acting in a form of circular displacement
which reproduces the threat of revolution harbored within the New World
enslavement of Africans, the three possible sources of authority are equal
to the extent that each requires abdication, reserve, or suppression in order
to maintain the semblance of control. Authority—like the drifting ship,
the simmering revolt, the guarded speech of the possible commanders,
and the language of the narrative which simultaneously unfolds and withholds the drama before us—is caught at a point of crisis and held in
precarious suspension.

Melville the "author" fully participates in the suspension of authority:
like Benito Cereno, "eating of his own words, even as he ever seemed
eating of his own heart," he checks his powers while displaying them and
renders his judgment in the very act of withholding it. Because Melville
seems to have taken his central metaphor for the relationship between
Benito Cereno and Babo from a passage in Delano's *Narrative* in which
he describes the original Cereno as a man "frightened at his own shadow,"
one could say that the narrative voice, which dictates to Delano as surely
as Babo does to Benito Cereno, is itself a kind of "shadow," at once
merged with but partially suspended above or outside his conscious point
of view. The merger of the two figures is continually suggested but never
realized, and the more accurate way of characterizing the narrative voice
would be to call it a voice of the unconscious, an embodied reservoir of
those impressions that spring momentarily to Delano's mind before laps-
ing back into the region from which they have emerged in a manner
comparable to the ghostlike ship: "The living spectacle it contains, upon
its sudden and complete disclosure, has, in contrast with the blank ocean
which zones it, something of the effect of enchantment. The ship seems
unreal; the strange costumes, gestures, and faces, but a shadowy tableau
just emerged from the deep, which must directly receive back what it
gave."[21] The story we read is therefore as completely "dictated" to us as
the "fictitious story" of fevers and calms is "dictated" by Babo to Benito
Cereno for presentation to Delano, and as completely as Cereno's account
of the revolt aboard the San Dominick is dictated to the court for presen-

tation, in ceremonious indirect speech, to the public. We are as cunningly manipulated by the narrator as Benito Cereno is by Babo, to such an extent that the last tormenting image we are presented as Delano leaves the *San Dominick,* joined hand in hand with Cereno across the supporting and mediating figure of "the black's body," is appropriate as well to the tenuous relationship between the reader and Delano, joined but separated by the conspiring voice of the narrator exercising his authority in the very act of holding it in abeyance.[22]

Eating its own words in near mimicry of the haunted Spaniard, the narrative voice lures the reader in only to discount suddenly the perceptions it has projected, insidiously displacing the possibility of a rebellion by the slaves onto Delano's suspicions of a malicious plot engineered by Benito Cereno—concealing the central drama of black liberation behind the shadow play of the contest between the American and the European, representatives of New World political and economic power built upon the common crutch of African slave labor. The arena of enchantment and suspense in which Melville's narrative unfolds strips the tale of vertical temporality; all historical dimensions are versions of one another, just as the primary tropes—of Jacobin terror, the Spanish Inquisition, the Haitian Revolution, American slavery—flow into one another in a kaleidoscope of figurative displacements. Delano's theater of consciousness contains the history of New World slavery in a skewed simultaneity such that the clues rising to the surface of his awareness appear to come at once out of personal memory and the hemispheric past. As the constant eruption and imperfect, incomplete containment of clues allowed by the regulating voice of the narrator suggests, the "shadowy tableau" does not entirely take back what it reveals; memory is not complete, but neither is repression. Likewise, the regulating mechanisms of slavery—both the physical and legal regime of southern chattelism and the comprehensive ideology of racial superiority that had no regional boundary—were imperfect in their containment: neither could they stop slave resistance, escape, or revolts, nor could they fully repress within the discourses of inequality the fear that more African Americans, like Nat Turner and Madison Washington, might violently seize the right of revolution as their own. Melville's account of the "enchantment" of Delano, then, is also a means to examine the mystifications by which slavery was maintained, as Europe and the United States, South and North, Benito Cereno and Amasa Delano are supported arm in arm across the physical pain and laboring energies of "the black's body."

Melville borrowed the rudiments of Amasa Delano's trusting disposition and generosity directly from the captain's own self-serving account, which records that the *"generous captain Amasa Delano"* much aided Benito Cereno (only to be poorly treated in return when he tried to claim his just salvage rights) and was himself saved from certain slaughter by his own "kindness," "sympathy," and "unusually pleasant" temperament. A passage earlier in Delano's *Narrative* might also have caught Melville's eye: "A man, who finds it hard to conceive of real benevolence in the motives of his fellow creatures, gives no very favourable testimony to the public in regard to the state of his own heart, or the elevation of his moral sentiments."[23] The self-serving nature of Delano's remarks aside, what is notable is the manner in which Melville may be said to have rendered perversely ironic the virtue of "benevolence," the central sentiment of abolitionist rhetoric since the mid-eighteenth century. Delano's response to the blacks is not "philanthropic" but "genial," it is true—but genial in the way one responds to Newfoundland dogs, natural valets and hairdressers, and minstrels performing "to some pleasant tune." In this passage Melville eviscerated less the American captain than northern liberalism for its profound indulgence in racialist interpretations of black character. *Uncle Tom's Cabin* was the rhetorical masterpiece of northern racialism, but William Ellery Channing's statement in *Slavery* (1835) is succinct: "The African is so affectionate, imitative, and docile that in favorable circumstances he catches much that is good; and accordingly the influence of a wise and kind master will be seen in the very countenance of his slaves."[24]

Melville's depiction of Delano is a parody of such sentiments. Although it may have had no particular source, his conception of Delano's stereotyping could have been drawn from a *Putnam's* essay, "Negro Minstrelsy—Ancient and Modern," appearing in January 1855 (the time at which he was composing his tale). In the course of a complimentary portrait of black minstrelsy as an art form, the writer observed: "The lightness and prevailing good humor of the negro songs, have been remarked upon. A true southern melody is seldom sentimental, and never melancholy. And this results directly from the character and habits of the colored race. No hardships or troubles can destroy, even check their happiness and levity." Of course, such a view of African American levity and docility, stock ingredients of the romantic racialism willfully played upon by Babo, was also but a thin cover for apprehensions that something more dangerous lurked behind the facade.[25] Like Delano's consciousness, however, the racialist argument, which was nothing less than the fundamental ideology of minstrelsy that would rule white America's view of blacks long past the Civil War, bespoke a national mission in which political regulation and racial hierarchy were raised to such a pitch that calculated manipulation cannot be divorced from naiveté. That, it may be, was Melville's America.

Melville's distillation of Delano's racialism and his manic benevolence into tropes of minstrelsy empties him of moral authority. An example of the mind at work in the *Putnam's* essay, Delano's offensive stereotypes allow us to see that the trope of African American docility and gaiety was generated as much by sympathetic liberalism as by the harsh regime of slavery. Minstrelsy—in effect, the complete show of the tale's action staged for Delano—is a product, as it were, of his mind, of his willingness to accept Babo's Sambo-like performance. Melville in this way nearly collapses the distance between proslavery and antislavery, South and North, so as to display the combined stagecraft that preserved slavery. Paternalistic benevolence is coextensive with minstrelsy, on the plantation or on the stage. As Saidiya Hartman argues, minstrelsy, like the orchestrated amusements of slaves arranged by the master for his own pleasure, called attention to the artifice of racialism but at the same time aggressively asserted the black subject's given place in the social order. Resolving the tension between domination and intimacy, violence and pleasure, Hartman writes, "the grammar of sentiment and the rhetoric of minstrelsy together enabled a performance of slavery which wed cruelty and festival." At the same time, blackface minstrelsy also offered the potential for a critique of southern slaveholding and a marginal preservation of some elements of African American cultural expression. The farce of the minstrel show, deeply informed by an American spirit of anarchy that resisted hierarchical social structures and forms of authority, routinely clothed mild subversion of the masters—or the economic stratum that they represented to working-class audiences—within its racist caricatures. By the mid-1850s, however, such tendencies in favor of antislavery or more complex theatricalizations of racial issues were overwhelmed by the cultural politics of Union and Compromise that necessitated northern acquiescence in proslavery sentiments.[26] Already carefully controlled in the degree of its rebellion against the masters, blackface minstrelsy was now entirely contained by the national agenda. Melville placed his tale on this dividing line: Babo's subversion is apparent to Cereno but hidden from Delano. Revolt has occurred but has been recontained within blackface stereotypes, and it will ultimately be entirely suppressed by the politics of Union represented by the New England captain.

One can hardly lose sight of the fact that Babo, as Melville was at pains to show, is not a white man in *blackface* on a stage but a *black man*, an African, on a slave ship—nonetheless playing the part of a slave. Babo's act terrorizes Benito Cereno but thoroughly beguiles Amasa Delano. Paradoxically, Delano watches Babo's performance without ever seeing it. Although it is Benito Cereno and Babo whose feigned intimacy, undergirded by terror, displays the essential relation of master and slave, it is Delano and Babo who most effectively enact the dynamics of artifice, the construction of the natural, on which both minstrelsy and the defense of slavery are built. When Babo, in the wake of the shaving scene, goes so far as to slash his own cheek with the razor in order to deceive Delano— holding forth the great power of his deceit by inflicting terror as though in a mirror—the American captain's response also mimics the confusion of domination and intimacy that Babo has staged: his first thought is that "slavery breeds ugly passions in man," but the sight of Benito Cereno supported by Babo "as if nothing had happened" leads him to conclude that the staged punishment was "but a sort of love-quarrel."[27]

It is Delano, not Benito Cereno, for whom the slave's disfiguration could signify a love quarrel, and in whom the grammar of sentiment and the rhetoric of minstrelsy are most clearly united. In his foolhardly but carefully calibrated benevolence, the character of Delano represents both the founding fathers, who sanctioned slavery even as they recognized its contradiction of the Rights of Man, and the contemporary northern accommodationists, who too much feared sectional strife and economic turmoil to bring to the surface of consciousness a full recognition of slavery's ugliness in fact and in principle. San Domingo, like Nat Turner, was a lesson in racial fears as often for the North as for the South, for antislavery as for proslavery. The fundamental relation of terror that underlies the artificial levity of Babo's ministrations to his master constitutes Melville's devastating critique of such widespread northern racialism, of which Delano is merely a representative. Delano's "old weakness for negroes," surging forth precisely at Melville's greatest moment of terrifying invention, the shaving scene, is the revolutionary mind at odds with itself, impassioned for freedom but fearful of continuing revolution, energized by the ideals of paternalistic humanitarianism but blind to the recriminating violence they hold tenuously in check.

The Play of the Barber

The secrets of slavery are concealed like those of the Inquisition.

Harriet Jacobs, *Incidents in the Life of a Slave Girl*

The "dread of tautology," Melville remarks at one point in *Pierre,* is "the continual torment of some earnest minds,"[28] and though nowhere in *Benito Cereno* does tautology reach the enervating pitch it does in Melville's incest romance, it is nonetheless important to the narrative unfolding of evidence about the mystery with which Delano and the reader are confronted. Unlike irony, which by deception, insinuation, or bald presumption revolts against the authority of one meaning to proclaim the authority of another, tautology asserts the virtual equivalence of potentially different authorities or meanings. It does so by rhetorical mimicry—by an actual or fully implied reproduction of phrases and gestures—or by bringing two meanings into such approximation as to collapse the distinction between them without literally doing so. It should be evident from this characterization that tautology may be taken to be the governing figure of Melville's narrative method as well as his historical vision in *Benito Cereno,* where phenomena both in temporal sequence and in visual space are routinely shown to be on the point of collapse into something else. By failing to understand the ironic import of his own remarks to Benito Cereno—for example, in his remarks about the symbolism of Cereno's padlock and key, or his reflections about Aranda's remains being aboard the ship—and by unwittingly articulating, through the narrative voice suspended in his consciousness, suspicions that move closer and closer to the literal truth of events aboard the *San Dominick,* Delano participates in a continued act of suppressed revolt against belief in the appearances presented to him and consumes irony in the rhetorical gesture of tautology.

The central marker of Melville's deployment of tautology in *Benito Cereno* is the dizzying array of double negatives ("not unwilling," "not unaffected," "not unbewildered," and so on) that act as localized versions of the effect generated throughout by the precarious relationship between the narrative voice and Delano, in which a suspicion or interpretation is created but then withdrawn, creating in short compass an irony that is allowed neither completion nor any "handle for retort." Just as altruism and racism are virtually indistinguishable in Delano's character, so suspicion and reassurance coexist within virtually the same gesture, the same moment, as in scene after scene "the same conduct, which . . . had raised the alarm, served to dispel it," and "innocence and guilt . . . use one seal—a hacked one." Punning on the many scenes in which things both *are* and *are not* what they appear, and offered to Delano as a clue that he must untangle or cut if he is to interpret the mystery play before him, the famous symbol of the knot is a concentrated representation of tautology itself. "Knot in hand, and knot in head," the transfixed Delano defines a situation in which presented meanings or signals are both the "same" and yet separated or suspended so as to act in a fashion one might call taut or tense (the archaic noun *taut* means precisely "mat" or "tangle"). The knot that comprises the events aboard the ship and the story's convolutions, like the shadowy tableau, offer and swallow up meaning at the same time, offering no handle for retort. Because it suggests but prohibits identity, tautology offers an absurd paradox that necessarily "contains" irony by subverting its revolutionary intent (to mock or overturn authority), stifling its import and suspending its achieved effect, leaving the reader, finally more so than Delano, caught in the impasse of resistance and containment that governs Melville's tale no less than its antebellum historical moment.[29] Tautology therefore defines not just the perceptual apparatus that occludes Delano's recognition but also the relationship of Benito Cereno and Babo, whose enacted revolt has been contained as something that *is* and *is not*.

According to *Benito Cereno,* tautology is also the appropriate rhetorical figure for the Hegelian paradox of slavery, which can be seen, as I argued in chapter 1, to structure the idiosyncratic "authorial" relationship between Nat Turner and Thomas Gray as it is reflected in the "Confessions." The master's domination slides into slavery when he understands his parasitic dependence on his slave; the slave's subservience slides into mastery when he understands that his very consciousness of freedom is a mode of liberation. In the Hegelian paradox, mastery (like slavery) both *is* and *is not*. Granting Babo a true mastery that has simply been reconfigured as the artifice of bondage, however, Melville takes this one step further. Babo's power, like that of Nat Turner, is exercised less in the violence of revolt—which is first concealed from view and finally put down by violent counteraction—than in his uncanny manipulation of the revolt's linguistic and visual *narrative.* In Turner's case this takes the form of a published "confession" destined to carry the subversion of slaveholding authority onto a new and far-reaching political and cultural plane; in Babo's case it takes the form of a masquerade that humiliates the masters and a legal proceeding that further mystifies the slaves' intellect and cunning, both events sending to Melville's audience a comparable "confession," as it were, of the slave's hidden potential for inverting the relationship of power. In *Benito Cereno,* as in the "Confessions," the subtle distance between *is* and *is not,* as between master and slave, is one of conjoined parasitism and communion. Mastery becomes a mournful liability, while the condition of slavery conceals an indulgence in the most terrifying power. Specifically, European rule in the New World is eaten away from within, as the economic and political costs of slavery diminish its capacity to survive; in signal instances outright revolt has demolished the regime of the masters and threatens the same in the United States.

The figure of tautology functions in the temporal dimension as well, forcing into single explosive textual tableaux the simultaneity of revolutionary moments and historical frames that the narrative suspends within one another. Although it is Babo and Benito Cereno who enact the drama of tautology, it is Delano who witnesses that drama, himself drawn into parasitic relationship with, and approaching a dangerous equivalence to, Benito Cereno. At its extremity the text brings Delano and Cereno into a mirroring relationship while at the same time driving them apart. Delano becomes at one point involuntarily almost as rude as Don Benito; begins more and more to respond with coldness and reserve to the Spaniard's own apparently ill-bred reticence; is overcome by the "dreamy inquietude" and "morbid effect" of the mysterious calm; and at length feels himself to be the victim of some sort of recurrent "ague" or "malady" that he strives to get rid of by "ignoring the symptoms." Cereno's "black vapors" seem slowly and surely to have infected Delano, bringing him involuntarily closer to the posture of the ruined captain, whose "simulation of mortal disease" springs from the malady of black revolution that has overtaken the ship.[30] Joined but separated by the mediating power of Babo, the communion of Benito Cereno and Amasa Delano is one of frequent double negatives in which the historical has become symptomatic. Delano is an American in relation to Cereno's European colonial rule, and a northerner in relation to Cereno's southern planter rule, in each case drawn into the contagious risks of servile rebellion. The reflexive contagion that threatens Delano, like the contagion of revolt that has consumed the *San Dominick* and its captain, serves to bring the narrative closer yet to the breaking point of suppressed rebellion; and like the brutally mimetic action of Melville's greatest moment of invention, the shaving ritual, it defines an involuntary form of communication that at once merges and separates the captains by bringing them into a mirroring or tautological relationship, locked in a stance of communion and isolation that mimics the respective histories they represent. Themselves held in suspense, both captains are variously ignorant of the African social and political world that surrounds them on the *San Dominick,* and whose course of resistance is being played out by enigmatic signs and masked communications periodically revealed.

No scene more effectively comprehends the power of tautology than the shaving of Benito Cereno,[31] which brings to a climax of terror the "juggling play" that Babo and Benito Cereno have been "acting out, both in word and deed," before Delano. Revealing Babo's role as a trickster at the height of ostentation, the "play of the barber" compresses Delano's blind innocence, Benito Cereno's spiritual fright, and Babo's extraordinary mastery of the scene's props and actors into a nightmare pantomime symbolic of the revenge of New World slaves upon their masters. The cuddy, with its "meagre crucifix" and "thumbed missal," its settees like an "inquisitor's rack," and its barbering chair that seems "some grotesque engine of torment," is a scene defined by symbols of Spain's violent Catholic history. Babo's use of the Spanish flag as a barber's apron, which through his agitation unfolds "curtain-like" about his master, heightens Delano's playful affection for "the negro" and coordinates the personal and historical dramas of vengeance that are acted out—dramas that De-lano, as he often does, unwittingly or unconsciously glimpses but fails fully to comprehend:

Setting down his basin, the negro searched among the razors, as for the sharpest, and having found it, gave it an additional edge by expertly stropping it on the firm, smooth, oily skin of his open palm; he then made a gesture as if to begin, but midway stood suspended for an instant, one hand elevating the razor, the other professionally dabbling among the bubbling suds on the Spaniard's lank neck. Not unaffected by the close sight of the gleaming steel, Don Benito nervously shuddered; his usual ghastliness was heightened by the lather, which lather, again, was intensified in its hue by the contrasting sootiness of the negro's body. Altogether the scene was somewhat peculiar, at least to Captain Delano, nor, as he saw the two thus postured, could he resist the vagary, that in the black he saw a headsman, and in the white a man at the block. But this was one of those antic conceits, appearing and vanishing in a breath, from which, perhaps, the best regulated mind is not always free.

The "antic conceit" of decapitation—uniting Jacobin terror, the Inquisition, and slave vengeance—has more actuality here than the literal barbering that is taking place. To begin with, it exposes the rebellious potential within every slave. As Thomas Wentworth Higginson said in an 1858 address to the American Anti-Slavery Society: "I have wondered in times past, when I have been so weak-minded as to submit my chin to the razor of a coloured brother, as sharp steel grazed my skin, at the patience of the negro shaving the white man for many years, yet [keeping] the razor outside of the throat." The American slave might soon act on his own, Higginson warned. "We forget the heroes of San Domingo."[32] Like Higginson's suggestion that the black heroes of San Domingo are both forgotten and yet held on the brink of consciousness, Melville's scene aboard the *San Dominick* evokes a revolutionary paradigm but quickly returns it to the shadowy tableau of memory. The conceit of decapitation, merging the French Revolution's ethos of deposed power with the terror of black insurrection and issuing suddenly from a relaxation of control in Delano's otherwise "best regulated mind," acts as a form of revolt against perceptive and rhetorical constraint which imbeds historicity within the aesthetic, making literary form an instrument of political consciousness. As a revolutionary gesture—moreover one that is nearly involuntary—the conceit Delano imagines parallels the actual revolt that has occurred but is held temporarily in abeyance. Likewise, the suspension or deferral of completion in the revolt that Delano's presence aboard the ship provokes is echoed in his own deferred acceptance of the conceit presented so boldly to him. It epitomizes Melville's masterful employment throughout the tale of metaphors whose submerged meaning momentarily exceeds in truth their literal contexts, only to be forced—repressed—once again beneath the conscious surface of Delano's mind and the story's narrative. The suggested metaphor falls into such close equivalence with the actual event as to be nearly synonymous with it. And in fact the drawing of "Babo's first blood" rather than dissipating the suspense only increases it, as Benito Cereno's nervous fit on the one hand forces Delano to dismiss his suspicions of the Spaniard but on the other again leads him to articulate, in blind incomprehension, the very truth of the scene: "Is it credible that I should have imagined he meant to spill all my blood, who can't endure the sight of one little drop of his own? . . . Well, well, he looks like a murderer, doesn't he? More like as if himself were to be done for."

Their conversation about the *San Dominick*'s peculiar voyage resumes "between the intervals of shaving," as Babo keeps the razor at Cereno's neck in close check on his every word, his "dusky comment of silence" reciprocating something suspicious in Don Benito's manner and once more leading Delano momentarily to the suspicion that the two are "enacting this play of the barber" for some malign purpose. The last image of the scene, Babo the sculptor surveying his master as "the creature of his own tasteful hands," merges the imminent decapitation of Cereno with the artistry of Babo and calls our attention to the resemblance between Melville the narrator and Babo the tormenting master artist. The scene's irony is held at the point of utmost suspense, the metaphoric on the absolute verge of becoming literal to such a degree that the tension can be expressed only in a series of tautological statements that blindly bring Delano face to face with the literal and bring the narrator, dictating Delano's conduct as completely as Babo dictates Benito Cereno's, into virtual equivalence with the slave, both carrying out plots and expressing in mimic action their mutual authority through a suspended and agonizing ritual. The "play of the barber" both *is* and *is not:* it is a play, and yet the theatrical performance does not begin to characterize the lines of force and reversals of hierarchy that go into this play; Babo is a barber, but such a role fades beyond memory next to the flow of blood that could begin at any moment. The scene is not simply ironic, but revels in the luxury of Babo's tormenting control. It verges on tautology in such a way that the act of shaving is less a symbol of Babo's usurped authority than its virtual embodiment, one that releases and contains its significance in the very act of holding it poised at razor's edge, like Babo's blade "suspended for an instant" near the "Spaniard's lank neck," with the gentle, terrifying admonition, "Now, master . . . now, master."

In his delicate physical mannerisms and his verbal solicitude, Babo replicates the fawning care attributed to slaves in the propaganda of the master class, now tautologically emptying proslavery's claims of all meaning except terror. His masquerade of devotion to Benito Cereno concisely portrays the layered qualities of rebellion and submission—the complex intersection of "Nat" and "Sambo" roles acted out for the white masters— that historians have detected among the accounts of slave behavior, and it is a virtual parody of Higginson's observation in his 1861 essay on Turner: "In all insurrections, the standing wonder seems to be that the slaves most trusted and best used should be the most deeply involved."³³ Like other simulations of intimacy scattered throughout the tale, the ministering care of Babo in the cabin scenes explodes the mystifications of proslavery argument. In *Cannibals All!* (1857), for example, George Fitzhugh developed the quasi-Hegelian view that benevolence was regulated by a law of hierarchy that was natural and divine; that dependent slaves therefore exercised as much control over their superiors as their superiors did over them; and that "the interests of master and slave are bound up together, and each in his appropriate sphere naturally endeavors to promote the happiness of the other." In the intimacy of slaveholding relations for which the family was the best model, Fitzhugh argued, "inferior and superior act and re-act on each other through agencies and media too delicate and subtle for human apprehensions." The least sign of insurrection, however, destroyed the cherished southern fiction of the tranquil plantation "family," revealed it as a charade. Likewise, the stagecraft of Melville's tale theatricalizes slavery, exposing its supposedly "natural" relations of mastery and racial supremacy as conventions of power. What is more, the "love-quarrel" that Babo goes on to stage between the "childless married couple" of master and slave so as to throw off Delano's suspicions heaps one tautology upon another: the pretense of devotion gives way to the pretense of punishment, only to return once again to devotion. Babo, having made paternalism his weapon, goes beyond a mere demonstration that Fitzhugh's appeal to a hierarchy of natural affections was an arrangement of social and political power. "Revenge possesses some properties in common with love," wrote the propagandist "Nero" in the wake of Nat Turner's revolt.³⁴ Affection and hatred, love and terror are now virtually one in Melville's play of the barber.

Both the physical scene and the suggested metaphors of threat conspire to form a concentrated ritual that has the partial look of the domestic minstrelsy Delano has witnessed time and again. Here, however, Melville so layers the scene with allegorical props as to make the cuddy nearly an archaeological site in which times past and present have entered a single frame. (An analogous effect is achieved by Charles Chesnutt in his story "The Doll," in which a black barber has the opportunity, during a scene of shaving, to cut the throat of the white racist responsible for his father's murder.) The scene in brief recapitulates the torturous drama aboard the *San Dominick* and defines a scene of judgment at once psychological and historical. As Philip Fisher has astutely suggested, the room of the shaving scene "suffers from simultaneity." Like a museum in its display of antiquated furniture and devices, the separating partitions of its former officers' quarters torn down, the cuddy is "built over an abolished world," a room "marked by revolution, its very openness a sign of the canceling of some previous power." This, of course, is the mode of Melville's narrative in its totality. Enforcing for us the recognition that this terrifying ritual has been acted over and over, "shaving-time," as Babo calls it, is a moment of temporal suspension when epochs merge and the course of imperial history is threatened with reversal.[35] Shaving-time is the reconfiguring of time: all historical motion is suspended in the timeless present—Babo's "Now, master . . . now, master"—and pointed toward a future of black ascendancy. And yet that reconfiguration remains only potential in *Benito Cereno*. The cuddy's simultaneity includes not just the layering of the feudal past upon the democratic present, for the doubleness of the scene— what *is* and *is not* at the same moment—is the very sign of revolutionary paralysis, which conceals alongside revolt the countersubversive threat of reversal, of a restoration of the old order. The simultaneity of historical moments—for example, the layering of Caribbean upon southern United States history—can never be complete. The forces of restoration and regulation that sweep through Delano's mind to put down the revolt in consciousness recall the countersubversive exposure of Gabriel's and Vesey's plots, and the vengeful suppression of Turner's short outbreak, just as they anticipate the restoration of order and racial hierarchy that he will make possible by the conclusion of the tale. Melville's containment of the revolt of slave against master reveals the power relation to be one of artifice rather than nature; in making power the only index of rule, however, he accentuates rather than dismantles the struggle to maintain clearly marked hierarchies.

Yet the destruction of Benito Cereno—the titular character of the story and a figure who by the point of the shaving scene has reached the station of a ruined king from classic tragedy—can hardly be construed as an act from which Melville flinches. If his attitude is at last one of mercy, he nonetheless participates in the attack on slavery and slaveholders through his sympathetic portrait of Babo's brilliance. The shaving scene, of course, is directed not just at Cereno but also at the reader. The same could be said of the entire machinery of Babo's ritual control, which, if Hegel is correct, continually maintains the reversed semblance of order while, at razor's edge, destroying the regime of slavery in a grand act of consciousness of freedom. Trickster and confidence artist, Babo stands outside the servile and animalistic metaphors that Delano requires to comprehend him. His artistry may be traced in the cunning authority he has established over the *San Dominick* well in advance of those scenes, such as the shaving ritual and the luncheon, where, alongside Melville, he pushes his theatrical, even gaudily ostentatious political torment of the deposed master to the outer reaches of possibility.

Ashantee Conjurors: Africanisms and Africanization

> They called for the instrument that they had brought to America in their skins—the drum—and they played upon it. With their hands they played upon the little dance drums of Africa. The drums of kid-skin. With their feet they stomped it, and the voice of Kata-Kumba, the great drum, lifted itself within them and they heard it. The great drum that is made by priests and sits in majesty in the juju house. The drum with the man skin that is dressed with human blood, that is beaten with a human shin-bone and speaks to gods as a man and to men as a God. Then they beat upon the drum and danced. It was said, "He will serve us better if we bring him from Africa nameless and thing-less." So the buckra reasoned. They tore away his clothes that Cuffy might bring nothing away, but Cuffy seized his drum and hid it in his skin under the skull bones. The shin-bones he bore openly, for he thought, "Who shall rob me of shin-bones when they see no drum?" So he laughed with cunning and said, "I, who am borne away to become an orphan, carry my parents with me. For Rhythm is she not my mother and Drama is [he not] her man?" So he groaned aloud in the ships and hid his drum and laughed.
>
> Zora Neale Hurston, *Jonah's Gourd Vine*

For the reader, as for Benito Cereno, the "heroes of San Domingo," Toussaint and Dessalines in particular, are present in the shaving scene—likewise the slave rebels Joseph Cinque, Madison Washington (the leaders of the revolts aboard the slave ships *Amistad* and *Creole*), and Mure, the original of his own Babo, as well as the conspirators involved in Gabriel's and Vesey's plots and Nat Turner's revolt. The *San Dominick*, like Dumas's ark of bones, is a ship of ghosts. Melville's portrayal of Babo might have aroused memories of all these notorious slave rebels, all of them in one faction of the white mind artful and vicious men prompted to their deeds by madness, dreams of San Domingo, or abolitionist propaganda. Babo too is full of that "art and cunning" the real Delano attributed to all

African slaves; and Melville's depiction of his ferocity and cruelty, Delano's perception of Babo as a snake and his followers as wolves (in this he echoed typical white assertions, for example, that Turner and his band were "monsters" and "blood-thirsty wolves"), and most of all the attribution to him of great powers of deception—these characteristics make Babo fearsome and commanding at the same time.[36] Nonetheless, most judgments of Babo as a heroic character (or, what is often the same thing in such inquiries, judgments about the degree of Melville's purported racism), have remained locked into Delano's perceptions to such an extent that the revolt itself and the mechanisms holding it in place throughout the tale are lost to view.

On the face of it, Babo is most like Turner in the fact that his revolt is put down and he is executed. As in the case of the Southampton revolt, however, one must look for the success of Babo's revolt not in its duration or its spread. From the perspective of some American readers in the 1850s, the revolt aboard the *San Dominick* would in one sense have been long ago and far away, despite Melville's efforts to suffuse it with contemporary reference, and it therefore cannot be said to work in the immediate realm of propaganda occupied by Turner's "Confessions." Nevertheless, Babo's control and artistry, his capacity both to wield power and to uncover its structural sources and festive trappings, is the most certain sign of Melville's high estimation of the black rebel. As I have suggested, his tale— that is, the masquerade performed for Delano and, by implication, that of Melville for his own audience—is in this respect comparable to Turner's "Confessions" in being a means to carry the strategic purpose of the revolt beyond the execution of the rebel slaves. More to the point than Melville's approval of Babo, however, is his dramatization, despite the obscuring haze of Delano's regulating ignorance, of Babo's own manner of superior regulation.

Perhaps the most significant aspect of Babo's ritual control, an inversion of the policing regulation necessary to the maintenance of the plantation, is to be found in the discipline of the oakum pickers and the hatchet polishers. Like the operation of Delano's own vague suspicions, the near eruption into violence of the black crew at several critical moments appears in a series of hints that flash forth and are just as suddenly concealed. Once, for example, Delano, after being jostled, bids "the blacks stand back . . . making use of a half-mirthful, half-menacing gesture," whereupon the oakum pickers quickly and silently quell any deadly reaction. Such incidents alert the reader, if not Delano, to the threat of the sudden realization of a new revolutionary order, one that has already been called into existence, in fact, but over which a mask of docility has been thrown. The routine of the ship's work is in this way equivalent to the entire regime of slavery's labor and its simmering resistance. The elders act the part of sentinels over the hatchet polishers, who themselves act under the pretense of orders, dictated by Babo to Benito Cereno, to overhaul and clean the cases of knives and hatchets supposedly impaired by the storm's flooding of the hold. Their routine, that is to say, resembles actual labor and mocks it at the same time:

> [The elderly oakum pickers] each had bits of stranded old junk in their hands, and, with a sort of stoical self-content, were picking the junk into oakum, a small heap of which lay by their sides. They accompanied the task with a continuous, low, monotonous chant; droning and drooling away like so many gray-headed bag-pipers playing a funeral march.
>
> The quarter-deck rose into an ample elevated poop, upon the forward verge of which, lifted, like the oakum-pickers, some eight feet above the general throng, sat along in a row, separated by regular spaces, the cross-legged figures of six other blacks; each with a rusty hatchet in his hand, which, with a bit of brick and a rag, he was engaged like a scullion in scouring; while between each two was a small stack of hatchets, their rusted edges turned forward awaiting a like operation. Though occasionally the four oakum-pickers would briefly address some person or persons in the crowd below, yet the six hatchet-polishers neither spoke to others, nor breathed a whisper among themselves, but sat intent upon their task, except at intervals, when, with the peculiar love in negroes of uniting industry with pastime, two and two they sideways clashed their hatchets together, like cymbals, with a barbarous din. All six, unlike the generality, had the raw aspect of unsophisticated Africans.[37]

Screened though our vision of the oakum pickers and the hatchet polishers is by Delano's racialism, we recognize here a further scene of exhausted yet tense simultaneity encompassing the whole of New World slavery. The ritual of labor describes a scene of revolutionary violence held in check—an apt description of slavery itself. The economic order of this plantation, however, is in a state of pathetic decay, its cargo damaged or discarded altogether, its work force in arms and engaged in a clever charade. The scene reminds us, well before the shaving scene, with what ease the instruments of labor could become the instruments of revenge. What Delano interprets as the uniting of "industry with pastime," the mournful songs of the oakum pickers and the periodic cymbaling of the hatchet polishers, describes another level of the ambiguous mask of cultural expression that could be an index of subversion as well as control.

Echoing Frederick Douglass's analysis of holidays and amusements but granting them, in fact, a greater reservoir of insurrectionary potential, Melville's ritualized scene of black labor puts "pastime" in a richly energized cultural context. In Delano's interpretation, work veers toward minstrelsy, as in his perception of Babo at the outset of the shaving scene as a typical Negro who takes "to the comb and brush [as] congenially as to the castanets." The castanets here, however, are hatchets. Similarly, music is communication and conspiracy. Melville's scene of labor exemplifies the fact that the sounds of slave culture could become a form of—indeed, be born of—resistance. Both the black spirituals and the heavily rhythmicized music of the work songs have sometimes plausibly but incorrectly been interpreted as forms of simple diversion, the mark of accommodation (as planters sometimes imagined) or of imposed control. As Melville recognized, however, black music was a sign of the continuity of African culture and was easily transfigured into a vehicle of protest that reversed the regime of power seemingly represented in the songs. The sounds produced by the hatchet polishers in *Benito Cereno* clearly bear both the communicative and the threatening power of African drumming, transferred as it frequently was in the New World into a range of percussive instruments such as claves, scrapers, and chachás (cymbals).[38] Like the "monotonous chant" of the oakum pickers, the language of the hatchets, which is a "barbarous din" to Delano's uncomprehending ears, has the pragmatic value of regulation and signal. Arising at crucial moments in the enactment of Babo's masquerade, the percussive sounds are, in fact, the language in which the Africans' communication occurs during the suspended duration of Delano's presence. Such sounds are nothing less than a kind of speech—in this respect an elaboration of drumming in African tradition as a mode of synthetic vocalism based on pitch and rhythm—and they carry, too, a resonance of sacred power that was retained and developed throughout the Caribbean and among some blacks in the American South.* Whether

---

* Among other valuable remarks on the language of African drumming, including Hurston's landmark observations in *Jonah's Gourd Vine,* some of which appear in the epigraph to this section of the chapter, Janheinz Jahn's more analytic depiction is useful: "The Africans . . . did not need

or not drumming in America retained its explicit African power to summon the gods or the spirits of ancestors, as it did in San Domingo, it was
frequently linked to actual rebellion or to the incitement of less forthright
resistance among slaves throughout the New World, including the American South. (It was reported, for example, that in the large uprising of
slaves near New Orleans in 1811, the rebels were driven into a militarized
frenzy by reed instruments and the beating of drums and iron kettles.)
Revolution aside, African American drumming, which had a significant
role in the formation of black cultural languages in the United States,
carried strong religious and social significance, and was often banned on
plantations as a consequence.[39] Drumming thus epitomized resistance and
can be distributed along a scale running from the retention of African
cultural practices antagonistic to the masters' social regime to outright
assault on that regime.

Because the Ashanti were among those Africans who had developed a
highly sophisticated drum language, with complex rhythms and tonalities
that both accompanied and extended the range of the human voice, it
seems certain that Melville, in his careful attention to the communicative
and regulatory function of the hatchets' cymbaling, meant to probe not
just the supposed "savagery" of African culture (note his ironic rendering
of Delano's mental characterization: their "raw aspect of unsophisticated
Africans") but also the links between rebellion and cultural community.
Even so, the portrait of the slaves, their relations to one another and their

---

an alphabet to convey information; instead they developed the drum language, which is superior
to writing for that purpose. It is quicker than any mounted messenger and it can convey its
message to a greater number of people at one time than telegraph or telephone. . . . Both western
and African culture possessed writing, one an alphabetical script, the other a drum script. . . .
The young European learns in school to connect optical phonetic signs with their meaning, and
in the same way the young African had formerly to learn the art of understanding the acoustical
phonetic signs of the drums." See Janheinz Jahn, *Muntu: African Culture and the Western World*,
trans. Marjorie Grene (1961; rpt. New York: Grove Weidenfeld, 1989), pp. 187–88. Cf. Rudi Blesh,
Shining Trumpets: A History of Jazz, rev. ed. (1958; rpt. New York: Da Capo, 1976), pp. 25–46,
and Paul Oliver, *Savannah Syncopators: African Retentions in the Blues* (New York: Stein and Day,
1970), pp. 30–37, 81–82. On the sacred dimension of drumming in the New World, see especially
Maya Deren's description of the drums and rhythm themselves, rather than the drummers, as
sacred: "It is the drums and the drum beats, *per se*, which are the sacred sound, and although
one man may articulate the drum's voice more fluently, brilliantly and invocatively than another,
he is but a minor part of the mechanism of that speech. . . . It is as if the drums were understood
as the moral *organism*, whereas the drummer was a *mechanism*, a necessary material accessory to
their activity." See Maya Deren, *Divine Horsemen: The Living Gods of Haiti* (1953; rpt. Kingston,
N.Y.: McPherson and Co., 1989), p. 246.

ability to act together, remains fragmentary and somewhat mysterious, perhaps explicitly by Melville's design. Because both Babo's and an omniscient perspective are precluded in *Benito Cereno*, the action of the revolt and the overall workings of the African community remain largely embedded in a network of enigmatic cultural signs.* Babo's precise and nuanced

---

* Melville's Babo, like the original, is Senegalese, whereas the four oakum pickers (Mure, Nacta, Yola, and Ghofan) and six hatchet polishers (Matinqui, Yau, Lecbe, Mapenda, Yambaio, and Akim) named in the deposition in *Benito Cereno* are native Ashanti, which allows Melville to focus much attention on the most feared group of West Africans brought to the New World. Babo, it is also worth recalling, is represented as a man who had already been enslaved in Africa, perhaps by someone like Atufal, the fallen African king who now plays the mock role of humiliated servant. Although Babo and Atufal are leagued together in the revolt, there is the further indication in Melville's version that Babo's dictatorship over Atufal, as well as Benito Cereno, has its source in his own history of enslavement by whites and blacks alike. It is also noteworthy that Babo—both the real Babo and the fictional—has been some years among the Spaniards and that he obviously speaks Spanish well. Babo and Benito Cereno drew up a written agreement governing the voyage to Senegal, signed by Babo in Spanish and possibly in an African language. (Delano's own text is somewhat ambiguous in its reference to "their language." If Babo and Atufal signed in an African language, it may have been Arabic, and Sterling Stuckey and Joshua Leslie speculate that there were more literate Africans than Spaniards on board the *Tryal*, a fact that is supported indirectly by Melville's many allusions to Muslim influences.) In any case, the language he uses is of less consequence than the fact, as it indicates, that Babo was *ladino*—a term applied to Africans who had lived in the New World a considerable length of time or, in some usage, been born there of slave parents, although the term *creole* (or *criolle*) was typically reserved for those born in the New World—and that the Spanish court considered the revolt to have been led by *ladinos*. In this respect Babo, as Stuckey and Leslie argue, represents a historical epoch, joining in his single life several generations of slave experience. As Martin Delany would suggest in his analysis of the potential for slave revolution in Cuba in *Blake*, however, there was considerable contention about whether *ladinos* or *bozales* (recently enslaved native Africans, like Melville's hatchet polishers, whom he and Delano refer to as "raw Africans") were more likely to lead revolts. That is, whites wondered whether those closer to a "savage" state or those more influenced by the forces of "civilization" were more likely to revolt. The argument was bound up as well with the fact that trading of *ladinos* was legal, whereas the importation of *bozales* by the trans-Atlantic slave trade was outlawed by Spain in 1817, however common it remained under false colors in Cuban and American practice. It became a significant legal issue in the *Amistad* trial (see my discussion later in this chapter) whether the slaves were *ladinos* or *bozales*. With the exception of Babo and Atufal, the Spanish court may have been mistaken in its assessment of the revolt's leadership, and Melville's dramatization seems to indicate that *ladinos* and *bozales*, both different African ethnic groups and different "generations" of those enslaved, as it were, could work effectively together toward the same revolutionary goal. As Stuckey writes, "slave ships were the first real incubators of slave unity across cultural lines, cruelly revealing irreducible links from one ethnic group to the other, fostering resistance thousands of miles before the shores of the new land appeared on the horizon—before there was mention of natural rights in North America." See Amasa Delano, *Narrative of Voyages and Travels in the Northern and Southern Hemispheres* (Boston: E. G. House, 1817), p. 337; Herman Melville, *Benito Cereno: Great Short*

command of Spanish, as well as his ability to communicate in West African languages and possibly in Arabic, is notable. In addition, Melville's array of Islamic symbolism suggests a distinct counterpoint to the world of European culture. Not only did Melville's symbolism invoke an Islamic-Christian conflict predating by some seven hundred years the introduction of African slaves into America and locate the pageant of New World slavery and slave revolution against the fact that, at the time Columbus sailed to the New World, Islam was the dominant world religion and the ideological ground of an extensive empire. It was also a means to invoke the strength of a contrary source of revolutionary power; throughout parts of Latin America, Muslim teaching, assimilated to African and African American religions, had been influential in slave rebellions, and Islam in the New World was easily construed as a religion of resistance.[40] Yet, because the Islamic allusions are not widespread and not always attached to the African slaves, it is hard to infer such a direct influence on Babo, except by implication. Melville's specific focus on the Ashanti, however, may offer a more clearly delineated cultural matrix in which to read the revolt.

Commentary on the Ashanti frequently mentioned their brilliance as imperial warriors, their practice of slave sacrifice, and their propensity to act as leaders aboard slave ships or in slave communities and thus their likelihood to instigate revolts. In white accounts drumming itself was associated not just with rebellion but with primitivism and ritual sacrifice by the Ashanti, a fact accentuated by one of Melville's most radical deviations from Delano's original text—the apparent "cannibalizing" of Aranda, or in any event the stripping of his skeleton for presentation in place of the Columbus masthead. The risk Melville ran in such an invention took to its furthest reaches the more general risk that his antebellum readers would see only the brutality of the slave revolt (or, like some of his later readers, interpret such actions as the embodiment of an abstract evil) without comprehending the dynamic that derived violence from violence,

---

Works of Herman Melville, ed. Warner Berhoff (New York: Harper and Row, 1969), pp. 301, 305; Joshua Leslie and Sterling Stuckey, "The Death of Benito Cereno," *Journal of Negro History* 67 (Winter 1982), 297–301; Leslie and Stuckey, "Avoiding the Tragedy of Benito Cereno: The Official Response to Babo's Revolt," *Criminal Justice History* 3 (1982), 128–31; Eugene D. Genovese, *From Rebellion to Revolution: Afro-American Slave Revolts in the Making of the New World* (1979; rpt. New York: Vintage Books, 1981), pp. 98–99; and Sterling Stuckey, *Slave Culture: Nationalist Theory and the Foundations of Black America* (New York: Oxford University Press, 1987), p. 3.

terror from terror. We have no way of knowing, of course, whether cannibalism is the means by which Aranda's skeleton is prepared. The preparation may involve methods vaguely comparable to those that R. S. Rattray recorded in the case of Ashanti kings, whereby decomposition of the corpse was hastened by scraping the bones bare before reassembling the skeleton with gold wire and talismans. The royal skeletons, housed in mausoleums, then became objects of periodic ritual propitiation involving human sacrifice and drumming ceremonies.[41]

Aranda, of course, is not likely to have been done the honor of a king; but his murder and stripping down could well be read as an inversion of his mastery, and the "shaving" away of his flesh may inform the shaving scene of Benito Cereno, whose witness of the skeleton of Aranda as the ship's new figurehead would thus certainly augment his own horror. That cannibalism is only implied by Melville's concealed ritual is important in its own right. For contemporary readers cannibalism was the extreme mark of the "savage," and Irving's *Life of Columbus* was not alone in pointing out that European explorers were predisposed to believe that Africans and Native Americans would be cannibals. What matters from the perspective of Babo's poetics of terrorism, then, is only that the treatment of the skeleton *implies* some grisly ritual, whether it be the eating of the master's flesh or its removal by tools. The crucial ritual is enacted not below deck but above, where Babo forces the Spanish crew to view and testify to his act, such that the ritual that is hidden participates in the one that is not.[42] Like other shadowy tableaux that rise up in nightmare eruption from beneath the surface appearances of the *San Dominick,* the imagined ritual rises into the form of Aranda's skeleton, only to be shrouded in canvas and held from view until the moment of climactic revelation; in the meantime, its work of terror goes on. When the skeleton is exposed in the place of Cristobal Colon's image, it is the Columbian myth itself—the entire story of New World history told from the European American point of view—that is stripped down to the rudiments of its own carnage: the master becomes the sacrificial emblem of his own vicious system of power.

In a minor but perhaps most striking inversion of conventions, those associated with gender roles and domesticity, *Benito Cereno* further undermines the comforts of ruling ideology by overturning Delano's misinterpretation of the slave women's docility ("naked nature . . . pure tenderness and love") to reveal the fact, apparently well grounded in the actual revolt itself and the significance of matrilineal authority in Ashanti culture, that the women are every bit the equal of the men in the strength of their resistance. In the final battle they raise "a wailing chant, whose chorus was the clash of steel," and generally encourage the rebels in their violence, even preferring a more brutal torture, one may surmise because of the sexual abuse slave women were often compelled to endure on ship and plantation alike.[43] The black women, merged in Delano's perceptions with the amorphous background of the "natural," the prime cultural sign of racism's disguise, turn out to be central to the revolt itself and its subsequent regulation. Like the percussion of the hatchets, their "wailing chant" infuses the steel of insurrection with added linguistic power. The war songs of the women, the rhythmic control of the hatchet polishers, the prominent role of the elders in managing the concealed revolt, and everywhere Babo's ritualized manipulation of the ship's reconstituted theater of revolutionary terror—all these elements indicate Melville's transfiguration of the inert materials of Delano's own account into a subtle commentary on the hidden presence of African culture within an unsuccessfully suppressive European American regime.

That is to say, there is a complex cultural language at work behind the scenes of our first perceptions of the *San Dominick*. Not only does the narrator's tale become more controlled and suffocating on subsequent readings, but, more important, Babo's control and the array of African presences are highlighted. Most of all, Melville emphasizes the links between Babo's language and his own in his conversion of the rhythms of resistance into an explicit mechanism of ritual control. As Benito Cereno delivers his halting, dictated tale of the *San Dominick*'s calamitous voyage, all the while "painfully turning in the half embrace of his servant" and driving Delano deeper into suspicion of his utter incompetence as a mariner and captain, the cymbaling of the hatchets (which "had anything but an attractive look, and the handlers of them still less so") periodically erupts. The intervention into the tale of the menacing sounds of the hatchets reinforces Babo's quiet, even silent pressure of dictation, controlling Benito Cereno's narrative and momentarily arousing Delano's alarm, which quickly subsides in his characteristic perception that the file of hatchet polishers is nothing but "so many organ-grinders, still stupidly intent on their work." What Cereno recognizes, Delano ignores. And yet Melville takes care to indicate that Delano too is regulated by the ritual charade staged by Babo, who plays upon the American's own self-regulation by racist assumptions and blind "innocence." The labor of the "Ashantee conjurors," as Delano designates them, thus promotes and conceals revolutionary order; the Sambo mask, conditioned by Delano's expectations, overlies not just the single Nat Turner, with his potential for the isolated spree of antislavery terror, but a pervasive conspiracy and politicized social organization of the sort that the letter from "Nero" threatened in Virginia or that had to be imagined latent within any segment of the slave population. As he reviews the suspicious questions put to him about his own ship, Babo's manipulation here coming yet closer to merging itself with the narrator's, Delano momentarily gives over the regulation of his consciousness to Babo: "By a curious coincidence, as each point was recalled, the black wizards of Ashantee would strike up with their hatchets, as in ominous comment on the white stranger's thoughts." Here it is Delano who is the stranger, the Other, and the reader is briefly transported outside his point of view and required to see the action from an opposing perspective. Before once more dismissing his suspicions of Benito Cereno's piratical designs as an "incredible inference" not to be credited since he assumes it would require the allegiance of Cereno's entire crew, white and black alike, Delano articulates to himself the unrecognized truth of the situation: "Upon gaining that vicinity [of his own ship at anchor], might not the *San Dominick,* like a slumbering volcano, suddenly let loose energies now hid?"[44]

Indeed, Delano's misconception aside, Babo does plot the release of revolutionary energies spreading to Delano's ship, just as it was feared that the black revolution in San Domingo, frequently characterized by southern and northern writers as an impending volcanic eruption, conflagration, or hurricane, might spread to other slaveholding territories. By framing his revelation of the allegorical significance of the tale with the "ominous comment" of the hatchet polishers, Melville exposes the haunting gap between the mind of New England and the mind of African America. The cultural divide is also a political divide fashioned by the history of New World slavery and its simmering turmoil. Melville's brilliant transfer of revolutionary regulation out of the consciousness of Delano and into that of Babo, underlain by his scant but systematic allusions to African cultural practice as a New World language of resistance, also had more than general significance for his midcentury audience. It would surely have reminded readers of mounting anxiety not over expansion alone but over the risk that present Caribbean nations would be the cradle for revolutions aimed at the United States and its southern slave economy. In fact, Babo's juggling play, with its razor aimed at the throat of the South, had a more specific reference than the legacy of San Domingo's

long-standing menace to southern slaveholding. In the wake of the dip-
lomatic crisis over the slave revolt aboard the *Creole* in 1843, Daniel Webster
wrote to the American consul in Havana to beware a British plot to invade
Cuba and put in power "a *black Military Republic* under British *protection.*"
With 600,000 blacks in Cuba and 800,000 in her West Indian islands,
Britain could "strike a death blow at the existence of slavery in the United
States" and seize control of the Gulf of Mexico.[45] Webster's concern
anticipated by ten years the magnified apprehension about the Caribbean
to which both Melville's tale and Delany's *Blake* respond, and it throws
into relief the split between revolutionary ideals and revolutionary sentiment that perennially compromised and postponed the question of slavery.

A symptom of his own ambivalence about the tortured relationship
between union and slavery, Webster's warning about Cuba sheds a different light as well on Babo's symbolic role. Not only might Babo evoke
Toussaint, Nat Turner, Madison Washington, or Joseph Cinque; he likely
also brought to mind in Melville's audience the current ruler of Haiti,
Faustin Soulouque, who came to power in 1847 and had himself made
emperor on the model of Dessalines in 1849. His empire was renowned
for its gaudy displays of pomp and feared for its brutality. He employed
voodoo, priests, assassination, torture, and massacre to put down any
threat of revolt; and in 1849 he mounted the first of several attacks on
Santo Domingo (that is, the Dominican Republic, independent since 1844)
that were sometimes perceived abroad as a campaign to exterminate the
white race. An article in the *Democratic Review* in 1853 declared Soulouque
"the dark image of Louis Napoleon" and ridiculed the reluctance of the
United States, France, and England to join together in putting down this
"despot of a horde of black savages, whose grandfathers murdered their
masters, and whose fathers murdered their brothers . . . and [who] would
as readily exterminate every white man, as would their ancestors in the
jungle of Africa."[46] The fear that a black empire would spread throughout
the Caribbean was in turn countered by (or acted as a cover for) southern
calls for American intervention which were spurred on by the arrival of
Franklin Pierce's expansionist administration.

Among the constellation of historical and contemporary issues Melville
invoked in the drama of the *San Dominick*, present concern over the
sporadic war between Haiti and the Dominican Republic is central for
several reasons. From the mid-1840s on, claims had been made by Frederick Douglass and others that Haiti would be annexed to protect American (slaveholding) interests. Now threats to the Dominican Republic—

another Texas, it was said—seemed to offer a suitable excuse. The significance of the whole island was heightened by the simultaneous crisis over the Kansas-Nebraska Act and the "Africanization of Cuba," a purported plot by Spain and Britain to free slaves and put blacks in power. In retrospect, the fact that the South spent energy on the battle for Kansas that it might otherwise have directed toward Cuba, a territory of greater value to it, does not contradict the fact that at the time acquisition of *both* seemed possible. Pierce's May 1854 interdiction against filibustering in Cuba was based on his reports that Cuba was too well protected, and on northern pressure brought to bear on him as a result of his conciliation of the South in signing the Kansas-Nebraska Act the day before. Cuba, in addition, would have been too much. If the South, in David Potter's words, "sacrificed the Cuban substance for the Kansas shadow," it did not do so intentionally. Besides, the fears of endless slave expansion that Theodore Parker voiced in "The Nebraska Question" were still echoed a year later in an essay, "The Kansas Question," appearing in the October 1855 issue of *Putnam's* in which *Benito Cereno*'s serialization began. Kansas, the essay maintained, was but the next step in the spread of slavery to Mexico, the Amazon, and eventually back to Africa. In the long run, the conjunction of Kansas and Cuba devasted both the Democratic party and the idea of popular sovereignty; crushed the South's dream of a Caribbean empire; lost a territory destined to be of strategic importance to the United States in later years; rekindled fears about the spread of Haitian terror and counterbalancing proslavery plots against that republic; and at the same time sparked premonitions of the greater domestic convulsion to come. "The storm clouds of [war over] slavery were gathering so fast in the South," wrote John Bigelow to Charles Sumner after an 1854 visit to Haiti, "that writing letters about Hayti seemed like fiddling while the country was burning."[47]

The threat posed by an "Africanization" of the colonial New World, which would play a key part in Delany's linkage in *Blake* between plots of slave resistance in the United States and those in Cuba, remained plausible, not likely—but perhaps less unlikely than the "incredible inference" Delano imagines such a plot to require. Melville does not allow us inside of Babo's rebellion, and our view is at times as nearly veiled as Delano's. And yet, of course, we see far more. Most of all, we see the array of Africanisms that constitute Babo's own weapons of resistance and exist as a distinct shadow play behind the overt theatricalization of power that Babo's minstrelsy presents to Delano, providing an "ominous comment on the white stranger's"—and the white reader's—"thoughts." Africanization, as *Benito Cereno* portrays it, is not a Spanish plot but a force of African resistance to New World slavery. Bigelow's letter to Sumner makes San Domingo the shadow play of coming American civil war, but *Benito Cereno* brings the portent of Caribbean revolution more strongly into the foreground, more firmly yokes it to America's paralyzed revolutionary moment. The two worlds are layered upon each other, made simultaneous, as the black revolutionary world may be said to be layered upon the revolutionary world of the American and French political fathers. The play of the barber is thus extended into a grander historical dimension by Melville's pantomime of New World conflagration at the hands of black slaves. Held in check at a point of explosion and contagion, the Africanization of the slaveholding New World may well have seemed no less real to Melville's audience than a bloody, divisive civil war in the United States.

The Law of Nature or the Hive of Subtlety

The counterpointed plots at work in the political context of America's Caribbean interests is matched by the counterpointed actual or imagined plots that circulate throughout *Benito Cereno*. In his construction of slave revolution, however, Melville gave no easy quarter to the rights of black freedom; rather, he measured pragmatically the likely operation of the law and of race politics in America. Moreover, his fascination with revolt and mutiny, as *White Jacket* and *Billy Budd* remind us, was tempered always by his equal fascination with the mechanics of repression. Captain Vere's combined paternalism and rigid justice refine qualities found in both the fictional and the actual Captain Delano. Even for the good captain, like the good master, benevolence may be no barrier either to rebellion or to its consequences. "I have a great horror of the crime of mutiny," wrote Delano in a discussion of the case of the *Bounty* in his *Narrative*, for it leads only to greater abuses against the mutineers. "Vengeance will not always sleep, but wakes to pursue and overtake them." A virtual reign of terror against blacks followed Turner's insurrection. Likewise, Delano had to prevent the Spanish crew and Benito Cereno himself from "cutting to pieces and killing" the blacks after the *Tryal* had been retaken. But legal retribution followed the same instinct. At Concepción, as graphically as in Melville's tale, five of the rebels were sentenced to hanging and decapitation, their heads then "fixed on a pole, in the square of the port of Talcahuano, and the corpses of all . . . burnt to ashes." Justice here echoes revolution: among more gruesome brutalities, both sides in the San Domingo Revolution displayed the severed heads of their opponents; similarly, the heads of defeated black insurrectionists in Charleston in 1739, New Orleans in 1811, and Tennessee in 1856 were fixed on poles or carried in parades, while in the wake of Nat Turner's revolt, as I have discussed in chapter 1, the head of a black man was impaled on a stake outside Jerusalem at an intersection that henceforth became known as Blackhead Signpost. Babo's head, "that hive of subtlety," gazes across the plaza toward St. Bartholomew's Church, where the recovered bones of Aranda lie, and beyond that the monastery where Benito Cereno lies dying, soon to "follow his leader."[48]

The repressive mechanisms of justice—legally authorized or not—worked swiftly to contain slave insurrection in the United States when it occurred. But full-scale insurrection was only the most extreme form of slave resistance, which appeared in many guises. In the atmosphere of crisis in which Melville wrote, it is important to add, simple escape from slavery had come to seem a potential revolutionary act, with its suppression guaranteed by the Fugitive Slave Law. Melville's investigation of revolt in *Benito Cereno* extrapolates from the controversial decisions upholding the Fugitive Slave Law rendered by his father-in-law, Massachusetts Supreme Court Chief Justice Lemuel Shaw, to more difficult and germane instances of revolt at sea.[49] Despite the fact that he held antislavery views while adhering to what he took to be the overriding primacy of the rule of law, Shaw is no doubt burlesqued alongside Webster as a man blinded by the ideology of Union. Delano appears to have none of the conscience of Justice Shaw, but in any case his mind is rendered by Melville not as a moral repository but as a sieve for the cascading dialectic between racial psychology and political power. The most difficult decision to make about *Benito Cereno,* in fact, is whether there is in Delano any difference whatsoever between blind ignorance and a calculating assertion of hierarchical power that hides behind ostensible ignorance.

But this tautological conundrum also resonates with contemporary ideological significance. Aside from the revolt of Turner, the instances of slave uprising that most drew public attention in the late antebellum period took place aboard ships and involved international rights entailing long court disputes. Like the revolt aboard the *San Dominick,* however, they also set the questions surrounding slaves' "right of revolution" in a framework at once terribly ambiguous and crystal clear. The case of the slave revolt aboard the *Creole* was the subject, as we have seen, of Frederick

Douglass's short story "The Heroic Slave," which played ironically on the name of the revolt's leader, Madison Washington, to highlight the shadowed vision of the founding fathers. Indeed, Douglass himself once anticipated the climactic scene of *Benito Cereno,* in which Delano, echoing the satyr of the ship's sternpiece—"holding his foot on the prostrate neck of a writhing figure"—grinds the black rebel beneath his own foot. Speaking to a Boston antislavery audience in 1848, Douglass proclaimed: "There are many Madison Washingtons and Nathaniel Turners in the South, who would assert their rights to liberty, if you would take your feet from their necks, and your sympathy and aid from their oppressors." But the more famous case of the *Amistad,* whose slaves revolted in 1839 and were eventually captured off Long Island after an abortive attempt to sail to Africa, is even more likely to have been on Melville's mind—not least because the enactment of the revolt resembled that aboard the *Tryal–San Dominick,* and because the slave leader, Joseph Cinque, was viewed by a contemporary white writer as an intriguing combination of guile and humanity, a man whose "moral sentiments and intellectual faculties predominate considerably over his animal propensities," but who "killed the Captain and crew with his own hand, cutting their throats."[50]

Henry Highland Garnett, Douglass, and other abolitionists celebrated Cinque's heroism, even considered him an American patriot; and when John Quincy Adams won freedom for the slaves before the Supreme Court (much to the embarrassment of President Van Buren and the outrage of the Spanish authorities, who had demanded their return to Cuba), he appealed to "the law of Nature and Nature's God on which our fathers placed our own national existence."[51] What, though, was the "law of Nature," and what evidence was there that it was synonymous with the law of the fathers? The Supreme Court rulings in both the *Creole* and *Amistad* cases were fraught with ambiguity, and as Robert Cover points out, Adams's appeal in the *Amistad* case contained what was perhaps a deliberate double entendre, a kind of tautology: Adams "could be saying that nature's law applied because there was no other law or that there was no other valid law because nature's law applied." Justice Joseph Story's opinion in the slaves' favor rested on the first side of this razor-sharp distinction; that is, he ruled that the *Amistad* slaves, because they were shown to be *bozales* (not *ladinos,* as the Cuban ship masters had claimed in their false documentation), were never legally enslaved (rendering both Spanish law and treaty inapplicable) and therefore had the right to embrace the law of nature, rebel against their captors, and attempt to sail to Africa.

In the absence of positive law, the purportedly eternal principles of justice prevailed. Abolitionist celebration of the victory and of Adams's eloquent brief lost sight of the fact that Story's decision had done nothing to dislodge the notion that "legal" slaves were property and that they had no rights under American law. In the similar 1843 case of the American slave ship *Creole,* the inspiration for Douglass's "Heroic Slave," the slaves revolted off the coast of Virginia, en route to New Orleans, and sailed to Nassau, where they were freed by British authorities, despite the fact that they had been legal American slaves when they left port, sailing under the American flag to an American destination. Daniel Webster among others had celebrated the *Amistad* decision but refused to recognize the same rights in American slaves aboard the *Creole.* The perceived threat of the spread of black rebellion in the Caribbean was one difference, enduring contention with England another. Arguments by Joshua Giddings and William Jay to the effect that natural law superseded American law on the high seas were ignored by the arbitrator, who later decided that the United States' claims of remuneration were justified, and Giddings was censured in Congress for encouraging slave revolt.[52]

For a theory of emancipation, neither the *Amistad* nor the *Creole* provided particular solace. In both instances the freedom won by the slaves was undermined by the fact that no "right of revolution" had been recognized; the technical definition of legal slavery and the ambiguity of legal rights on the high seas interferred with clear enunciations of African American rights. Both the law of slavery and the proslavery ideology on which it was founded (in the North as well as the South) were so permeated with notions of nature's hierarchy—the distribution of sentiments and powers according to an imagined set of "natural" or divine ordinances—that no other conclusion seemed possible. Recognizing just this fact, Melville had to demonstrate that the very notion of the law of nature was itself riddled with assumptions that could as easily authorize racism as contravene it. Although Babo acts according to the laws both of nature and of the revolutionary fathers, Delano cannot conceive of such action in black slaves. Like the "naked nature" of the slave mothers aboard the *San Dominick,* which turns out to conceal in them a rage for torture and brutality surpassing that of the men (a feminine brutality corroborated, it might be added, by accounts of the San Domingo rebellion), the "natural" relationship of master and slave defined by the fathers, despite their inclusive dream of freedom, remained a disguise and a delusion.[53] Like many such delusions, however, the racialized law of nature was one of considerable force. The elaborate minstrel charade of Babo, with its regulating torment and display of intellectual prowess, entirely shatters the paternalistic benevolence and the law of nature governing proslavery. The master, Benito Cereno, is stripped of his soul as Aranda was stripped of his flesh. But this does not prevent the restoration of a regime of benevolent rule by Amasa Delano, the American captain. Tautologically, the law of nature is itself a "knot": it both *is* and *is not;* its application, as the opposing decisions of the *Amistad* and the *Creole* indicate, hinged upon the applicable artifices of human power, not on an abstract moral principle. Like the court decision, Delano's actions and his restorative narrative tell us that the law of nature is the law of power.

Although some readers have dismissed the legal documents at the conclusion of the tale as an aesthetic miscalculation or an unnecessary flaw resulting from Melville's hasty composition or his attempt to stretch his commercial reward from *Putnam's,*[54] a majority have seen in those documents an approximation of the full moral burden of the story, a burden that Delano escapes and to which Benito Cereno succumbs in the muted finale. In them is embedded the final account of the law of slavery in *Benito Cereno;* in them the revelation that the law of nature is an artifice of expediency leads only to the conclusion that artifice and nature form a tautology. Returning the tale to the actual historical narrative from which it emerged, like a "shadowy tableau" from the deep, and at the same time reconstituting the social and political conventions threatened by the revolt aboard the *San Dominick* and held in suspension by the play engendered in Delano's consciousness by Babo's masquerade and Melville's cunning narrative form, the legal deposition acts retrospectively to explain and endorse, in stately legal phrases, the urgent suppression of the slaves' revolt. Insofar as the depositions define the historical character of *Benito Cereno,* they do so by the virtually silent dictation of indirect speech reproduced in documents "selected, from among many others, for partial translation," but about which the suspicion arises in the tribunal that the deponent "raved of some things that could never have happened."[55] The flawed and cold-blooded depositions recount the rebellion selectively and retrospectively, and in doing so they reenact and respond to an escalating pressure to cure the disease aboard the *San Dominick,* restore regulation and order, and suppress the rebellion by legally deposing the fallen black king Babo.

It is on the authority of these markedly fragile and questionable legal documents that we are asked to reconstruct, in imagined memory, the black revolution that they formally suppress, and to distinguish between the voice of the tale, which engages in a rebellious creation of fiction, and the voice of the deposition, which apparently recites and reproduces the historical texts of the actual trial of the actual Captain Delano's actual account. The "fictitious story" dictated by Babo to Don Benito that the deposition alludes to but fails to reproduce thus points toward and in retrospect allies itself with the fiction of the mystery story created by Melville, itself suppressed and overturned by the stately, ceremonial, and "literal" language of the court. As a "key" that "fit[s] into the lock of the complications which precede it," the deposition ironically reverses these significant symbols of lock and key earlier ironically attached to Benito Cereno's mock power; for while it explains the mystery, unlocks it, the deposition also publicly and legally locks up the significance of the revolt in chains and sentences that are as immune to subversion and irony as Delano's consciousness.[56] In its extreme act of countersubversion, the deposition overthrows the suspended irony that momentarily makes master slave and slave master, undoes roles and scenes in which rebellious metaphors have come dangerously close to becoming literal, restores the good weather and smooth sailing of a racially hierarchical "natural" world, and retrospectively suppresses the revolt of Melville's fictional version of Delano's history. The law of slavery, Melville seems to say, is the law of history.

And yet the final conversation of the tag ending, deferrred by Melville and presented retrospectively, suggests that the authority of the deposition, riddled with lapses and obscured by "translation," is not complete, that in fact the hull of the *San Dominick,* "as a vault whose door has been flung back," does not lie completely "open to-day," but rather, like the enchanted deep, takes back what it gave while leaving a shadow of meaning suspended between revolt and deposition, subversion and countersubversion. The black right of revolution left suspended outside the confining chains of legal language is not more "natural" than social or political, nor does Melville come close to granting its moral authority anything like beneficence. It is simply one form of power standing behind the mask of another, waiting in the shadows for its turn. The full character of *Benito Cereno*'s ironic suspense and draining silence about crucial matters thus comes into proper perspective only at the end—not just the end of the mystery tale, when in a "flash of revelation" the truth of the revolt is revealed to Delano and the skeletal figurehead of the *San Dominick* is exposed, but in the end of the entire tale, when the two captains, in the scene given "retrospectively, and irregularly," stand once again in confrontation and the narrator proceeds to describe the spiritual wastage and death of Don Benito, and the "voiceless end" of Babo, his severed "head, that hive of subtley, fixed on a pole in the Plaza."[57] The silence that follows the last conversation of Delano and Cereno, echoing the moments of suspended or suppressed power that animate Melville's whole tale, leaves the American and the Spaniard poised once again in that posture of flawed communication and failed communion that defines their relationship throughout the story of the slave revolt aboard the *San Dominick,* divided yet merged by the shadow play of Babo's revolt, which holds the New World history they together summarize in a state of haunting crisis.

The suspension of authority that envelopes the *San Dominck* and its tale is a form of mutual *abdication,* a silence or refusal to speak and act that both expresses and withholds authority by keeping it readied for possible implementation. The link between Babo as artist and Melville as narrator— both silently engaged in the scheming of plots and the dictating of roles to their captains—that is suggested in the shaving ritual is reinforced in the scene of Babo's execution by the fact that the narrator's exposition has been a "hive of subtlety" all along. In a tale whose concealed "plot" characteristically proceeds by "whispering" and the exchange of "silent signs," Melville's own authorial abdication, like that of his characters, serves to form a moral riddle that deepens even as it is solved by fully participating in it. Like the "dusky comment of silence" that accompanies Babo's razoring, cunningly inserted between the talking and listening of the two captains, the silence that pervades Melville's tale in its atmosphere of suppressed articulation and failed communication is itself a form of expression that makes the ground the reader treads in *Benito Cereno,* a ground "every inch" of which, to borrow one of Cereno's final remarks to Delano, has been "mined into honey-combs," as perilously brittle as the decaying ship's balustrade, which at one point gives in to Delano's weight "like charcoal." After the confrontation of Delano and Cereno that produces the "shadow of the Negro," there is "no more conversation."[58]

In between rebellion and suppression, or between the creation of authority and its exercise of mastery and decay into enslaving conventions, lies silence. Frozen in indecision, the law derived from the *Creole* and *Amistad* cases, like the logic of the Fugitive Slave Law, was silent on the only issue that mattered to Babo. His silence, in turn, is the most powerful articulation of those unrecognized rights, no matter that they in turn may lead to the creation of a new racial hierarchy grounded in naked power.

Babo's aspect seems to say, "Since I cannot do deeds, I will not speak words," and, when Don Benito faints in his presence, he forces Babo's legal identity to rest on the testimony of the sailors. Melville's characterization of Babo recalls the "martyr-like serenity" attributed to Cinque; it also recalls Denmark Vesey's co-conspirator Peter Poyas in his admonition to his comrades, "Do not open your lips! Die silent, as you shall see me do," as well as the language that John Beard used, in his then authoritative 1853 account of Toussaint and the San Domingo Revolution, to describe the rebels' reaction to extreme torture: "On the countenance of those who were led to death shone an anticipation of the liberty which they felt was about to grow on a land watered with the blood of their caste. They had the same firmness, the same resignation, the same enthusiasm as distinguished the martyr of the Christian religion. On the gibbets, in the flames, in the midst of tortures scarcely was a sigh to be heard; even the child hardly shed tears."[59]

Babo's silence also gathers together the powerful instances of silence articulated in the narrative—his own "dusky comment of silence" during the shaving, the Spanish sailor's "silent signs," the "unknown syllable" communicated among the hatchet polishers, Cereno's "mute dictatorship," the contagion of silence that overtakes Delano as well, Don Benito's terror that is "past all speech," and so on[60]—compressing all of them into the overwhelming *abdication* of his own silent death, which renounces power while at the same time reserving its volcanic energies in a radical shadow play staged within the legal theater of his own execution. Like Nat Turner and Gabriel Prosser, who refused to plead guilty to crimes that were crimes only within the narrow rule of law, not within the realm governed by the "law of nature," Babo will not speak within the language of a law that does not apply to him. As the paradoxical *Creole* and *Amistad* cases suggested, the rebels might legally *be slaves* by rule of law, according to the state code of chattelism that could be adduced in certain circumstances; but in truth they were, no matter, *not slaves*. The law of slavery, the law of "man" and "thing," was a pure tautology in which *is* and *is not*, mastery and bondage, were entangled in a spiraling dialectic. In such a world violence followed by silence was enough to count as freedom.

Caribbean Empires

Benito Cereno circles continually around a plot against himself that Delano vaguely suspects Benito Cereno to be contemplating, perhaps with the aid of Babo and the slaves. As Melville's working out of Delano's New England anxiety suggests, fears of purported plots of slaves against their masters were matched or outstripped at the time by fears of the two other "plots" I have touched on—that of the South to expand its power and that of Cuba to be "Africanized." The supposed conspiracy of 1853 between Spain and Britain to end slavery and the slave trade in Cuba and promote armed black rule produced calls from Cuban and American slaveholders for American intervention. New Spanish policies liberalizing slave laws, combined with the seizure in February 1854 of the American steamer *Black Warrior* on a violation of port regulations, accelerated both legal and extralegal maneuvering to obtain Cuba before it became, as a State Department agent, Charles W. Davis, wrote in March 1854, another "Black Empire" like Haiti, "whose example they would be proud to imitate" in destroying the wealth of the island and launching "a disastrous bloody war of the races." The height of imperialistic rhetoric came after the crisis had passed and attempts to force a purchase of Cuba had failed, in the notorious Ostend Manifesto of October 1854, which declared that Cuba belonged "naturally to that great family of States of which the Union is the providential nursery" and that the United States would be justified "in wresting it from Spain . . . upon the very same principle that would justify an individual in tearing down the burning house of his neighbor if there were no other means of preventing the flames from destroying his own home." The issue of Cuba, that is to say, was couched in the familiar rhetoric of domesticity that ruled debates over slavery. It also brought together just those threats Delano perceives aboard the *San Dominick:* Spanish misrule and deterioration, and threatened black insurrection and liberation.[61]

The more telling literary meditation on the specific clash over slavery in Cuba was to appear on the very eve of the Civil War in Delany's novel *Blake; or the Huts of America.* Calling for the exercise of black revolutionary force, Delany replied to Stowe, to Douglass, and conceivably to Melville in *Blake,* some of whose ideas and verse date to Delany's service as co-editor of the *North Star* with Douglass from 1846 to 1848, and which was probably written between 1852 and 1858 before being published serially in part in 1859 and probably in full in 1861 and 1862. Because it is rather awkwardly crafted as a novel and more often resembles a manifesto or a political anatomy of slave culture, *Blake* has seldom been read with much attention to its remarkably potent message, its array of the language and song of early black American life, and its interesting formal devices. The novel advocates slave revolution and depicts a leader, Henry Blake, who combines the vision of Nat Turner with the commanding intelligence and authority of Toussaint; like *Benito Cereno,* however, the novel also concludes in a state of paralysis. Identifying divine deliverance with violent revolution and associating the plotted insurrections of Gabriel Prosser, Denmark Vesey, and Nat Turner with the spirit of the American Revolution, Blake, born Henrico Blacus in Cuba, is a free man who spreads a plot for "terrible insurrection" throughout the South after his wife, a slave who rejects the attentions of her owner-father, is sold to a planter in Cuba. Blake then follows her trail to Cuba, buys her freedom, and becomes the leader of the "Army of Emancipation" that will free the slaves of Cuba and, presumably, spread the fire of revolution to the United States. The *Anglo-African Magazine* advertised that *Blake* would run to eighty chapters, but the serialization that survives breaks off in an unresolved state of tension, on the brink of black revolution, at chapter 74—not, however, without an extraordinary force gathered precisely into that threatening truncation.[62] Whereas Melville charts the suppression and containment of slave rebellion, Delany brings rebellion to the point of outbreak without actualizing it.

The interest of the novel, however, lies less in its craft, which is often rudimentary, than in its compelling portrait of a revolutionary ethos. Although *Blake*'s own dramatic action is unified, the historical characters and events to which Delany alludes lay several spheres of action upon one another, ranging from the significant series of Cuban slave uprisings in the early 1840s (climaxing in the conspiracy and severe repression known as La Escalera) through the calls for American annexation and the filibustering of the 1850s. At the conclusion of Delany's novel, the poet Placido, who in reality was executed in 1844 for his part in a major revolt, is still alive, awaiting the coming revolution, whereas Narciso Lopez, who commanded several private American attempts to annex Cuba by military force before being executed in 1851, has just been led to the garrote. Likewise, the Dred Scott decision of 1857, the Fugitive Slave Law of 1850, and Cuban political events of the 1840s all seem to be telescoped into the much shorter time frame of the novel. Although not so dramatic as Melville's symbolic compression of the Age of Revolution into the antebellum decade, the effect is to create a fictive world in which Cuban and American slavery are yoked together in historical simultaneity. *Blake* is neatly divided into two parts, but the temporal movement is not forward, toward the moment before the Civil War, when the novel was published, but back and forth; and the relationship between United States expansionism and Cuban revolution is implicit from the outset before being brought to a white heat at the conclusion of the novel. In this respect the stark division into halves may be seen less as a mechanical device than a means to accentuate the fact that the Cuban situation was a kind of twin, a shadow play, of the American South for masters and slaves alike.

The demise of San Domingo as a slave state propelled forward the slave economies of both the United States and Cuba, the first because of the expansion into Louisiana and eventually Texas that it facilitated (by means of the Louisiana Purchase), the second because of the marked rise in sugar production that occurred when planters shifted their attention to the island, followed by the influx of African labor supplied in American and Portuguese slave ships. By the 1850s southern expansionist sentiment, though it was hardly univocal, was often predicated upon glamorous visions of an empire that reached beyond the United States' continental borders. The South's—and the Pierce administration's—plan to "rescue" Cuba from black rule presupposed the decay of the Spanish empire and its replacement by an Anglo-Saxon empire in the western hemisphere. Peculiar to the South's version of manifest destiny, of course, was the extension of slavery and the shift of national power geographically to the south. The appearance of *Blake* at what came to be the tail end of the antebellum expansionist period is closer to prophecy than to confirmation, for the outcome of slaveholding expansion could not easily be foreseen at the time. The proslavery dream of a Caribbean empire reached its most extreme formulations in documents such as Henry Timrod's "Ethnogenesis," William Walker's *War in Nicaragua,* and Edward Pollard's *Black Diamonds Gathered in the Darky Homes of the South* (published in 1861, 1860, and 1859, respectively); but it was based on sentiments expressed throughout the decade, for instance in *The Amazon and the Atlantic Slopes of South America* (1853) by Matthew Maurey, which advocated the export of southern slaves to colonize the Amazon basin. Pollard was representative in his claim that southern expansion was not a sectional issue but one involving "the world's progress, and who shall be the founders of its greatest empire of industry." Eventually, he maintained, the seat of the South's empire would be in Central America; control of the West Indies, the isthmuses of Central America, and the production of the world's cotton and sugar would complete America's destiny:

What a splendid vision of empire! How sublime in its associations! How noble and inspiriting the idea, that upon the strange theater of tropical America, once, if we may believe the dimmer facts of history, crowned with magnificent empires and flashing cities and great temples, now covered with mute ruins, and trampled over by half-savages, the destiny of Southern civilization is to be consummated in a glory brighter even than that of old, the glory of an empire, controlling the commerce of the world, impregnable in its position, and representing in its internal structure the most harmonious of all systems of modern civilization.

Walker, too, in one chapter of the account of his filibustering career in Sonora and Nicaragua, celebrated the destined rejuvenation of Central and South America. The effort the South wasted on the "shadow" of Kansas, Walker wrote, could have brought her the "substance" of Central America, a territory necessary to protect slavery, to raise the African from spiritual darkness and teach him the "arts of life," and to forestall the spread of the economic and political degeneracy that he said had occurred in Haiti and Jamaica.[63]

Walker among others adopted in his rhetoric a new ideology of progress that paternalized the remnants of Spain's American empire. He believed that popular sovereignty could be applied as effectively to the Caribbean and Central America as to Kansas, and that expansion was necessary to complete the republican defeat of dying European monarchism. (Paranoia was not wanting in the argument. In an 1852 article, "The Cuban Debate," the *Democratic Review* attacked Louis Napoleon as a puppet of the "Holy Alliance"—the pope; the czar; the queens of Spain, Portugal, England, Greece; the kings of Prussia and Denmark; the emperors of Haiti, Austria, Morroco; and so on—who were plotting to seize Haiti and Cuba as the prelude to an assault on the principles of democracy in the United States. So refined did this idea of conspiracy become in the early 1850s that at one point Louis Kossuth, the enthusiastically courted hero of the 1848 Hungarian revolution, became embroiled in a southern plot to invade Haiti on the pretext that Faustin Soulouque was a czarist agent.)[64] Needless to say, the engine of expansion was economic. California gold, the dream's prevalent symbol in this period, would soon so enrich the nation, claimed *De Bow's Review* in 1854, that no possible investment would be equal to it but the cultivation (by slave labor) of the entire western hemisphere. Lying between two of the great valleys of the world, the Mississippi and the

Amazon, the gulf would link the most productive regions of the earth, and by unlocking trading access to the wealth of the Pacific basin (China, Australia, California) make the Atlantic in the modern world what the Mediterranean was "under the reign of the Antonies in Rome." Given the continued dissolution of European political power on the one hand and possession of Cuba, Santo Domingo, and Haiti on the other, the United States might control the gulf and through it the world: "Guided by our genius and enterprise, a new world would rise there, as it did before under the genius of Columbus." This new Columbian vision had a price, however, one which the circular argument of the writer for *De Bow's* did little to hide: "Heretofore, the great difficulty in civilizing the barbarian races of the world has been to procure cheap and abundant clothing for them. A naked race must necessarily be a wild one. To Christianize or civilize a man, you must first clothe his nakedness. In the three millions of bags of cotton the slave labor annually throws upon the world for the poor and the naked, we are doing more to advance civilization and the refinement of life than all the canting philanthropists of New and Old England will do in centuries." As the author noted: "Slavery and war have [always] been the two great forerunners of civilization."[65]

And of freedom: "empire" became a common word in discourse about the region—not only among slave interests such as the Knights of the Golden Circle, which promoted a gulf circle of power drawing together New Orleans, Havana, Yucatán, and Central America, but remarkably also among black American colonizationists such as J. Dennis Harris, who proposed to build an "Anglo-African Empire" in Haiti, a mulatto utopia, and James T. Holly, who imagined a similar regeneration originating in Haiti, "the Eden of America," and overspreading the whole world.[66] In his own philosophy of emigration Delany, who worked with Holly in the mid-1850s on plans to found such a black empire in the tropics, eventually turned his attention to Africa, with the more concrete and politically dramatic goal of establishing a cotton empire to counter that of the slaveholding South. Although Delany at the outset of the decade had envisioned Africa as the most appropriate site of black aspirations, his influential nationalist paper, "The Political Destiny of the Colored Race," prepared as a report for the Cleveland National Convention on emigration in 1854, adhered to the convention's narrowly defined program and advocated emigration to the West Indies or South American as a means of establishing the territorial base necessary to black economic independence. Delany argued that the rights of citizenship and participation in national rule would always be denied African Americans, that their population was too sparse to mount effective resistance to white oppression, and that their unique racial traits could be developed, and made visible to the world, only in a separate national arena. (Delany's nationalist pride was reflected in the names of his children, both his sons—Toussaint L'Ouverture, Faustin Soulouque, and Rameses Placido among them—and his daughter, Ethiopia Halle Amelia.) In his call for the cultivation of the Negro's "inherent traits" and "native characteristics," Delany anticipated Du Bois in bending his apparently racialist argument toward a recognition that blacks, as well as whites, could instruct the world in the arts, in philosophy, in political economy, in jurisprudence, and in metaphysics. His more detailed account of his trip to Africa in 1859–60, *Official Report of the Niger Valley Exploring Party* (1861), set forth a plan for emigration that included one of the first strong articulations of an Ethiopianist or Pan-African political philosophy. Arguing that "Africa is our fatherland and we its legitimate descendants," Delany thought that emigration would regenerate both African and American blacks. Coining a phrase that would later become the watchword of modern Pan-Africanists (although they used it in a variety of ways), Delany inserted into a discussion of the manufacture of African cloth and the availability of navigable rivers an explicit nationalist challenge: "Our policy must be—and I hazard nothing in promulgating it; nay, without this design and feeling, there would be a great deficiency of self-respect, pride of race, and love of country, and we might never expect to challenge the respect of nations—*Africa for the African race, and black men to rule them.* By black men I mean, men of African descent who claim an identity with the race."[67]

Blake was composed before Delany's visit to Africa; the onset of the Civil War made moot the planned emigration. The philosophy of racial pride, however, and more particularly the vision of a modern black state that unites the splintered aspirations of the peoples of the African diaspora, is built into Delany's protonationalist novel. Between his nationalist essays and his unique fictional narrative, Delany offered perhaps the most comprehensive literary treatment of Pan-Africanism from an American perspective, and on American soil, prior to Du Bois in *Darkwater* and *Dark Princess*. As Vincent Harding has argued, in *Blake* Delany maintains a striking "revolutionary tension" in his ability to "express an African nationality based on the homeland experience, yet at the same time participate responsibly in struggle against the bondage of African people in the Americas."[68] More than that, he wrote in *Blake* a virtual chronicle of the black revolutionary moment of the Americas, which together with *Benito Cereno* presents a panoramic spectacle of New World slavery in its climactic phase. But unlike Melville he wrote, as it were, from inside the laws of slavery (though Delany himself was never a slave) and from inside the race. He wrote, that is to say, from Babo's point of view.

"It Is Wrote in Jeremiah": American Maroons

> Solomon, General John, and Ditcher lay on their bellies in the hut. They were whispering with their faces near the dirt floor. Gabriel and Blue came in with Ben. No greetings, no useless words passed. The three got down and made a circle. An eery blue light pierced a crack in the wall, separated the dull silhouettes. No preliminary words, no Biblical exten-uations preceded the essential plans this time. . . . They all murmured. Their assent, so near the ground, seemed to rise from the earth itself. H'm. There was something warm and musical in the sound, a deep tremor. It was the earth itself that spoke, the fallen star.
>
> Arna Bontemps, *Black Thunder*

Against the visionary prospect of slaveholding power extended throughout the Southwest and the Caribbean, even Latin America, *Blake* arrays its own power to depict slave resistance on a vast and coherently organized scale. The novel opens with a meeting devoted to the joint interests of Cuban and American slave traders, the latter group including the master of Maggie, Henry Blake's wife. As Delany suggests, there is little to choose between Havana and Baltimore as suitable locations for such a meeting, since the illegal trade in slaves has flourished with Baltimore's participation (along with New York, the city was the leading fitter of the American ships used in the trade between Africa and Latin America) as much as Havana's. In part two of the novel, when Blake becomes involved in a plot to seize a slave trader on the high seas, Delany takes occasion to look in more detail at the mechanism of the trade itself; but the opening scene serves to situate *Blake*'s successive action in the web of economic interest that Delany saw binding the United States to the Caribbean. Bound together, too, are the interests of North and South, a fact made clear in the relations between the family of Colonel Franks, the Natchez planter and owner of Maggie, and their northern relatives, the Ballards. Judge Ballard, recently involved in a court case upholding the Fugitive Slave

Law, and his wife, a cold, condescending woman who insists on having
Maggie as her servant at the Ballards' own Havana country seat, epitomize
the guilty involvement of the North in the crimes of southern slaveholding.* The surreptitious sale of Maggie, which sets in motion Blake's life
as a rebel conspirator, recapitulates the by then archetypal scene of slave
narratives and antislavery fiction, the separation of slave family members,
but it also acts as the linchpin for Delany's critique of the far-flung,
politically and economically complex regime of New World slavery.

The radical southern crusade to reopen the legal slave trade in the 1850s
is a latent topic in *Blake*. The argument of the novel suggests that a revival
of legal trade is at best a sideshow to the more complicated issues of illegal
slaving and the legal internal trade; but it is relevant that southern opinion
in favor of a revived international trade accelerated over the decade. Even
though it was a minority opinion (calls for a revived trade inevitably
alienated northern Democrats, and they were anathema to the upper
South, which had an economic stake in supplying slaves to the cotton
states, and to those who feared rebellion among an increased black population, especially among a fresh concentration of native Africans), the
clamor for revival had a philosophical basis in the view that the South was
the cradle of a new world economic order. Leading ideologues of the
trade, such as Leonidas Spratt, whose "Destiny of the Slave States" (1853)
was the opening salvo in the new war, agreed with George Fitzhugh and
others that slave labor was morally superior to the hired labor of northern
capitalism; and they contended, not without logic, that the integrity of a
slaveholding political economy depended upon a willingness to expand it.
Most southerners opposed a revived trade, but many did so for practical
reasons alone. Jefferson Davis, for example, opposed the trade because he

---

* Judge Ballard's qualifications as a true southerner in spirit do have a limit. On the one hand,
he is shown to be a shrewd investor in Cuban and southern plantations, and his delivered opinion
on the law, which fuses the Compromise and the Dred Scott decision, is impeccably proslavery:
"Persons of African descent have no rights that white men are bound to respect." Moreover, he
believes that the rights granted free blacks and mulattoes in Cuba make the colony "a moral
pestilence, a blighting curse," which can be cured only by American annexation. On the other
hand, when forced to watch a poor slave boy whipped into a grotesque and painful Jim Crow
performance ("Bringing the lash down upon a certain spot on the exposed skin, the whole person
being prepared for the purpose, the boy commenced to whistle almost like a thrush; another cut
changed it to a song, another to a hymn, then a pitiful prayer"), Judge Ballard begins to weep
and halts the cruelty. As Franks remarks to him, in a certain echo of *Uncle Tom's Cabin*: "Not
quite a Southerner yet Judge, if you can't stand that!" See Martin R. Delany, *Blake; or the Huts
of America* (Boston: Beacon Press, 1970), pp. 61–62, 67.

feared a sudden influx of blacks into Mississippi, not because of a theoretical quarrel with the idea. His objection, he added, "is not supposed to
be applicable to Texas, to New Mexico, or to any *future acquisitions* to be
made south of the Rio Grande." One point of Delany's novel, however,
is that a revival of the legal trade was hardly necessary, so porous were
the legal blockades to existing importation of slaves from Cuba to the
lower South.* Cuba itself imported more than half a million African slaves
between 1820 (the date Spanish law supposedly outlawed the international
trade) and the 1850s, and the United States coast from South Carolina to
Texas received thousands of these each year.[69]

When Henry Blake's wife is sold, he manfully confronts Franks and
refuses to serve him. (Presumably one reason for his reluctance physically
to assault Franks, who purchased Blake, once a free man, through chicanery, lies in the fact that Franks is not only Maggie's master but also her
father. Although the complex race-mixture laws of Cuba turn out to play
a role in *Blake,* Delany does not develop the themes of patrimony and
miscegenation with much rigor.) Colonel Franks, echoing the language of
contemporary political apprehension about "Africanization" and simmering black rebellion in the Caribbean, interprets Blake's threat as a "rebellion! A plot . . . but the shadow of a cloud that's gathering fast about us,"
and Delany's orchestration of Blake's consequent activities lends support
to this view. Like the anonymous "Nero," whose threatening letter to
Governor Floyd hinted at a vast conspiracy of southern slaves waiting to
rise in rebellion in the wake of Nat Turner's revolt, Delany's novel outlines
the possibility of such a conspiracy set in motion by the leadership of

---

* As antislavery authors and polemicists were quick to point out, moreover, the moral advantage in America's internal trade was, if anything, minimal. David Turnbull, the famous antislavery
British consul to Cuba whose activities led to his deportation and whose work is almost certain
to have influenced Delany, thought otherwise: "This practice of selling men and women by
auction in the public streets [in the United States], and the indecent personal examination to
which it gives rise, surpasses in shamelessness all the atrocities of . . . Havana, where the sales
are made within doors, and are comparatively private. The purchasers at these slave auctions are
mere dealers or traders who are only not pirates under the American law, because their transactions
are completed on shore. The planters in Louisiana, and along the banks of the Mississippi are
pretty much on a par with those of Cuba and the Brazils; with this difference, that as the prime
cost is greater [in the United States] compared with the food and maintenance of the slave, they
cannot afford to work him to death in so short a time. As to the men of Maryland and Virginia,
who push the *auri sacra fames* so far as to raise negroes like other stock for the market, we must
go to the interior of Africa to find their parallel." See David Turnbull, *Travels in the West: Cuba,
with Notices of Porto Rico, and the Slave Trade* (London: Longman, 1840), pp. 64–65.

Henry Blake. Two narrative plots work side by side over the course of the first half of the novel: the rescue and leading to Canada of Blake's son, Maggie's parents, and a group of other slaves from the Frankses' and surrounding plantations; and concomitantly Blake's travels throughout the slave states, where he lays the groundwork for a shadowy rebellion. Both plot lines have sources in Delany's own life. Throughout the 1850s, as I have suggested, Delany espoused a nationalist philosophy of emigration, and he himself, unable to practice medicine in the United States, moved to Canada in 1856 as a first step toward what he hoped would be a more permanent emigration to Latin America or Africa. Delany helped organize the convention of blacks who met with John Brown at Chatham in 1858; but in his own account of the meeting, he would claim that only Brown's plans for redirecting the Underground Railroad to Kansas were discussed, not the violent insurrection that was to surface at Harper's Ferry. By the time of Brown's action in 1859, Delany was in Africa on his expedition to explore territory for African American emigration. Nevertheless, *Blake,* much of it written in Canada in a house called "The Hut" (in this case the term designates the home of a free, respected black man rather than, as in the subtitle of the novel, the miserable conditions of American and Cuban slaves), is clearly animated by a similar spirit of resistance, with Canada serving in Henry Blake's case as a way station to the final act of revolution that will be launched in his native Cuba.[70]

The more specific basis for the outline of Blake's activities in the first half of the novel lay in travels that Delany himself had made throughout the slave Southwest in the late 1830s. Drawn by the possibility that a large black emigration to the new republic of Texas might open the door to a free black nation, Delany traveled extensively, down the Mississippi, through Louisiana, Texas, Oklahoma, and Arkansas. Although he became persuaded that Texas was destined to become part of the slaveholding South, Delany worked many of his observations and conversations with southwestern blacks into the fabric of *Blake* twenty years later. As Blake travels from state to state, leaving behind him "the consequences of a deep-laid scheme for a terrible insurrection," he also offers Delany the opportunity to survey slave conditions and receptivity to ideas of rebellion.[71] Cunningly playing upon the genre of the travel narrative made popular by Fanny Kemble and Frederick Law Olmstead, Delany's narrative shows slave culture from the inside, from the perspective of resistance. As Delany demonstrates, slave culture is not always visible to the masters, and resistance can take many forms. A Saturday holiday of feasting and merrymaking among the slaves, for example, turns out to be a cover for Henry's escape with his young son; and Mammy Judy's melodramatic expression of religious anguish serves to disguise, before Franks, her knowledge of the boy's whereabouts.

Most important in Delany's analysis, however, is his depiction of the sources in African American slave culture of a readiness for organized political resistance that can be called into action by proper black leadership. Among other reflections on the presiding example of *Uncle Tom's Cabin,* Delany bypasses Stowe's split between the mixed-race George Harris's adherence to the principles of revolutionary democracy (said to result from his white blood) and black Tom's Christian subservience to Legree's brutality by making Blake both fully black and nearly opportunistic in his willingness to manipulate Christian doctrine for his own revolutionary purpose. Indeed, Blake refutes Stowe's racialism in his own attack on the "Brown Society" of Charleston's mulatto elite, who, far from leading the African American revolution, openly castigate darker Negroes. Whereas Mammy Judy and many of the slaves Blake visits in his travels are apparently cowed by the religion of the slaveholders, Blake, like Nat Turner, sees religion as an instrument of struggle. He calls for a prayer before announcing to his maroon comrades his plan for the overthrow of slavery. Blake's "secrets" of organization are never spelled out; but they are no doubt consistent with the natural rights philosophy alluded to in his claim—later explicitly echoed in Arna Bontemps's comparable portrait of Gabriel in *Black Thunder*—that "the trees of the forest or an orchard illustrate [a plan for insurrection] . . . tobacco, rice, or cotton, the whistling of the wind, rustling of the leaves, flashing of lightning, roaring of thunder, and running of streams all keep it constantly before their eyes and in their memory." The natural law underlying Blake's appeal to the right of revolution is consistent, moreover, with his admonition to "make your religion subserve your interests, as your oppressors do theirs . . . we must begin to understand the Bible so as to make it of interest to us."[72]

Blake's repeated reception as a savior and his blessing by the elders among the slaves corroborates the jeremiadic quality of the slave songs and verses that are reproduced throughout the text:

> It is wrote in Jeremiah,
> Come and go along with me!
> It is wrote in Jeremiah,
> Go sound the jubilee!

And, in stark contrast to the pacifying role assigned to Christianity by proslavery advocates and by northern moderates such as Stowe, Blake's prophetic role answers the prayers of the community, as in the case of the eighty-year-old slave who, after meeting with Blake and agreeing to spread the conspiracy himself, declares: "My eyes has seen, and meh yeahs heahn, an' now Laud! I's willin' to stan' still an' see dy salvation!" Deriving his example from Nat Turner rather than Uncle Tom and coming like "a thief in the night" (1 Thessalonians 5:2), Blake unites Christ's Second Coming with the potential terror of slave violence; he seizes the opportunity for a novelistic version of Turner's message that Stowe had thrown away in *Dred,* where the black rebel hero is killed and the maroon community dissolves into the background of her otherwise penetrating cross-racial incest romance. Blake's intention is to convince his followers that a good master is the worst of masters, because of his guile, and to persuade them that slavery at its best has brainwashed them. As one follower, Andy, realizes, after thinking about his former servitude to a relatively decent master: "I could chop 'is head off sometime, I get so mad. I bleve I could chop off Miss Mary' head; and I likes hur; she mighty good to we black folks." Perhaps the lesson of Turner's "Confessions" that Delany most absorbed was that the propaganda of proslavery—its claims of affection and benevolence—was a strong ground on which to build a counterstructure of African American conspiracy and terror. Or, as "Nero" had written in his insinuating terrorist declamation to Governor Floyd: "Revenge possesses some properties in common with love. We cannot enjoy either in full fruition unless the object of affection, or vengeance be conscious of being loved, or punished."[73] The slaveholding "family," Andy says, must not simply be made to repent; it must be executed, mangled.

Blake's prophecy is seen by some survivors of an earlier era as a reanimation of the insurrectionary spirit of Gabriel, Vesey, and Turner, and it is in Virginia and the Carolinas, in fact, that Delany sets his novel's striking conjunction of revolution, conjure, and maroon life. Gamby Gholar and Maudy Ghamus, conjure men and supposed former comrades of Turner and Gabriel, are treated skeptically by Blake (and Delany); but at the same time, their maroon life is also made a sacred preserve (a hush harbor, as it were) of the revolutionary ethos. In the "fearful abode" of the Dismal Swamp, where for years "some of Virginia and North Carolina's boldest black rebels" have lived, writes Delany, "the names of Nat Turner, Denmark Veezie [*sic*], and General Gabriel were held by them in sacred reverence; that of Gabriel as a talisman. With delight they counted the many exploits of [those] whom they conceived to be the greatest men who ever lived, the pretended deeds of whom were fabulous, some of the narrators claiming to have been patriots in the American Revolution." The elderly conjure men confuse the battles of the Revolution with instances of slave resistance (insisting that Gabriel was a general first in "de Molution"), and the episode noticeably distances Blake from the folk army who make up his most likely recruits, much as Douglass detached himself from slave culture even as he drew inspiration from it and much as Bontemps would portray Gabriel as intellectually detached from the folk and the world of conjure in *Black Thunder*. Likewise, in what appears a clear transfiguration of the millenarian signs of Turner's revolt, *Blake* emphatically rationalizes its hero's response to a display of potentially prophetic meteors and comets: Henry is tempted to read allegorical significance into the blazing stars, but Delany, displaying his *own* scientific training and faith in rationalism, emphasizes that "the mystery finds interpretation in the fact that the emotions were located in his own brain, and not exhibited by the orbs of Heaven."[74]

Even though Delany clearly puts little stock in visionary prophecy or conjure (Blake is a pragmatist, recognizing that money is far more effective than conjure in aiding escape from slavery), this unusual episode nonetheless ties Blake to a tradition of resistance that has past heroes and has survived, in the maroon communities and elsewhere, uninhibited by the peculiar institution. Whatever Delany's own skepticism about the folk beliefs of slave culture, his novel pays tribute to those who, in their retention of some mode of an African philosophy and in their existence either on the edge or outside of plantation slavery, have made their own culture. The maroon slave world in which revolt is nurtured is exemplary of the liminal community whose marginalization and subjugation produce manifestations of the sacred or the prophetic by virtue of its inherent transgressions of governing institutions.[75] As Nat Turner had demonstrated with cataclysmic power, liminality could be exploited to controvert the law and philosophy of chattel slavery, and it is this latent reservoir of sacred cultural power that Blake's (and presumably Delany's) travels through the margins of southern slave culture are meant to galvanize.

Blake himself seems a sufficient "warrior" to meet the criteria of the conjure men; and conversely, the maroon community of the swamp, if they are not a large enough number to take the whole United States, as Maudy Ghamus believes, are nonetheless figured as a band of brothers equal to Blake's conspiratorial plans. Delany recognized that maroon com-

munities represented one of the most significant threats to planters—
simply by encouraging other slaves to run away, by staging periodic raids
on plantation supplies and robbing whites, or by more openly engaging
in violent uprising. Cases of arson, attack, and plunder were common in
areas with significant maroon communities, and assaults by white militia
were typically met with harsh resistance. In the United States, nevertheless,
rebellion inspired by maroons was for the most part peripheral and sporadic. Over the course of the antebellum period—until the Civil War,
when organized resistance rose sharply—maroon activity decreased in the
upper South and shifted to the Gulf Coast, but nowhere did it ever have
a presence comparable to the *cimarron* communities of Latin America,
which would become part of Delany's subject in the second half of *Blake*.[76]

Like "Nero's" letter, however, the threat of maroon activity, and the
threat of conspiracy generally, was one measure of the blind inadequacy
of paternalist theories of slave contentment. As it happens, the plans for
insurrection disseminated by Blake, though they correspond in some degree to the trip taken by Delany in 1839, also have an intriguing resemblance to a widespread panic about slave insurrection that swept through
the South in the fall of 1856, while Delany was probably composing his
novel. Reports of mild insurrection were commonplace in other years as
well, but in 1856 the fears took on a momentarily compelling pattern.
Rumors of a plot extending from Delaware to Texas, set for Christmas
Day, ran like wildfire for a time, exacerbated by sectional tensions over
Bleeding Kansas, the Cuban crisis, the reopening of the slave trade, and
particularly the Buchanan-Frémont presidential contest. Despite the fact
that John C. Frémont lost the election, the most severe panic, which
erupted *after* the election, was still blamed by some on abolitionist propaganda or the Republican campaign itself. One Virginian, assembling an
unoriginal set of clichés to explain the panic, asserted that suspicious
whites, reacting to ignorant blacks, who had themselves been seduced by
the misleading rhetoric of the Republican campaign, had become convinced that "they were standing on a volcano, almost ready to burst forth
with fury and destruction . . . momentarily expecting to hear the cries,
groans, and shrieks of women and children who were being murdered by
the hands of slaves." But similar fears were aroused by plots of violent
attack upon slaveholders or municipalities, or plans of plunder and escape,
uncovered in Kentucky, North Carolina, Georgia, South Carolina, Alabama, Florida, Arkansas, Tennessee, Mississippi, Louisiana, and Texas—
in short, in all the states that Henry Blake visits, plus others. Some of the

conspiracies, like those in Texas and Arkansas, purportedly involved hundreds of armed slaves, while others were weakly linked, isolated incidents of resistance or insubordination. The conspiracies discovered in Kentucky and Tennessee appear to have been based on the most substantial evidence of concerted insurrectionary plans. Punishment of implicated slaves, any number of whom were forced into confessions that have to be treated with some skepticism, ranged from whipping to execution. The best accounts suggest that, although the panic was fueled by rumor and unfounded political fears in many instances, the prevalence of the discovered plots was too powerful to overlook. Not without reason, the *Richmond Enquirer* commented: "These are not the wild and visionary projects with which negroes may be disposed to amuse themselves in the most quiet communities but the maturely prepared, and, in some instances, the partially executed plans of a deliberate and widespread purpose of revolt."[77]

Even before he shifted the locale of his revolutionary plot to Cuba, then, Delany had grounded it not in a fantasy of slave revolt but in the substantial evidence of conspiratorial actions among the black communities of the slaveholding South. Such a threat was, in fact, far more likely to arouse apprehension among slaveholders than the manic, futile rebellion led by John Brown, which also gave point to *Blake* after its serialization had already begun in the *Anglo-African Magazine*.* The 1856 panic was unique in the fact that, although the connections are now impossible to piece together, it seems undeniable that some of the conspiracies were linked and that a Christmas rising (perhaps modeled on the great Christmas rising of 1831 in Jamaica) was intended in many quarters. What this suggests, of course, is that there were effective networks of communication hidden from the masters—hardly a surprise but remarkable, in this case, for their seeming extent and complexity. In his journey Blake plants the seeds of such a widespread conspiracy in slave quarters and in the further liminalized world of maroons alike, and it is this tactically astute political message, rather than his decided skepticism about supernatural visions and conjure, that constitutes his prophecy. If it is implausible that the 1856 conspiracies were motivated by a single insurrectionary leader, an orga-

---

* One issue of the *Anglo-African Magazine* that carried the serialization of *Blake* also reprinted Turner's "Confessions" and compared Turner to Brown in an admonition that found little difference between the two: "So, people of the South, people of the North! men and brethren, choose ye which method of emancipation you prefer—Nat Turner's or John Brown's?" See *Anglo-African Magazine* 1 (December 1859), 386.

nized uprising across numerous state lines need not, of course, be the outcome of one person's plotted subversion. The spirit of resistance (to the slaveholder, the spirit of terror) portrayed in *Blake* is most effectively embodied in the suggestion left behind by its hero that local units have been inspired and prepared to act with independent force on their own.

Henry Blake, one could add, is the incarnation of an idea and his story an allegory of retaliation that borrows from Delany's nationalist philosophy as well as his own travels. Nat Turner did not travel, but his message did. The text's own lack of specificity about the nature of the plan and its "secret" organizational strategy underlines the fluid nature of the conspiracy that Blake envisions, as well as the amorphous character of the threat of slave uprising that periodically haunted southern planters. In a world governed by illusion and deception, a world where transgressions of the law of slavery ranged across the broadest spectrum of resistant behavior, what Delany may most have borrowed from Turner was the recognition that propaganda was among the most effective weapons of resistance African Americans could employ. The inevitable risk that fears of slave revolt would bring about cruel repression and diminish slave mobility was countered by the necessary articulation of a philosophy of liberation, even if the form it took was bound to induce terror and a consequent counter-subversion on the part of slaveholders. Like Turner's "Confessions," *Blake* is a work in which radicalism is first of all an act of consciousness—the slave's consciousness of his or her power to act, to resist, and the master's consciousness that his illicit power will always be under siege. The language of resistance could overturn the language of bondage; the literacy denied slaves would be their initial instrument of revenge. Literature that could accomplish this would have entered dramatically into history.

Delany's novel itself was incendiary, and it may be that he got no response from William Lloyd Garrison when he requested help in finding a publisher for the novel in volume form because Garrison, a radical pacifist, found its propositions too extreme.[78] The novel extended the lessons of Douglass's autobiography, especially its formative events of resistance such as the defeat of Covey or the plot for an Easter uprising, and it wrenched apart the racialist sentimentality of *Uncle Tom's Cabin*. If Stowe's novel was considered profane and politically dangerous enough to be censured and banned in the South, *Blake*, though it is highly unlikely that it would ever have found a comparable audience (had the war not cut short its potential effect), might have seemed a text of outright insurrection. Writing in the early to mid-1850s when sectional tensions were moving toward a crisis but when the prospect of civil war was not yet in evidence, Delany projected a far more elaborate version of the threat outlined by "Nero's" letter—the threat not of secession and disunion but of African American resistance on a grand scale. Henry Blake spreads among the slave population of the South the simple belief that revolution is possible, that slave culture can nurture an African American identity invisible to the masters, and that organized insurrection is not unthinkable. In this alone *Blake* is set apart from every other black text of the period, many of which advocated (or, in the case of the slave narratives, recounted) individual acts of resistance but none of which suggested that large-scale nationalist political action was possible apart from emancipation and emigration—certainly not that it was possible, and had to be nurtured, within the most oppressive confines of the slave community.

Sugar, Conspiracy, and the Ladder

Blake would be worthy of attention even if it ended after the slaves' escape to Canada and Henry Blake's planting of the seeds of revolution throughout the slave South. In carrying his action next to Cuba, however, Delany displayed a profound understanding of the interlocked histories of the two countries. Like Melville, he wrote at a moment when the joint destinies of the Caribbean and the United States were very much in contention, and he offered an anatomy of slaveholding that compressed the triangular relations of Africa, the West Indies, and the United States over a broader historical period into a single moment. More than that, he provided, alongside his analysis of the crisis over expansionism, a portrait of Afro-Cuban culture in the throes of revolutionary fervor, as Blake is revealed to be a native Cuban, born Carolus Henrico Blacus, and matures into the leader of an organized political revolutionary movement. Both Delany's hero and his novel, then, open to view the underpinnings of a later nationalist ethos in African culture as it survived in rich transfigurations throughout the Americas. Delany once again wrote from inside the culture of slavery, but in this case too the narrative plot is primarily an occasion for various observations about Cuban society and a means to advance his hero toward the revolutionary moment. Blake's wife, Maggie, is recovered, after further sufferings that take such a toll on her that Blake does not at first recognize her; Blake brings over from Canada the group of slaves that had escaped with him; and he is reunited with his cousin, represented to be the famous revolutionary poet Placido. Blake merges his resistance philosophy with Placido's lyric poetry, the two of them together representing the dual aspect of Delany's own career and express- ing the "great question" of racial destiny Blake puts to Maggie: "Whatever liberty is worth to the whites, it is worth to the blacks; therefore, whatever it cost the whites to obtain it, the blacks would [should] be willing and ready to pay, if they desire it."[79]

Blake's plot to capture a slave ship en route from Africa to Cuba, which he considers a necessary weapon in their plan for revolution, brings the novel's action back to its point of origin; for the ship he intends to capture (the American *Merchantman*, appropriately renamed the *Vulture* when shipping out of Cuban port for the coast of Africa) is the very ship that Colonel Franks and his partners had fitted in Baltimore at the outset of chapter 1. Flying American colors as soon as it leaves port in Cuba, the *Vulture* is the very symbol of the intersecting forces that keep slavery in existence yet at the same time poised for destruction, and Delany's chapters on the trade and the stymied revolt aboard the ship are a means of probing the central mechanism of New World slavery. Cuba had the longest- standing slave trade in the Americas. Free trade in slaves, authorized in 1789 in order to stimulate the island's economy, was hardly hampered by the treaties of 1817 and 1835 outlawing it, which were seen by Spain as diplomatic concessions to Britain that could be, and were, easily circum- vented in fact. A continued supply of slaves was crucial to Spain's retention of power in the region, and the high tide in the import of "black ivory" came, in fact, in the 1830s and 1840s, beginning under the rule of Captain- General Miguel Tacón, when close to 200,000 African slaves, carried on some sixty to eighty ships a year, were landed in a ten-year period. Dip- lomatic machinations and guile at sea alike operated to frustrate what minimal attempts were made to stop the trade. American slavers flying under a Spanish or Portuguese flag could not be searched by American cruisers; and ships under American flag could not be searched by British cruisers. The cat-and-mouse game of trading made a mockery of treaties, and flags became transparent conveniences in a political charade. In ad- dition, a significant number of the slaves shipped for Cuba were ultimately destined for illegal landing in the United States (probably some 300,000 between 1808—the date the slave trade was outlawed in the United States—and the early 1860s), particularly in Texas; and the great majority of slave ships were owned and outfitted by Americans, with the result, as Du Bois wrote in his landmark study, that "the American slave-trade finally came to be carried on principally by United States capital, in United States ships, officered by United States citizens, and under the United States flag."[80]

Delany's trading sequence is no more effectively dramatized in literary terms than the rest of the novel, but it offers powerful vignettes of the cruelties of the middle passage and a futile chase by a British cruiser (to lighten the ship for escape, 600 of the 1,800 slaves are thrown overboard), and of the slave factories on the African coast. Delany's Portuguese factor, Ludo Draco, was perhaps modeled on the Brazilian-Portuguese figure Francisco Feliz de Souza, the leading factor of the 1840s and, like Draco, an intimate friend of the tyrannical Dahomean King Ghezo, who made a fortune in the slave trade. (When de Souza died in 1849, several slaves were sacrificed in his honor, including a boy and girl who were decapitated and buried with him to be his servant and wife in the next world.)[81] In addition to demonstrating that the United States is the current best market for Draco's slaves, *Blake*'s African chapters, borrowing a strategy from *Uncle Tom's Cabin,* depict the preparation and packing of the slaves for the middle passage through the sympathetic eyes of Draco's young daughter. Like Stowe's Little Eva, Draco's Angelina, his daughter by his African wife, is intended to be a barometer of sentiment for the reading audience. Horrified to discover that the excruciating sounds coming from the barracoons where the slaves are whipped and branded ("a sacrifice of burnt offering to the god of Portugal and Spain") are part of her father's business, Angelina falls into a grave swoon. As the girl lies on what appears to be her deathbed, Draco resolves never again to trade in slaves, whereupon Angelina is miraculously revived.[82] The episode, stilted though it is, serves the purpose of deploying one form of sentimentality to undermine another; that is, by shifting the emotional burden to an African girl, Delany at once makes evident the full reach of American slavery, truthfully implicates Africans in the moral burden of the trade, and demonstrates that Little Eva's black counterpart is not the minstrel sprite Topsy, a racialist doll, but an African girl whose moral intensity (and saccharine characterization) is the equal of Eva's.

The shipboard revolt plotted for the *Vulture*'s return course to Cuba never comes to pass. The mutinous mood of the black crew that was evident in the voyage to Africa, led by the sailing master Blake, rises to a higher pitch with the brutal destruction of the new slaves during the middle passage; but a severe storm intervenes to contain the energy of revolt until, apparently, the opportunity has passed. Although Delany may have intended the storm as an allegorical enactment of the international contentions between Europe and the United States that forestalled black revolt in the New World, his purpose in sidestepping the intended rebellion at this point is obscure, to say the least. Still, the final result of the voyage achieves something of the same purpose. Because the "cargo" of slaves is known to have been mutinous, its value is lowered and the majority are thus passed at sale into the hands of mulattoes friendly to the island's growing black revolutionary movement. Instead of becoming a part of the massive African labor force imported to work the Cuban sugar fields under extremely harsh conditions, these new Africans, then, will be part of the "Army of Emancipation" that Blake and Placido are raising.

The revolutionary context that Delany relies on in constructing his action in the Cuban half of *Blake* was more complex and volatile than that in the United States. The existence of a national independence movement that in some cases overlapped, but was hardly synonymous with, a slave liberation movement created conflicting allegiances among the large free black and mulatto populations. Cuban slavery itself was marked by more extreme racial paradoxes than that in the United States. The rapid growth in sugar production during the nineteenth century required large outlays both of capital and of slaves; the former came primarily from United States investors, southern and northern alike (hence Delany's focus on Judge Ballard's Cuban holdings), the latter from the illegal African trade. The large class of free blacks, along with many Cuban-born mulattoes and creoles (in this usage Cuban-born Spanish, that is to say, Cuban whites),* tended toward a liberal democratic ideology. The significant free black and mixed-race population, along with the prevalence of slaves who, through the agency of *coartación,* had arranged to purchase their freedom through hire, made racial and class boundaries quite fluid and created a social situation that had no equivalent in the United States, except to a degree in New Orleans. Even though their own livelihood frequently depended on it, many free blacks opposed slavery; and most mulattoes and creoles, if they defended slavery, nonetheless opposed the slave trade. Defended by the colonial Spanish government, by most American investors, and by some creoles, however, the trade flourished—in part because, contrary to what one might expect and what has been argued by one contingent of

---

* In Cuba the terms of classification by demography and race generally followed these groupings: Spanish; creoles, or Cuban-born Spanish; free mulattoes and free blacks; *bozales* (recently imported African slaves); *ladinos* (slaves imported before the 1821 prohibition of the slave trade); and *criolles* (slaves born in Cuba).

modern historians, slavery in Cuba was especially ruthless and thus required constant infusions of new labor from Africa (in contrast to the United States, where higher domestic reproduction rates fostered not just stability but population growth, which made possible the internal trade from the upper to the lower South). The injury and mortality rate on sugar plantations was very high (up to 10 percent yearly), punishment for insubordination or resistance was severe, and loss to maroon communities and to suicide exceeded that in the United States. Cuban planters had a saying that succinctly told the story: "Sugar is made with blood." Like the rest of Latin America, Cuba could keep its slave population numerically stable only through continual imports; but this had the politically destabilizing effect of introducing a younger, more recalcitrant population that could more easily become the focus of revolutionary designs.[83]

Whether it was a function of Delany's awkwardness as a novelist or his choice to lay the ideological groundwork for revolution within a mixed-race social structure that was far more fluid—and thus amenable to political association and conspiracy—in Cuba than in the United States, the role of plantation slaves, the black masses among whom he spread his revolutionary message in the American South, is drastically diminished in Blake's Cuban resistance work. It is barely implicit in the novel, even though Cuban maroon communities, like those formed from other Latin American slave populations, were larger and had a much more active role in defining a black political subculture than their counterparts in the United States. Blake travels throughout the Cuban countryside spreading his philosophy of revolution among rural slaves and maroons, but the dramatized conspiracy in the second act of the novel arises among the urban mulatto elite in league with slaves, cutting across color lines to unite all "Africans" in a nationalist brotherhood that includes sympathetic creoles as well. The Grand Council meeting at Madame Cordora's is thus the occasion for Placido and Blake jointly to articulate Delany's philosophy of liberation. The poem ascribed to Placido, one of several in *Blake* borrowed without acknowledgment from the African American poet James M. Whitfield,*

---

* Delany borrowed several poems from Whitfield, whose writings had appeared in the *North Star* and other antislavery publications, and whom Delany knew as a fellow advocate of African American emigration. The poem here ascribed to Placido (Delany, *Blake*, pp. 259–60) is Whitfield's "Prayer of the Oppressed," which was collected in his volume *America and Other Poems* (Buffalo, N.Y.: James S. Leavitt, 1853), p. 61. Other poems borrowed from Whitfield include "To Cinque" (which introduces Blake to the Grand Council as the leader of the Army of Emancipation), "Yes! Strike Again the Sounding String," and "How Long" (Whitfield, *America*, pp. 20, 59, 29; Delany,

is a benediction upon the conspiracy that has just been formalized according to military regulation. An Ethiopianist hymn that resembles Placido's own poetry to a degree but is more overtly antislavery in spirit, Whitfield's verse is at once a jeremiad and a political statement:

> How long, O Lord! ere thou wilt speak
> In thy Almighty thundering voice,
> To bid the oppressors' fetters break,
> And Ethiopia's sons rejoice?
> How long shall Slavery's iron grip,
> And prejudice's guilty hand,
> Send forth like bloodhounds from the slip
> Foul persecutions o'er the land?[84]

The discussions that follow, both in this meeting and in the later one at the home of Blake's father, make evident that the revolutionaries include all colors within their definition of Ethiopia; and, congruent with Delany's philosophy of emigration spelled out in "The Political Destiny of the Colored Race" and the *Official Report of the Niger Valley Exploring Party, Blake* projects not just revolution but the founding of a modern black state of the sort Delany envisioned in his political writing. Because the African race, under New World slavery, was already "the principal producer of the greater part of the luxuries of enlightened countries," it was arguable that their industry and skill, along with the wealth of territory, population, and climate granted to Africa, could make their native nations a great force in world industry. Delany's philosophy combined several important elements: a theory of industrial uplift and missionary zeal; a rejection of the prevailing legal philosophy of race announced most bluntly in the

---

Blake, pp. 250, 286, 308). The dedication of *America* reads: "To Martin R. Delany, M.D. This volume is inscribed as a small tribute of respect for his character, admiration of his talents, and love of his principles, by the Author." For his part, Delany had recognized Whitfield as "one of the purest poets in America," a near equal of John Greenleaf Whittier and Edgar Allan Poe, but his appropriation of Whitfield's compelling verse in *Blake* may have been a more sincere, if unidentified, tribute. See Delany, *The Condition, Elevation, Emigration, and Destiny of the Colored People of the United States* (1852; rpt. New York: Arno Press, 1969), p. 132. On Delany and Whitfield, analyzed in the broader context of Delany's strategic use of poems and songs in *Blake*, see Allan D. Austin, "The Significance of Martin Robison Delany's *Blake; or the Huts of America*" (Ph.D. diss., University of Massachusetts, 1975), pp. 179–203; on Whitfield, see Joan R. Sherman, "James Monroe Whitfield, Poet and Emigrationist: A Voice of Protest and Despair," *Journal of Negro History* 57 (April 1972), 169–76.

Dred Scott decision; and an early Pan-Africanism. Delany's citation of the influential Scripture from Psalms 68 ("Ethiopia shall yet stretch forth her hands unto God; Princes shall come out of Egypt") put the novel's politicization of Christian doctrine into a powerful proleptic form.[85] Although Delany might have taken his Ethiopianist doctrine from Robert Alexander Young's "Ethiopian Manifesto" (1829) or other texts that cited the same Scripture, his philosophy here, as in his formulation of the concept of "Africa for the Africans" in the *Official Report,* looked ahead to ideas that were to be key to a later generation of Pan-African nationalists such as Edward Blyden, Henry Turner, and Du Bois. Blake's immediate revolutionary project has not Africa as its goal, however, but the founding of a modern black state in Cuba.

Blake's final declaration of war, at a subsequent meeting of the conspirators, portrays him as a combination of Christ and Toussaint:

You know my errand among you; you know my sentiments. I am for war—war upon the whites. "I come to bring deliverance to the captive and freedom to the bond." Your destiny is my destiny; the end of one will be the end of all. On last Sabbath, a day of rest, joy and gladness to the whites, I was solemnly and sadly impressed with our wretched condition. While passing through the great cemetery amidst the busy throng of smiling faces and anxious countenances of the whites; the soul-impressing odors of the flowers and inspiring song of birds; the sound of the unfettered rolling sand on the beach and untrammeled winds of heaven; and then beheld the costly ornaments and embellished tombs erected at the expense of unrequited toil, sweat and blood wrung from our brother slave still laboring on in misery, inexpressible suffering and wailing, though Sabbath it be, sending up to heaven in whispers of broken accents, prayers for deliverance, all in the sight of these happy throngs and costly catacombs—I could not suppress the emotion which swelled my breast, nor control my feelings when I cursed their bones as they lie mouldering in their graves. May God forgive me for the wickedness, as my conscience admonished and rebukes me. In contemplation of our condition, my heart is sorrowful to sadness. But my determination is fixed; I will never leave you. An overwhelming power of our oppressors or some stern adversity, brethren, may force you to forsake me, but even then will I not leave you. I will take me to the mountains, and there in the dreary seclusion of the wilderness, though alone, will I stand firmly in defence of our cause. Buckle on your armor then, and stand ready for the fight! Finally, brethren, I may eventually go down to a disappointed and untimely, but never to a coward's or a traitor's grave! God's will be done.[86]

This remarkable speech far outstrips the language that Frederick Douglass would attribute to Madison Washington, for example, and its invocation of the black slave fathers, with resonant overtones of messianic deliverance, recalls Garnet's similar gesture in "To the Slaves of the United States of America." Between Blake's oratory, Placido's (and Whitfield's) poems, and the philosophy articulated by the two of them together, one has the full range of Delany's thought. In its lucid combination of literary and political strategies, *Blake,* whatever its weaknesses in narrative structure and characterization, is among the most compelling statements of black transnationalist ideology in the nineteenth century.

Not just an independent black nation but the revolution necessary to secure it was far easier to contemplate in Cuba than in the United States. At the time Delany was writing, as I have already suggested, the volatile political situation between the United States and Cuba held the potential for many different resolutions; that a black war for independence, as in Haiti, did not materialize in the 1850s does not detract from Delany's millenarian vision. By exploring in detail the Afro-Cuban culture that made possible broad conspiratorial alliances of a sort difficult to imagine under American slavery, with its stark racial distinctions, limited free black population, and geographic obstacles, Delany also wrote a significant chapter of hemispheric African American cultural history that has seldom been appreciated. Even so, his chronological confusion in *Blake,* however purposeful it may be, obscures the fact that the machinery of repression could be just as severe in Cuba as in the United States. Although the novel's Placido is in part Delany's alter ego, he was also a historical character—with the attendant problem for *Blake*'s representational strategy that the historical Placido was already ten years dead, the martyr of a revolutionary conspiracy virtually destroyed by a campaign of government terror in 1844. The Conspiracy *de la Escalera,* also known in some accounts as Placido's Conspiracy, stands not just in the background of Delany's novel, however, but also in its foreground. Both the double-layered chronology of *Blake*—its superimposition of the 1840s upon the 1850s—and the fact that it breaks off on the eve of a revolution that may or may not succeed, may or may not also be crushed by government suppression, makes the relevance of the historical event acute.

The conspiracy, which appears to have been unraveled on the basis of the betrayal of a slave woman involved in it, took its name from the notorious method of punishment officials employed to extract information and confessions, or simply to mete out torture: prisoners were strapped to a ladder *(escalera)* for what in many cases was reported to be excruciatingly brutal whipping. Some four thousand conspirators were initially arrested. Close to eighty were executed publicly and perhaps another one to three hundred killed by excessive torture; twelve hundred were imprisoned; and four hundred were exiled. An article in the *North American Review*, typical of the reaction in the liberal press of the northern United States, appropriately compared La Escalera to the Inquisition.[87] In addition to the indiscriminate executions and torture, the colored (mulatto and black) militia, charged with complicity in the conspiracy, was disbanded. There is, indeed, evidence that secret meetings were taking place among rebel slaves and free blacks committed to a program of abolition; but many early American observers, and some historians since, have tended to dismiss the purported plot as a charade engineered by Captain-General Leopoldo O'Donnell, a corrupt governor who profited mightily from the slave trade, to crush liberal and abolitionist sentiment. However much O'Donnell exaggerated the threat, both the rising unrest among slaves, in part in reaction to the institution of a harsher slave code in 1842, and the growth of a free colored class that favored independence and limited emancipation are clearly documented. Fuel was added to the fire by charges against David Turnbull, the outspoken abolitionist (alluded to in fictional disguise by Delany) who had been appointed British consul in 1840 and was almost immediately charged with inciting slave insurrection. The British withdrew Turnbull as consul, but he returned in 1842 as superintendent of *emancipados* (liberated Africans, many of whom had been illegally imported from Africa), whereupon he was quickly accused of organizing a rebellion and imprisoned before being deported.

Rebellions had flared repeatedly for several years running, including a significant rising in Cárdenas in 1843 and another in Matanzas the same year. But the conspiracy of La Escalera discovered early the following year, for which Turnbull was widely and plausibly blamed as one of the masterminds, became an occasion for repression of the most outrageous dimensions. (Turnbull was one thing, but Delany himself seemed to discount the risk that the British government would actually instigate any black revolution, as those who feared a British-backed "Africanization" of Cuba held. The planter who manumits Maggie remarks: "If the Negroes rise and take off our heads, declaring their independence, the English will be the first to acknowledge it. But they'll never come and cut off our heads, politely handing them to the Negroes.") What mattered was not the certain prospect of black violence but the mere implication of it, a fact captured well in the account of an American resident of Cuba, the southern physician J. G. F. Wurdemann:

> It is needless to state, that all the horrors of the San Domingo massacres were to have been repeated [by the conspirators]. Many of the whites were to have been flayed and broiled while alive, and with the exception of the young women, reserved for a worse fate, all, without discrimination of age or sex, were to have been massacred. The plans were, however, so ill organized, that the insurgents could only have presented an inert mass before even the armed monteros of the island, and their insurrection could only have drawn down destruction upon themselves. A civil war between the two races must necessarily be one of extermination, as is ever the case when the savage contends with the civilized man.

What O'Donnell, operating with the impunity granted by such views, accomplished in his massive suppression was the systematic destruction or intimidation of not just slave leaders but more important, so far as the success of any independence and emancipation movement might be concerned (and so far as the accuracy of Delany's representation might require it), of much of the middle-class free black population as well.[88]

The role of Placido, its anachronism aside, is interesting in part as a reflection upon Delany's belief in the ideological function of literature. Because he was considered a martyr to the revolutionary conspiracy, Placido's poetry was relatively well known in the United States in the decade after his execution in 1844 and was translated by William Cullen Bryant and others. An article in the *North American Review* of 1849, for example, gave an account of his heroic demeanor in the face of the firing squad (when the first volley barely wounded him, Placido supposedly directed the squad to fire at his temple) and translated a number of his poems, including the famous "Prayer," which he was to have composed the night before his death and chanted on the way to his execution, and the "Hymn to Liberty," written the same morning:

O liberty! I wait for thee
    To break this chain and dungeon bar;
I hear thy spirit calling me
    Deep in the frozen North, afar,
With voice like God's, and visage like a star. . . .

Yes, liberty! thy dawning light,
    Obscured by dungeon bars, shall cast
Its splendor on the breaking night,
    And tyrants, flying pale and fast,
Shall tremble at thy gaze and stand aghast!

Born Gabriel de la Concepcion Valdes, Placido was an orphaned mulatto, not a slave himself, whose career as a romantic poet drifted further and further into politics following Captain-General Miguel Tacón's suppression of an independence movement among creole liberals in the mid-1830s. Placido's political poems, though they frequently focused on independence movements in other parts of the world (for example, in Greece and Poland), were transparently about Cuba as well.* The facts of his life remain sketchy, but it appears that he was arrested on charges of sedition on several occasions before the climactic year 1844. Charged with a central role in La Escalera, Placido, whatever the degree of his guilt, was without question a convenient object lesson for the government since his revolutionary sentiments, if not his actions, were widely known by the populace, who loved his poetry.[89]

Delany's adoption of Placido as a central character in his novel thus has two functions: to demonstrate Delany's belief in the political function of literature, and hence the place of revolutionary politics in his own writing; and to provide a basis for the plausible construction of a revolutionary movement with the degree of cooperation across class and color lines that

---

* On occasion—for example in William Wells Brown, *The Black Man, His Antecedents, His Genius, and His Achievements* (1863)—Placido was confused with another Cuban poet, Juan Francisco Manzano, a former slave whose poems were translated by R. R. Madden and published in London under the title *Poems by a Slave in the Island of Cuba* (1840). Manzano was the author of an autobiographical narrative and of long poems such as "The Slave-Trade Merchant" and "The Sugar Estate," and although Delany seems to have intended his fictional Placido to resemble the real one, he may also have intended a composite figure who would evoke recollections of Manzano among his readers. See Juan Francisco Manzano, *The Life and Poems of a Cuban Slave,* ed. Edward J. Mullen (Hamden, Conn.: Archon, 1981), and Philip S. Foner, *A History of Cuba and Its Relations with the United States,* 2 vols. (New York: International, 1963), I, 191–93.

he envisioned. At the same time, a peculiar ambiguity is introduced by the example of La Escalera, and what makes it especially relevant to Delany's conception in *Blake* is the disagreement, extending to modern accounts, about whether or not any significant conspiracy existed. Delany, one must surmise, had no doubts about the existence of a conspiracy, just as he apparently had no trouble imagining that something like the 1856 panic in the United States was based on legitimate plots among slaves. But if the conspiracies were true, the slaveholders' reaction and suppressive terror were natural consequences: theorists of benevolence notwithstanding, slavery *was* a state of controlled racial war. In the case of La Escalera, the terror of the first several months of 1844 effectively annihilated the threat of slave revolt and of free colored political radicalism, giving Spain a reprieve of several decades from such internal pressures. In collapsing together the decades of the 1840s and the 1850s, Delany conveniently intertwines the fate of his political hero and the martyred poet, but he also reanimates a potential for allied Afro–New World revolt that had, in fact, been severely undercut even as paranoia about the "Africanization" of Cuba by other means grew more intense.

In addition, of course, Delany contended that so long as slavery existed, the suppression of revolts or the execution of leaders such as Placido or Nat Turner could provide only temporary peace for the regime. The principal strategy of revolutionary resistance need not be full-scale revolt; continual agitation, conspiracy itself, and surges of violent outbreak were themselves enough to place the slaveholders' order under such economic and political strain that it might eventually be destroyed by external forces or crumble from within. As in the first half of the novel, devoted to spreading an ideology of African-American resistance, the representation of Afro-Cuban politcal action, though it has the greater potential for climactic insurrection, depends equally on Delany's portrait of its operation in the arena of propaganda and cultural resistance.

El Día de los Reyes

Blake's oratorical declaration of war, made at the third meeting of the conspirators, occurs on the day of Special Indulgence granted the colony by the Spanish bishops. Indeed, all of the significant movements toward revolution, as Delany dramatizes them, take place in the context of national festivals, which have in *Blake* a duplicitous meaning comparable to holidays such as the Fourth of July in the cases of Nat Turner and Frederick

Douglass. Festival moments are typically conservative in their reverence for an ancestral or nationalist past, but they are also frequently laced with a subversive energy derived from the temporary abridgement of social codes or hierarchical structures. Holidays for Douglass and Turner enclosed such a potential inversion in the very myths—most of all the primacy of the founding fathers' revolutionary bequest—that held social disorder in check through a process of ritual veneration. At least in the sphere of ideology, slaves' appeal to patriotic violence, whatever the extent of its irony, would thus inevitably be parricidal in nature. For Gabriel, Vesey, and Turner, less so for Douglass, the ideology of the American Revolution had also become suffused with an Afro-Christian dimension that implied an equal identification with, and a drawing of sacred power from, the teachings of the *black* fathers. Both the more pronounced syncretism of African with European cultural forms that marked the black Caribbean world generally, and the relatively freer access to political association by mulattoes and blacks in Cuba, offered Delany a much more flexible context in which to examine the function of holidays and festivals in building a revolutionary ethos. The festive or holiday moment in the case of African Cuba would thus provide an even better example of ritual as it is defined by Renato Rosaldo—as the space or "crossroads" where the trajectories of diverse social processes (in this case diverse cultural traditions) intersect without being contained in a single encapsulated form.[90] As it happens, the same concept illuminates the simultaneity of chronological moments, and of contesting political interests, that Delany also builds into his archly historicized narrative structure.

Delany recognized that the character of Afro-Cuban society made possible a degree of political organization among blacks implausible, if not entirely counterintuitive, in antebellum America. His representation of the meetings among the insurrectionists drew on the institution of the *cabildo,* long-standing social clubs that were typically reflective of the common African ancestry of their respective members. *Cabildo* members were both free and slave (the latter predominantly in urban areas), and their activities ranged from land investment to funeral provisions to the purchase of freedom for slaves. Most of all they served as reservoirs of African tribal culture, however transformed by New World forces, and were marked by a syncretic blending of African religious practice with Catholicism. In some cases they may have been associated with the secret societies of the Ñáñigos, a ceremonial brotherhood, apparently derived from Nigerian traditions, whose rites were devoted to maintaining venerative links with the magic world of the dead. Even if it once played a central role, such a secret ritual dimension of African origin may have faded into the routine paraphernalia of male freemasonry (initiations, codes, regalia, and the like) in most *cabildos* without losing its power to inform their political potential. The revolutionary age of 1789 to 1848, as Eric Hobsbawm contends, was one in which secret brotherhoods had a significant influence in European social upheaval.[91] Whatever their syncretic structural sources in European brotherhoods, the *cabildos* in any case bore such a relation to Spanish power, and their essential African tribal character, whether or not it drew on so overt a practice of sacred drama as Ñañiguismo, added a code of cultural practice that would have been dangerously subversive. In *Blake* Delany does no more than imply such a secretive African dimension by his focus on festival masquerade; but in doing so he provides an indigenous account of "Africanization" that powerfully reorients the role of Afro-Cubans among the various factions pitted against the Spanish slave-holding regime.

The point at which the members of *cabildos* interacted with the mixed-race elite which Delany makes the crucible of Blake's revolutionary movement is difficult to establish. To the extent that prosperous mulattoes identified with creole society and depended on the slave economy, they separated themselves from the activities of the *cabildos,* particularly the raucous street celebrations of festival days. But Delany's construction of the revolutionary group, borne out by the suppression of La Escalera, suggests that lines were drawn politically and culturally rather than racially. Also, although it is possible to interpret both the *cabildos* and the festive activities for which they were known as part of the government's method of controlling the black population (much in the way that Douglass argued that slave holidays were a safety valve used by planters to police their slave populations), the evidence points in the opposite direction as well— namely, that the *cabildos* were a means of promoting nationalist solidarity, a fact indicated by their decimation by the colonial government during La Escalera.[92]

The most pronounced manifestation of the cultural significance and potential political effectiveness of the *cabildos* appeared in their holiday celebrations, particularly their festive parades on January 6, El Día de los Reyes (King's Day), which probably originated as a transfiguration of African celebrations of the winter solstice into the New World observance of the Epiphany. Led by *cabildo* elders in parades whose costumes and banners displayed their tribal groupings, Afro-Cubans joined the ritual veneration of African ancestors to the often highly secularized engagement in Catholic liturgy, each *cabildo* electing its own king and queen as part of the celebration. Related, as Sterling Stuckey as shown, to similar, if less highly organized and less common, celebrations among black communities in the United States such as John Kunnering and Pinkster festivals, El Día de los Reyes was typically a day of unrestrained license which contrasted with the officious control of such public demonstrations on the part of blacks by Spanish authorities on almost all other occasions.* In 1838, in fact, King's Day provided the occasion for a small-scale rebellion in the Trinidad Valley.[93] In pointing his novel toward a climax on that festival day, then, Delany sought out a symbolic event that at once gave expression to survivals of African culture, demonstrated the necessary syncretism that infused any Afro–New World society, and provided, in its ritual breaking down of the regulating power of the slave regime, a model for the eruption of revolution.

Masquerade and ritual mark the maturing of the black revolution from the beginning. The first step in the conspiracy coincides with the "gala day" in honor of the nativity of Isabella, queen of Spain. The national fete, in Delany's representation, bears numerous signs of the impending threat to Spanish rule, beginning with the necessary solidarity across class

---

* In *Incidents in the Life of Slave Girl* Harriet Jacobs provides a valuable description of the incorporation of John Kunnering (also known as John Canoe, Jankunnu, John Conner, and so on) into their Christmas celebrations by African American slaves: "Every child rises early on Christmas morning to see the Johnkannaus. Without them, Christmas would be shorn of its greatest attraction. They consist of companies of slaves from the plantations, generally of the lower class. Two athletic men, in calico wrappers, have a net thrown over them, covered with all manner of bright-colored stripes. Cows' tails are fastened to their backs, and their heads are decorated with horns. A box, covered with sheepskin, is called the gumbo box. A dozen beat on this, while others strike triangles and jawbones, to which bands of dancers keep time. For a month previous they are composing songs, which are sung on this occasion. These companies, of a hundred each, turn out early in the morning, and are allowed to go round till twelve o'clock, begging for contributions." Any whites who refused to make such contributions, Jacobs adds, were regaled with satiric songs. The passage bears comparison to Delany's representation of King's Day in its details and in its display of ulterior purpose. In Jacobs's narrative this particular Christmas Day is also the occasion for her grandmother to employ her own kind of masquerade and deceit in the face of the masters, by inviting to her house the men who have been searching for the runaway Harriet, now hidden in her grandmother's garret. The John Kunnering described as part of the same occasion is thus joined to the network of subversion and trickery, in this case largely the work of women, by which slaves resist the plantation regime. See Harriet Jacobs, *Incidents in the Life of Slave Girl*, ed. Jean Fagan Yellin (Cambridge, Mass.: Harvard University Press, 1987), pp. 118–19; and see pp. 277–78n.1, n.2 for further references, as well as Stuckey, *Slave Culture*, pp. 68–73, 78–79, 227.

and color lines: "Never before had the African race been so united as on that occasion, the free Negroes and mixed free people being in unison with each other." Whereas the customary brutal sport of the dog chase, which demonstrated the use of dogs in running down slaves, had once prompted indifference or encouragement from the free blacks and mulattoes, it now produces murmuring, anger, and vengeful looks; and the parade of troops provides an opportunity for the blacks to study the soldiers against whom they will have to contend in the event of revolution. The festival ball held by the Captain-General, Count Alcora, has a mirror image in the ball at Madame Cordora's, at which the first full-scale organizational meeting of the rebels is held. Placido, as poet laureate to the Captain-General, is only one of several rebels who live within the world of the masters while plotting their destruction. The signs of insubordination that are everywhere evident and point to the danger of revolt are summed up in Countess Alcora's prophetic dream "of being in the interior of Africa surrounded entirely by Negroes, under the rule of a Negro prince, beset by ambassadors of every enlightened nation, who brought him many presents of great value, whilst the envoy of her Catholic Majesty sat quietly at the foot of the African Prince's throne."[94] The dream reverses the direction of the slave trade, as it were, carrying the countess into the interior of Africa, where she is surrounded by blackness and subordinated to an African prince. One could also argue that the exchange of imperial roles, like Delany's portrayal of the slave trade in Africa itself, is intended incidentally to show that both Europeans and Africans profited from the trade. More dramatically, however, the dream inverts imperial power on the very occasion of Isabella's gala day, revealing the latent ambiguity in black participation in such festive days and, like Babo's ritual display in *Benito Cereno*, subjecting the monarch to mock humiliation bordering on racial terror.

The ambivalence of this festive syncretism was captured well by Wurdemann in his description of King's Day itself, which included, in the attire and accoutrements he observed, a tribute to Isabella that could scarcely have had univocal meaning:

Each tribe, having elected its king and queen, paraded the streets with a flag, having its name, and the words *viva Isabella,* with the arms of Spain, painted on it. Their majesties were dressed in the extreme of the fashion, and were very ceremoniously waited on by the ladies and gentlemen of the court. . . . But the chief object in the group was an athletic negro, with a fantastic straw helmet, an immensely thick girdle of strips of palm-leaves around his waist, and other uncouth articles of dress. Whenever they stopped, their banjoes struck up one of their monotonous tunes, and this frightful figure would commence a devil's dance, which was the signal for all his court to join in a general fandango, a description of which my pen refuseth to give. . . . Havana is on this day in a perfect hubbub, and the confusion that seems to reign among its colored population is indescribable. On all the plantations the negroes, also, pass the day in dancing to the music of their rude instruments; and the women, especially, are decked out in all the finery of tinsel and gaudy clothes. Songs are often combined with the dance, and in their native dialects they ridicule their owners before their faces, enjoying with much glee their happy ignorance of the burthen of their songs. Their African drums are then heard far and near, and their sonorous sounds, now falling, now rising on the air, seem like the summons to a general insurrection.

Delany himself, quoting from an unidentified American periodical of the day, offers a comparable extensive description of the music, rumba dancing, costumes, and display of ritual magic on King's Day which likewise makes clear the dangerous implications of the festival:

On this day they were allowed to use their own language and their own songs, a privilege denied them on other days, lest they might lay plans for a general rising.

As it is[,] the sights, the sounds, the savage shrieks, the uncouth yells suggest very uncomfortable thoughts of Negro insurrection. One cannot help thinking of the menace of the Spanish Government that Cuba shall be either Spanish or African, and when we see these savages in their play more like wild animals than human beings, the idea what their rage would probably be, makes the boldest shudder. It would be easy on King's Day for the Negroes to free themselves, or at least to make the streets of Havana run with blood, if they only knew their power; Heaven be praised that they do not, for who can count the lives that would be lost in such a fearful struggle.[95]

As Wurdemann's description makes clear, King's Day may have been unique in the unleashing of energy allowed by Spanish authorities, but it was only a more extreme expression of the antagonism implicit in Afro-

Cuban cultural forms generally. Like every other New World black community, slave or free, Afro-Cubans made dancing and drumming a means of cultural resistance, in this case one that was ostentatiously ranged against the more decorous dances that were a passion among the planters. The "devil's dance" described by Wurdemann was likely a reference to the *diablitos* (little devils) who were portrayed in Ñañiguismo as the dead who have returned to life, creatures from the other side who always coexist invisibly with the living but whose forms are made ceremonially visual on the occasion of El Día de los Reyes. But such masquerade, reanimating the dead with priapic powers, extends mere ridicule of the masters into a potentially stronger form of resistance. As an instance of the subversive force incorporated within carnival festivity as it has been studied by Bakhtin and others, King's Day in Delany's text brings the ritual overthrow of reigning authority, its parodic displacement by satyr figures and travestied leaders, to the verge of actualization.[96] Summoned by the drums and authorized by the ancestors' presence, even by their sacred power, the living are infused with the spirit necessary to mount an armed insurrection. The mockery of the masters coincides with the ritual—and quite likely the deliberately parodic—display of Isabella's image, which, like the flag of Spain ceremoniously draped around Benito Cereno as he receives his terrifying shave at the hands of Babo, is here potent with the tropology of subversion. By his libidinously charged human form, the "athletic negro" (compare Jacobs' "athletic men") who leads the dance usurps the place of the mock Spanish royalty, and in so doing, one might guess, especially subordinates the queen—perhaps in implied sexual conquest or humiliation—much as Countess Alcora's dream surrounded her with African Negroes and prophesied Isabella's envoy sitting at the feet of an African prince. In his account Delany offers a description that is less elaborate but even more frank in its assessment of the subversive power of King's Day—this despite the fact that, correct in his view of the rebellious power of language and song, he strangely argues that the planning of a revolution can occur only in the midst of public festivity. Before we look more closely at the interplay between King's Day and Delany's conception of the revolution, however, it is necessary to recognize that in *Blake*, as in the Cuba of the 1850s, there was more than one revolution in the offing.

The final episodes of Delany's novel place the notion of a conspiracy on a still more complicated footing, one that indicates the vexing crosscurrents of political contention that surged through colonial Cuba in the

1850s. Captain-General Alcora, although he has reliable evidence of sub-version, dismisses much of it as irrelevant or impossible to separate from propaganda aimed at Spanish authority—not by black revolutionaries but by creoles and Americans. Thus, the report by a planter near Matanzas that his wife has been reduced by her fears of insurrection to hallucinations of black serpents and ghosts (although, paradoxically, she calls on a black chief for protection) is shunted aside by Alcora as the product of schemes by American "patriots," a large number of them planters near Matanzas who seek the annexation of Cuba by the United States.[97] The woman's dream is a counterpart to that of Countess Alcora, but Alcora's attribution of it to white propaganda is not so much a mistake as a partial truth that obscures the complexities of the conspiracies operating at the time.

Although a number of them favored outright independence for Cuba (increasingly so in the 1850s), the creoles and resident Americans feared black revolt more than Spanish authoritarianism—a fear that dated from the revolts of the early 1840s—and sought annexation as a protection from both. But they were rightly unable to separate the two, charging that Spain and Britain were promoting abolition or its threat—the Africani-zation of Cuba—as a means to undermine their interests. By the same token, creole and American slaveholders, supported by a strong contingent of Cuban exiles in the United States, the Junta Cubana, also exploited the fear of Africanization in order to strengthen their calls for annexation by the United States, whose proslavery officials in particular were quite will-ing to decry the threat of another "black empire" like Haiti off the coast of the southern states. To advocates of a Caribbean extension of American empire, pro- and antislavery alike, Cuba seemed the vital key. Calls for annexation proceeded from different motives but reflected in miniature the frequent confluence of southern and northern versions of expansion-ism. The characteristically proslavery *Southern Quarterly Review* argued in 1852, for example, that "Cuba will be Americanized—will own the sway of our race, as will St. Domingo, the West India Islands, generally, and all Mexico, in the course of time." On the other side of the coin, the characteristically antislavery *Putnam's Monthly,* suggesting that legal slavery could be ameliorated by the moral influence of Anglo-American "civili-zation" (unavailable under Spanish rule), proposed in the lead article of its first issue the following year that "the extension of empire by CONQUEST will soon be superseded by the irrepressible desire of states to become united to each other by the NEW LAW OF ANNEXATION." Cuba in either case was seen to be a key test case as well as a desirable possession. As

Richard Kimball wrote in *Cuba and the Cubans* (1850), "Cuba locks up in a closed ring, the whole sweep of the Mexican Gulf. . . . Whoever holds her, commands the great highway to Mexico and South America, to Oregon, California, and the Pacific." Threats of black conspiracy from within were thus met with even more concrete threats from without, such as those led by the filibusters Narciso Lopez and John Quitman (head of the "Order of the Lone Star") which resulted in futile attempts to invade and liberate Cuba lasting for six years after 1848, until the failure of efforts to purchase the island and the return of a more conservative regime under the second Captaincy-General of José de la Concha.[98]

The Africanization fears of creole and American planters (and of planters in the American South) were not entirely without ground. Because the creole and American slaveholders desired the benefits of United States rule but lived in mortal fear of black liberation, the Spanish government, itself exceedingly anxious about subversion of its rule, was willing to risk slave emancipation in order to forestall either independence or annexation. Delany's description of King's Day includes the indication that "Roncall"—Federico Roncali, the Captain-General who succeeded O'Donnell and preceded Concha and then Juan de la Pezuela (whose policies of liberalization set off even greater fear of Cuba's Africanization)—had already seized the countersubversive offensive. Here again Delany was accurate in his depiction of Roncali's willingness to hold up the threat of black emancipation (and its implied devastation of planter life) as a counter to creole or American support of plans for United States annexation. Roncali took advantage of King's Day, Delany writes (borrowing from the periodical account), "to give the Creoles of Cuba a significant hint of what they might expect from the government if they gave any alarming degree of aid to the revolutionary operations of General [Narciso] Lopez." Prolonging for three days the festival privileges of the Lucumis, the "most warlike of the tribes of the African slaves of Cuba," the Captain-General calculates to leave the creoles shuddering "at the fearful illustration thus exhibited under their eyes of the standing threat that Cuba must be Spanish or African."[99]

Roncali, whose title was Conde de Alcoy and who was thus perhaps also a model for Delany's Count Alcora, had already made clear his willingness to consider radical moves as a means to counter plots of annexation, writing to Spain soon after his arrival that "the conviction of this terrible weapon [a decree of emancipation] could in the last extreme prevent the loss of the island, and if the inhabitants convince themselves that it will be used, they will tremble and renounce every illusion before bringing upon themselves such an anathema." In this, however, Roncali was responding legitimately to the specter of the French Revolution of 1848, which had created a sensation in Cuba (not least, presumably, among the *cabildos* and other Afro-Cuban groups that may have nurtured plans of black rebellion) and been seized upon as a forewarning of the demise of slavery by the "patriots," who used it as yet another pretext for annexation. Once more superimposing the 1840s upon the late 1850s, Delany thus compressed the French renewal of radical republicanism into America's own 1848, its prospect for imperial expansion through war with Mexico toward a more profound dominion over Latin America. The volcanic energies of revolution in *Blake* therefore arise not from slavery alone but from the fact that colonial rule (or imperial expansion) fueled by slave labor increased the pressure of servile insurrection exponentially. Roncali's emancipation threat was the other side of the coin Melville had dramatized in *Benito Cereno*—the deliberate relinquishing of colonial power to a slave population rather than its decay into impotence. In both cases the resulting threat appears the same. Spreading Benito Cereno's private terror throughout the slaveholding class of the New World, Delany enshrouds the planters in a limitless nightmare:

> Few people in the world lead such a life as the white inhabitants of Cuba, and those of the South now comprising the "Southern Confederacy of America." A dreamy existence of the most fearful apprehensions, of dread, horror and dismay; suspicion and distrust, jealousy and envy continually pervade the community; and Havana, New Orleans, Charleston or Richmond may be thrown into consternation by the idle expression of the most trifling or ordinary ignorant black. A sleeping wake or a waking sleep, a living death or tormented life is that of the Cuban and American slaveholder. . . . The inhabitants of a house on the brow of a volcano could not exist in greater torment than these most unhappy people.

Conspiracy and countersubversion—among slaves; free blacks and mulattoes; the Spanish government; the creole and American "patriots" in Cuba; pro- and antislavery annexationists in the United States and their filibustering mercenaries, to name just the primary factions—answered each other in a complicated endgame whose time was running out. With even more immediacy than *Benito Cereno*, the brittle antebellum political world in *Blake* is one in which the intersecting axes of the geographical and the historical concentrate all defining forces of the New World into an imminent cataclysmic event soon to break forth in the "Southern Confederacy of America."[100]

On the evening of King's Day, the American and creole patriots, in order to divert Captain-General Alcora's suspicions from themselves, contrive an act of apparent sedition among the blacks. When the plot backfires, Alcora immediately aims at the white rebels a series of suppressive orders of the sort that followed on the heels of the failed expeditions of Lopez (whose execution is announced as part of the novel's action but is not dramatized) and Quitman. The patriots in turn unleash their wrath upon the blacks, including an attack on Placido and the horsewhipping of Madame Cordora's daughter. Just as rage for revenge among the black rebels has been kindled to a burning point, however, Delany's novel breaks off with its enigmatic admonition: "Woe be unto those devils of whites, I say!" Whether or not Delany's truncation of the novel was deliberate, the effect is to suspend the course of revolution in a crisis comparable to the historical moment at which *Blake* first appeared. Perhaps the incompletion of the novel was an accident, the result of personal or editorial events; or perhaps, like Melville, Delany took proslavery countersubversion to be more potent than black rebellion; or, perhaps the most interesting possibility, he saw that such a surprising eclipse of the novel's revolutionary import augmented its threat. In any case, the stymied narrative is a fitting representation of slavery in the Americas at the point of explosion. King's Day might be a screen for the promotion of black liberty; but it might also conceal an antithetical colonial repression. Delany knew, nonetheless, that the rule of the masters, whether Spanish or American, was not eternal. His use of El Día de los Reyes to show contending cultures as well as contending political forces in a state of final tension put in ritual form the truth that Melville had staged in *Benito Cereno*'s ceremonial shaving scene. Where Melville saw the wheel of revolution and repression turn full circle, Delany, putting Hegel's psychology of bondage on the practical plane of political action, saw something more: "Of the two classes of these communities, the master and the slave, the blacks have everything to hope for and nothing to fear, since let what may take place their redemption from bondage is inevitable. They must and will be free; whilst the whites have everything to fear and nothing to hope for."[101]

The revolution against slavery could take many forms—not least the form of a African American novel devoted to outlining a historical philosophy of Afro–New World liberation and kindling a terror of slave revolution among the masters. Delany's neglected novel—like his unfortunately neglected career as a writer and African American political leader—adds a most significant dimension to the complex rewriting of the slave narrative to be witnessed in Douglass's autobiographical revisions, in such a striking hybrid of memoir and novel as Jacobs's *Incidents in the Life of a Slave Girl,* and in later fictive historicizations of resistance to slavery and Jim Crow such as Frances Harper's *Iola Leroy,* Bontemps's *Black Thunder,* William Melvin Kelley's *A Different Drummer,* or Toni Morrison's *Beloved,* to name just a few. For all its significance as a precursor and a point of reference in the record of African American literary and intellectual history, however, *Blake* was unique in its day, standing midway between the sharp testimony of slave revolution in Turner's "Confessions" and its diffusion in endless layers of ironic containment in *Benito Cereno.* In Delany are united Turner's authentic witness, if not his millenarian sacrifice, and Melville's hemispheric and epochal vision, if not his storytelling craft. Appearing almost without notice on the eve of the Civil War and strangely apocalyptic in its narrative inconclusion, *Blake* is a most appropriate final account of New World slavery—and of the antebellum world of slaves and masters alike—at the moment of its revolutionary cataclysm.

II

The Color Line

· 3 ·

Mark Twain and Homer Plessy

The carnivalesque drama of twinship and masquerade that constitutes *Pudd'nhead Wilson* and its freakishly extracted yet intimately conjoined story "Those Extraordinary Twins" is likely to remain misread and controversial in estimations of Mark Twain's literary achievement as long as the work's mimicry of America's late nineteenth-century race crisis is left out of account. Readers have, of course, often found a key to the novel's interpretation in the notorious "fiction of law and custom" that makes the "white" slave Roxy legally "black" by allowing one-sixteenth of her blood to "outvote" the rest.[1] Like so many parodic moments in the book, however, Twain's joke about voting speaks not simply to general anxieties about miscegenation but more particularly to the deliberate campaign to disfranchise blacks and strip them of legal protections gained in the Reconstruction amendments which was under way by the early 1890s. Built upon the brutal artifice of racial distinctions, both American law and American custom conspired to punish African American men and women in the post-Reconstruction years, and Twain's bitter, failed fiction, verging on allegory but trapped in unfinished burlesque, has typically been thought to participate in the black nadir without artistically transcending it or, conversely, without reaching its broader historical implications.

In fact, however, no literary work of the late nineteenth century more accurately embodied the erosion of promised racial equality in the age of Jim Crow, not least because its own powers of representation and philosophical inquiry seem continually on the point of collapse. The world of *Pudd'nhead Wilson* (1894) is a world of chaos, error, and deceit—a world of elegant pretension layered upon criminality and lies. In this respect in particular, the novel reiterates the moral structure of slavery (in the time frame of the plot) and of postbellum racism and segregation (in the implied allegorical time frame of the narration), bringing into the foreground in both instances the hypocrisy, violence, and racial loathing that *Adventures of Huckleberry Finn* (1885) had kept barely in check by the constraining good conscience of Huck and his authorial double, Mark Twain. *Pudd'n-head Wilson,* in contrast, unleashes in extravagant form the world of Tom Sawyer, Twain's other double—a world of painful burlesque in which Jim's humanity is exchanged for the minstrel play of his reenacted liberation from the cabin of slavery. Raised to a great height of achievement but everywhere in peril in *Adventures of Huckleberry Finn,* Twain's narrative style and compositional control seem to crash down in *Pudd'nhead Wilson:* Jim is a "nigger" again; Tom Sawyer is in control.

My attention in this chapter is focused on Pudd'nhead Wilson's story at the expense of Huck Finn's, which is of course the better-known tale and has for good reasons long been recognized as Twain's masterpiece. I do not mean to overturn that judgment so much as to suggest that, to the extent *Adventures of Huckleberry Finn* is taken to be the preeminent novelistic commentary on American race relations in nineteenth-century literature, it can be understood only in light of *Pudd'nhead Wilson,* which refracts the earlier book's key elements, most of all the moral wreckage of its last chapters, in a merciless critique. In its devotion to issues of doubling and twinship, *Pudd'nhead Wilson* must be counted a dark double of *Adventures of Huckleberry Finn,* Twain's nightmare measurement of both the failed vision of the masterwork and the further and seemingly irremediable decline, by the 1890s, in the prospects for African American civil rights. Judged by its capacity to represent the perversions of justice and the nearly hallucinatory structures of pseudoscientific theory that coursed through nineteenth-century intellectual, political, and legal debate about race in the United States, *Pudd'nhead Wilson* extended *Adventures of Huckleberry Finn* to a new level entirely, its apparently grave artistic flaws the true sign of wisdom.

It is not necessary to make a choice between the two novels or, against all odds, to elevate *Pudd'nhead Wilson* too high. Nevertheless, recent critical interest in the novel—rather extraordinary in comparison to its traditional estimates—is an indication that fresh questions are being asked about the text's engagement with the history of post-Reconstruction race relations and the rise of segregation. It is not insignificant, moreover, that African American authors have responded powerfully to *Pudd'nhead Wil-son*—Charles Chesnutt's *House behind the Cedars* and *The Marrow of Tradition,* Pauline Hopkins's *Of One Blood,* James Weldon Johnson's *Auto-*

biography of an Ex-Coloured Man, and George Schuyler's *Black No More,*
for example, all appear to show its influence—for they have arguably been
more alert to the book's iconoclastic break with just the modes of verisimilitude that have long been said to prove the greatness of *Adventures
of Huckleberry Finn.* Both in their ramifications for a reconstructed canon
of American literature and their own historical reference, then, *Pudd'nhead
Wilson* and its germinal short story, "Those Extraordinary Twins," may
serve equally well to place Twain at the center of critical contention over
how best to evaluate a national literature of race.

Nevertheless, the case in favor of this peculiar Siamese twin of a novel
is far from self-evident. It has been persuasively demonstrated that Twain's
chaotic process of composition and his unconcerned interchange of various
manuscript versions make it impossible to place much weight on authorial
intention narrowly defined.[2] Yet this hardly leads to the conclusion that
Twain's vision had no coherent meaning or that his own comic rationale,
contained in the opening of "Those Extraordinary Twins," reveals nothing
of significance about the text's critique of contemporary race theory or
Twain's authorial involvement in that critique. Indeed, one might rather
argue that the confusion and seeming flaws in the manuscript and the
published text, while largely attributable to his haste to produce a book
that would ameliorate his financial problems, are also a measure of the
social and psychic turmoil that Twain, not least as a liberal southerner
living and working in the North, felt in the post-Reconstruction years.
The key phenomena in late nineteenth-century race relations have just as
much place in determining the text's range of implication, its meaning, as
do such mechanical factors as compositional sequence and manuscript
emendations. Preoccupied with relevant but improperly construed issues
of aesthetic unity and verisimilitude, readers have often missed the primary
ways in which *Pudd'nhead Wilson* and its attached tale of the Italian
Siamese twins involves itself in the dilemma over national discrimination
against blacks that would reach its authoritative constitutional expression
two years later in the Supreme Court ruling in the case of *Plessy* v. *Ferguson,*
while mirroring as well the equally volatile issue of anti-immigrant nativism.

Although the Court's landmark ruling in favor of the doctrine of "separate but equal" was not handed down until 1896, Homer Plessy's case
had been pending since January 1893, after being carried up from the
Louisiana State Supreme Court to the high court on a writ of error.
Despite the manifold thematic and figurative entanglements between *Plessy*

v. *Ferguson* and *Pudd'nhead Wilson*, it is not necessary to argue that Twain
had specific knowledge of the case as it came before the Court. It is quite
likely for several reasons that he did; but more critical is the fact that *Plessy*
brought to a climax the series of Supreme Court decisions, legislative
maneuvers, and developments in sociological theory that had already created the atmosphere in which Twain's wrenching text was composed. The
central irony of Homer Plessy's deliberately staged challenge of Louisiana's
segregated train car law lay in the fact that he was seven-eighths "white"—
like Twain's Roxy and her son Tom, he was thus "black" only by the
fictions of law and custom—and his case therefore tied together the radical
decline in black civil rights that had occurred since Reconstruction and
the fanatical adherence to "one-drop" definitions of blackness that had
begun to engulf not just the South but most of the nation by the mid-
1890s. Twain's tale, in which color hallucination, separation and reversal,
and the freakish alliance of bodily selves play such crucial roles, is a fitting
gloss on the nation's rush toward racial extremism in law, in science, and
in literature, and its propensity to define equal protection under the
Constitution in such a way as to render the African American population
invisible or, what was more fantastic, to define color itself not by optical
laws but by tendentious genetic theories that reached metaphysically into
a lost ancestral world. Whereas Melville, in *Benito Cereno*, had judged that
race slavery was an exercise of political power that masqueraded behind
the supposed "laws of nature," and Chesnutt and Du Bois, among others,
were soon to argue vigorously that "race" was itself a metaphysical notion
constructed of cultural, not biological, inheritances, Twain fused both
arguments in his idiosyncratic text.

The Second Slavery

Midway into his story, having rather lamely joined his two plots of Tom
Driscoll's imposture as a white man and the visit to Dawson's Landing of
the Italian twins (no longer Siamese twins except in those textual moments
where Twain forgot to disconnect them), Twain offers a scene of minstrel
banter between Roxy and her ostensible son Chambers. The latter tells
Roxy that Tom, her real son, who has by now usurped the place of master,
is in debt through gambling and likely to be disinherited by his uncle,
Judge Driscoll. "Take it back," retorts the furious Roxy, "you misable
imitation nigger dat I bore in sorrow en tribbilation." Although it is not
the first such scene, this exchange offers the strongest evidence that Roxy,

a slave both in body and in mind at this moment in the tale, has trained herself to forget that Chambers is not really her son but rather her rightful master doomed through machinations of her creation to a life of slavery. More telling, however, is her identifying him by a doubly ironic phrase as the "imitation nigger." For Chambers *is* unknowingly a white man imitating a slave, a reverse of the standard fictional situation of the "tragic mulatto" whose discovery of "black blood" destroys personal and professional aspirations. As Tom's virtual white double, Chambers is, as it were, imitation black; and in his speech and actions he, like Roxy, imitates the role of "nigger" defined for him by the white world of enslavement. "If I's imitation, what is you?" Chambers replies, speaking in his own voice and that of Twain, his creator. "Bofe of us is imitation *white*—dat's what we is—en pow'full good imitation, too—Yah-yah-yah!—we don't 'mount to noth'n as imitation *niggers*." Or, as George Walker, one of the period's most famous African American minstrels, put it in a comment that obviously reached beyond the minstrel stage to define a range of prescribed racial roles, the popular "darky" performances of white minstrels in blackface doomed black actors to what he called the "fatal result" of double imitation: "Nothing seemed more absurd than to see a colored man making himself ridiculous in order to portray himself."[3] Twain both reverses the issue and turns it inside out. Roxy, a black in whiteface, and Chambers, presumed to be a black in whiteface, play minstrel roles as "imitation niggers," Roxy by law and Chambers ironically by means of Roxy's act of rebellion; whereas the legally black Tom passes in whiteface for one of the masters until he is unmasked by Wilson as both murderer and slave, reduced to inventoried property, and sold down the river.

"Imitation," in Twain's usage, had multiple ramifications. It pointed to the ironies that miscegenation introduced into any variable doctrine of equality; it governed the shadowy middle ground between nature (genetics) and nurture (environment) on which Twain staged his inquiry into the behaviors of mastery and subservience; and it defined, again, the shared territory of his narrative's own "fiction" and the racial "fiction" of American constitutional law and social custom. The intersection between the literary and the historical, between the double role reversals that permeate *Pudd'n-head Wilson* and the nation's descent into proliferating forms of social and legal racism in the late nineteenth century, was for Twain the point at which discourse itself could best display the workings of power and domination. Grounded in "fictions" and dressing in the elaborate masquerade necessary to authorize racial hierarchy across the broadest spectrum of human sciences, the discourse that Twain exposed to view while indulging was anything but "fictive" or powerless. It was, instead, the very incarnation of power and mastery, and for that reason rendered the promise of equality all the more an illusion. When Twain returned to the slave's revenge against his master, the culminating feature of *Pudd'nhead Wilson,* in his late unpublished narrative "Which Was It?," he once again placed the motive for his black character's humiliation and enslavement of the white master along the axis of post-Reconstruction legal history. Having purchased his freedom through years of hard labor, Jasper is immediately reenslaved when his freedom papers are destroyed in a fire and his master-father refuses to issue him a duplicate. Jasper's "second slavery,"[4] as Twain calls it, was not his alone but referred to all African Americans, whose rights were lost, case by case, in courts hard-pressed by their few dissenters to deny that the logic of *Plessy* was not equivalent to a new, "second" black slavery that imitated the first.

If repetition and duplication became the governing tropes of Twain's mind and art from *Adventures of Huckleberry Finn* forward, it was not least because he found that those tropes perfectly described America's betrayal of African American freedom—in the legislatures and courts, in the press, on stage, and in literature. The minstrel show, from which Twain borrowed profusely in constructing *Pudd'nhead Wilson,* forced blacks into humiliating comic roles that had their counterparts in other arenas of national life. In the legal rise of Jim Crow, the South received the blessings of a predominantly northern court; in the cultural rise of Jim Crow, the North adopted southern plantation ideology. The sections fed imitatively upon each other's racist inclinations, as did the dual erosion of civil rights under federal and state jurisdictions that in the aftermath of Reconstruction became increasingly separate and *unequal.* The imitative exchange of identities that the minstrel tradition exploited, at just the historical moment when the nation was engaged in a vast articulation of structural racism under the disguise of sectional reunion and Old South nostalgia, perpetuated the masquerade of the plantation tradition and at the same time revealed it to be (as Marx said of revolution) tragedy replayed as farce. The national popularity of minstrel shows in the 1880s and 1890s spilled over into nostalgic depictions of the antebellum South and "darky" characters in magazine fiction, theater, the novel, and the essay, testifying to a widely felt need, spurred by economic and political crises, to resurrect a romantic image of the Old South. At times oblivious to the significant differences among southern writers, influential northerners such as William

Dean Howells enthusiastically promoted the work of ideologically diverse authors, including Joel Chandler Harris, George Washington Cable, and Thomas Nelson Page. Romantic magazine fiction and novels regularly featured mended family ties or the marriage of northern to southern mates as a sign of sectional reconciliation. Exploiting this strategy, but in a way manifestly more racist than other southern romance, Thomas Dixon's saga of the Ku Klux Klan, especially *The Clansman* (1905), was widely popular just after the turn of the century in fiction and on stage, and of course a few years later became the basis for D. W. Griffith's famous film *The Birth of a Nation*. The tremendous success of Dixon's and Griffith's version of American race mythology would have been unthinkable without the sociological and legal underpinnings of Jim Crow. As Albion Tourgée noted as early as his well-known 1888 essay "The South as a Field for Fiction," American fiction and culture were becoming "distinctly Confederate in sympathy."[5]

Without question *Pudd'nhead Wilson* and "Those Extraordinary Twins" are implicated in the dangerous burden of minstrel humor, and the theme of the plantation masquerade pervades the entire novel in parodic but nonetheless serious forms. For the moment it is enough to say that the immediate challenge for *Pudd'nhead Wilson* was to define the meaning of the phrase "imitation nigger" in late nineteenth-century America and to suggest, as Twain always did in portraying American race problems, that it is imitation, training, practice, and habit that created the category of "nigger" and all modes of hierarchy said to be natural or divine in origin. While the Supreme Court, along with politicians and social scientists, appealed to abstruse but scientifically resounding categories of "racial instinct" and behavior rooted in the "nature of things," Twain, despite evident traces of "racism" left behind like the undeleted fragments of the conjoined twins' story, subverted the category of instinct and portrayed race as a role—but one that he, an actor in his own setting and age, had great difficulty throwing off.

Changing "itself from a farce to a tragedy" during his process of composition (as Twain, not quite honestly, explained his method of composition), *Pudd'nhead Wilson* and the story of the twins comically dramatized national policy in which farce and tragedy were indistinguishably conjoined, like black and white in the mulatto body or like the Italian "freak of nature"—separate but equal in name and by law but hardly so in fact. The story's endless play on the problems of doubling reflects Twain's own interest in questions of identity, dream selves, and dual personalities, which readers have rightly connected to his long psychosexual fascination with miscegenation and racial doubles.[6] More specifically, it corresponds to an array of dualisms making up the contemporary American racial trauma: theories of miscegenation and "blood" contamination that polarized the races and both divided and blurred mixed-race identity; sectionalism and the evident cultural, economic, and legal reunion of North and South that was under way by the 1890s; the conservative drift in constitutional law that created distinct notions of national and state citizenship, with a consequent decay in legal protection of civil rights; and pervading all, the dual layering of antebellum and post-Reconstruction (or Old South and New South) ideologies, the recreation of the dynamics of slavery in new masquerade that Twain adumbrated here, as he had in *Adventures of Huckleberry Finn,* by imposing upon antebellum dramatic action an allegory of the 1880s and 1890s.

By the time of *Pudd'nhead Wilson,* the painful attempt by Huck and Tom to "set a free nigger free"—as Huck described the charade of Jim's mock liberation into which Twain cast his initial penetrating critique of the collapse of Reconstruction ideals—had become a nightmare of tautology. The "second slavery" of the nadir was already embedded in Twain's bitter humiliations of Jim in *Adventures of Huckleberry Finn* as Huck acquiesces in Tom's ludicrous imprisonment and parodic torment of a man already legally free. What ranks as one of the most notorious debates in the history of American literary criticism—the success or failure of the last chapters of *Huckleberry Finn* after Jim and Huck have drifted past the cross-route to freedom in a dense white fog—can be properly adjudicated only by reference to the renewed crisis over sectionalism and black rights that accompanied Twain's periods of composition and this struggle to redeem, even simply to conclude, his deteriorating pastoral novel. "Now, old Jim, you're a free man again," says Tom, "and I bet you won't ever be a slave no more." At last finishing a draft of his famous novel in 1883, when the Supreme Court decided the landmark *Civil Rights Cases,* which cut the heart out of "equal protection" and led directly to *Plessy,* Twain knew otherwise. His obsessive return to the same farcical theme of Jim's liberation in *Tom Sawyer Abroad* and other late fragments indicates that even the despair of *Pudd'nhead Wilson* had not drained Mark Twain of his compulsion to work through the problems of Jim's freedom and Huck's conscience, which were also the nation's, again and again.[7]

African Americans were free according to the law; but the law, in ways that Melville had prophesied in his vision of tautology, was year by year binding them in new chains. Reflective of, if not overtly caused by, growing northern concern about the freed black population, the sequence of court rulings that prepared the way for the decision in *Plessy* broke down the legal gains African Americans had made during Reconstruction largely by giving southern, states-rights rule precedence over national civil rights protection. The "dual" citizenship that in effect allowed the reconstitution of aspects of chattel slavery in a system of segregation subverted African American freedom at the same time that it fired the debate over whether it was environment (the world of social construction) or instinct (the laws of "nature," of biological heredity) that created seemingly separate racial characteristics. Both in Twain's novel of racial crisis and in the rising national penchant for Confederate nostalgia, doubling was rampant: the 1850s and the 1890s, the South and the North, and white and black became freakishly twinned in the failure of freedom. Taking on the voice of corrupted legalism that rules his tale of artificial identity, Twain himself, southern imposter and pudd'nhead author, stood in mocking yet deadly serious judgment over materials that refused to cohere—materials that, like the destructive constitutional decisions from which they undoubtedly borrowed part of their grim energy, were themselves a "monstrous 'freak,'" a "twin-monster" of skewed intentions and betrayed ideals. A full understanding of *Pudd'nhead Wilson* must therefore trace the intricate relationship between Twain's fascination with questions of psychological and racial doubling, and the pervasive dualisms in race theory and the laws of segregation—laws that required an African American man or woman, as Chesnutt would write of Jim Crow train car regulations, to be "branded and tagged and set apart from the rest of mankind upon the public highways like an unclean thing."[8]

The Badge of Servitude: Homer Plessy and the Rise of Segregation

> "But what is this group; and how do you differentiate it; and how can you call it 'black' when you admit it is not black?"
>
> I recognize it quite easily and with full legal sanction; the black man is a person who must ride "Jim Crow" in Georgia.
>
> W. E. B. Du Bois, *Dusk of Dawn*

When he boarded a Louisiana railroad car in 1892, Homer Adolph Plessy played a deliberate role—the role, as it were, of "imitation nigger." Light enough to pass for white, Plessy had conspired with his cohorts—among them the former black Reconstruction governor and grandfather of author Jean Toomer, P. B. S. Pinchback, and a prominent black New Orleans physician and attorney, Louis A. Martinet—to challenge the state's segregated railroad car law. Enacted in 1890, the law entailed that railway companies carrying passengers within the state "shall provide equal but separate accommodations for the white, and colored, races" by providing separate coaches or by dividing a single coach with a partition "so as to secure separate accommodations." Although plans to contest the Jim Crow law had been formulated almost as soon as it passed the legislature, little headway was made until the former Reconstruction jurist and literary figure Albion Tourgée, known both for his contentious career as a carpetbagger judge in North Carolina and for his novels of the postwar South, was asked to oversee the legal challenge. Despite Martinet's opposition, Tourgée advised, for reasons that would become apparent but were riddled with irony, that the challenge be made by a mixed-race person light enough to pass for white. One attempt by a light-skinned black man named Daniel Desdunes failed in its final effect after an interstate railroad was chosen and the state supreme court in the meantime ruled that the commerce clause prohibited Jim Crow regulation of interstate travel. In the second attempt, by Homer Plessy, an intrastate train was chosen. As soon as he sat down in the whites-only car, Plessy announced himself a Negro to the conductor and was arrested according to prearranged plan. Plessy's argument when his case was brought to trial, predominantly the work of Tourgée, rested in essence on the twin claims, by this time rather familiar, that Jim Crow laws violated the rights and privileges of national citizenship guaranteed by the Fourteenth Amendment and the prohibition of involuntary servitude stated in the Thirteenth Amendment.[9]

Plessy's appeal of the lower court ruling against him to the Louisiana State Supreme Court brought forth from Justice Charles Fenner the key ingredients of the eventual United States Supreme Court ruling. Like Justice Henry Billings Brown, who wrote the majority opinion in *Plessy,* Fenner chose the path of anachronism, for his decision was based on cases admittedly prior to the enactment of the Thirteenth and Fourteenth Amendments, and also prior, in one instance, to the Civil War. He appealed to a Pennsylvania Jim Crow railroad regulation upheld in the immediate wake of the Civil War amendments by a court that referred to racial differences "resulting from nature, law, and custom" and declared that, "following the order of Divine Providence, human authority ought not compel these widely separated races to intermix." For his most important precedent, however, Fenner looked past the amendments and the war entirely. In *Roberts* v. *City of Boston* (1849) Lemuel Shaw, chief justice of the Supreme Court of Massachusetts and Herman Melville's father-in-law, wrote in a decision upholding school segregation that racial "prejudice, if it exists, is not created by law and probably cannot be changed by law." (The plaintiff's attorney, Massachusetts politician and abolitionist Charles Sumner, would be heard from again in postwar civil rights cases.) Two years later, in the famous case of the fugitive slave Thomas Sims, Shaw took on further aspects of Captain Amasa Delano, Melville's satirically portrayed New England commander in *Benito Cereno,* and struck a blow for sectionalism and states' rights when he adhered to the letter of the Fugitive Slave Law and ordered Sims returned to the South. Yet by 1855, the year of Melville's enigmatically volcanic story of slave subversion and its repression, the Massachusetts legislature had countered Shaw's opinion in *Roberts,* the burden of which rested on his view that segregation was a reasonable exercise of the state's police powers, and outlawed school segregation.[10]

Even so, Fenner and Brown had no trouble citing the case as precedent some four decades later. Indeed, as Fenner pointed out, no paradox was involved so long as one interpreted the Fourteenth Amendment in such a way as to conclude, as "is well settled," that it "created no new rights whatever, but only extended the operation of existing rights and furnished additional protection for such rights." He argued, not without justification, that Shaw's interpretation in *Roberts* contained the speculation that segregation might lessen rather than promote prejudice; and he also noted that the Massachusetts constitution contained guarantees of equality before the law comparable to those of the Fourteenth Amendment and that these had not prevented Shaw from deciding that equality need not be adjudicated in a single interpretive context but could be judged in dual contexts, white and black. Following a line of reasoning similar to Fenner's, Brown too circumvented the Civil War, the Massachusetts legislature, and the federal civil rights amendments in his eccentric appeal to *Roberts.* In doing so, the Massachusetts-born justice brought to life in the legal world the plantation myth that was then enjoying such a renaissance in the literary world. As C. Vann Woodward notes, he likewise doubled the Melvillean irony that the opinions of "two sons of Massachusetts . . . should have bridged the gap between the radical equalitarian commitment of 1868 and the reactionary repudiation of that commitment in 1896," while the lone dissenter in *Plessy,* Justice Harlan, was a former slaveholding southerner whose progressive vision and opinion would turn out to bridge "the greater gap between the repudiation of 1896 and the radical rededication of equalitarian idealism" in the 1954 *Brown* v. *Board of Education* decision. In 1896, however, Harlan's voice was drowned out. Like Lemuel Shaw, Henry Billings Brown appealed to "established usages, customs and traditions of the people" in his *Plessy* opinion and held that "legislation is powerless to eradicate racial instincts or to abolish distinctions based upon physical differences," that whatever equality is afforded in political and civil rights, "if one race be inferior to the other socially, the constitution of the United States cannot put them upon the same plane."[11]

In this construction, Brown also harked back implicitly to *Dred Scott* v. *Sandford* (1857), in which Roger B. Taney had codified in constitutional theory the view that African Americans were of "an inferior order," indeed, "so far inferior that they had no rights which the white man was bound to respect" and therefore were not Americans at all. Despite casting his opinion in terms of a natural racial hierarchy, Justice Taney rested his notorious opinion about African American noncitizenship on customs and traditions that had created dual legal systems for both southern and northern blacks. Virtually spelling out the artifice of which racially discriminatory laws were made, even as he appealed to the wisdom and the high literary intelligence of the framers of the Constitution, Taney spoke of the "unhappy black race" as one "separated from the white by indelible marks, and laws long before established," and moreover as "a class of beings" upon whom the state laws of the framers had "impressed such deep and enduring marks of inferiority and degradation." Taney's argument was not, strictly speaking, biological, but it blurred the biological into the constitutional in an even more unsettling and philosophically rigid way. The legal justification of racial inferiority, that is to say, was constructed and discursive; the law of slavery was branded into African American beings by "indelible" marks that, having been already "impressed" on blacks at the time the Declaration of Independence and the Constitution were drafted, could not, according to Taney's logic, be erased except by constitutional amendment.[12]

Leaving aside the incoherence of Taney's argument—its contradictory but strategic figures of speech—and its perverse view of citizenship, long refuted by scholars, it had in any event been superseded by the Civil War amendments, and the recurrence to it by Fenner and Brown is therefore all the more disturbing. In his *Plessy* opinion Brown claimed that race instincts and classifications, because they belong to the "nature of things," could not be altered by law; the Civil War amendments could not have been intended to alter natural law, Charles Lofgren comments, because according to Brown's logic their framers and ratifiers "would not have sought and intended the impossible." Although it was perfectly in tune with the leading sociological thought of the day, the essence of which would be summarized in William Graham Sumner's famous dictum that "stateways cannot change folkways," Brown's ruling nevertheless ignored the fact that congressional debate surrounding the equal protection clause of the Fourteenth Amendment made it very difficult (though obviously not impossible) to construe as not intending to prohibit color classifications of the kind authorized in *Plessy*. Like the language of the amendments themselves, the debate left a less than univocal record, but it can hardly be doubted that the flexibility built into the notions of equal protection and due process was meant to give courts the strongest means to combat discrimination rather than promote it. Besides being wrong about the power of legislation, moreover, Brown's circular reasoning historically lost sight of the fact that, from the Civil War to the 1890s, some portions of the South had survived without the established customs and usages of Jim Crow. Social equality was rare, of course, but Brown's introduction of the issue was irrelevant to the fact that political equality had been enjoyed by blacks with at least measured success in parts of the South.[13]

The majority opinion in *Plessy*, which Robert Harris has styled "a compound of bad logic, bad history, bad sociology, and bad constitutional law" that would rule American civil rights legislation and judgments for the next half century, summed up the degradation of black rights that had occurred over the previous two decades. Like *Pudd'nhead Wilson*, a text preoccupied with problems of legal rights, evidence, codes of authority, and the interplay of "natural" and artificial laws, and culminating in a melodramatic burlesque of a trial that sets right subverted racial roles and boundaries, *Plessy* v. *Ferguson* was at once a mockery of law and an enactment of its rigid adherence to divided, dual realities. What *Plessy* brought to fruition was the long assault on the Fourteenth Amendment that had begun with the *Slaughterhouse Cases* of 1873, in which the Supreme Court first held, in a verdict on the surface not pertaining to African American civil rights but in a manner critically destructive of those rights, that the amendment provided "dual" citizenships—national *and* state, a principle reaching back to the very constitutional beginnings of the United States—and so carefully circumscribed federal protection of rights transcending state oversight as to make national citizenship virtually meaningless. By proposing a reading of the privileges and immunities clause that, in Loren Miller's words, was nothing more than a "judicial fiction," the Court's decision in the *Slaughterhouse Cases* denied that the amendment had been intended—as clearly it had—to protect freedmen from such ignominious regulation as the postwar Black Codes.[14] But of course "judicial fiction" is very much to the point. *Slaughterhouse* and subsequent cases leading up to *Plessy* reinvoked the notion of duality so crucial to Taney's landmark opinion abrogating black citizenship in *Dred Scott,* thus—as in Fenner's and Brown's later citation of Lemuel Shaw's verdict in *Roberts*—carrying forward antebellum constitutional theory, grounded in the "indelible" and "enduring marks of inferiority and degradation" that stigmatized African Americans, into an arena in which it should have had no place.

For the next two decades the struggle continued between a Congress generally intent on furthering the reach of federal law and a conservative Court intent on limiting centralization. Because the curtailment of governmental reach grew out of a complex debate over federalism and applied as well to cases having nothing to do with race, it would be wrong to insist that the rulings that led to *Plessy* were always mere covers for racist policy. Still, the correspondence between the Court's conservative bent and the national rise in segregationist sentiment allowed states, and individuals or bodies under state jurisdiction, the greatest freedom to legislate and act in patent bad faith on the question of race. For example, *United States v. Reese* (1876), *United States v. Cruikshank* (1876), and *United States v. Harris* (1883) all undermined federal jurisdiction in cases involving southern mob violence against blacks, in particular those attempting to exercise voting rights. Separating national from state rights, the Court insisted that, while it could prevent a *state* from abridging civil rights, only states themselves could prevent *individuals* from denying blacks their rights. Corresponding to the end of Reconstruction, the establishment of such a federal-state duality had the effect of drawing a stark color line. As Frederick Douglass noted in 1880, "The citizenship granted in the Fourteenth Amendment is practically a mockery, and the right to vote, provided for in the Fifteenth Amendment, is literally stamped out in the face of government."[15]

Most far-reaching and destructive was the Court's overturning of the critical civil rights legislation of 1875 in the *Civil Rights Cases* verdict of 1883. The original sweeping legislation, which governed equal access to accommodations, public conveyances, restaurants, theaters, and the like, had been brought to pass largely through the efforts of the aging Charles Sumner, in his words "so that hereafter in all our legislation there shall be no such word as 'black' or 'white,' but . . . one shall speak only of citizens and of men."[16] The Court's rebuke of Sumner's vision and its extension of racial dualism onto a new plane of significance is evident in the contrasting views represented on the one hand by the majority opinion, and on the other by Harlan's lone dissent, which prefigured his role in *Plessy*. The Court (in Justice Joseph Bradley's majority opinion) denied that in finding the federal prohibition of segregation unconstitutional it was "reinventing" slavery. To discover the vestiges of the peculiar institution in acts of "mere discrimination on account of race or color" undertaken by private individuals, Bradley wrote, would be "running the slavery argument into the ground" and unfairly singling out the Negro not as a "mere citizen" but as "the special favorite of the laws." This resuscitation of the *Dred Scott* view that the Constitution still accepted racial distinctions rightly struck Harlan as "subtle and ingenious verbal criticism" that ignored the intent of the Thirteenth and Fourteenth Amendments to purge concepts of superiority and inferiority, the touchstone of *Dred Scott,* from the eyes of the law. Harlan insisted, moreover, that personal views of racial matters—his own included—had no bearing on the legal issues embodied in the amendments. In even more forcefully returning power to the states, he argued, the *Civil Rights* verdict ushered in "an era of constitutional law, when the rights of freedom and American citizenship cannot receive from the nation that efficient protection which heretofore was unhesitatingly accorded to slavery and the rights of the master."[17] The Constitution had originally counted the African American slave as three-fifths of a person; the Supreme Court now emasculated the amendments that had made blacks whole, once again guaranteeing that the South could number blacks among their population for political representation, while reducing them before the law, and at times literally in body, to human fragments.

In defining a dual *constitutional* citizenship that in practice was easily translated into dual *racial* citizenship, the cases leading up to *Plessy* defined the privileges and immunities and equal protection clauses negatively. That is, the Court consistently denied that anything positive had been added by the process of amendment to the protection of rights already lodged in the state. In the language of Justice Morrison Waite's opinion for the majority in *United States* v. *Cruikshank* (1876): "The only obligation resting upon the United States is to see that the States do not deny the right [of one citizen against another under the Constitution]. . . . The power of the National Government is limited to the enforcement of this guaranty." In separating national from state rights and declaring that only states themselves could prevent individual citizens from denying African Americans their rights—for example, white mobs bent on disfranchisement through intimidation—the Court completed the deal struck in the Compromise of 1877 and left equal protection, like Twain's mulatto and even more like his Siamese twins, monstrously lodged in two bodies, neither of which had full responsibility for its legal or moral guarantee. The notion of dual citizenship and the reinvention of slavery exfoliated in *Plessy* into Justice Brown's extrapolation of further distinctions between the law and nature, and between narrow political rights and broader social rights, which were routinely distinguished in discussions of race, to be sure, but which were then, and were long to remain, a mechanism to mystify political rights themselves.* The object of the Fourteenth Amendment, in Brown's view, "was undoubtedly to enforce the absolute equality of the two races before the law, but, in the nature of things, it could not have been intended to abolish distinctions based upon color, or to enforce social, as distinguished from political, equality, or a commingling of the two races upon terms unsatisfactory to either."[18] Here nature was made to merge decisively with custom—the long-standing custom of racism— and the commingling that Brown intended to prevent in the arena of democratic life likewise created a theoretical closed circle excluding blacks from all equal rights. The "laws of nature," in Twain's world as in Melville's, moved toward tautology. "Nature" was the court of last appeal in matters of racial hierarchy and segregation, but its saturation in social practice, training, custom, and usage served to empty the term of all but variable interpretive constructions. The very syntactical placement of Brown's phrase "in the nature of things" revealed, in fact, that "nature" was consciously a product, in his mind as in Taney's, of legislative and judicial debate. Whatever the intention of Brown's distinction, moreover,

---

* As Kelly Miller would later write, the slogan "social equality," "like a savage warwhoop, arouses the deepest venom of race, which slumbers only skin deep beneath a thin veneer of civilization. This expression cannot be defined according to the ordinary import and weight of words. Whoever coined it possessed a genius for summoning the evil spirit. . . . 'Social' and 'equality' are two excellent words; but 'social equality' must not be pronounced in good society, like two harmless chemical elements uniting to make a dangerous compound." See Kelly Miller, *Radicals and Conservatives and Other Essays on the Negro in America* (originally published as *Race Adjustment,* 1908; rpt. New York: Schocken, 1968), pp. 123–24.

legal theory and practice alike showed that social and political rights, like the Siamese body, could not be separated without grave risk to both.

Because the Louisiana railroad car statute was not simply a form of private discrimination but rather a state action and thus potentially liable to the Court's by then weak enforcement of equal protection, the idea of a negative guarantee of rights, with its consequent definition of citizenship as dual, might seem to have been of particular import in the case of *Plessy.* Brown and the majority, however, did not just ignore this fact; instead, consistent with the evisceration of the Fourteenth Amendment in *Slaughterhouse,* they found it irrelevant to the central issue of *Plessy*—that of "equal" protection. That a state action of segregation was involved in this case in fact became the predicate whereby the Court was able to judge that Homer Plessy's segregation was authorized by the dual citizenship inherent, one could say, in the constitutional "nature of things" and that his treatment was equal under a constitutional Louisiana law. What was clear by 1896, though, was that dual citizenship and negative enforcement of equal protection, even if they were not primarily masks for naked racial discrimination, made it increasingly easy to cover pernicious intent with the cloak of law. *Plessy* was a landmark case not because it drastically altered the direction of legislation and judicial thought but because it concluded the process of transfiguring dual *constitutional* citizenship into dual *racial* citizenship which had unfolded since the end of Reconstruction. Although reaction to *Plessy* among journalists outside the South was largely negative, the most striking thing about newspaper coverage was the mundane, even slight notice given the decision. The economic and cultural reunion of North and South necessitated political and legal separations that turned the "Negro problem" over to the South, thereby using the South to further what in reality were national inclinations. After the Supreme Court decision in the *Civil Rights Cases,* one historian has argued, there was throughout the North "not only acquiescence among the white population in the 'Southern Way' of solving the race problem but a tendency to imitate it in practice."[19] The national courts both launched and themselves imitated the circular law of imitation. As the mob cases of *Harris* and *Cruikshank* had indicated, however, the essential division was not necessarily that between federal and state jurisdiction but between black and white skin—or rather, black and white "blood." The complex theory of imitation set forth in *Pudd'nhead Wilson,* comprising law, political and social ideology, and a theory of representation, referred all other arguments to the paradoxical cultural consequences of a racial code founded on "one-drop" rule, which recast the rule of slavery into increasingly nuanced but at the same time stark forms.

John Marshall Harlan's famous dissent in *Plessy* built on his view, already articulated in the *Civil Rights Cases,* that federal allowance of discrimination did indeed constitute a "badge of servitude" and a resurrection of "slavery" in the form of the "sinister legislation" states were able to pass. He dismissed the issue of social equality as a red herring, noting on the one hand that political equality and the guarantee of civil rights did not promote it, but arguing on the other that the denial of such rights certainly *did* promote racial antagonism and violence. Most important for Harlan, however, was the central fact that the Civil War amendments had annihilated *Dred Scott,* while *Plessy* reconstituted its most invidious implications. "We boast of the freedom enjoyed by our people above all other peoples," Harlan stated; yet that boast was hard to reconcile with the "brand of servitude and degradation" retained in Jim Crow laws, whose "thin disguise" of "equal" accommodations "will not mislead any one, nor atone for the wrong this day done."[20] But the meaning of such slavery was more effectively spelled out in Albion Tourgée's brief, which distinguished in antebellum terms between simple chattelism and the black person's "legal condition of subjection to the dominant class, a bondage quite separable from the incident of ownership." As a "defenceless and despised victim of the civil and political society," Tourgée argued, the slave was "in bondage to the whole white race as well as to his owner." (In this he echoed Frederick Douglass, who had reflected on the threatening precedent of *Dred Scott* when he asked in an 1862 article: "Shall [the freedmen] exchange the relation of slavery to individuals, only to become the slaves of the community at large, having no rights which anybody is required to respect, subject to a code of black laws?") Chattelism might be gone, Tourgée concluded, but the Supreme Court decisions culminating in *Plessy* would clearly have reestablished black bondage to the dominant class. Just as Henry Billings Brown recurred to Lemuel Shaw in writing the majority opinion, Harlan echoed the plaintiff's argument advanced by Charles Sumner in the *Roberts* case—that Boston's Jim Crow schools violated central American principles. "We abjure nobility of all kinds," said Sumner, "but here is a nobility of the skin. . . . We abjure all privileges of birth; but here is a privilege which depends solely on the accident [of] whether an ancestor is black or white."[21]

Superimposing 1849 on 1896, the arguments of *Plessy* v. *Ferguson* recreated caste distinctions that violated American principle, the legacy of the Civil War, and the process of constitutional amendment. Likewise super-imposing the 1840s–1850s on the 1890s, Twain's Tom Driscoll, a disguised aristocratic master exposed as a slave, echoes Charles Sumner in asking the pertinent question: "Why were niggers *and* whites made? What crime did the uncreated first nigger commit that the curse of birth was decreed for him? And why this awful difference between white and black?"[22] Not just the caste division enunciated in *Dred Scott* but the more insidious aspects of slavery itself would reappear under the forms of segregation that began to flourish in the 1890s as the words *white* and *black* acquired newly powerful, separate meanings and "nobility of skin" took on subtle-ties in some respects more extreme than those regnant in the Old South.

In point of fact, the racist underpinnings of the New South and post-Reconstruction America generally, as Twain dramatized with such passion in *Pudd'nhead Wilson*, required the creation of an Old South myth that in most ways exceeded historical reality. By 1890 the myth had received the blessing of the North; the Republican party had given up attempts to break the Democratic "Solid South," and the largely northern, Republican Supreme Court ruled consistently on the side of the capitalistic develop-ment that the New South hoped to attract.[23] In Twain's recreated ante-bellum world, replete with the gaudy aura of nobility and fabricated genealogies worshipped not only by the white masters but ludicrously by their black slaves as well, the code of southern gentlemen appears to be at odds with, or to despise recourse to, law, and in this it belongs to the elaborate system of honor that governed much antebellum southern social interaction. In the New South, however, the code and the law were approaching identity to the extent that the code was based on racial or genealogical purity, and mob pressure dictated the legal suppression of African American political rights. Twain's focus on southern codes of honor and patrilineal right, moreover, demonstrates his apprehension of the degree to which contemporary race law was itself based on social codes—on the consensus of behavior and opinion, on "customs and usages," rather than the careful rule of law, which seemed to disappear from view even as both the majority in *Civil Rights Cases* and *Plessy* and Harlan in his dissents claimed it as their guide. Indulging an extreme mode of legal realism, however, Twain declared law the province of per-sonal predilection and discriminatory social codes. *Pudd'nhead Wilson* can be understood as a despairing reply to the principles supporting Harlan's dissent in the *Civil Rights Cases* and an anticipation of his further dissent in *Plessy*, one that pessimistically portrays the perilous collapse of the rule of law under the burden of race prejudice that permeates received social custom and usage.[24]

The aristocratic code of the Old South, part of the stage machinery of *Pudd'nhead Wilson*, was central to the "fiction" created by the New South, not least because it imagined a time when the question of black legal rights had been virtually meaningless. In the new order white supremacy "outvoted" black rights at the polls and in the courts until, in *Williams* v. *Mississippi* (1898), the first state disfranchisement case to come before the Supreme Court, the legal definition of duality gave a free hand to individual and communal racism. Confronted with Mississippi's 1890 suffrage law, which excluded various convicted criminals, required a poll tax, and finally demanded that the prospective voter read and interpret a section of the state constitution—an act clearly liable to official abuse—the Court replied that such codes did not deny equal protection or, "on their face, discriminate between the white and Negro races." Specifically, Justice Joseph McKenna wrote, it was not shown that the administration of such laws "was evil but only that evil was possible under them."[25]

As James Weldon Johnson would wryly remark several decades later, the black man going before the Supreme Court, "unable to prove that the committee which had met him at the polls with shotguns was actuated by any such base and unconstitutional motives" as might inhere in the illegal abridgment of his rights by the *state*, inevitably "found his case thrown out." Twain, however, had anticipated both Johnson and the Supreme Court. In the figure of Huck Finn's father, he had, in fact, already painted his darkest portrait of the crude, illiterate white racist authorized by the disfranchisement decisions to vote at the expense of qualified black (male) voters. Pap Finn's drunken tirade about the free mulatto ("most as white as a white man") from Ohio, whom Pap is astonished to learn can vote in that state, again conflates antebellum and post-Reconstruction racial politics. Pap's frustration that under 1850s Missouri law the "free nigger," with no protective freedom papers, cannot be seized and sold for six months points ahead in the novel to Jim's extreme jeopardy, turned to painful comedy by Tom's charade of liberation. The antebellum setting of Pap Finn's harangue also barely hides the fact that it is the man's capacity to vote, guaranteed by the Fifteenth Amendment, that is the appropriate touchstone for racist reaction in the postwar allegorical time frame of *Adventures of Huckleberry Finn*. In addition, the episode would seem a deliberate reflection on Dred Scott, whose landmark case turned on the question of whether or not, because he had once been taken *out* of Missouri by his master, he could claim his freedom under Illinois or territorial laws prohibiting slavery. The Court's denial that African Americans had any rights of citizenship that whites were "bound to respect" left Dred Scott the pawn of a "govment" with which Pap Finn would have been pleased. The post-Reconstruction decay of black rights, epitomized by the disfranchisement decisions and the Supreme Court's disinterested characterization of the racial "evil" left to state jurisdiction, revived Dred Scott in such a way as to define any potential black voter as, in Pap Finn's words, "a prowling, thieving, infernal, white-shirted free nigger."[26]

At the same time, blackness outvoted whiteness in the blood, and "one-drop" ideology drove mulattoes toward blacks—or, in the case of those who were light enough to pass, toward a masked existence among whites. Lynching peaked in the early 1890s, as Twain was writing, and national campaigns against it were sparked by Ida B. Wells's powerful 1892 editorials on lynching for the *Memphis Free Speech* and the *New York Age,* reprinted as a pamphlet entitled "Southern Horror: Lynch Law in All Its Phases." Revived schemes for the deportation of blacks to colonies in Africa or Latin America were further evidence of the white desire for permanent separation. Fears of increased black criminality and so-called degeneration created the paradoxical situation in which racist exclusion and black alienation fed imitatively upon each other, creating—as Twain a few years later would write of lynching—a "mania, a fashion; a fashion which will spread wider and wider, year by year, covering state after state, as with an advancing disease." In Twain's imagined world of *Pudd'nhead Wilson* the danger of mob rule latent in *Adventures of Huckleberry Finn* has become nearly an enshrined principle of law—so much so that the power of imitative behavior, as in Roxy's case, can even destroy the slave's awareness of her own oppression or her recognition that her son has been transformed by her own hand into her abusive master. The conflation of mobs and courts in the "United States of Lyncherdom," as Twain called it, allowed the power of imitation to define roles of black submission, roles of black segregation, and ultimately roles of black destruction. The imitative behavior that spread disfranchisement laws to state after state during and after the 1890s, and decimated African American economic and social rights in the process, thus gave to lynching a figurative dimension that made it all the more virulent. In the words of Joel Williamson: "One could lynch just as effectively by genteel means as crudely by rope and faggot. Negroes could be lynched by account books. And they could be lynched by written history," so as to open "the way for an honorable reunion of North and South."[27] The rewriting of Confederate myth and Reconstruction fact gives the "fiction" of race relations special meaning in the 1890s, and it is such a mode of "lynching" that Twain's novel comes close to joining even as it plunges into the darkest satire on southern life and American racial practice since Tourgée's 1879 novel of Reconstruction, *A Fool's Errand*.

When Tourgée went before the Supreme Court to argue the case of *Plessy v. Ferguson*, an observer remarked in the *Washington Post* that he was on "another fool's errand." The allusion to Tourgée's novel rightly foresaw that the arguments of his brief for Homer Plessy were as doomed as his previous hopes for racial harmony in Reconstruction North Carolina, where he served as a superior court judge from 1869 to 1879. A man of principle but decidedly an outsider (perhaps even a pudd'nhead to the locals), Tourgée in retrospect styled his idealistic venture the dream of a foolish man, but the kind of man who is "both fool and genius,—a fool all his life and a genius after his death, or a fool to one century and a genius to the next, or a fool at home and a prodigy abroad."[28] The respective implications of their fiction were only approximately allied, but both Twain and Tourgée nevertheless played the fool with dead seriousness on the issue of race, Twain not least because the role of his main fool, attorney David Wilson, was so clearly caught up in the performance of Mark Twain the author. Even though Twain had long been fascinated by the combination of farce and brutality latent in legal systems, the sequence of critical civil rights rulings after Reconstruction was beyond question crucial to his novel's mad ridicule of laws, evidence, courts, and trials, all failing in their primary duty to bring about justice, much as Tourgée discovered that the weight of military occupation and legal proscription could not properly restore order or create racial justice during Reconstruction.

Even though he may not have deserved the unqualified description of either genius or hero, the history of the legal battle for black civil rights culminating in *Brown* v. *Board of Education* would recognize John Marshall Harlan as the "fool" half a century ahead of his time. In his goals, if not in his argumentation, Tourgée sided with Harlan in his allegiance to the rule of law rather than the rule of custom and privilege. Perhaps more clearly than Harlan, however, Tourgée saw that the two were inseparably entangled, and it is his arguments that bear most precisely on the legal and racial figurings of *Pudd'nhead Wilson*. His attempt to drum up national support for Plessy's case with a vigorous newspaper campaign primarily in the North and through the efforts of the National Civil Rights Association (which he had established in 1891, with George Washington Cable among others on its executive board) met with strong and immediate early success. Given Twain's relationship with Cable, strained though it was by the early 1890s, and given too his general interest in the promotion of African American rights, it is probable that Twain was well acquainted with Tourgée, his writings, and his civil rights efforts. Disagreement among various race leaders over tactics, conservative attacks, and southern physical intimidation of blacks undermined the organization, however, and by the time *Plessy* was heard, the NCRA hardly existed, the atmosphere of race hatred had heightened, not abated, as Tourgée had hoped, and his errand before the Court seemed more foolish than ever. Nevertheless, Tourgée's arguments were of great, if sometimes ironic, import. In addition to detailing the mechanisms by which Jim Crow reconstituted the essence of slavery—the slave being in "bondage" to the entire white race, not just the property of a single owner—Tourgée turned the property argument on its head (and explicated his choice of a very light mulatto such as Homer Plessy to challenge the law) by insisting that the Louisiana segregation law had deprived Plessy of his property, which in this instance was vested in his "reputation of being white." "Indeed," Tourgée asked, is whiteness "not the most valuable sort of property, being the master-key that unlocks the golden door of opportunity?"[29] Apparently hoping to fool the property-minded justices into recognizing an element of color that would destroy Jim Crow by rendering it chaotic, Tourgée opened himself to the irony that such an argument would in reality protect only those who could pass—the mulatto elite—and define equal protection just as restrictively and negatively as the Court already had, only locating it at a different mark on the color line.

Tourgée's argument is hardly as far-fetched as it might appear, for color clearly did govern property rights. With the advent of increased power among African Americans during Reconstruction and the passing of the Fifteenth Amendment, there had been a significant drive, successfully resisted, not only to legalize interracial marriage but more particularly to make white fathers legally responsible for their mixed-race offspring and their property inheritable by those children. Even with the demise of Reconstruction and the subsequent pressure to adopt a "one-drop" definition of blackness, the law governing mixed-race property rights and color itself as a kind of property was somewhat fluid and ambiguous, varying over time and from state to state. For example, the Supreme Court in *Pace* v. *Alabama* (1882) anticipated the logic of *Civil Rights Cases* the following year by upholding Alabama's harsher punishment of *interracial* fornication as opposed to intraracial on the specious Fourteenth Amendment grounds that the law punished both the black and white member of the couple equally. Interracial marriage fell under the same construction, but with the additional burden that because marriage was the medium for the transmission of property, miscegenation threatened white property rights. As Eva Saks has argued, miscegenation law used blood "to control the legal legitimation of social unions and the legal disposition of property to the children of these unions," in the process creating out of "blood" a metaphor that signified race but that also pointed to a physical phenomenon that could remain utterly invisible. In transforming race into an intrinsic and changeless entity signified by blood, miscegenation jurisprudence defined it as inheritable property. The tracing of genealogy, as Saks suggests, was the search for an authoritative legal representation of race that in the end had no conclusive proof except for the unstable category of reputation, since visible evidence counted for nothing against the imputation of hidden blood. At the same time, however, courts relied on the rule of degree. In *Ferrall* v. *Ferrall* (North Carolina 1910) a husband's attempt to disinherit his children by declaring his wife Negro "within the prohibited degree" was soundly rejected on the grounds that the marriage had been legal and his wife was visibly white. Referring to *Pudd'nhead Wilson* (which had been cited by the husband's attorney), the court compared the man's attempt "thus to bastardize his own children" to Tom Driscoll's selling of Roxy "down the river." (Twain himself, as we will see, initially included a passage that made Tom's "bastardy" a humiliating augmentation of the desire for revenge sparked by Roxy's revelation of his hidden "blood," but he apparently decided that in the legal context of the novel Tom's "nigger illegitimacy"—as Tom himself thinks of it in his meditation—was virtually redundant and needed no explication.) However much it showed that race and blood were fluid constructions—semiotic fictions—*Ferrall* did nothing to dislodge the fact that "whiteness" was property and "blackness" its negation. The disingenuous logic of *Pace*, which also underlies the formal theory of *Plessy* and which is parodied most conclusively in Twain's burlesque of hanging only "one" of the Siamese twins, replicates this epistemological circle. The separate bodies (the black and the white), although they appear to be punished equally, are in fact punished as one miscegenous (black) body: their crime is that they threaten to pass black "blood" into the body of an offspring, contaminating or destroying the inheritable property of whiteness, and hence the inalienable property rights, lodged in the white partner.[30]

The mixed-race figure thus concentrated the problem of racial doubling insofar as he could be said to *imitate* or parody but not to *own* the property of whiteness. The de jure dual citizenship that made for de facto racial dualism left the mulatto a "freak" of natural law, while the spread of segregationist thought and policy made the light-skinned black an uncanny reminder that blackness both *was* and *was not* visible and whiteness both *was* and *was not* a form of property with legal significance. Whatever its merit in protecting the rights of at least the mulatto elite, the brevity of the portion of Tourgée's argument devoted to color as a form of property suggests that Tourgée had, by 1896, recognized its "foolishness," or its rank paradoxicalness, in this instance. Even so, it underlined the hallucinatory character of the Jim Crow laws that were ushered in by *Plessy,* which over the next half century would reach such extremity that Tourgée's further speculations on the color line were not in the least foolish: "Why not require all colored people to walk on one side of the street and the whites on the other? Why may [the state] not require every white man's house to be painted white and every colored man's black?" Tourgée foresaw that there was no logical end to such discriminations, and Justice Brown's reply that they must be "reasonable" was nothing to the point. The primary question, in Tourgée's view, was "not as to the *equality* of the privileges enjoyed, but *the right of the State to label one citizen as white and another as colored.*" In holding indeed that "a single drop of African blood is sufficient to color a whole ocean of Caucasian whiteness"—to *outvote* it—the Supreme Court called Tourgée's bluff and exposed the nadir of the new segregationism, demonstrating that the nation itself was now the freak, separated and rejoined over the black body—like Amasa Delano and Benito Cereno linked by the crutch of Babo—which was now conclusively separated from and unequal to the white.[31]

Blaspheming Colors, Extraordinary Twins

It was in this world that Twain wrote and within this particular legal discourse that his tale of miscegenation, doubling, and legal fictions of color, ownership, and identity must be read. For in their opposition to radical racists, liberal politicians and writers were likewise compelled toward fantasy or, in any event, toward significant accommodation of racism.

A good example would be George Washington Cable's controversial essay written in reply to the *Civil Rights Cases* of 1883, "The Freedman's Case in Equity," which Cable delivered regularly on the lecture circuit with Twain and published in *Century Magazine* in 1885 before including it that same year in his volume *The Silent South*. (Among other things, Twain regularly read the passages from *Adventures of Huckleberry Finn* recounting Jim's mock liberation by Tom and Huck, and it may be that the grim comedy of David Wilson's courtroom theatrics embrace Twain's reflection on this and other instances in which the success of his platform humor, which also included some minstrel comedy and unpleasant racial jokes, was likely to depend on the racist inclinations of his audience.) Driven from the South because of the power of his message in favor of African American political rights and against segregation, Cable nonetheless paradoxically pointed out that his essay did not touch the domain of social privileges and asserted that "social equality is a fool's dream." He intimated, more-over, that the real risk of miscegenation now resided not among identifiable Negroes but among light-skinned African Americans who might success-fully mix with the white population—the "joke," as his narrator would call it, that Johnson would soon exploit in *The Autobiography of an Ex-Coloured Man*. Before professional jealousy spoiled their friendship, Twain and Cable discussed the problem of miscegenation and the purported threat of black supremacy in the South, the tempestuous issues that were said to underlie the foolish dream of social equality and that soon found release in Twain's fiction.[32]

Cable's lectures and essays on behalf of blacks brought forth not only the scorn of the radical South but also the advocacy of Jim Crow by reunion-minded northerners. As tolerance for any sign of equality evap-orated in an obsession with racial purity, the specter of "invisible black-ness" put mulattoes—indeed, anyone suspected to be of tainted ancestry or, like Homer Plessy, willing to admit it—increasingly into the peculiar position outlined by Charles Dudley Warner, Twain's collaborator in his first novel, *The Gilded Age*. Warner wrote sympathetically of the relative racial harmony that existed in mid-1880s New Orleans despite the city's inconsistent mix of segregation customs and regulations. Yet because "society cannot be made or unmade by legislation," Warner noted, in anticipation of Justices Fenner and Brown, the "instinct in both races against mixture of blood" had better be heeded by blacks as well as whites, for it is "they who will see that there is no escape from the equivocal position in which those nearly white in appearance find themselves except by a rigid separation of the races."³³

Warner's lecture was delivered at the World's Industrial and Cotton Exposition of 1885, one of numerous expositions in the 1880s and 1890s jointly sponsored by North and South to promote sectional reconciliation and southern industrialization, and it therefore signals a common intellectual subcurrent in the drive toward reunion.³⁴ The most prominent crusader who crossed the Mason-Dixon line in the other direction was Henry W. Grady, the editor of the *Atlanta Constitution,* whose appearances before northern audiences and whose posthumous volume *The New South* (1890) trumpeted Dixie's vision of racial and sectional harmony through segregation and northern investment. Like Cable and Warner, Grady similarly appealed to barely latent northern fears of miscegenation and increasing black population, and he maintained, somewhat incoherently, that there was in both whites and blacks a natural aversion to mixing that had been broken down by mulattoes. Falling just between the critical years of *Pudd'nhead Wilson* and *Plessy* v. *Ferguson,* what might now be considered the most revealing instance of the spread of the segregationist thesis occurred in Booker T. Washington's famous 1895 address to the Atlanta Cotton States and International Exposition: "In all things that are purely social we can be as separate as the fingers, yet one as the hand in all things essential to mutual progress."³⁵ In a contemporary atmosphere charged by physiological race theory, Washington's metaphor of the hand neatly balanced cooperation and segregation, giving unspoken support to *Plessy's* doctrine by appealing to an image of separate but equal brotherhood composed of both social and natural law.

In addition, Washington's metaphor has an oblique echo in *Pudd'nhead Wilson,* where fingerprints paradoxically demonstrate Tom's inviolable individuality and the fact that he belongs to a group scorned for racial identity alone; and Tom, recognizing that "a man's own hand is his deadliest enemy" and provides "a record of the deepest and fatalest secrets of his life," hides his palm from David Wilson to keep the "black-magic stranger" from reading therein the sign of his guilt as well, it seems, as the sign of his invisible color. Sir Francis Galton, the father of Pudd'nhead Wilson's "black-magic" science and author of *Finger Prints* (1892), speculated—incorrectly—that supposed signs of differing racial characteristics such as intelligence would appear in the prints themselves. What is more, Galton went on to achieve his greatest renown as a promoter of eugenics, which advocated the progressive breeding of an improved society and which in the American climate of the early twentieth century automatically took the form of nativist theories of protection against the threat of race suicide through miscegenation and immigration.[36] It is possible that Twain, following Galton, harbored the suspicion that racial characteristics could be detected in fingerprints. But his use of the metaphor of the revealing hand in *Pudd'nhead Wilson* seems rather to mock the theory that segregation was rooted in organic laws susceptible to proof by the new scientific and sociological study of heredity. Wilson's triumphant display of Tom's identity as a "negro and slave" shows rather that those two categories are social constructions that have been wrongly construed as natural, much as courts had read race prejudice, equally a social construction, to be rooted in the "nature of things." Twain's anachronistic introduction of fingerprinting science into an antebellum story served to enforce the critique of post-Reconstruction appeals to antebellum legal findings and race ideologies, the means for "reinventing" slavery as rigid segregation. Booker T. Washington's similar metaphor, while it may be said to have carefully calculated the social construct of a biracial society as organic, nevertheless demonstrated the power of those appeals in its acceptance of segregation as necessary to political harmony and economic progress.* The theory of an organic society that nonetheless allowed for racial seg-

---

* Although it is possible to read a good deal of Washington's writings as a sly commentary on the need for blacks to submit to the ideology of Jim Crow, to "wear the mask," if they were to combat racism and win civil rights most effectively, some key episodes in his work are difficult to reconcile. Washington's seemingly most overt comment on *Plessy*, for example, appears in an anecdote about Jim Crow train cars in *Up from Slavery*. After taking note of Frederick Douglass's dignified response to being ejected from a white passenger car ("the soul that is within me no man can degrade"), Washington launches into a humorous anecdote about a southern conductor's inability to tell whether a light-skinned man riding in a black passenger car is truly black. Not wishing to insult the man by asking him outright (in case he *is* white), the conductor examines him in detail, without conclusion, but finally surreptitiously studies the man's feet. As Washington says to himself: "'That will settle it'; and so it did, for the trainman promptly decided that the passenger was a Negro, and let him remain where he was. I congratulated myself that my race was fortunate in not losing one of its members." Washington's glib account may be extraordinarily deadpan, and his account of the conductor's physiological examination a cunning exposure of the absurdity of one-drop ideology and, in fact, the pseudoscientific constitution of race itself. If so, however, protest is buried so deep as to be virtually indistinguishable from accommodationism. See Booker T. Washington, *Up from Slavery* (1901; rpt. New York: Penguin, 1986), pp. 100–101. On Washington's "minstrelsy" as a signifying critique, see Houston A. Baker, Jr., *Modernism and the Harlem Renaissance* (Chicago: University of Chicago Press, 1987), pp. 25–36.

regation disguised the vertical axis of racial hierarchy within the horizontal axis of segregation and the controlled "progress" of the race. Fingerprints, which should be adduced as signs of nonracial individuality, instead convict Tom of being black. In Wilson's usage, Tom's prints are a sign of his individual guilt; but they remain identified, in Wilson's theatrical exposure of Tom as an invisible mulatto, as "nigger paw-marks," physiological markers that condemn him to return to the category of slave.[37] Like Washington's figurative fingers (or the feet of his "white" passenger consigned to the Jim Crow car), they conceal racial hierarchy within "equal" protection.

Segregation into dual halves of society, as in dual standings before the law, left blacks and whites in significant ways more divided than they had been during slavery, with blacks, as Tourgée argued, again in bondage to a dominant white class. "Equal" and "separate" were twinned by law but arranged in a paradox—in theory tautological but in practice contradictory. Likewise, the widening gulf between colors swallowed into an abyss those whose very bodies were marked by the violation of racial barriers. Escape from what Warner rightly called the "equivocation" of the mulatto's dual status lay not in identity or unity but in segregation, not in "equal" but in "separate" existence as it came to be defined by mob rule and by courts of law. Thus, when Pudd'nhead Wilson translates mob opinion into the rule of law at the conclusion of Twain's novel, he simultaneously reveals the hidden "nigger," the white man with black blood, and moves to the apex of the townspeople's values. Recasting his joking irony about the halves of an "invisible dog" into the final revelation of racial law, Wilson reverses the "election" and "verdict" that early on voted him a fool and carries out his original threat against that dog—to kill his half. Exposed at last as the "miserable dog" to which he has been compared by Roxy, Wilson, and even himself throughout the novel, Tom is condemned for the crime of murder but punished for the crime of being black when he is sold down the river as part of the estate's inventory.[38] His sale depends on his identity, not his crime, on the "custom and usage" of his color rather than on his standing as an acting, willful human subject. The rule of law gives way to outright theater, the court becoming an explicit domain of staged opinions and prejudices that burlesque the drift in constitutional law. As chattel, Tom, like Dred Scott, has no rights that white people are bound to respect. And his other half, Chambers, is left radically "unequal" under the supposedly equal treatment of the law. Like the innocent but nonetheless dead half of the hanged freak in "Those Extraordinary Twins," he is "killed" as well by being thrust into a ruling class to which he does not by habit belong.

The fear of "mongrelization" that pervaded radical rhetoric about miscegenation imputed bestiality to African Americans but suggested also that, in their rise toward political or social equity with whites, they were at best able only to "imitate" the requisite manners and intelligence of civilized society. Playing on the imitation of "forms" and "habit" that Twain said could be concretized into "automatic," "unconscious," and "natural" behavior, both stock minstrel scenes and racist literature denied the priority of environment in forming character and satirized black pretensions to manners, learning, or political sophistication.[39] Imitation was, in fact, one of the most charged issues in contemporary social theory. In developing theories of behavior, a number of American commentators wrote in answer to Gabriel Tarde's influential volume *The Laws of Imitation* (1890), in which Tarde had stated the extreme theory of code-governed, imitative behavior in a fashion that would have been most attractive to Twain in his deep pessimism: "The social like the hypnotic state is only a form of dream, a dream of command and a dream of action. Both the somnambulist and the social man are possessed by the illusion that their ideas, all of which have been suggested to them, are spontaneous."[40] In two telling instances I would like to return to—Roxy's trance and Pudd'n-head Wilson's dream—Twain forces imitation into just such a somnambulistic corner, suggesting that Tarde's view accorded with his own skepticism about free will and his increasing preoccupation in his late work with fantastic dream states in which will and identity are entirely occluded.

It was the racial use to which Tarde's general theory might be put, however, that has most bearing on Twain's examination of imitation in *Pudd'nhead Wilson*. Contemporary American theorists modified Tarde's views but often did so in order to describe a hierarachy of racial distinctions and to theorize that the Negro's imitativeness, as a tool of assimilation, was at best superficial, constrained by supposedly inferior mental capacity and primitive instincts. Limited by "instinctive impulses" that become fixed by natural selection ("certain coordinations of nerve cells and muscle fibers which tend to discharge in one way rather than another"), Charles Ellwood argued, imitation varies racially such that a Negro raised by Caucasians would fail to take on their "mental and moral characteristics." In Ellwood's semi-Lamarckian account, the possibility of modification of behavior by imitation is burdened by race and the risk of reversion: "His [the Negro's] natural instincts, it is true, may be modified by training, and perhaps indefinitely in the course of generations; but the race habit of a thousand generations or more is not lightly set aside by the voluntary or enforced imitation of visible models, and there is always a strong tendency to reversion." That is, the "nigger" in him, according to Ellwood, would prevent the black person from adapting by imitation to a "higher" moral model. Likewise asserting that the laws of social imitation were racially determined, but giving it a different twist, Jerome Dowd suggested that racial assimilation was tied to social assimilation through imitation and the availability of models for emulation. Dowd thus argued that black slaves, because of their close personal association with their white masters, had higher moral standards than postwar blacks: the law of imitation established the "superiority of the antebellum Negro," and only racial intermarriage, unlikely to be condoned by society, could counteract the likely moral and physical disintegration of contemporary African Americans. Philip Bruce's account of black "degeneration" along these lines was typical in its claim that the Negro is "eager to ape the habits and customs of the whites, and yet reveals in his own infirmities that he is incapable of adopting anything but the form." In Bruce's view there was no solution but the extinction or withdrawal of one or the other race: "The South cannot remain permanently half black and half white."[41]

Bruce's deliberate updating of Lincoln's language in his House Divided speech recast the crisis over slavery (the nation cannot remain half slave, half free) in the new language of segregation. Bruce's statement was itself a form of imitation; he parodied Lincoln, one could say, so as to draw dire implications from the achievement of African American freedom, much as the post-Reconstruction Supreme Court cases parodied the language of antebellum decisions that should have lost their standing as precedent. The Court's inability to separate political from social inequality (even as it claimed to draw a clear line between them) left it caught in the same quagmire of assumptions that underlay theories of African American "reversion" and "degeneration," and that reappears in Twain's garbled, unsatisfactory representation of the sources of Tom Driscoll's behavioral traits.

Twain's inquiry into imitation as a component of character reaches no very satisfactory judgment about the ratio between instinct and training in the case of Tom, and he seemed unable to decide how exactly to construct his model of behavior or what degree of Lamarckian influence he cared to set forth. The laws of imitation that defined the era's promotion of racist stereotypes in minstrelsy and its proliferation of legal sanctions against "black blood" were intended to prevent the acquisition of political and social graces or economic gains. Inevitably, those laws became uncanny in the figure of the mulatto: was he "white," or did he, like Tom Driscoll, adopt a pattern of imitative behavior that suppressed the "'nigger' in him"?[42] In his original manuscript Twain had allowed Tom to realize, when Roxy reveals to him his true identity, that the "nigger" in him was the Lamarckian result of "decades and generations of insult and outrage," whereas his "white blood" was "debased by the brutalizing effects of a long-drawn heredity of slave-owning." But such rational meditation is deleted from *Pudd'nhead Wilson,* where the pared-down focus on the hidden mark of blackness, the "nigger" in Tom, is placed before Twain's readers as a stringent test of their capacity to differentiate social construction from "nature." Whereas the deleted passage depicts Tom as more humiliated by his illegitimacy than by his hidden color, the text Twain published swallows both into Tom's fear that the "curse of Ham was upon him," which is shown to be a mythically inscribed idea (though one bearing the weight of biblical injunction) rather than a fact of nature. Because the "main structure of his character was not changed, and could not be changed," Tom quickly throws off his "nigger" behavior, leaving only "one or two very important features" altered and waiting for activation: namely, his realization of a form of racial consciousness and consequently his avenging hatred of his "uncle," Judge Driscoll. Although the deleted passage offers a more precise account of the cultivation of racial behavior, it also suggests more clearly with what ease custom can become naturalized.[43] Twain's stark canceling of the category of the natural was a straightforward assault on imitation theories such as those advanced by Dowd, Ellwood, and Bruce. At the same time, however, it demonstrated that the naturalization of custom (witness the language of the law since *Dred Scott,* as well as the "natural result" of Roxy's practiced servility to Tom) led inexorably to the exercise of hierarchical power and hence to forms of segregation, racial or otherwise, whose authority was always circularly displaced.

The theme of imitation, which defines patterns of behavior, violence, and judicial practice throughout *Pudd'nhead Wilson,* is lodged most provocatively in the thematic dialogue between the Italian "freaks" and their Jim Crow counterparts, Roxy and Tom, the "imitation niggers." The "two stories tangled together," producing "no end of confusion and annoyance," Twain would claim in comic defense of his flawed tales, until the "doings" of Pudd'nhead and Roxy "pushed up into prominence" the character of Tom and the three of them took over a "tale which they had nothing at all to do with, by rights." The result was the notorious "literary Caesarian operation" by which Twain separated his two stories, pulling the freak story "out by the roots" and thus himself giving twin birth to the freak tale and to its racial double. The figure of the maternal body unites Twain and Roxy in the "doings" that produce both Tom—Roxy's son apparently by the shadowy, offstage aristocratic figure, Colonel Cecil Burleigh Essex—and Tom's story, a fantasy union in which Twain recapitulates the sins of the white fathers within the authorial body of the black mothers.[44] While Roxy saves one son, her own, only to become his slave, she also condemns another man to slavery; her power, like Tom's blithe willingness to continue the role of white master, collapses into a haunting imitation of the essential tenets of racial hierarchy. Roxy's pride and pleasure in seeing "her son, her nigger son, lording it among the whites and securely avenging their crimes against her race" turns mastery into a house of mirrors but accomplishes no such vengeance. (Tom will do so, but only after he knows his identity, and only then when driven by desperation.) Because she can only parody the violence of slave society in her attempt to subvert it, Carolyn Porter notes, Roxy exemplifies the double bind of the slave mother, "not only the victim, but also the reproducer of social death."[45] Twain, one could add, does the same thing, imitating Roxy's plot in his own by locating both the white fathers and the black mothers (or the "imitation" black mothers) within himself and generating in the double chronological fields of his novel the reconstituted social death of the post-Reconstruction racial world.

Tom's blackness, like Tom's very existence as a character, is revealed by Twain's participation in the "tragedy" of miscegenation, by his willingness to incarnate in his act of writing the coupling of slave and master while at the same time standing judicially, ironically detached in the role of his foolish hero, Pudd'nhead Wilson. Becoming (black) mother as well as (white) father to his illegitimate mulatto heir, Twain brings to the surface of consciousness apprehensions he had once intimated in his well-known response to William Dean Howells's review of *Roughing It*. "I am as uplifted and reassured by it," Twain wrote Howells, "as a mother who has given birth to a white baby when she was awfully afraid it was going to be a mulatto." Drawing perhaps on his recorded dream fantasies about black female sexuality, Twain's authorial imitation of master-slave miscegenation lodges in his own body the sexual and racial doubleness at the heart of his story, and it provides a double connection—a Siamese linkage—to the two imperfectly separated tales, illuminating the double imitation in which Tom and Roxy themselves are engaged as actors in the stage play of Twain's social critique. In Roxy and Tom is centered the paradox of alienation and imitation. They strive to, and physically *do*, imitate the white masters, Tom by actually becoming one—to such an extent, in fact, that he is willing to sell Roxy *down*river to raise money for his debts. But the tautological subtleties of the color line render them all the more different for being nearly the same in their possession of the property of whiteness. Like the ironic outsider, Puddn'head Wilson, who in his first encounter with the townspeople appears an "uncanny" spectacle, and even more like the "uncanny apparition" of the Siamese twins, the imitation niggers Roxy and Tom literally embody a violation of the "laws" of nature and call forth the uncanny fright that Freud assigned to the double: "something which ought to have remained hidden but has come to light."[46] Brought to light, so to speak, Tom's blackness is ruthlessly efficient: it deprives him of property and at the same time turns him into property. In the plot's terms he is part of the creditors' inventory; but in terms of the novel's contemporary frame of reference, the sudden exposure of Tom's hidden blood puts him, as Harlan and Tourgée argued, in bondage to the entire white race—whose very features he reflects in an even more uncanny apparition of mastery enslaved.

The mulatto's imitation of the white "master" race played upon the central trope of minstrelsy, which was that African Americans on stage, whether they were blacks or whites performing in blackface, had to caricature African American features so as to make them conform to white custom. By reversing that caricature, mixed-race figures revealed the logic connecting one-drop ideology and minstrelsy that was crystallized in the 1896 popularity of Ernest Hogan's hit "All Coons Look Alike to Me."[47] Appearing in the same year that *Plessy* was handed down, Hogan's lighthearted love song on the face of it had nothing to do with Jim Crow. But enthusiastic audiences and critics of Hogan alike were quick to sense its implications: that all "coons" are coons, no matter what their color. Or, as James Weldon Johnson would put it two decades later, in the endlessly polarized, bifurcating world of American racial ideology, there can be no such thing as an "ex-coloured man." Hogan's hit song revealed the deep anxiety, also exploited by Johnson's novel, that black and white could not be distinguished without the accepted markers of color and physiognomy. What was most uncanny about mulattoes, then, was that they threatened to display the category of nature as an act of artifice and political control, and segregation as arbitrary. Like Twain's freak twins, a pair of dandies, the mulatto Tom sports equally "blaspheming colors" that are meant to be separated but have become freakishly, uncannily merged.[48]

Soon after the war minstrelsy had incorporated freaks and female impersonation into its repertory, as did Twain in his novel, in both instances collapsing boundaries on stage that were rigidly drawn in other forums of public life. In the uncanny status they came to have in American racial politics, persons of mixed race could be said to combine minstrelsy and the physical "abnormality" of freaks; that is, by crossing "natural" boundaries and violating taboos of purity and differentiation, the mulatto put them under intense pressure. Like the freak, the mulatto was held by some social theorists to be an unnatural hybrid, a "mongrel" destined to die out through a failure of reproduction—a perversion of the organic development toward higher, more pure racial forms—while to others he represented an aggressively contaminating danger to those forms. A monstrous hybrid that powerfully condensed race theory and popular racial stereotypes, the figure of the mulatto in effect became the scapegoat for contemporary Confederate apologists, the master's conjunction of property and reproduction. Yet the mulatto also therefore symbolized the "enslavement" of the white race to its past sins, an enslavement that Twain's authorial involvement in the process of miscegenation through the Siamese twins' story self-consciously doubled. Thematizing the specter of doubles, Twain's twins and his uncanny mixed-race figures thus offer a running theoretical commentary on one another. Through its fluid disruption of "natural" laws and "instinctual" prejudices, the figure of the twins yokes antebellum chattel slavery to post-Reconstruction neo-slavery in particularly compelling ways. In one of the shreds of their Siamese form left unrevised in *Pudd'nhead Wilson,* Twain designates their sideshow exploitation in Europe as "slavery." In the twins' story itself Angelo finds normal men to be "monstrosities" and "deformities," and their separateness an "unsocial and uncanny construction," but he still desires "that he and his brother might become segregated from each other."[49]

In their reflection of both the dilemma and the demise of Twain's invisible mulatto hero, the twins point to that crisis in the loss of distinctions that René Girard has made central to the process of ritual sacrifice whereby a community restores a threatened order by the mechanism of victimage. Because they threaten to augment radically the disappearance of hierarchical or representational distinctions on which cultural order is based, Girard argues, twin figures, like rival brothers, portend the loss of degree and differentiation in its most visible form, suggesting a monstrous double that subsumes all difference into itself and at the same time radiates outward: "Any violent effacement of differences, even if initially restricted to a single pair of twins, reaches out to destroy a whole society." If twins augur indiscriminate violence and the danger of pollution across boundaries that cannot be recognized, the mulatto, himself a twin, and even more certainly twin figures whose race is in doubt represent an acceleration of the uncanny erasure of distinctions and the likely appearance of what Girard refers to as "sinister repetitions, a dark mixture of unnameable things."[50] The law of the "second slavery" was nothing if not a law of sinister repetition, and the rising white fear of a hidden, racially mixed population contaminating the white race showed that the true threat of imitation lay in its destructive effacement of the authorized, legislated racial differences of segregation. The moral hallucination that takes over *Pudd'nhead Wilson* when it is paired with "Those Extraordinary Twins" arises not just from Twain's exposure of the nadir's callous reinvention of slavery but from his driving the philosophy of Jim Crow to the brink of an undifferentiated chaos. A politics of racial hierarchy stipulates order; but a world without any of the distinctions that have been codified as naturally ordained unleashes dangers that must be abolished or ritually proscribed. The mechanism of sacrifice can work by the erection of uncrossable boundaries and margins into which the oppressed can be cast; or it can lead to ritual expulsion and execution—to lynchings, mutilations, or less grisly state punishments, spreading, as Twain said, like a mania. Twain's two stories contain the whole array of racial sacrifice, acted out certainly in Tom's pardon and sale downriver and represented with more than figurative exactness in Twain's subjection of the twins to the process of legal judgment. In *Pudd'nhead Wilson* the twins are separated (the liberal segregationist solution), but in "Those Extraordinary Twins" they are hanged (the radical racist solution).

Twain's twins were Italian, and he modeled them to some extent on the Tocci brothers, late nineteenth-century Siamese twins who, like Angelo and Luigi, had two heads and four arms but only two legs. Yet he drew as well for the meaning of the twins in his novel on his 1868 comic sketch about the famous Chang and Eng, "Personal Habits of the Siamese Twins." In Twain's postwar imagination the twins became a mock replica of sectional strife: Eng fought on the Union side and Chang on the Confederate, they took each other prisoner, and were exchanged for each other as prisoners by an army court. Their marriages and drinking are subject to Twain's comic eye, as in "Those Extraordinary Twins," and although he fails to mention that the real Chang and Eng were also slaveowners, the irony of that fact had obviously become far more suggestive by the 1890s when the uncanny spectacle of the freak came back into his writing.[51] By then the twins' bodily servility pointed not just to the conjoined intimacy of white and black but also to the resurgence of antebellum manners and social theory in late nineteenth-century life, the freakish doubling of reactionary myth in contemporary postures. The fratricidal conflict that Twain turned into burlesque in 1868 had by 1894 become organized along racial lines, with the white South and North increasingly allied against African Americans—tied to them as though by physiology (as in many cases they were) yet anxious to be cleanly separated. The explicit return of latent Civil War models of fratricidal intimacy to Twain's consciousness, along with his authorial embodiment of miscegenation itself, paralleled the uncanny practice of imitation in race law whereby the courts, as in *Plessy*, appealed to antebellum case law that should have been long dead and buried but now returned from repression to reinvent slavery under new legal sanction.

Chang and Eng were Twain's original model for the figure of twinship that yokes the extraordinary twins to Tom and Chambers or to Tom as mulatto, but the more physiologically apt Tocci brothers were an even better model. In addition, the fact that Angelo and Luigi are Italian is far from insignificant. In anti-immigrationist thought of the 1880s and 1890s, Italians were widely believed, on the basis of their "color," their reputed criminal activities, and their comparatively low standard of living, to be among the most degraded of immigrants, and their willingness to mix with blacks brought forth excited nativist charges that new immigrants would further "mongrelize" America's racial stock. The Italian twins' blurring of the color line has an even more specific force in *Pudd'nhead Wilson*. Besides satirizing the aura of nobility and culture that surrounds the gentleman twins, Twain also capitalized on the common stereotype of Italians as criminals especially adept in the use of knives and prone to impassioned violence and vengeful assassination. The climax of such anti-Italian feeling, in fact, came in New Orleans just the year before Homer Plessy set out to test the segregated train car law. When a jury failed to convict a group of Italians on trial in 1891 for the murder of a New Orleans police superintendent, allegedly caused by his efforts to bring Mafia members to justice, a rioting mob of several thousand attacked the prison and lynched eleven of the suspects. The case created a national sensation, with the prosecution complaining that it was impossible to get convictions against the Mafia because of their strict code of honor, while politicians and periodicals lined up to defend or attack the mob's makeshift execution of the "assassins" and the atmosphere of lawlessness and "bloody duels" that some said had made it possible. Most important, the lynchings ignited a diplomatic crisis when Secretary of State James Blaine refused to grant redress to the families of the victims, some of whom were Italian citizens, or guarantee the indictment of the mob (President Benjamin Harrison finally offered redress some months later). The administration's logical but unsatisfactory contention was that the controversy came about because of the Italian government's inability to understand the "dual nature of our government"—that is, its division into federal and state jurisdiction. The incident grew briefly into a serious war scare and dramatized the entire question of immigration as few incidents had since the sensational Haymarket Affair.[52]

The government's appeal to the notion of "dual" citizenship of course made the Italians liable to state oversight in the same way that the Supreme Court had said blacks such as Homer Plessy were liable to state, not federal, laws for their protection. The incident demonstrates, moreover, the fact that lynching in the 1890s was not reserved for African Americans alone but had spread like an epidemic across many racial lines. By the same token, however, the fervor of anti-immigrant thought that was demonstrated in the New Orleans violence proved that there was no paradox involved when the most radical of southern racists, such as South Carolina's Benjamin Tillman, turned out over the course of the decade to be outspoken anti-imperialists. Fearing further contamination by mixing with alien peoples, they sought the expulsion of blacks from America, or at least their political and economic suppression, rather than increased "paternal" responsibilities for the colored races of the world. Neither anti-imperialist arguments nor anti-immigrationist ones achieved ascendancy in the 1890s, but the New Orleans Mafia lynchings and the subsequent national outburst of militant patriotism had a significant effect on the process of reunion between North and South which would reach its peak in the Spanish-American War at the close of the century. In dramatic demonstrations of loyalty, Union and Confederate veterans' groups pledged cooperation against the Italian enemy if war should come. Journalists and politicians alike called for sectional unity in the face of the seeming threat from abroad and the purported fifth-column danger within.

The lynchings and their aftermath therefore gave South and North alike a further opportunity for reunion—linked again over what was perceived to be the criminality of "lower" races.[53]

A Whisper to the Reader

> Because I am the white man's son—his own,
> Bearing his bastard birth-mark on my face,
> I will dispute his title to the throne,
> Forever fight him for my rightful place.
> There is a searing hate within my soul,
> A hate that only kin can feel for kin,
> A hate that makes me vigorous and whole. . . .
> When falls the hour I shall not hesitate
> Into my father's heart to plunge the knife
> To gain the utmost freedom that is life.
>
> Claude McKay, "Mulatto"

Writing most of *Pudd'nhead Wilson* and its appended burlesque at his villa in Italy or on trips back and forth to the United States, Twain might be imagined to have deliberately cultivated the deadpan voice of his protagonist and the detached irony evident in his opening "Whisper to the Reader," with its bogus rhetoric of authentically rendered courtroom scenes and legal language, and its absurd mockery of antique cultural traditions. Reducing genealogy and law alike to the self-interested repetitions of custom and usage, Twain gives us his novel "under my hand this second day of January, 1893."[54] In foreshadowing the language of wills and testaments which suddenly leaves Tom Driscoll without inheritable property and without the property of whiteness that could save him from sale as chattel, Twain lays the groundwork for his critique of the genealogy of legal precedent to which the Supreme Court had recourse in its elevation of the custom of prejudice into the rule of law. The tone and setting of the "Whisper" initiate an ironic distance on the problems of American race relations and the New South that is certainly present in the tale (one might compare Johnson's writing of much of *The Autobiography of an Ex-Coloured Man* at his consular post in Venezuela), but it is inconceivable that Twain was not also impressed by the Italo-American crisis and the light it cast on the blurring of the color line caused by non–Anglo-Saxon immigrant races. The Italian twins, in their Siamese version, define the conjunction of black and white that Twain located in the bodies of Roxy and Tom. As immigrant figures they simultaneously bridge the gaps between white and black and between North and South, further segregating one pair while unifying the other.

The rhetoric of ironic distance with which Twain opens *Pudd'nhead Wilson* must be taken as his defense against direct implication in the emotional pain of the tale, a disguise, like Tom's color, that covers a latent and incriminating truth that will be revealed at the end of the tale. Provisionally separated from America (and his own personal financial troubles), Twain nevertheless employed the figure of the foreign twins to study the very American problem posed by his own black changeling, lodging the trope of doubling not only in the now separated twins but also in the now "Negro" Tom and his slave Chambers. But the short story and the novel are, of course, never adequately segregated—never separate but equal. Angelo and Luigi, both of them charged with the crime of kicking Tom Driscoll when only one is guilty, are exonerated in confusion by a court that refuses to "imitate other courts"; but when their paralyzing double election to the board of aldermen cannot be resolved by court after court, the citizens lynch "one" of the twins.[55] Lynching, that is, takes the place of or approximates the justice of the courts. Twain, as we have seen, would later claim that lynching thrives on imitative behavior, something his novel had already shown to apply to the whole range of human attitudes and actions, including his own authorship, and something the Supreme Court cases that provided the foundation for his satire had shown to be key to its own decisions, as one after another the civil rights cases destroyed the gains of Reconstruction by mimicking antebellum law and carefully dividing black from white.

"Imitation is the bane of courts," remarks the judge in "Those Extraordinary Twins" before condemning the hung jury for failing to convict Angelo-Luigi and thus setting free a being with "a hidden and grisly power for evil," by which crime after crime may be committed with no way to separate the guilty one from the innocent. In *Pudd'nhead Wilson* it is the Siamese-like secret mulatto Tom, the monstrous double who, disguised as a woman and finally donning blackface, commits crimes undetected.[56] His ultimate crime, the murder of the judge, is committed with the knife of the Italian twins against a man whom Twain had originally thought to cast as Tom's actual father (he may still be taken as such, given the resemblance between Tom and Chambers) and whom he loosely modeled on his own father, John Marshall Clemens, both a slaveholder and a sometime judge—his name, like that of John Marshall Harlan, an echo of past heroic justice. Judge Driscoll, in any case, is the book's symbolic father in his relationship to Tom, Chambers, and Roxy, as well as in his upholding of the *code duello* and the laws of aristocractic prerogative. Despite Twain's own suppression of evidence, as it were, the murder thus follows a logic of revenge that is perfectly forecast in the crisis scene when Tom discovers his own "blackness" from Roxy and momentarily begins to behave like a "nigger." He feels "as secret murderers are said to feel when the accuser says, 'Thou art the man!'" and finds that "hatred of his ostensible 'uncle' was steadily growing in his heart; for he said to himself, 'He is white; and I am his chattel, his property, his goods, and he can sell me, just as he could his dog.'" At that time the "nigger" in him is once again resubmerged into his characteristic "white" behavior, but it now breaks forth with uncanny force, having become in Twain's conception a political rather than a biological element. The murder is not exactly premeditated, but the seeds of Tom's vegeance lie in his recognition scene with Roxy. Although the impulse to murder arises as an instinct to prevent discovery when Tom, now in blackface, is caught by his uncle, the act resonates with the deeper implications already brought to the surface and then resubmerged, like a shadow from regions of the uncanny, in the earlier scene: "Without hesitation he drove the knife home—and was free." In James Cox's words, Tom becomes "the avenging agent who carries back across the color line the repressed guilt that has gathered at the heart of slavery." More than that, he carries the antebellum world into the post-Reconstruction world in yet another way. In playing out the parricidal rebellion of the African American slave against his master-father—or, if his disguise as a woman or his role as Roxy's son is taken into account, as a female slave avenging the master's sexual abuse—Tom fuses the Old South and the New by dramatizing the reversal in meaning miscegenation underwent after emancipation. Between 1865 and 1890 the fact of slaveholding miscegenation by white masters and the fear of black slave rebellion were together transformed into the specter of black crime and contamination—the Negro as mongrel or "beast."[57] The imitation white Tom, now like a minstrel performer masquerading in the disguise that parodies his hidden slave status, becomes in effect the mulatto killer of contemporary race theory.

Tom's crime with the knife momentarily implicates the Italians, already considered "assassins" because of his slander of them. As in late nineteenth-century America, however, it is the black man who is found to be most liable to criminal guilt. Twain leaves unsettled the question of whether it is the "nigger" in Tom that leads to the killing, though as allegory it can be read no other way. In that case, however, the epithet "nigger" resonates with a paradoxically positive value. Tom's murder of Judge Driscoll, a latent possibility ever since he discovers that, as a legal slave, he has no rights that the judge is bound to respect, is to be read allegorically as a just act of moral revolt. But Twain's characterization of Tom is hardly so simple. Tom's traits of laziness, criminality, and cowardice, which Roxy herself ascribes to his hidden race, may be a sign of either aristocratic degeneration or blackness as defined by the radical thesis and the minstrel stereotype. (The stereotype is enforced by a disturbing instance of imitation in the scene where Tom's newly acquired eastern mannerisms are burlesqued by a black bell ringer: the black man plays the minstrel to mock the white man who, secretly black, is playing a mannered role that he does not yet know to be a role.) Tom's blackface disguise at the moment of the killing renders the artifice of racial identity absurd in a more profound way. The blackface mask raises Tom's secret "Negro" self to the surface, at last visible but at the same time wildly mutable. Blackness becomes part of Tom's performance even as it begins, under the constraint of custom and usage, to slide toward habit, instinct, and "natural" law. As Twain says of Tom's remorse over the judge's killing: "He was playing a part, but it was not all a part."[58]

Twain was still revolving the scene of revenge in his mind a decade later when he composed the unpublished narrative "Which Was It?" When he gains ascendancy over Harrison, his master (by discovering Harrison's guilt in a murder), the slave Jasper subjects him to all of his own previous humiliations and to a course of training that will make him a proper slave. Reduced to slavery, Harrison, says Jasper, is going to settle the "long bill agin de low-down ornery white race," a bill that includes his own cruelty as well as the previous betrayal by Harrison's uncle, Jasper's own father, of Jasper's claim to manumission and his sale of Jasper's mother downriver. Studying the countenance of his new white slave, Jasper sees a spectral "duplicate" of the father who had betrayed him and is galled by the recognition that "the hated blood was in his own veins!" But both the natal racial identities of the two men and the training as a slave that Harrison receives from Jasper are relatively incidental next to the simple fact that one has power over the other. After Jasper forces Harrison to sign a confession that seals Jasper's control over him, the reversal of roles is complete:

> [Jasper] held up the fateful paper and contemplated it a long minute, his nostrils faintly dilating; and when at last he ceased from this contemplation he was visibly a changed man. The meek slouch of the slave was gone from him, and he stood straight, the exultation of victory burning in his eyes; and not even his rags and tatters could rob his great figure of a certain state and dignity born in this moment to it of the pride of mastership and command that was rising in his heart. He looked the master; but that which had gone from him was not lost, for his discarded droop and humble mien had passed to his white serf, and already they seemed not out of place there, but fit, and congruous, and pathetically proper and at home.[59]

The confessional document turns Harrison into Jasper's slave as completely as the loss of his manumission papers had once left Jasper caught in a "second slavery" to Harrison's ancestor, his very own father. Whereas the conclusion of *Pudd'nhead Wilson* places a great deal of weight on the inculcation of behavior by training in its depiction of Chambers's pathetic inability to adapt to the role of white master, "Which Was It?" casts back to much earlier notebook entries in which Twain speculated about eventual black dominion in the United States and suggests that the habits of mastery (or of slavery) are rather easily acquired. Like most of his late work, Twain's story trailed off into inconclusion. In so radically foreshortening the reversal of roles, he did not change the direction of *Pudd'nhead Wilson* but distilled its vertiginous dialectic into a few rudimentary motions in which genealogy and law alike are shown to be matters of habitual power and slavery a function principally of opportunity and profit.

Even before the bleak inconclusion of "Which Was It?," however, there were few psychic recesses in the regime of mastery, including his own, that Twain had left unexplored in his anatomy of segregation. His recognition that there was no way out of the dialectic of mastery and slavery, even if race could be expunged from it, finally paralyzed Twain's writing. But the fact that, both in America and in his work, race had never yet been expunged from the rule of law and the consequent hierarchy of cultures played no small part in his extreme moral pessimism and his grotesquely ambivalent expression of it in *Pudd'nhead Wilson*. In blackface and women's clothing at the time of his murder of the judge, Tom in his masquerade includes the maternal authorial disguise adopted by Twain himself, divided as ever between exposing Tom as a "nigger" and participating in his revenge against the aristocratic southern fathers. Twain's double participation in the plot of his novel everywhere imitates the Siamese-like entanglement he attributes to his characters. Separate but equal, his twin, paradoxical inclinations toward both black vengeance and racist suppression must be said to lie at the heart of his novel's flawed form as well as its dangerously comic representation of Reconstruction's tragic failure.

Tom's identity belongs neither to his whiteness nor to his blackness; and the novel, like the law of the land in Jim Crow America, leaves him unprotected, stranded between dual worlds of jurisdiction neither of which is responsible for his acts or for his rights. The hero of the novel has no trouble convicting Tom—convicting him both of murder *and* of pretending to be a white man. Tom's sale down the river indicates which is the worse crime, or at any rate demonstrates that the murder follows from the masquerade. The value of Tom's whiteness as a kind of "property" does him no more good than it did Homer Plessy; the court and the governor recognize only his blackness, in which property is not self-possession or identity but a sign of the rights of others. In the aftermath of Reconstruction, as in classical comedy, disguises were removed, order restored, degree reinstituted where it had threatened to break down under the offer of a form of equality that was perceived as "Negro domination." Likewise in *Pudd'nhead Wilson* masks are removed and order restored where an inversion in the hierarchy of mastery has momentarily left the community in a state of crisis. Consciously tying his own flawed art to the courtroom theatrics of David Wilson, Twain engaged in a ghostly reduction of the world of the novel to a stage play of parodic codes and habits in which the law dressed as one more player, and in his identification with Wilson Twain admitted his complicity in restoring to order the plantation myth provisionally subverted by Roxy's act and Tom's role.

The road to reunion of North and South required both the reinvention of the Confederate myth in the cultural domain and the reactionary readings of constitutional law carried out by legislatures and the Supreme Court. In his reply to Cable's "Freedman's Case in Equity," the popular southern writer Thomas Nelson Page had argued, at just the time Twain was writing *Pudd'nhead Wilson,* that in the encroaching struggle against a rising Negro population, "the only thing that stands today between the people of the North and the negro is the people of the South." Page's plea for states' rights and southern control of the "Negro problem" met with increasing favor in the North during the 1890s. It needed and received the assent and support of figures like Pudd'nhead Wilson, who can be read both as an outsider to the South and, ultimately, as its most admired representative, the one who most embodies its cherished codes and racial values. Forsaking the last remnants of good conscience left his title character at the conclusion of *Adventures of Huckleberry Finn* in favor of the antics of Tom Sawyer's mock performance of liberation, now replayed with reference to the national legal theater, Twain embodied the disintegration of African American rights in his own disintegrating text. Taken "on trial" by Twain as a "fool" who exposes the town's pretensions and failure of ironic insight, Wilson, it might be said, matures into an eloquent spokesman for Jim Crow.[60] If Tom Driscoll was Twain's Homer Plessy, Twain's pudd'nhead representative of the law was no Albion Tourgée or John Marshall Harlan but rather the rising voice of segregation. Convicting the black man of imposture as a white gentleman, Wilson's miraculous revelation of Tom's identity restores the community's subverted aristocratic order and saves it from mongrelization by the monstrous double, much as the overturning of Reconstruction and its accompanying civil rights legislation and antimiscegenation theory restored an antebellum racial hierarchy in the new dress of Jim Crow. Crossing geographic as well as chronological boundaries, Wilson is the sign of sectional reunion in law and in culture. His voice of irony, not unlike Twain's own deadpan voice, modulates from critique to accommodation. Both separated from and yet intimately tied to the story whose conclusion he creates, Pudd'nhead-Twain freakishly twins in himself both the racist inclinations bred in him since birth and the countering condemnations of racism that are the better part of his conscience.

In Twain's novel fiction and law imitate each other, and the greatest challenge, in the end, is to separate "racism" from its parodic critique. Like *Benito Cereno* before it or like Faulkner's *Absalom, Absalom!* or *Go Down, Moses* after it, however, *Pudd'nhead Wilson* comes close to being debilitated by its suffocating racial crisis, which is concurrently a crisis in novelistic representation. The question with which one is left is whether such a critique is capable of breaking free from its own disorienting, self-incriminating circles—or what, exactly, such "freedom" would entail. For although *Pudd'nhead Wilson* might be compared to the equally bizarre and inventive satire of later African American writers such as George Schuyler or Ishmael Reed, Twain's parody, published as the destructive power of legal segregation came into full swing, might also be construed as the luxury of a white writer who, unlike Douglass or Du Bois, would never himself have to ride Jim Crow. If post-Reconstruction America's racial crisis had its most enervating critique in *Pudd'nhead Wilson,* only those on the other side of the color line could truly measure the great costs and, indeed, the great cultural achievements of that crisis. No career better embraced both than that of Charles Chesnutt, in whose work was written the entire history of nineteenth-century African American life.

· 4 ·

Charles Chesnutt's Cakewalk

> Not to mention how he was forever turning guitar strings into train
> whistles which were not only the once-upon-a-time voices of storytellers
> but of all the voices saying what was being said in the stories as well.
>
> Albert Murray, Train Whistle Guitar

At a significant moment in the development of the conspiracy hatched by
white supremacists to regain political and economic control of the fictive
city of Wellington, North Carolina, Charles Chesnutt inserts into *The
Marrow of Tradition* (1901) a seemingly diversionary episode in which a
young white aristocrat successfully mimics a black servant in a cakewalk
performed for visiting northerners. Tom Delamere's parodic imitation of
Sandy Campbell anticipates the more serious incident in which Tom will
dress as Sandy while commiting the robbery of his own aunt that results
in her death, and it therefore functions as one of several careful links
between the political plot of the novel—the disfranchisement of black
voters and accompanying white violence—and the melodramatic plot of
family romance and generational, cross-racial conflict. But the chapter
entitled "The Cakewalk" also signals to the reader a larger constellation
of issues that are bound together by Chesnutt's tightly woven meditation
on the race crisis at the turn of the century, and it offers a striking gloss
on some of the most pressing concerns of Chesnutt's career as a writer of
racial fiction—a career in which he found himself caught, as he did in his
professional life as an aspiring attorney, between two worlds and responsive to a multitude of problems marked by a color line that was drawn as
starkly through the practice of literature as through American society at
large.

Because its argument is germane both to the novel's dramatization of the theme of sectional reunion and to the matters of color and African American culture as they exfoliate in Chesnutt's career, his description of the masquerade performed for the northern visitors is worth quoting at length:

> The gentlemen of the party were concerned in a projected cotton mill, while the ladies were much interested in the study of social conditions, and especially in the negro problem. As soon as their desire for information became known, they were taken courteously under the wing of prominent citizens and their wives, who gave them, at elaborate luncheons, the Southern white man's views of the negro, sighing sentimentally over the disappearance of the good old negro of before the war, and gravely deploring the degeneracy of his descendants. They enlarged upon the amount of money the Southern whites had spent for the education of the negro, and shook their heads over the inadequate results accruing from this unexampled generosity. It was sad, they said, to witness this spectacle of a dying race, unable to withstand the competition of a superior type. The severe reprisals taken by white people for certain crimes committed by negroes were of course not the acts of the best people, who deplored them; but still a certain charity should be extended towards those who in the intense and righteous anger of the moment should take the law into their own hands and deal out rough but still substantial justice; for no negro was ever lynched without incontestable proof of his guilt. In order to be perfectly fair, and give their visitors an opportunity to see both sides of the question, they accompanied the Northern visitors to a colored church where they might hear a colored preacher, who had won a jocular popularity throughout the whole country by an oft-repeated sermon intended to demonstrate that the earth was flat like a pancake. . . . In order to give the visitors, ere they left Wellington, a pleasing impression of Southern customs, and particularly of the joyous, happy-go-lucky disposition of the Southern darky and his entire contentment with existing conditions, it was decided by the hotel manangement to treat them, on the last night of their visit, to a little diversion, in the shape of a genuine negro cakewalk.[1]

As Chesnutt's pungent sarcasm here and elsewhere in the novel makes clear, the "white man's views of the negro" constitute a charade of several dimensions, in which the "best people" often played the most responsible roles, as they did, for example, in the 1898 Wilmington riot on which *The Marrow of Tradition* is based.

The passage's allusions to generational change, racial degeneracy, and white vigilantism sum up the central problems of the novel. Those problems in turn are gathered into the revealing trope of the cakewalk, which may be taken as a figurative key (but not a pejorative one) to the construction of *The Marrow of Tradition* and to much of Chesnutt's writing across a range of modes from folk culture to the political novel. More than that, the cakewalk, as an equivocal trope derived from African American folk arts *and* from blackface minstrelsy, functions as a key to the operation of racial prejudice in American culture, the arts, the law, and social practice, all bound together in the intricate rituals of segregation. Like Twain, Chesnutt reached back into the decayed world of antebellum law to find the origins of modern racism; but he also reached into the vibrant world of slave culture to find the origins of modern African American cultural resistance to racism.

The cakewalk, as a performative dance and as a cultural event, evokes the complex dialectical process by which African American culture defined itself in relation to the paradigm of white mastery that lingered—and from the perspective of linguistic and social custom perhaps accelerated—in the aftermath of Reconstruction. In Chesnutt's use here the cakewalk functions first as a metaphor for the South's "performance"—its often disingenuous display of racial harmony and black progress, or its calculated explanations for the lack of either—before a northern "audience," whether in the press, in Congress, in business and industry, or in literature. Landmark events such as the Atlanta Cotton States and International Exposition in 1895 demonstrated that the South had economic and political, as well as cultural, reasons to promote the plantation mythology of kind masters and contented slaves—or, in the modern guise, benevolent white employers and happy, subservient black laborers. Featuring facsimile recreations of plantation life, complete with performances of black spirituals and folk dances, events such as the Atlanta Exposition did not, of course, deceive the North so much as display an image comforting to whites of both sections and to both political parties. Such "Old Plantation" installations, with their advertised cakewalks, breakdowns, and fiddle and banjo music, had a double aim: to entertain, and to instruct visitors that the region's blacks were under control.[2] One highlight of the Atlanta Exposition was Booker T. Washington's famous "Atlanta Compromise" address, the most succinct and rhetorically effective articulation of Washington's conservative views on black education, suffrage, and civil rights, which became for most of white America a measure of the degree to which African Americans were eager to hasten sectional reconciliation by willing participation in the plantation myth, or at least in its resulting postbellum economic structure. Although Washington was accused by many of being the white man's spokesman, he was no minstrel; as Paul Laurence Dunbar's poem might have put it, he "wore the mask" in order to create an arena of black power (in addition to personal power) where it was possible to do so.[3] Nevertheless, his famous speech stood in the charged field where politics and cultural typology intersected, and the scathing criticism directed at Washington by Du Bois and other black leaders was a measure of his paradoxical performance at the very boundary of Jim Crow.

Because it had reached something of a peak of popularity in the United States at the end of the nineteenth century (albeit in new forms that were to lead directly to the black musical stage), the blackface minstrelsy of Tom Delamere is an apt metaphor for the South's projection of a "happy darky" legend. As Chesnutt well knew, the legend was no less pervasive, even if historically dislocated, in the North. Although he maintained a longtime friendship with Booker T. Washington that is reflected variously in his fiction, their serious correspondence dates from the years after the publication of *The Marrow of Tradition,* when Chesnutt cordially but vigorously disagreed with Washington on a number of issues, black suffrage in particular. It is not evident that one should read the cakewalk episode in *The Marrow of Tradition* as a deliberate reflection upon Washington's Atlanta speech, but it is incontestable that Chesnutt's novel may be read as a critique of, among other things, the Washingtonian ethos. This is certainly the construction that his novelistic portrait puts on the issues of black professionalism, the disfranchisement of black voters by intimidation and violence, as well as by law, and the southern attempt to attract northern investment. Tom Delamere, like many talented blackface performers of the day, burlesques a black man in order to entertain his audience. Imitating the unknowing Sandy (although with "grotesque contortions" that seem to the observing Lee Ellis "somewhat overdone"), Tom wins the prize cake with his partner, thanks his audience in a speech that "sent the Northern visitors into spasms of delight at the quaintness of the darky dialect and the darky wit," and finally caps his masquerade with a sensational "buck dance."[4] What happens to Sandy as a result of this burlesque and the more serious one that follows it is central to the political message of Chesnutt's novel; presumably, however, Tom's brilliant masquerade works here to help attract northern money for southern cotton and northern good will toward southern race problems.

Chesnutt's own experience of discrimination in the North made him realistic about the sometimes small, sometimes significant sectional differences in racism. But the novel takes as its starting point the fact that the vaunted "reunion" of North and South at the close of the century was predicated upon northern acquiescence in southern control of the "Negro problem." The nation became Confederate in sympathy, as Tourgée had phrased it, to the degree that the more blatant acts of white supremacist assault occurring in the South, whether individual or communal, were often winked at in the North. Minstrelsy was the cultural mask for a national reunion built upon an escalation of racial discrimination and violence. As we have seen, it was also a complex trap for the white literary artist, such as Twain, in whose exploration of racial problems personal guilt, genealogical burdens, and social critique were antagonistically entangled. More obviously, it ensnared the African American artist in a constant awareness and estimation of the effect of the color line upon his professional aspirations and his literary materials—a dilemma exacerbated in the case of Chesnutt, whose very light skin emblematically incorporated the essence of the race crisis and dictated the perspective of much of his fiction.

The Marrow of Tradition is the leading literary assessment of that crisis during the turn-of-the-century decades, touching as it does every important social, political, and personal aspect of the problem of segregation and color prejudice. Some of the novel's contemporary readers—foremost among them William Dean Howells, who had promoted Chesnutt on the basis of his short story collections and his first novel, *The House behind the Cedars*—found its message bitter, a harsh increase in Chesnutt's skepticism about American racial equality. Writing in the *North American Review* in December 1901, Howells admired the novel but felt that Chesnutt had stood up "with a courage that has more justice than mercy in it"; and early black critics, among them Benjamin Brawley and J. Saunders Redding, also lamented the novel's "propagandistic" tone and considered it a lesser achievement than *The House behind the Cedars* and the color line stories.[5] Modern readers, by contrast, have tended to find the novel melodramatic or artificial in its style and construction, or not harsh enough in its denunciation of racism. But Chesnutt's apparent ambivalence about the proper (or most practical) black response to the white supremacist terror in the Wilmington riot, along with the melodramatic structure that fuses the political and the personal, the social and the familial planes in the novel, is precisely what marks *The Marrow of Tradition* as an acute representation of its era's racial turmoil. He would later write to Booker T. Washington that, in counterpoint to the plantation fiction of Joel Chandler Harris and Thomas Nelson Page, he was committed to what he termed a "literature of necessity."[6] The definition may be aptly applied to almost all of Chesnutt's writing, which is infused with the double moral necessity of racial justice and African American cultural consciousness. But Chesnutt's obvious ambivalence about color and class, and what at first glance seems his attenuated relationship to a separate black folk culture, are serious issues to be confronted. They go to the heart of his magnificent work and constitute his own curious literary cakewalk. At the risk of putting undue weight on a single element, I begin by looking at the cakewalk itself as a means to estimate Chesnutt's development of an African American aesthetic that was capable of engaging the most serious issues of the nation's racial politics. As cultural event and as cultural trope, the cakewalk provides a succinct entry into the work of one of the most important—and least understood or appreciated—American writers of the early modern period.

The Origin of the Cakewalk

It would be a mistake to assume that the cakewalk was simply another act of minstrelsy destructively imposed upon African American life by exploitive white entertainers and audiences. Its history is more complex, and from slavery through freedom it had the potential to represent a stage of transition in black public artistry, from the playing of assigned parts—typically imitative of or subservient to whites in blackface—to the creation of unique, culturally distinct black roles. When Chesnutt chose the cakewalk as his metaphor for the resurrection of white supremacy and the cultural transmission of a plantation ideology, he chose a figure appropriate to the historical moment in which the nation found itself with the rise of Jim Crow. Black civil and political rights were crumbling, but a new generation of African Americans, those who had been born and come of age after the Civil War, had the opportunity to reverse the dangerous momentum. The post-Reconstruction generation, however, had to throw off the heavy burden of roles prescribed by sociological stigma, judicial or legislative decree, and cultural stereotype in order to create new ones.

Against the white racist recreation of a mythic antebellum idyll, in which the loyal "old-time darky" was adamantly projected as a type superior to the lazy, degenerate, or criminal postbellum blacks, the "New Negro" of the late nineteenth century had to create a counterforce of self-definition and achievement. Like black politics, black culture was everywhere marked by the difficult ambiguities of that challenge.

The cakewalk, though it had borrowed white elements from the outset, and became a white dance craze that ushered in the explosive popularity of ragtime at the turn of the century, was a dance with clear African American and shadowy African origins. It derived in its stage form from the "walk-around" that concluded many minstrel shows, a grand prome-nade in which couples dancing in a circle competed with fancy improvised steps and struts, but its popular public appearance in the form known at the turn of the century dates from closer to the end of Reconstruction. The Centennial of American Independence in Philadelphia in 1876, for example, included a plantation set with ex-slaves singing spirituals and work songs. An added attraction was a cakewalk, or walk-around, done in the original plantation style. The following year, as part of a variety bill that featured an "Exquisite Picture of Negro Life and Customs," the white minstrel team of Harrigan and Hart presented a promenade number entitled "Walking for Dat Cake." Within twenty years the cakewalk would become the most popular element of the minstrel and early black theatrical stage, usually a grand finale with elaborate choreography and costumes.[7] It could easily be made to correspond to the stereotype of black buffoon-ery, whether danced by whites in blackface or by blacks, themselves likely to be masked in exaggerated blackface as well. Yet it is also the case that the cakewalk occupied a liminal territory with a significant potential for resistance, a psychological and cultural space in which the racist appro-priation of black life in offensive mannerisms gave way to an African American reversal of the stereotype. Although the cakewalk could be performed as a burlesque of black freedom and cultural integrity, it de-rived, as some of its participants obviously knew, from the distinctive survivals of slave culture—the work songs, dance, spirituals, and verbal and material arts in which African retentions, a consciousness of resistance to white subjugation, and the creation of a new African American culture were uniquely combined. Like the folktales that provided the foundation for Chesnutt's superior work in short fiction (or the spirituals that were to provide the foundation for Du Bois's landmark statement of modern

African American culture in *The Souls of Black Folk*), the cakewalk necessarily fused African elements and New World acts in a conscious reaction to the world of the masters.

According to the black musician and former slave Shephard Edmonds, the cakewalk was a Sunday dance performed for their own pleasure by slaves, who "would dress up in hand-me-down finery to do a high-kicking, prancing walk-around. They did a takeoff on the high manners of the folks in the 'big house,' but their masters, who gathered around to watch the fun, missed the point." The cake, Edmonds related, would be awarded by the master to the "couple that did the proudest movement." Edmonds's claim notwithstanding, it seems unlikely that many masters missed the satire on their own manners. Especially those who were less harsh in their discipline might have been liable to accept a limited attack on their pretensions and foibles and might have been willing to acknowledge to their slaves that they saw themselves burlesqued in the dance. The variations in plantation discipline and the lack of extensive documentation of the cakewalk among slaves make useful generalization on this score nearly impossible. More to the point, however, are the intentions of the slaves. From the beginning of its transposition to the New World aboard slave ships, African American dance was entangled to some degree in the regime of slavery. Subject to discipline and regulation, at times even deployed by masters as a species of entertainment or humiliation, black dance, like black song, black story, or black worship, always thrived partly in the world of secrecy and masquerade.[8] What the slaves danced for the masters by coercion were not necessarily the African-inspired dances that remained hidden in their own communities. By the same token, because dancing could be coded with the expression of cultural preservation and political resistance from its beginning in African America, satire of the masters was never far from the surface in public performance.*

---

* Although he too, probably mistakenly, asserts that white masters always missed the satire at their expense evident in such slave dances as the cakewalk, Ralph Ellison, drawing an analogy to Duke Ellington's satiric retort when he was denied a Pulitzer Prize, provides a succinct account of the cultural formation of African American dance: "[The slaves,] looking through the windows of a plantation manor house from the yard, imitated steps so gravely performed by the masters within and then added to them their own special flair, burlesqueing the white folks and then going on to force the steps into a choreography uniquely their own. The whites, looking out at the activity in the yard, thought that they were being flattered by imitation and were amused by the incongruity of tattered blacks dancing courtly steps, while missing completely the fact that before their eyes a European cultural form was becoming Americanized, undergoing a meta-

Whether or not the masters detected the full range of parodic or rebellious nuance in the plantation cakewalk, the role of satire in the dialectic of cultural formation is of utmost significance. It points here to a reversal of roles—more properly an exchange of roles—that informs the late nineteenth-century evolution of minstrelsy toward increased black artistic control, as well as to the more comprehensive and long-standing argument about the origins of African American folktales and songs. The complicated cross-currents of expression, appropriation, and parody that go together to constitute the modern cakewalk offer an excellent instance of the survival and transformation of the satiric function of performance in African culture under the circumstances of American slavery. As a dance version of the "songs of allusion" or "songs of derision" ("signifying songs," as they came to be known among New Orleans Creoles) in which the tricksterlike attack on authority or social position is central, the cakewalk of the slaves, and later that of black stage performers, is an example of the principles of subversion and indirection essential to the evolution of African American cultural expression in the nineteenth century.[9] Because satire itself—or, to use a term from black folk vernacular that I will explore in relation to Chesnutt's writing, "signifying"*—is thus a central

---

morphosis through the mocking activity of a people partially sprung from Africa. So, blissfully unaware, the whites laughed while the blacks danced out their mocking reply." See Ellison, "Homage to Duke Ellington on His Birthday," in *Going to the Territory* (New York: Random House, 1986), p. 223–24.

* I use the idea of signifying, a concept and a term dating from the nineteenth century, primarily in the senses defined by Henry Louis Gates, Jr., and Roger Abrahams. Gates characterizes signifying as a rhetorical strategy through which "a second statement or figure repeats, or tropes, or reverses the first." In his analysis of the folk figure of the Signifying Monkey, for example, Gates ties the concept of signifying to deconstruction but also attributes it specifically to the rhetorical improvisation of black language: "Signifyin(g) epitomizes all of the rhetorical play in the black vernacular. Its self-consciously open rhetorical status, then, functions as a kind of writing, wherein rhetoric is the writing of speech, of oral discourse. . . . The mastery of Signifyin(g) creates *homo rhetoricus Africanus,* allowing—through the manipulation of these classic black figures of Signification—the black person to move freely between two discursive universes. This is an excellent example of what I call linguistic masking, the verbal sign of the mask of blackness that demarcates the boundary between the white linguistic realm and the black, two domains that exist side by side in a homonymic relation signified by the very concept of Signification." In a more practical definition that is especially relevant to Chesnutt's manipulation of the category of "nonsense" in his conjure tales, Abrahams argues that black signifying refers to the capacity of linguistic formations to elicit deep meaning while casting doubt on conventional meaning: "To the outside world, such signifying is sometimes regarded as a mark of irresponsible irreverence; it may make serious matters seem playful, the subject of banter. But this is exactly what is intended in the world of *nonsense,* to use the West Indian term for signifying; it provides

part not just of African American culture but of the African sources of that culture as well, the cakewalk offers a resonant instance of the subversion from within that defines the place of much African American cultural work with respect to the prevailing mainstream and typically exclusive norms of white culture. It is therefore emblematic of the fact that, over several crucial decades in the development of American music (less so in the other arts), the nation became not just more Confederate in sympathy but also, consciously or not, more black and southern in the inflections of its cultural languages.

Symbolic of a fact little noticed in the interpretive arguments about the relationship between African American and European American cultural materials, the cakewalk subverted not by parodic attack alone but by replacement, by recalling in performative expression a cultural meaning separate from and prior to enslavement. The fact that it derived from the

---

a context in which the community encourages its wits to test the limits of meaning by exploring the edges of believability, all of this in the service of expressive resilience and improvisational creativity." As Abrahams puts it in an earlier definition, signifying may cover a range of linguistic forms and verbal games (toasts, the dozens, sounding, and so on) common in black vernacular and thus refer "to the trickster's ability to talk with great innuendo, to carp, cajole, needle, and lie," as well as to a "propensity to talk around a subject, never quite coming to the point," or to parody or satirize friends and enemies alike. Such tactics of indirection, frequently remarked in African oral culture, took on special characteristics of cultural and political resistance (and survival) under American slavery. The rhetorical function of signifying in black language would thus include a register of exclusion, what Claudia Mitchell-Kernan, Geneva Smitherman, and others have analyzed as the coded dialect influenced by conditions of enslavement and racism but reaching creatively beyond them in modern linguistic formations, including literature. I will draw primarily upon the troping dimension of signifying—its capacity to revise a given text (indeed, a given tradition or frame of thought) by revising or subverting its cultural assumptions. Gates gives a very useful example when he notes that "the intertextual relationship between the slave narrative as a body of discourse and its counter-genre, the Confederate romance or the plantation novel, is also a relation of Signifyin(g) structures." Although I would dispute the idea that signifying is "a uniquely black rhetorical concept," as Gates argues, and that it "can exist only in the realm of intertextual relation," his definitions are exemplary. See Henry Louis Gates, Jr., *The Signifying Monkey: A Theory of Afro-American Literary Criticism* (New York: Oxford University Press, 1988), pp. 44–88, quotes at pp. 52–53, 75; Roger D. Abrahams, "Introduction," in *Afro-American Folktales: Stories from Black Traditions in the New World* (New York: Pantheon Books, 1985), p. 6; Abrahams, *Deep Down in the Jungle: Negro Narrative Folklore from the Streets of Philadelphia* (1963; rpt. New York: Aldine, 1970), pp. 51–52; Gates, *Figures in Black: Words, Signs, and the "Racial" Self* (Oxford University Press, 1987), pp. 49, 53. See also Claudia Mitchell-Kernan, "Signifying, Loud-Talking, and Marking," in Thomas Kochman, ed., *Rappin' and Stylin' Out: Communication in Urban Black America* (Urbana: University of Illinois Press, 1972), pp. 315–35, and Geneva Smitherman, *Talkin' and Testifyin': The Language of Black America* (Detroit: Wayne State University Press, 1986), pp. 47–49.

minstrel show walk-around may obscure a most significant fact about the cakewalk. Because the walk-around was itself a secularization of the slaves' spiritually powerful ring-shout, it inevitably concealed within it African cultural elements that would perforce be reawakened in the later staged cakewalk or in the slaves' own performance of it on the plantation. An intricate genealogy typical of African American cultural forms in the aftermath of slavery thus informs the evolution of the cakewalk. In this respect, Roscoe Lewis's history of Virginia slavery, part of a WPA history project based on the oral testimony of former slaves and their descendants, is especially helpful in locating the precise black roots of the cakewalk. Lewis's informants recalled that the cakewalk was a festival dance connected to harvest time. In their Sunday dress, sometimes lighting the night with torches, the slaves competed for a prize cake awarded for the best "cuttin' of figgers," sometimes by the plantation mistress, sometimes by the slaves themselves (when the slaves awarded the cake, it would be made of cornmeal and cabbage leaves, baked in ash). The cakewalk on the plantation, accompanied by banjo music, clapping, and foot tapping, could include the motions of labor, but without any tools or load, and typically involved an exchange of partners that eventually eliminated all but the two judged by the crowd to be the best couple. Marked by cheerfulness and grace, the cakewalk as Lewis interprets it could be traced in form, if not in particulars, to African tribal celebrations. Because it was related distantly to the African circle dance and more immediately to the slaves' ring-shout (which would itself eventually be incorporated into a black Broadway revue, *The Darktown Follies,* in 1913), the cakewalk combined ritual festivity and the cycle of plantation work. Like other dances of slave culture, the cakewalk frequently incorporated the pantomime of labors such as shucking corn or pitching hay, but here too its subtle signifying character can be seen. As Sterling Stuckey observes, such a dance allowed the slaves to review "the labor performed on the plantation that made it possible for the master to exist and to prosper." The plantation cakewalk was thus "a means of distancing slaves from the purely exploitative reality of work, of extracting from the experience spiritual and artistic rewards, which helped slaves affirm their dignity through labor."[10]

The cakewalk's original meaning, then, lay in its combination of satire and cultural celebration, and in the resulting complexly layered consciousness—at once derivative and original, subordinated and resistant—that marked the evolution of much African American literary and material expression. White minstrels (and sometimes black) put on grotesque makeup and outlandish clothing in order to caricature black life; even less offensive and purportedly more affectionate representations were likely to result in the same humiliations. In the plantation cakewalk, however, it was black slaves who donned exaggerated finery to parody their masters. Their power to do so was no doubt carefully circumscribed, but the public expression of such potentially liberating caricature—commonplace in the life of the slave community hidden from the master's eyes—is a striking inversion of the culturally damaging set of minstrel stereotypes that would survive far past the end of slavery. Like the minstrel performances that fed the imaginations of Stowe, Melville, and Twain, the cakewalk in later white performance risked the aggrandizement of false emotion and fabulous sentimentality. For the black performer, however, the cakewalk always had within it the potential subversion and rearrangement of white models, a subtle reflection upon the role of black labor within the American economy, and thus an index of the unique tensions of African American culture. In addition, the dance carried with it the remembered and transmitted patterns of a festive celebration of life, not of enslavement and death, the echoes of an inherited African beginning.

Nevertheless, Chesnutt's use of the trope and its capacity to inform the culture of Jim Crow more generally depend not just on the cakewalk's evocation of slave culture but also on its role in the development of the African American musical stage in the late nineteenth century. As it was performed in the age of segregation, the cakewalk evolved out of minstrelsy, whose large touring companies, both black and white, spread the popularity of the dance across the nation. The cakewalk's first important performance on the black stage was as the finale of the 1890 *Creole Show,* which, significantly, eliminated blackface and added women to its cast; likewise, *The Octoroons* (1895), another mixed-gender black show, concluded with a "Cakewalk Jubilee." (Three other black stage shows of the 1890s, although modeled on minstrel show formats, discarded the cakewalk. In 1896 *Oriental America* concluded instead with a medley of operatic selections; the same year *Black Patti's Troubadours,* starring the concert singer Sissieretta Jones, experimented with a combination of opera, farce, dance, and short musical numbers; and in 1898 *A Trip to Coontown,* the first show entirely produced and managed by blacks, superimposed upon a continuous story line about a con artist an array of specialty numbers like those of earlier revues.) Built in part on the proto-ragtime and frequently racist "coon songs" that propelled the dance, the vogue of the cakewalk served, ironically enough, both to integrate women into the majority of black minstrel companies and to catapult to fame a number of black performers, male and female alike (Sissieretta Jones, for instance, first came to attention because of her performance at an 1892 Jubilee Spectacle and Cake-Walk at Madison Square Garden). Fascination with the dance reached its peak of popularity in 1898 with the opening at New York's Casino Theatre Roof Garden of *Clorindy, the Origin of the Cakewalk,* by Will Marion Cook and Paul Laurence Dunbar. Set in Louisiana in the 1880s, the musical deceptively portrayed the origins of the dance as a relatively contemporary phenomenon. Because Dunbar's dialogue was largely done away with in the course of rehearsal, what remained was less a stage musical than a variety bill with music by Cook and lyrics by Cook and Dunbar in collaboration. As Cook would recall in 1944, *Clorindy,* even though its notoriety came from a featured array of coon songs such as "Who Dat Say Chicken in Dis Crowd?," "Hottest Coon in Dixie," and "Darktown Is Out Tonight," represented a real step forward. With twenty-six gifted black voices singing a new style of music, an "anthem in rhythm," Cook observed, "Negroes were at last on Broadway, and there to stay. Gone was the uff-dah of the minstrel! Gone the Massa Linkum stuff! We were artists and . . . nothing could stop us, and nothing did for a decade."[11]

Cook's claim was warranted but misleading. Even though it provided far wider employment for blacks in American musical theater than ever before, the rise of the cakewalk and coon songs came at an obvious price. It was an age of black caricature on stage and in print, from the crude racism of white supremacist propaganda to stand-up comedy (including that of Mark Twain) to the manifold racist representations of blacks in song-sheet illustrations, advertisements, and southern memorabilia. Magazines and newspapers that catered to both lower-class and more genteel audiences were filled with caricatures in image and in language of black social, political, and cultural life.[12] In this atmosphere African American artists were hardly immune to the adoption of stereotypes. For example, the initial fame of *Clorindy's* star, the gifted black singer and comedian Ernest Hogan, rested on his composition and performance of "All Coons Look Alike to Me," a song whose title, far more offensive than its actual lyrics (which tell the story of forlorn love), became emblematic of "coon" stereotypes. Although the generic title "coon song" was indiscriminately applied to virtually any new ragtime number, produced by the hundreds during the era, those most stereotypically popular utilized the long-standing minstrel figures of the shuffling old-time darky or the ostentatious Zip Coon dandy and provided them with lyrics devoted to gambling, razor fights, caricatured social and political aspirations, the consumption of booze, watermelon, chicken, ham, or pork chops, and other similarly demeaning reductions of African American life. As in the case of cakewalks, "coon shouting" contestants, both black and white, vied for audience approval and vaudeville roles, with mimicry of pretended black manners— the proper way to eat a watermelon, for example—an essential part of the portrayal. Despite the relatively innocuous lyrics of "All Coons Look Alike to Me," Hogan's title alone therefore summed up the fierce irony of African American success in the American musical theater. One of his stage achievements had been to discard the exaggerated blackface makeup and rely instead on his own expressive features, billing himself as the "great unbleached American," but his "natural" appearance only made the irony more biting. Often soundly criticized by contemporaries and especially by succeeding generations of black performers for the offensive image projected by his song, Hogan later regretted its fame, particularly its accentuating of the "coon" epithet. But he noted, too, that he included the term (inserting it into a rag he had stolen from a Chicago pianist) because "the coon is a very smart animal"—a justification found in instances of African American folklore as well—and he argued that the ragtime characteristics of the song, which gave "a new musical rhythm to the people," were of direct financial benefit to black performers. Reflecting on the rise of black musical theater in the 1890s, Hogan concluded, in the manner of Will Cook, that "we came along in leaps and bounds after weighing the good with the abuse."[13]

The fact that on the opening night of *Clorindy* Hogan was required to sing ten encores of "Who Dat Say Chicken in Dis Crowd?," a coon song with patently offensive dialect lyrics, points succinctly to the painful paradox of the show's success and to the potential risks involved when writers such as Chesnutt incorporated the dangerous tropes of black minstrelsy into their own signifying satire. The song voices the racial hierarchy of society through the comic stereotype of the darky chicken thief. At a "great assemblage of the culled population," with "culled swells" from various southern states called together to discuss the black political situation, an errant rooster breaks up the meeting:

Who dat say chicken in dis crowd?
Speak de word a-gin and speak it loud.
Blame de lan', let the white folks rule it,

> I'se a lookin' fu a pullet,
> Who dat say chicken in dis crowd?

African American political concerns are swept away by a minstrel gag that is commensurate with the depiction of black identity in the illustration for the song's published sheet music, in which a group of rag-clothed adult blacks are depicted in the diminutive postures of children, facing an enormous chicken. Although it is conceivable that Cook and Dunbar intended a critique of black civil rights paralysis, Hogan and others clearly capitulated to the coon role and played the song for laughs. Cook's mother apparently thought the song nothing but ugly minstrelsy: upon hearing Cook and Dunbar rehearse the song at home, she called out to her son, a classically trained musician, "Oh, Will! Will! I've sent you all over the world to study and become a great musician, and you return such a nigger!"[14] To be a "nigger" in this instance, for Cook and Dunbar alike, was to sacrifice the class distinction and economic success that a classical education seemed to make possible; but it was also to recognize that, at a moment when few professional doors were open to the talented black artist, the burlesque stage, like dialect literature, was one of the best paths to independence. Two of Charles Chesnutt's most bitter tales, "A Victim of Heredity" and "Dave's Neckliss," would reconstruct the elements of coon humor in a signifying but bittersweet critique of the stereotypes' pervasive presence in American life and the consequent difficulty of the black artist's escaping their denigrating influence; and the best of his conjure and color line stories would frequently draw on the racist figures of popular culture in order to seize and invert their cultural power. Likewise, his insertion of the cakewalk into *The Marrow of Tradition*, as we have already seen, would elevate the paradigm to the more powerful stage of American judicial and political life, which in turn could be said to reflect the elaborate trope of minstrelized race relations that soon swept through virtually all American popular arts.

A theatrical piece about origins, *Clorindy* displayed in small the peculiar mix of authentic retention, white distortion, and responding satire that appears in much African American performance of the late nineteenth and early twentieth centuries. In this respect the evolutionary course of the cakewalk, from slavery to stage, is a compact symbol of minstrelsy worth further examination. In both instances black song, dance, and manners—in short, elements of black cultural identity—were appropriated by white performers (as Tom Delamere appropriates the behavior of Sandy Campbell), only to be taken back, but now with a double layer of parodic form, by African American performers. Not only did the addition of black performers and black cultural elements such as jubilee music revitalize minstrelsy, but blacks on stage were also able to combat the "old-time darky" image and play the trickster, infusing their performances with legitimate African American cultural expressions and including, surreptitiously or not, ideas and routines that protested plantation mythology and contemporary racism. As Rudi Blesh argues, the vicious prejudice fostered by white minstrelsy was schizophrenically answered by canny black minstrels, who turned their "version of the burnt-cork divertissement into a subtle but devastating caricature of the white *Ubermensch,* employing the blackface like an African ceremonial mask, and through the whole thing insinuated [their] way onto the white stage."[15] The mask, then, was not just a facade behind which the true intentions of the black performer, like those of the dissembling slave or the dissembling black writer or his fictive interlocutors, could be hidden; rather, it was an intricate example of that cluster of behavorial acts and attitudes that, as we have seen in the case of Twain, went under the heading of "imitation" in current racial theory as it spilled over into literary practice. If blacks, according to the racial bias of contemporary sociology, could survive only by imitating white customs and culture, then any distinct African American culture, it was argued, was doomed to assimilation and erasure. There were other means of cultural survival, of course, but black minstrelsy's reappropriation of significant elements of African American folk life, surviving from slave culture and early blackface minstrelsy alike, signified on the racist theory of imitation. African American minstrelsy was imitation with a vengeance.

What lived behind the mask of minstrelsy was the shadow life of African culture, as distinct a retention as rhythmic dancing and drumming, or blue tonality in vocal music. The syncretic development of black-voiced culture survived censorship and distorting appropriation in the antebellum period, and it would survive, even more remarkably perhaps, the most invidious caricatures of the nadir. Such a serpentine record of cultural survivals is hardly surprising, for the 1890s witnessed the coalescence of seemingly polar contradictions in white racial attitudes. America, white as well as black, became engrossed by the preservation of black folk life at the same time harsh new forms of segregation were being enacted. The cakewalk and *Plessy* v. *Ferguson,* one could say, were bound together by the racial logic of America's segregated culture. The white public view of black life was mostly channeled into plantation stereotypes, but folklorists, historians, and entrepreneurs—black and white alike—sought to recover, or record before its passing, the substance of African American oral and material folk arts, a fact with crucial implications for the writing of Chesnutt among others. To one degree or another many white (and even some black) efforts to record the passing of slave culture were framed by a nostalgia for the world that had been destroyed.[16] Although they seldom evinced an explicit desire to return to the days of white supremacy, novelists and ethnographers together displayed regret for the loss of slave culture comparable to that displayed for the apparent passing of American Indian culture, a duplicitous act that frequently combined idealization and subjugation. Such ethnographic romanticism in some instances amounted to a kind of mourning for the African American population whose original African cultures had been severely altered, if not actually destroyed, but who remained excluded, despite emancipation, from participation in the epistemological and imaginative domains of white American culture— excluded, that is to say, from the recognized public creation of knowledge and beauty. The recreated plantation was a perfect topos for lamenting the loss of legitimate white mastery but also for demonstrating that, though legal slavery was gone, the forms and hierarchies of a clearly defined racial order, with its consequent economic privileges, could still be maintained. Plantation literature and culture did not simply demand a febrile return to the past; it was the deceptive screen for keeping contemporary African Americans in bondage to the whole white race, as Albion Tourgée had said in his brief for Homer Plessy.

Panoramic recreations of antebellum life played a special role in Jim Crow culture, and modern minstrelsy increasingly featured "authentic" workaday scenes and "real" southern blacks, fresh from the experience of plantation slavery. Al G. Field's minstrel troupe mounted a gigantic traveling show entitled *Darkest America,* which purported to employ only Negro performers and displayed a sugar plantation, a steamboat race, the South Carolina State House at the time of the Hayes-Tilden election crisis, and a Washington, D.C., Negro ballroom scene, among other tableaux. In the recreation of plantation life and so-called black history, the stage and the political forum easily merged; theater and politics extended each other's capacity to drain African American culture of both original values and civil rights while mapping it onto an idealized display of racial supremacy that transported pastoral nostalgia into a violence-ridden present. The recreated plantation at the Atlanta Exposition was only one of many similar attempts in the public arena to preserve an idyllic southern past through the use of life-size replicas and "authentic" Negroes, but it was fitting that Booker T. Washington's own willingness to play a prescribed role, for which he was lauded and embraced by northern and southern whites alike, should be set against the backdrop of the new plantation.[17]

Like the cakewalk itself, however, the plantation spectacles no more completely obliterated African American cultural retentions than Washington completely sacrificed the prospects for black American economic and political gain, whatever the cost in humble subjugation he was willing to pay. The most extravagant of such spectacles was the 1894 *Black America,* an outdoor pageant of plantation life staged in New York and Boston by an ex-minstrel and a former impresario with Buffalo Bill's touring show. Touted by its producers as an "ethnological exhibit" in which the audience would see "no imitations, nothing but what is real," and continually extolled in the press as a "genuine" recreation of black plantation life, *Black America* was a fantasia of stereotypes played by an "authentic" black cast of hundreds. The singing of spirituals was mixed with archetypal feasting on watermelon, and a grand cakewalk capped a show that recreated African episodes of dance and song alongside examples from the European and African American traditions. Because of its mammoth proportions, Robert Toll has asserted that *Black America* "symbolized the final culmination of the minstrel show."[18] At the same time, however, one may note, first, that it was staged in that terrain of cultural ambiguity where professional blacks first worked in great numbers, and second, that African and true African American elements, however distorted, were precariously preserved. Du Bois and Langston Hughes, for example, would borrow from and attempt to correct the errors of *Black America* and similar shows in staging their own historical pageants of black American life; and the assertion of *Black America*'s program that the cakewalk was not a theatrical invention but the representation of an "original" dance from the days of slavery had a powerful double meaning that cannot be ignored. Both political accommodation and cultural assimilation were sharp, two-edged swords.

By the mid-1890s Madison Square Garden was holding national cakewalk championships for competing hometown couples from around the country, and by the turn of the century the dance had become popular in both American and European high society. Indeed, one means of the cakewalk's wide dissemination, the effects of which are still evident today, lay in its basic rhythm, a grand promenade in two-step march form that was easily popularized by, among others, John Philip Sousa, who introduced the cakewalk to Europe at the Paris Exposition in 1900. Coinciding with the rise of community bands and a significant brass band literature, exemplified by Sousa's compositions, cakewalk music entered the realm of a more explicitly military nostalgia. In the evolution of ragtime out of these different strains in American popular music, the two-step of the cakewalk occupies a peculiar position. To cite a representative example: in a song entitled "At a Georgia Campmeeting" (1897) by Kerry Mills, the most prolific composer of popular cakewalks, the basic march structure is overlaid with walk-around rhythms and banjolike sounds, and applied to a folk tune, "Our Boys Will Shine Tonight," guaranteed to evoke a militarized plantation nostalgia. Through the brass band compositions of Sousa and other adaptations of the cakewalk to conventions of European American musicality (Igor Stravinsky's "Ragtime for Eleven Instruments" and Claude Debussy's "Golliwog's Cakewalk" were two instances of the continental incorporation of the form), the remnants of its cultural uniqueness threatened to disappear for good into a plantation vision of "oldtime Negroes" on the one hand, and a vivacious but colorless instrumental literature on the other. By this point in its assimilation to white culture, it would seem, the cakewalk more often than not resembled a burlesque exaggeration of the quadrille that climaxed high-society dress balls, and its relation to slave society, not to mention African festival dance, was grossly attenuated.[19]

It is clear, however, that something outside the tradition of European ballroom dancing—something African American and southern—remained in the cakewalk, just as something alien to European rhythms appeared in the advent of ragtime, a culturally ambiguous form of music. In the same way that the form of ragtime was characterized by more than improvised syncopation, so the cakewalk remained more than a two-step promenade.*

---

* Ragtime in its classical form was either a written music or one in which a relatively static regime of embellishment, not improvisation as such, was employed, and it therefore lacks central characteristics associated with the evolution of black jazz. The separation between the written and the improvised may be crucial to conceiving of the orality of a black aesthetic, but it would be too simplistic a mechanism for defining African American expression. Ragtime in this respect occupies a middle ground, as James Weldon Johnson would insist when he made it the presiding metaphor for his protagonist's racial self-examination in *The Autobiography of an Ex-Coloured Man*. Although it does not seem so rhythmically challenging to the modern ear, ragtime at the turn of the century displayed striking syncopation, essentially the result of a transfiguration in African American culture of the march or quickstep. The "ragging" of standard tunes (and later the more overt improvisation characteristic of jazz) or the creation of new ones with shifted accents and multiple rhythms can be likened to the broader act of signifying, the parodic

It remained "black," its meaning deriving from the ability to preserve a black dance out of slave culture even as it thus became entangled in the long and contentious debate over African American origins and survivals which ensued. As Henry Edward Krehbiel, the foremost early professional commentator on African American song (and an advocate of the African origins thesis despite his own racialist assumptions), would soon remark, the "rhythmical intoxication" of ragtime dance, from the cakewalk to the turkeytrot and the tango, partakes of African "primitivism." Even though he admired black music intensely and was instrumental in creating a theory of its development, Krehbiel still considered contemporary American dances an African-influenced regression from refinement. "The dance which is threatening to force grace, decorum and decency out of the ballrooms of America and England," he wrote in 1913 of the tango and related dances derived in part from the cakewalk, "is a survival of African savagery, which was already banished from the plantations in the days of slavery. It was in the dance that the bestiality of the African blacks found its frankest expression." Krehbiel's judgment was echoed by a number of observers who found contemporary music and the dance it accompanied, especially black dance inspired by African and Caribbean forms of move-ment, to be brutal or obscene. However it might be "cleansed" by high-society white participants who performed it in a more decorous setting, the cakewalk was a link to popular jazz dance of the early twentieth century and therefore a vehicle for the preservation and dissemination of African-ized elements of cultural expression. Both the improvisatory character and the physical energy of the cakewalk, a mark especially of those perfor-mances that claimed to be "authentic," must have been partly responsible for the pronouncement by the elite *Musical Courier* in 1899 that the cake-walk was a "sex dance . . . an African *danse du ventre,* a milder edition of African orgies."[20] The *Courier's* prissy critique no doubt derived from the particular Victorian element of American racism that held blacks to be overly licentious; but the observation would have appealed as well to those among the black middle class who were eager to distance themselves from

---

appropriation of a cultural or linguistic "standard" by a differently styled voice. See Ben Sidran, *Black Talk* (1971; rpt. New York: Da Capo, 1981), p. 27; Gunther Schuller, *Early Jazz: Its Roots and Musical Development* (New York: Oxford University Press, 1968), pp. 32–33, 65–74; William J. Schafer and Johannes Riedel, *The Art of Ragtime: Form and Meaning of an Original Black American Art* (1973; rpt. New York: Da Capo, 1977), p. 9; and Wilfrid Mellers, *Music in a New Found Land* (New York: Alfred A. Knopf, 1964), p. 277.

minstrelsy and any black folk art that could be linked either to slave culture or to Africa.

What was at stake in such a judgment—what became a point of contention for many turn-of-the-century African American leaders and created a central ambivalence about the sources of his inspiration in the case of Chesnutt—was perhaps the most pressing racial question of the era: Could the race advance culturally or ever be accorded equal political and social rights without discarding the traces of its enslavement and African origins? The post-Reconstruction years put African American culture under intense pressure as the work of preservation and historical legitimation was set against the eroding forces of suppression. Corresponding to the question of civil rights, then, was another: What life and what historical memory were "authentically" black? What was "genuine" in the tradition and what not? *Black America*'s claim to represent an "authentic" portrait of black slave life was one measure of this conundrum. It was reported that the show's numerous chorus was recruited among farm and mill hands of the South, so as to secure "perfect Negro types" to be trained by a black manager who built on their "inborn imitative aptitude."[21] How the chorus could both be genuine and yet need professional stage training to imitate true Negro music is a paradox essential to the role of minstrelsy in black cultural life in the 1890s and to the greater problem of imitation, the theoretical cornerstone of racial, as well as artistic, assimilation.

The paradox crystallized in the careers of the period's most famous black minstrel team, Bert Williams and George Walker, who in 1903 would make the cakewalk an international fad by their seven-month London engagement with Cook's musical *In Dahomey,* and who took over *Clorindy* after its first few months and traveled with the show to other major eastern cities. Promoting themselves as "two real coons," Williams and Walker were exemplary of the generation of black performers who threw off the main trappings of minstrelsy, in costume and manner alike, in order to broaden the conception of black stage art. Walker's 1906 article in *Theatre Magazine* (cited earlier in chapter 3 for Walker's well-known remark that "nothing seemed more absurd than to see a colored man making himself ridiculous in order to portray himself") traced the course of their success in part to a curious incident in 1893. When the actual Dahomeans who had been engaged to appear in an exhibit at the San Francisco Midwinter Fair were late in arriving, black Americans, including Williams and Walker, were hired as "sham native Dahomians" to play their parts. Once the real Africans arrived, the two performers stayed on to study the Dahomeans so as better to delineate their mannerisms (giving a more precise meaning to the timeworn description of minstrels as "Ethiopian Delineators"). Because the Dahomean exhibit in San Francisco was borrowed directly from the more famous one at the Chicago World's Columbian Exposition, Williams and Walker's study raises a more explicit question. The Chicago Exposition had been the site of strong black protests, led by Frederick Douglass and Ida B. Wells among others, over its initial exclusion of African Americans from taking any part in the exhibits. That the Dahomeans simply counted for all blacks in the minds of many white fairgoers is evident in published comments about them, for example that in *Frank Leslie's Popular Monthly:* "Sixty-nine of them are here in all their barbaric ugliness, blacker than buried midnight and as degraded as the animals which prowl the jungles of their dark land. . . . In these wild people we easily detect many characteristics of the American negro."[22] The delineation of "authentic" Africans by Williams and Walker thus ran the obvious risk of more deeply ingraining in the white public's mind the stereotype of the "savage" that middle-class blacks sought to obliterate. The significance of black American imitations of African culture should in any case be tested against the curious "back-to-Africa" shows, such as *In Dahomey,* which were staged in the early twentieth century and bore a relation to renewed interest in colonization as a response to heightened white racism. Walker's assertion that such songs as "My Zulu Babe" and "My Dahomian Queen" were Americanized *African* songs is hardly creditable. Nonetheless, his pride in the team's "radical departure from the old 'darky' style of singing" must be taken seriously, and his claim to derive inspiration from African sources rather than from the conventions of blackface minstrelsy gives a special weight to the billing of Williams and Walker as "real coons." In Walker's conception the label was a ploy to get the attention of theater managers, and his complaint that there was nothing "natural" about whites' performances as coons suggests that the term itself was virtually neutral for him, meaning little more than "Negro." Nonetheless, the idea of "real coons" modeled on imported Africans perfectly captures the narrow range of movement left open for the black artist when the ideology of Jim Crow had permeated all arenas of American life.

Because it was more publicly visible than the rise of the blues and jazz, the entrance of blacks into minstrelsy and stage shows displaced into seemingly ephemeral modes of cultural work a central issue: the capacity to define the behavior of "real coons" was nothing less than the capacity to take control of one's culture, one's ancestral history, and one's racial identity, all of which were under assault at a most precarious moment as the slave generations passed away and promised black rights were put more and more at the mercy of state and local controls. What happened in the national public eye was therefore of magnified importance. In January of 1898, when cakewalking was at the crest of its American vogue, Williams and Walker, in a publicity stunt, called at the home of the tycoon William Vanderbilt, who had achieved some notoriety as a cakewalker. Humorously maintaining that "the attention of the public has been distracted from us on account of the tremendous hit which you have made," the pair left a letter challenging Vanderbilt to a public competition for the title of champion cakewalker of the world and a fifty-dollar prize— the low stakes, so the story goes, because Williams reminded Walker that it was a shame to take the money.[23] The challenge, unanswered by Vanderbilt, was a joke. But whatever the immediate intentions of Williams and Walker, it contained resounding dimensions of satiric cultural politics as well. Whereas the plantation slaves had lampooned the social airs of the master while understanding well his volatile power, Williams and Walker lampooned Vanderbilt's presumably diluted performance of a "genuine" black dance within the context of his obvious social power. In effect they challenged Vanderbilt, in meeting them on their own ground, to give back that which he had taken. He could not be made to do so. If Nathan Huggins is correct to argue that the pretensions of turn-of-the-century white high society were themselves so close to travesty as to mirror the deliberate excesses of minstrelsy, associated from its antebellum beginnings with a populist assault on class distinctions, the challenge by Williams and Walker can be taken as a sign of the lingering gulf between the two racial worlds.[24] White American pretenders might ape their notion of European gentility; but black Americans were locked into a nearly impossible defense of their own cultural lives.

At this remove, what could be left in the cakewalk of its origins in the plantation ring-shout or the African circle dance? The "authenticity" of black culture, preserved as much by exploitation as by devoted preservation, was undeniably hybrid. Although the ethnologist Harold Courlander claimed to have seen versions of the cakewalk in Africa,[25] they were nonetheless much different from the antics of white ballroom dancers or even the best struts of black stage players. The most powerful argument advanced for the survival of true African dance in American forms places great emphasis on the centrifugal hip motion and propulsive rhythms of African dance, which distinguish it from the more erect, leg-driven European style, and derives the cakewalk from dancing juba and a loose set of African forms.[26] African dance, that is to say, appears to unschooled white observers as abrupt, contorted, overtly sensual, a "primitive" counterpoint to the more linear motion of European dance. It may be, then, that the satiric import of the plantation cakewalk—its physical burlesque of the masters' Europeanized dance forms—is its most African feature. If this is true, the ostentation of African American theatrical dance—its superadded burlesque of minstrel forms largely popularized by whites—may also be related to African modes of satiric allusion in song and dance. Like folktales and spirituals, the more prevalent forms of cultural survival, black dance personified in the cakewalk from this perspective was still "African," but the masks that covered such a discovery were multiple. Familiar to white America largely as "coontown," African American authenticity nonetheless survived, even prospered among, its misrepresentations. What belonged specifically to black cultural life—in the case of dance a bodily motion, in the case of music a tonality, in the case of folk literature a satiric inflection akin to dialect—had to be looked for by means of indirection, by means of a deviation from, or subversion of, a dominating set of cultural standards that transferred the regulating discipline of the plantation into a new, more subtle but comprehensive cultural space continuous with the political and economic realities of Jim Crow America.

Word Shadows and Alternating Sounds: Folklore, Dialect, and Vernacular

> Who knows but that, on the lower frequencies, I speak for you?
>
> Ralph Ellison, *Invisible Man*

In 1901 Chesnutt contributed to *Modern Culture* an essay, "Superstitions and Folklore of the South."[27] What is remarkable about it, especially in light of Chesnutt's conjure tales, is his apparent degree of skepticism about black folk beliefs. In charting the background of his Uncle Julius stories, Chesnutt carefully records methods and instances of "conjuration" practiced by purported conjure doctors, both women and men. But the emphasis falls decidedly on the various rational explanations that can be put forward to account for the apparent success of any curse or cure. Old Aunt Harriet, who claimed to have extracted a snake from her own arm (inhabitation by reptiles is one of the most common signs of conjure in the folk records of the day), is represented by Chesnutt as "lying" or "merely self-deluded." Her religion is probably little more than "superstition," and her belief that a mystic voice brought her a cure for an ankle sprain appears to be written off by Chesnutt: "She is not the first person to hear spirit voices in his or her own vagrant imaginings." Old Uncle Jim, another informant, is but a "shrewd, hard old sinner, and a palpable fraud." As Chesnutt records it, conjure thrives on "delusion" and the "credulity of ignorance," signaling the "relics of ancestral barbarism" that have not yet been shaken off as African Americans become more civilized. In these animadversions Chesnutt seemed to be little different from the majority of ethnologists and folklorists who had begun in earnest to collect material about conjure at the end of the nineteenth century. The overwhelming reliance on theories of racial hierarchy and the progress of civilization, fueled by the twin engines of science and Christianity, made any response but skepticism unlikely. Most ethnography about conjure (or "hoodoo") stigmatized such elements of slave culture and its aftermath as superstition or delusion—of interest from an anthropological point of view but nonetheless irrational and regressive—and implicitly cooperated with sociological theory and legal proscription to identify the potential for "reversion" and "degeneration" to forms of primitivism among contemporary African Americans who did not aspire to a more assimilated American middle class.

Given his own precarious position straddling the color line, and given his clear aspirations to middle-class professional respectability, it is not surprising that Chesnutt would detach himself from the irrationality of conjure. For this reason alone, his characterizations of conjure would be central to any estimate of his role as a writer committed to the notice and preservation of distinct black American traditions at an especially difficult historical moment when the legislated "superstitions" of Jim Crow held full sway. If the conjure tales in particular are evidence of such a commitment, they are nevertheless tales in which Chesnutt's curt personal belief that conjure was "superstition" is marked and in which his own imaginative transformation of the folk material, not its original substance, is predominant. Or so it seems: Chesnutt no doubt identified to some degree with the skepticism voiced in the white narrative frames of his own conjure stories; and yet it is the black liminal voice of the trickster, immersed in the strategies if not the actual secrets of conjure, whose historical memory and cultural values are most at stake in these stories. Chesnutt, that is to say, may himself have been signifying in "Superstitions and Folklore of

the South" (the essay's several oblique allusions to the barbarity of segregation and the fetish of race purity are one kind of evidence), adopting
the isolating voice of contemporary ethnography while working inside it
in order to preserve African American cultural forms and to make them
instruments of his own gain, much as his character Uncle Julius does in
the tales. Chesnutt, one could say, was doing a literary cakewalk that
assumed ever grander and yet more detailed, subtly argued forms over the
course of his writing career.

Preservation and transformation exist in a taut balance in the nineteenth-
century ethnographic record of black folktales, and Chesnutt's focus on
his *literary* appropriation of folk forms exacerbates rather than diminishes
that tension. Seeming to remove himself as far as possible from the "original" tales of slave culture, Chesnutt pointed on several occasions to the
privilege of authorial license, most notably in his late essay "Post-Bellum—
Pre-Harlem," in which he remarked that with one exception his conjure
tales were "the fruit of my own imagination, in which respect they differ
from the Uncle Remus stories which are avowedly folktales." And other
critics have followed his lead in differentiating him from Joel Chandler
Harris, who, as Chesnutt put it in the 1901 conjure essay, "with fine literary
discrimination collected and put into pleasing and enduring form, the
plantation stories which dealt with animals."[28] Chesnutt's relationship with
Harris is complex and worthy of extended discussion, which will follow.
The difference between them, however, here asserted by Chesnutt on the
spurious basis of an opposition between folklore and imagination, is no
simple one but must instead be read within the overarching problem of
African American cultural origins and African retentions. His account of
the origins of his own versions of conjure tales was extremely canny and
was dedicated to the promotion of his own career as a writer. But one
must begin with the fact, as Robert Hemenway has demonstrated in his
landmark essay on Chesnutt's folklore, that there are numerous sources—
or, at any rate, analogues—for many of the central features of his conjure
tales. This fact alone places Chesnutt in a strikingly complicated relation
to the issue of African retentions, for whatever his ultimate assessment of
the cultural value of African American folk beliefs in the late nineteenth
century, Chesnutt appears to have followed Harris and others in their
view that, though many black stories were part of the world's stock of
wonder stories, appearing throughout racially distinct cultures or reflecting
European origins, some of the tales had specific African beginnings. Although they are related to animal trickster tales and to other story para-

digms such as the Master-John cycle, conjure tales were constituted, for Chesnutt, by a relatively distinct body of imaginative structures that were at once more amenable to narrative transfiguration and more precisely traceable to the ancestry of slave culture. The belief in conjure, he observed, was rooted in "African fetishism, which was brought over from the dark continent." Lacking the "sanctions of religion and custom" that supported them in Africa, such beliefs became, "in the shadow of the white man's civilization, a pale reflection of their former selves."[29]

This "pale reflection" that African beliefs became under the pressure of enslavement and American acculturation corresponds, moreover, to the explanation that Chesnutt offered of his own imaginative processes. Whereas he first thought—or remembered—that only "The Goophered Grapevine" came directly from black folklore, his interviews with elderly blacks, including a conjure man, reminded him that some of his seemingly imaginative innovations were "but dormant ideas, lodged in my childish mind by old Aunt This and old Uncle That, and awaiting only the spur of imagination to bring them again to the surface." Chesnutt's eminently Hawthornian account of his creativity—a literary influence that is evident in the tales themselves—puts a limit on the liberty exercised by the artist: ideas must already exist "somewhere in his consciousness," ready to be subjected to the "power of rearrangement."[30] Yet Chesnutt's admission (or his recognition, as the case may be) about the sources of his tales is interesting not for what it takes away from his artistry but for what it adds. By locating elements of his stories in the childhood tales told him by elders of the generation of slavery, Chesnutt placed himself closer to those originating beliefs that had become only a pale reflection of their former African selves, and he made the remembrance of slave culture a foundation for modern African American culture. More pointedly than Harris or other white folklorists, Chesnutt found himself at a demanding double remove—separated from the generations of slavery as they were in turn separated from all but the most resilient elements of African culture. But he made of this distance a powerful instrument to demystify the positivist constructions of primary material by folklorists, blurring the line between redaction and creation in a most profound way. The literary category of the imagination, which at first appears to separate Chesnutt's work from the "folktales" of Harris and the conjure beliefs collected by professional ethnographers, circles back, by the path of personal and historical memory, to merge his narrative art with the stories of the black ancestors. Chesnutt's theory suggests, too, that the distinction between the rearranging power of the imagination and the bequest of folklore is a tenuous one. Just as Harris's Br'er Rabbit tales must be seen as the product of the transforming forces of folk storytelling, long before Harris set them in his own problematically imagined plantation frames, so Chesnutt's consciously fabricated tales contain materials that were far from stagnant but instead were structured according to particular cultural pressures and belief patterns that had evolved generation after generation, from Africa to the New World, absorbing new European American elements along the way.

Chesnutt was resolutely middle class, and the majority of his published fiction, especially his color line stories and *The Marrow of Tradition*, reflects in some measure his genteel literary tastes. At the same time, however, his fiction also reflects his concern that the rise of a black middle class could jeopardize racial cohesiveness in the very act of uplifting the race and sacrifice a distinctive strain of African American art whose record lay in the oral narratives. Leroi Jones (Amiri Baraka) is thus widely off the mark in his claim that Chesnutt subscribed to the proposition, a sign of "slave mentality," that the Negro "must completely lose himself within the culture and social order of the ex-master," and counted himself part of that black middle class that "wanted no subculture, nothing that could connect them with the poor black man or the slave."[31] The black middle class often ignored or ridiculed the folk culture that survived in trickster stories and plantation tales, in minstrelsy, and on the black stage, or that was preserved in the spirituals and was beginning to flourish in jazz, but Chesnutt incorporated those folk voices into his writing in the most remarkable ways. Indeed, he made such a rift within African American culture the very subject of his writing because it was, in perfectly visible ways, the subject of his life as a man of mixed race light enough to pass for white. One could say that his exploration of class and color divisions produced in Chesnutt an uneasy adherence to a "subculture" that was part of, not separate from, the middle class; the lower class, the "folk," and the reminders of slavery itself were contained "somewhere in its consciousness," just as the folk beliefs of African origin were contained somewhere in Chesnutt's own imaginative reservoir. The tension between the two realms, and the signs of Chesnutt's honest recognition of his moral obligation to keep them united, appear throughout his fiction. Not the best, perhaps, but the most classic statement is found in his famous story "The Wife of His Youth."

First appearing in the *Atlantic Monthly* in 1898, the story was collected the following year in *The Wife of His Youth and Other Stories of the Color Line.* The plot, of course, concerns the dilemma confronted by a northern, upper-middle-class mulatto, a member of the best "Blue Vein" society of Groveland (modeled on Chesnutt's own Cleveland), when he must decide whether or not to acknowledge the validity of his marriage during slavery to a dark-skinned, illiterate woman from whom he was separated but who reappears on the eve of his engagement to a beautiful light-skinned woman of his own class. The story has a place in the larger structure of concerns examined in the color line stories as a group; but one can notice here several aspects of the story that illuminate Chesnutt's relation to his conjure stories as part of the "subcultural" content that had to be similarly acknowledged in his own career. By her coincidental appearance upon the scene, Ryder's wife, Liza Jane, interrupts his idyllic visions of increased assimilation of European cultural standards and upward progress through a further lightening of his children's dark skin. Standing in stark contrast to his fantasy of a social world represented by Tennyson's poem "A Dream of Fair Women," Liza Jane, who is "very black,—so black that her toothless gums, revealed when she opened her mouth to speak, were not red, but blue," looks "like a bit of the old plantation life, summoned up from the past by the wave of a magician's wand." She is undeterred by the slim chances of finding the husband of her youth and tells Ryder, apparently without knowing yet who he is, that "de signs an' de tokens" have guided her search.[32]

In addition to its role in Chesnutt's critique of color consciousness and intraracial racism, "The Wife of His Youth," written at the same time he was organizing a collection of his conjure stories, represents a meditation upon the complexities of his own acknowledgment of a past—not the literal past of his youth (although that is part of it as well) but rather the symbolic past of his race. Liza Jane seems summoned up as though by conjure, a reminder of Ryder's as well as Chesnutt's obligation to confront and, as Ryder finally does, to embrace a painful past and the culture that is carried with it. The embrace is nothing if not ambivalent. As Alice Walker reminds us, Ryder's black wife is too old to bear children, and his declaration that "our fate lies between absorption by the white race and extinction in the black" (complete with its bitingly ironic allusion to Lincoln: "with malice towards none . . . ") therefore does not present to him quite the moral dilemma that it appears to. But Ryder's choice operates on other levels as well. Included within his recognition of Liza Jane are several implicit indications of Chesnutt's own cultural obligations:

to join with the lower classes in the struggle for rights; to put the good of the community before the advances of the few who are able to enter directly into the white social and cultural mainstream; and to take control of the popular conceptions of "the old plantation life" that are being generated by racist commentary and unscrupulous artistry. In an age dominated by literary accounts of sectional reunion symbolized by North-South romantic alliances, Chesnutt's stories of reunion were typically dedicated to the postbellum reunification of scattered or racially divided black families. Marriage was a sign of communal healing, just as it remained, in the color line plots, a sign of continuing racism. In either case it was for Chesnutt also a metaphor for his art and for his place within an American literary community that was at best only tolerant of, and usually antagonistic toward, any but the mildest portraits of racial conflict. When Ryder narrates the story of his wife to the gathered throng of his middle-class peers, he speaks "in the same soft dialect, which came readily to his lips," that his wife had used earlier. What they hear in his story and in his voice are those "wrongs and sufferings of this past generation" that they usually ignore but that all of them "still felt, in their darker moments," as a "shadow hanging over them."[33]

Werner Sollors has suggested that "The Wife of His Youth" is a story in which the conflict between cultural "consent" (choice of a culture defined outside inherited ethnic or racial boundaries) and cultural "descent" (acceptance of inherited categories based on race) is marked. One must add to this that it is not Ryder alone who is the storyteller here but Chesnutt too. Like Ryder, he speaks in a dialect that is not his own but that comes readily to his lips, and in doing so he instantly casts in a critical light the post-Reconstruction vogue of dialect plantation literature by authors such as Thomas Nelson Page and Joel Chandler Harris, who wrote from the other side of the color line.[34] Chesnutt's pun on "darker" is a reminder that color is a fluid category, a mask that can hide but cannot obliterate a cultural past—and a mask that, as the rise of "one-drop" segregation made evident, could easily be punctured. The story self-consciously adopts a kind of mask, however, for although we are told Ryder reproduces Liza Jane's dialect in retelling her story, the text itself does not do so. One of the era's favorite literary devices and a necessary focal point for any interpretation of Chesnutt's relation to race writing at the turn of the century, dialect remains a sign of difference, a part of the past that Ryder accepts, even imitates, but that Chesnutt does not actually reproduce. It is a sign, that is to say, of Chesnutt's own very subtle acknowledgement of his complex "blackness" alongside his own membership in the best mulatto society. Liza Jane, a bit of the old plantation conjured up in his middle-class imagination, speaks in an alien voice, but one that Chesnutt knows to be bound indissolubly to his own cultural life. "The Wife of His Youth," then, may be read in part as an emblem of Chesnutt's divided sensibilities. His recognition of his own "wife" lay in the tribute his first book of stories, *The Conjure Woman,* paid to a world that was at once hindered by degradation and ignorance according to the standards of white middle-class society, but at the same time alive with powerful knowledge and cultural meaning generated on hidden but distinguishable African American planes of discourse.

The metaphor of the shadow, as Chesnutt uses it in "The Wife of His Youth," is not unlike Melville's "shadow of the negro" in *Benito Cereno:* both suggest a haunting black (African) presence within the structure of Euro-American civilization. But the "shadow of the white man's civilization" which Chesnutt in his essay on conjure sees to have fallen over African beliefs reverses this signification, and his work devoted to the color line (which for Chesnutt is also a shifting language line) frequently alternates between these two forms of veiling in order to show the perspectival character of cultural assumptions. The easy exchange of places between the "savage" and the "civilized" is a reiterated theme in *The Marrow of Tradition* and other stories devoted to race violence. But Chesnutt's fiction plays even more broadly with the possibility, not widely accepted in his day, that cultural values are relative, fundamentally a function of political control and economic superiority. The metaphor of the shadow is therefore alive with signs of threat to the established racial order (or, what may seem the same thing, aspirations to join the established order). More than that, the "shadow" represents an amorphous, liminal realm between two worlds, neither dark nor light, neither past nor present, in which the language of cultural assimilation and resistance are in combat.

In "The Wife of His Youth" the gulf between Ryder's elevated language, laden with idealized notions borrowed from European culture, and Liza Jane's thick dialect must be bridged by his (and Chesnutt's) telling of her story, his virtual authentication of her existence. Which language, however, is it that casts a shadow over the other? An anonymous writer for the *Atlantic Monthly* in 1891, arguing that the language of ex-slaves and their descendants is a kind of mystified jumble of misunderstood English, provides a useful gloss on this problem:

> If shadows of material objects are grotesque, even more so are the shadows cast by words from fairly educated lips into the minds of

almost totally ignorant people. Display in utterance of these quaint word-shadows, if one may so call them, makes dialect.

This grotesquerie, this quaint transformation of something well known, real, and admirable into something queer, fanciful, and awkward, yet bearing resemblance to the fair formation it shadows, gives to dialect writing and to dialect speech that piquant flavor that all the world favors. Especially is this true of that lately full fashionable style of literary production, song and story, in negro dialect. The words of our language that enter the mind of the old-time negro have indeed found their way into a dusky realm. Here is with us a race which has wholly forgotten its own language, or whatever methods of communication it made use of in its African home. The language of an utterly diverse race it must perforce employ, since it has lost the tongue of its own people. Into the minds of the individuals of this race, a people hardly a century out of barbarism, the light of civilization shines with dazzling effect. The language they must use is the growth of centuries of civilization, its roots reaching to even older civilizations, its branches grafted with luxuriant word-growths of almost every nation on earth. It is little wonder that this language of ours assumes in these startled brains most fanciful shapes. To take down some of these shadowy effects, with our language for cause, would be to make a dialect dictionary, a glossary of plantation patois, a work for which, happily, there is no need.

The author goes on to list numerous examples of highly metaphoric transformations in black English—for example, a giant is a "high-jinted man"; to keep down grass is to "fight wid Gen'al Green"; to join a church is to "put on a shine-line gyarment"—of just the sort that Zora Neale Hurston would later say were characteristic of the "adornment" and "angularity" of black speech but which the author reads simply as the bizarre result of sophisticated discourse colliding with ignorance and pretension.[35]

The *Atlantic* author's analysis is more noteworthy, however, for the range of its prejudicial but revealing commentary on the question of black language, which is assumed to occupy a dark, fanciful, grotesque realm, a deep linguistic substratum of American culture that cannot be coincident with Africa (since black America "has lost the tongue of its own people") but is instead a strange limbo of queer dialect. Like William C. Elam, writing about black literary "lingo" a few years later, and like educators for generations to come, the author unflinchingly considers black dialect to consist of "vulgarisms" derived from the incorrect use of standard English. Following the influential model of blackface minstrelsy, where nondialect parts might indicate grandiloquent "white" speech or be employed in a segment that needed to be inoffensive to whites (for example, a blackface performer singing an Irish ballad), many linguists and popular writers polarized language into forms marked clearly by color alone or considered the seeming malapropisms of black speech to be *only* arcane errors. In their collection of black folk song, for instance, Howard Odum and Guy Johnson lamented the difficulty of recording dialect because "there is no regular usage for any word in the Negro's vocabulary." In spite of depicting black dialect as a gothic shadow cast by the civilized illumination of white English, however, the author of the *Atlantic* article still manages to preserve within a welter of racialist errors and clichés a sense that the "lost" tongue of Africa has some bearing on the forms of English spoken by American blacks. Nevertheless, the writer pays no attention to the Africanisms that constitute the most significant concrete retentions of African culture in America, which ethnologists would soon begin to find characteristic of black and, increasingly, white southern speech. Nor does he note that there was, in fact, another point of view—namely, as L. W. Payne argued in 1903, that southern white dialect (his example was Alabama) was "more largely colored by the language of the Negroes than by any other single influence." As Chesnutt would put it with more than a little irony in *The House behind the Cedars*: "The corruption of the white people's speech was one element—only one—of the Negro's unconscious revenge for his own debasement."[36]

Modern distaste for dialect writing—in particular the justified contempt for the use of racially stereotyped dialect as a means of denigration in stories, cartoons, advertisements, and the like—has made both critics and readers reluctant to look closely at its cultural significance. The "jingle is a broken tongue," as Dunbar wrote of the constraints placed on black vernacular in his poem "The Poet," and dialect has too often been read only as a capitulation to minstrelsy, the sign of debasement and cultural "Uncle Tomism." What is of immediate interest in the relationship of the *Atlantic* essay to the dialect writing of Chesnutt, however, is its elucidation of the cultural barriers against which he and other black writers of the period worked. The great flowering of regional as well as racial dialect writing during the realist period corresponded to significant changes in the nation's sectional allegiances, its networks of transportation and communication, and its sense of cultural singularity. Dialect was one marker of class and regional alienation from the centers of power and at the same time a sign of anxiety about passing phases—reputedly simpler, more humble pastoral phases, as both the plantation and the agrarian mythologies held—of American life.[37] For black writers, the best-known example being Dunbar, the use of dialect was fraught with the tension between capitulation to stereotypes and the desire to find an audience for African American literature, whether one took that desire to be rank minstrelsy or a literary act of cultural consciousness akin to the publication of dialect verse by nationalist poets such as Robert Burns and John Synge. James Weldon Johnson's ambivalence on this point is instructive. In the preface to his 1922 anthology *The Book of American Negro Poetry* and then again in that to *God's Trombones* (both written after he himself had published stereotypical dialect verse), Johnson argued that African American writers needed to find "a form that will express the racial spirit by symbols from within rather than by symbols from without, such as the mere mutilation of English spelling and pronunciation." But Johnson himself would largely repudiate this statement ten years later in his preface to Sterling Brown's *Southern Road,* which employed dialect in a masterly way.[38] Moreover, Johnson's contemporaries proved that for the African American writer another argument was equally important: the use of dialect could also signal, as it did for Chesnutt, the shift into a mode of cultural discourse that deliberately signified upon stereotypes. As it gained prominence in the black folklore revival of the 1890s and was made more clearly capable of honoring forms of black language (the spiritual, the sermon, the folktale), dialect took on a distinctive power with respect to the "coon" language of plantation and minstrel stereotype.

Because he understood dialect to mean not just accent or intonation but also figurative diction, the *Atlantic* author is somewhat closer than most writers of the day to recognizing that African American language represented a creative as well as a necessary merger, over a number of generations, of native linguistic survivals and the language of the masters, usually assimilated in oral forms. Increasingly in the early twentieth century, black writers recognized that the elaborate metaphoricity and what seemed the unfixed character of African American language could also be construed positively as a linguistic medium whose fluidity and capacity for improvisation were akin to the development of improvisatory arts in black vocal and instrumental music. Once the living memory of slavery had receded and the postslavery generation of writers had passed through the furnace of Jim Crow, the generation of Hughes, Hurston, and Brown could return comfortably to dialect as a sign of African American cultural strength. Dialect, in this reading, is both a salvaged speech that pays tribute to those who have gone before and an index of what has been kept alive in the evolving cultural memory of song, folktale, and everyday language. Writing from the vantage point of 1925, in Alain Locke's classic collection *The New Negro,* Charles S. Johnson described the necessary process well:

> The generation in whom lingered memories of the painful degradation of slavery could not be expected to cherish even those pearls of song and poetry born of suffering. They would be expected to do just as they did: rule out the Sorrow Songs as the product of ignorant slaves, taboo dialect as incorrect English, and the priceless folk lore as the uncultured expression of illiterates,—an utterly conscious effort to forget the past, and take over, suddenly, the symbols of that culture which had so long ground their bodies and spirits in the dirt. The newer voices, at a more comfortable distance, are beginning to find a new beauty in these heritages, and new values in their own lives.[39]

The only shortcoming of Johnson's charactertization, of course, lies in the fact that he attributes the revival and theoretical reassessment of African American folk forms to the "newer voices" of the Harlem Renaissance generation. In fact, Du Bois and Chesnutt, to name only the most prominent, had waged the battle for African American cultural integrity a full generation earlier—though not without marked anxieties about the painful double consciousness any legitimation of slave culture required. And they did so by making their own literary acts not distinct from but continuous with the unwritten, signifying "word-shadows" of the black spirituals and black folktales.

Dialect, to put it differently, became the language of the folk trickster— both the protagonist and the author—transferred to literary narrative, and Chesnutt's use of dialect must therefore be taken in part as a subtle, self-conscious examination of his relation to both the white plantation tradition and to those black writers who may have pandered to the public taste for "darky" language. More than that, however, it was a means for him to explore the ways in which language is perspectival and coded with assumptions of hierarchy and power. Like the language of James Fenimore Cooper's Indians, Negro dialect was frequently defined by its highly "poetic" style, a two-edged characterization that usually indicated natural spontaneity on the one hand, and the lack of civilized traits of order and control on the other. Dialect's Rousseavian communication by the visual language of metaphor (a standard account of primitive language in the eighteenth and nineteenth centuries) and its appeal to fantasy (in trickster and conjure tales, for instance) set it apart from refined language and pointed toward an animist or animalistic order of precivilization constructed beneath or within the order of high culture. What the American folklorist Newbell Niles Puckett heard as the "altiloquent speech" of blacks, on which minstrelsy was based—or, indeed, which minstrelsy created as the form that any black speech took in the white mind—led him to judge that "the Negro is constantly being lost in a labyrinth of jaw-breaking words full of sound and fury but signifying nothing."[40] "Signifying nothing," however, might turn out to be just right: African American dialect, in high culture no less than in slave culture, is in a constant condition of signifying on the power of the linguistic masters, appropriating and depleting that power, at least provisionally, and thus turning it into "nothing." (The category of "nothing," as it is employed in black folklore and Chesnutt's conjure tales, is one to which I will return.) Far from being the obvious sign of regression or the inadequate comprehension of civilized cultural forms, dialect might be the linguistic tool best able to show that the bondage of language can also be liberating.

At the point where literature blurs into folklore—precisely the territory occupied, of course, by Harris and Chesnutt—the issue is even more problematic: too problematic, one is tempted to say, to be left to the folklorists and literary critics. For example, Roger Abrahams's decision to eliminate dialect in his 1985 collection of African American folktales, so as to remove the "stigma" of "racist resonances" still attached to the vernacular that flourished in the minstrel tradition and its literary descendants, must be respected. As Abrahams points out, much dialect writing left behind the authenticity of oral rendition and conformed only to the worst traits of racially stereotyped speech. Nevertheless, Abrahams's decision raises several issues similar to those that unfold in Chesnutt's tales. Because the line between folklore and literature is difficult to establish in black oral narrative, only a reader interested solely in the reduced "content" of the tale could be satisfied by the even more enervating translation into textbook prose. In addition, Abrahams admits that he is flattening out the historical dimension, at times eliminating terms that have "lost their currency" and modifying styles that modern readers "would find difficult to read." This seems a very peculiar sacrifice of historicism in the name of convenience—not least because dialect, precisely because in many instances it *does* belong to the act of imagination that at a particular time created, or at least passed on, the folktale, has the capacity to locate the vernacular imagination in history and to embody the unique features of a separate culture, in this case the culture of African America. Altogether, one would prefer to have more precision, rather than less, when tracing the formations of multicultural traditions. No written record of dialect is entirely adequate, of course, but Joel Chandler Harris's admonition in his "apology" for the use of dialect in *Nights with Uncle Remus* is worth careful attention: "The discriminating reader does not need to be told that it would be impossible to separate these stories from the idiom in which they have been recited for generations. The dialect is a part of the legends themselves, and to present them in any other way would be to rob them of everything that gives them vitality."[41]

Many renderings of dialect intended to be "authentic" have exacerbated racist interpretations of African American culture, however, and Abrahams's decision therefore must also be weighed against the long years of white denigration of black language in any form whatsoever. At the end of the nineteenth century, when Chesnutt wrote, even those who granted that black diction or pronunciation had had some influence on white speech patterns were reluctant to recognize African American vernacular as anything but primitive. A paper delivered at the International Folk-Lore Congress held at the World's Columbian Exposition in 1893 succinctly stated the prevailing view, with some remarkable sidelights. Repeating the racist claims that the Negro is closer to the savage than any race other than the American Indian and that Negroes are no more advanced mentally than children, Annah Watson argued that these facts accounted for black culture's rich store of oral legends. Those slaves who were well treated (and the implication is that the majority were treated well) had few worries and thus developed imaginative romantic natures, influenced in part by lingering pantheistic African beliefs in a spirit world that had been diluted in America into the superstitions of conjure. This perfect exposition of plantation literary ideology made the proper recording of dialect a crucial part of the folklorist's obligation in the field: "The speech of the people is inseparable from their thought. So long as they think in dialect and talk in dialect, the form of speech will remain an important factor in all representations of them which are in any sense faithful." This part of Watson's language theory is no doubt correct, and her view of African retentions is valuable. Indeed, her racialist intention—to show that black speech and thought are both primitive—need not obscure the potential of dialect to figure forth just what is "inseparably separate," as it were, within African American culture. Defined in relation to a dominant culture, dialect might function as an index of the power of signs to exclude and oppress; but it might at the same time indicate a powerful mode of cultural self-preservation and determination. As Henry Louis Gates, Jr., argues, dialect can turn the "metaphor against its master." Hovering between the two poles of white English and an African language "lost in some mythical linguistic kingdom now irrecoverable," black dialect is the only available key to that unknown tongue. Moreover, Gates's view that successful dialect writing is inherently musical and approaches the metaphoric richness of black spirituals—a level that dialect poetry or prose has, however, seldom reached, notably in the cases of Hurston and Brown—points to the necessity that dialect be understood as more than tone and pronunciation.[42] Metaphor would have to include not just the semantic plenitude and singularity of folk speech but also its oral legends, its material and psychological space, and the implied sources of its language and beliefs. The "shadow language" of black dialect may have been—and may still be—perceived by whites as a garbled version of standard English or a haunting, potentially destructive presence within the kingdom of culture. More appropriately, however, it should be recognized as a signifying alternative, another cultural language that has historically conditioned and transfigured white English while drawing force from its own liminality.

In the same way that the cakewalk fused its African roots with a satiric commentary on big house fashion, dialect writing and the folk sources of its intonations contained within it African sounds propelled into a unique black American vernacular that was to remain a kind of crossroads of cultural languages. For Annah Watson and even for Chesnutt that imaginative territory might be termed "superstition," but it was also another form of the "irrecoverable" kingdom that at once remained hidden behind the mask of dialect and became shadowed forth within it. From Watson's perspective, the contemporary "curio-hunter" had to work to preserve the disappearing lore of the ex-slaves. (One compelling reason for this task lay in her speculation that America was the meeting place of the two great branches of the human family: from their origins in central Asia one group went east, across the Bering Strait; the others divided, going south to Africa or west to Saxony, before being united in their movement west to America.)[43] If one sets aside her ethnographic racialism, the argument does not much diverge from Chesnutt's demonstration that the conjure tales were a foundational territory of the black dialectical imagination, which he explored with an equal, if morally distinct, sense of its lapse into less and less recoverable forms.

I have placed such emphasis on the definition of black dialect in Chesnutt's day for three reasons. First, African American writers who chose to write in dialect—especially if, like Chesnutt, they drew clear lines between different forms of black speech according to class—faced the challenge of overcoming the racialist attitudes maintained about dialect by their readers, even sympathetic ones. Second, in a related issue, the conscious use of dialect by the black writer (and here it merges with the significance of vernacular dance and early jazz) points to the elemental role of sound itself in language and therefore allies the problem of proper dialect to the heated turn-of-the-century debates about the African origins of black music, the influence of unique tonality in that music, and the consequent possibility that certain "sounds" of a culture could not be "heard" or reproduced (imitated) by members of another culture. Third, the controversy over dialect is symbolic of questions about what unique materials or qualities in black culture could be recorded in literature and preserved with a degree of authenticity. Chesnutt met all of these issues head on in his conjure tales, and together they constitute the most astute expression and theoretical analysis of African American vernacular and its accompanying folk beliefs during the ascendancy of segregation.

Chesnutt once complained to his editor, Walter Hines Page, that it was a "despairing task" to write dialect. The problem was not just orthographic. Rather, Chesnutt argued, echoing an increasing tradition of fieldwork, "there is no such thing as a Negro dialect. . . . What we call by that name is the attempt to express, with such a degree of phonetic correctness as to suggest the sound, English pronounced as an ignorant old southern Negro would be supposed to speak it, and at the same time to preserve a sufficient approximation to the correct spelling to make it easy reading."[44] Chesnutt's blithe, condescending detachment from the rural southern folk is rather dismaying—it is difficult to believe that here, as in his remarks on conjure as superstition, Chesnutt is signifying—but it does not distort the theoretical importance of his views (or of his dialect writing). Leaving aside the point that all speech is dialect measured against some hypothetical standard, Chesnutt sums up the dilemma of transcribing dialect into literature. At the level of writing mechanics, Chesnutt's problem with dialect was shared by all writers who adopted the form; his statement points to the sacrifice in authenticity (of an "ignorant old southern Negro's" talk) necessary to communicate to a literate middle-class audience. Nonetheless, his argument that printed dialect of the kind adequate to capture the language of a figure such as Uncle Julius can at best only approach the actual sound of his voice also repeats verbatim comparable observations made by those who recorded African American spirituals with the intention of publishing them for a general audience, and it therefore raises a thornier theoretical issue with broad cultural implications for the location and preservation of black culture.

The problems of transcribing black language and black music are not, in fact, separable in the evolution of African American culture. Since the antebellum period collectors of music had noted the difficulty of properly annotating the spirituals, and Du Bois would make that fact integral to his use of them in *The Souls of Black Folk*. The issue was not one of annotation alone, however, but of preservation and public dissemination. It was often remarked, for example, how the jubilee singing of choral groups such as those from Fisk University and Hampton Institute modified African American spiritual music to suit public taste; indeed, transplantation into a more formal concert setting itself affected the character of the music. As Hampton arranger Thomas Fenner admitted, there were various pressures at work. The fact that the group sought a harmony between the "rude simplicity" of plantation song and a more regularized concert sound meant a certain loss in quality (although Fenner clearly thought his arrangements could improve the music). "Half of [the music's] effectiveness, in its home," he wrote, "depends upon accompaniments which can be carried away only in memory." The inspiration of numbers, the overpowering chorus, the swaying of the bodies and the stamping of feet, and "the wild enthusiasm of the Negro camp meeting—these evidently can not be transported to the boards of a public performance." In addition, he noted, many blacks who had survived slavery or grown up outside its influence were inclined to despise the music "as a vestige of slavery." Most illuminating, though, was Fenner's observation, one repeated by a number of musicologists, that the intonations of the black spiritual were inherently difficult to annotate according to conventional scalar paradigms: "Another obstacle to its rendering is the fact that tones are frequently employed which we have no musical characters to represent. . . . These tones are variable in pitch, ranging through an entire interval on different occasions, depending on the inspiration of the singer." Such singing amounted, for Fenner, to a foreign language, its tones impossible to express in familiar words. To hear the true spirituals, he said, *"go listen to a native."*[45]

I will return to the role of the spirituals and their complex turn-of-the-century cultural and ethnographic history in chapter 5; but debates about the character of black vocal music bore a close relation to discussions of dialect in African American folklore and literature, both of which can be seen to be animated by an essential aural aesthetic. Like black dialect, the record of black vocal music—its concert performance, but especially its scored representation—was an inadequate embodiment of its sound source; it failed to bring forth the tonal meaning of the singer, just as the inadequate transcription of dialect failed to bring forth the tonal meaning of the speaker. More than that, according to one musicological interpretation, the record of black music in the spirituals, whether performed on stage or written in the songbooks that flourished at the end of the century, was paradoxically destroyed even as it was being preserved. Whereas the *African* appropriation of Protestant mission music Africanized it into jubilees, original songs of praise, the "purification" of African American spirituals by touring black choirs eliminated or reconfigured any residual elements of African folk art and the unique sounds forged in slave culture as characteristic tonalities and rhythms were made to conform more closely to European standards.[46] Black sound, to borrow the metaphor of the *Atlantic* writer, lived in a "shadow" world that could not be completely transcribed. Such a language, if it cannot be fully heard, cannot be fully understood. Whereas ethnologists were prone to characterizing black language as the sign of a world that failed to meet civilized standards, there was the counterpossibility, exploited by Chesnutt (and, in fact, by Harris as well), that black language was also the sign of a secret world kept out of range of the middle-class mind, much as the coded languages of slavery had been deliberately kept out of the range of the masters. In Ralph Ellison's powerful metaphor, it was a language that spoke on "lower frequencies."

Chesnutt stands in a critical position in the theoretical development of the aesthetics of cultural separatism which has generally been the concern of ethnomusicologists and linguists but has now entered literary studies in a more profound way in theories of vernacular and debates about Afrocentrism. His conjure tales and the dialect of Uncle Julius represent his need "to preserve fidelity to the sound of African ancestors and the phonics of their descendants," Houston Baker argues. The sound of dialect, embodying the transformative power of conjure and reaching toward the language of Julius that the narrator John and his wife, Annie, at critical moments take to be "nonsense," is the hidden sound of the "ignorant old southern Negro's" real language (to recall Chesnutt's seemingly deprecating phrase), operating at an "effective register *behind* the mask of the narrational dialect" and modifying "the dynamics of lordship and bondage."[47] Baker's brilliantly suggestive remarks, the most probing reading of the theory underlying Chesnutt's conjure tales, go far toward explaining how those stories operate and how we are to read Julius's own "folk" tales and his dialect, or that of a character such as Liza Jane, in relation to Chesnutt's middle-class frameworks and settings. Baker finds Chesnutt's deployment of Julius's subcultural role to be one of masked signification, with Chesnutt signifying upon his audience (and editors) just as Julius is signifying upon his carpetbagger employers. Given Chesnutt's ambivalence about black class distinctions and his published skepticism about the "superstitions" of black folk belief, as we have seen, his act of signifying in the arena of literature must be even more complex. Yet the importance of "sound" as a marker of dialect—what cannot be adequately printed on the page, what cannot be annotated or, indeed, "heard"—goes to the heart of the drama of African retentions and black cultural survival which Chesnutt, emblematic of his age, played out in his fiction.

In our experience of Chesnutt's conjure tales, Uncle Julius's language conceals several things at once: trickster that he himself is, Julius usually has an ulterior motive, one of material benefit to himself; with sometimes comic or neutral deadpan narration not always penetrated by John or his wife, he often recounts incidents that portray the harsh cruelty of slavery (and its aftermath); and his tales of conjure, as well as the hidden resonances of his speech itself, preserve and record, if in fragmented echoes, the culture of African survivals—what is framed as "superstition" but what clearly articulates something more. At extremity, what is "more," what survives, may be, like the ring-shout hidden within the cakewalk, nearly invisible; or it may be transparently present but impossible to capture in available (standard) cultural language. That is, the conjure tales—like the larger debate about African survivals or the authentic preservation of slave culture—foreground the role played by ignorance or bias (or outright racism) in cross-cultural interpretation.

In an 1889 essay I took note of in my introduction, Franz Boas set forth a theory of language that had profound implications for his field and has equally profound significance for the historical study of literary forms, as well as any interpretation of narrative in dialect. After a careful study of his own faulty methodology, Boas argued in "On Alternating Sounds" that there were no such phenomena as alternating sounds. What the fieldworker took to be phonetic variations were in fact examples of his own "sound-blindness," his inability to perceive the subtleties and actual semantics of the speech he was hearing. Thus, transcriptions of the same sounds often proved to be at great variance with one another. Because the hearer perceives "unknown sounds by the means of the sounds of his own language," imposing his own culturally conditioned paradigms upon ones unfamiliar to him, Boas concluded, "alternating sounds are in reality alternating apperceptions of one and the same sound."[48] Boas's break with the tradition of evolutionary philology, which anticipated his mature theories of cultural relativism, offers a compactly formulated means of understanding both the difficulties of writing dialect, broadly understood, and the cultural differences it may represent. The widespread argument that black language either resembles music or contains within it forceful elements of musical form, distantly inherited from Africa, is especially relevant here; for it is precisely the musicality, the implied phonetics lying outside the range of white cultural hearing, that is at issue in Boas's thesis. Just so, the bearing of musical tonality on the cultural role of black dialect is a key issue in one of Chesnutt's most suggestive but least studied conjure tales.

"Tobe's Tribulations," an Uncle Julius tale not included in *The Conjure Woman* but published separately in *Southern Workman* in 1900, is at once straightforward and circuitously allegorical. The fact that it appeared in *Southern Workman,* a black magazine published at Hampton which initiated a "Folk-Lore and Ethnology" section in 1894 (following an editorial invitation to readers to submit their materials), may itself be significant, because the story is one in which the black folk elements are stronger, less clearly subordinated to the imaginative retelling of Chesnutt himself, and in which the tale's political message is overt if nonetheless complicated. The story is notable for its inclusion of one the fullest statements, through the voice of John the narrator, of the significance of Julius's folk imagination. John's views do not, of course, always represent Chesnutt's, and he is most often deliberately characterized as naive, obtuse, or culturally blind. In this instance, however, his language is close to that in Chesnutt's own essay about conjure, approaching a kind of ethnography while at the same time displaying the clear bias of his cultural perspective. (If Chesnutt *is* signifying in "Superstitions and Folklore of the South," then perhaps it is the voice of John as well that we hear bound up in his own seemingly deprecating remarks about conjure as superstition.) As in other tales, John's ethnographic statement appears in the context of his prefatory remarks about the strange but entertaining stories old Julius can summon up. His account of black folklore is similar to Harris's and includes notice of the mixed African and European (especially Scottish) sources of the tales:

> [Julius] had seen life from what was to us a new point of view—from the bottom, as it were; and there clung to his mind, like barnacles to the submerged portion of a ship, all sorts of extravagant beliefs. The simplest phenomena of life were to him fraught with hidden meaning—some prophecy of good, some presage of evil. The source of these notions I never traced, though they doubtless could easily be accounted for. Some perhaps were dim reflections of ancestral fetishism; more were the superstitions, filtered through the Negro intellect, of the Scotch settlers who had founded their homes on Cape Fear at a time when a kelpie haunted every Highland glen, and witches, like bats, darkened the air as they flew by in their nocturnal wanderings. But from his own imagination, I take it—for I never heard quite the same stories from anyone else—he gave to the raw material of folklore and superstition a fancifulness of touch that truly made of it, to borrow a homely phrase, a silk purse out of a sow's ear.[49]

Here is virtually the whole of Chesnutt's folk aesthetic. Although the compliment goes to Julius, it is Chesnutt whose imagination works over the raw materials of folklore. Like Thomas Fenner, the Hampton arranger, he looks for a harmony between the original and the "developed" forms but pays tribute at the same time to the transforming powers of the black storyteller, the arranger of the folktale. The metaphor of the submerged ship recalls Chesnutt's remark in his conjure essay that the folklore lying behind his published stories had been put into his childhood unconscious by elderly storytellers, and his description of their sources in African fetishism appears here as well. Let me bypass for the moment the slight racial tension in John's narrative voice and Chesnutt's characterization of the mixed origins of the tales and note instead how completely, despite his own seeming skepticism about such "superstitions" (to the degree that Chesnutt shares John's voice), he portrays Julius as living in the spiritually saturated world characteristic of much African belief. Although there is no way to know whether or not Chesnutt was aware of it, Tobe's name derives from the Kongo term for good luck charms.[50] Himself a *tobe* or *toby,* as the term was translated into African American usage, Tobe is thus himself inherently a figure of conjure, a kind of living material matrix, and in any event his point of view, in a figure that combines social, political, psychological, and cultural import, is given from the "bottom."

"Tobe's Tribulations" conforms to the typical format of the Uncle Julius stories. John proposes or initiates some enterprise—in this case catching frogs from his marsh for a frog leg dinner—and Julius counters it with a story calculated to dissuade John (and serve Julius's self-interest) or to instruct him and Annie about southern history, usually both. Julius's story in this instance concerns Tobe, the slave of Julius's own former owner, Mars Dugal McAdoo. When a neighboring slave escapes and (like Frederick Douglass) sends a "sassy letter" back to his master, Tobe is inspired to follow suit. He enlists the aid of the conjure woman, Aunt Peggy, who gives him a "goopher mixtry" that will turn him into a bear and allow him to escape; but instead of escaping, he accidentally hibernates for a month. Aunt Peggy tries turning him into a fox, but Tobe, succumbing to minstrel stereotype, gets waylaid eating chickens and ends up pursued by foxhounds. Aunt Peggy then turns Tobe into a frog so that he can hide for a day, but she gives him too much goopher and he remains a frog for life. Tobe, says Julius, is one of those frogs in John's marsh, his voice (as Annie hears it) "like the lament of a lost soul," still waiting after forty years to be turned back into a man. Therefore, Julius dislikes frog legs; but feeling a bit of "mis'ry" come on because of the sad tale he has told, he asks instead for "a drap er dem bitters out'n dat little flat jimmy-john."[51]

Like other animal transformation tales in Chesnutt's repertoire, "Tobe's Tribulation" plays upon the degrading effects of slavery and contemporary racist laws of natural hierarchy: Tobe is still waiting after forty years to be turned back into a man. Julius underlines this allegorical plane of the story by his ironic remark: "Co'se ef [Tobe] had waited lak de res' un us he'd a be'n free long ago. But he didn' know dat, en he doan know it yet."[52] Like Twain, Harris, and Melville, Chesnutt uses one historical plane to explore another, registering the survival not just of slave culture but of the "second slavery," as Twain called it, in the postbellum decades. Julius, the conjure tales tell us over and over, may be many things—witty, intelligent, dignified, cunning, proud—but he is not yet free.

It is not the ending of the tale, however, but the beginning that is most relevant to Chesnutt's exposition of a theory of black culture. Although

Annie hears Tobe's voice as the "lament of a lost soul," John characteristically cannot hear it because he cannot imagine what "the vocal expression of a lost soul" sounds like. What he has heard is detailed at the beginning of the story:

> As soon as the red disk of the sun had set behind the pines the performance [of the frogs in the marsh] would begin, first perhaps with occasional shrill pipings, followed by a confused chattering; then, as the number of participants increased, growing into a steady drumming, punctuated every moment by the hoarse bellowing note of some monstrous bullfrog. . . . For a while after we went to live in the neighborhood, this ceaseless, strident din made night hideous, and we would gladly have dispensed with it. But as time wore on we grew accustomed to our nocturnal concert; we began to differentiate its notes and to distinguish a sort of rude harmony in these voices of the night; and after we had become thoroughly accustomed to it, I doubt whether we could have slept comfortably without their lullaby.

There is no doubt that this descriptive passage operates first on the literal level to introduce a natural scene that will be the basis for Julius's tale of conjure. Nonetheless, because in Chesnutt's stories the action of magical transformation is always bound up with the process of political signification, the secondary level is equally telling. The concert in the marsh—its din and bellowing, chattering and drumming, that produce at best a "rude harmony" of alien sounds—invokes the music of the slave quarters heard from the big house. Yet its hideous, frightening "noise" becomes, after a certain period of acculturation, a "lullaby." As is often the case in Chesnutt's tales (likewise in Harris's), two temporal frames are merged here, for the sounds, like Tobe's story itself, link antebellum and postbellum life. One can imagine John and Annie transported back into the days of slavery, witnessing the expression of black culture (and, like visitors such as Fanny Kemble, startled by it); yet they are also post-Reconstruction carpetbaggers who hear the frogs' concert of voices transfigured within the framework of plantation mythology. The "lullaby" is the message of antebellum tranquillity, the essence of the Old South myth that operates in both historical registers. The pastoral melody disguises the fact that slave music—for instance, its threatening drumming, alluded to here— was often the subject of planter scrutiny because of its potential to conceal messages of resistance or, at the least, evidence of dissatisfaction or trickery; and, like the trope of the cakewalk in *The Marrow of Tradition*, it designates the ease with which the new northern partners in the postwar southern economic venture can become accustomed to the contemporary music of the quarters, the music of peonage, without grasping its continued language of pain and resistance. The "lament of lost souls," what can truly be heard within the frogs' chorus, is the message of slavery, the surviving essence of African American life in the black spirituals and work songs whose vital meaning lives into Reconstruction and beyond.[53]

John does not hear Tobe's voice (there is no concluding frame to contain his response, skeptical or otherwise, in this tale), and I will return to Tobe's "lullaby" in a further discussion of Chesnutt's use of "nonsense" as a marker of the indirection and concealment historically encoded into African American language. The point of the story, however, is to make the reader hear Tobe's voice—hear the voice of failed emancipation as well as the surviving voice of Africans in America, scarred so deeply by the experience of slavery and expressed from the "bottom" of life. The "bottom," as John describes Julius's point of view, thus becomes not just a metaphor of racial hierarchy but one that also has geographical and spiritual significance. The choral sound from the "bottoms" of the marsh, the slaves' terrrain of gathering and celebration, must come also from "beneath" existing layers of cultural prejudice in order to be heard. As John Wideman writes of the conflict between Julius's dialect and John's language in his interpretation of "A Deep Sleeper," Chesnutt "explores the forms and uses of language where the seams of intelligibility burst."[54] "Tobe's Tribulations" is a stunning rendering of that liminal realm, of the seams between two cultures that are not just linguistic or epistemological in nature but also deeply, harshly inscribed by political and economic domination, and consequently by cultural ignorance. Like the problematic "alternating sounds" described by Boas, the voices of African American slavery, the tale reminds us, are easily misheard (and mistranslated into a comforting "lullaby") or not heard at all by the master class. Paradoxically, however, it is the essence of those voices that they be virtually beyond articulation in the standard forms of the dominant culture and that their characteristic sound occupy the margins of tonality.

At extremity, such cultural sound passes into another language—in this case the several languages of Africa likely to have influenced any given slave population's black English—and "Tobe's Tribulations" (for reasons to which I will return) might also be construed as a story about African retentions and the vexing question of African American cultural origins. Chesnutt's ascription of the origins of Uncle Julius's tales first to his own imagination, then to childhood stories by former slaves, and finally to the obscure past of African fetishism shows his own indecision—or his own cunning—on this issue. It is not necessary to rehearse here the labyrinthine debate among folklorists and ethnomusicologists about retentions. The most persuasive positions are those that stress at least a syncretic theory in which African American cultural expressions can be understood as a blend of sometimes competing, sometimes corresponding idioms, with the stress on African influence.*

---

* The long debate among scholars has produced no consensus. Melville Herskovits's landmark argument in favor of the African origins of black American culture, *The Myth of the Negro Past* (1941), is supported by the more specialized folklore studies of J. Mason Brewer, Alan Dundes, and Daniel Crowley, to cite just a few, and opposed by the work of Richard Dorson and others, who argue that the vast majority of tales appear in (or derive from) European or Asian traditions as well. In the more extensive musicological debate that often overlaps that about folktales, Newman White, George Pullen Jackson, and D. K. Wilgus (the last in a valuable summary article) have maintained that the seemingly distinct features of African American music appear also in Anglo-American styles and that the melodic core of the black spiritual is borrowed, in one degree or another, from white traditions. Their arguments have been variously countered by those of James Weldon Johnson, Rudi Blesh, Marshall Stearns, Gunther Schuller, Richard Waterman, and others. The modified views of Winthrop Sargeant, Paul Oliver, and John Lovell, who argue for pronounced but carefully circumscribed African retentions in African American music, are the most compelling. Although a syncretic view dominates all serious discussion today, the weight seems clearly to have shifted toward the African origins argument in the case of music and probably in that of the folktales. It is evident as well that more than a few of the European origins arguments are still marked by a cultural bias of just the sort Boas's paper on "alternating sounds" had meant to eliminate. See Melville J. Herskovits, *The Myth of the Negro Past* (1941; rpt. Boston: Beacon, 1952); J. Mason Brewer, *American Negro Folklore* (Chicago: Quadrangle Books, 1968); Alan Dundes, "African Tales among the North American Indians," in Dundes, ed., *Mother Wit from the Laughing Barrel: Readings in the Interpretation of Afro-American Folklore* (1973; rpt. New York: Garland, 1981), pp. 114–25; Daniel J. Crowley, "Introduction," in Crowley, ed., *African Folkore in the New World* (Austin: University of Texas Press, 1977); John F. Szwed and Roger D. Abrahams, "After the Myth: Studying Afro-American Cultural Patterns in the Plantation Literature," in Crowley, *African Folklore in the New World*, pp. 65–86; Beverly J. Robinson, "Africanisms and the Study of Folklore," in Joseph E. Holloway, ed., *Africanisms in American Culture* (Bloomington: Indiana University Press, 1990), pp. 211–24; Richard M. Dorson, *American Negro Folktales* (New York: Fawcett, 1968), passim, and *American Folklore*, rev. ed. (Chicago: University of Chicago Press, 1977), pp. 166–98; Newman I. White, *American Negro Folk-Songs* (Cambridge, Mass.: Harvard University Press, 1928); George Pullen Jackson, *White and Negro Spirituals* (New York: J. J. Augustine, 1943); D. K. Wilgus, "The Negro-White Spiritual," in Dundes, *Mother Wit from the Laughing Barrel*, pp. 67–80; James Weldon Johnson, preface to *The Book of American Negro Spirituals* (New York: Viking, 1925); Rudi Blesh, *Shining Trumpets: A History of Jazz*, rev. ed. (1958; rpt. New York: Da Capo, 1976), pp. 3–80; Marshall W. Stearns, *The Story of Jazz* (New York: Oxford University Press, 1958), pp. 3–33; Gunther Schuller, *Early Jazz: Its Roots and Musical Development* (New York: Oxford University Press,

Although I emphasize this perspective, one can do without a strict account of origins in analyzing the evolution of African American cultural forms in the aftermath of slave culture. For example, in discussing plantation songs in his famous 1893 challenge to Americans to use their native folk materials in artistic productions, Antonin Dvořák correctly noted that from one perspective the exact origin of folk materials finally mattered very little. "The important thing," he argued, "is that the inspiration for such music should come from the right source, and that the music itself should be a true expression of the people's real feelings." (Dvořák responded in part to the conservative—and incorrect—argument that Stephen Foster had composed many "slave" songs, while others were not of American origin at all but imported from Africa. He anwered his own challenge the same year in his symphony *From the New World,* which employed black and American Indian folk melodies; and although it also resulted in significant work by Harry Burleigh, Rubin Goldmark, Clarence Cameron White, and a few other composers, the aesthetic principles underlying the advocacy of such nationalism gained little acceptance among American classical musicians.) In the case of both African American music and narrative, what mattered was the firing transfiguration of African heritage into American custom during slavery, which made the black spirituals, and to a less obvious degree the tales, the preeminent American art. What mattered, that is to say, is what happened in African *America,* as memory and adaptation merged into a single expressive force under a regime that punished or stigmatized significant elements of African American life.[55] My argument is in favor of the survival of transfigured African elements in black American culture; but like conjure itself, the reality of survivals may be less important in this case than the belief in them. The acceptance of a syncretic theory of the folktales and music leaves ample room for appreciating the powerful African elements in the tales themselves and in the sensibility that informs their telling without requiring that they all be traced to an African rather than a European, American Indian, or Asian origin. Even so, the characteristic African American forms

1968), pp. 3–62; Richard Waterman, "African Influence on the Music of the Americas," in Dundes, *Mother Wit from the Laughing Barrel,* pp. 81–94; Portia K. Maultsby, "Africanisms in African-American Music," in Holloway, *Africanisms in American Culture,* pp. 185–210; Winthrop Sargeant, *Jazz: Hot and Hybrid,* 3rd ed. (1938; rpt. New York: Da Capo, 1975), pp. 147–220; Paul Oliver, *Savannah Syncopators: African Retentions in the Blues* (New York: Stein and Day, 1970), passim; and John Lovell, Jr., *Black Song: The Forge and the Flame* (New York: Macmillan, 1972), pp. 18–128.

of cultural expression, though they may continually blur into the forms of the dominant culture, remain unique in ways that can be best understood by recourse to those features of African culture that were taken to be distinctive by ethnographic writers of Chesnutt's era.

In her 1920 book of African folklore, Natalie Curtis tells an anecdote about C. Kamba Simango, a young man from Portuguese East Africa who had come to Hampton Institute to study. Simango, an expert player of the *mbi'la* (thumb piano), once improvised at the conventional piano using his fingers as drumsticks, as though he were playing the marimba. He found, as Curtis recounts it, that the available tones of the piano did not correspond to the range to which he was accustomed: "'This note is too high and the next one is too low and there is none in between!'—an unconscious commentary on the limitations and crude inflexibility of our European tonal system." There has been much discussion of the differences between the tempered scale of European music and the typically more expressive tonal scale of African (and African American) music, which, particularly in vocal form, utilizes interpolated notes, glissandi, wavers, falsetto, and the like to achieve greater flexibility of sound. Whether or not the pentatonic blues scale is particularly African (a dubious commonplace), what nineteenth-century commentators noted from the outset was that the "blue tonality" of black music (a concept that must include more than just the flatted thirds and sevenths of the classic blues scale, as the phrase is sometimes narrowly used) was difficult to annotate by conventional methods; its sounds, its tonal "dialect," did not correspond to the available cultural sound map. Writing in the *Journal of American Folklore* in 1903, for instance, Charles Peabody gave the example of a black Mississippi man's work song periodically "intoned" as he plowed behind a mule for fifteen hours a day, a song that "melted into strains of apparently genuine African music, sometimes with words, sometimes without. Long phrases there were without apparent measured rhythms, singularly hard to copy in notes." Similarly, Peabody found a black woman's lullaby "quite impossible to copy, weird in interval and strange in rhythm; peculiarly beautiful."[56]

Beginning with the slave songs set down by William Allen and his colleagues, and Thomas Wentworth Higginson, through the comments of Krehbiel, Fenner, Peabody, and others later in the century, and on into various commentaries on jazz in the twentieth century, the question of capturing the exact sound of black music and language has been baffling, not least because the boundary between language and music blurs in the

African heritage. Allen's landmark collection of spirituals, *Slave Songs of the United States,* opened with what was to become a characteristic admission that "the best we can do with paper and types . . . will convey but a faint shadow of the original. . . . The intonation and delicate variations of even one singer cannot be reproduced upon paper."[57] Here, then, was a signifying reversal of the denigration of black language as a mere "shadow" of traditional English. As Allen's caveat suggested, the convergence of musicality and meaning in African American speech meant that the recorded sign, not the act of signification, would be the "shadow," the inadequate container for a meaning that slid away in the act of performance. The challenge arose not just on account of an unfamiliar vocabulary or mode of intonation but also because of the black tradition, evident in slavery and surviving after it, of sometimes dissembling and hiding its communications within a culturally distinct, necessarily private language. The political level of circumspection in black language that slavery entailed has survived on through the twentieth century in the vernacular forms of speech, language games, signifying, and sermonizing analyzed by Roger Abrahams, Geneva Smitherman, Claudia Mitchell-Kernan, and others.[58] Both in its capacity for linguistic analysis and in its primary expressive forms, black language can be joined to the principal strategies of indirection that ethnomusicologists have found to be characteristic of African and African American music, and the tight fusion of aural and semantic qualities in African American language.

Commentary on the forms of African music that have been carried into American culture uniformly stresses the contours of tone in African language and, conversely, the vocalized quality of tone with which African instruments are played.* These complementary elements of sound reappear

---

* Two related features of African music and language are especially important here—the preeminence of rhythm and the fusion of tonal and semantic characteristics. The preeminence of rhythm over melody and harmony, as well its special communicativeness in African tradition, gives the role of drumming a special bearing on the quality of black musicality. The dependence of much African language on pitch and timbre facilitated the convergence of drumming and speaking or singing, each form amenable to expressive changes in pitch and tone. Those elements, as we have seen in the case of antebellum music and dance, were translated and transfigured in the American setting of slavery in such a way as to determine the shape of black culture, at least in its forms closest to folk expression, after emancipation. At the same time, however, drumming and other forms of African music were often deliberately censored on the plantation, a fact of key importance in the development of black musical forms. The African practice of communicating by talking drums depended on the drummer's ability to reproduce the tonal inflections and rhythms of spoken sentences, which was facilitated, in the case of West African languages, by

in African American music (where the instrumentation of jazz has an unerring component of voice) and language (where meaning bends into the domain of sonority). Both the talk-singing of black church and secular music and the distinct improvisatory musicality of black language games in folk performance would be modern examples of what Geneva Smitherman has called the "tonal semantics" of black speech. The vocalism of language and the linguistic expressiveness of music, based on tones that signify upon the limits of the tempered scale and regular rhythm, constitute a cultural sound that inevitably diverges from the European American standard. Such a "recomposing [of] America in terms of Africa," as Ben Sidran remarks, required both recourse to hidden meanings, to the double entendre of signifying, and an exploration of the emotive level of expres-

---

their pitch structure. Despite its suppression on the plantation, the rhythmic component central to African music nonetheless survived in altered, indirect forms; if the drums were silenced, their percussive effects were translated into clapping, foot tapping, or patting juba. Like this heightened focus on rhythm and a polyrhythmic complexity, an inflected tonality also therefore entered into singing and instrumentalization in marked forms. Even though he is probably in error about the starkness of the distinctions and the relay of African elements into African American forms, Ernest Borneman, in his deservedly influential essay on the roots of jazz, sums up the range of these ideas and provides indications of how they may profitably be applied to the language of folklore and black literature: "While the whole European tradition strives for regularity—of pitch, of time, of timbre and of vibrato—the African tradition strives precisely for the negation of these elements. In language, the African tradition aims at circumlocution rather than at exact definition. The direct statement is considered crude and unimaginative; the veiling of all contents in everchanging paraphrases is considered the criterion of intelligence and personality. In music the same tendency towards obliquity and ellipsis is noticeable: no note is attacked straight; the voice or instrument always approaches it from above or below, plays around the implied pitch without ever remaining on it for any length of time, and departs from it without ever having committed itself to a single meaning. The timbre is veiled and paraphrased by constantly changing vibrato, tremolo and overtone effects. The timing and accentuation, finally, are not *stated*, but *implied* or *suggested*. The musician challenges himself to find and hold his orientation while denying or withholding all signposts." Borneman presents a rich statement of the possibilities for reading African American literature, particularly that written at the historical moment when black music takes on its characteristic modern forms, in a context in which the tonalities of a hidden language and the limits of cultural hearing are taken seriously into account. See Henry Edward Krehbiel, *Afro-American Folksongs: A Study in Racial and National Music* (1914; rpt. New York: Frederick Ungar, 1962), pp. 66–72; Blesh, *Shining Trumpets*, pp. 25–46; Eileen Southern, *The Music of Black Americans: A History* (New York: Norton, 1971), pp. 14, 200–214; Schuller, *Early Jazz*, pp. 42–47, 54–56; Leroi Jones [Amiri Baraka], *Blues People: Negro Music in White America* (New York: William Morrow, 1963), pp. 23–26; Stearns, *The Story of Jazz*, pp. 275–82; A. M. Jones, *Studies in African Music*, 2 vols. (London: Oxford University Press, 1959), I, 230–51; Dena J. Epstein, *Sinful Tunes and Spirituals: Black Folk Music to the Civil War* (Urbana: University of Illinois Press, 1977), pp. 45–60; and Ernest Borneman, "The Roots of Jazz," in *Jazz*, ed. Nat Hentoff and Albert J. McCarthy (New York: Holt, Rinehart and Winston, 1959), p. 17.

sion beyond the function of verbal interchange that brought out the "individualism of an otherwise destroyed personality."[59] Sidran's striking characterization has most immediate applicability in the vocalized presence of what could be construed as shouts, cries, or transfigured field hollers in the blues and in modern instrumental jazz. But the asemantic character of such vocalized sound also tells us a good deal about the workings of black dialect, which can be interpreted as both an assault on the authoritative diction of the master's language and a means of generating a secretive language in which linguistic and musical traces of African heritage survive.

It is not likely, of course, that one can find the whole repertoire of such African American expressive characteristics operating verbatim in Chesnutt, for example; but as "Tobe's Tribulations" makes evident, the tonal semantics of African American language have a critical place in Chesnutt's art. Julius's dialect language represents the blue tonality of African-American speech—the "galvanization of meaning and pitch into a single vocalization," as Sidran writes.[60] But dialect is also a sign, for Julius as well as for Chesnutt, of the double meanings and hidden semantic constructions, grounded in a signifying response to slavery dating from the origins of slavery, that are beyond the range of his auditor, John. What this provides us, moreover, is the linguistic equivalent of the dissolution of boundaries upon which conjure is based. The metamorphosis through indirection, inflected tonality, and improvisation appearing in black folk speech corresponds in Chesnutt's tales, through Julius's voice, to the metamorphosis of human into animal or inanimate forms. The conjure tales demonstrate that John lacks an ability to understand Julius's language. He hears certain satiric puns and moral messages, to be sure, but he cannot actually hear the sound of Julius's voice, whose canny dialect cajoles and plays upon John and Annie's sentiments while often bypassing their comprehension and signifying on the controlling discourse of white America. To understand what Chesnutt's stories accomplished in the conflicted atmosphere of the folklore and folk music revival of the 1890s, however, one must read him in relation to Joel Chandler Harris, the author most responsible for the initial popularization of African American folklore.

Uncle Remus, Uncle Julius, and the New Negro

"All that nonsense singing [along with a Dizzy Gillespie recording] reminds me of Cab Calloway back in the old *scat* days," I said, "around 1930 when he was chanting, 'Hi-de-*hie*-de-ho! Hee-de-*hee*-de-hee!'"

"Not at all," said Simple, "absolutely not at all."

"Re-Bop certainly sounds like scat to me," I insisted.

"No," said Simple, "Daddy-o, you are wrong. Besides, it was not *Re-Bop*. It is *Be*-Bop."

"What's the difference," I asked, "between *Re* and *Be?*"

"A lot," said Simple. "Re-Bop was an imitation like most of the white boys play. Be-Bop is the real thing like the colored boys play."

"You bring race into everything," I said, "even music."

"It is in everything," said Simple. . . . "Be-Bop was certainly colored folks' music—which is why white folks found it so hard to imitate. . . . The ones that sing tried to make up new Be-Bop words, but them white folks don't know what they are singing about, even yet."

"It all sounds like pure nonsense syllables to me."

"Nonsense, nothing!" cried Simple. "Bop makes plenty of sense."

"What kind of sense?"

"You must not know where Bop comes from," said Simple, astonished at my ignorance.

"I do not know," I said. "Where?"

"From the police," said Simple.

"What do you mean, from the police?"

"From the police beating Negroes' heads," said Simple. "Every time a cop hits a Negro with his billy club, that old club says, 'BOP! BOP! . . . BE-BOP! . . . MOP! . . . BOP! . . . That's where Be-Bop came from, beaten right out of some Negro's head into them horns and saxophones and piano keys that plays it. Do you call that nonsense? . . . Them young colored kids who started it, they know what Bop is."

Langston Hughes, "Bop"

Mark Twain's well-known compliment to Harris that the framework of narration in his Uncle Remus tales was more important than the content of the tales ("The stories are only alligator pears [avocados]," wrote Twain in 1881, "one eats them merely for the sake of the dressing") goes against the grain of modern readings, which tend to value the tales' mythic action—their black folkloric kernels—but lament the stereotypical plantation mythology generated by old Uncle Remus's storytelling to the little white boy. For his part, Harris repeatedly insisted that he was only the "editor and compiler" of the tales, that they were not "cooked" but "given in the simple but picturesque language of the negroes, just as the negroes tell them."[61] Nevertheless, Harris's narrative frame is important not just for its enforcement of plantation mythology but because there are certain signs that, in his own sometimes confused and contradictory way, he went behind Remus's mask more frequently than some readers have suspected. Welding his own imagination to that of Remus, Harris used him to critique a range of southern problems and to comment on a time before slavery—an African time. The imaginative framework in which the animal tales of African American folklore are set, whether by the most rudimentary collector or by a publishing author such as Harris or Chesnutt, cannot always be firmly distinguished from the tale itself, for the fabrication of storytelling is the essence of both. It is this aspect of Uncle Remus's own role and his tales that Chesnutt would take further, turning it back on Harris, in his creation of Uncle Julius.

The manifold relations between Harris and Chesnutt can perhaps best be measured by a look at Harris's original portrait of Uncle Remus and the Chesnutt story that most directly responds to it. "A Story of the War" established Remus's position within the southern family that first owned him and then, following the Civil War, employed him. As it appeared in *Uncle Remus: His Songs and Sayings* (1881), the story also fixed the "faithful darky" characterization of Remus that Harris would have great difficulty throwing off. But what happened to the story between its first publication in the *Atlanta Constitution* in 1877, under the title "Uncle Remus as a Rebel," and its inclusion in the first Remus volume is even more noteworthy. The central action of the story is Remus's shooting of a Yankee sharpshooter who is about the kill his master, "Mars Jeems." In the newspaper version the Yankee, John Huntingdon, is killed; in the volume version he is only wounded (and loses an arm), thus allowing him to be nursed back to health, marry Jeems's sister, Miss Sally, and move with her to Atlanta after the war, taking with them Uncle Remus as an employee. In his reworking of the tale into a classic example of the North-South reunion theme so prevalent by the 1880s, Harris's most brilliant structural stroke was to make John and Sally's son the "little boy" to whom Uncle Remus tells his wealth of animal stories.

These features of the story are familiar to any reader of Harris, and critics have often enough taken Remus's shooting of John to be the best evidence of Harris's reactionary mythology. Yet not only were there such instances of slave allegiance in the war's history available to Harris, if he needed a model, but also Remus is shown to be markedly ambivalent: "It sorter made cole chills run up my back" to shoot a Union soldier, Remus tells John's visiting northern sister in his own narration of the incident, "but w'en I see dat man take aim, en Mars Jeems gwine home ter Ole

Miss en Miss Sally, I des disremembered all 'bout freedom en lammed aloose." The fact that it is John, his new employer, who was shot by Remus and lost an arm, is withheld until the last lines of the story, where Remus has an opportunity to tell us that in return for taking John's arm, he has given his own arms, to work for John. The theme of reconciliation thus operates on several levels. Remus pays tribute to his northern savior after shooting him in order to save his own southern master, and his story, during which he speaks "from the standpoint of a Southerner," is directed at an additional northern audience (not just John's visiting sister but by implication Harris's wider circle of readers who eagerly purchased his volume after the explosive popular reaction to his serialized Remus tales). A fine example of sectional reunion in literature, "A Story of the War" portrays the white South, in the immediate aftermath of Reconstruction, as restored to a loving, benevolent relationship with "the Negro." Despite his own liberal philosophy and demonstrable despair about purported racial progress in the South, Harris's stories seldom broke free from the careful containment of the "Negro problem" represented by Remus's narration of his participation in the war. Moreover, at the moment we meet him, in Atlanta in the 1870s, Remus is fed up with the "sunshine niggers" of Reconstruction (who beg his tobacco, borrow his tools, and steal his food) and longs to move back to the plantation with Mars Jeems.[62] Divided between the animal tales and the Atlanta sketches, *Uncle Remus: His Songs and Sayings* temporally displaces the "legends of the old plantation" and their narrative setting with urban satire, thus creating a structural nostalgia that corresponds to Remus's conservative opinions. In *Nights with Uncle Remus,* Harris not only moves Remus irrevocably back to the plantation (along with John, Sally, and the little boy) but in fact appears to transport the entire structure and setting of his storytelling into a vague antebellum past.

The second volume's remarkable elision of the two temporal frames of Remus's life, antebellum and postbellum, surpasses even Twain's deliberate narrative collapse of the two frames as a mechanism to reveal the persistence of slaveholding beliefs and actions. Still, the presence of a doubled temporal perspective is implicit in the Remus tales (and in Remus's own animal stories) from the very beginning. One suggestion of this lies in the concluding lines of the last tale told by Remus in the first volume. Offering to carry the tired little boy into the house after the conclusion of his story, a particularly gruesome one, Remus says: "I speck I ain't too ole fer ter be yo' hoss fum yer ter de house. Many and many's de time dat I toted yo' unk Jeems dat away, en Mars Jeems wuz heavier sot dan what you is."[63] Remus is still the beast of burden for the new generation of white men (by the last Remus volumes it is the "little boy's" little boy—a fussy, spoiled representative of the New South, in Harris's imagination—who is listening to Remus's fireside tales). As this allusion to Mars Jeems as the boy's uncle (one of several throughout the Remus volumes) reminds us, however, Remus was Mars Jeems's protector *and his slave* even when Jeems was a boy. Remus is not the "little boy's" slave in *Uncle Remus: His Songs and Sayings,* but he is in *Nights with Uncle Remus;* the second volume, as I will note, literalizes Remus's figurative slavery in the first through the retrogressive act of Harris's imagination. Although he has a very small, offstage role in the volumes, then, Mars Jeems represents plantation slavery in a very specific way: he remains the one saved by Remus's shooting of the Yankee, and he is the little boy's most direct male link to the past of slaveholding, as Remus is his link to the past of slavery.

If "A Story of the War" and Mars Jeems's role in it may be taken as constitutive of central structural features of Harris's mythological world, what relationship to it may be discovered in Chesnutt's story "Mars Jeems's Nightmare," which appeared as one of the seven stories in *The Conjure Woman?* "Mars Jeems's Nightmare" stands out among the conjure tales for several reasons. To begin with, it is one of the few that involve the conjuring of a white person, and it therefore occupies a more charged, potentially subversive political ground. In addition, the self-interested purpose of Julius's recital is more transparently figurative in this instance and the layering of the antebellum and postbellum time frames more instructive. In form the tale resembles a widely distributed African American folktale in the Master-John cycle, a group of stories in which the slave John (or Jack) and Master (ole massa, marster, and so on) square off in some kind of contest of wits; and as a tale of physical metamorphosis, it belongs with those that move in the direction of magic realism and can be allied to similar strategies in African folklore. But the story is also an example of Chesnutt's signifying upon Harris, for although Chesnutt might have taken his name from many sources, this Mars Jeems seems undeniably to be a reimagining of Harris's symbolically evocative character.

In the same letter, cited earlier, in which Chesnutt complained to Walter Hines Page about the difficulty of writing effective dialect, he remarked that he did not find the story of metamorphosis in "Mars Jeems's Nightmare" entirely novel but felt that his treatment of it was. "I have thought a good title for the story would be 'De Noo Nigger,'" he continued, "but I don't care to dignify a doubtful word quite so much; it is all right for Julius [to use the phrase], but it might leave me under the suspicion of bad taste unless perchance the whole title's being in dialect should redeem it."[64] This added insight into the issue of dialect on Chesnutt's part is important; but more striking here is the alternate title itself, which underlines the two-pronged action of the story. In "Mars Jeems's Nightmare" there are two "new niggers"—first, Mars Jeems himself, who by conjure is turned into a slave, brought to his own plantation, and made to undergo the cruelties of his overseer's regime; and second, Julius's grandson, a lazy, incompetent worker, representative of that postwar generation of "new niggers" about whom Uncle Remus often complains. John fires the grandson after a short trial period, but Annie rehires him after the moral of Julius's tale sinks in. Chesnutt's alternate title, "De Noo Nigger," thus addresses a contemporary sociological issue, yet it does so by forcing us to locate the roots of that issue in slavery and racism.

Although Julius may tell his tale in order to gain a more charitable attitude toward his grandson, his tale is powerful in its own right. Stopping at a spring to fill their water jugs, John, Annie, and Julius observe a man riding his horse with furious brutality. It turns out that he is the grandson of the subject of Julius's ensuing story of Mars Jeems McLean, who ran a harsh, hardworking plantation in the old days. Suppressing black folk culture ("dey wa'n't 'lowed ter sing, ner dance, ner play de banjo"), denying slaves any right to court and marry ("said he wuz n' raisin' niggers, but wuz raisin' cotton"), and giving his mean overseer, Nick Johnson, a free hand for cruelty, Mars Jeems is every inch the bad master. When one slave, Solomon, is whipped and his girlfriend sold because of their courting, he employs the conjure woman, Aunt Peggy, to "wuk her roots" and put a "goopher" on master so as to get his girlfriend back. Even though Aunt Peggy admits that she "has ter be kinder keerful 'bout cunj'in' w'ite folks," she agrees to conjure Mars Jeems. His experience of slavery under Nick Johnson is a nightmare lesson in the reversal of roles, but it is also an allegory of the phenomenon of the "noo nigger," as Mars Jeems is called throughout his period of magical transformation. Mars Jeems's incompetence as a laborer and his astonishment at the overseer's brutality reflect two things at once: his own acculturation as a white master and his figurative representation of the new generation of blacks locked into the ambiguities of the post-Reconstruction years, those who feel pride in living and working freely on the one hand, despair at the failure of civil rights and pitiful educational and labor opportunities on the other. Julius's characterization of the new Mars Jeems applies in both cases: he "could n' 'pear ter git it th'oo his min' dat he wuz a slabe en had ter wuk en min' de w'ite folks." Of course, when the conjure is removed and Jeems recovers from his "monst'us bad dream . . . a reg'lar, nach'ul nightmare," he has undergone at least a limited moral renovation. He fires his overseer, initiates a more humane regime for his slaves, and prospers personally and financially.[65]

"Mars Jeems's Nightmare" stops a good deal short of undermining plantation slavery. Jeems does not free his slaves but only models his new plantation on the extended "family" advocated by proslavery idealists such as George Fitzhugh. In this respect, however, Julius's depiction of the slaves as recognizing Jeems's right as "de marster" to do as he pleases while despising Nick as "nuffin' but a po' buckrah" offers only a beggar's choice between between benevolent and cruel subjugation. Similarly, his assertion that "in dem days any 'spectable pusson would ruther be a nigger dan a po' w'ite man," while it purports to illuminate the complex psychology of class on the plantation, more directly points to the half-truth of the postbellum southern contention that racial violence was a manifestation of lower-class white backlash. It cannot be proved that Julius is speaking entirely ironically in his statements. But his specious signifying on the rights of the master is clearly calculated to reveal the racist genealogy of John's naive framing comment about Julius's personality. Julius, he observes, had been so long accustomed to think of himself a slave that in the postwar years "he had been unable to break off entirely the mental habits of a lifetime, but had attached himself to the old plantation, of which he seemed to consider himself an appurtenance."[66] It is Chesnutt who is speaking ironically now. Julius, although he is no Remus, is indeed an appurtenance of the plantation myth, inscribed by the habits of white thought into the southern (and national) consciousness. As a commentator on black attitudes he here repeats a "darky" view whose implications are scarcely less unsettling for the post-Reconstruction years than for the antebellum, no matter how certain we are that Chesnutt intended Julius's remarks as a test of his audience's moral acuity. The story, that is to say, employs Julius both as a character and as a symbol, the two forces not always in perfect congruity.

Before looking in more detail at Chesnutt's reworking of Harris's points of view, I would like to turn briefly to a second informing feature of "Mars Jeems's Nightmare" that will serve to characterize that difference more sharply. Chesnutt's tale, as he recognized, is novel in its treatment but not in its general plot. Although the story may have a number of antecedents, it strongly resembles a common example of the Master-John stories generally entitled the "Philly-Me-York" tale. In the tale's typical outline, Master pretends to go away on a trip (to "Philly-Me-York" or "Phillynewyork," as the slaves confusedly, or creatively, understand it) but dons a ragged disguise and returns to his plantation, where he catches his trusted slave John, as he had suspected, throwing a big "frolic" for the slaves, dancing, drinking, butchering Master's hogs, wearing his clothes, and so on. When Master reveals himself, John is caught and punished, or runs away, or, alternatively, talks his way out of the trouble. Some versions of the tale have John escaping to the next county, getting whipped, or begging forgiveness at the end. But Zora Neale Hurston's version in *Mules and Men* (1935), which essentially combines two Master-John tales, is far more intricate and complimentary to John. When Master threatens to hang John for "killing up all my hogs and havin' all these niggers in my house," John engages his friend Jack to hide in the hanging tree and strike matches while John prays for God to throw bolts of lightening if he is willing to grant John's prayer that Master and his family and plantation will be destroyed. The trick works, of course. Master is so frightened that he gives John "his freedom and a heap of land and stock" before running away himself: "and that's how come niggers got they freedom today."[67] Hurston's tale traces emancipation not to patient subservience but to cunning and aggression.

The Master-John stories are a strong influence on Chesnutt's tales generally (the form seldom appears in Harris's Remus tales), and they are one of the most powerful examples of African American folklore. Sometimes Master wins the contest, and sometimes John; but the strategies at work make it clear that from John's black perspective they constitute a methodology of rebellion and a means of attacking the master directly, in deeds or more often in words. More than occasionally the tale ends with Master's defeat, even his death, as in a combination animal-John trickster tale recorded by Hurston in which Master is tricked into drowning himself. For the most part, however, the tales maintain a taut balance of power (an "uneasy partnership" in a "harsh and lethal conflict," as Richard Dorson remarks), and John is able to gain only limited victories through his verbal cunning and exploitation of the masked roles of slave existence. In this respect they measure the price of power and subjugation in more human terms, displaying both the rewards and the hazards of the trickster role. The Master-John tales were written down far less often than the animal trickster tales, suggesting a self-censorship by black informants more stringent than usual. Because they do not disguise their meaning in the costumes of animal mythology and are typically narrated as though they were memories rather than fantasies, the Master-John tales are more overtly threatening but also more pragmatic and balanced in their dramatization of the struggle for control. They demonstrate effectively that the great majority of slaves did not internalize the rules or humiliating postures of slavery but engaged, at the level of imagination as well as that of action, in outright rebellions against the master's power.[68]

Insofar as a number of the Master-John stories supplied by postbellum informants scrutinized "values and beliefs of an old-fashioned country Negro, an Uncle Tom, [as] seen through the eyes of a cynical, disillusioned Negro," in Harry Olster's formulation, one may analogously configure Chesnutt's relation to Harris—or rather, the relation of Julius to Remus. In the post-Reconstruction era the Master-John tales inevitably transfigured the master-slave relationship, either literally or figuratively, into a boss-laborer relationship. Even more strikingly than Harris's animal tales, which were by their very nature projected into a mythic past, whether antebellum or African (or extrapolated into a timeless realm that has made their message appear universal), the Master-John stories could easily be modernized. As is more often the case, they could be made to exist in two time frames at once, thus offering a critique of contemporary race relations and of plantation mythology. For example, a tale entitled "De New Nigger an Eh Mossa," which was collected in Charles Jones's *Negro Myths from the Georgia Coast* (1888), appears to utilize the same play on the phrase "new nigger" as does Chesnutt in order to signify upon the lingering effects of slavery. The gist of the simple story, rendered by Jones in a very thick dialect, is this: when the New Nigger complains that he works in the field while Mossa sits around, the latter explains that he works with his head. The New Nigger soon thereafter stops working; when Mossa confronts him, the slave tells Mossa a riddle, which Mossa cannot solve; he laughs at his own error and neglects to punish him.[69] Jones's tale is notable less for its plot—those recorded by Hurston and others are far more complex—than for its proof that the black man can also "work with his head." We cannot know if Jones's informant (or Jones himself) intended the complex pun or not, but his translation of the idea of the "new nigger" out of the colloquial legacy of slave folklore and into the political present, where the phrase New Negro would soon take on a range of

connotations generated by African Americans rather than white southerners, allies it with the more contemporary Master-John tales that are echoed
in "Mars Jeems's Nightmare" and other of Chesnutt's conjure tales.

The Master-John paradigm in general, and the Philly-Me-York story in
particular, give special meaning to "Mars Jeems's Nightmare"—and to its
relatively conservative resolution. As in the folktale Mars Jeems goes away
on a trip and comes back in an unrecognized disguise, here one of actual
blackness (also, after he is turned back into a white man, he is so ragged
and unkempt that Solomon does not recognize him). He discovers not
the festive cavorting of his slaves but the grim daily realities of his own
regime. Chesnutt, in an act of signifying that perhaps called forth from
his subconscious a Master-John story told by "old Aunt This or old Uncle
That" (as his blithe account of the interaction between memory and
creativity had put it), thus transfigures the rudiments of the folktale into
a vehicle for the critique of slavery and of post-Reconstruction race relations. In making the tale the "fruit of his own imagination," Chesnutt also
lends it a moral dimension missing from most of the Master-John tales:
Master is not only defeated in this case; he also undergoes a moral transformation.

The conservative import of the ending—the fact that Mars Jeems does
not go so far as to free his slaves—must be measured against the image
of the family that Chesnutt intended to create here. Throughout his work
Chesnutt came back obsessively to the figure of the family, once divided
and destroyed by slavery (and often by miscegenation), now attempting
some form of reconciliation. In doing so he countered two prevalent
literary forms of the day. Plantation mythology crushed out the reality of
slave suffering and family trauma by highlighting the loyalty of black
"servants" to their white southern masters before, during, and after the
Civil War. Even when fictional and stage minstrelsy took note of the slave's
escape from cruel bondage, his postwar return to his family on the plantation was the vehicle of a new racialist ideology. For example, a skit
entitled "Uncle Eph's Return," included in Edward Marble's 1893 minstrel
handbook *The Minstrel Show, or Burnt Cork Comicalities,* portrays its hero
returning to his plantation family of wife, children, and grandchildren
forty years after his escape. Proclaiming that "Massa Lincum took de one
load off dese shoulders" while he joins in a concluding dance of "merry
darkies," Uncle Eph is the sign of ideological reunion, at once celebrating
the end of slavery and representing black racial subordination to minstrel
typology. Likewise, the flourishing of literature devoted to the reunion of

North and South, which frequently turned on the theme of cross-sectional marriage, whether in the maudlin stories of numerous magazine writers and novelists or the radical racist productions of Thomas Dixon, depicted a white view of the war's effects that typically subsumed the black family within its protective mythological bonds of affection.[70] Chesnutt, by contrast, wrote throughout his tales of the destruction of black family ties by punishment and separation, and he satirized not just the deceitful historiography of slavery but also the genre of "darky" romance in a number of stories, most famously in his intricate trickster narrative "The Passing of Grandison." The tales of *The Conjure Woman* are filled with instances of the fracturing of slave families (as in "Sis' Becky's Pickinniny") or the master's forbidding of courting and marriage altogether (as in "Mars Jeems's Nightmare"). "The Wife of His Youth," I have suggested already, embeds the reunion theme in Chesnutt's theory of African American cultural production; while in stories such as "Aunt Lucy's Search" or the comic "Uncle Wellington's Wives," Chesnutt also wrote specifically of postwar black reunion, a further way of exposing the underlying racism of sectional reconciliation. The stories of both the color line and conjure, that is to say, are driven by plots of family separation, and the predominant purpose of ironic judgment in the one case and of conjure in the other is to repair the family disintegration caused by slavery. "Mars Jeems's Nightmare" brings both of these possibilities together in one tale.

The "lived happy ever after" ending of Julius's narrated tale, as John characterizes it, appears saccharine: "W'en de niggers see how fine Mars Jeems gwine treat 'em, dey all tuk ter sweethea'tin' en junseyin' [courting] en singin' en dancin', en eight er ten couples got married, en bimeby eve'ybody 'mence' ter say Mars Jeems McLean got a finer plantation, en slicker-lookin' niggers, en dat he 'uz makin' mo' cotton en co'n, dan any yuther gent'eman in de county."[71] Still, despite its conservative posture within the ideology of antislavery, the ending must be seen to heal the broken family ties of the plantation and to operate within a post-Reconstruction context as well. The harmonious plantation family was hardly Chesnutt's ideal of social relations. His lesson for John and Annie, and for his readers, was that the generation of New Negroes must be given opportunities to prosper and that the sense of the southern as well as the national family must become truly interracial. Whereas Harris sometimes tentatively held forth plantation slavery, in its most humane forms, as a plausible labor relation (his ideal was a yeoman agrarianism) and a potentially fine realization of paternal society, Chesnutt maintained no such illusion. As always, Julius, playing the "John" role in a Master-John confrontation with his boss, gets the best of his own master, John. Even though the carpetbagger John has not yet undergone the moral transformation that affects Mars Jeems, Julius's grandson gets a second chance, while Remus's grandson, by contrast, will go to jail.

The fact that the narrated story ends not with freedom but with a more humane slavery, then, is misleading. For Julius's tale does gain from John a more lenient attitude toward his grandson, part of the new generation born after slavery; and in the nearly mad laughter of Mars Jeems as he interrogates his overseer about his cruelty toward the "noo nigger" who was "puttin' on airs, des lack he wuz a w'ite man," it registers a double frenzy, signaling both Jeems's vengeful hatred of the overseer (the emotion Chesnutt could easily imagine in a slave but could not, apparently, afford to portray except through dislocation) and the mad laughter of his own self-recognition as a master. Julius is so forward with the moral of his tale in this case—white folks must make allowances for "po' ign'ant niggers w'at ain' had no chanst ter l'arn"—that the discrepancy between John's and Annie's separate recognitions of it hardly matters.[72] As the other "noo nigger" in the story, Julius's grandson represents the generation, Chesnutt says, for whom allowances must be made, economic opportunities and education carefully provided. For this reason the significant place of the concept of the New Negro (the "noo nigger") in "Mars Jeems's Nightmare" and the Harris stories it alludes to is worth examining more closely.

Because of its association with Alain Locke's famous 1925 anthology of black writing by the same name, the New Negro has often been associated by modern readers solely with the generation of creative and culturally independent black intellectuals and artists who appeared in the aftermath of the First World War, a period loosely described by Locke as the Negro Renaissance and by subsequent critics as the Harlem Renaissance. The term has earlier and more diverse uses, however, and it is tempting to speak of two New Negro periods, differentiating between the more economically successful, politically active generation of the later period and the generation associated with Booker T. Washington, many of whom also invoked the term. The New Negroes of the 1920s were likely to define themselves self-consciously as progressive and politically radical in comparison to the seemingly more accommodationist "Old Negroes" of Washington's era; their postwar philosophy was one of race pride, even separatism, absolute economic and political equality, and cultural integrity. Yet when it came to such generational distinctions, reality was often difficult to separate from stereotype. As Locke wrote in the introductory essay of his collection, the Old Negro was "more of a myth than a man," "a stock figure perpetuated as an historical fiction partly in innocent sentimentalism, partly in deliberate reactionism" to which the Negro himself contributed a share through the "protective social mimicry forced upon him by the adverse circumstances of dependence." The New Negro, by contrast, was achieving a "spiritual emancipation" and appeared to be slipping out "from under the tyranny of social intimidation and to be shaking off the psychology of imitation and implied inferiority."[73]

Although Locke's essay found the rebellious spirit of the New Negro to be a relatively recent phenomenon, elements of a comparable "radicalism" are evident within the first phase of the New Negro movement, whose proponents, as though in serial regression, similarly differentiated themselves from the Old Negroes of an earlier postbellum generation. The spirit of rebellion against the old racial order appeared in a variety of forms. The turn of the century saw a great flourishing of black historical writing variously infused with a sense of nationalistic purpose and committed to describing a continuity between African civilization and the history of black Americans. The phrase New Negro proliferated during the 1890s, and distinct signs of cultural race consciousness were in evidence. Du Bois's *Souls of Black Folk* appeared in 1903, for example, and the song that became the popularly accepted Negro national anthem, "Lift Every Voice and Sing," by James Weldon Johnson and Rosamond Johnson, was composed in 1900. Washington's volume of historical sketches and prose portraits of successful blacks, *A New Negro for a New Century* (1900), can be seen as a necessary precursor to the social and intellectual activism of Du Bois and the cultural independence associated with Locke's anthology. But signs of the new racial spirit can be traced back further. Charles Jones's folkloric use of "New Nigger" in 1888 has already been noted. Washington entitled an 1895 essay "The New Negro Woman," and the phrase appeared again that same year in an editorial in the *Cleveland Gazette*—where Chesnutt might have seen it—devoted to African American civil rights and the rise of a class with education, refinement, and money, to cite two examples. In his nationalist novel *Imperium in Imperio* (1899), Sutton Griggs announced that "the cringing, fawning, sniffling, cowardly Negro which slavery left, had disappeared, and a new Negro, self-respecting, fearless, and determined in the assertion of his rights was at hand." A few years earlier, in 1895, J. W. E. Bowen had defined the consciousness of the New Negro in *An Appeal to the King* (1895) as "a racial personality under the blaze of a new civilization," and as far back as the early 1880s, in an address entitled "Right-Mindedness," Alexander Crummell had spoken of the special needs of "a new people, running a race which they have never before entered upon; and undertaking civilizing achievements, from which their powers and capacities have been separate for long centuries."[74]

The concept of the New Negro is thus relatively fluid over at least a forty-year period. Indeed, the turn-of-the-century generations flow so much together that Wilson Moses has argued that the Harlem Renaissance grew from a conception of the New Negro that not only existed as early as the immediate post-Reconstruction era but could be traced ultimately to "a Christian black nationalism, with its roots in the African Civilization movement of the antebellum decade."[75] Be that as it may, the idea everywhere suggests the dawning of a consciousness that looked toward the new century as a time when the debilitating effects of slavery would at last be left behind. But it was a consciousness nonetheless formed as well by the current bleak prospects for any large-scale black advance, and the positive concept of the New Negro had to counter the negative meanings with which it was loaded in the discourse of racism. For instance, the image of the New Negro had to confute southern lamentations for the passing of the "old darky" such as those in Thomas Nelson Page's stories in *In Ole Virginia* (1893) or his essays in *The Negro: The Southerner's Problem* (1904), where he regretted that the "old-time Negro" had become "so rare that even now when a gray and wrinkled survivor is found he is regarded as an exceptional character, and he will soon be as extinct as the dodo."[76] The intention of Washington's illustrated volume and similar books and essays (devoted not just to achievement but often to gentility, self-respect, and cultural refinement) was to counteract the racist image of blacks as regressive, infantile, or animalistic and to restructure the race's own image of itself. Even works of avowed protest and nationalism depended on a relatively homogenous set of ideals borrowed from the middle-class culture of white America.

This generation, then, was itself "new" in comparison with the "old" generation of slaveholding days, but it remained to be seen what progress was to be permitted. In racist ideology the "old-time darky" of the plantation was superior to the Negro of the New South, and emancipation, it was argued, had ushered in an age of childlike loss of direction, mental and physical decline, and a propensity for violence on the part of blacks. For African Americans, to rise or progress by means of the idea of the New Negro therefore meant not so much inventing a new idea as appropriating and inverting one that was already being used—especially in the South, but in the North as well—to control and demean the generation of blacks who grew up after slavery. With comparatively few exceptions white (and some black) sociological accounts of the race problem identified retrogressive and criminal tendencies in the "new" generation of blacks. As a typical 1903 essay in *Harper's Weekly,* "The Negro Problem and the New Negro Crime," put it, "the new negro at the South is less industrious, less thrifty, less trustworthy, and less self-controlled than was his father or his grandfather."[77]

These generational differences and variable conceptions of the New Negro, inscribed into the tentative moral pedagogy of "Mars Jeems's Nightmare," are explored in a number of Chesnutt's works, at length in *The Marrow of Tradition.* As I have already indicated, it was Joel Chandler Harris whose representations of the "old" and "new" Negroes Chesnutt had most to answer in *The Conjure Woman.* Harris was a man of multiple writing personalities. Many of his essays were directed against his contemporaries' racist caricatures of the new generation of blacks, while his Atlanta sketches allow Remus himself to participate in such regressive judgments. Likewise, Harris's animal tales are one of the richest records of African American culture set down with remarkable authenticity. Again, however, it is not the stories but the storyteller who has aroused the most animosity against the Remus tales. Bernard Wolfe's influential essay on Harris characterizes his tales as a monument to the South's ambivalence, an "unconscious orgy of masochism" in which love and hatred of blacks is mixed. Wolfe's essay drew on a notorious self-characterization of Harris's authorial personality in which he described his writing self as the "other fellow" inside him who came forth and took charge in his fiction, burning off otherwise potentially damaging internal energies. In Wolfe's flamboyant interpretation, Remus is this suppressed artist within Harris (the "other fellow"), and his recital of the animal tales is the creation of a counterweight to the "tottering racial myth of the post-bellum South," one in which "blackness becomes black magic."[78] In fact, both characterizations, though important, are nonetheless too simplistic. On top of the editor-author split that Harris admitted and Wolfe explored in separating Harris from Remus, remarkable duplicities multiply in the fiction itself.

Although the narrative frames of Harris's animal tales sometimes clearly depict Remus in the darky stereotype, it was the historical sketches and sayings of the volumes, where Remus was a contemporary urban figure, not a remnant of the agrarian plantation world (whether antebellum or not), that were most obviously governed by prevailing racial assumptions and played for minstrel comedy. In *Uncle Remus: His Songs and Sayings,* for example, Remus is the butt of watermelon humor; he jokes with the editors at the *Atlanta Constitution* (that is, with figures such as Harris himself) that news of the black community can always be found in "de calaboose," where some "new nigger mighter broke into jail"; and he adopts a belittling attitude toward black education: "Hit's de ruinashun er dis country. . . . Put a spellin'-book in a nigger's han's, en right den en dar' you loozes a plow-hand." In a sketch entitled "Race Improvement," the potential irony in Harris's view of the aftermath of Reconstruction dissolves into Remus's reactionary characterization of the creation of a "new nigger":

> Dey er sorter comin' 'roun'. Dey er gittin' so dey b'leeve dat dey ain't no better dan w'ite fokes. W'en freedom come out de niggers sorter got dere humps up, an' dey staid dat way, twel bimeby dey begun fer ter git hongry, an' den dey begun fer ter drap inter line right smartually; an' now . . . dey er des ez palaverous ez dey wuz befo' de war. Dey er gittin' on solid groun', mon. . . . You slap de law onter a nigger a time or two, an' larn 'im dat he's got fer to look atter his own rashuns an' keep out'n udder fokes's chick'n-coops, an sorter coax 'im inter de idee dat he's got ter feed 'is own chilluns, an' I be blessed ef you ain't got 'im on risin' groun'. . . . An' den ef you come down strong on de p'int dat he oughter stan' fas' by de fokes w'at hope him w'en he wuz in trouble de job's done. W'en you does dat, ef you ain't got yo' han's on a new-made nigger, den my name ain't Remus.[79]

Remus's textbook paternalism here underscores rather than undermines the prevailing white southern view of the "new nigger." Predisposed to loafing, stealing, and effrontery, the post-Reconstruction Negro must be cut down to size and made to "stand fast" by his white friends if he is to get on "rising ground." The current alternative is illustrated by the story Remus tells of his own grandson, William Henry, in *Uncle Remus and His Friends* (1892), a comic account of the futility of William Henry's education, with a Washingtonian message about the value of manual labor over book learning. To Remus, William Henry is an "owdacious" "wall-eyed Affikin" who has just enough "new issue nigger" in him to guarantee a trip from jail to the gallows. Unable to master the agricultural skills that would give him suitable employment under a white boss (while delivering milk, for example, he absurdly mistakes a man's ear-trumpet for a pitcher and fills it with milk), William Henry has, according to Remus, been ruined by his "town nigger blood": "Ef eve'body wuz votin' fer 'im, he could n't be gwine no straighter ter de chain-gang."[80] (Voting, however, is something Remus finds equally mystifying. The same volume includes "Intimidation of a Colored Voter," in which the actuality of violent intim- idation of blacks attempting to exercise their rights is reduced to a burl- esque, with Remus confusing the candidates for national election with participants in a cakewalk and using his rheumatism as an excuse to avoid voting. Harris, by contrast—and schizophrenically, one could say—wrote essays in support of black suffrage.) The burlesque of Remus's grandson William Henry, however one construes the place of white responsibility for his social and economic dilemma, is governed by deep skepticism about the progress of the New Negro, which for Harris was principally tied to the industrialization of the South that he feared but that was inevitably generalized in the minstrel humor of the sketches to result from ineradicable racial characteristics.

The contrast between Remus's attitude toward William Henry and the sympathy generated for Uncle Julius's grandson in "Mars Jeems's Night- mare" is pronounced—and all the more peculiar given Harris's often progressive racial views. There is no question that Harris's attitudes toward blacks were very complicated; that he was sympathetic to the plight of William Henry's generation in the New South; that he outran most of his contemporaries in his advocacy of black civil and political rights; and that he used his writing as a form of private psychotherapy and coded revolt against the extremity of southern racial customs. Even though his essays show him to be an unapologetic paternalist, when measured against the southern demonology of his day Harris was often and obviously liberal. But his views are hardly predictable. He editorialized often against racism but also felt that black Reconstruction proved the Negro to be "no more than . . . a little child who had wandered, quite by accident, into the halls of legislation." "Like a novice learning to play chess," Harris wrote in a 1904 essay, "The Negro of Today," "he moved whatever pieces he was told to move, and when no one was observing him closely he moved others for his own amusement." In this essay and others, Harris, despite his condemnation of slavery as an institution and his increasing advocacy of African American rights and education, continued to glorify an ima- ginary plantation life of the antebellum past. As in his 1877 essay "The Old Plantation," he called into memory a moonlit feudal world of beneficent masters and plaintively singing Negro slaves, now "hushed into silence by the necessities of a new dispensation." The "green and gracious" antebellum world "has passed away," wrote Harris in a tribute applicable as well to his own storytellng, "but the hand of time, inexorable, yet tender, has woven about it the sweet suggestions of poetry and romance, memorials that neither death nor decay can destroy."[81] Unable to sacrifice his own recreated childhood memories to a frank acknowledgment of slavery's corruption and brutality, Harris thus often projected a utopian vision in which kind masters oversee the needs of, and in turn are cared for by, thankful slaves. The Harris who wrote the essays was largely the Harris who wrote the minstrel sketches of Remus in contemporary society, a fact evident enough in the later volumes, where Remus is more and more Harris's mouthpiece for his attacks on the New South.

And yet there was the "other fellow" who wrote the animal tales, with their wealth of comically nuanced commentary on the race of the masters and their haunting evocation of an African American mythic world. As Wayne Mixon has contended, Harris's utopian vision did not derive from a misapprehension of historical or contemporary racial realities. Subordinated in Harris's fiction to his critique of the New South and to his exposé of white racism, the idealized portrait of antebellum life was more often an atemporal, mythic construction in which an imagined childhood and a fantastic "creetur time" blotted out the unpleasant truths of southern history for black and white alike. Indeed, when he obscured the harshness of slavery, it was often to indulge a nostalgia for a black world, not a white one. In an era of the most radical racism, Mixon persuasively argues, Harris waged war on "a white world characterized by materialism, scientism, and disdain for the imaginative sensibility" by predicating human harmony on "an appreciation of the worth of the black experience."[82] There is no better way to understand the meaning of the African American folklore revival of the late nineteenth century as a phenomenon of racial politics or as a means for writers such as Chesnutt to reconfigure the available white stereotypes than to see clearly the importance of Harris's own idiosyncratic but marked contribution to black cultural life.

Consider the complicated role of Brer Rabbit himself in Harris's tales. Harris called attention to what he took to be the Negro's selection as "his hero the weakest and most harmless of all animals" but attempted disingenuously to write off Brer Rabbit's trickery as "mischievousness," not malice. As Harris would clearly have known, however, it is plain to every reader that the rabbit's victories over the fox and other strong animals are motivated by the most transparent aggression and obsequious mocking contempt of the slave for his master, or the black man for his white boss. Harris, one could say, masked his own mockery in order to drive its lesson home. On the hotly contested question of the folktales' origins, Harris also showed a subtle sense of the power of indirection. Whether or not the figure of the animal trickster could be traced to Africa was important to cultural archaeology, to be sure, but it was irrelevant to its immediate significance in the black American imagination. More than half of Harris's animal tales can, in fact, be traced to African origins; but their precise genealogy is less important than the fact that Harris himself invoked an African ancestral dimension in his devoted act of literary recreation while at the same time pushing the archetypes in directions that were specifically American.[83] That is to say, he wrote with a pronounced consciousness of the dense layers of resistance to slavery and signifying upon the masters built into the tales, but also of a legitimate African heritage that could counteract routine racist denigrations of African American culture as one rooted in ignorance and barbarism. If Chesnutt signified upon Harris—and he certainly did—he also had much to learn from him.

Disguising his own account of American slavery and race relations in the costumes of animal lore, Harris was the first to pay careful tribute to the great complexity of inherited African American folklore. Even so, he came perilously close to perpetuating the sentiment that blacks were indeed closer to the animal kingdom or, at the least, savage in their naturally determined behavior. Part of Harris's popularity, an unavoidable dissonance between intention and effect, no doubt came from such an identification in the minds of many white readers. Folklore analysis itself more than a few times corroborated this view, even with the best of intentions. Although it is widely separated in its assumptions from racist diatribes such as *The Negro a Beast* by Charles Carroll, W. S. Scarborough's folkloric argument that "the primitive negro is on intimate terms with the wild animals and birds, with the flora and fauna of the wild stretches of pine woods among which for generations his habitation has been pitched," could easily lend support to racist evolutionary theory. (Both Scarborough and Carroll were black.) As Frantz Fanon remarks, in a psychopathological reading inspired by Wolfe's essay, Harris's white audience could easily tell themselves that the the black man is "in closer touch with the 'lower animals' than with the white man, who is so far superior to him in every respect." But while Scarborough's definition of Negro primitivism conforms to one construction of pastoral possible in racist theory, Harris's tales go in a different direction. Harris made the mask of animal lore a means to explore not the plantation world of contemporary social science and neo-Confederate literature but the antipastoral world of chicanery and violent revenge staged in the subculture of slavery and its aftermath.[84] The two worlds were separated by the color line of Jim Crow which cut a jagged path through American culture as much as it did through American political and social life; but they were also interlocking, superimposed worlds in which could be set the most powerful explorations of America's defining moral dilemma.

It is possible, of course, to read the animal tales as an account of violence contained within the slave community or its precursor African societies. It is also possible to read them outside a racial framework altogether, as their variable appearance in different forms throughout world mythology would suggest, or to question Harris's most basic assumption about the material he utilized. In his contribution to *The New Negro,* for example, Arthur Huff Fauset charged that the Remus tales were contorted adaptations, not the pure records of folklore that Harris claimed. Attacking Harris for his creation of a mythic plantation figure in Remus himself, Fauset also disputed the identification made by Harris and others between the rabbit and the slave. The African American would not choose Brer Rabbit as a prototype of himself in slavery, contended Fauset, for the rabbit of African folklore is a strong, notable figure, not the weak one imagined by Harris, who "transgress[ed] so far from the true ways of the folk spirit and the true lines of our folk art."[85] Nevertheless, Fauset's essay, though its focus on Harris's "distortions" is warranted, draws too stark a boundary between the so-called folktales and the framework in which they are set. In addition, its thesis is contrary to almost all other commentary about the equivalence between the slave and the rabbit, which Harris in any event took directly from the black storytellers at Turnwold plantation, where he lived as an adolescent printer's apprentice, imbibing the African American culture that would form the core of his Remus tales.* As the

---

* The question of Harris's own sources aside, sufficient evidence existed before the turn of the century to identify the rabbit with the slave trickster. Abigail Christensen argued in the preface to her *Afro-American Folk Lore* (1892), for instance, that "the Rabbit represents the colored man. He is not as large, nor as strong, as swift, as wise, nor as handsome as the elephant, the alligator, the bear, the deer, the serpent, [or] the fox, but he is 'de mos' cunnin' man dat go on fo' leg' and by this cunning he gains success. So the negro, without education or wealth, could only hope to succeed by strategem." Some collected tales, such as Mary Owen's *Old Rabbit, the Voodoo, and Other Sorcerers* (1893), moved the rabbit closer to a human conjurer, while others

preeminent trickster of African American folklore, Brer Rabbit need not always represent the black man or woman; like other trickster figures, he may be read as the generalized symbol of anarchic revolt against limiting controls and suppressive power, whether moral, political, or social. Yet his message of violent conquest over the larger, more powerful animals and over Mr. Man serve to place him specifically in the liminal realm of enslavement, where victory often occurs only in a fantasia of amoral destructiveness.

Just as it has become commonplace for literary critics and historians to lament Harris's popular influence, which is seen to be so laden with elements of racism, so it has become a commonplace for folklorists to lament quietly that Harris has been eliminated from reading lists because of his "racist" portrait of Remus as a plantation darky, and to advise instead that his animal tales should nonetheless be studied in isolation for their record of authentic black folklore. On the face of it both objections are reasonable, at least for schoolroom pedagogy. But both views likewise

---

simply saw him as a rather pedestrian black trickster, whether slave or freedman, interested in daily survival. In a Georgia folktale about the origins of the rabbit's foot as a good luck charm recorded in 1899, to take one example, the rabbit defeats Ole Mammy Witch Wise, who bewitches the animals so they cannot get their meals out of the garden. Two African American work songs recorded in the early twentieth century (the first also with a variant featuring "coon" instead of rabbit) repeat the identification of the slave and the rabbit:

> Rabbit is a cunning thing
> Rambles in the dark,
> Never knows what trouble is
> Till he hears old Rover bark.

> In the garden
> Stealing cabbage.
> White man's gun,
> Rabbit run.
> Rabbit stew,
> That'll do.

See Christensen quoted in Lawrence Levine, *Black Culture and Black Consciousness: Afro-American Folk Thought from Slavery to Freedom* (New York: Oxford University Press, 1977), p. 112; Emma M. Backus, "Tales of the Rabbit from Georgia Negroes," *Journal of American Folklore* 12 (1899), 108–15 (Backus's essay is also of interest for the fact that its dialect writing is much closer to modern forms of black English than to the stereotypical Negro dialect of nineteenth-century foklore and literature); and White, *American Negro Folk-Songs*, pp. 233–35. On the rabbit as a common trickster figure in East African folklore (as opposed to West African, where the tortoise is more common), see Alan Dundes, "African Tales among the North American Indians," in Dundes, *Mother Wit from the Laughing Barrel*, pp. 124–25.

ignore the fact that the nightmare effect of the tales, as racial commentary, resides precisely in the contrast between the animal violence and the false pastoral tranquillity of old Remus's avuncular affection for the little white boy. Following the practice of many collectors of folklore and songs in the period, Harris no doubt rigidly censored the language and content of his tales. Like Howard Odum and Guy Johnson, who refused to set down folk songs they considered vulgar (a rather significant number, as Abrahams and other more recent collectors have shown), Harris suffused his tales with an air of Victorian propriety that must be counted as a large share of Remus's problematic character. Nevertheless—or perhaps because of such necessary censorship—the level of violence embedded within the wry comedy of Remus's tales is extreme: to take only the duels of Brer Rabbit with the other animals, especially his nemesis Brer Fox, is to find an abundant catalogue of atrocities. In complimenting Harris for the power of his narrative form, Mark Twain must have shrewdly recognized that it was the plantation frame that in fact heightened the effect of such violence. Think for a moment of Remus's invocation of his own Mars Jeems in the concluding animal story of *Uncle Remus: His Songs and Sayings,* where Remus carries the sleepy little boy back to his plantation comfort. He performs this calming, sentimental act, so in keeping with Harris's mischievous announcement that Remus "has nothing but pleasant memories of the discipline of slavery," after concluding his cycle with a tale of extreme mayhem and racial threat. In "The Sad Fate of Mr. Fox," the last tale, Brer Rabbit first tricks Brer Fox into getting killed by Mister Man; he then serves Brer Fox's head to his wife and son as if it were a piece of beef, and escapes from their revenge; finally, as Remus tells the boy, some folks say Brer Rabbit married ole Miss Fox, while others say the Rabbits and Foxes are still quarreling.[86]

Not least because it follows a tale devoted to a monogenetic theory of the origin of races, in which Remus argues that "way back yander" "de time wuz w'en we 'uz all niggers tergedder," the story of Brer Rabbit's ghastly trickery of the Fox family, followed by the implied threat of his mixing blood with them, heightens the unnerving anxiety that is built into the nostalgic framework of the tale. The violence of the trickster tale reminds us that a black man is speaking to a white boy, and Remus's allusion to Mars Jeems further underscores the pulse of ambivalence that his own submission to bondage—whether to the little boy or, in an earlier day, to his uncle—always has running beneath it. As Abigail Christensen observed in the case of her own collection of tales: "If we believe that the tales of our nurseries are as important factors in forming the characters of our children as the theological dogmas of maturer years, we of the New South cannot wish our children to pore long over these pages." To what degree Harris saw through the extraordinary tension submerged in the ending of his first collection or, indeed, deliberately created it is hard to measure. Both his own neurotic personality and his allegiance to the ideas of southern racial paternalism inscribed his writing with a deep ambivalence. In a letter asserting the veracity of his tales, Harris said that his "sole purpose in this was to preserve the stories dear to Southern children in the dialect of the cotton plantations," and most of his contemporary readers appear to have agreed with Thomas Nelson Page's view of Harris, that for the real language and habits of "all American Negroes of the old time, his works will prove the best thesaurus." But should we not assume that this is Harris the double-voiced trickster speaking? His frequent claims about authenticity and veracity, about being a mere compiler and editor, and about the simplicity of Remus's tales ("There is no pretense that the old darkey's poor little stories are in the nature of literature, or that their re-telling touches literary art at any point," he wrote in the preface to *Uncle Remus and His Friends*) form part of the central deceptive trope of the volumes—the wily implication that they are specimens of pure plantation mythology.[87] In the trickster tales dating from the antebellum years, masters may have glimpsed the doubled visage they feared lay within every slave—Nat Turner hidden behind the mask of Uncle Tom. In layering the minstrel world of Remus's commentary on the politics of the "new nigger" upon the magic world of the animal trickster, burgeoning with the libidinous energy of revenge, Harris tore apart the plantation myth even as he contributed to its generation in wildly popular forms.

Brer Rabbit is a trickster disguise for Remus, who in turn is a trickster disguise for Harris himself. This superimposition of created selves that Harris offers the reader is clarified in those moments where he self-consciously comments on the multiple layers of Remus's stories and the boy's near-recognition of the deeper truth they can reveal. On two occasions in *Nights with Uncle Remus,* for example, the little boy asks embarrassing questions about Brer Rabbit's tricking of Mr. Man, once when Brer Rabbit steals a wagonload of Mr. Man's money, and earlier when he steals Mr. Man's meat. In reply to the boy's question about the theft, Remus answers: "In dem days de creeturs bleedzd ter look out fer deyse'f, mo' speshually dem w'at ain't got hawn and huff [horn and hoof]." Further questions are forestalled by the arrival of the little boy's father, upon which

Remus, rubbing his hands and looking serious, reflects: "Dat little chap gitin' too much fer ole Remus—dat he is!" Insofar as the tales in which Mr. Man is Brer Rabbit's antagonist represent a more marked intrusion of the world of the masters into the dream world of the animal tales, this truncated scene invites the reader to reflect upon the evident revolutionary function of Harris's tales.[88] Just as Remus's statement brings him closer than usual to spelling out the allegory of slavery, so the little boy, presumably, is getting too close to recognizing the underlying truth of the tales. Paradoxically, of course, this is just what he is supposed to do—or what Harris's reader is supposed to do. Moreover, the seeming antebellum setting of the volume heightens the significance of the boy's questioning, for Remus, as a slave, cannot admit that Brer Rabbit actually stole from Mr. Man, nor can he explain to the boy why it should not be considered stealing. The boy is not his intellectual match, by any means, but the simple moral challenge traps Remus in the vise of enslavement, separating him from the white boy, like Jim from Huck Finn, by a wide cultural gulf.

In placing his second volume of tales in a plantation setting whose antebellum dimension was more pronounced, I would argue, Harris accomplished a brilliantly challenging act of self-examination, one that clarifies his relation to Chesnutt. While the motion of Harris's imagination was backward, that of Chesnutt was forward. Julius's tales continually hark back to antebellum times, but the lesson of his signifying always lies in the present—something given greater weight by the fact that his audience is not a little southern boy but an adult northern couple. The thematization of literary reunion allows Chesnutt to situate the problem of the "noo nigger" in a more self-consciously national light. As Robert Bone has perceptively argued, Chesnutt "used Harris as a mask," subverting the mythology of the Remus legend (at least as it had been interpreted by Harris's white audience) with the "demythologizing spirit of antipastoral."[89] Harris remained beholden to public approbation of his views on race progress and was too internally divided to speak forthrightly except from behind the cunning facade of the folktale, but Chesnutt had the advantages of relative anonymity, of color, of residence in the North, and of a privileged vantage point on Harris himself, his precursor. Moreover, although Chesnutt's formal relationship with African culture—that is, his adoption of significant cultural forms of narrative indirection, semantic intonation, and signifying, all of them summed up, as we shall see, in the concept of conjure—was finally the stronger one, he, unlike Harris, did not rely directly on collected oral testimony. Such tales lingered in his unconscious, as he at last recalled, but his creative relation to that material could be more fluid, less tortured than Harris's. He too became an authorial trickster, but he did so by subverting the figure of Remus with that of Julius and by replacing the changeless, allegorical dreamworld of animal contention with the spirit world of conjure. This is nowhere more evident than in the two authors' respective treatments of mythic time and the origins of African American folk culture.

"De Ole Times," Slave Culture, and Africa

In his essay on conjure Chesnutt admitted that he did not know where the term "goopher" came from, and he said he was not sure whether any other writer had used it, though it was in common oral use in the South. As a matter of fact, William Wells Brown had used it in *My Southern Home* (1880), a book with which Chesnutt was certainly familiar. We know, moreover, that the term usually referred to graveyard dirt and probably derived from the Ki-Kongo verb *kufwa*, "to die".[90] Chesnutt could easily enough have found out more about the term (and perhaps he did), but he hardly needed to be aware of its distant African origins to make use of it in his tales, any more than a conjure man or woman needed to know its etymology to apply its powers. The point here is that the thorny issue of origins (whether of folktales or of black music, the two so often in close linguistic proximity) bears closely on our understanding of Chesnutt and on the articulation of an African American aesthetic in the late nineteenth century, though resolution of the debate is neither possible nor necessary. The theory of the African origins of black American culture forms a significant part of both Harris's and Chesnutt's tales; concurrent evidence of European sources or influence in that culture hardly negates the African argument, and in any case, as I have already contended, what matters most is the transfiguration of received materials in the African American cultural imagination.

Even though within a decade he would disgustedly renounce arguing about the question after professional folklorists had mistakenly attacked him, Harris confidently asserted the African origin of his animal tales in his first two Uncle Remus volumes, offering in the preface to *Nights with Uncle Remus* a fairly elaborate comparative study of African, South American, and African American folklore. The dominant view of the 1890s and the subsequent few decades remained in favor of the African uniqueness of black American folktales, with a number of folklorists specifically tracing the Uncle Remus tales to West Africa. Harris took his inspiration to write the Uncle Remus tales from a now famous essay by William Owens appearing in *Lippincott's Magazine* in 1877, in which the author called attention to the animal tales of black American folklore (especially the Tar Baby story) and declared that they were "purely African." Even though the tales were condensed from a variety of African tribal traditions and inevitably "complicated by the frequent infusion into them of ideas evidently derived from communication with the white race," Owens argued that the "predominant traits of negro character" could be perfectly collated with the "predominant traits of African folk-lore." Owens's thesis represents a strong version of the African origins argument; and the first essay to be devoted to Harris himself as a folklorist, by T. F. Crane writing in *Popular Science Monthly* in 1881, corroborated this argument. Other folklorists writing in the *Journal of American Folklore,* the *Southern Workman,* and *Popular Science Monthly,* among other journals, tended to follow suit, even when they argued for a more syncretic theory.[91] But the key issues were hardly to remain so simple.

One of the paradoxical elements in Bernard Wolfe's essay on Harris (first published in 1949) lies in his contention that the Remus tales are not African in origin but predominantly European. Wolfe has been proved wrong, but he argued that what he took to be Harris's erroneous claim of African origins in fact counted *against* their racial radicalism: "If they came from the Congo, they offered no symbolic blows to the Americans." In Harris's fragmented psyche, torn between a desire to find "the venomous American slave crouching behind the rabbit" and a countering defensive insistence on the "Africanism" of the rabbit, Wolfe saw a mirror image of the South. Because ethnology and the folklore revival were embroiled in theoretical battles over the links between cultural evolution and theories of socioracial hierarchy, the discrediting of an evolutionary theory in which the African origins of black folktales was crucial, Wolfe contended, might have led Harris to identify a notion of black consciousness that was threatening to him as a southerner.[92] What is interesting today about Wolfe's interpretation, aside from his error about the tales' origins, is its assumption that the African and African American features of the tales could not form a continuum or work in harmony. Africa, in this view, paradoxically became a kind of "Sambo" disguise. For Wolfe, Africanism was itself a mask for Harris, a means of dodging worrisome questions about the rebellious threat contained in his tales; if the tales were African, then they dealt with nature or with distant mythology or perhaps with the quaint beliefs of savage religion. The fact is, of course, that the African origin of the tales—the vital remembrance of ancestral narratives shadowed forth in however fragmented a form—can be seen to be perfectly in keeping with the subversive, even the violent radicalism of their message. That is to say, the racist assumptions of ethnology in Harris's day and beyond ironically inverted the content of the tales most germane to a nationalist African American cultural politics. The adaptation of the animal tales to an American setting no doubt stripped them of much original meaning; but what the process of retelling and transformation preserved could awaken latent narrative "sounds" such as the tonalities and rhythms of banned or censored music on the plantation or the signifying indirection of trickster storytelling. Whether or not Harris's assertions about the African origins of his tales were based on the remarks of his Turnwold storytellers or those he spoke with later—and there are strong hints to be found in Remus's own opinions that go beyond the technical questions of ethnology—Harris's intuition was uncanny.

In the face of the challenge of readers and professional folklorists, Harris abandoned his claim to know the origins of the animal tales (of his elaborate preface to *Nights with Uncle Remus* he wryly remarked in *Uncle Remus and His Friends,* "I knew a great deal more about comparative folklore then than I know now") and contemptuously dismissed folklorists as hindrances to his simple task of collecting the tales.[93] This disclaimer may, however, represent the height of cunning on Harris's part. He was convinced that what he heard from his ex-slave informants came from the other "old world"—not from Europe but predominantly from Africa. At the same time, it served Harris's purpose to blur the question of origins, for nothing is more peculiar about the tales and the effect they would have had on a contemporary reader (or listener, since they were so widely read to children) than the absolute dreamlike fluidity of narrative temporality that the volumes taken together create.

The general scheme is perplexing: the sketches of *Uncle Remus: His Songs and Sayings* locate Remus, as I have noted, in the employ of John and Sally Huntingdon, living in Atlanta during Reconstruction, though the animal tales in the same volume place him on a plantation of indistinct historical moment; *Nights with Uncle Remus* and *Daddy Jake, the Runaway* (in part) seem clearly to transport the storytelling Remus back to an antebellum period, but leave him still employed by—rather, as he makes clear, enslaved to—John and Sally (for he still speaks, now anachronistically, of past incidents with the little boy's "Unk Jeems," who of course is the master Remus purportedly saved in "A Story of the War," before the little boy's birth); *Uncle Remus and His Friends* continues the conceit that Remus is an antebellum storyteller, but, like the first volume, this one also contains the urban sketches in which Remus delivers comic (and racist) jeremiads about the the modernization and racial upheaval of post-war Atlanta; *Told by Uncle Remus* adds another twist in its suggestion that Remus has returned to plantation life—but now certainly a modern plantation—after living in Atlanta with John and Sally, once the little boy is grown and married, the father now of the new "little boy" to whom Remus tells his tales. (Other volumes published at or after Harris's death— *Uncle Remus and Brer Rabbit* [1907], *Uncle Remus and the Little Boy* [1910], *Uncle Remus Returns* [1918], and *Seven Tales of Uncle Remus* [1948]— continue in the same vein.) Because Harris did not set out to write a series of volumes when his sketches and tales of Remus first ran in newspaper serialization, one cannot find premeditation in the puzzling time scheme. Harris simply changed Remus to suit his developing sense of narrative strategy. Although a great deal could be inferred from a close study of the transformation in Remus and his tales volume by volume, two matters are of primary interest: Harris's imaginative fusion of the postbellum and antebellum frames, and his exploration, by a further temporal disorientation, of a black distant time in the prehistory of Africa (the time of "my great-grandaddy's great-great-grandaddy," as Remus epochally projects it on one occasion in *Told by Uncle Remus*)[94] or at least well before the world of enslavement.

At odds with the logic of its relationship to the first Remus volume, *Nights with Uncle Remus* is cast ambiguously back into an antebellum time whose nearly mystic ambiguity is no mistake. As Harris states in the preface, repeating the fact three times in the space of two sentences, he "endeavored to project [the tales] upon the background and to give them the surroundings which they had in the old days that are no more." The "old days that are no more" turns out to be an amorphous idea, but its immediate reference in the book's context is to "plantation life in the South before the war." The conclusion of the volume, in contrast with the unsettling combination of violence and nostalgic comfort of *Uncle Remus: His Songs and Sayings,* expresses the most oppressive sentimentality of the plantation myth. In a Christmas Eve serenade by the slaves gathered in the quarters, to which the white men and women at the big house listen "with swelling hearts and with tears in their eyes," Harris offers a virtual hymn to paternalism entitled "My Honey, My Love." The words of the seemingly nonsensical song of animal courtship are at first glance less important than its symbolic effect on its audience, especially the little boy. Lulled to sleep by the plantation chorus, the little boy is again carried home to the big house by Remus, who continues

> singing softly in his ear all the way; and somehow or other the song seemed to melt and mingle in the youngster's dreams. He thought he was floating in the air, while somewhere near all the Negroes were singing, Uncle Remus's voice above all the rest; and then, after he had found a resting place upon a soft warm bank of clouds, he thought he heard the songs renewed. They grew fainter and fainter in his dreams until at last (it seemed) Uncle Remus leaned over him and sang.
>
> *Good night.*[95]

This extraordinary conclusion, complete with Harris's own benevolent salutation, could not fail to type him for later readers as the most egregious of Old South mythographers. (It is not clear whether the song itself is essentially African American or one of Harris's stylized adaptions, suited to his predominantly white audience. The effect on the listeners, in any event, is the same.) The song, especially as it is extended by Harris's depiction of its performative context, resembles the most saccharine verse being composed by white and black dialect poets of the day, and it corroborates the overweening image of the mammy (here fixed in an emasculated Remus) that was recorded by Dorothy Scarborough in the section of her black folk song study devoted to lullabies: "One discerns in [the melodies] something more than ordinary mother-love,—as marvelous as that is,—a racial mother-heart which can take in not only its own babies, but those of another, dominant, race as well. What other nation of mothers has ever patiently and with a beautiful sacrifice put alien children ahead of its own—in outward devotion if not in actual fact?"[96] Scarborough's last phrase unravels her heartwarming portrait. The mythology of the black mammy drew in some instances upon the facts of devoted service, of course, but its most diligent proponents often failed to admit that the role of the mammy was built, too, of outright oppression or grim economic necessity. Harris takes this mythology to its limit. In its deliberate blend of black choral music, then being popularized by groups of singers such as those from Fisk or Hampton, with the angelic portrait of the faithful retainer bending over the slumbering boy, like

Uncle Tom over the heaven-bound Little Eva, the passage seems almost parodic. Harris pays an awkward compliment to black music in his suggestion that the masters compare it favorably to European classics. The dominant impression created here, however, is that of a post-Reconstruction South that still feels itself enveloped within the soothing embrace of black tenderness, the warm heart of slaveholding's most skewed, painful dreamworld.

The Remus of the conclusion is perfectly in keeping with the "old-time darky" portrayed in Harris's most prominent race essay, "The Negro as the South Sees Him," which would not appear until 1904, when Harris's own skepticism about the New South had reached its height and his own sketches of Remus in modern Atlanta had become more obviously cast in fixed minstrel molds. Foreshadowing the later thesis of the Agrarians, Harris represents the dream world of plantation mythology as a "romance," a less ideal world than yeoman agrarianism but one nonetheless set in direct contrast to the unfeeling, money-getting world of the New South. Remus, in this view, is not servile or sentimental but humble, dignified, and loving toward his good masters. Perhaps, Harris admits, he is putting forward a plea for slavery, but only because "in some of its aspects it was far more beautiful and inspiring than any of the relations that we have between employers and the employed in this day and time. That, however, is a fact for the poets and the romancers to deal with." As for the "old family servants" who are either "gone or going fast," he adds, "we shall never behold their like again. May their souls rest in peace."[97] Harris's resurrection of the Old South's feudal defense of slavery as a labor system was directed as much against whites as blacks, but neither the conclusion of *Nights with Uncle Remus* (the work of the poet and the romancer) nor much of the framing characterization of Remus in subsequent volumes could gainsay its tempting fantasy.

Unless, of course, it is a trap, truly a parody. Harris's complicated psychology leaves the possibility uncertain at best, but the pacific lullaby may conceal within it the strains of resistance that are evident in some songs of the first Remus volume.* Just as Harris maintained that Stowe's unintentional defense of slavery in *Uncle Tom's Cabin*—its portrait of

---

* Two of the songs in *Uncle Remus: His Songs and Sayings* are of particular note for their introduction of a voice that counters plantation archetypes. "A Plantation Serenade," for instance, is an incipient blues that speaks of theft, mobility, drinking, and sexual pleasure as responses to

beautiful characters and tender black-white familial relations—would "not be found in the text of the book" but rather in the sentimental dreamworld to which it gives rise, the reverse may be true of Harris's work. The ending of *Nights with Uncle Remus,* with its perhaps less-than-unconscious allusion to Uncle Tom and Little Eva, is not so thoroughly contradictory as that of *Uncle Remus: His Songs and Sayings,* where Brer Rabbit's terrifying violence against the Foxes lies just behind the soothing murmur of Remus's good-night voice. "My Honey, My Love," however, conveys a double message. Its pacifying, hymnodic, yet decidedly black sound, which Harris remarks is "ridiculous enough when put in cold type, but powerful and thrilling when joined to the melody with which the negroes had invested it," covers and at the same time reveals a world beyond that of

---

white dominance; like Frederick Douglass's "We Raise de Wheat," it makes clear the hierarchy of the racial economy:

> De ole bee make de honey-comb
> De Young bee make de honey,
> De niggers make de cotton en co'n,
> En de w'ite folks gits de money.

Another of Harris's song transcriptions, "A Plantation Chant," is excerpted and attributed to Remus, his voice once more comforting the little boy at the conclusion of "A Plantation Witch," a tale of black conjure. The boy goes to bed frightened, but it soothes him "to hear the strong, musical voice of his sable patron, not very far away, tenderly contending with a lusty tune":

> Hit's eighteen hunder'd, forty-en-eight,
> Christ done made dat crooked way straight—
>   En I don't wanter stay here no longer;
> Hit's eighteen hunder'd, forty-en-nine,
> Christ done turn dat water inter wine—
>   En I don't wanter stay here no longer.

The chorus that is added in the more extended transcription in the "Songs and Sayings" section of the volume underlines the specific element of protest against enslavement that is here woven into traditional folk hymnody:

> You ax me ter run home,
>   Little childun—
> Run home, dat sun done roll—
>   An' I don't wanter stay yer no longer.

In addition to laying a somewhat dissonant tranquillity on top of a frightening bit of black folklore, Remus's serenade conceals a message that, to the boy and perhaps to Harris's less astute readers, is lost amidst the comforting melody of old Remus's voice. See Joel Chandler Harris, *Uncle Remus: His Songs and Sayings* (New York: Viking Penguin, 1982), pp. 171, 146, 170.

the white boy and the white masters.[98] Composed of fragmented, puzzle-like invocations of a threatening nighttime world that mixes the animal lore of Remus's tales, the night world of the slaves themselves (*their* time, as opposed to master's time), and the journey toward the nighttime world of death, "My Honey, My Love" subtly undermines the tranquillity it creates, much as Harris's entire output of Remus lore did. The effect is magnified in the context of *Nights with Uncle Remus* itself, for as the volume's title implies, its storytelling is set in a nighttime world, one that infuses the simplicity of childhood with the potential for fear and night-mares of the kind revealed often enough in the brutal anarchy of the animal lore. With the introduction of the Gullah storyteller Daddy Jack and other slave narrators, moreover, the volume alludes to a more fully realized black world and, in the case of Jack's tales, one closer in spirit to African times.

Because the tales themselves can be shown to have African sources in most instances, it would be possible, following Wolfe, to argue that Harris's appropriation of them, which became increasingly secondhand over the course of his career, was further evidence of the white manipu-lation of African American culture that would take more public and commercial forms in coming decades. Harris's insistence that the tales had not been "cooked," however, and his demonstrable respect for the "times" from which the tales had come, indicate not just a desire to satisfy the demands of professional ethnology but also an actual faith, contrary to his view of the "old-time darky," in the separateness and dignity of African and African American culture. The "times" of the tales, then, are of utmost importance to Harris's view of black culture and to the final effect of the Remus volumes. On the one hand, Harris invoked the African "times" in which men and animals lived in one continuous, culturally articulated world, the world that many black folk and some folklorists (Newbell Puckett, for example) felt pulsing through the tales;[99] but, on the other hand, he also invoked a more complex set of temporal levels that refracted African times through the times of slavery and of postwar black experience.

"Dem times" can be an atemporal realm in which animals are the same as people ("mo samer dan folks" or "same like folks") or, in virtually the same narrative breath, a preslavery world in which Brer Rabbit and "dem yuther creeturs" do not have to do the work of fetching buggies and horses. At moments "dem ole times" appear to be antebellum times seen from the perspective of Reconstruction or after, a time that the white folks might know as well as the blacks—a time coincidental with the plantation myth. "Dem days" can also be an allusion to the slaves' own world, even within slavery, as when Remus alludes to the animals' courting while slyly looking at Daddy Jake (who is courting Aunt Tempy). And it can stand in signifying contrast to "dese days" of slavery, as when Remus, telling the story of Brer Rabbit and Mr. Man's wagon of money, reverses the power relation of master and slave: "In dem days folks had ter keep out der way er ole Brer Rabbit." In addition, however, it can point to a specific African world before slavery, when "de creeturs wuz bossin' dey own jobs," or when everything was larger and stranger: "Folks is lots littler now dan what dey wuz in dem days, an likewise de creeturs." More particularly, it can describe a world of African American folklore in the act of creation. When the little boy begins one tale by describing a dream in which he imagined Brother Fox had wings and flew after Brother Rabbit, Remus responds positively by describing his own vision, in which the creatures gather together in his cabin to "run over de ole times wid one er n'er, en crack der jokes same ez dey uster," or "git up a reg'lar juberlee" with makeshift musical instruments. Giving his storytelling voice "a gruesome intonation quite impossible to describe," Remus recreates the world of slave music, itself a memory of African music:

> Dem creeturs dey sets dar . . . en dey plays dem kinder chunes w'at moves you fum 'way back yander; en many's de time w'en I gits lonesome kaze dey ain't nobody year em ceppin' it's me. Dey ain't no tellin' de chunes dey is in dat trivet, en in dat griddle, en in dat fryin'-pan er mine; dat dey ain't. W'en dem creeturs walks in en snatches um down, dey lays Miss Sally's pianner in de shade, en Mars John's flute, hit ain't nowhars. . . . W'en I shets my eyes en dozes, dey comes en dey plays, but w'en I opens my eyes dey ain't dar. . . . I des shets my eyes en hol' um shot, en let em come en play dem ole time chunes twel long atter bedtime done come and gone.[100]

This brilliant passage from *Nights with Uncle Remus,* in which Harris reflected upon the sources of his own creativity, works on several levels at once. In contrast to the sentimental plantation song that concludes the volume, this music offers a plain tribute to the music of the slave quarters— the music made after dark on the instruments that could be found or fashioned from homely utensils such as a trivet, a griddle, and a frying pan. "Juberlee," in Remus's phrase, mixes *jubilee* and *juba,* the freedom spiritual and the African-born clapped and patted rhythm of slave folk music. That it was night music, created in the slaves' own secret time, is underlined by Remus's dreamlike evocation of it. What his dreamworld also signifies, however, is the layering of temporal frames available in the passage. Because *Nights with Uncle Remus* is set in antebellum times, the world of music invoked is also specifically African, "way back yander" (a fact also suggested by the little boy's dream of the flying fox); but because Remus's narrative frame always includes an implied postwar present, an implied dimension of plantation mythology, the earlier time of the dreamworld is also that of slavery—not the torment of enslavement itself but the world made by the slaves beyond white control, a world continuous with but characteristically after "de ole times" in Africa. From Harris's perspective, there was inevitably some component of nostalgia and racist misrepresentation in that world. For Remus, however—and this seems one of many places where Harris most fully projected himself into his black character—this is the world of memory, of creativity, of African origins and living African American culture. Readers who have missed this dimension of Harris's work have missed all the best in it—everything he most wanted to say and preserve for a better time.

When the editors of the *Southern Workman* issued a call in 1893 for the collecting of black folklore and instituted a new department of "Folk-Lore and Ethnology" in their journal, they cautioned readers not to try to "improve" the stories or songs they submitted. They assumed, moreover, that their black audience would have far greater success than whites in collecting authentic folk material. No doubt the editors benefited from the popularity of Harris's volumes just as much as they may have doubted the complete legitimacy of his stories. Explicitly calling for material that would authenticate black Americans' cultural links to Africa and counteract the argument that the middle passage and the rigors of slavery had annihilated such cultural memory, the editors sought to "make out of the scattered, unwritten history which now lies in the brains and the hearts of the old folks an ordered and comprehensive whole that will show to all who have an interest in it the past of the Afro-American." Whatever his disability as a collector, Harris was frankly confident that he participated in such an enterprise. That "de ole times" could also include a frank reference to Harris's own art is evident in the last clear allusion to them in his published works. As Remus says to the little boy in the opening tale of *Uncle Remus Returns*: "De ol' times is done gone, an' ef' 'twan'n't fer deze ol' tales nobody wouldn't know dat dey yever wuz any ol' times."[101] The tales do that service, as folklorists have always pointed out; but they also offer a running commentary both on the meaning of preserving "de ole times" and, what is more, on the paradoxical fusion of temporal modes that made the generation of white plantation fantasy the very means by which Harris could help set down for history the African roots of black American life.

Charles Chesnutt, whether he liked it or not, wrote against the backdrop of Harris's great popularity. Too much his contemporary to be a precursor with whom Chesnutt might struggle in filial conflict, Harris was an object of Chesnutt's signifying even as he was, one might guess, one of his best teachers. Although it is known that he read the Remus tales to his children, Chesnutt left little clear evidence of his thoughts about them—except the evidence we may deduce from the conjure tales themselves. I have suggested already how "Mars Jeems's Nightmare" can be read as a reply to Harris's own Mars Jeems; that signifying relationship is prototypical of the larger relationship between the two writers, and between the animal tales on the one hand and the conjure tales on the other. In an 1890 letter to George Washington Cable, Chesnutt bluntly placed Harris among those plantation writers who "give us the sentimental and devoted negro who prefers kicks to half-pence." Chesnutt did not doubt that black persons of such "dog-like fidelity" existed (he gave the recent example of a Negro who wrote the governor of North Carolina offering to serve the seven-year prison sentence of his old master), but he added, "I don't care to write about these people; I do not think these virtues by any means the crown of manhood."[102] Black manhood would remain a key element of Chesnutt's fiction, as it had been throughout black male literature from Walker, Douglass, and Delany forward. *The Marrow of Tradition* takes up the transition from the generation of "faithful" servants to the independent New Negro in a nearly bewildering array of examples that place the trope of manhood very much at the novel's center, and there is nothing in Chesnutt approaching a hint of adherence to the doctrines evident in Harris's essay "The Negro as the South Sees Him." The implication in Chesnutt's letter, on the contrary, is that Harris's blacks, like those actual "old-time darkies" who were still living out the debilitating effects of slavery, are not men. As Remus is drawn, this judgment would apply in some instances but not in others. In any event, Uncle Julius would have few signs of the "darky" about him except those he might put on as a deliberate mask. But Chesnutt's own evocation of the "de ole times," like that of Harris, employed an analogous superimposition of historical time frames that allowed him to explore both the resurgence of plantation typology in post-Reconstruction history and the countering origins of modern African American culture in the "ole times" of slavery, the middle passage, and Africa.

Not that Chesnutt was incapable of "darky" humor. In one of his first published stories, "An Eloquent Appeal" (1888), the appeal on behalf of black civil rights turns out to be a black sharper's prelude to selling a "Magic Corn Cure." Such humor disappeared quickly from Chesnutt's stories. Another in apparently the same mold, "A Roman Antique" (1889), has a surprising twist. An old black panhandler, claiming to be the former servant of Julius Caesar, begs a quarter for rheumatism medicine from the narrator. Momentarily entranced by a vision of imperial Rome, the narrator mistakenly gives the man a twenty-dollar gold piece. The difference between the con man and the conjure man, that is to say, is a relatively small but very important one. Julius, in his tales, is certainly a trickster, and one could say that he is a con man of sorts, his tales carefully calculated to serve his own interests. But he is not literally a conjure man; conjure belongs to another world, to "de ole times" that Chesnutt in his essay on conjure represented, perhaps coyly, as times of bewildering "superstition." Later he would self-effacingly describe the conjure tales as "naive and simple stories, dealing with alleged incidents of chattel slavery, as the old man had known it and as I had heard of it." Perhaps we should not find surprising such detachment from the "superstitions" of slavery in the author who had confided years earlier to his journal that he considered country people's belief in ghosts, luck, cloud signs, witches, and the like to be ignorant "nonsense."[103] According to these statements, as well as the subliminal self-portrait in "The Wife of His Youth," one might conclude that Chesnutt felt compelled to write on behalf of the less educated, less properous black folk descended directly from slavery, even if he could not accept some of their beliefs. Nonetheless, such seemingly unambiguous assessments by Chesnutt put into doubt neither the belief in conjure nor, as a consequence, its psychological power as an instrument of resistance or revenge when turned against the white world, or when transfigured into a narrative strategy by Uncle Julius or Chesnutt himself.

The efficacy of conjure lay principally in the belief in it, and such "nonsense," for Chesnutt (as, occasionally, for Harris in his portrait of Remus as well) was a potent reservoir of meaning and linguistic power. Conjure, as it is usually defined in Chestnutt's stories, entails a transformation or metamorphosis in physical form, across two levels of animate or inanimate existence—the human and animal being the most obvious. Likewise, the stories appropriate the figurative power of conjure: operating on confluent levels of antebellum action and post-Reconstruction action, conjure is the allegorical component that bridges the seeming discrepancy between the levels of temporality, casting the two time frames into a simultaneous event. In this respect the stories are magic realism not just in their utilization of fantastic elements but more centrally in their narrative capacity to dissolve and rearrange the reader's historical sensibilities and racial assumptions, bringing "de ole times" of slavery forward into the post–Civil War present and splintering the prevailing structure of plantation mythology. Like the conjure woman working her roots, Chesnutt employs the power of linguistic metamorphosis to work his own "roots"— the pun seems quite deliberate—recovering the past of slave culture and beyond it echoes and retentions of the middle passage and African life. Such a power, drawn from conjure while remaining different from it, did not diminish the force carried within the African American oral narrative tradition but rather augmented it by casting back to an even older time, an inchoate ancestral time, and inserting into the literate, published form of white American culture surviving African traditions of eloquence and verbal inspiration.

Talking Bones: Conjure and Narrative

When he first proposed a volume of conjure stories to Houghton Mifflin in 1891, Chesnutt hesitantly called attention to his race (despite the fact that "the infusion of African blood is very small—is not in fact a visible admixture") and spoke of his submitted manuscript, whether out of slight ignorance or slight arrogance, as "the first contribution by an American of acknowledged African descent to purely imaginative literature." He added that the people he wrote of "have never been treated from a closely sympathetic standpoint" by "a writer with any of their own blood." Although Chesnutt also said that he would not necessarily want his color advertised if the book were published, letting the book stand or fall on its merits, his color, once it had been mentioned, could not be ignored, as his own letter indicates. With extreme caution but also with extreme canniness, Chesnutt wrote as a man of African descent and wrote of people whom he thought had not been well represented in the plantation tradition of Harris and Page. If he was guarded about announcing his own race, he also furnished his publishers lists of African American newspapers so as to guarantee that he would reach a black audience.[104] Chesnutt, one could say, carried the trope of conjure, if not a personal belief in it, into the very stratagem of his own career. He wore the necessary mask of whiteness (and, like Homer Plessy, could have worn it without detection), but he claimed his African American heritage in promoting the authenticity of his literary voice. In doing so, he inserted tricksterism into the calculated game of the American literary market, much as Uncle Julius regularly inserts the tricksterism of his tales (a rational form of conjure) into the calculated game of his own economic relationship with John, Annie, and other whites.

As a result of Chesnutt's ambivalence and his similar erasure of the boundary between his own storytelling and the tales of Julius, his portrayal of "de ole times"—he too used the phrase—was no less complicated than that of Harris. Like Harris, he superimposed commentary about current race relations and the rise of the New South upon allegorical tales of the antebellum period; the conjure tales, like Remus's animal tales, always exist on these two planes at once. But whereas Harris invoked a further temporal dimension, that of an African prehistory shadowed forth in the "creetur" time of many of Remus's tales, Chesnutt invoked through Julius's concept of conjure less a temporal than a psychospatial representation of a separate cultural world of blackness horizontally coexistent with the crushing world of slavery but also reaching by implication into an African past. Even though belief is critical to conjure's effectiveness, the literary artist need only believe in the belief, as it were. Both Julius's belief in conjure and the trust we as readers are seemingly asked to put in him are radically unstable. Robert Hemenway, moreover, is misleading in his suggestion that Julius himself believes that all his conjure stories are true. What he believes in, rather, is the *legitimacy* of conjure and in the power and "truth" of his stories' moral implications. The stories themselves, as they are deployed by Julius in his contest of wits with John, function as "lies" in the classic African American folkloric sense—as tales that destroy the barrier between redaction and invention in order to place all discourse in the realm of manipulation and power. Julius's tricksterism exposes the world as a web of linguistic pathways conditioned by various hierarchies, most of all in this case the economic and political dominance of white over black. Like the slave tricksters of the animal tales and the conjure tales, Julius's narrative work unravels the web of language that supports the racial order, revealing it to be not a natural arrangement but a construct of political artifice.[105] The marginal world between redaction and invention that Julius's narratives bring into the foreground of storytelling is also the marginal world between slavery and freedom, whose geography was more pronounced than ever in the wake of emancipation. Moving conjure into the realm of the imagination, Chesnutt did not undermine its legitimacy but preserved it in the only way that he thought possible. As a result, his tales were more than fine reconstructions of folklore; they became a probing theoretical statement about the transition between oral and literary forms in African American culture.

The lead story of *The Conjure Woman* and Chesnutt's most anthologized tale, "The Goophered Grapevine," though it is not his best, is perhaps the most striking commentary on Chesnutt's role as storyteller and author. In addition to being one of the tales most heavily saturated with demonstrable folk motifs, it is also the clearest expression of the place of the conjure tales within American culture. The tale, in fact, takes culture as its subject, and perhaps it is for this reason that Chesnutt attempted to cloak his debt to preexistent folklore materials in commenting on the volume. At an ambiguous but apparently post-Reconstruction date, John moves to North Carolina because of his wife's ill health and there takes up "grape-culture," which, like most southern industries, "had felt the blight of war and had fallen into desuetude." The ruined plantation that he takes over anticipates the blighted landscape of the South ("the Egypt of the Confederacy") that was to be given such power by Du Bois in *The Souls of Black Folk*. Because the general premise of the narrator's move to North Carolina deliberately echoes that of Albion Tourgée in *A Fool's Errand* (Chesnutt's fixation on the success of Tourgée's novel, which he noted on at least two occasions, supports the likelihood that the trope of settling in the South combined Tourgée's experience with Chesnutt's own life as a displaced southerner), the tale also looks backward in its literary genealogy.[106] Like Tourgée's autobiographical narrator, John from the beginning is locked into the mode of foolish naiveté that characterizes his perspective in many instances throughout the tales; and his position as an outsider to the South, even when it is treated sympathetically, is the means for Chesnutt to scrutinize both his moral pretensions and his cultural, racial blindness.

Like other of the conjure tales, "The Goophered Grapevine" drew not just on the archetypes of folklore but also on typecast roles of popular culture. In particular, Chesnutt may have borrowed several key tropes, puns, and dramatic elements from the minstrel show. John is the interlocutor, or straight man, in the show staged in the conjure tales, with Julius functioning as the end man, given the job of cracking hidden jokes or satirizing John's politics and his ignorance (a function perhaps strengthened by the fact that Julius was a fairly common name for minstrel figures).

Also, even though Chesnutt no more identified with John's obtuse morality than did Melville with Delano's, John also stands to a degree for Chesnutt's own entry into the South as a northern author, though in his case one with distinctly southern roots. Like John, he may have suffused the tale with an air of Victorian propriety. In his version Henry's hair grows lushly every spring, whereas in the analogous folktale cited by Hemenway the man who eats the goophered grapes finds that each season his penis gets larger. (The cycle of exploitation is the same in both tales. In "The Goophered Grapevine" Henry's master resells him as a prodigious laborer every spring; in the folktale the slave's master starts "advertising that he had a nigger that could beat any man in bed and make any woman cry for him to stop.") And, like Aunt Peggy, who here and elsewhere in the tales sells her power to white masters as well as to slaves, Chesnutt may have felt that his own imaginative engagement of conjure bifurcated between commercial profit in the world of white culture and the preservation of distinct strains of African American culture. The enterprising narrator John intends to revive the once-luscious scuppernong vines, but he also intends to "introduce and cultivate successfully a number of other varieties." Julius, of course, spins a tale calculated to dissuade John from purchasing the land and thus undercutting his own black market business in grapes. His claim, that some of the old vines have indeed survived and that only he can distinguish the conjured vines from the new ones, completes the figurative framework of the story. Grape culture is a trope for culture itself here. John's revival of the old vines and his introduction of new varieties makes the vineyard flourish, so that he derives considerable income from his shipments to the North. Yet although Julius's production goes underground and he is reduced to something of a Washingtonian retainership, he stays on as a spinner of tales and as the obvious voice of the other culture—that of the slaves—which has also been displaced.[107]

The whole structure of "The Goophered Grapevine" mimics a post-Reconstruction social and cultural economy, not least in the story of the goophered slave Henry. Identified here as another "noo nigger," Henry is sold over and over again, much to his white master's profit, before finally withering away once the Yankee stranger "bewitches" Mars Dugal with his shortsighted advice for raising a bigger crop of grapes. The intrusion of the Yankee, who "dug too close under de roots, en prune de branches too close ter de vine" and burned the life out of them with "lime en ashes," can be read as the military invasion during the war itself or as the military occupation of Reconstruction; but it also contains a Remus-like reflection on the invasion of northern technology into the fragile agrarian economy of the New South of Chesnutt's own day. Most of all, however, the Yankee's bewitching advice is poised against Aunt Peggy's conjure, just as John's rational language and pragmatic view of the world are poised against Julius's signifying language and his view of the world formed by an African American experience. The hidden magical world of Julius is marked by unfamiliar words such as "goopher," by a dialect that enchants John and Annie but produces a cultural language that they will at key moments construe as "nonsense." In his experience of the South, the story suggests, John eventually delves beneath its "somnolent exterior" and finds that "the deeper currents of life—love and hatred, joy and despair, ambition and avarice, faith and friendship—flowed not less steadily than in livelier latitudes." The same is true, of course, of Julius's world, despite the contrary weight of contemporary white sociological theory about black life and history, but John does not so easily discover this fact. At one point in his tale, Julius reels off a list of minstrel items—"ef dey's anything a nigger lub, nex' ter 'possum, en chick'n, en watermillyums, it's scuppernon's"—one purpose of which is to conjure John into a stereotypical interpretation of Julius's motives. The items inhabit the marginal world of blackface in which culture blurs into a false racial typology. This tricksterish scene, in which Chesnutt himself skirts dangerous stereotypes, anticipates the comparable scene in *Invisible Man* where Ellison's protagonist relishes a hot buttered yam as an iconographic moment on the way to his embrace of black folk culture: "What a group of people we were, I thought. Why, you could cause us the greatest humiliation simply by confronting us with something we liked." Likewise, Julius's foods exist in a liminal territory between psychological freedom and psychological slavery—between authentic cultural preservation and its betrayal by the forces of popularized racism—which Chesnutt's readers are challenged to interpret correctly. In Julius's narrative deployment the icons of minstrelsy enter into the story's dialogue about culture. As in the more powerful stories, "Dave's Neckliss" and "A Victim of Heredity," to which I will return, Julius's list takes elements out of black culture, signifies upon their potential for cultural denigration, and in doing so points to defining characteristics of John's moral and cultural blindness.[108]

It is on this plane that Chesnutt conducts his most interesting critique of the dominant culture even as he reveals his own deep anxieties about moving beyond its boundaries or "speaking" in a subcultural voice. Relegating dialect and belief in conjure to a "venerable-looking colored man" who is not entirely black and who has a "shrewdness in his eyes" that "was not altogether African," Chesnutt may be said to keep his distance while at the same time he explores crucial, "blacker" dimensions of his own self. Once the "current of his memory—or imagination" is revived, Julius's language flows "more freely," and the story acquires "perspective and coherence"; he takes on a dreamy expression and seems "to be living over again in monologue his life on the old plantation." The revitalization of Julius's oral culture, parallel to the revival of the grape culture of the ruined plantation, is Chesnutt's as well. He cannot relive a plantation experience that he never had, but like the narrator of "The Wife of His Youth," and more directly than Harris, he can begin to speak in the dialect of the past, with its surviving rhythms and meanings of the African American experience hidden within the deceptively "dreamy" language of plantation mythology. Like all the stories, Julius's story is oral. Dialect is the marker not of regression, however, but of preservation; it is the marker of a distinct intonation, as Chesnutt refers to it, in which memory *and* imagination flow together out of the past and into the present. John and Annie often accuse Julius of inventing his tales, of lying; he denies such charges but does so obliquely, typically responding that he has heard the tale many times. Yet imagination and memory are deceptive, shape-shifting categories in Chesnutt's use, as indeed they must be in the transmission and collection of folklore that put the great body of African American oral culture in printed form. As stories are recounted, improvised in successive renderings, "memory" itself, both individual and collective, is necessarily transfigured, as lying and reiteration join together in founding a tradition. In the context of "The Goophered Grapevine," Chesnutt's declaration that the stories were the "fruit of my own imagination" thus appears now in a slightly different light and should not be taken as a denial of the legitimacy of the conjure stories as oral events or as embodiments of supernatural belief. Instead, as the first comments on Julius as a storyteller in the tale suggest, imagination is the form that memory may take. Although John may not see the significance of that duality for the creation of an African American cultural record, Chesnutt certainly did.[109]

Perhaps because of his own marked ambivalence on so many fronts, Chesnutt was able, like Harris, to bring his tales alive in two worlds at once—the magic world of antebellum conjure and the contemporary world of deteriorating racial justice. But not without strain. If conjure was the survival of an African belief, it was easy enough for nineteenth-century observers (whether planters, slaves, or others, including Chesnutt, in his strategic fashion) to dismiss it as savage or irrational, even though conjure in black America was richly infused with widely held European American superstitions and magical beliefs as well. Accounts of conjure, as I have already noted, were almost invariably treated by ethnologists as outright superstition, at odds with scientific evidence and a hindrance to the progress of the race. Chesnutt himself would have agreed with Newbell Puckett, one of the greatest of early collectors of African American folklore (despite the pronouncd racialism of many of his interpretations), who argued that "Negro race pride" was gradually suppressing the old beliefs of illiterate blacks. Yet the irony for Puckett the ethnologist, as for Chesnutt the author, could not have been more striking. As Puckett noted, a prominent black college had refused his request for collected superstitions since current "race consciousness," a professor informed him, necessarily included the temporary "desire to forget the past in pressing toward the future."[110] In the cultural circularity imposed upon blacks in Jim Crow America, race pride might entail recovering the past, but only a past— whether of Africa, or slavery, or both—that could not be used in any way to embarrass or to hurt the race.

The argument that Harris's theory about the African origins of his animal tales threatened to rob them of their disturbing political immediacy as *African American* vehicles of protest thus has its counterpart in the problem of conjure. The latter problem was more complex, however, for belief (or disbelief) in conjure was a part of slave psychological and spiritual life, whereas belief in the world of Remus's animal tales belonged, at least chronologically, more transparently to myth. Wolfe's mistake about the implications of an African origins theory would be even more serious if it were applied to Chesnutt. Without the legitimacy of a belief in conjure, and one grounded in survivals of an African tradition at odds with the European Christian paradigm into which slave religious beliefs had been thrust, the meaning within Julius's tales, as well as the mechanisms of ironic differentiation that set his world apart from that of his carpetbagger employers, would be undermined. Julius's whole mode of storytelling— his working by indirection and "nonsense," his different set of tonal semantics, the entire psychological domain of his narration as one of magic, pulled up from Chesnutt's subconscious memory where it had been lodged by the elderly slaves—all of this depends on the accepted legitimacy of conjure. And yet, of course, the legitimacy of conjure on the plantation itself was always in question, certainly among the masters. This fact gave it the problematic status that Chesnutt exploited so well, reproducing the tension between skeptical master and believing (or at least pretending) slave in the relationship between the skeptical John and the trickster Julius.

Conjure by its very nature stood on the margins of belief as that concept was normally understood by literate white or black Americans. One of the earliest essays to study conjure, that by Leonora Herron and Alice Bacon in *Southern Workman,* accurately summed up the prevailing interpretation of the late nineteenth century in stating that conjure was "a relic of African days, though strange and incongruous growths rising from association with the white race, added to and distorted it from time to time, till it became a curious conglomerate of fetishism, divination, quackery, incantation and demonology." According to plantation history, the conjurer (root doctor, hoodoo, goopher, and two-head were other names applied in different forms to the conjure man or woman, or to the act of conjuring) had the power to charm or curse or heal individuals. By the use of bags or balls filled with various secret incredients (a trick, mojo, toby, hand); by using roots or animal parts made into a potion or poison, or other common items such as hair, pins, bones, cloth, feathers; by a hex or a look that could cast a spell such as a reptile infestation; by turning into a witch and riding the victim at night—by all manner of arcane and mystic activities in which the aura of secret power was requisite, conjure maintained an enduring presence within many slave communities and many black communities after slavery. Deriving from African fetishistic belief, conjure created a merger between the spirit and physical worlds such that the fetish could become the bearer of good or evil spirit, acting as a conveyance of one charm or protection against another. Because their conjure often did appear to work—by whatever ratio of actual power, chicanery, psychological suggestion, homeopathy, coincidence, or luck— conjurers could become figures of significant power on or near the plantation, and many remained powerful in the years after. Combining the "malevolence of the witch with the benevolence of the African medicine man or priest," as Mary Berry and John Blassingame write, the conjurer was often not just a spiritual figure but also a hero in the community who combined spiritual and secular roles.[111] The conjure man or woman could be, in the broadest sense, the carrier of African American folk culture. Articulating the suppressed religious beliefs of African spiritualism, the conjurer can be seen as the embodiment of the "word" as *nommo,* a living force of supernatural power uniting conjure and oral force strikingly compressed into epigrammatic form by Hurston: "Belief in magic is older than writing. So nobody knows how it started." Well before ethnographers took an interest in it, conjure had been inscribed into the work songs, blues, and folktales of slave culture.[112] Alongside Christianity, but often in place of it as well, African religion revived in the form of conjure flourished in part as an answer to the hardships of bondage and the slavemasters' deliberate stripping away of long-standing African cultural and spiritual practices. Conjure in this respect created a vehicle for the retention of African beliefs in which resistance and heroism alike were possible, as well as the separate creation of an African-based identity apart from the censorship of slavery. Like the animal tales that Harris transmitted, tales of conjure were thus a vital component of a culture passed on orally, a culture of circumspect voicing that was not "literate" until collectors began to record the tales that flourished among the slave generations and their descendants.

The fact that conjure seldom worked on whites—to put it another way, the fact that most whites did not believe in it—gave its cultural uniqueness a corresponding practical liability. In fact, because those slaves or free blacks who did not believe in conjure—Frederick Douglass and Martin Delany, to cite two examples—might also dismiss it as a psychological game practiced upon the ignorant and gullible, conjure belonged to a doubly circumscribed world. Some masters, moreover, may have exploited conjure as part of the larger group of "superstitions" that they themselves encouraged among slaves as a means of psychological control. As Gladys-Marie Fry has demonstrated, for instance, the masters' inculcation of a fear of ghosts among slaves aided the work of patterollers (slave patrols) and provided a point of departure, eventually, for the terrorizing regalia of the Ku Klux Klan. Despite such limitations on its power, however, a significant proportion of slaves believed that conjure could influence the lives of their masters and by extension their own treatment as slaves (conjurers commonly attempted to influence the forthcoming punishment of slaves, their marriages and separations, and similar events governed directly by the master's capricious will); but its effects were far more often felt directly only by African Americans themselves. This was more emphatically true by the end of the nineteenth century. Citing the contemporary example of a young man who believed himself conjured by a jilted sweetheart, Julien Hall pointed to what he took to be the obvious psychosomatic dimension of conjure. The young man's health had gone into such a severe decline that he was expected to die, Hall said, "a victim of a relic of barbarism and the dark ages." But what mattered most, after emancipation as before, were the mesmerizing power of the conjurer and the psychological willingness of the community to believe. In a discussion of conjure in her 1893 collection of folktales, *Old Rabbit, the Voodoo, and Other Sorcerers,* Mary Alicia Owen provided a strong clue to the source of its power in a prevailing substructure of belief in a world in which the spiritual and the physical are in constant intersection. Conjure depended, she said, on "daring that which is horrible and repulsive, and, above all, in a perfectly subjective iron *will.* It also acts greatly by the terror or influence inspired by the conjuror himself."[113]

If conjure operated secretly, as part of the hidden language of the African American world set apart from the white command of slaveholding, it also posed no direct threat to the plantation regime and seldom changed the balance of power in the slaves' favor. The power of the conjurer was thus localized within the slave community, where, although it might have little practical consequence for the everyday hardships of slavery, its symbolic power could still be significant. Conjure represented the fact, as Lawrence Levine contends, that whites were not necessarily omnipotent, that there were "forces they could not control, areas in which slaves could act with more knowledge and authority than their masters, ways in which the powers of the whites could be muted if not thwarted entirely." What mattered, then, was not that conjurers had power over the masters but that they appeared to have powers that the masters lacked.[114]

With significant African history only beginning to be written and embraced by blacks, and with African retentions stamped by many sociologists and ethnologists as the relics of savagery and gross superstition, conjure could hardly have been the most obvious literary topic for a middle-class mulatto with the refined European American literary tastes of Charles Chesnutt. The mystery, in fact, is that the tales are so strongly felt, so completely steeped in the reality of conjure, despite their deliberate containment within a skeptical frame that pits oral and written cultures in ironic combat. As in the case of Harris, however, where the seeming contrast between the frame narrative and the animal tales is finally what generates the true power of the folklore, so in Chesnutt's case the framing skepticism—which is partly Chesnutt's own conscious evaluation of the shadowy world created by Julius's narratives and partly his means of entering fully into Julius's provocative, signifying voice—is in fact what generates the exceptional originality and force of his transfigured folklore.

The multiform cultural contrast on which Chesnutt's tales are built may be briefly suggested by two instances in which he subverts not just his narrator but the tradition of European American literate culture in which he himself chose, or was compelled, to work. "The Conjurer's Revenge," a story whose title turns out to have significance for Chesnutt's artistic intentions as well, begins with deliberate allusions to the accoutrements of white culture with which John and Annie surround themselves—newspapers and magazines, library, piano and vocal music. As the frame opens into the occasion for Julius's story, Annie is reading a missionary report and John is following the "impossible career of the blonde heroine of a rudimentary novel." Julius's story—a "plantation legend" that relieves the "monotony of Sabbath quiet"—is, of course, far more fascinating; it also offers a direct challenge to the entire system of religious and cultural belief with which John and Annie support their lives. Similarly, "The Gray Wolf's Haunt" opens with John reading a preposterously tedious philosophical tract whose jargon Annie labels "nonsense." This "nonsense" stands in direct contrast to the beliefs in conjure that Chesnutt labeled "nonsense" and to what Annie considers to be Julius's "nonsense" in "The Conjurer's Revenge." Throughout both tales, as in most others, John is either duped by Julius or naively blind—that is, duped by Chesnutt. But readers concentrating on the trickster qualities in Julius's self-serving tales have often entirely ignored the fact that the "deceitfulness of appearances" also invites a closer look at Chesnutt's own signifying language. The conjure tales are not only an artful, effective form of protest literature against racial injustice but, more important, a recapitulation of the generative playfulness upon which black cultural language depended. Julius's trickster tales are "double lies" of the kind described by Daniel Crowley, for they belong to the signifying "lies" of African American storytelling but include as well the prevarication of Julius's ulterior motives *and* Chesnutt's own signifying upon the American cultural matrix, shot through with racism, in which he had to perform.[115] Uncle Remus's alter ego, Brer Rabbit, was Harris's revenge upon the propriety and racism of his culture's governing mythology; Brer Rabbit's "nonsense" of trickery and combat brought African cultural weapons into play against the imminent destruction of black culture, even if Harris could not always make himself articulate a true identity with Remus as a black man. The refutation of Jim Crow culture by black storytelling—by the "lies" and "nonsense" of folktales—is far more obvious in the case of Chesnutt. Uncle Julius, less removed from his creator, is Chesnutt's revenge upon the pale cultural theology of his day and its undergirding of racial arrogance. His "nonsense" links together African and African American traditions in a cultural struggle that Chesnutt, drawing his own artistic identity from Julius, carried out by means of a more public circumlocution.

John's culture is depicted as literate printed nonsense, collected commodities of language and thought that are presented as a lifeless contrast to the vocalized stories of Julius, compounded so explicitly of memory and improvisation, the central features of the African American oral tradition. Harris was more straightforward in his evocation of "de ole times" as a survival of African thought and spirit. But Chesnutt, too, in his masterly placement of his own authorial voice within that of Julius the storyteller and his creation of a historically resonant setting for the *telling* of African American culture, also evoked an African past. Julius's dialect, as I have already argued, is the vocalization of that past, in all its ironies of representation on the page and in the tradition of literary plantation speech. Whereas Harris heard slave music as something of a distant memory in which the true sounds of the quarters merged with a grown-up little white boy's recollection, Chesnutt, as in "Tobe's Tribulations" and like celebrations of nonsense, remembered it as the music of his own culture, strangely distant but belonging to him all the same. To recall or respect conjure was not enough, however; Chesnutt's achievement was to embody it formally in his literary strategies.

One of the essential features of conjure in slave culture was its work by counteraction. It was often employed to prevent or to stop evil action by a personal antagonist, by another conjurer, or by someone of superior force, the slaveholder for example. The comforting platitudes of proslavery argument and the plantation revivalists notwithstanding, slaves recognized bondage as an evil against which conjure might be ranged. Even if conjure could not literally halt slavery or the cruelty that permeated it, slavery nevertheless directly shaped conjure, as it shaped African American culture, by providing the context in which it would flourish. Similarly, although few of the folktales of conjure collected at the turn of the century or few of Chesnutt's own conjure tales directly concern the conjure of white people ("Mars Jeems's Nightmare," as we have seen, is one; "A Victim of Heredity" and the remarkable late story "The Marked Tree" are other examples in which conjure victims are white), the stories make clear that the effects of conjure were felt throughout plantation life. Chesnutt for his part demonstrates this most effectively by allowing conjure to operate in the narrative integuments of the stories themselves, joining physical metamorphosis to allegorical metamorphosis and insinuating the verbal arts of oral tradition into acts of writing and publication.

One of the remarkable things about "Mars Jeems's Nightmare," again, is its combination of unique features—the conjure of a white man, the incorporation of a Master-John plot, the commentary on the New Negro, and the clear moral drawn by Julius. Julius's ulterior motive, another reprieve for his lazy grandson, is in this case nearly coincidental with the story's secondary moral, namely, the story's commentary on the plight of the "noo nigger" of post-Reconstruction America. More often in the conjure tales, Julius's ulterior motive functions as much to camouflage as to reveal the interior significance of the conjure, which appears in symbolic language. But such interior significance is also present to a degree even here, for "Mars Jeems Nightmare," in spite of its moderate resolution, tells a tale of great psychological and cultural violence. Like the most subversive of Harris's Remus tales, it resorts to the physical punishment of the master in order to achieve its purpose, combining nuanced indirection and frontal assault. When Mars Jeems is turned into a slave, the most obvious sort of irony that could be visited upon a slaveholder is yoked to the definitive feature of conjure—its ability to transform or influence the physical world by spiritual means. Conjure's power of transformation in the tales is in turn connected, as Houston Baker has noted, to the African American's mastery of narrative form, the "sound" inside black dialect as it opens up a "drama of African spirituality challenging and changing the disastrous transformations of slavery."[116] In the momentary imaginative space of this story, Mars Jeems is made a slave. Whipped and brutalized in recompense for the history of his own plantation brutality, he is also stripped of his name (he is beaten for denying that his name is "Sambo," a generic slave name) and of any memory of where he has come from. He speaks in slave dialect and is everywhere referred to as "de nigger." In other words, Mars Jeems's nightmare—though he refuses to be broken by the overseer—is a recapitulation of both the physical and cultural denigrations of slavery, a lesson that escapes John even though he claims to find the moral of the story transparent. Unlike Mars Jeems, John cannot be conjured and cannot, therefore, be made to learn the tale's desperate lesson.

The act of transformation, the metamorphosis of physical forms, is relevant not just to Mars Jeems's short-lived enslavement by conjure (and to his rescue by conjure as well: Aunt Peggy prepares a goophered yam for him to eat in order to change him back into a white man). It also illuminates the psychological and formal properties of the story itself. Nightmare and actual transformation are blurred, so as to suggest the ambiguity of conjure; and Julius's tale is characterized by John, in his typical way, as something "made up," while Julius, wearing what exact storytelling mask we do not know, says he heard the tale in his childhood from his mother. This difference in views corresponds, of course, to the one Chesnutt located in his own craft, the "fruit of my own imagination" balanced against the eruption of folkloric, ancestral memories. In this way the blurring of distinctions that governs the etiology of the story parallels, or works in conjunction with, the action of Mars Jeems's conjure. Because Chesnutt was apparently reluctant to credit black folklore with legitimacy even as he felt compelled to give a "voice" to those who had been so misrepresented in the plantation tradition, it may be correct to say that the transformation was internal as well. Conjure operated beneath the level of Chesnutt's full and conscious approbation, but it operated nonetheless. The subcultural materials of "superstition" came forth in the real voice of Julius's dialect.

Like Julius, Chesnutt signified in the manner of signifying *nonsense* as defined by Abrahams: he tested "the limits of meaning by exploring the edges of believability." The fluidity built into the language of signifying— both its improvisational flexibility and its inherent decimation of fixed forms and beliefs, as noted previously—allies it with conjure's similarly transformative power. Because it enfolds the tricksterism of the animal folktales into a specifically human agency, at once abridging and heightening the allegorical dimension, the conjure story may be seen as a cultural intensification of the metamorphic power of the animal tales. If the animal trickster and his tale inhabit the border world, the liminal zone, in which the verbal artifice of the human passes into hypothetical "nature"—a world of "ole times" or a magically transformed present where animals speak and act—the conjurer and his or her tale may be taken even more decidedly to represent the state of liminality itself, a state of constantly regenerative power in which one sees, to borrow Robert Pelton's phrase, "hermeneutics in action." The conjure tale explores the very ground of what is culturally intelligible—the simultaneously shared and contested ground between two cultures in which the ideological (in this case the politics of racial domination) may be diffused or deflected into indirection or emblematic behavior but remains nonetheless a potent determining force. The language of conjure is the language of signifying and cultural struggle.[117] It is

through such language, made both instrumental and thematic in the conjure tales, that Chesnutt defined his own partial allegiance to an originating
African American cultural voice by making the category of transformation
or metamorphosis, central to conjure, coincident with the movement
across allegorical levels of temporality in the formal structures of the tales.

Virtually all the tales involve the metamorphosis of persons into animals,
birds, trees, or other objects, often with the intent of helping them escape
punishment or slavery itself, at other times to torment them for some
contrary act, or further to demonstrate the elision between human and
animal, or human and "thing," in the philosophy of chattelism. Tales of
metamorphosis or metempsychosis were among those commonly collected
by folklorists of the 1890s.[118] But Chesnutt's most powerful tales symbolically historicize the action of metamorphosis as well, and I would like to
begin an examination of the interaction of storytelling and narration in
Chesnutt's conjure stories, as well as their ultimate appeal to a linguistic
power with explicit African retentions, by looking at three tales in which
metamorphosis is the mechanism for a symbolic critique of slavery and its
post-Reconstruction aftermath. In "The Conjurer's Revenge," the metamorphosis of Primus into a mule contains a small catalogue of commentary
on American race relations. As in other cases, Julius's ulterior motive—to
persuade John to buy a horse rather than a mule (a horse, it turns out, in
which he has some financial interest)—is something of a red herring. That
is, the tale's apparent ulterior motive, Julius's gain, contains another motive
in Chesnutt's act of narrative signifying. Julius's "duplicity" in telling the
tale, and his "more than unconscious part in [the] transaction" of the sale,
thus point instead to the strategic operation of conjure itself. His story of
Primus, turned into a mule by a conjure man after he steals the conjure
man's shoat, is where the story's true tricking and transformative power
lies concealed. To take the most obvious fact, Primus, as a mule, is
emblematic of slavery itself and at the same time a special case of the role
played by animals in nineteenth-century racial mythology. Zora Neale
Hurston and William Faulkner were among a number of writers who
appropriated the colloquial analogies between slaves and mules; and Chesnutt, light-skinned enough to pass, was certainly aware of the parallels
that racist commentary often drew between mules and mulattoes (the
words have the same etymology) as sterile or "degenerate" species. Both
the labor of slavery and the ideology that supported it had intentionally
blurred the boundary between the human and the animal, but the problem
was contemporary as well—a certain complication, as we have seen, for

the animal tales of Harris. The Negro, as Charles Carroll's notorious racist tract had it, was a "beast," and bestial imagery pervaded white supremacist doctrine of Chesnutt's day. Julius's suggestion that he cannot help but think that any given mule might be "some er my own relations, er somebody e'se w'at can't he'p deyse'ves," therefore asks the reader, with a doubled vision, to see Primus the "metamorphosed unfortunate" as a slave, the whole of his tale undoubtedly signifying upon the broader figure of enslavement made famous by Stowe—"how a man was made a thing." Furthermore, the plot of Chesnutt's story, whereby Primus is only partially turned back into a man by the contrite conjure man on his deathbed, leaving him a clubfoot, situates the antebellum tale more specifically in a post-Reconstruction context.[119] Crippled by generations of bondage, not yet fully a "man," first legally defined as a laboring animal and still characterized as "bestial" by postbellum racist theory, the Negro has not yet fully escaped the white man's legal conjure known first as slavery and now as Jim Crow.

The tale's instance of conjure does not directly relate to slavery, then, but its effects nonetheless ironically reproduce the condition and results of slavery. In addition, the strategic operation of conjure is shown to be formed by slavery and to contain its essential dialectic between dehumanization and cultural survival. As in Chesnutt's tale, so in the narrated world of slave culture, conjure operates along the borders and across the boundaries between two cultures. Primus, for example, is conjured after he has slipped off the plantation to attend a dance given by free blacks; returning home he cuts across the cotton fields so as to escape the slave patrol and comes upon the tempting shoat (which itself seems to "charm" him). Once he is conjured into a mule, but has presumably escaped, dogs and "niggerketchers" go after Primus until his trail gives out. Also, it is the conjure man's conversion to Christianity at a camp meeting that is responsible for his change of heart and decision to restore Primus to human form; but his conversion, Julius relates, also symbolizes the gradual, certain decay of an African-based faith, for it distances the conjure man from his own father, a king "ober yander in Affiky what de niggers come fum," where he was stolen and sold to "de spekilaters." Such elements locate conjure within the ambiguous borderland between slavery and freedom, and more specifically the assimilating cultural borderland between the world of the slaves (and their ancestors) and the world of the masters. Annie labels the story "nonsense," lacking a moral and the "pathetic" quality she usually finds in Julius's tales; for his part Julius replies that he cannot make out

"dem wo'ds you uses" and swears the story is "nuffin but de truf," a story
that he has heard for some twenty-five years.[120]

But as Julius ironically adds: "Dey's so many things a body knows is
lies, dat dey ain' no use gwine roun' findin' fault wid tales dat mought des
ez well be so ez not." Truth and lies blur—in the story as in the political
life of black Americans. Conjure might be true or not; freedom might be
true or not. The analogy that Julius introduces at this point to support
the veracity of his tale—the young New Negro attending school who tries
futilely to convince Julius that the earth revolves around the sun rather
than the reverse—is complex. On the one hand, it seems an example of
the sort of minstrel humor one finds in Harris's sketches of Remus in
Atlanta, where the old-time Negro's ignorance and distrust of modern
knowledge are played for comedy. On the other, however, it points to
what can be considered the Copernican revolution constituted by emancipation, a revolution in thinking similarly invoked by James Weldon
Johnson in *The Autobiography of an Ex-Coloured Man* to demonstrate that
the world of black civil and social rights no longer revolves around the
southern white man. ("By a complex, confusing, and almost contradictory
mathematical process, by the use of zigzags instead of straight lines, the
earth can be proved to be the centre of things celestial . . . [likewise] the
white race assumes as a hypothesis that it is the main object of creation.")
Julius insists that one must believe one's eyes: but the riddle is not for
him but for John and Annie to solve. Julius may play the Remus darky
here, yet he lives, as he knows, in a world that is undergoing a revolution
still to be completed.[121] Like the black world of conjure, the superstition
of white supremacy is slowly giving way, perhaps, to a more rational
discourse. But Julius's nonsense is morally superior to that of his literate
but ignorant listeners, and Chesnutt poses to his own audience a simple
challenge to recognize that fact.

A second tale in which metamorphosis is clearly bound up with the
transformation from slavery to freedom is "Po' Sandy." Conjured into a
tree by his wife, Tennie, so that he will not continually be sent off the
plantation to work for the master's kinfolk, Sandy is inadvertently cut
down and and milled into lumber for the mistress's new kitchen. As in so
many of the tales, Sandy's predicament is a function of the slave family's
destruction. His first wife is traded to a speculator ("Sandy tuk on some
'bout losin' his wife, but he soon seed dy want no use cryin' ober spilt
merlasses," Julius laconically remarks), while his second has been sent
away as a nurse at the time Sandy is cut down, just before they had

planned to turn into foxes and run away. When Tennie returns, she finds "de stump standin' dere, wid de sap runnin' out'n it, en de limbs layin' scattered roun'," and at the mill, where she tries to beg Sandy for forgiveness, the screaming Tennie is so distracted by grief that she has to be tied to a post while she watches the saw "cut de log up inter bo'ds en scantlin's right befo' her eyes." The extraordinary violence of the story, which rivals the grimmest of Remus's tales, mimics the agonies of family separation and the human mutilation of slavery. The dehumanizing metamorphosis of slavery broke families apart at the same time that it was capable of systematically destroying individuals, virtually turning them into the products created by their own labor. In a double act of transformation, one in which Tennie's black conjure cannot protect Sandy from the white economic conjure of slavery, he is turned into a material part of the plantation. Reversing the direction of Chesnutt's first story, "Uncle Peter's House," a parable of building property in the face of great post-Reconstruction odds, "Po' Sandy" puts its hero literally into the house of bondage. Although the workmen must labor mightily to subdue Sandy the tree (their axes can barely cut his trunk; the saw sets off a frenzy of "sweekin', en moanin', en groanin'"), the machinery of slavery ultimately reduces Sandy to a tractable object.[122]

His revenge, of course, is to haunt the kitchen, rendering it useless, so that it is eventually torn down and turned into an equally useless schoolhouse. Tennie is left mad, eventually found dead one winter morning on the floor of the schoolhouse, where she has gone to talk to Sandy's spirit. Revenge and grief are yoked in the world of spirit; conjure cannot save Tennie and Sandy, but it can withdraw them from bodily submission to enslavement. Julius's story, which "Kyars [his] 'memb'ance back ter ole times," operates in part as a subterfuge to dissuade John from using the lumber for his own new kitchen (although it is Annie, not John, who is affected by the tale) so that his church can use it for meetings. But again, its more vital ulterior message works at a hidden level, beneath the "pathetic intonation" that strikes a "responsive chord" in his auditors' hearts. As Julius remarks to John, the lumber of the schoolhouse "is gwine ter be ha'nted tel de las' piece er plank is rotted en crumble' inter dus'." Likewise, the ghosts of slavery will haunt the South (and America) until its last remains have disintegrated. Moreover, Julius has a right to the created property of slavery—produced by his own labor and that of his ancestors—while John does not. Annie's remark—"What a system it was . . . under which such things were possible"—refers first of all to the brutalities of slavery; but John's skeptical denial to the contrary, it also refers obliquely to the authenticity of conjure. In "Po' Sandy" conjure and slavery are surprisingly bound together in responsibility for Sandy's destruction. It is significant that Tennie, before she agrees to transform Sandy, has given up conjure because of her conversion to Christianity. The story suggests that the language of the Bible could easily be made an instrument of slavery; but conjure in this instance can only counteract the ideology of enslavement—cruel labor protected by the pieties of religion—through a metamorphosis that leads to ironic annihilation. As in "Dave's Neckliss," Chesnutt's most intricate instance of reification, however, Sandy's being rendered into a material object of the plantation economy indicates also a metamorphosis in his role in the story. Delivering him from the deadly cycle of enslavement—"Before I'll be a slave / I'll be buried in my grave" ran "O Freedom," a famous African American spiritual cited by Du Bois and others as a song of resistance—Tennie's conjure returns to an Africanist power that fails to save Sandy but does render him, by joining in Chesnutt's own imaginative conjure, a powerful symbol of both the lingering effects and the cultural inheritance of slavery. In her own eventual insanity—she appears to Mars Marrabo "de wuss 'stracted nigger he eber hearn of," carrying on "ter herse'f wid some kine er foolishness w'at nobody could n' make out"—Tennie manifests the extreme effects of the alienation of enslavement. Conversing with Sandy's spirit in the schoolhouse and turning inward the power of conjure to induce insanity, Tennie in her own "nonsense," which bewilders and threatens the master, speaks a symbolic language that signifies on the white conjure of slavery.[123] And her madness has a legacy: haunting the church built of this tragic drama and bequeathed now to John and Annie, Sandy's spirit is at once the incarnation of Tennie's grief and a reminder of those who have gone before. As in Toni Morrison's *Beloved,* so in Sandy's story memory is fixed, not obliterated, in the act of mourning, and conjure ties the violent, painful ancestral world of slave culture to the precarious world of contemporary African America.

Although it is a tale published late in Chesnutt's career, "The Marked Tree" (1924) may be read as a companion piece to "Po' Sandy." Reflecting on the problem of genealogy that would so absorb him in his color line stories and in *The Marrow of Tradition,* Chesnutt entwines the ruin of the South's physical landscape with the ruin of its familial and economic history. When her own son is sold to pay for the wedding of her mistress's son, a slave mother "marks" the symbolic family tree with a curse, so that the tree becomes a kind of "Upas tree, the fabled tree of death," and subsequently destroys all family heirs in a series of freak accidents. The elements of the story echo common folktales and bear comparison to *The Marrow of Tradition,* in which the possibility of a contaminated genealogy leads to two related forms of white racial hysteria. Zora Neale Hurston, moreover, records an instance of conjure that is just as frightening. After an "unreconstructed" Georgia planter strikes and kills one of his servants for sassing him, the conjure man stalks the planter, driving his wife, son, and daughter one after another into fits of homicidal madness in which they attempt to kill the planter and must be institutionalized. Hurston's story suggests a concomitant means of avenging white brutality and of signifying upon the nightmare of the racial nadir. Likewise, "The Marked Tree," in its relation to "Po' Sandy," rests upon a signifying reversal of the trope of the family tree. Whereas Sandy is destroyed by the mutilations of the slave machine, unprotected by Tennie's conjure, the marked tree, symbolic of the "rotten heart" of the genealogy of the south (conceivably of Chesnutt's veiled hostility toward his own white ancestors as well), asserts the hidden power of conjure's revenge.[124] Explicitly reaching generation after generation into the present, conjure here travels across the antebellum and postwar time frames in its ability to tear apart, as though by a mysterious force within, the property and refined traditions of the aristocratic white South. "The Marked Tree" accomplishes its own reconstruction of black integrity, worn down by judicial and illegal assault in the post-Reconstruction years, by an act of vengeance. Like "Mars Jeems's Nightmare," "The Marked Tree" is one of the few tales in which conjure is practiced upon whites—and one of the few in which it accomplishes its purpose with complete success. Its late appearance is a sign both of Chesnutt's angry despair over the course of black civil rights through the early 1920s and, perhaps, of his resentment about the failure of his own career.

Madness of the sort that afflicts Tennie, or that momentarily seizes Mars Jeems in the aftermath of his experience of slavery, or that threatens to descend upon the Spencer family in "The Marked Tree," is a figure for the pitched struggle between the destructive power of enslavement and the assertion by the slaves of their own psychological strength. The mythology of conjure includes the madness of grieving as a language of cultural crisis, a language in which mourning operates simultaneously as social critique and as a strategic kind of cultural memory. In one of Chesnutt's most disturbing and remarkable Uncle Julius tales, "Dave's

Neckliss," madness in fact displaces conjure as the articulation of the liminal realm in which slavery is overcome. Tricked into being accused of stealing a ham by a fellow slave jealous of his courtship of a woman, Dave suffers a humiliating punishment at the hands of his master by having a ham chained around his neck. The punishment, and the fact that his antagonist takes up with his former lover, drives Dave mad. He has visions of ham trees, talks to himself, and even after the ham is removed from his neck feels "des lack he'd los' sump'n" and continues privately to wear a lightered-knot (fat pine) around his neck. At length he feels he has turned into a ham and hangs himself in the smokehouse.[125]

This brilliant, grisly tale, which Frances Keller rightly compares to Kafka's story "The Metamorphosis," appeared in 1889, and Chesnutt proposed to include it in the first collection of stories that he offered Houghton Mifflin. When *The Conjure Woman* finally appeared a decade later, the story had been dropped (Chesnutt also chose to exclude "Tobe's Tribulations" and "A Victim of Heredity"), probably because conjure as such is not present—but perhaps because it was simply too unsettling.[126] Nevertheless, "Dave's Neckliss" perfectly illustrates the convergence of conjure and the black psychological realism that appeared in Chesnutt's greatest creative moments. The tale's haunting magnificence rests only partly on its inventive dehumanization of Dave into an inanimate form. In addition, it fuses slavery and its subsequent history, for Dave's inability to give up the icon of the ham chained around his neck functions as a reminder of the lasting debilitation of slavery. Minstrelsy and chattelism are joined in the ham, a sign of labor, of stereotyped behaviors of consumption, and of the underlying theory of animality that linked the two in the subliminal, or even the tendentiously public, discourse of racism. In being turned into a ham, however, Dave also signifies upon one of the stereotypical foods of coon songs, which figuratively dehumanized blacks by making them into pathetic buffoons who are addicted to watermelons, hams, chickens, and the like. In fact, the story itself plays upon that stereotype in its frame: Julius's story this time earns him the rest of John's Sunday dinner ham, of which he has already had a large serving. But "Dave's Neckliss" is one of the clearest representations of the fact that Julius's own tricksterism, his ability to obtain a material advantage, is often a screen for the more radically penetrating message of the tale. "Dave's Neckliss" turns the minstrel caricature into an inheritance from slavery that is productive of madness, figuring in it a revolt against type that takes the form of internalized frenzy and shock. Hanging himself, Dave turns his suicide into a self-inflicted act of cultural lynching in which he dramatizes not only the dehumanization of racism but also the self-destructive effects of African Americans' own acceptance, whether on the minstrel stage or in the arena of politics and economic struggle, of debasing minstrel stereotypes.

A comparable story that combines the critique of minstrelsy and an act of revenge against white masters is "The Victim of Heredity," which offers us a further way into the comprehensive narrative power of "Dave's Neckliss." Having caught a chicken thief, John asks Julius why "his people" cannot resist chicken. Julius's answer takes the form of a parable that John, as usual, misunderstands. With his peculiar "prejudices in favor of the colored people," it is the carpetbagger John, as much as or more than his "colored neighbors," who cannot entirely "shake off the habits formed under the old system." John suggests that chicken stealing must be "in the blood," and Julius agrees that it is, but the account that he gives is an allegory of slavery's deprivations as well as a signifying reversal of them. When Mars Donald MacDonald attempts to cheat his nephew Tom out of his rightful inheritance, the conjure woman, Aunt Peggy, comes to Tom's rescue. Deceptively allowing MacDonald to work a conjure on his slaves, so that he can successively reduce their rations and realize more profit (an act that can also be taken to represent the post-Reconstruction treatment of black labor through the inequities of sharecropping and convict lease), Peggy then turns conjure to salvation, reversing the trick so that MacDonald must spend his fortune buying thousands of chickens to revive his starving slaves. Having bought up all the state's chickens, Tom makes a killing and avenges his uncle's misdeeds. All North Carolina blacks, theorizes Julius, must therefore have some of the MacDonald slaves' blood in them and thus have an irresistible craving for chicken. Most straightforwardly, the story, as Annie interprets it, is a parable: blacks learned dishonesty and theft under the regime of slavery, and as victims of the "influence of heredity" they must be excused until they have had time to outgrow such habits. (She therefore has the sheriff release the thief.) Habits in the "blood," that is, are actually the effects of an impoverishing environment. But the story also brings into view the stereotype of chicken thieving itself, which was common in minstrelsy and became the basis, as we have seen, for Ernest Hogan's great encore piece in *Clorindy, the Origin of the Cakewalk*, "Who Dat Say Chicken in Dis Crowd?" As in the musical number, the general stereotype of the chicken thief and chicken eating borrowed a motif, one also appearing in a genre of black folk songs, and rendered it ludicrous in order to undermine if not destroy legitimate black social and political aspirations. In one of the modern Atlanta sketches of *Uncle Remus and His Friends,* for example, Remus ridicules the current rise of black interest in African emigration. Joking about the large influx of blacks into the city, he says that he will have to "tighten up de chicken-house en de stor'room twel dish yer Affkin move is blowed over." It was possible, however, for blacks to seize the stereotype in order to subvert it. As Houston Baker has demonstrated, Booker T. Washington manipulated the minstrel trope of chicken thieving in *Up from Slavery,* appropriating the image from his slave familial past as a groundwork for his own achievements and thus speaking in "a cultural voice won from slavery's victimization and silencing."[127] The same may be said of Chesnutt's story. "A Victim of Heredity" attacks the stereotype at the fundamental conjunction of heredity and training; it asserts not just that environment, rather than "blood," is the cause of behavior, but also that the cultural origins of such stereotypes in racism can be rooted out and overturned. Even though it is another, more generous, white man who benefits, conjure here works to undermine the master's economic security and revitalize his abused slaves. Julius's story at first glance appears to exploit a bit of "darky" humor, but the act of conjure, although it may be said merely to transpose the slaves into a more liberal regime—perhaps that of postwar neo-slavery—turns the accepted typology inside out, making it the vehicle for a ridiculing assault on commonly held views of inherited racial traits. Like "Dave's Neckliss," the story revels in the exploration of a culturally destructive image in order to appropriate its power in an act of figurative metamorphosis. Chesnutt's fictive seizure of the image, that is to say, is itself an act of cultural conjure that reclaims and transforms its significance.

The authorial act of metamorphosis is at once more transparent and far-reaching in the case of "Dave's Neckliss." Given the gruesome form of Chesnutt's critique in Dave's tale, it is all the more striking that the story initially identifies Dave as a preacher whose interpretation of Scripture seems to offer no threat to the ideology of plantation slavery. The punishment for his supposed theft of the ham includes the suppression of his religious role. Stripped of his religion and Bible—but more than that stripped of his role as a community leader by the false accusation against him—Dave represents slavery's threatened reduction of plausible black leadership, often to be found in the nineteenth century and after in the African American church, to minstrelsy and insanity. Whether one reads that reduction as part of the calibrated controlling power of proslavery

Christianity itself, as the story allows, or as a reference to the more rigid suppression of slave literacy and worship that followed Nat Turner's abortive revolt, as it may also imply, "Dave's Neckliss" displaces authentic African American culture with a series of intellectual strictures and punitive burdens metonymically symbolized by the ham chained around Dave's neck. For one thing, the "ham" evokes the proslavery argument that African Americans were the descendents of Ham, condemned to be the progenitor of servants for looking upon his father, Noah's, nakedness (Genesis 9:23–27). Casting a withering look at the potent mythology of Scripture by literalizing its absurd injunctions, Chesnutt found a further way to suggest that Dave's religion, which had the potential to make him a community leader, even a Nat Turner, also had the potential to emasculate him. Indeed, both possibilities are fused insofar as Dave's metamorphosis makes him into a sacrificial object. The Sunday ham that opens the story—"from which several slices had been cut, exposing a rich pink expanse that would have appealed strongly to the appetite of any hungry Christian"—and prompts Julius's rendering of the tale is transformed over the course of Chesnutt's narrative into the body of Dave, placed in the service of his master as no more than smoked meat and finally driven to a suicidal act of self-lynching. When Julius eats heartily of John and Annie's Sunday ham ("w'eneber I eats ham, it min's me er Dave . . . but I nebber kin eat mo' d'n two er th'ee poun's befo' I gits ter studyin' 'bout Dave"), his story tells us, he eats the body and blood of Dave in a ritual of remembrance in which comedy cloaks his identificaiton with a legacy of suffering.[128] Mocking the failed deliverance of proslavery theology, as well as its contemporary transfiguration into the degrading chains of minstrelsy that still hang around the necks of African Americans, Chesnutt linked the madness of racism to Dave's inculcated grief and insanity, once more deriving cultural memory from a harrowing act of sacramental mourning.

As Chesnutt's frame ironically adds, such chains are still present in the form of John's cultural blindness to the meaning of Dave's tragedy. Julius's tale is the occasion for one of John's most interesting meditations upon the function of Julius's storytelling and upon the lingering effects of slavery. Noting Julius's "undeveloped nature" and "childish" moods, John sees nonetheless that Julius never indulges in any of the "regrets for the Arcadian joyousness and irresponsibility" that characterize plantation mythology. And yet Julius's judgment of slavery's cruelty seems to John closely circumscribed. Julius appears to speak with a furtive disapproval which suggested to us a doubt in his own mind as to whether he had a right to think or to feel, and presented to us the curious psychological spectacle of a mind enslaved long after the shackles had been struck off from the limbs of its possessor. Whether the sacred name of liberty ever set his soul aglow with a generous fire; whether he had more than the most elementary ideas of love, friendship, patriotism, religion—things which are half, and the better half, of life to us; whether he even realized except in a vague, uncertain way, his own degradation, I do not know. I fear not; and if not, then centuries of repression had borne their legitimate fruit.

John's absurd and demeaning misunderstanding of Julius's character is one of the things that has led a few readers to assume that Chesnutt himself, speaking obliquely through John, finds Julius's "old-time darky" mask to be less than an act. Chesnutt was fascinated by the middle ground of historical transition on which such a character might stand; but such a reading of John's remarks is entirely misleading. It is Julius's tale of Dave— a tale that John obviously fails to comprehend in any but the most superficial way—that signifies the cultural destructiveness of slavery that John purports to find in Julius himself. The telling of the tale is a denial that the destruction of African American culture was complete or that the master's proscriptions were not recognized and resisted. Part of that resistance lies in the very telling of the tale, the ongoing act of cultural cognition, remembrance, and creation that the orally transmitted stories have become. To put it another way, the telling is evidence that what was partly destroyed was *African* culture: *African American* culture in turn recreated itself generation after generation. As John's frame puts it (and here it *is* Chesnutt as well as John speaking), Julius's tales offer the opportunity for the reader "to study, through the medium of his recollection, the simple but intensely human inner life of slavery." Manipulating John much as Melville manipulates Delano, Chesnutt penetrates John's obtuse misreadings of Julius, as well as the deceptive screens of Julius's ulterior motives (which John frequently does recognize), to let the reader provisionally relive the physical pain and potential psychological derangement of enslavement and its aftermath in the "medium of his recollection."[129]

Recollection is also the medium of Julius's oral culture, a culture of memory or reconstructed ancestral wholeness in which the voice of dialect, full of subtle intonation and deceptive planes of signification, breaks away from the destructiveness and rigidities of cultural misreading into a vocal act that operates, as Ellison might say, on another frequency. Like Harris and other adapters of the folktales, Chesnutt gave his ex-slave narrator a rich voice in which vocal properties are of special significance. Chesnutt set forth not just an alternative to literate culture, the power of the book, but rather a dimension of spirituality itself—a survival of the strong African traditions of speech and song in which auditory space is perceived as a physical field of action and speaking well is a sign of authority. The *griot,* the communal and historical storyteller, in particular may be recognized as an exemplary artist in African tradition—a "blacksmith in words," according to a Bambara formulation—and his command of circumlocution and oratorical wit are taken to be extensions of the primal energy of sound itself, the force of *nommo* harnessed to the medium of communal memory.[130] In the case of Du Bois, the retentions of such African practice were formative in his use of the black spirituals in *The Souls of Black Folk;* for Chesnutt, Julius's narrative voice, a dialect of preserved memory and ineradicable cultural difference, is at once an artistic mask and a form of racial political commentary.

At times Julius's storytelling voice takes on characteristics of performance in the plantation tradition, as when, in "Po' Sandy," the "pathetic intonation with which he lengthened out the 'Po' Sandy' touched a responsive chord in our hearts." The guile of tricksterism here enters into public performance. Julius's most characteristic voice, however, is represented as a fusion of tonality and narrative, as in "The Marked Tree": "His low, mellow voice rambled on, to an accompaniment of night-time sounds—the deep diapason from a distant frog-pond, the shrill chirp of the cicada, the occasional bark of a dog or cry of an owl, all softened by distance and merging into a melancholy minor which suited perfectly the teller and the tale."[131] In this case Julius's voice is closer to that evident in "Tobe's Tribulations," a tale, I have argued, in which what cannot be heard by John is critical to our conceptualization of Julius's voice. Like Primus turned into a mule in "The Conjurer's Revenge," Tobe turned into a frog makes the act of metamorphosis an allegory of slave culture. Speaking becomes thematized not only in the sense that the quality of intonation is separated, by way of dialect, from the cultural standard that it comments on, but also in the sense that speech is made a reservoir of the hidden and the unarticulated. The suggestions by Baker, Gates, and others that dialect should be read as a mask can thus be pushed further on the basis of Chesnutt's conjure tales. The voice of African American culture is itself a voice of metamorphosis and transformations: it is the liminal voice of conjure in which dialect marks, but does not fully contain, the historical record of slavery and its transcendence.

A prominent feature of "Tobe's Tribulations," which must be interpreted as a reflection upon the tonal semantics of African American culture, indicates precisely this multilayered meaning of conjure in the tales. Just as "Mars Jeems's Nightmare" resembles the Master-John cycle of African American folktales, "Tobe's Tribulations" is related, by analogy, to a series of folktales of speaking animals or objects that took on special resonance in their American form and have been shown by William Bascom to constitute one of the most striking African-derived sequences in black American folklore.[132] In one form of the story a slave discovers a talking turtle, but when he takes his master to hear the turtle, it refuses to talk. After the slave is beaten for lying to his master, he asks the turtle why it would not talk for the master; it repeats what it had said to him before: "Well, that's what I say about you negroes, you talk too much anyhow."[133] The point of the story, as it was rendered in versions shaped by the African American experience of slavery, is political: because the life of slavery is a life in which survival depends upon secrets and hidden languages, the slave talked too much in telling the master of the turtle's power. Secondarily, of course, the tale suggests a parallel significance in African American culture generally—that it will thrive on the surreptitious and must remain built upon elements of thought and language that amount to a kind of conjure against the dominant culture.

But this variant of the tale is less powerful than that in which the speaking object is a skull or a set of bones. In a version from Africa recorded by Leo Frobenius, for example, the Nupe hunter who discovers a talking skull learns that its message ("talking brought me here") soon applies to himself. When the skull refuses to speak for the king, the hunter is killed, and it is then his own head that can say to the skull, "Talking brought me here." The talking skull tales as a group focus attention on the importance of verbal economy and the control of language in African oral culture, more specifically on the magical or spiritual properties of speech that create its great potential for power held in reserve or acting in disguise.[134] Severed from the physical body yet nonetheless able to articulate the lesson of warning, the skull itself occupies the domain of magic speech that is a prerequisite of good storytelling, but a domain not to be entered upon without regard for the power of story. Memorialized in Meta Fuller's profound 1937 sculpture *Talking Skull,* the figure harbors the threat of destruction for an indiscriminate use of language, while at the same time reiterating in its own message the kind of linguistic economy and concealment that the hunter should have practiced in the first place.

Richard Dorson notes African American examples in which the speaking animal is either a turtle or a mule (in this latter case, where the slave is to be shot for insisting that a mule can talk, the equivalence between mules and men under slavery is further underlined), but his more haunting instance of talking bones resembles the Nupe tale. Related to the common folk motif in which speaking bones reveal a murder, the "Talking Bones" tale refers to the indiscriminate killing of slaves by masters, who then dump the bodies in the woods. When the slave John discovers the bones of one victim, they say: "Tongue is the cause of my being here." The bones refuse to speak when John returns with his master, so John himself is beaten to death and left in the woods: "And then the bones talked. They said, 'Tongue brought us here, and tongue brought you here.'" Speaking in these tales is allied with danger and the threat of death; it becomes a guarded category of life in which articulation must remain very private or at the least work on several levels simultaneously. As Herskovits and others have argued, the principles of subterfuge and concealment that could be found to operate in the language of any oppressed group were strengthened in the case of black America by the fact that "indirection" was such a strong part of the language and social etiquette that Africans brought with them to the New World, transferring it, for example, into the animal folktales, where circumlocution and indirection are of paramount importance and constitute, in fact, the allegorical nature of the tales themselves. Whether in everyday speech, in tales, in work and worship songs, or in other cultural arts, slave secrets cannot be spoken directly for fear of betrayal. Because of its constant and various pressure of protection, resistance, and dissembling, slave language—the act of talking, the trope of the tongue—came to be one riddled with ambiguities and defined by silence or indirection.[135]

"Tobe's Tribulations" does not, of course, exactly reproduce the common folk motif of the talking animal or the talking bones. Were Julius to insist that he has discovered a talking frog, John would not kill him, but only think him insane or superstitious. But the point of the story is that Julius hears a language that John does not; the story exists within the very borders of believability that define conjure as a phenomenon of belief and signifying as a linguistic act. Something in Julius's language always remains secret. In terms of the marking of dialect itself, we have seen, this can be figured variously—as the "word shadows" defined by ethnology to belong to a primitive language at odds with standard English; as the echoes of a lost and now unspeakable African tongue; or as the rediscovery for a middle-class narrator such as the hero of "The Wife of His Youth" of the subcultural dialect of his own slave past. John and Annie's characterization of Julius's stories as "nonsense" is therefore not without justification. Julius's language approximates "nonsense" in that it requires a reconceptualized framework of being in the world in order to be fully understood. Julius's beguiling language recapitulates the sounds of Tobe's language that are inaudible to John—the "confused chattering," "hoarse bellowing," "drumming," and "strident din" that only after prolonged exposure form themselves into a kind of "rude harmony"—in the tale's folk motif of the talking animal. As I argued earlier, the "noise" coming out of the "bottoms," pressed through John's perceptual screen of plantation mythology, is turned into a "lullaby" rather than a "lament of lost souls."* The slave's indirection and the master's bias meet in the liminal realm of "noise" and "nonsense" that constitutes the ground—the "bottoms"—of slave culture on which both Julius's and Chesnutt's stories are built. Like Tobe's tribulations, Julius's narrative inhabits a liminal terrain between worlds, where

---

* Chesnutt may have had in mind a comparable opening in Harris's Uncle Remus story "A Plantation Witch," in which Remus's voice merges with a chorus of frogs: "The serious tone of the old man caused the little boy to open his eyes. The moon, just at its full, cast long, vague, wavering shadows in front of the cabin. A colony of tree-frogs somewhere in the distance were treating their neighbors to a serenade, but to the little boy it sounded like a chorus of lost and long-forgotten whistlers. The sound was wherever the imagination chose to locate it—to the right, to the left, in the air, on the ground, far away or near at hand, but always dim and always indistinct. Something in Uncle Remus's tone exactly fitted all these surroundings, and the child nestled closer to the old man." Here as elsewhere, of course, the dynamics of narration, and their implied promulgation of, or signifying upon, plantation mythology, differ markedly in the cases of Harris and Chesnutt. Although his trickster tales have their own dimension of ideological critique, Remus's voice, as it appears in the frames of the tales, is typically an extension of Old South nostalgia, whereas Julius's voice speaks more often in cunning antagonism. At the conclusion of "Mr. Bear Catches Old Mr. Bull-Frog," however, Remus sings a nonsense song that replicates the mildly mocking song sung by the frog when he escapes the axe of Mr. Bear, in this case apparently adding his own voice to the signifying nonsense of black language. When the little boy remarks that it is a "might funny song," Remus replies, "Funny now, I speck . . . but 'twern't funny in dem days, en 'twouln't be funny now ef folks know'd much 'bout de Bull-frog langwidge ez dey useter." The passage seems to register Harris's characteristic ambivalence, at once indicting whites for their ignorance of black culture and transposing the lost language into the vague liminality of "dem days." See Harris, *Uncle Remus: His Songs and Sayings,* pp. 142–43, 123–24.

the survival tactic of verbal economy and indirection, the capacity to carry on secret communication within the master's disciplinary regime, is elevated into a definition of culture itself. "Nonsense" in its very essence offers an implied threat to social order, to the hierarchy of intelligibility; for that reason it also raises our awareness of the artificiality of the controlling modes of discourse, moving speech out of the realm of nature and toward the realm of performance.[136] As it passes into *non*sense according to white ears or white cultural standards, then, black language passes into the borderland of sound; its aural semantics, whether carried in a countervailing vocabulary or dialect, or in the registers of hollers, chants, and melody, evade the mapping of white cultural practice just as the apparent "alternating sounds" evaded the cultural mapping of the ethnographers described by Boas.

Beyond the boundaries of the intelligible, the cultural "nonsense" of African America asserts its necessarily subordinate power as one of secrets, a power that reflects on the fact that power itself is a mutable discursive construction. Tobe, Julius, and Chesnutt, in a kind of triad of verbal concealment and indirection, make nonsense the sign of cultural difference even as they load its sound with disarming powers of verbal insurrection. Reconfiguring the necessity of secret language and deceptive actions on the plantation, black language, coded in alternative sound and diction, like the motifs of the folktales that are an integral part of that language, follows a path of development that can be printed as dialect but cannot be adequately represented by such indices. Chesnutt's critique of culture thus operates on several levels. His tales offer an acute analysis of the devastating effects of racism, as the antebellum world is shown continually to live on into the world of the postwar South and as the northerner John is subjected to harsh ironizing. More broadly, Chesnutt offers a penetrating investigation of the tradition of American literature and its resistance of African American forms (or its appropriation of them in the plantation tales of Harris and the collections of folklorists). And specifically, Chesnutt offers the most extraordinary theoretical account to date—rivaled only by *The Souls of Black Folk* in the same era—of the fundamental characteristics of African American cultural expression. Both Julius's stories and Chesnutt's tales are satiric in their approach to Reconstruction and its aftermath. Yet the function of satire as Chesnutt uses it must include reference to the bardic function of African storytelling in which ritual insult and attack on authority through tricksterism or "songs of allusion" is a characteristic feature.[137] Satire functions as a part of the social language itself, and radical indirection, an improvisatory freedom to move around and under an authoritative structure of significance, is one of its manifestations. To hear the conjure tales properly—both Julius's tales and Chesnutt's encompassing tales—requires an apprehension of what is implied or silent, of the "talk" that is dangerous or subversive but is, nonetheless, a key element in the retrieval of history.

The themes of inflected articulation and political silence in Chesnutt's tales reach an apogee in "The Dumb Witness," which is a conjure tale without conjure and a Julius tale without Julius. Later incorporated into Chesnutt's last published novel, *The Colonel's Dream,* the tale takes on additional resonance as a commentary on the precarious racial future of the New South. In its own right, however, "The Dumb Witness" is remarkable for its interweaving of the problems of inheritance, language, and miscegenation, the tripartite core of Chesnutt's most overtly political fiction, which comes to full maturity in *The Marrow of Tradition.* The tale is simple but compact with the structure of classical tragedy that so galvanized Chesnutt's imaginary portraits of the southern miscegenation complex that lay embedded in his own familial history. Malcolm Murchison is a slaveholder who surprises Viney, his slave mistress of fifteen years, with the news that he is to marry a white northern widow. Some "passionate strain of the mixed blood in her veins," Chesnutt remarks, provokes Viney into a reaction of "hysterical violence" and pleading. Distraught, she seeks out Murchison's fiancée and drives her away with a covert communication; Murchison responds to Viney's "power to dip your tongue in where you are not concerned" with a merciless physical attack on her that leaves her tongue mutilated. One week later he receives news of a large inheritance from his uncle, but it is Viney alone who knows the money's secret hiding place. Her subsequent refusal to speak, over a period of decades, drives Murchison into debt, into madness, and at last to his death. Her revenge complete, Viney tells Murchison's nephew the secret, and the plantation is restored to its former glory.[138]

The proliferation of secrets and silences throughout the tale passes beyond the achievement of Viney's revenge into Chesnutt's entire handling of the act of storytelling. Viney's oral capacity for vengeance is presented ironically as a function of her enslavement: "Slaves were not taught to write, for too much learning would have made them mad." Chesnutt here collapses the danger of slave literacy (its potential for catalyzing resistance and revolt) and the hatred generated by such disadvantage into the sort of mental derangement likely to be held forth by the masters as the result of education. But to be illiterate is not to be unintelligent, or "dumb," but only to be denied an important instrument of liberation and cultural power. Chesnutt thus makes silence and illiteracy into a single "dumb" instrument that turns the diagnosis of madness back on the masters. Murchison attempts without success to employ a colored man to teach Viney to write, but her inability to learn is obviously a part of her vengeful strategy. Viney is "of our blood" (as Murchison's uncle writes in his letter naming him as heir) and is thus a victim of the twin tragedy of incest and miscegenation; moreover, her segregated cultural world marks her as mistress but never wife, property but never heir. Because Viney's silence lasts beyond emancipation and the era of Reconstruction, it works also to separate more markedly the culture of slavery from the surviving culture of enslavement. The "meaningless inarticulate mutterings," the "discordant jargon" deriving from "no language or dialect, at least none of European origin," which at last pours forth in "a flood of sounds that were not words," represents a very particularized form of power.[139] Like Melville's Bartleby, Viney speaks the forceful language of rebellion in both her silence and her valuable inarticulate speech.*

The intimation of an African language (or perhaps American Indian, given her "dash of Indian blood") hidden within Viney's array of sounds suggests, moreover, that Chesnutt intended the tale to operate as a critique of American culture's exclusion of the folkloric oral world of black culture. This is underlined by the very form of the tale and its utilization of the trope of silencing within the larger context of Chesnutt's own production of tales. Although Julius is the source of most, but not all, of the story's facts in this case, he does not narrate the tale. John absorbs the tale, which is first told in Julius's "own quaint dialect," into his own voice—his own dialect of standard English, one could say—and contentedly comments

---

* When Chesnutt wrote the story of "The Dumb Witness" into the plot of *The Colonel's Dream,* a skeptical exposé of a New South dominated by poor white arrivistes who lack both the grace and the paternalistic protective attitudes toward blacks displayed by their aristocratic forerunners, he diluted its import. Now it is the overseer, not the master, who physically abuses Viney; the incestuous implication of their affair is discarded; and a deathbed scene of confrontation allows the forgiving white man a moral ascendancy over the vengeful, somewhat more stereotypical tragic mulatto. But the novelistic version also makes a further adjustment in the opposite direction: there is, in fact, no hidden money. Whereas the short story concludes with the prospect of renewal in the next generation of the southern dynasty, the novel does away with the inheritance, leaving the youngest heir (again a nephew) to abandon the bigoted, blighted South and seek his fortune in New York.

that it is a story "of things possible only in an era which, happily, has passed from our history." Insofar as John's comprehension of the tale turns out to be painfully inadequate, the transformation of Julius's story into refined literary language might be read as a form of conjure or theft—the act of cultural dissociation and incorporation by which the plantation mythology of post-Reconstruction white writers was created. Speaking in his own narrative voice here, Chesnutt thus engaged in a thickly conflicted cultural action. To begin with, he explored a solution to the limitations of dialect writing. As Robert Stepto has persuasively argued, Chesnutt's first four conjure tales—"The Goophered Grapevine," "Po' Sandy," "The Conjurer's Revenge," and "Dave's Neckliss"—represent something of a cycle in their own right, one in which John is shown to be an increasingly (but never fully) reliable narrator and in which Chesnutt measured his own reluctance to found a career on the narration of dialect stories. Simply from the perspective of narrative strategy, the next step was to be located in "The Dumb Witness," where conjure itself is eliminated (as in "Dave's Neckliss") and John speaks in his own voice. That such a step might symbolize the completion of John's "apprenticeship," as well as Chesnutt's desire to speak in his own literary voice, is supported by Chesnutt's complaint in a letter to Tourgée that he was uncomfortable with the limits of Julius as a narrator, and also by the fact that he then turned to color line stories before resuming his Uncle Julius stories over the course of the 1890s.[140]

But "The Dumb Witness," especially if one reads it in the context of those color line stories, such as "The Wife of His Youth," that offer explicit commentary on Chesnutt's ambivalence about "black" culture, is an even more complex meditation on the politics of narration. It unites language and miscegenation on two fronts: language is linked here to property, to the material wealth and social power that is the functional expression of the literate control of language; and language is linked at the same time to questions of literary power, to the voice of culture as it is ranged along the color line. John's telling of Julius's tale and his orderly improvement of it with information he says was not available to Julius constitute his own silencing of Julius's voice and of Viney's story. Given the ironies and satire characteristically hidden in Julius's narrative vocalization, one can hardly take Chesnutt's choice of John's voice as a confirmation of his having become a reliable narrator. John's blithe remarks about Viney's story belonging to another era show that his sensibilities have not advanced much, and he must in the end turn to the grinning Julius to discover, of course, that Viney has never truly lost her voice, but, like Julius himself, has played "dumb" all along. Rather, one must judge that John's voice is also the voice of cultural suppression—or, from the middle-class, light-skinned Chesnutt's point of view, the voice of cultural miscegenation and assimilation. Dialect is stripped away from the tale and with it the sound of Julius's voice—the very sound that was as commercially valuable to Chesnutt as to Harris. Julius's silence is the contemporary inversion of Viney's; but whereas her act may be read as one of revenge and a denial of the master's property through language, John's appropriation of Julius's voice converts the property of African American culture into a literary commodity even as it erases that voice from the page. Chesnutt himself thus became the "dumb witness" to a crisis in cultural transmission. Standing on the border of color formed by the legacy of slaveholding miscegenation, denied his rights and split by the violent segregation of American cultural forms, Chesnutt would soon enough feel silenced by the public's lack of interest in his fiction. In "The Dumb Witness" he composed a tale in which the elimination of the dialect voice of black culture was its strongest sign of presence: the silent, indirect language of African American life, "subcultural" in the material resonance of muffled sound itself, ran beneath the language of Chesnutt the published author, who spoke predominantly in the refined voice of the majority literary culture. Like Viney, who is "of our blood," Chesnutt crossed the boundary of color and culture in an act of articulation. The voice of slave culture was silent, was "dumb," but it had its revenge.

White Weeds: The Pathology of the Color Line

> The lesson on segregation was only a logical extension of the lessons on sex and white superiority and God. Not only Negroes but everything dark, dangerous, evil must be pushed to the rim of one's life. Signs put over doors in the world outside and over minds seemed natural enough to children like us, for signs had already been put over forbidden areas of our body. The banning of people and books and ideas did not appear more shocking than the banning of our wishes which we learned early to send to the Dark-town of our unconscious.
>
> Lillian Smith, *Killers of the Dream*

"The Dumb Witness" links the conjure tales to the rest of Chesnutt's career, which can be understood as an elaboration upon the questions posed in the early color line stories. The central question, simply stated, was: What is a white man? Chesnutt's 1889 essay of that title, which surveyed the varying legal definitions of whiteness offered by different states and sarcastically dismissed the hypocritical theories of racial "purity" put forward by promiscuous white racists, did not provide a very satisfactory answer, but then neither had *Plessy* v. *Ferguson* or countless other legal and supposedly scientific attempts to resolve the issue. Because its decision rested on the case of a man black only under "one-drop" law, *Plessy*, as I argued in chapter 3, carried segregation into a metaphysical domain, though one that had the backing of scientific, sociological, and legal theory to support it. Chesnutt understood from intimate personal experience, however, that theories of segregation amounted to no more than a kind of superstition. As the carefully coded language of his folklore essay seems to imply, the philosophy of race purity and the laws of segregation were part of the white world's conjure:

> Relics of ancestral barbarism are found among all peoples, but advanced civilization has at least shaken off the more obvious absurdities of superstition. . . . The means of conjuration are as simple as the indications. . . . It may be a mysterious mixture thrown surreptitiously upon the person to be injured, or merely a line drawn across a road or path, which line it is fatal for a certain man or woman to cross. I heard of a case of a laboring man who went two miles out of his way, every morning and evening, while going to and from his work, to avoid such a line drawn for him by a certain powerful enemy.

Black men and women, no matter how dark or light, were those who could not cross the superstitious racial lines drawn everywhere for African Americans by a powerful enemy. Given the irrationality of segregation and the widespread hysteria about miscegenation, both of which long outlived Chesnutt, the more important question, as *Plessy* ironically proved, was: Who can *appear* to be a white man? A 1908 study of American segregation by the eminent progressive journalist Ray Stannard Baker included in its section on mulattoes and race mixture the judgment that "no one, of course, can estimate the number of men and women with Negro blood who have thus 'gone over to white'; but it must be large." (One 1921 estimate suggested that between 1900 and 1910 anywhere from 10,000 to 25,000 passed each year—statistics whose gross margin of error is an index of the complete ambiguity of mixed-race life.) Within a few years James Weldon Johnson would exploit the nation's anxiety about the invisible mulatto population in his masterpiece of combined pathos and satire, *The Autobiography of an Ex-Coloured Man*. The theme, however, was already a common property of literature when Chesnutt came to it, predisposed by the history of his own family and his personal position on the color line to find in it a perfect vehicle for the literary attack on segregation. He recorded in a journal entry of 1875 that he considered passing as white; but there is no evidence that he ever did so. His color became, instead, his means of examining the doubleness of American racial life from within its most vexing liminal role. As he would understatedly remark in accepting the Spingarn Medal in 1928, mixed color had for Chesnutt "more dramatic possibilities than life within clearly defined and widely differentiated groups."[141]

The conjure tales, the color line stories, and his first novel, *The House behind the Cedars* (1900), all portray families torn apart by slavery and racism, and in some instances reunited by perseverance and subterfuge, during slavery or in the wake of emancipation. No writer before Faulkner so completely made the family his means of delineating the racial crisis of American history as did Chesnutt. His fictional family was more often than not interracial, and it therefore functioned as a social embodiment of prohibitions and fear, of the taboo against the "monstrous" that was everywhere visible but just as bluntly denied in American racial life. In a nation governed by harsh proscriptions against intermarriage and given to fanaticism about black sexuality, the family itself was a nebulous, overly politicized concept. Academic and popular sociology alike proclaimed the black family to be inherently or environmentally corrupt. No fact was more often or more scurrilously claimed by racist commentators than that the "failure" of the black family was a sign of racial degeneration. Whether or not the fault was said to lie in the history of slavery, the archetype of the black rapist, the assertion that black women were licentious, and the charge that black families were "naturally" at home in squalor and filth were all common pronouncements in the post-Reconstruction interpretation of so-called black family pathology. It could be confidently noted, for example, that "there is little knowledge of the sanctity of home and marital relations" among blacks, with children raised to "show the superlative of filth and indecency"; each black community, it was argued, "is but an aggregation of ignorant homes, and each home is but a circle of thoughtless individuals"; and yet another observer reported that a "family sense remains to be developed among the negroes. In a long and intimate connection with this folk, I have never heard a [Negro] refer to his grandfather, and any reference to [his] parents is rare."[142] In his color line stories and in *The House behind the Cedars,* and then again in *The Marrow of Tradition,* Chesnutt answered such destructive charges in detail. As he was able to document by firsthand experience, it was the legacy of white dissipation, and in some instances of forbidden love, that left the most visible mark of pathology—white pathology—on the black family.

It is difficult now to conceive of the overwhelming acceptance through-out the scientific and sociological world of Chesnutt's day of theories expounding the inevitability of black racial degeneration, in particular the degeneration and eventual extinction of mixed-race people. Without question, such work had a profound impact not just on Chesnutt's career but also on his literary strategies. The great bulk of evidence against the "myth of the mulatto demise," as Joel Williamson calls it, counted for little, and combined with the cruel realities of segregation, the myth itself helped drive significant numbers of light-skinned African-Americans across the color line.[143] Indeed, mulattoes themselves were on occasion the pro-pounders of the most virulently racist tracts, as in the case of *The Negro a Beast,* by Charles Carroll, noted earlier. In a similar pseudoscientific work of great self-loathing published in 1901, William Hannibal Thomas argued that "negro nature" is so "thoroughly imbruted with lascivious instincts" and "so craven and sensuous in every fibre of its being that a negro manhood with respect for chaste womanhood does not exist." In a rare show of open disgust with American publication of racist theory, Chesnutt wrote several harsh letters to Thomas's publishers, protesting the disas-trous effect such a book could have for the 9 million black men and women of the United States whose freedom, as he argued, had not yet been made secure.[144] By the time he rebutted Thomas, the glaring cen-trality of the sexual component in American racism had become ever more evident in the violent disorders of the Wilmington "race riot" upon which *The Marrow of Tradition* was based.

Chesnutt's contribution to the literature of race mixture and the color line rests less in *The House behind the Cedars* or in the stories devoted specifically to the theme, which are not necessarily his best work, than in his general conception of miscegenation as both a social and a cultural issue. Because his ancestry provided the framework in which he might study his own pronounced sense of injustice, Chesnutt's most powerful uses of the theme of miscegenation make secrecy, denial, or evasion central to its dramatic function. As in his conjure tales, moreover, it is those cultural-ideological elements that most distinguish his work from the bulk of turn-of-the-century passing literature. Such melodramatic elements as ancestral sins, lost inheritances, and revelations of blood mixture, far from typing Chesnutt's fiction as derivative, gave him the means of exposing cultural segregation at work. "The Dumb Witness" is concerned with the denial of voice and subsequent revenge; but as the story makes clear, Viney's revenge is against Murchison not only as a lover but also as a master—and not just a master but one to whom she is related by blood, in what precise degree we are not told. Yet as African American slave narrators had announced some time in advance of Faulkner, miscegenation was also frequently enough literal incest of just the sort described in Chesnutt's tale, where the the quadroon slave mistress and her lover are both descended from the same patriarchal, ancestral tree. In accomplishing her revenge, Viney does not destroy the entire family (as does Phillis in "The Marked Tree"), but she does destroy the prospects of Murchison's cross-sectional marriage and his continuation of the plantation dynasty in the new regime of the postwar South. Her revenge encompasses the two basic tropes of American race literature, blood and language, embedding the one within the other by converting the unspoken secret of her lineage into the unspoken secret that avenges it.

It would not be plausible, perhaps, to say that Chesnutt, too, wrote in an act of revenge; but his fascination with genealogy grew directly from his own experience of the "marked tree"—what he once referred to as his "ragged family tree"—of southern miscegenation. Born in 1858, Charles Waddell Chesnutt was the son of Andrew Jackson Chesnutt and Anna Marie Sampson. Both were free blacks who left North Carolina in 1856 to settle in Cleveland, where they were married and Charles was born, before returning to Fayetteville in 1866. The evidence that is available, although it is in part a matter of speculation, indicates that both Chesnutt's mother and father were the illegitimate offspring of white men, Waddell Cade and Henry Sampson, and their black mistresses, Ann M. Chesnutt and Chloe Sampson Harris (she later married a black man named Moses Harris). Like Alexander Manly, whose famous antilynching editorial would play a crucial role in the Wilmington violence dramatized in *The Marrow of Tradition*, Chesnutt was descended from white men of property but deprived of the paternal name and the full inheritance that went with that lineage. In both instances, it should be noted, the white paternal grandfathers provided a certain amount of property for their black off-spring, but far less, of course, than went to their legitimate white heirs. That Chesnutt bore the family name of his grandmother—in an era, and coming from a region, preoccupied with patrilineage—may be an additional reason that his fiction, most notably *The House behind the Cedars,* often dwelled on the lives of black women and their mulatto children. (Apropos Alexander Manly's editorial, which scandalized the South by suggesting that white women sometimes had voluntary affairs with black men, one might also add that a cousin of Chesnutt, John P. Green, claimed that his mulatto mother was the daughter of a white woman who, along with her sister, had had illicit affairs with the same black man, thus giving birth to mixed-race children who were both sisters and cousins. In view of the ultra-Faulknerian possibilities open to him, then, it is clear that Chesnutt simplified, rather than complicated, the tangled family melodrama he might have built into his fiction.)[145]

One sees most clearly the emotional dimensions that lie behind Chesnutt's use of the family as a metaphor for the crisis in American racial politics in *The Marrow of Tradition,* which revolves around the twin axes of sexual conduct that link the antebellum and postbellum worlds: on the one hand the doubled racial legacy of the slaveholding patriarch Samuel Merkell, a family of white descendants and a parallel family of black descendants; and on the other the hysteria about "Negro domination" that has its most virulent expression in the thematics of rape and lynching. Although in *The Marrow of Tradition* the genealogical "secret" is subordinated to the ideological significance that can be attached to it, whether privately in the form of inherited property or publicly in the form of economic and political power achieved through racial intimidation and violence, the novel's network of masquerades and covert plots and its scenes of melodramatic revelation suggest that the underlying structure of nineteenth-century American race law and social prejudice was the "ragged tree" of patrilineal sexual exploitation and disinheritance. Before he made miscegenation the wellspring of Jim Crow in *The Marrow of Tradition,* however, Chesnutt had probed its phenomenology in one novel and a set of stories that borrow from the strategies of the conjure tales.

Like a great deal of the literature of miscegenation and passing, Chesnutt's color line stories (which he once described as "sermons")[146] are dominated by melodrama, and their fundamental trope is irony. The moral level of Chesnutt's anatomy of miscegenation is easily recognized, and the stories often point toward the exposure of the shame and guilt that inhere in race denial and that can exist on both sides of the color line. But the epistemological level of the stories is no less important, for the stilted narrative operations of melodrama—revealed ancestral sins, secret communications, extraordinary coincidences in plot—constitute a perfect structure for the crisis of racial identity. If the sins of the past, most of all the original sins of miscegenation, exist as silent mechanisms that govern behavior for generations to come, identity itself becomes a social construct of the most brittle, coincidental kind. Under the taboo of miscegenation which had become ingrained into the highest law of segregation, in fact, identity itself, either in an act of self-recognition or in the attribution of identity to another, had become a radical act of imagination. Despite the flood of racial theory that posited incontrovertible biological proof of racial differences, race remained, for all to see, a tormenting philosophical abstraction. In case law color was a construct codified, for example, in the utterly unstable notion of "reputation," the form of property (that of "whiteness") that Tourgée tried in vain to capitalize upon in his brief for Homer Plessy before the Supreme Court. The yoked concepts of reputation and property, to which Chesnutt would return in *The Marrow of Tradition,* fused the moral and epistemological planes, requiring the mulatto—or allowing him the opportunity, as the case may be—to prove himself white. Such proof, with all its attendant and conflicting ramifications in law, social theory, and cultural membership, was inevitably derived through adjudication within a liminal realm of difference no less peculiar and tortured than the liminal realm of metamorphosis—the transformation from one animate form to another—in conjure.

It is just this ambiguity of racial proof that the young John Walden seizes upon in *The House behind the Cedars,* when, contemplating his future career as an attorney, he decides to pass, appropriately changing his name to Warwick, a character from a Bulwer-Lytton novel. His mentor, Judge Straight, reads to him passages out of applicable North and South Carolina law, the latter instructing that juries may judge race not just by an admixture of black blood not exceeding one eighth but also "by reputation, by reception into society, and by the exercise of the privileges of the white man." (Because Chesnutt chose not to pass and went on to become an attorney whose law practice was not halted but was certainly hindered by his admission that he was "black," John's insistence on the color of his skin rather than the abstract issue of a color-blind justice surely sprang from Chesnutt's rueful reflection upon the consequences of his own act of conscience.) But it is precisely John's acceptance of the logic of racial identity enunciated in such a law that draws his sister Rena into the novel's formulated tragedy of passing and its proto-Faulknerian world, where the "sins of the fathers shall be visited upon the children." Like Henry and Bon in *Absalom, Absalom!,* John Warwick and his white friend George

Tryon, Rena's fiancé, are held together by a semi-incestuous bond that ensures Rena's destruction. John and George are made brothers by the psychological union produced "when one loves some other fellow's sister." But that love in turn is based, for both of them, on the idea of Rena's whiteness. John feels "something more than brotherly love" that is motivated by Rena's "Greek sense of proportion, of fitness, of beauty." Her presence in his world of passing gives him psychological security, we are told; but the novel's necessary unfolding of racial sins also implies that, as in Faulkner's world, only an act of incest could finally protect the family secret. For his part, George, when he discovers her racial strain, sees not the beautiful white woman of the novel's transparent Victorian masquerades but a shameful and corrupt misrepresentation: "He had seen her with the mask thrown off. . . . With the monkey-like imitativeness of the Negro she had copied the manners of white people while she lived among them, and had dropped them with equal facility when they ceased to serve a purpose." Because it reveals the secret of Rena's blood and exposes to view the bittersweet relation of Molly Walden and her white lover, the novel is governed by the conventional requirement that Rena and John must, as Molly fears, do "penance for her sin" and "expiate as well the sins of their fathers."[147]

The House behind the Cedars is limited by the conventions of white beauty that define the genre of tragic mulatto fiction, and the power of its melodrama to produce a serious challenge to racialist cultural assumptions is constrained by Chesnutt's own fundamental ambivalence about a story that he had worked on for a decade and to which he felt an extraordinary emotional attachment. In Chesnutt's significant public statements about racial mixing, "The Future American: A Complete Race Amalgamation Likely to Occur" (1900) and "Race Prejudice: Its Causes, Results, and Cures" (1904), he scoffed at black racial separatism as little more than a mirror image of white Jim Crow and instead idealized a physically homogenous social order. In *The House behind the Cedars,* nevertheless, Rena is brought to a recognition that she belongs not in the white world but with "her people," even though, having crossed the color line, she must pay the ritual sacrifice for the sins of her ancestors. To the degree that it capitulates to conventions of racialized, gothic sexuality, the novel, although it tentatively invokes the hidden promise of mixed-race "new people," thus fails to forecast a new generation of "future Americans."[148] However much he satirized the South's rituals of aristocratic and pure genealogy (the chivalric tournament and the social ball of the Clarence

Social Club at which the newly passing Rena first charms George Tryon are a more elaborate representation of the Victorian poetic taste evinced by Ryder in "The Wife of His Youth"), Chesnutt was hemmed in by his own anxiety. John and Rena may act unconscionably in passing; but they also act pragmatically and in service of the mixed-race elite to which Chesnutt belonged. Although the epistemological plane is engaged in the novel's frequent recourse to the radically ambiguous language of the law and especially to coincidental epistolary revelations as a means to advance the downward spiral of Rena's fall, there are, finally, no secrets, and "sin"—whether of the black mother or the white father—is left in an undisturbed category of governing genealogical facts. Passing issues in tragedy, but tragedy does not issue in significant self-scrutiny. Frank, the novel's darkest-skinned character, is its most ethical, though he remains a minor figure; by the time of *The Marrow of Tradition,* however, some of Chesnutt's most venomous sarcasm is directed at the black Jerry Letlow, who would bleach his skin and straighten his hair in order to appear more white, and his rage of futile protest against the color line would be lodged not in the mulatto hero William Miller but in the angry, destructive black laborer Josh Green.

At least two of Chesnutt's short stories make the secrecy of blood a more compelling phenomenon than did his first novel, and they therefore provide a more interesting pathway from the conjure stories to *The Marrow of Tradition*. In "Her Virginia Mammy" the heroine's obsession with proving her unsullied racial stock is ironized in the most extraordinary ways. The plot is simple: raised an orphan by adoptive German immigrant parents after a steamboat accident kills her family, Clara is reluctant to marry John Winthrop, a descendant of Mayflower pilgrims, until her newly discovered black "Virginia mammy" persuades her that she too is descended from the best First Families of Virginia lineage. Mrs. Harper, the woman she takes to be her mammy, is of course in reality her mother, an olive-complexioned former slave whose love affair with Clara's white father violated all public standards of southern decorum despite its common occurrence. The story, however, carefully preserves the secret of Clara's racial mixture in the sense that her mother knows the truth, her fiancé guesses the truth (but conceals it himself), and the reader knows as well; Clara alone remains under the precious social and psychological illusion that she is the descendant of the best white blood of Viriginia on both sides of her family.

What is of particular interest in the story is the manner in which

Chesnutt handles the epistemology of Clara's hidden mixed blood, which is fused with the ironic language of his narrative. Clara's passing is embedded in the text itself, for example in the conversation with Mrs. Harper that at once reveals and conceals her true origins. Crucial moments at which Mrs. Harper might tell the truth but instead creates the fiction of Clara's aristocratic mother are marked by dashes ("I knew your father—and your mother"; "Your father and mother were on the boat—and I was on the boat"; "Your mother—also belonged to one of the first families of Virigina"; "Yes, child, I was—your mammy . . . and my heart loved you and mourned you like a mother loves and mourns her firstborn"). The dash is the sign of passing, the orthographic representation of secrecy written into textuality, which, one might argue, is the only domain of its existence in the story. In this case, however, it is not Clara who passes but rather her mother who lets her pass. In an appropriate paradox, the dash thus links mother to daughter but while also eradicating their most crucial bond. Ironizing blood, it turns mother into mammy and replaces the most telling relationship of human regeneration with a fictive construct consonant with the social order of segregation. Mrs. Harper protects her daughter, but she does so by the perpetuation of a tragic illusion. If John's magnanimity derives from untold knowledge of his own tainted past, the story offers no explicit evidence. Rather, he seems to speak generously, and for Chesnutt, when he remarks that "we are all worms of the dust, and if we go back far enough, each of us has had millions of ancestors."[149] John's remark evacuates the genealogical justification of American segregation of any philosophical meaning, but it does nothing to touch the practical effects of coding inherited "blood" with the power of law.

Clara Hohlfelder, "a Miss Nobody, from Nowhere," becomes Clara Stafford, who, because she can now marry John and take his name, "shall have nothing left of all that I have found." "Nothing" is correct: emptied of significance, Clara's past constructs the truth of racial identity as an artifice, as it is so constructed by the law's own fictions, but one she herself construes as natural. Her earlier intimation that "the blood of my ancestors seems to call to me in clear and certain tones" is verified by ironic inversion. The trope of sound, so critical to Chesnutt's imagined delineation of a distinct black culture, and frequently represented in his fiction by the racial marker of dialect, is echoed once again in Clara's dance studio. Her class of colored professionals, who distance themselves from darker Negroes yet appear to display "a natural aptitude for rhythmic motion, and a keen susceptibility to musical sounds," makes up the social family that Clara is not allowed to recognize. She feels "perfectly at home among them"—an intuition further confirmed textually but not dramatically in John's far from unintentional pun when he replies to Clara, "It is a great thing to have faith in one's self" and "to be able to enjoy the passing moment"—but for Clara both the colored professionals and the musical sounds to which they respond by "natural aptitude" exist strictly across the dash of the color line.[150] Because she is not put in a position to hear the sounds properly, Clara misconstrues them. Like Boas's "alternating sounds," the "certain tones" of her past are so far from Clara's imagination as to be inaudible except by an ironic reversal in which she is deceptively reassured of her whiteness. The plenitude of whiteness replaces the "nothing" of her black heritage, but in the process Chesnutt's canny manipulation of the phenomenological category of race reduces it to nothing more than an idea—a biased perception, a coincidence, a lie.

"Her Virginia Mammy" is Chesnutt's most provocative investigation of the social ironies of the American color line, but "White Weeds," a remarkable story unpublished in his lifetime, offers a more overt presentation of race as an epistemological problem. It does so by rendering the question of racial mixture altogther secret—almost. Once again the male protagonist, Professor Carson, is represented to be of old and distinguished southern ancestry, while the woman he is to marry, Marian Tracy, has no parents or close relatives living and is shrouded in mystery. An anonymous letter informs Carson that his fiancée has black blood, but his sense of prudence and honor will permit him neither to ask her outright nor to cancel his wedding plans. Although Carson has overcome much of the racial antipathy he has imbibed as a postwar southerner, his belief that the "touch of a Negress" is "pollution" remains "bred in the bone." Because of his paralyzing fear lest his "children show traces of their descent from an inferior and degraded race," he is unable to restrain himself from asking his wife to deny the anonymous charge immediately after their wedding. Her refusal to answer his question one way or the other, a striking reconceptualization of the trope of silence employed in "The Dumb Witness," drives Carson to madness and an early death. In an extravagant act of public revenge that has meaning, ironically, only to herself, his wife conducts his funeral as though it were her true wedding, arranging fitting secular music from Wagner and Hoffman, and entering "clad not in widow's weeds but in [white] bridal array" to the accompaniment of *Lohengrin*'s "Wedding March."* The mockery of her "white weeds," which

* In this detail the story bears comparison to Du Bois's "Of the Coming of John" in *The Souls of Black Folk,* in which the "Wedding March" from *Lohengrin* is symbolic of the transcendence

provokes most of the spectators to think of the madness of Ophelia, compresses the secret of her blood into its essential form. Exchanging the black dress of mourning for the purity of white marriage garments, Mrs. Carson empties color of its significance without revealing to the reader any evidence upon which to make the required choice of segregation.[151]

The story insists on an answer, however, and the storytelling narrator, who explains what lay behind Mrs. Carson's bizarre behavior, insists that Carson's tragedy was all for "nothing, absolutely nothing," since his own knowledge of Marian Tracy's family proves that "her line of descent for two hundred years is quite as clear, quite as good, as that of most old American families."[152] The story, that is to say, will not let the heroine's ambiguous silence speak for itself. Chesnutt himself forces her secret blood to appear white. To be sure, we are meant to take the narrator's assurance of her family's "clear" blood line to be open to question, perhaps like that of "most old American families." But more to the point is that fact that Chesnutt was compelled to answer—was compelled to draw the color line at all. The moral authority of the story resides in Marian's act of silent witness against racial definitions of identity. Silence modulates from a trope indicative of slave culture's concealment and subversion to an index of resistance to the very foundations of American race law. Chesnutt's violation of that witness in the form of assurance that it was all for "nothing" does not undercut the meaning of silence but rather calls our attention to it, insisting, as the conventions of law and language itself required, that one choose between white and black. "Nothing," like nonsense or dumbness, is a trope that harbors strong but utterly nebulous expressivity in Chesnutt's use: it renders a moral judgment about Carson's need to know his wife's "color," but it also forces the reader to participate in Carson's need, and in doing so to construct an invisible racial division in which "nothing," emptied of legal rights and humanity itself, reverts to the black side of the color line.

The closer that Chesnutt came to the order of symbolic representation in his fiction of miscegenation, the greater his distillation of blood itself into an idea that is finally best articulated in figures of silence or emptiness.

---

that John experiences as he is about to be lynched for killing a white man, his former childhood friend, in the course of protecting his sister from rape. Chesnutt's use of music "ranging from Mendelssohn to ragtime" in the Carsons' actual wedding likewise brings to mind the signifying trope of music as a mode of cultural "miscegenation" in Johnson's *Autobiography of an Ex-Coloured Man,* whose protagonist makes his name by composing a rag version of Mendelssohn's (rather than Wagner's) "Wedding March."

An observation by Peter Brooks about the nature of melodramatic representation is helpful here. "Mute gesture," he argues, "is an expressionistic means—precisely the means of melodrama—to render meanings which are ineffable, but nonetheless operative within the sphere of human ethical relationships. . . . Yet of course it is the fullness, the pregnancy, of the blank that is significant: meaning-full though unspeakable."[153] Blood, for Chesnutt, could theoretically be reduced to "nothing," to a kind of blank without philosophical or moral import; but in the practical terms of law, language, behavior, and the operative structure of knowledge itself, race was continually constituted by difference. Race *was* difference, and the act of passing, the metamorphosis of color, was its sign. "The Dumb Witness" links language and miscegenation in an act of silent revenge, as Viney, bound to Murchison both by incest and by acts of love that could be condoned outside the recognition of the law but not within it, turns a special form of vocalization into a weapon. Suddenly converted into property by Murchison's plans to take a white wife, Viney in her silence takes back what she has given. Likewise, in "White Weeds" Marian Tracy's silence is a weapon; whether or not she is "black," she passes by withholding a secret that she may not even know with certainty. One could construe silence in both of these instances as a form of protest, but Chesnutt saw that it was something more. Silence was the fullest inflection of an African American cultural language that depended upon secrecy and indirection for survival; yet it was also a form of communication in which difference might be expressed even as it was erased. To be forced into the choice that Marian Tracy refuses to make, the choice authorized by *Plessy* v. *Ferguson,* was also to be left, as "Her Virginia Mammy" suggests and as Johnson would argue in *The Autobiography of an Ex-Coloured Man,* with the moral equivalent of "nothing." It was to find that property was lodged in an invisible genealogical imperative that might or might not be salvaged in the pathetic recourse to the "reputation of being white," and it was therefore to be returned once again—like Jim returned once again to Huck and Tom's derisive cabin of slavery—to an anachronistic world of masters and slaves that was far from dead.

Chesnutt takes such a reification of the phenomenon of color to its extreme state of liminality in "Lonesome Ben," a conjure tale in which an escaped slave's clay eating renders him mulatto, thus alienating him from his family and his master alike. The tale is also a variation on the Philly-Me-York Master-John story with which Chesnutt had experimented in "Mars Jeems's Nightmare." In this case, Ben, whipped by his master for drinking, decides to run away. When clouds obscure his vision of the

North Star, he ends up going in a circle; without food, he begins eating clay—and then begins to turn to clay, so much so that first his own wife does not recognize him and then his master, who sees only a "mis'able lookin' merlatter" when he comes upon Ben lying in the road and leaves him, as Julius remarks, with "no wife, no chile, no frien's, no marster." Ben's failed escape from slavery and his turning to clay superimposes the circular bondage of postwar southern blacks, perhaps like Ben unable to escape and yet symbolically bereft of family and masters, upon the greater alienation of mixed-race people. In turning to clay—an inventive attenuation of Dave's turning into a ham—Ben is an incarnation of the "state of non-differentiation" that Mary Douglas finds represented by dirt, which begins as the symbol of contaminating danger to order and purity, the threat of "boundary transgression," but ends as the symbol of dissolution, of "total disintegration." That is to say, Ben's bodily dissolution acts out miscegenation's threat to racial order in a doubled, paradoxical way: both the decay that white racism predicted through black "contamination" and the eradication of social and psychological identity suffered by mixed-race people are expressed in his ordeal. In a terrifying instance of metamorphosis that comes not from conjure as such but from the contradictory forces of "blood" manifesting themselves in his objectified body, Ben disintegrates: "He laid dere 'til he died, an' de sun beat down on 'im, an' beat down on 'im, an' beat down on 'im, fer th'ee or fo' days, 'til it baked 'im as ha'd as a brick. An' den a big win' come erlong an' blowed a tree down, an' it fell on 'im an' smashed 'im all ter pieces, an' groun' 'im ter powder. An' den a big rain come erlong, an' washed 'im in de crick."[154] "Lonesome Ben" is no doubt an expression of Chesnutt's private agony about life on the color line, a life in which the invisible "admixture" of blood stripped his whiteness of meaning and reified his blackness, threatening at any moment to reduce any act of achievement to a mere function of his "race." Also a tale devoted to the creation of cultural memory in an act of narrative mourning, "Lonesome Ben" elevates the reification of the human under slavery, which Chesnutt had already explored in "Po' Sandy" and "Dave's Neckliss," to a new level in order to move it beyond the register of labor to that of psychology and legal identity. Smashed to pieces, Ben is not even a man made into a "thing." In the logic of race superiority, from which America had not recovered but rather had translated into more irrational, bewildering forms in the era of Jim Crow, objecthood first displaces subjectivity before being obliterated in a nightmarish return to pure physicality.

To be African American under the rule of segregation, said Chesnutt, was to risk being made to be "nothing." Ben performs no act of revenge comparable to those of Viney or Marian Tracy. In his case the inherited signature of slavery's originating acts of miscegenation leeches his body of its humanity, its capacity to think and act. The successive reification and disintegration produced by Ben's mixed blood portrays nothing less than the phenomenon of race suicide—not the suicide of Anglo-Saxon America through the contamination of "alien races" so feared by turn-of-the-century race purists but rather the suicide of humanity inscribed in the law of Jim Crow.

Fusion: *The Marrow of Tradition*

> Man the sum of his climactic experiences Father said. Man the sum of what have you. A problem in impure properties carried tediously to an unvarying nil: stalemate of dust and desire.
>
> William Faulkner, *The Sound and the Fury*

It was to the pervasive law of Jim Crow, entwined in the genealogical secrets of miscegenation and the inherited burdens of racially coded cultural difference, that Chesnutt turned in his political masterpiece, *The Marrow of Tradition*. Chesnutt's hope that he had written "the legitimate successor of *Uncle Tom's Cabin* and *A Fool's Errand*," the two works that were his idea of America's most influential literature, indicates an admiration for Stowe's and Tourgée's capacity to render political arguments in the form of fiction. Chesnutt's novel is built on the twin fortunes of the Miller and Carteret families, separated by color but bound together by the entanglements of antebellum miscegenation. The novel begins and ends in family crisis. At the outset the newborn Carteret heir, Dodie, defines the professional color line that the black Dr. Miller cannot cross; but in the end, an innocent victim of the racial violence unleashed by his own father and other white supremacists, Dodie owes his life to William Miller and to the forgiving generosity of his wife, Janet. The atmosphere of drugged, funereal apprehension surrounding Dodie's birth with which *The Marrow of Tradition* opens is representative of the nebulous restoration of sectional autonomy that had taken place by the end of the century. Major Carteret has attached his future hopes to his wife's estate after the war's ruin of his own, while she has been reduced to periodic hysteria by the proximity of her black half-sister, Miller's wife, who now lives with her husband in the former family mansion of the Carterets. Olivia's hysteria, the female counterpart to the male hysteria of racial violence that governs the novel's political plot, results both from the young heir's fragile health and from her own deep anxiety and guilt about her "twin" sister Janet's place within the family's genealogy. The problems of property inheritance, generational conflict, and genealogy, carried across chronological as well as racial boundaries, thus form the integuments of Chesnutt's plot. As an overt symbol of the New South's perilous racial situation—"There's time enough, but none to spare," Miller is told in the novel's last line as, now crossing the color line, he rushes to save the child's life—Dodie is heir not only to the family's estate but to the burden of its sins as well.[155]

Dodie belongs to a new generation whose fate hangs in the balance at the conclusion of the novel. *The Marrow of Tradition* tells the harrowing, historically acccurate story of the Wilmington race riot of 1898, an event that should more rightly be styled a revolution (as Chesnutt does), a rebellion or a coup (as several historians have), or a massacre (as did its other chronicler in fiction, David Bryant Fulton). The white supremacist rebellion in Wilmington could have been invented in Chesnutt's imagination, but it came to him virtually ready-made. Engineered by white Democrats and radical racists who had seen their control of the city slip into the hands of Fusionists, an upstart political party composed of Republicans and dissident Populists, many of whom were black, the revolution restored power to white Democrats by completely subverting the principles of free democratic election. Some of Chesnutt's relatives lived through the violence, and he traveled to Wilmington in 1901, as part of a tour of southern states, to collect material for his novel. He was stunned by the revolution's flagrancy and the federal government's inability, or unwillingness, to respond, writing to Walter Hines Page that it was "an outbreak of pure, malignant and altogether indefensible race prejudice, which makes me feel personally humiliated, and ashamed for the country and the state."[156] In making Dodie a symbol of the complex knot of property, genealogy, and racial politics that Chesnutt found to be at the heart of segregationist theory, and in allowing Miller to save his life, he put an optimistic gloss on the future that was hardly justified by contemporary events.

Heir to the South's appropriation of the "Negro problem," Dodie Carteret is born into a world of crude bigotry, lynching, and race hysteria. Thomas Dixon's Ku Klux Klan sagas would soon be among the nation's favorite race literature, powerfully translated onto stage and screen, and pronouncements such as those of William B. Smith would adequately summarize the prevailing white view of segregation's necessity: "If we sit with negroes at our tables, if we entertain them as our guests and social equals, if we disregard the colour line in all other relations, is it possible to maintain it fixedly in the sexual relation, in the marriage of our sons and daughters, in the propagation of our species?" The threat of interracial sexuality is at the center of Chesnutt's novel in the near lynching of Sandy after his false accusation of murder, in the fictive use Chesnutt makes of Alexander Manly's famous editorial reply to Rebecca Latimer Felton's speech on rape, and in the entangled genealogical destinies of the Millers and the Carterets, as well as in a variety of subthemes and figures. *The Marrow of Tradition,* one could say, is devoted to the question of "propagation"—or, to use the novel's more frequent words, to "generation" and "degeneration." In this respect in particular, it represents a complex deepening of the moral analysis of miscegenation that Chesnutt had undertaken in the color line stories and *The House behind the Cedars.* Against the common charge that postbellum blacks and especially mulattoes were a retrogressive or "degenerate" species, likely without careful regulation by white civilization to revert to the purported savagery of their African ancestors, Chesnutt ranges the obvious degeneration of the Old South's aristocratic descendants, particularly Tom Delamere, while rendering everywhere ambiguous the concept of pure blood. Olivia's panic about her resemblance to Janet Miller and her fear that discovery of her father's actual marriage to his African American lover, Julia Brown, might lead people to "assume that she, Olivia Carteret, or her child, had sprung from this shocking *mésalliance*" form part of the novel's continual interrogation of the fear of racial pollution. Although the "weed" of slavery has been cut down, Chesnutt writes, "its roots remained, deeply imbedded in the soil, to spring up and trouble a new generation."[157]

Converging with a national interest in the purity of racial stock and the ancestral sources of contemporary fitness to survive the Darwinian social struggle, southern worship of genealogy was driven specifically by the need to recreate the aura of aristocratic greatness supposedly smashed by the Civil War. The South's "mistake," however, as Thomas Sutpen would have it in *Absalom, Absalom!,* corrupted all dreams of genealogical purity: not just in the haunting sin of slavery that remained visible in the war's long aftermath, but in the effluvium of black blood, long mixed into white whether visibly or not, which reappeared to "trouble" succeeding generations. Modern Jim Crow, Twain had shown, was built on the utter legal fiction of "blood," but it was left for Chesnutt to tie together genealogy and the politics of racial violence. His ideal metaphor for that coupling was latent in the historical circumstances of his plot, for "fusion" had colloquial usage as a term for miscegenation in addition to designating the maverick political party that controlled much of North Carolina politics in the 1890s before being swept away in a statewide frenzy of racial intimidation and violence. For example, after the Fusion-dominated North Carolina legislature had called an adjournment to mark Frederick Douglass's death in 1895, a *New York Times* editorial, in somewhat confusing diction, yoked his mixed marriage to the upstart political party: "Fusion is a marriage of two parties having no principles in common. The indorsement of [that is, the memorial for] the miscegenation leader is the legitimate heir of [this political] union." Fusion might represent progress or the idealized harmony of American democracy; but it was anathema to proponents of white racial superiority.[158]

In order to see clearly the way in which Chesnutt merged politics and genealogy in *The Marrow of Tradition*, it is necessary to understand the mechanism of the revolution itself and the range of historical details that he expertly reworks into the fabric of his narrative, writing what was up to that time perhaps the best political novel in American literature. The trope that binds the genealogical plot of the two families to the political plot of the Wellington revolution is rape—rape understood in the condensed double sense that everywhere animates its usage in the American racial context as the antebellum sexual rights of the white masters were converted into the postwar specter of the black rapist. Philip Bruce contended in a typical statement of Jim Crow theory (published not by any means as a speculative or incidental work but rather in his contribution to a multivolume history of the United States) that rape had become a daily occurrence in the South, perpetrated by a new generation of Negroes "brutalized by a life in which there is no self-discipline and no self-restraint, and without any anticipation of the legal consequences to curb their brutal passion." Thomas Dixon's great popularity (as well as that of the sensational film made from his work, D. W. Griffith's *Birth of a Nation*) depended upon a leering, propagandistic portrait of the black rapist. Taking a page directly from Dixon, Senator Benjamin Tillman of South Carolina advocated lynching and thundered melodramatically against rape in the halls of Congress: "I had rather find [my daughter] killed by a tiger or a bear and gather up the bones and bury them, conscious that she had died in the purity of her maidenhood, than to have her crawl to me and tell me the horrid story that she had been robbed of the jewel of her womanhood by a black fiend." As studies of lynching by Ida B. Wells, Walter White, and others would show, what Wilbur Cash would later call the South's "rape complex" was detached from contemporary as well as historical reality, a free-floating trope of attack that could be used with virtual impunity on any political occasion and in support of any racial cause. Even those commentators who condemned white rape of black women, during slavery and after, remained convinced that the threat of black sexual assault needed to be met with instantaneous and violent retribution. Thomas Nelson Page's argument was representative of this point of view. He condemned lynch mobs but explained that their "ferocious rage" was motivated by the shock brought on by "the ravishing and butchering of their women and children" at the hands of Negroes to whom freedom meant only one thing—"the opportunity to enjoy, equally with white men, the privilege of cohabiting with white women."[159] On a different and more unusual plane was the revived Jeffersonian argument of the sociologist Lester Ward, who held that the evolutionary character of racial conflict by which states and nations progressed naturally produced a corollary law that drove black men to rape white women. Whereas Jefferson had asserted that black men showed a sexual-aesthetic preference for whites comparable to "the preference of the Oranootan for the black women over those of his own species," Ward put such an argument in the neo-Darwinian framework of species preservation. Just as whites might respond violently to the crime of rape according to a biological law of race preservation, the black man commits the act in the first place because he is driven by the "imperious voice of nature commanding him at the risk of 'lynch law' to raise his race to a little higher level."[160]

Ward's thesis might have existed on a continuum with Chesnutt's portrait of the "Blue Vein" elite, who will marry only lighter mates and who distinguish themselves from "niggers," or with his sardonic comment that the "infusion of white blood has certainly toned up the Negro immensely."[161] But as Chesnutt well knew, the charge of rape that accompanied nearly every lynching of a southern black man, whatever the evidence, ironically reversed the visible historical fact that had created the mulatto elite—namely, that a significant portion of the African American population were the descendants of acts of white rape of black women. More important, it grossly ignored the prominence of white rape or interracial passion that remained evident in the mixed-race population of the day. What was denied was the possibility of a white man's or woman's sexual expression of love for a black person. Chesnutt put such a possibility to work in the central scenes that bind together the familial and the political plots of his novel. Moreover, the most brilliant stroke of the Wilmington white supremacists, and the incident that provides the key to Chesnutt's novelistic rendering of the revolution, came in the *Wilmington Messenger*'s manipulation of an editorial against lynching by the African American editor Alexander Manly. The offensive editorial appeared in Manly's newspaper, the *Wilmington Record,* a relatively prosperous paper supported by much white advertising. But its source lay in the remarks made before an 1897 agricultural meeting in Tybee, Georgia, by Rebecca Latimer Felton, the wife of former congressman W. H. Felton and later famous as the first woman to become a United States senator. Commenting upon the seeming decline in rural security and a rising fear of black criminals, Felton rallied her audience with a forthright call for lynching: "When there is not enough religion in the pulpit to organize a crusade against sin, nor justice in the court house to promptly punish crime, nor manhood enough in the nation to put a sheltering arm about innocence and virtue . . . [and] if it needs lynching to protect woman's dearest possession from the ravening human beasts—then I say lynch, a thousand times a week if necessary." After Felton's speech was reported and attacked in the *Boston Transcript,* Felton responded in the *Macon Telegraph,* charging that northern newspapers, with their misguided liberal sentiments about black civil rights, were responsible for encouraging black crime.[162]

Entitled "Mrs. Felton's Speech" and apparently published for the first time in August 1898, Alexander Manly's reply condemned the indiscriminate practice of lynching and the role of white journalism in fanning the flames of racist attack. His sober argument—that if whites would only deal fairly with blacks and treat crimes by all races equally, then blacks could be counted on to join in the campaign against both sexual attack and vigilante justice—was completely ignored by the Democratic press, which instead responded vociferously to his sarcastic suggestion that whites should

> guard their women more closely . . . thus giving no opportunity for the human fiend, be he white or black. You leave your goods out of doors and then complain because they are taken away. Poor white men are careless in the matter of protecting their women, especially on the farms. They are careless in their conduct toward them and our

experience among poor white people of the country teaches us that women of that race are not any more particular in the matter of clandestine meetings with colored men than the white men with colored women. Meetings of this kind go on for some time until the woman's infatuation or the man's boldness brings attention to them, and the man is lynched for rape. Every negro lynched is called a Big Burly Black Brute, when, in fact, many of those who have been dealt with had white men for their fathers, and were not only not black and burly, but were sufficiently attractive for white girls of culture and refinement to fall in love with them, as is very well known to all.

Although the Democratic press quoted only this part of Manly's editorial, clearly calculated to elicit a visceral response, he had included the further admonition to Mrs. Felton to "tell your men that it is no worse for a black man to be intimate with a white woman than for a white man to be intimate with a colored woman. . . . You cry aloud for the virtue of your women while you seek to destroy the morality of ours."[163]

White newspapers throughout the South denounced Manly's impudence and reiterated Felton's argument. The *Wilmington Weekly Star* reprinted her speech immediately, and the *Atlanta Journal* ran it under the headline "Lynch 1000 Weekly Declares Mrs. Felton."* Manly's opinions were no

---

* Felton's prominence because of her speech lasted well beyond the events of 1898. When a black man named Sam Hose was accused of rape and murder in a notorious case in April 1899, Felton and others were employed by the *Atlanta Constitution* to write opinions for a symposium devoted to the prevention of such crimes. The day after his arrest Sam Hose was castrated and burned alive in a ghastly public ritual attended by some two thousand people; his body was mutilated and cut into souvenirs for the jeering crowd. Du Bois was to recall that he canceled an appointment to meet Joel Chandler Harris rather than pass by the grocery store where Hose's knuckles had been placed on display (on another occasion he claimed that he had canceled the appointment after seeing the knuckles himself); and it was perhaps the Hose case that Chesnutt had in mind when he wrote in *The Marrow of Tradition* of the white savagery that led lynchers to carry off "fragments of [the victim's] mangled body as souvenirs, in much the same way that savages preserve the scalps or eat the hearts of their enemies." When the Emory College professor Andrew Sledd attacked lynching in the *Atlantic Monthly,* citing the Sam Hose case, Felton replied in the *Constitution* that Sledd was a traitor to the South, deserving of tar and feathers. The ensuing letters to the editor favored Felton's position. Felton's racism also accommodated a peculiar form of feminism. As part of a later work in favor of women's enfranchisement, she attempted to bolster her argument in favor of the matrilineal descent of political power and rights by noting that, whereas white fathers of mulatto children in the old South typically left them slaves, the "degenerate white woman who sunk herself beneath the pity of her sex, and outlawed herself beyond recovery [in giving birth to mulatto children] . . . gave them freedom, no matter how dark complexioned." See John E. Talmadge, *Rebecca Latimer Felton: Nine Stormy*

more shocking than those expressed earlier in the famous antilynching writing of Ida B. Wells, who argued in one trenchant *Memphis Free Speech* editorial of 1892 that the "thread bare lie" of the rape charge would eventually bring about a reaction in public sentiment "very damaging to the moral reputation of their [white] women." Wells's offices were burned as a result of her frankness and she was driven from Memphis; but in her subsequent national campaign against lynching she did not hesitate to defend "the poor blind Afro-American Samsons who suffer themselves to be betrayed by white Delilahs" and to focus on the hypocritical fact that "any mesalliance existing between a Southern white woman and a colored man is a sufficient foundation for the charge of rape." For Manly as for Wells, it was the truth of his assertion that some white women might take black lovers or husbands and willingly bear their children that most violated the sacred taboo of white womanhood. As Philip Bruce had put it in his influential volume *The Plantation Negro as a Freeman,* "The few white women who have given birth to mulattoes have always been regarded as monsters . . . who have sunk to the level of beasts of the field."[164]

Although North Carolina whites were virtually unanimous in their condemnation of Manly, prominent Wilmington and Raleigh black leaders were split; some bravely defended Manly's statement of the obvious truth while others disassociated themselves from his scandalous views. In the aftermath of the revolution, when thousands of African Americans had been driven from Wilmington and New Hanover County, those blacks who did not see that Manly was only a convenient scapegoat complained, as did one woman in a letter to President McKinley, that many innocent people had been made to suffer for the sins of Manly.[165] Such a division of opinion, perhaps little surprising in an era dominated by the views of middle-class accommodationists, would also be reflected in the structure of Chesnutt's novel, which is built in large part on the contesting opinions of William Miller and the darker-skinned, poorly educated rebel figure Josh Green. Manly's editorial, however, played directly into the hands of his opposition. Although it would have made a strong impression in virtually any part of the South or, indeed, the nation in 1898, the Manly

---

Decades (Athens: University of Georgia Press, 1960), pp. 113–18; James M. McPherson, *The Abolitionist Legacy: From Reconstruction to the NAACP* (Princeton: Princeton Unversity Press, 1975), pp. 304–5; W. E. B. Du Bois, *Dusk of Dawn: An Essay toward an Autobiography of a Race Concept* (1940; rpt. New York: Schocken, 1968), p. 67; Charles Chesnutt, *The Marrow of Tradition* (1901; rpt. Ann Arbor: University of Michigan Press, 1969), p. 296; and Rebecca Latimer Felton, *The Subjection of Women and the Enfranchisement of Women* (Cartersville, Ga., 1915), unpaginated.

editorial could have had the exaggerated impact that it did only in the heated context of North Carolina politics that forms the arena of Chesnutt's novel.

The Wilmington revolution had its roots in the overthrow of Reconstruction and the destruction of black civil rights in the last two decades of the century. The more immediate cause was to be found, however, in the elections of 1894 and 1896, in which Democrats throughout the state, as well as in Wilmington, lost their positions to Republicans and Fusion party candidates, some of whom were African American or who had appointed African Americans to various civil service positions. There were eleven black legislators in the North Carolina general assembly in 1897, the largest number since the previous decade and at a time when black political participation was being suppressed throughout the South. President McKinley also appointed twice as many blacks to federal positions as any previous president, including, for example, John Campbell Dancy as customs collector for the port of Wilmington. An outsider who replaced a white Democrat in the post, Dancy was routinely referred to in the *Wilmington Messenger* (the leading Democratic newspaper and the primary model for Carteret's paper in Chesnutt's novel) as the "Sambo of the Custom House." The rapid Fusion renaissance of black political fortunes may thus have left the ardent Democrat feeling, as one historian remarks, "like a man who had gone to sleep by a dim, guttering fire, only to awake in a house ablaze."[166] The campaign of intimidation and violence launched by white supremacists in Wilmington thus had causes specific to the city, but it also partook of a statewide climate of racial outrage on the part of whites.

The charge of "Negro domination" at the center of the Democratic campaign referred in reality less to actual numbers than to the sense on the part of whites that they had lost economic and political control of certain cities. In Wilmington, for instance, where black voting had remained at a higher level than in some other parts of the South in the aftermath of Reconstruction, the numbers were typical: three of ten aldermen were black, and one out of three on the school committee; there was a black coroner, a black deputy superior court clerk, and a black justice of the peace; the health board was all black, as were two out of five fire stations; fewer than half the city's policemen were black, but there were various black mail clerks and a number of black professionals and craftsmen. If one were to judge only by racial balance, the numbers were not inappropriate in a city where the majority population was black (11,000 to 8,000; 14,000 to 10,000 in New Hanover County altogether). More telling, though, were the objections of whites to being summoned before a black judge, to being arrested by black police officers, to having their homes inspected by black sanitation officers, and so forth. The governor and the mayor, who had himself been elected after a special election act amended the city charter in favor of opposition aldermen, were held responsible for the rising crime rate, the influx of black population, and what was alleged to be the insolence and corruption common among black officials. Domination, that is to say, was a code word for a loss of power or economic clout, and a fear of granting to African Americans any but the most minimal forms of authority. In 1898 an answer to the threat of black domination was swiftly formulated. In Wilmington a group of leading white Democrats who called themselves the "Secret Nine" (Chesnutt reduced it to the "Big Three") began to plot a counteroffensive in the early months of 1898, eventually forming a group of clubs that went under the banner of the White Government Union and merged with the growing statewide white supremacy movement.[167]

Nowhere was the campaign against "Negro domination" more virulent than in the North Carolina press, a fact that Chesnutt exploited to great effect in his novel. During an era in which leading national magazines and newspapers were prominent in the creation of black minstrel caricatures and routinely ran inflammatory headlines and stories about black crimes and lynch mobs, the newspapers of Wilmington and Raleigh, the greatest offenders in the North Carolina campaign, were perhaps not extravagant. The *Raleigh News and Observer*, edited by Josephus Daniels, ran a series of articles vilifying black leaders under sometimes ludicrous headlines such as "Unbridled Lawlessness on the Streets," "Greenville Negroized," "Chicken under His Arm," or "Negro on Train with Big Feet behind White," and charging blacks with such social "outrages" as refusing to observe Jim Crow seating during a circus performance. In addition, the *News and Observer* promoted white supremacy effectively through Norman Jennett's cartoons, which depicted absurd caricatures of black politicians towering over whites or crushing them under gigantic shoes. In September 1898, two months before the watershed election, the *Kinston Free Press* published an article listing black officials in numerous counties and towns emblazoned with the headline "Nigger! Nigger! Nigger!"[168] Running throughout such propaganda were explicit or implicit fomentations to race violence on the basis of alleged black sexual crimes. With such statewide support the *Wilmington Messenger*, edited by Thomas Clawson, had little difficulty making itself the primary mouthpiece of the Wilmington revolution.

Manly's editorial therefore brought an already heated atmosphere to the point of conflagration. Even though some accounts have speculated that Manly did not even write the offending editorial or that it was a Democratic ploy, the best evidence shows that he was the author. Manly, it may be said, was only speaking the truth and only following a line of argument already advanced by outspoken southern black congressmen such as South Carolina's Thomas E. Miller and North Carolina's George H. White. Still, if Manly's act was heroic, it was also foolhardy in its provocation. The *Wilmington Messenger,* like Chesnutt's white supremacist paper in *The Marrow of Tradition,* led the charge against Manly with headlines such as "Negro Editor Slanders White Women" and "Infamous Attack on White Women." Papers throughout the South and some in the North reprinted or excerpted Manly's editorial in order to attack his views, and journalists nationwide later held the editorial responsible for the Wilmington "riot." More important, however, was the use to which the editorial could be put. The lynching fever that broke out upon the appearance of Manly's editorial was deliberately held in abeyance; the Democratic campaign kept alive the passions awakened by Manly but also directed them toward election day. In a speech before an enormous Fayetteville rally in October, led by the Klan-like white supremacist organization known as the Red Shirts, Benjamin Tillman asked: "Why didn't you kill that damn nigger editor who wrote that?" But Manly, for the moment, was worth far more alive than he would have been dead. As Chesnutt would write in fictionalizing the episode: "A peg was needed upon which to hang the *coup d'état,* and this editorial offered the requisite opportunity."[169]

Because the campaign against Negro domination capitalized so blatantly upon the supposed threat to white masculinity posed by black political activism, the irony of Manly's name and his public aspersions against white manhood cannot have escaped many Democrats. The pun latent in his name (and recognized by Manly's son Milo in his later conversations with Leon Prather) was one crucial to his reply to Felton and subsequently to Chesnutt's deployment of Manly's thesis in *The Marrow of Tradition.* Whereas Felton longed for the "manhood" necessary to protect virtuous white women from violation at the hands of black beasts, Manly's editorial subverted the concept of manhood by leveling racial distinctions in the commission of sexual crimes, and by attributing control of their own sexual lives and racial preferences to white women. As Richard Yarborough has argued, it therefore provides a framework in which to interpret the concepts of manhood and manliness as they were expressed in the racist rhetoric of the Wilmington campaign.[170] The concept of manliness, and puns upon the term, function literally and figuratively throughout Chesnutt's novel—in the behavior of both black and white men under the pressure of racial crisis, in the use of the charged symbol of white womanhood to organize racial antagonism, and in the origins of the Carteret family crisis in the antebellum sexual liason of Samuel Merkell and Julia Brown.

Certainly, the irony in Manly's name was not likely to have escaped Alfred Moore Waddell, who became a leader in Wilmington's white supremacy campaign. The explicit model for Fulton's Colonel Moss in *Hanover* and one of the models for Chesnutt's aristocrat of racism, General Belmont, Waddell, though he did not belong to the Secret Nine, was instrumental in the provocation of the Wilmington revolution. Defeated in 1878 in his own bid for reelection to Congress by Daniel Russell, who by 1898 had become governor and was despised by white Democrats, Waddell focused his anger on Wilmington's African American leaders and professionals. Fulton's fictive delineation of Waddell's sentiments was in fact little different from Waddell's recorded public statements: "We are going to elevate the white man to his place and regulate [*sic*] Sambo to his sphere, if the streets have to flow with blood to accomplish that end. . . . 'Nigger root doctors' are crowding white physicians out of business; 'nigger' lawyers are sassing white men in our courts; 'nigger' children are hustling white angels off our sidewalks." In an actual speech commended by the *Messenger*, Waddell proclaimed that "we will never surrender to a ragged raffle of negroes, even if we have to choke the Cape Fear River with [black] carcasses," and it was primarily on account of his electrifying speeches that he was appointed chairman of a public committee created by the Secret Nine to oversee the implementation of a "White Declaration of Indepedence" (or the "Wilmington Declaration of Independence") drawn up on the eve of the 1898 election.[171] (Waddell's allusion to the Cape Fear River, repeated in other speeches, may have been one source for the later rumor, not true, that in the revolution the river *was* choked with bodies.)

Colonel Waddell was a classic southern aristocrat, proud of his lineage and Confederate military record, and his sense of the Wilmington revolution was in keeping with the proslavery interpretation of secession as authorized by the American Revolution, a view that was explicitly carried over into the language of the white Democrats' "Declaration of Independence." As Waddell would later write to Walter Hines Page, the revolution was but "the good old Anglo-Saxon way of patiently waiting until government becomes intolerable and then openly and manfully overthrowing it." Waddell devoted one of his pre-election speeches to Alexander Manly and took up the reverberating cry of injured southern manhood in hinting that Manly should be lynched. The "White Declaration of Independence," presented publicly on November 9, the day after the election, still focused attention on Manly, by now an icon of Negro domination that yoked professional achievement to the specter of criminality. After a preamble that declared black suffrage unconstitutional and rejected the notion of any African American political rule, the declaration insisted that the reins of government be taken by those whites who owned 90 percent of Wilmington property and paid commensurate taxes; called for jobs currently held by blacks to be turned over to whites; and demanded that Manly, the author of "an article so vile and slanderous that it would in most communities result in the lynching of the editor," be driven from town.[172]

Alfred Moore Waddell is of special note, moreover, because of his possible relationship to Chesnutt's grandfather, Waddell Cade. Frances Keller implies that there may have been some family relationship that would entangle Alfred Waddell in Chesnutt's imaginative treatment of his family tree, but no clear evidence has been unearthed. The name alone, however, would have reminded Charles Waddell Chesnutt of his own mixed heritage. Some ten years before the Wilmington revolution, Chesnutt had already had the opportunity to challenge Waddell's view of the post-Reconstruction South. In a letter circulated to the Cleveland Open-Letter Club in 1889, Chesnutt took the occasion of a reply to Waddell's anti-Negro stance to formulate a statement of his developing views not just of Reconstruction but also of the rising racism of the New South. Chesnutt's moderate statement was a prelude to the more bitter reaction that Wilmington would provoke:

> The white people of the South do not want to be governed by the Negro at all, whether well or ill; more than that, they do not want the Negroes to share with them the power which their numbers justly entitle them to. They prefer to curtail their own liberties very materially, as Mr. Waddell's letter admits, in order that they may entirely eliminate the Negro from political significance. I do not believe that

this is necessary. One half of the time and ingenuity spent in conciliating the Negroes, in winning their friendship and confidence, that
is now spent in subverting their rights, would enable the white people
of the South to govern by the influence which superior wealth,
station, intelligence, and experience in public affairs would naturally
give them.[173]

There was nothing offensive in this proclamation, but the flamboyant
racism of Waddell evident in his leadership at the end of the century would
call forth the more radical reply of *The Marrow of Tradition*. Although it
is not certain how much primary material or firsthand testimony Chesnutt
utilized in his novelization of the Wilmington revolt, it seems more than
likely that the intertwining of the careers of Manly and Waddell (especially
if Chesnutt was, or believed himself to be, related to Waddell) would have
struck him with a singular intensity.

A dimension of Manly's role that has not been noticed and one that
makes Chesnutt's interest in him all the more likely is his family's genealogical resemblance not only to the Carteret-Miller family but also, strikingly, to the Chesnutt family. The very light-skinned Manly was the grandson of Charles Manly, governor of North Carolina from 1849 to 1851.
Governor Manly, not so unusually for a white man of his station at that
time, had more than one family, his legal wife and children and his several
slave mistresses and their children. Born in 1866, the son of one of his
black children whom Governor Manly had manumitted with small property grants, Alexander Manly attended Hampton Institute and, after moving to Wilmington, became a house painter and served as registrar of
deeds before responding to the need for a black newspaper by starting his
own with a used press purchased, ironically, from the editor of the *Messenger*. Driven from Wilmington by the racial violence that surrounded
the election and that became fixated on his editorial, Manly moved to
Philadelphia, where Ray Stannard Baker would encounter him as an
apartment house janitor and an example of the tormenting ambivalence
of mulatto life. Unable to find work because of his race, Manly decided
to pass as white, whereupon he immediately got a job as a union painter.
But his new life "finally became unbearable," he reported. "No decent
man could stand it. I prefered to be a Negro and hold up my head rather
than to be a sneak."[174] As one who toyed with the idea of passing himself,
as some of his relatives had done, Chesnutt would have found the last

episodes of Manly's life just as poignant as his ancestry and his role in the Wilmington revolution.* Not least because Chesnutt's situation paralleled Manly's, Chesnutt's own descent from white grandfathers, men of property, on both sides of his family was a principal reason for his searching use of genealogy and inheritance in *The Marrow of Tradition*. Like Manly, moreover, Chesnutt was clearly haunted by the exact character of the relationships between his grandparents on both sides. It seems evident enough that Chesnutt considered neither an instance of rape. He saw, rather, that the conventions of slaveholding miscegenation allowed for interracial passion but destroyed its legal foundations and thus the fullest emotive and economic legacy that might flow from it. His representation of such an alliance at the heart of *The Marrow of Tradition* constitutes a return to the basic autobiographical plot elements of *The House behind the Cedars*. At the same time, however, his juxtaposition of the genealogical plot with the plot of revolution, wherein interracial sexuality took the form of outrage over the threat of black rape, was a way of continuing Manly's argument in another, far more personal form.

Manly's editorial and Waddell's ascendancy provided the spark for the pre-election intimidation and terror that guaranteed white Democratic victory in Wilmington and throughout the state in the November 1898 election, as well as for the postelection violence that wrote that victory in blood, driving thousands of African Americans out of their homes and jobs, out of the county and state. Chesnutt subtly collapsed the two actions, placing the riot before the election and thereby revealing the violent logic of disfranchisement and Jim Crow as it was bound up with the existing legal processes of United States racial justice. Like Twain, Chesnutt exposed the legal framework of segregation as a fiction of violence, greed, and power, attempting to undermine the crude propaganda

---

* A few other facts about Manly's later life are especially notable. Some of Manly's family did pass, one brother becoming the captain of one of the country's largest trans-Atlantic steamships. When Manly bought a house in a working-class neighborhood of Philadelphia, he was not taken for black until his darker, part–American Indian wife, Carrie Manly, a former singer with the Fisk Jubilee Singers, arrived; they faced significant bigotry until Carrie one day saved the life of a neighbor child. The building that housed Manly's painting business also contained a boxing gym. Manly persuaded a young brothel bouncer who appeared to be a natural boxer to take the sport seriously and train at the gym. The young man's name, which would become synonymous with black manhood for the next generation, was Jack Johnson. See Leon Prather, *We Have Taken a City: The Wilmington Racial Massacre and Coup of 1898* (Cranbury, N.J.: Associated University Press, 1984), pp. 161–63.

of Dixon, Bruce, Felton, and others who created and exploited the caricature of black crime and sexual violation. He did so by weaving together his political and genealogical plots in one especially important incident: the specious charge that the black servant Sandy has assaulted and murdered a white woman, which plays into the escalating plot for revolution by the white supremacists. Tom Delamere's second "cakewalk," his caricatured disguise as Sandy during the act of robbery and murder, thus has the specific rhetorical effect in the novel of merging the fear of contamination of genealogical purity—a contamination that of course had taken place long ago, despite Polly Ochiltree's denial of its legitimacy—with fear of "Negro domination."[175] The question of Samuel Merkell's legacy, his "will" to his two children, one white and one black, is thus bound to the political will of the white Democrats who are determined to retake control of their city.

Wilmington white supremacists, along with those of a like mind throughout the state, had begun to seek the disfranchisement of black voters well in advance of the November election. Disfranchisement, as we have seen in the previous chapter, revived the racist assumptions of *Dred Scott* and carried to extremity the "lynching," one might say, that was legally authorized by state legislatures and the United States Supreme Court. Mississippi and South Carolina had already disfranchised African American voters by amendments to their state constitutions in 1890 and 1895, respectively; Louisiana would follow in 1898 and North Carolina in 1900. The rationale that was provided for amended franchise requirements obscured the racial motivations in name only; although a large number of poor whites also lost the vote, black men were clearly the primary targets in all cases. As the language of the decisive Supreme Court case *Williams* v. *Mississippi* put it in 1898, it had not been demonstrated that the implementation of such state suffrage laws "was evil but only that evil was possible under them." The unintentionally revealing language of the Court had special relevance in the case of North Carolina, which followed Louisiana's lead in making the infamous "grandfather clause" the key element in its amendment. (A ruse to ensure that whites, even if they failed other qualification requirements, could still vote, the grandfather clause allowed any man to vote who had done so before 1867 or who was the son or grandson of someone who had voted then. Because former slaves had been denied the vote at that time, the grandfather clause excluded almost all contemporary African American voters.) Even though the grandfather clause was a transparent charade, it survived court review until the Supreme Court struck it down in 1915. As North Carolina historian John Spencer Bassett wrote in 1899, with the Wilmington revolution fresh in his mind, the grandfather clause represented "one more step in the educating of our people that it is right to lie, to steal, & to defy all honesty in order to keep a certain party in power."[176]

In North Carolina's 1900 campaign against the black franchise, Waddell, made mayor of Wilmington in the aftermath of the revolution, remained a key player, telling whites to warn away any black voter they encountered at the polls: "If he refuses, kill him, shoot him down in his tracks." Such violence, after the bloodletting of 1898 and restrictions upon black voting put in place then, proved unnecessary. North Carolina blacks lost their vote by a margin of 59 percent to 41 percent. Whether or not Chesnutt kept track of Waddell's leadership role in completing the revolution started two years earlier, he took the keenest interest in African American disfranchisement. Perhaps on no other topic was he aroused to such continued passion. Reflecting on the proposed North Carolina amendment in an 1899 letter to Walter Hines Page, he wrote: "The Supreme Court of the United States is in my opinion a dangerous place for a colored man to seek justice. He may go there with maimed rights; he is apt to come away with none at all, and with an adverse decision shutting out even the hope of any future protection there, for the doctrine of *stare decisis* is as strongly entrenched there as the hopeless superiority of the Anglo-Saxon is in the Southern states." Chesnutt also contributed an essay, "The Disfranchisement of the Negro," to *The Negro Problem,* a volume edited by Booker T. Washington in 1905; he regularly took more openly radical stands than many other black leaders; and he carried on a continued argument over the franchise in correspondence with Washington in particular during the next several years. Although he protested the grandfather clause for the lie that it was, Washington favored property and education restrictions that inevitably put African Americans at a disadvantage. In one of his replies to Washington, Chesnutt argued against all such roadblocks to black voting and, with unusual venom and also unusual race consciousness, condemned white southerners as generally "an ignorant, narrow and childish people. . . . I make no pretense of any special love for them. I was brought up among them; I have a large share of their blood in my veins: I wish them well, and first of all I wish that they may learn to do justice. . . . I admire your Christ-like spirit in loving the Southern whites, but I confess I am not up to it."[177] In light of Chesnutt's white ancestry, the symbolism of the "grandfather" clause must have struck him, as it would have Alexander Manly, with special irony. At the North Carolina polls, as in the Jim Crow train car, Chesnutt would not have qualified as the legitimate grandson of a white man.

Given Chesnutt's perspective on the black vote, one is able to see more clearly why he violated historical fact in *The Marrow of Tradition* and placed the riot before the election. In our very first glimpses of Carteret as editor, we find him joining the essential rhetorical themes of North Carolina's antiblack campaign in an editorial arguing that "the ballot in the hands of the negro [is] a menace to the commonwealth" just as great as the "commingling" of the blood of "two unassimilable races." When their campaign for white supremacy flags, unable to generate sufficient momentum on the issue of disfranchisement alone, Carteret, Belmont, and McBane retrieve the Barber (Manly) editorial but reserve it for more effective use later in the campaign, when it will appear in the sensational context generated by the sexual hysteria surrounding Polly Ochiltree's apparent murder and Sandy's near lynching. The two incidents are not causally joined in *The Marrow of Tradition,* yet they partake of the same appeal to primitive emotions and form a unified action signified by Tom Delamere's cakewalk. After Sandy's arrest, Carteret once more proposes to use the Barber editorial as a pretext for his crusade, but again draws back, writing instead a generic harangue about the strenuous efforts "necessary to protect the white women of the South against brutal, lascivious, and murderous assaults at the hands of negro men." Although Sandy is exonerated, his innocence is not as useful news as his guilt. The charges against Sandy, as Chesnutt writes, borrowing Manly's own language, were in effect "made against the whole colored race. All over the United States the Associated Press had flashed the report of another dastardly outrage by a burly black brute,—all black brutes it seems are burly,—and of the impending lynching with its prospective horrors." In contrast, news of Sandy's innocence, like knowledge of Tom Delamere's guilt, is buried. (Writing in the wake of the Atlanta riot of 1906, Kelly Miller would make the same point. The South, he argued, makes it "appear that 'Negro,' 'rape,' and 'lynch' are connotative terms." Whenever a Negro is accused of rape, newspapers and weekly journals "rehash the same gruesome particularities until the whole nation becomes inflamed against the race on account of the dastardly deed of a single wretch.") Outstripping the facts of the case, the sensational journalistic representation of Sandy as a brutish criminal is the only alternative to the minstrel image also favored by the press. Forty years before Richard Wright would make the journalistic caricature of Bigger Thomas a central feature of *Native Son,* Chesnutt put the power of the white press under scrutiny. In its treatment of African Americans, the national press, as Julius puts it in a powerful dialect pun that describes ads for runaway slaves but also signifies upon contemporary lynching, publishes "noospapers."[178]

Sandy's misrepresentation in the press is in keeping with the misrepresentation of Alexander Manly's editorial, both texts subsumed into the statewide and nationwide efforts to strip African Americans of political and economic power. The conjunction of the two events calls attention to the fact, as General Belmont puts it, that it was an "age of crowds" conducive to revolution and capable of promoting race purity by the abridgment of the political process and the law.[179] As the postwar civil rights amendments were dismantled in the succession of legislative acts and court decisions leading to *Plessy*—among them *United States* v. *Reese* (1876), *United States* v. *Cruikshank* (1876), and *United States* v. *Harris* (1883), all of which dealt with mob intimidation of black voters—the separation of federal from state control sacrificed the individual's most basic civil rights to equal protection and a fair trial. Segregation unleashed the mob, which in turn furthered segregation by disfranchisement. No novel of the period represented the combined legal and illegal mechanisms of segregation more powerfully than *The Marrow of Tradition.*

When the Big Three finally reprint the scandalous editorial, they do so expressly to bypass the political process. Belmont suggests that because it would be two years before North Carolina's "nigger amendment"—that is, the grandfather clause that would guarantee black disfranchisement— could go into effect, the white supremacy campaign needs to resort to tactics of intimidation to swing the upcoming election. Chesnutt here too adjusts chronology to a slight degree, since the amendment was not actually passed until 1900. As we have seen, however, the violence of 1898 effectively stopped black voting, and this is precisely the point of Chesnutt's novelistic manipulation. Carteret reproduces the editorial as a means to mobilize support for the violent revolution. By having Carteret discover Barber's editorial, then twice hold it in reserve to be used in a calculated way once the statewide election campaign has opened, Chesnutt echoed the rather deliberate deployment of the Manly editorial in Wilmington's actual politics. (Chesnutt may have borrowed the name Barber from that of the journalist J. Max Barber, who was to become an editor of the *Voice of the Negro,* published in Atlanta; coincidentally, he and his magazine would also be forced out of the city by the Atlanta riot of 1906.)[180] In reality, the violent massacre occurred after the election had already achieved its initial purpose of turning Republicans and Fusionists out of office. But in placing the fictional riot before the election, Chesnutt did more than consolidate the resulting violence with its primary intent. He also manipulated the use of Manly's editorial so as to underline the rhetorical fictions of the attack on Manly—the fact that the proclamation of endangered white womanhood, which could be used to even better effect in the aftermath of Polly Ochiltree's death, was an obvious charade to mobilize white hatred of black jobholders and black voters. Both the timely use of Manly's dangerous editorial and the backdating of the riot itself allowed Chesnutt to dramatize the blatant racism of disfranchisement.

The mirroring images of male and female hysteria that Chesnutt employs in *The Marrow of Tradition* spring in part from the loss of economic and political power suffered by the South in the aftermath of the war and felt keenly by male leaders, and in part from the instability of gender relations that resulted. "Negro domination" did, in fact, threaten the manliness of the white southerner, though not in the way it was often represented. Male hysteria was not primarily about rape; it was about votes and the feared loss of white southern virility, which in turn sprang from the region's prolonged economic deterioration which had reached the stage of depression by the end of the century. Rape was the mask behind which disfranchisement was hidden, but it was part of the larger charade of plantation mythology that set out to restore southern pride and revive a paradigm of white manliness that the legacy of the war and the economic and political rise of blacks during Reconstruction had called seriously into question. The post-Reconstruction discourse of southern masculinity, as the reaction to Manly made evident, provided a particularly compelling context for Chesnutt's dramatization of the personal and sectional impotence that race hysteria sought to counteract in proliferating images of heroism and ancestral veneration.

By the 1880s ceremonial bereavement had begun to give way to ceremonial celebration of southern heroes in an attempt to revive the failed image of heroic masculinity that was so much a part of sectional culture. Monuments to the dead appeared now in town squares rather than in cemeteries. A significant literature on combat heroism, magazines such as the *Confederate Veteran,* speaking tours by Jefferson Davis and other deposed leaders, veterans' parades, reunions, and festivals organized by the United Confederate Veterans and similar organizations—all of these means were employed to adulate the heroic efforts of the Lost Cause. The worship of iconic heroes was foremost a means of restoring a psychically acceptable sense of the manhood lost in military defeat, in the extraordinary sacrifice of young men's lives, and in the vast northern appropriation of southern wealth. The neo-Confederate romance cast an aura of greatness over minor heroes (such as Alfred Moore Waddell) and, in the form of a sudden flood of biographical and artistic representations, elevated true sectional heroes such as Robert E. Lee and Jefferson Davis to saintly status. On the model of heroes of the American Revolution, Confederate officers, especially the dead, were shrouded in the myth of Christian knighthood, and the United Daughters of the Confederacy, for example, yoked Christian service to patriotism in awarding the Cross of Honor to aging veterans. Confederate sacrifices were memorialized in stained-glass installations; evangelical songs were given Confederate lyrics; and the hagiographic search for heroes assumed overt theological dimensions, with the sacrifices of Davis, Lee, and others compared to the Passion of Christ. By the 1890s, moreover, sectional reunion, fueled by northern complicity in the production of the plantation myth and the destruction of African American civil rights, made the restoration of southern masculinity a national enterprise. The revival of a Confederate ethos provided at once a necessary healing, a further mechanism for sectional reunion, and a distorted reconceptualization of antebellum life.[181]

At extremity, as in Thomas Dixon's novelistic celebrations of Confederate heroism and modern racism, the soldier and the Klansman were blurred into a single image of Christian manhood called forth in preparation for a new war against African Americans. Womanly purity, the idealized embodiment of genealogical regeneration and of racial segregation, had antebellum roots but contemporary demographic meaning. The decimation of the white male population by the war had created a generation in which both the pressure and the opportunity for white women to take black lovers had increased; combined with the South's political and economic weakness, such a threat to white masculinity created unbearable pressures. Lynching and castration were the denial of white degeneration and negative assertion of a hollow, furtive masculinity that thrived on the collection and display of black "souvenirs." Central to the creation of that mythology was the glorification of genealogical dynasties and heroic patriarchs, or the erection of false ones as surrogates for questionable contemporary manliness. What Dixon recognized, however, was that the entire nation was ready to participate in the sexual sacrifice of the black man, and that it was nationalism rather than sectionalism that benefited most from the triumph of the Old South mythology.[182] Genealogy and politics met in the media's glorification of the historical Ku Klux Klan and their moral whitewashing of the new Klan, revived after the turn of the century. Plantation mythology required a concomitant glorification of fragile and pure womanhood. The image of noble knighthood riding to the rescue of women and family that Dixon and D. W. Griffith exploited with such precision ran throughout much southern mythology of the last two decades of the nineteenth century but quickly became fixed in national archetypes. Directly connected to revisionist histories of Reconstruction was the artificial image of the prostrate family and female vulnerability, which fed the racial mythology of rape—hardly distinct in many representations from intermarriage itself—as it was exploited by artists and politicians alike. Rebecca Latimer Felton's speech was notorious primarily because of her prominence and because of Alexander Manly's rebuttal, but its sentiments were in fact commonplace and were part of the political drama of gender relations by which southern manhood had been restored to psychological vitality.

Waddell's claim that the Wilmington revolution was a means of "manfully overthrowing" an intolerable tyranny on the order of the American Revolution thus linked all the elements of the Confederate revival: the reanimation of revolutionary proslavery principles; sectional autonomy and the revisionist view of Reconstruction; and the assertion of white southern "manliness" through the emasculation of black Americans. "Fusion," whether political or interracial, was a threatening affront to any such revival of white masculinity. As Chesnutt saw, the Wilmington revolution was a small-scale version of the southern restoration by the conjoined means of cultural manipulation and the naked application of force. Its gender politics were of the utmost importance to a national ethos of segregation, and his novel's use of the Wilmington violence would stand in precise contrast to that in Dixon's book *The Leopard's Spots,* which predictably castigated Manly for "defaming the virtue of white women in the community." On the advice of his friend Congressman Theodore Burton, Chesnutt sent copies of *The Marrow of Tradition* to several members of the House of Representatives who had already received copies of Dixon's novel; but his correspondence indicates that most officials were willing to see *The Marrow of Tradition* as at best another view, rather than a refutation of Dixon's negrophobia.[183]

Dixon was the master of racial hysteria, but it was Chesnutt, perhaps because of his own double heritage, who provided the most devastating critique of that hysteria. His representation of it relied upon the repeated trope of doubled gender and race relations. Olivia Carteret may belong to that generation of American women whose experience of hysteria registered a larger social crisis over gender roles.[184] But she is also in the tradition of Stowe's Marie St. Claire and Faulkner's Mrs. Compson—a specifically southern victim of the neurosis of female generativity inflected by racial fear. Olivia Carteret's paranoia about Janet Miller springs in part from their relationship itself and their twinlike appearance; in part from her jealousy that Janet has been blessed with a son while she has no child until Dodie is born (and her subsequent fear that Janet has conjured Dodie); and in part from the fact that William Miller, through the effort and dignified labor of his father, the son of a slave, and his own hard study of medicine has achieved comparative material success. Living in the house formerly owned by the Carteret family, Miller and his wife are the symbol of black usurpation and, in the novel's terms, of the ascendancy of black genealogy over white. The crisis of conscience that Olivia undergoes when she learns the truth about her father's marriage to Janet's mother, and hence the legitimacy of the will and the marriage certificate that divides his property between them, puts her in what Chesnutt calls a "moral pocket." The novel's intricate plotting of the discovery as Olivia first burns the will, then burns the marriage certificate, only to realize that she is now worse off than before, unable to reveal the legacy to Janet without revealing as well her father's "unpardonable social sin" of marriage to a black woman, puts melodrama in the service of a wrenching movement toward racial understanding. Olivia is left faced with the last installment of the penalty of conscience that has accumulated over generations of slaveholding injustice. After a symbolic dream that seems to prophesy Dodie's death, she chooses to swallow the past in silence and salve her conscience by planning one day to give an appropriate amount of money to Miller's black hospital, which is soon to be destroyed in the election violence.[185]

Olivia Carteret must admit to herself the fact that her father loved and married a black woman. Because the evidence that she has is more incontestable, it is not necessary for her, like Faulkner's Ike McCaslin, driven into the ambiguous web of Carothers McCaslin's incest and misgenenation with mistress and daughter, to insist desperately that *there still must have been love. . . . Some sort of love.* Olivia knows that there was love: what she cannot bear is the possibility that she herself will be tainted by that love, that she or her child will be thought to have "sprung from this

shocking *mésalliance*."[186] Her moral crisis thus also refers to the genealogical mixture of Chesnutt's own family, as well as that of Alexander Manly,
for the two families of Samuel Merkell closely parallel those of Manly's
grandfather and Chesnutt's two grandfathers. The novel's absorption in
the use to which a sacrilegious assault upon white womanhood can be
put receives its most radical critique in Olivia's hysteria, where not just
white miscegenation but also white interracial love must be repressed. The
New South's corrupt masculinity, as Tom Delamere's story makes clear,
was a legal and political masquerade. Olivia's story suggests additionally
that it required too a simple denial of love. Major Carteret made Manly's
charge a weapon of political scandal; but his own wife's ancestry (the
source of the inherited wealth off which he now lives) proves the truth of
Manly's assertions.

The "moral pocket" in which Olivia finds herself is an emotional one,
to be sure, but it is thus also legal, and her act participates in the revolution's illegal attack on black rights. In Olivia's hysteria, the emotive and
legal levels are perfectly integrated. The ambiguity of blackness that Chesnutt explored in all of his color line stories and in *The House behind the
Cedars,* where he takes explicit account of the category of "reputation"
upon which much state law was based, is brought to a pitch in *The Marrow
of Tradition.* As we have already seen in the previous chapter, significant
rulings governing the law of miscegenation which paralleled the rise of
segregation law held that blood could be conceived of as property. During
Reconstruction there were attempts to make white men responsible for
their mulatto offspring and thus make their property inheritable by those
children. Nonetheless, the pervasive illegality of interracial marriage that
accompanied the rise of segregation left many mulattoes bereft of such
property rights. Absent a legal obligation in the form of a marriage
contract, inherited white blood might well prove meaningless to a "black"
person; but the presence of such a contract, as I indicated in chapter 3,
could guarantee the legitimacy of white blood. In the North Carolina case
of *Ferrall* v. *Ferrall* (1910), for example, a white man attempting to evade
a property settlement with his wife because she was "negro within the
prohibited degree" was rebuffed by the court. In conceiving of blood as
a kind of property that accrues over time or in a defined contractual
relation, and finding that the wife was thus "white" according to the
marriage contract, the court, though it had no quarrel with the theory of
segregation and race superiority, put that contract on a higher legal plane
than the law defining admixture. "The law," the court concluded, "may

not permit [a man] thus to bastardize his own children." As Eva Saks comments, the ruling in *Ferrall* v. *Ferrall* showed explicitly that blood was social rather than biological and that it was, like other property boundaries, the creation of the law. The ruling therefore exacerbated the task of miscegenation law—to define the boundaries of a family and to make property stable by making it inalienable: "Tracing the defendant's genealogy became the equivalent of a title search, the search for an authoritative legal representation of race."[187]

Although Chesnutt obviously could not have drawn upon *Ferrall,* Olivia Carteret's discovery of Janet Miller's legal rights rests primarily on the legitimacy of the marriage contract, which turns out to be of more importance than Samuel Merkell's will. Because the marriage occurred during the military occupation of Reconstruction, it was valid by North Carolina law. But Chesnutt's novel had contemporary resonance as well, for one could say that the law as it came to be construed in North Carolina within a matter of years would have left Janet Brown Miller the legitimate, legally "white" heir of Samuel Merkell absent any will to the contrary. Riddled with ideological burdens in an age of rising segregation based on legislation and judicial decision, the law is of crucial importance throughout Chesnutt's fiction and infuses nearly every aspect of *The Marrow of Tradition*. Chesnutt was trained as a lawyer, passing the Ohio bar in 1887, but hemmed in by the constraints of prejudice he spent most of his professional energies as a stenographer and court reporter. His alter ego, John Warwick in *The House behind the Cedars,* passes in order to pursue the career for which he is qualified. Combined with his ancestral history, Chesnutt's experience with the law left it, for him as for Twain, a discursive field charged with ideological ambiguity. Cognizant of his own father's illegitimacy and the fact that his parents' families (like the ancestors of Alexander Manly) had received legacies out of generosity rather than recognized legal right, Chesnutt in his conception of Samuel Merkell's estate and his double legacy measured the limits of North Carolina's recognition of blood as property. He had argued against the prevalent equation of mixed blood with illegitimacy in his essay "What Is a White Man?," and both *The House behind the Cedars* and *The Marrow of Tradition* put the question of legitimacy in the context of legal inheritance.

As *The Marrow of Tradition* portrays it, the law is a barrier to the free exercise of racism and therefore must be overridden. Merkell's marriage and will are legitimate and must be destroyed; old Delamere's will, which leaves much of his estate to Miller's hospital, must also be destroyed by his executor Belmont in order to consolidate the coverup of Tom's crime and protect the revolution; and the revolution itself must be launched so as to bypass the slower process of disfranchisement based on constitutional amendment. That is to say, Chesnutt's representation of the law is less responsive to the nightmarish inadequacies of judicial process than is Twain's; but his pessimism about the results of segregation's moral acceptability in the national conscience is no less deep. The two chapters describing Olivia Carteret's crisis of conscience stand in a pivotal position: preceding them is the chapter devoted to the final deployment of Manly's editorial as the linchpin of the revolution; and following is the chapter in which the revolution's violence finally breaks forth on the eve of the election. The question of legal inheritance—a question of racial identity as well as one of human compassion and love—stands at the center of racist conflagration. *The Marrow of Tradition,* as its title suggests, is consumed by questions of legal and familial tradition—by questions, as I remarked earlier, of "generation." Olivia's manic hysteria about her heir, Dodie, and the possibility that she or he will be mistaken for the contaminated black heirs of Samuel Merkell's scandalous marriage to Julia Brown is the counterpart to her husband's promotion of racial hysteria. Both acts employ deceit and violence as means to preserve property and political right, not only reviving the rights of a slaveholding past but betraying them as well.

In this respect, the fact that it is Tom Delamere who commits the crimes with which Sandy is charged is very significant. Clearly echoing Twain's Tom Driscoll in *Puddn'head Wilson,* in both his weak character and his overt role as a racial double, the young Delamere is an archetype of the New South in the dress of a dissolute southern aristocrat. In the scene of Dodie's christening party, he is immediately distinguished by his lack of masculine character: "No discriminating observer would have characterized his beauty as manly. It conveyed no impression of strength, but did possess a certain element, feline rather than feminine, which subtly negatived the idea of manliness." Even if one were to discount the explicit puns on Manly's name, the picture of Tom's degeneration is put forthrightly in terms of gender, and in his dissipation in gambling Chesnutt likens him to a "well-bred woman who has started on the downward path," whereby "sin," once his servant, has become his "master." After he has gotten Sandy in trouble with his church congregation by his first cakewalk charade, Tom needles Sandy, telling him to "brace up . . . and be a man, or, if you can't be a man, be as near a man as you can." It is

Tom Delamere, of course, who is only the shell of a man. He also stands in marked contrast to his grandfather, Sandy's employer and a gentleman of traditional southern manners and breeding. To the paternalistic old Delamere, Sandy is a "gentleman in ebony," whereas to Tom he is a "darky," as Tom insulting calls him to his face.[188]

Tom and Sandy are doubles: they resemble each other to the degree that Tom's cakewalk charades can be successful, and given old Delamere's fondness for Sandy and Sandy's apparent devotion to him, there is more than a hint that there may be a blood relation between them. This possibility is less important, however, than their figurative relationship. Tom can be interpreted as the racial conscience of the New South, which depends upon generating through a charade epitomized by the staged plantation revivals, where minstrelsy and economic exposition coalesced, a contemporary panorama of humble, devoted black servants and laborers. Both old Delamere and Sandy are presented sympathetically by Chesnutt, but their paternalistic relationship has become undermined by irony as it survives into the contemporary era of Jim Crow. In contrast to Carteret, Belmont, and McBane, old Delamere is a man of character, despite his overt paternalism. Yet character is not enough. When Delamere's insistence that Sandy is innocent of the crime fails to move Carteret, he declares that there was a time "when the word of a Delamere was held as good as his bond." As Carteret remarks, however: "This man is no longer your property. The negroes are no longer under our control."[189] The paradox is critical: Sandy is no longer Delamere's slave property, but his resulting freedom places him at the mercy of lynch law.

Old Delamere barely succeeds in saving Sandy; he cannot prevent Carteret, Belmont, and McBane from fabricating an image of "family honor" that will protect Tom from prosecution and, once he dies, from betraying his written will on the grounds that his "property belonged of right to the white race, and by the higher law should remain in the possession of white people."[190] The subversion of his will, which would have left three thousand dollars to Sandy and the rest of his estate to Miller's hospital, brings the trope of violated inheritance into the present day. Linking Delamere to Samuel Merkell, the violation of the will constitutes an elaboration on Chesnutt's skepticism about the value of the law in racial matters, but it is also his most obvious endorsement of a strain of benevolence in the kind of southern white gentleman, among the generation of the grandfathers, from whom he must have felt himself to be descended. Chesnutt's admiration for the paternalistic principles of old Delamere is restrained, to be sure, but it stands in obvious counterpoint to his contempt for the white men of the New South.

Sandy too is a man of honor, refusing even to save himself by violating his trust to Tom, who is ready to let Sandy die in his place. Like Delamere, Sandy exhibits a quality of "manliness" that belongs to his character rather than his race. By the same token, he is to some degree the "darky" that Tom calls him. That is to say, he is represented as belonging to the passing generation that included some blacks whose devotion to their old masters, or to their old style of life, outweighs their remembered hatred of slavery. Sandy's place among the range of black characters that Chesnutt presents is worth more attention; but with respect to Tom he functions as a inverted image of the white man's degeneration. He is ironically the better man than Tom, but Tom's cakewalk imitation of Sandy suggests the more subtle and powerful symbolic bond that Chesnutt forged between the two. Tom, as the New South, feeds upon the weakness of Sandy's generation, creating of him a comforting image of plantation benevolence while at the a same time demeaning such benevolence as did exist in his racist caricature. Tom is not directly involved in the revolutionary plot to seize political control of Wellington, but his crime provides a rallying point for the Big Three. Because Polly Ochiltree is a surviving antebellum embodiment of racism, in her case filtered through her bitter jealousy of Samuel's affection for Julia Brown, her apparent murder, though it turns out probably to have been accidental death by fright, is ironically just. The representative of the New South's pathetic degeneration of breeding, character, and moral responsibility kills the embodiment of white southern womanhood, casting the blame onto an innocent and humble black retainer.

The cakewalk Tom performs for the northern visitors, I suggested at the outset of this chapter, has a political function in the novel. The northern visitors are shown the best of plantation mythology in action on their carefully composed tour that concludes with Tom's cakewalk, and they are easily persuaded, Chesnutt writes, that "a certain charity should be extended towards those who in the intense and righteous anger of the moment should take the law into their own hands and deal out rough but still substantial justice; for no negro was ever lynched without incontestable proof of his guilt." Tom's doubling of Sandy splits the cakewalk function perfectly in two: Tom portrays Sandy on the one hand as the minstrel darky, and on the other as the black criminal. When Tom mocks Sandy the first time, Sandy is comically cast out of his congregation for his sinful follies; when Tom mocks him the second time, Sandy is arrested for murder and nearly lynched. The revolution in Wilmington/Wellington accomplishes precisely the same purpose. As Chesnutt argues, "a new Pharaoh" had risen in the North who was oblivious to the civil rights of blacks. Governed by falsified statistics of black crime, by "coon song" images of African American culture, by purportedly scientific arguments about black physical and moral "degeneration," by imperialist conceptions of race superiority, and by the apparent necessity of lynchings, the new nation's racial conscience had been led to "a sort of *impasse,* a blind alley, of which no one could see the outlet."[191] Buoyed by judicial decisions and the necessary economic reunification of the nation, the North abandoned the South to Democratic control and a home-rule solution of the "Negro problem." The welcome creation of a plantation myth covered the underlying violence of southern (and American) life, both during and after slavery, so that when it burst forth in a violent torrent in November 1898, as well as in other so-called race riots at the turn of the century, such as those in New Orleans in 1900 and Atlanta in 1906, or in public lynchings, it could be written off as the necessary suppression of black criminality and "Negro domination." At once eviscerating the plantation tradition and working out his anger against the antebellum generation who would deny the legitimate union (and, perhaps, the true interracial love) of his own ancestors, Chesnutt showed the South's rape complex radiating throughout its culture.

Tom's first cakewalk ends with Ellis speculating about Negroes that "no one could tell at what moment the thin veneer of civilization might peel off and reveal the underlying savage." By the end of the novel, the truth of the metaphor is revealed in its reversal: the white supremacist massacre leaves many dead, while Miller's hospital lies "in smouldering ruins, a melancholy witness to the fact that our boasted civilization is but a thin veneer, which cracks and scales off at the first impact of primal passion." Likewise employing this widespread metaphor in an analysis of racial prejudice (which included an ethical defense of lynching), Harvard professor Nathaniel Shaler had warned that the strain of race conflict awakened primitive passions; under stimulus "the frail covering of civilization disappears in an instant before the strong ancestral passion of rage."[192] The savage South, spawned in *slaveholding,* not in *slavery,* was white, not black, said Chesnutt; the created caricature of the black rapist was made to incorporate a savagery that was mostly white in origin. As the mirror image of its black caricature, the white savagery expressed most horribly in lynching and sexual mutilation was compounded of inherited guilt, fear of change and lost power, and an irrational but not inexplicable aversion to pronounced cultural differences. Although they charged blacks with reversion to African savagery, and mulattoes in particular with species degeneration, it was racist whites who had degenerated from the comparative paternalistic manners of their fathers and, more to the point, from the dignity of human behavior. In the violence of Wilmington the charade no longer mattered, only victory. The further dimension of Chesnutt's cakewalk and the reason it is a revealing trope for his work, I suggest, lies also in Chesnutt's own ambivalence about the mixture of race and class that formed his genealogical inheritance and was reproduced in the contending African American moral forces at work in *The Marrow of Tradition*. It is here that the question of "manliness" takes on its greatest complexity in the novel. Indeed, it is not finally the whites whose manhood is most at issue for Chesnutt but rather the blacks.

A Great Black Figure and a Doll

> God told Noah by the rainbow sign,
> No more water, but the fire next time.
>
> African American spiritual

The exact course of the Wilmington coup is difficult to recreate, but its purpose and final meaning are crystal clear. The election itself was surrounded with the threat of violence throughout the state. Governor Russell's train was attacked on its way to Wilmington (where he had intended to vote), and he barely escaped being lynched himself. Many polling places were patrolled by armed white men to prevent blacks from voting; ballot boxes were stuffed at gunpoint. The election passed without any great violence, but the tension had not been dissipated, only increased. Masses of armed white men again gathered in Wilmington on the day after the election; and although blacks had been forbidden to buy ammunition and to meet in groups for weeks preceding November 8, there were also numbers of armed blacks. However the actual firing started—various accounts are available—there is no question that the white mob was intent upon furthering the suppression of black civil rights that began with the election itself. In particular, Alexander Manly was targeted for expulsion from Wilmington. Once the Secret Nine and their supporters had drawn up the Wilmington Declaration of Independence, the last resolutions of which blamed the city's crisis on Manly's editorial and demanded his banishment, a committee headed by Waddell met with thirty-two of Wilmington's leading blacks, many of them professionals in medicine, law, real estate, and the like. The white supremacists put the declaration's resolutions to the blacks on November 9 and demanded an answer by the following day—although only one answer, complete submission to white political and economic control, was acceptable. The black leaders drafted a heartbreaking but understandable reply to the white supremacists' ultimatum: "We, the colored citizens to whom was referred the matter of expulsion from the community of the person and press of A. L. Manly, beg most respectfully to say that we are in no way responsible for, nor in any way condone the obnoxious article that called forth your actions. Neither are we authorized to act for him in this matter; but in the interest of peace we will most willingly use our influence to have your wishes carried out." For reasons that have never become evident, Armond Scott, the attorney charged with delivering this reply to Waddell, mailed it rather than carrying it in person, and it therefore missed the deadline. Whether receipt of the formal reply would have made any difference to the white supremacists, however, is a fine question. On November 10 a mob led by Waddell armed itself at the Wilmington Light Infantry Armory and attacked the *Wilmington Record,* ransacking the press and burning the building to the ground. Within hours the "riot" was at full force.[193]

The reply to Waddell drafted by the Wilmington blacks could hardly be construed as an act of cowardice in view of the overwhelming odds they faced. The crowd of whites gathered in Wilmington included numbers of men from neighboring towns and farms who had appeared in a show of racial support, while numbers of blacks, including Alexander Manly, had already fled town, or were hiding in their homes or outside the city. (There is some evidence that Manly left before election day; but it was also reported that one of Chesnutt's cousins, who was Manly's printer's devil, went to the *Record* the night of November 9 and helped Manly bury printing equipment, in anticipation that the building would be burned.) In the outbreak of violence, those blacks able or willing to defend themselves by force were massively outgunned. Whites not only had a far superior supply of rifles, handguns, and ammunition; they also had the support of an activated state militia and the use of a rapid-fire Colt gun mounted on a carriage and at least two cannon. The fighting, which apparently started at the Sprunt Cotton Compress, spread throughout the city in a random, chaotic fashion, with many whites passing directly from vigilantism to criminality. As one Philadelphia editor was to write, "There was not one white man under arms who did not have some score to settle with a Negro rankling in his breast, which would have been fair excuse for a shot." The number of blacks killed was certainly greater than the figures of twelve or fourteen that were reported in official Democratic estimates. More important in the long run was the fact that thousands of blacks were driven from their homes (so that Wilmington and New Hanover County went from significant African American majorities to marginal white majorities within less than two years) and their property destroyed or illegally confiscated.[194] The outpouring of protest against the Wilmington violence by Du Bois and other black leaders (Washington was characteristically silent) met with little response from Congress or President McKinley. The long legislative and judicial implementation of Jim Crow had made mobs immune to federal control, and politicians and journalists alike succeeded in cloaking the truth of Wilmington under a disguise of legal necessity.

In one of his few obvious authorial intrusions into the narration of *The Marrow of Tradition*, Chesnutt remarks in the aftermath of the riot that "the negroes of Wellington, with the exception of Josh Green and his party, had not behaved bravely on this critical day in their history." Still, he continues, those who had fought were dead, while those "who had sought safety in flight or concealment were alive to tell the tale." In his biography of Frederick Douglass, Chesnutt had made a similar distinction between John Brown, whom he characterized as a foolish martyr, and Douglass, who prudently declined to follow Brown to Harper's Ferry.[195] Nonetheless, the Ishmael-like recompense granted those who, like Dr. Miller, counsel moderation and submission appears small in the face of Chesnutt's judgment. By the same token, however, the judgment hardly rings true. Whether or not he had in mind (or knew about) the accommodationist reply of the Wilmington blacks to Waddell's ultimatum, Chesnutt throughout the novel appears to identify with Miller in his ongoing argument with Josh Green about the wisdom of revenge or even resistance. Although he obviously reflects Du Bois's idea of the talented tenth in his philosophy of uplift by professional example, Miller in his political philosophy is closer to Washington's accommodationism, while Josh Green is a radical bent on vengeance, perhaps most analogous, in Chesnutt's day, to Robert Charles, the "outlaw" black figure at the center of the New Orleans race riot of 1900—a "riot" that, like the one in Wilmington, was more of a white rampage.[196] In this respect, and in the fact that Chesnutt carefully represents him as an illiterate folk hero, Josh introduces a dimension of thought rather at odds with Chesnutt's prevailing sensibility. Josh does not survive to tell the tale, as does Miller, but he represents a most important development in Chesnutt's artistic politics.

We meet William Miller and Josh Green in the same sequence at the outset of the novel, in the chapter entitled "A Journey Southward." With the great symbolic resonance of a ritual descent into the South that is repeated in *The Souls of Black Folk, The Autobiography of an Ex-Coloured Man,* and Jean Toomer's *Cane,*[197] to name only the most obvious, Chesnutt transports Miller, a physician trained in the comparatively egalitarian North, back to the land of his birth and his chosen field of work aboard a Jim Crow train. But color is not the only gulf felt by Miller. Like the light mulatto John Warwick in *The House behind the Cedars,* who similarly shows no signs of racial "degeneration," Miller is characterized as a mixed-race counterexample to both the racist theory of "degeneration which the pessimist so sadly maintains is the inevitable heritage of mixed races" and to the patent moral degeneration of Tom Delamere and the white supremacists. Like Warwick, Miller is also a man of the black middle class, pervaded by the class-bound racial philosophy that would receive its most notorious articulation in Hurston's chapter "My People! My People!" in *Dust Tracks on a Road.* His theory of uplift must be read in the context of his deliberate distancing of himself from the "noisy, loquacious, happy, dirty, and malodorous" lower-class blacks who are "just as offensive to him as the whites in the other end of the train." Here, however, we see not the model for but the limits of Chesnutt's identification with Miller. In his own journal of 1879, Chesnutt had described a train trip to Washington, D.C., during which the train took on a group of "fifty darkies" going to work at a truck farm near Norfolk. The lower-class blacks filled the car, "and as the day was warm and the people rather dirty, the odor may be better imagined than described. Although it was nothing to me," Chesnutt continued, "I could sympathize with my fellow traveler," apparently a white "gentleman" with whom Chesnutt had conversed, "who stuck his head out the window, and swore that he would never be caught in such a scrape again."[198] His use of the term "darkies" notwithstanding, Chesnutt's marginal identification with the lower-class blacks is far different from Miller's discomfort. By the turn of the century, moreover, and in the context of the racial violence recounted in *The Marrow of Tradition,* Chesnutt's racial solidarity, even if it was largely hypothetical, should have been even more pronounced.

Chesnutt's chapter in any event is a superior expostulation against Jim Crow located in the precise symbolic arena of *Plessy* v. *Ferguson*. Whereas Washington, in *Up from Slavery*, reduced the humiliation of Jim Crow train cars and the ambiguous status of the light-skinned mulatto to a kind of minstrel farce in which the trainman is forced to examine his passenger's feet to ascertain that he is a Negro—although one wants to allow for the possibility that Washington was judiciously signifying in this strange scene—Chesnutt's scene is filled with remarkable structural tensions. Like Plessy, Chesnutt might have passed for white on such a train; the slightly darker Miller cannot, and his anxieties allow Chesnutt a means to explore segregation in a very careful and symbolically rich way. Segregation aboard trains and streetcars, as Frederick Douglass had discovered in Massachusetts in the 1850s, was a distilled example of racial prejudice that knew no sectional boundaries. In the wake of *Plessy*, when the most extravagant kinds of segregated facilities became possible, the train car was easily one of the most charged symbols of racial politics in American culture, a field of ritual drama. The railroad's association with black labor in a segregated service economy and with the blues as an expression of African American cultural life must always include its explicit association with the system of American segregation itself. To cite just one relevant example in the political literature, Congressman Frank Clark of Florida, standing in support of a segregated street car measure proposed for Washington, D.C., spoke before the House of the necessity of such segregation in the South as he knew it. "The average negro is perfectly happy when he finds himself eating a watermelon or going on a railroad excursion," he said, and railroad companies cater to this need. But blacks require careful regulation: "Imagine a nice, new passenger coach, packed with dirty, greasy, filthy negroes, down South, in midsummer, and you can readily understand why that car does not long remain as good, as clean, and as desirable as a similar car occupied exclusively by white travelers." For Clark, such a situation did not demand an examination of why the black lower classes might dress or behave as they did but rather called forth a stereotypical harangue about God's created distinction between handsome, intelligent whites and Negroes with "black skin, kinky hair, thick lips, flat nose, [and] low brow" indicative of a "low order of intelligence." In rebuttal to a colleague who opposed Jim Crow facilities, Clark derisively asked him if, in the logical chain of experience that would result from a lack of segregation, he "would permit a negro to marry his daughter." America, he concluded, was "the country of the white man, not the country of the mongrel."[199]

Clark's radical rhetoric was not remarkable for its day, but it offers a useful counterpoint to Chesnutt's depiction of Miller's experience in the Jim Crow train car. For it is not only the "offensive" blacks against whom Miller must be measured but also the equally offensive whites. Aboard the train Miller is outraged by the "staring signs" labeled "White" and "Colored," the representations of white superstition that "would remind him continually that between him and the rest of mankind not of his own color, there was by law a great gulf fixed." But his own banishment to the Jim Crow car takes on special meaning for his moral position in the novel when he must endure the smoking, spitting, cursing, and offensive behavior of Captain McBane, the white racist who turns out to be a key player in the Wellington race revolution and the object of Josh Green's revenge.[200] Miller is scarcely more like Josh than he is like McBane; both inhabit a moral and personal geography that is unfamiliar and repulsive to him. Josh is introduced here as a "dusty tramp" and a "wet dog," a figure perhaps ordinarily good-natured but suffused with "a concentrated hatred almost uncanny in its murderousness" when he catches sight of McBane. He represents the next logical step beyond Ben Davis in "The Web of Circumstance," whose conviction for stealing a whip symbolizes his incarceration in the South's new chattelism. Although he is dragged down by white deceit and the racism of the convict lease system, Ben is on the verge of transcending the bonds of circumstance in an act of affection when he is shot dead by the white man who mistakes his kind intentions toward his young daughter. Unlike Ben, Josh has no kindness left in his heart. The more particular gulf brought forth in this chapter is thus the ideological one between Josh Green, set on revenge for the Klan's murder of his father, and Miller, the middle-class professional. Neither Miller's own philosophy of accommodation and invocation of biblical meekness, nor his anxiety about identification with "his people," will be overridden by the violent events of the Wellington massacre, but his identity as the book's hero will be stringently tested.[201]

The dialogue between Miller and Josh that runs throughout the novel defines a tension crucial to Chesnutt's structuring of the novel and to his own ambivalence about the identity of black culture. More than once Miller advises Josh to put away his "murderous fancies," while Josh replies that "ef a nigger wants ter git down on his marrow-bones, an' eat dirt, an' call [the white man] 'marster,' *he's* a good nigger, dere's room fer *him*. But I ain't no w'ite folks' nigger, I ain'. I don' call no man 'marster.'" From Miller's perspective, Josh's vengeance against McBane, however just, runs the obvious risk of being imputed to the entire race. The significance of Miller's apprehensiveness is spelled out quite exactly in the fact that the chapter that follows this conversation is "The Cakewalk." The chapter begins with the statement that "old Mr. Delamere's servant, Sandy Campbell, was in deep trouble."[202] The trouble, of course, springs from Tom's mimicry, which gets Sandy in trouble with his church congregation. But the greater meaning is evident: not only will Sandy get into far deeper trouble after Tom's second cakewalk when he is charged with the murder (and no doubt the sexual assault) of a white woman, but Chesnutt means as well to offer proof in support of Miller's moderate political views. Sandy becomes the scapegoat around whom Wellington's race violence referentially turns, his innocence nothing to the point beside his symbolic use as a means to stir white supremacist race hatred. With the exception of the obsequious Jerry and his mother, Mammy Jane, no black character is more different from Josh than Sandy; and yet, as Miller sees, their "crimes" can be put to just the same use. Each can be constituted as the "Negro problem" that Tom's cakewalk and the violent political charade of the white supremacists are meant to solve.

Because of Miller's dominant presence in the novel and Chesnutt's problematic identification with him as a middle-class professional with doubts about the wisdom of violent resistance to white supremacy, Josh Green is a figure difficult to interpret. Whereas his nemesis McBane had one partial real-life model in Mike Dowling, a leader of the Red Shirts (like Ben Tillman, moreover, McBane is one-eyed) Josh is a figure of folk consciousness apparently drawn from no actual participant in the Wilmington riot. (There was a Josh Green, identified as a wood and coal dealer, among the group of blacks constituted to answer Waddell's ultimatum, but there is no evidence that he resembled Chesnutt's Green in his radicalism. Likewise, there were several Millers among the black population, but none that closely resembles Chesnutt's character. Chesnutt himself also had relatives named Green, though none evident as any kind of a model.)[203] He is identified with the "Negro problem" even from Miller's point of view, and his dialect, which stands in sharp class contrast to Miller's refined conventional speech, aligns him with Chesnutt's other lower-class black "folk" figures in the color line stories, *The House behind the Cedars,* and the conjure tales. At the same time, Josh represents something very different and is set off from the other dialect-speaking characters of the novel. Mammy Jane's belief in conjure, for example, appears in *The Marrow of Tradition* as a kind of superstition at odds with Miller's classical medical training. It may participate in Olivia's hysteria and therefore signal a powerful form of folk belief that can work in counteraction to racism— that is, if the wicked conjurer Janet Miller really had conjured Dodie, casting her "evil eye" upon the baby, as the good conjurer Mammy Jane believes.[204] How Chesnutt handles conjure in this case is of special interest, but it is incidental to the political purpose codified in Josh.

Josh Green is not just a representative of the "Negro problem" as white Wellington defines it; he is also a "bad nigger" of the type that appears throughout modern black folklore and in literary adaptations such as George Washington Cable's Bras-Coupé in *The Grandissimes* or the protest heroes of Richard Wright, Chester Himes, and other naturalists. Josh Green would not by any means correspond to the whole range of characteristics ascribed to the "bad nigger" in modern folk mythology, where he may be a man of arrogance or insolence directed at white oppression, a braggart and exponent of rhetorical attack upon his enemies, or an outright criminal preying upon his own race. The element of revenge against racism is present in some form in all instances, however, and the "bad nigger" is in this respect a more radical development of the rebellious John figure of the Master-John tales. Likewise, Josh's dialect, far from marking any reversion to plantation mythology in Chesnutt's class distinctions, moves in the direction of Julius's linguistic power and passes into militancy. Josh's language is not the language of narrative irony but an explicit language of resistance and revolt, in which dialect is a countertype to the class-bound political moderation of Miller. As the medium of the "bad nigger" folk hero, dialect thus extends the verbal masking of the Master-John tales or of Julius's tales into a realm where blunt, "subcultural" language and violence are paired.

The mythic dimension underlying Chesnutt's characterization of Josh appears most saliently in such nineteenth-century black folk heroes as Railroad Bill (or Wild Bill) and Stagolee, whose stories were recorded in a variety of folkloric and musical versions and have been translated into more contemporary forms on through the twentieth century, for example in Sterling Brown's poem "The Last Ride of Wild Bill." Whereas Stagolee (Stackolee, Staggerlee, and so on) was typically depicted as an outright tough, a bully who might act as a black community leader even as he exercised his violence upon it in legendary fights and killings, Railroad Bill was modeled upon the exploits of Morris Slater, a black Alabama turpentine worker who killed a white policeman during an argument, escaped on a freight train, and lived the life of a desperado for the next three years before being gunned down by bounty hunters. His life and association with the charged mythic world of railroad travel linked Railroad Bill and comparable heroes to the many blues of railroad life; and the rapid growth of legends about his survival and combat against the white man in an era of rising segregation and black economic hardship tied the archetype of the "bad nigger" to folk trickster figures and the world of conjure while at the same time deriving from him certain stylized or charismatic modes of lower-class appeal in twentieth-century black politics.[205]

The "bad nigger" hero consolidated into the figure of Railroad Bill also no doubt derived in part from flourishing turn-of-the-century lore about railroad bandits in an age when the frontier was giving way to an increasingly homogeneous, technological society. But once again the significance of the train in a racial context cannot be overlooked. Railroad travel, especially as a means to migrate out of or return to the South, is the subject of numerous blues dating from the days of slavery but reaching a crest around the turn of the century. Because of its prominence in African American economic life and folklore, Albert Murray and Houston Baker have argued, the railroad became a cultural intersection or crossroads, a crucial site for vernacular expression. African drum talk reappeared in the "locomotive talk" of down-home folk arts, and the blues musician became "expert at reproducing or translating these locomotive energies" of labor mobility and travel out of the South. A sign of the possibility for migration and escape from the harshest conditions of racism, the railroad was at the same time the primary site of segregation in American public life—a ritually saturated location and an appropriately mobile sign of the proliferating regulation of Jim Crow. By including it within a song that mixes love and social commentary, the musician might reflect overtly on the relationship between Jim Crow and the tropology of the railroad, as in the blues collected by Odum and Johnson:

Well, I'm goin' to buy me a little railroad of my own;
Ain't goin' to let nobody ride but the chocolate to the bone.

Well, I['m] goin' to buy me a hotel of my own;
Ain't goin' to let nobody eat but the chocolate to the bone. . . .

She's long an' tall an' chocolate to the bone.
She make you married man, then leave yo' home.[206]

A field charged with the highest energy of racial meaning, the railroad is thus an appropriate site for Chesnutt's initial contrasting portraits of William Miller and Josh Green, separated by a gulf in class and political ideology that will remain to the end but united in the fact that each of them, "chocolate to the bone" according to American law, must ride Jim Crow. Josh Green, like Railroad Bill, may therefore be read as an alternative answer, one infused with folkloric power and rising toward violent resistance, to the culture of segregation.

The hero of black prose and poetry of the late nineteenth century was typically a figure caught between protest and assimilation. Frederick Douglass, who united the two tendencies with little sense of contradiction, could admire the violent assertion of black rights without abstracting that action from an "American" framework. The ideology of segregation that Douglass did not live to see in full flower made the gap between the two reactions more difficult to cross. The best-known public expression of that difference was the contest between Washington and Du Bois; Chesnutt's dramatization of the gap between Miller and Josh, far more stark than the public debate (and not exactly parallel to the Washington–Du Bois debate, of course), is its best literary expression, for it highlights explicitly the meaning of heroism in the formation of a cultural ideology. Miller, the advocate of restraint and moderation, gives an answer to the threatened racist violence consonant with the conciliatory answer that Wilmington's black leaders presented, however untimely, to Waddell. They disavowed Alexander Manly, and so does Miller, who thinks Barber's publishing of the editorial extremely ill advised so long as Wellington's blacks are living "in a sort of armed neutrality with the whites." When the riot breaks out, and Josh comes to Wellington's black professionals "lookin' fer a leader," Miller's practical advice against resistance is "not heroic," but it is, Chesnutt seems to say, "wise." By the same token, his resigned Washingtonian assertion that "our time will come" is answered harshly by Josh: "I'd ruther be a dead nigger any day dan a live dog!"[207]

The gap between the two views—symbolized by the gap that separates their language—presents an obviously melodramatic paradox that is played out over the remainder of the novel, leaving the reader to choose between equally painful alternatives. At stake, indeed, is the issue of "manliness" as it is dramatized on the African American side of the novel's equation. One might go so far as to say that Josh, as a version of the "bad nigger," comes close to the mythic power attributed to Stagolee by Molefi Asante, who places the mythic hero in the tradition of radical black nationalism and writes that he is the "uncensored, unselfconscious force" of freedom, the "ultimate projection of the black phallus into the white belly of America." Such a description is better suited to naturalistic heroes who come later in modern black literature; and any dimension of sexual revenge, which might conceivably strengthen the linking role between the genealogical and political plots played by white masculinity, is at best latent in the characterization of Josh's vengeance. Yet Josh's acting out of the criminal rage that the white press associates with the "Negro problem" and his explicit association in Miller's perspective with a dark, uncontrollable, primitive force—Josh appears to Miller on two occasions as "a great black figure" and "a black giant"—gives him the strongest right to a near-mythic status.[208]

The commitment to an ideology of violent resistance also virtually requires his death, just as middle-class anxiety about the "bad nigger" as a type who would jeopardize social progress created in folklore the necessity that the black outlaw pay for his moment of heroic glory. Even as he represents the justified retaliation against white oppression, he must be sacrificed to an assimilationist vision of racial harmony. To Miller, Josh is just such an incarnation of lower-class physicality that must be suppressed in favor of adherence to the law. Yet the law occupies a profoundly unstable terrain in *The Marrow of Tradition*. Chesnutt idealizes it as a power theoretically capable of justice but also subject to capricious subversion by racism, as it is in such compactly ironic color line stories as "The Web of Circumstance" and "The Sheriff's Children." An outlaw who has himself been created by the outlaw organization of the Ku Klux Klan, Josh personifies in his relationship to the law an increasing ambiguity that was characteristic of the African American folk hero in the 1890s as hopes for black political and civil rights crumbled and white supremacist violence became more frequent and publicly spectacular. In their mirror acts of killing each other, one might say, Captain McBane and Josh Green cancel each other out. In Chesnutt's terms, both are outlaws who represent a loss of control: on the one hand Carteret and Belmont's loss of control over the unruly mob, where the newspaper's "civilized" language of racist argument is finally stripped of its mask and, like the language of law as Twain saw it, reduced to the uncomprehending shouts of the mob that swallow up Carteret's unavailing attempts to restore order; and on the other Miller's loss of control over the forces led by Josh, who leap into suicidal confrontation with the white mob. The difference, nonetheless, is obvious: Carteret and Belmont, like the Secret Nine of Wilmington, already represent lawlessness. As Chesnutt puts it when McBane, with characteristic honesty, remarks that they need not hypocritically hide their intentions to drive offensive black professionals out of Wellington: "It robbed the enterprise of all its poetry, and put a solemn act of revolution upon the plane of a mere vulgar theft of power."[209]

McBane's honesty exposes the mechanics of racism in the white middle class in Wellington, for it shows in further detail what Chesnutt's collapse of the chronology of the revolution is meant to express—namely, that in the age of segregation the law became a cloak for violent seizures of power and, conversely, that the fabricated specter of black lawnessness was a cloak behind which white lawlessness might be hidden. It was no mistake that minstrel shows often exploited Negro "ignorance" of the law and made black judges and lawyers into buffoons, for the law itself had become an extension of blackface minstrelsy, a corrupting deception that had nothing to do with black innocence or intelligence but with the wholesale denial that those qualities even mattered in American courts or public life.[210] Made thoroughly an instrument of ideological pragmatism, the law was of a piece with Tom's cakewalk. Olivia Carteret must ignore the law in order to preserve her untainted legacy from Janet Miller; Belmont must ignore it to subvert old Delamere's will; Major Carteret must ignore it to accomplish his white supremacist goals and drive William Miller from occupying his own ancestral house. Captain McBane's blunt language merely tells the truth of the Carterets' more refined actions, frankly admitting the law to be the violent instrument of white racial supremacy. Likewise, one may look to Josh's language for a mirroring blunt articulation of truth—the truth, presumably, that Chesnutt, locked in a crisis of conscience that seems to reach an "impasse, a blind alley" in the novel, touched on when he declared that Wellington's blacks "had not behaved bravely on this critical day in their history."[211] If Miller was his more obvious alter ego, Josh spoke out of racial depths that Chesnutt had not experienced but could nevertheless fathom.

The novel leaves it for Janet Miller to throw back in her sister's face the personal recognition that she has neurotically coveted all her life (and the inheritance that she now finds is her due), and it ends with Miller, his own son sacrificed to mob violence, crossing the color line in order to save the white son of the New South. Whether he is able to do so is left appropriately unresolved. What is certain, however, is that the generosity of Janet Miller, alongside the implication that Miller's operation will succeed, indicates the utmost novelistic restraint on Chesnutt's part. He would have been within the bounds of artistic responsibility had he allowed Miller to pursue his own personal vengeance and cut Dodie's throat. Miller, as John Wideman notes, has his illusions about mulatto, middle-class existence stripped away and is left with the "bone-deep knowledge that men are either black or white and that nothing can occur between them that does not first take into account that dichotomy."[212] But Miller, of course, is also a figure of healing. With his hospital, the symbol of his commitment to "his people" of the South, destroyed in the riot, Miller remains a sign of forgiveness and reconciliation—both in his final act and in his mere survival. Leaving aside the Millers' son, whose death is emotionally necessary to the moral crisis of the conclusion, the others who die are deliberately sacrificed by Chesnutt in his own act of ideological healing. The extremists McBane and Green are killed. Mammy Jane (who dies calling out to her old white mistress in heaven) and her son Jerry (the gullible consumer of skin-bleaching products who futilely calls out to Carteret for help as violence breaks out), says Chesnutt, are representatives of a historical phase of subservient black accommodationism that must be overcome if leaders like Miller are to have any chance at successful "uplift."

Although they are not all developed as characters with equal effectiveness, the blacks of *The Marrow of Tradition* represent a wider range of class and type than any other such fictional group of the period, and they constitute a virtual anatomy of the complicated ideology of "progress" that surrounded the New Negro. Essentially three voices are represented— the less tractable working class; the aspiring professionals of the "talented tenth"; and an older, more meek servant class. Josh stands for the lower working class, prone to radicalism because of their more significant hardening at the hands of their white counterparts. The professional class to which Miller belongs, despite the fact that in 1900 they made up only 1.2 percent of the nation's black population, were the special target of the Wilmington revolution, as they were in some racist intellectual commentary. Arguing his theory of African American regression in *The Old South* in 1892, Thomas Nelson Page stated that the few Negro doctors and lawyers had achieved their small degree of success only because of a "considerable infusion of white blood in their veins." Nevertheless, in McBane's terms, they were the "smart niggers" who paradoxically set a bad example by making the others more difficult to control. If mulattoes in particular were scorned for their achievements, it was partly because they represented in their physiognomy the economic competition and contamination feared by the racist. As Carteret says to Jerry: "If you wish to get along well with the white people, the blacker you are the better,—white people do not like negroes who want to be white."[213] It is no coincidence, then, that Chesnutt places the ads for Jerry's whitening products on the same page with the Barber editorial in the *Afro-American Banner* before invoking them side by side with the white supremacists' republication of the strident column. Both texts, the one in painful cultural (and physical) self-mutilation, the other in brave protest, gloss the ambiguous terrain of miscegenation and passing; in an exception to Carteret's rule, however, Josh shows that "blacker" is not necessarily more tractable, that the rising New Negro was not confined by class or color.

Turn-of-the-century volumes devoted to the history of African Americans or, like Washington's *New Negro for a New Century*, to their social and professional achievements sought to overcome both racist theories of degeneracy and the plantation typology of the "darky." Nonetheless, some volumes by black authors participated in the myths of racial theory even as they promoted African American advances. H. F. Kletzing and W. H. Crogman's *Progress of a Race: Or, the Remarkable Advancement of the American Negro* (1897) made plantation melodies and portraits of loyal service to white masters part of the historical portrait, in essence casting the "old-time Negro" as an evolutionary type that would eventually give way to greater self-esteem and professional achievement. Introduced by an enthusiastic preface by Washington, which praised the "brilliant meteoric advance" of the Negro of the day, *Progress of a Race* accepted the theory of Anglo-Saxon leadership and superiority, and argued that blacks must "keep up with the procession" or else "get out of the way." Chesnutt would not, of course, have countenanced such a racial theory, but his characters Jerry, Mammy Jane, and (to a lesser degree) Sandy belong to a service class that he interprets in social (not racial) evolutionary terms. They have not yet joined the "chip-on-the-shoulder stage" represented by the Carteret's wet nurse or the professional aspirations of Miller.[214] Like old Delamere, Sandy, Jane, and Jerry belong to a passing world, one to which Chesnutt pays tribute even as he attempts to sweep it away. As he had remarked in his letter to Cable, quoted earlier, he knew that subservient "darky" characters in the mold of plantation mythology actually did exist, but he did not wish to replicate them in his work.

In *The Marrow of Tradition*, however, the "folk" and the "darky," though far from being equivalent, are put into uncomfortable proximity, and it is the middle-class physician, trained in the North, not Mammy Jane, with her seemingly outmoded superstitious beliefs in conjure, who will save

Dodie's life in the end. At the turn of the century, Chesnutt seemed to conclude, it is the Millers and the Carterets who must reach agreement on the future. For all the reasons I have indicated, it would be a mistake to draw too careful a parallel between Miller and Chesnutt. But it is certain that Chesnutt intended his novel to be conciliatory, that he intended it to contain an anguished cry of righteous protest moderated by the hopeful voice of compromise. He sent copies to Congress not as an act of intimidation but to provide a mechanism for telling the truth and restoring peace. Yet how are we to interpret the "folk" figures of the black lower class, and how reconcile the contradictory standoff between Miller and Josh? In the conjure tales and the color line stories, dialect and folk figures function as vehicles of indirect protest, subversion of the dominant culture through signifying language, and the creation of a "subcultural" voice of cultural integrity with African resonance outside the comprehension of mainstream white America. The reappearance of those figures is clearly marked in *The Marrow of Tradition*. The recourse to conjure has little effect, however, and Chesnutt's treatment of it does not diverge from his seemingly dismissive remarks in his 1901 essay on black "superstition." Josh, a folk hero of considerable significance, delivers a message of resistance laden with ambiguity; but his heroic resistance notwithstanding, *The Marrow of Tradition* drastically undercuts the powers, whether political or cultural, attributed to the folk in the conjure tales, consequently highlighting the skepticism in Chesnutt's published statement. In a book governed throughout by stark polarities, there seems little room for paradox: the new African American order, if it is to have a place in society at all, will of necessity pass beyond—forsake, perhaps—the world of the folk and its survivals of slave culture.

One means of understanding Chesnutt's dilemma and his deployment of the "folk" figures that had been a crucial element of his early writing career lies in the metaphor of the cakewalk which I have argued is at the center of the novel and, indeed, of Chesnutt's self-conscious understanding of his own profession as a writer. The cakewalk, as Chesnutt knew, was an ambiguous metaphor. It contained within it the expression of authentic African American culture, even African retentions, however distorted by the mimicry of white minstrel performance (like that of Tom Delamere) or by the white appropriation of the dance as a popular craze. In its performance by black artists, moreover, the cakewalk held, as it had on the plantation, the capacity for satiric commentary on the dominant culture. It stood as an embodiment of the painful entanglement between cultural self-determination and racist domination that may be said to have characterized the years in which Chesnutt lived and his art flourished. The reappropriation of cultural control that the African American performer expressed on the black stage, in musicals built around the problematic performance of coon songs and cakewalks, was a reversal of the roles of power. It was a return, one occurring on a grander and more lasting scale in vocal and instrumental music, to ancestral sources of creativity and a revival of those elements of plantation life that belonged not to the masters but to African American culture. In Chesnutt's own career the voice of such black cultural control belongs obviously to Uncle Julius and, more generally, to the conjure tales' ability to signify upon and destroy, even while wearing the disguise of, plantation literature and the racial conceptions that supported it.

The sharp dilemmas of such cultural negotiation are perhaps nowhere better depicted than in a story published in *Crisis* in 1912, which serves well to summarize the agonizing tension of Chesnutt's racial arguments and his own career. Rejected along with "White Weeds" by the *Atlantic* in 1904, "The Doll" is likewise a brilliant codification of racial conflicts whose controlled projection of anger may well have frightened the magazine's editors. The story portrays a southern white politician, in the midst of being shaved by a black northern barber, as he casually recounts having once killed a black man who protested the mistreatment (implied to be sexual) of his daughter. The barber, of course, suddenly realizes that the man killed by the colonel was his own father and that the moment of revenge he has often dreamed of is his to seize:

> In his dreams he had killed this man a hundred times, in a dozen ways. . . . He saw a vision of his father's form, only an hour before thrilling with hope and energy, now stiff and cold in death; while under his keen razor lay the neck of his enemy, the enemy, too, of his race, sworn to degrade them, to teach them, if need be, with the torch and with the gun, that their place was at the white man's feet, his heel upon their neck; who held them in such contempt that he could speak as he had spoken in the presense of one of them. One stroke of the keen blade, a deflection of half an inch in its course, and a murder would be avenged, an enemy destroyed.

But reminded of his obligations to others by the sight of his daughter's doll, the barber forgoes his revenge rather than jeopardize the future of his family and of his ten employees, as well as the larger black community, all of whom would suffer because of his single justified act. Because the colonel turns out to have known all along who the barber is, the balked revenge leaves an even more bitter taste at the story's end. Yet Chesnutt is clear about the allegory at work as the barber is caught in the struggle between homicidal impulse and restraint:

> For what white man, while the memory of this tragic event should last, would trust his throat again beneath a Negro's razor? . . . Indeed, [reasons for restraint] had presented themselves to the barber's mind in a vague, remote, detached manner, while the dominant idea was present and compelling, clutching at his heart, drawing his arm, guiding his fingers. It was by their mass rather than their clearness that these restraining forces held the barber's arm so long in check— it was society against self, civilization against the primitive instinct, typifying, more fully than the barber could realize, the great social problem involved in the future of his race.[215]

In this remark Chesnutt takes the side of restraint, the side of Miller, polarizing "civilization" and "primitive instinct" along not racial lines but pragmatic moral ones.

In asking, "What white man, while the memory of this tragic event should last, would trust his throat again beneath a Negro's razor?," more-over, the story disarms and humanizes the stereotype of the razor-wielding black criminal that had become rampant in racist cartoons, in minstrelsy, and even on the black musical stage.* In Tom Taylor's psychological turmoil and ultimate restraint, "The Doll" joins together the "coon" ste-reotype and the less comic threat associated with the weapon in the warning of Thomas Wentworth Higginson and others that slaves might cut their masters' throats, or in literary incorporations of the weapon such as those by Melville in *Benito Cereno* or Faulkner in *Light in August*. The

---

* To cite just one well-known example, the chorus of the grand finale of *Clorindy,* a raucous number entitled "Dere'll Be Wahm Coons a Prancin'," runs:

> And dere'll be wahm coons a prancin'
> Swell coons a dancin',
> Tough coons who'll want to fight,
> So bring long yo' blazahs,
> Fetch out yo' razahs,
> Darktown is out tonight. . . .

See Will Marion Cook and Paul Laurence Dunbar, *Clorindy* (New York, 1900).

razor here is a charged icon of African American resistance and revenge, and the black barber a simulacrum of the loyal retainer with mask torn off and revealed to be a murderous rebel—almost. Given that the third character in the story is a northern judge who acts as witness and moral conscience presiding over the drama of near retribution between Colonel Forsyth and Tom Taylor, it is hard not to believe that "The Doll" is a deliberate rewriting and condensation of some of the central features of *Benito Cereno*. Be that as it may, the terror of the story is not lessened but exacerbated by the fact that its violence remains latent and is in fact subjected to extreme psychological control on the part of Tom Taylor as, razor in hand—poised almost like Babo as he dabbles in the suds on Benito Cereno's lank neck—he listens to his father's murderer deliver a radical diatribe about black subservience and southern solutions to the "Negro problem." In the figure of the doll, moreover, is lodged the frightening ambivalence at the heart of the barber's hesitation, as well as Chesnutt's, for just as his attention is focused on "the upraised steel, and its uncompleted task," Tom's act of revenge is arrested by the sight of Daisy's broken doll, "hanging upon the gilded spike where he had left it."[216] He sees, that is, not just a reminder of his obligation to his daughter and the community at large but a miniature replica of his own probable lynching, if not in fact then certainly according to northern due process. (Tom's reflection that "he was black and not white, and this was North and not South, and personal vengeance was not accepted by the courts as a justification for murder" superimposes on Chesnutt's satiric view of southern law the studied irony that, as a black man, Tom would hardly qualify for such exoneration.) Further encoded in the drama of sexual abuse and contested patrimony that drives Chesnutt's best color line stories and *The Marrow of Tradition*, the action of "The Doll" thus joins its psychic ritual to the legal and political ritual of segregation and disfranchisement.

In Tom Taylor's choice the impulse of Josh Green is subjugated to the more agonizing restraint of William Miller, the compulsion to revenge and the violent achievement of justice subordinated to a mercy that is not a conciliation to racism but rather a recognition that the good of the community outweighs the right of personal retribution. "The Doll" itself stands on a razor's edge between unleashed violence and restraint, which is here the better part of valor, perhaps, but which also amounts to a kind of dignity that Chesnutt measured less persuasively but with more complication in the character of Miller. Like some of the conjure tales, the story turns minstrel stereotypes on their head, loading them with subversive, recriminating potential while at the same time keeping that violent counteraction in check. "The Doll" resituates the resisting voice of black culture in a character who sums up the range of characters in *The Marrow of Tradition,* combining the potential for revenge (both Josh's outbreak and Miller's implied opportunity to kill Dodie), a typecast servant's role, and the seeming race consciousness of the aspiring middle class. As Chesnutt manipulates the trope of the razor, moreover, Tom Taylor is at once a stage figure, a historical type, and a fully modulated psychological subject—a figure, like the story itself, who is representative of Chesnutt's concision and nuance at the height of its power. "The Doll" is screened through, and holds in perilous balance, the contending forces of plantation mythology and racial injustice at the turn of the century.

The form that such a crisis of racial tension takes in *The Marrow of Tradition* is less obvious but no less significant. It lies in what might be styled Chesnutt's authorial cakewalk. Tom Delamere's cakewalk exposes the South's political masquerade—its conjoined display of false minstrel images in the plantation tradition and the created specter of black criminality as a double mask to cover revolutionary violence. In the novel it is Chesnutt who exposes the charade of plantation mythology, openly displaying its rudimentary violence and its lies, and uniting the powerful tropes of disguise and white countersubversion delineated in such important precursors as *Benito Cereno* and *Pudd'nhead Wilson.* In both its narrative structure and its governing assumptions, *The Marrow of Tradition* is locked in the same posture of incompletely resolved, emotionally frustrating tensions that appear in "The Doll," and it is therefore likely to remain a difficult novel to judge and appreciate from the distance of a century. What Howells found too "bitter," most recent readers have found too indecisive or even complacent. Nevertheless, no novel of the period provides a better anatomy of the racial politics of the nation in the aftermath of Reconstruction or a more compelling portrait of the several ideological strands of class, color, and cultural inheritance that were being uneasily woven together to form the coming modern world of the New Negro. A masterpiece of political fiction—indeed, the most important protest against the painful descent of America into harsh segregation—*The Marrow of Tradition* is also Chesnutt's most searching reflection on the divided sensibilities of his own literary career. Both concluded in states of tension and irresolution commensurate with the nation's grave moral failure to make good the meaning of emancipation. For African American culture, as for the restoration of black political and civil rights that had eroded year by year since Reconstruction, there was time enough but none to spare: no more water, but the fire next time.

III

W. E. B. Du Bois:
African America
and the
Kingdom of Culture

· 5 ·

Swing Low:
The Souls of Black Folk

First off, he was a whisper, a will to hope, a wish to find something worthy of laughter and song. Then the whisper put on flesh. His footsteps sounded across the world in a low but musical rhythm as if the world he walked on was a singing-drum. . . . The sign of this man was a laugh, and his singing-symbol was a drum-beat. . . .

He had come from Africa. He came walking on the waves of sound. Then he took on flesh after he got here. The sea captains of ships knew that they brought slaves in their ships. They knew about those black bodies huddled down there in the middle passage, being hauled across the waters to helplessness. John de Conquer was walking the very winds that filled the sails of the ships. He followed over them like the albatross.

It is no accident that High John de Conquer has evaded the ears of white people. They were not supposed to know. You can't know what folks won't tell you. If they, the white people, heard some scraps, they could not understand because they had nothing to hear things like that with. . . .

So after a while, freedom came. Therefore High John de Conquer has not walked the winds of America for seventy-five years now. His people had their freedom, their laugh and their song. They have traded it to the other Americans for things they could use like education and property, and acceptance. High John knew that that was the way it would be, so he could retire with his secret smile into the soil of the South and wait.

Zora Neale Hurston, "High John de Conquer"

"In their fondness for eschatology, and the joy with which they anticipate the day of judgment and dwell upon its terrific and sublime features, the hymns are a fair echo and antiphone of the preaching which they accompany."[1] William Barton's portrait of African American spirituals selects only one of the many complex levels of allegory of which they, like the performative sermonic texts of the black church, are constituted. Not thoughts of Judgment Day alone but rather of earthly liberation and escape north, of a return to Africa or a revitalization of African beliefs, and the instilling of race consciousness—these are the forces that variously animate the spirituals' message of the freedom that will be found in a world beyond the veil of antebellum chattel slavery or, at a later historical moment, beyond the neo-slavery of post-Reconstruction peonage, legislated ignorance, and race violence. Barton's 1899 assessment was characteristic of his day in its subordination of the political dimension of the spirituals, but his recognition that they formed an antiphonal construct in which the preacher's voice could be a contrapuntal or harmonic accompaniment provides a useful vantage point from which to see their function as literature. What is more, it offers a fresh means to evaluate the strategy and structure of *The Souls of Black Folk,* the preeminent modern text of African American cultural consciousness. Du Bois's masterwork is a text of many dimensions—a first-rate, if unorthodox, history of post–Civil War race relations in the South; a trenchant essay in sociological and economic analysis; a brief for black education; and a study in comparative European American and African American cultures. Yet what is perhaps the most powerful feature of Du Bois's text has also been its least carefully regarded: his commentary on the transforming power, from slave culture through post-Reconstruction modernity, of the central expressive form of African America, the "sorrow songs."

In arguing for the centrality of the sorrow songs to *The Souls of Black Folk,* I mean to remedy a deficiency in critical evaluations of Du Bois without losing sight of the many modes of discourse that operate throughout the work. My emphasis will fall neither on the literary or musicological character of the spirituals as such, nor on Du Bois's relatively brief commentary on various elements of slave religion, but rather on the way in which he appropriated their core expression of African American culture, their *soul,* in order to create a foundation for modern African American culture as an extension of slave culture. His own comparative indifference to black churches and religious leadership during his maturity makes Du Bois's comments on the preacher in "Of the Faith of Our Fathers" seem rather isolated from his career's vast social and political argumentation. It would be a mistake, moreover, to confuse Du Bois's formal rhetorical style and narrative structure in *The Souls of Black Folk,* whatever its unusual generic accomplishment, with the cadences of the black preacher. If black religion did not provide him a language, however, it did provide the central matrix of his reconstruction of African American culture.[2]

In the sorrow songs, which both frame and carry forward the most resonant arguments of *The Souls of Black Folk,* Du Bois discovered a deep spiritual intonation for his cultural voice, one that would vivify his writing for at least three decades and make his work unique in its blending of poetics and politics, what he would eventually refer to as the necessary union of art and propaganda. If I concentrate on what initially seems a rather narrow topic within the available approaches to Du Bois's multivalent work, my purpose is to accomplish several things at once: to estimate the centrality of song to African American culture, both its extension of the folk traditions of slavery into a later era and its incorporation of the tonal semantics of vernacular culture into modern literary form; to trace Du Bois's own remarkably comprehensive theorizing about African American economic labor, political rights, and aesthetic endeavor in its continual reference to the grounding principles of survival and salvation articulated in the communal art of the spirituals; and, by extension, to argue that in the history of early twentieth-century American culture, traditional interpretations notwithstanding, few intellectual figures hold such a commanding presence as Du Bois. *The Souls of Black Folk* is one of the indispensable works of the early modern period, in literature and intellectual history alike; and yet, like Du Bois's work as a whole, it is not often carefully read and even less appreciated.

In the Kingdom of Culture

All of the key words in Du Bois's title ("souls," "black," "folk") retain a charged ambiguity. As Arnold Rampersad has remarked, "folk" verges on "nation" to such a degree in *The Souls of Black Folk* that it must be seen as an elaboration upon the idea of a racial nation as Du Bois had defined it in his landmark essay "The Conservation of Races" in 1897.[3] At the same time, however, "folk" moves toward a more specific geography, a stronger sense of soil and place not encompassed by "nation"—the geography of the black folk of the South, which could be the cradle of a black American nation (even, as would ultimately be the case in *Darkwater* and *Dark Princess,* the cradle of a Pan-African, diasporic, multicolored "nation") but could not be synonymous with it. The dividing line between "folk" and "nation" was one of many such liminal states upon which Du Bois rested his greatest and most characteristic arguments, not because his art was one of compromise but rather because it was one of constant encroachments and tensions. Like the line between colors (as in his famous aphorism "The problem of the twentieth century is the problem of the color-line") or the line between "American" and "Negro" cultures (as in his equally famous theory of "two-ness," of African American double consciousness) or the line between a post-Reconstruction Victorian world of imperial rule and scientific racism on the one hand, and the modern era of anticolonial revolt and the escalation of civil rights activism on the other, the line between "folk" and "nation" shifted and blurred in usage. "Folk" diminished and gave way to "nation" as Du Bois's Pan-African thought, latent in *The Souls of Black Folk,* came to the fore; but the voice of the folk rang with clarity in his early masterpiece, where it was grounded in "the Negro folksong—the rhythmic cry of the slave," which he, among others, considered "the sole American music" as well as "the singular spiritual heritage of the nation and the greatest gift of the Negro people."[4]

Nevertheless, when Du Bois, invited to collect some of his sociological essays into a book, "stepped within the Veil" of black America to compose his concluding chapters, he connected himself for the first substantial time to a folk with whom he did not have a great deal in common. His preface to *The Souls of Black Folk* is instructive in this regard. After the usual acknowledgment to publishers for permission to reprint previous essays that appeared in the *Atlantic Monthly,* the *Dial, Annals of the American Academy of Political and Social Science,* and elsewhere, Du Bois writes: "Before each chapter, as now printed, stands a bar of the Sorrow Songs,— some echo of haunting melody from the only American music which welled up from the black souls in the dark past. And, finally, need I add that I who speak here am bone of the bone and flesh of the flesh of them that live within the Veil?"[5] Du Bois forecasts the antiphonal relationship that would exist between music and text in the succeeding essays, a relationship in which the two forms gradually coalesce, as the volume unfolds, into an inseparable articulation of the tonal and the semantic dimensions of African American cultural expression. He also indicates his own peculiar relationship to that culture. His rhetorical question ("need I add . . . ") already contains the famous theory of double consciousness that would mark Du Bois's place within the Veil. But the question, surely, was addressed as much to himself as to his reader. His New England birth; his Harvard and Berlin graduate education; his love of European culture; his mixed-race identity, which was sometimes perversely charged against him by Garvey's circle as a sign of his disloyalty to black nationalist concerns; his reputation for a stiff, impersonal demeanor—in short, the range of characteristics that would remain a vague counterweight to the certain fact that he had to ride the Jim Crow car in America just like every other black person—all these things kept Du Bois from any sort of comfortable unification with the folk consciousness epitomized by the black spirituals.* Yet it was precisely that ambivalence, one that echoed the larger state of African-American culture, that allowed Du Bois to write so effectively in his volume and to do so primarily through the matrix of the sorrow songs.

The liminal, syncretic character of Du Bois's vision, although it was grounded in the circumstances of his birth and upbringing, should not be misconstrued as a simple dichotomy between "American" and "American Negro" of the sort Frederick Douglass continually expressed and which has typically been identified as the heart of Du Bois's sociological definition of black identity. Rather, the dichotomy embraced the broader cultural rift between "African" (or "Negro") and "American," and it was this tension, as much as his theoretical musings, that led Du Bois to an amorphous interpretation of the category of race that would have significant implications for his nationalist aesthetic. The unstable nature of race and nationality in Du Bois's thought appears as early as "The Conservation of Races," an extraordinarily elusive performance prepared for the American Negro Academy, which he founded with Alexander Crummell. Defining "race" and "nation" as virtually synonymous without fully collapsing the distinction between the two, Du Bois in this essay was unable to discard all traces of "race" as a phenomenon of color with biological roots and tie it resolutely to shifting environmental parameters. Race instead

---

* A stronger statement of this problem in Du Bois's perspective—one that, despite its kernel of truth, suffers from its own prejudice and loses sight of Du Bois's achievement—was made in 1935 by E. Franklin Frazier, who spoke of Du Bois as a "cultural hybrid" and a classic case of the "marginal man": "Once back in America and Atlanta [after his education abroad], he was just a 'nigger.' Fine flower of western culture, he had here the same status as the crudest semi-barbarous Negro in the South. In the *Souls of Black Folk* [*sic*] we have a classic statement of the 'marginal man' with this double consciousness: on the one hand sensitive to every slight concerning the Negro, and feeling on the other hand little kinship or real sympathy for the great mass of crude, uncouth black peasants with whom he was identified. . . . The *Souls of Black Folk* is a masterly portrayal of Du Bois's soul . . . [but] when he takes his pen to write of the black masses we are sure to get a dazzling romantic picture." Quoted in Tony Martin, *Race First: The Ideological and Organizational Struggles of Marcus Garvey and the Universal Negro Improvement Association* (Westport, Conn.: Greenwood Press, 1976), p. 298.

corresponds to a "vast family of human beings" infused with a common purpose or idea—a world-spirit or *Volksgeist,* to cite the German formulation that Du Bois had clearly appropriated. That "Negro" included a familial link to Africa is evident in Du Bois's optimistic challenge that black Americans are to take their "just place in the van of Pan-Negroism." The dichotomy, that is to say, is dynamic, and the choice as Du Bois represents it even here is between realizing a "distinct mission as a race" and "self-obliteration [as] the highest end to which Negro blood dare aspire."[6]

At times Du Bois's double consciousness left him open to accusations of Eurocentrism and blinded him to important elements of African life and the colonial situation. By the same token, however, it was just the reverse of debilitating: it made him acutely aware of the democratic implications of race theory. Finding neither a sound basis for a scientific definition of race nor a cultural-historical explanation that was not virtually open-ended, Du Bois returned again and again to quasi-mystic notions such as "genius," "strivings," and "common memory." Although he drew a far more romanticized picture of his double ancestry in *Darkwater,* in the later volume *Dusk of Dawn* he admitted that his speech, cultural patterns, and family customs were derived from New England. "My African racial feeling," as he calls it, "was then purely a matter of my own learning and reaction." Race, therefore, was not given to one but was to be acquired, absorbed, invented in a specific cultural circumstance that would be marked, yet not adequately defined, by color or other physical features. What Du Bois means by "reaction," however, is not far to seek. When he applied in 1908 for membership in the Massachusetts Society of the Sons of the American Revolution on the basis of his great-great-grandfather's war record, his application was denied because he could not produce a birth certificate of the man who had, of course, been a slave stolen from Africa. As Du Bois remarks, with a simplicity that overflows any theoretical barriers to his definition of race: "I felt myself African by 'race' and by that token was African and an integral member of the group of dark Americans who were called Negroes."[7]

The problem of where race was to be located, as much as the rise of invidious sciences of race, led to Du Bois's volksgeistian definitions. When he turned his attention to "real history" in "The Conservation of Races," however, one can see how little, in the end, it mattered to him that his central concern was so slippery. At first glance Du Bois seems aligned with his contemporaries who argued, for example, that "race is deeper than culture," that it is an "indwelling spirit" or "Will which is the force behind culture" and cannot be changed by environment or sucessfully copied (only deceptively "imitated") by other races.[8] On occasion Du Bois's definitions move in this direction, but increasingly over the course of his essays it becomes evident that what mattered to him was not race as such but "the race idea, the race spirit, the race ideal." The location—indeed, the incarnation—of such spirit was not in the liberal ego of the individual but in his representative nature: "We see the Pharaohs, Caesars, Toussaints, and Napoleons of history and forget the vast races of which they were but epitomized expressions." One can argue that this is the most revealing passage in Du Bois's essay, for it not only puts the question of race in more strictly nationalist terms and anticipates, in a grander form, Du Bois's notion of the "talented tenth" who would lead the race forward, but it also outlines Du Bois's own messianic conception of himself. To be the "epitomized expression" of African Americans would not override but would rather contain in vital tension the conflict between nation and race, and between American and Negro. The messianic leader was thus an Emersonian representative man like Toussaint in Haiti, Jefferson Davis in the South (on whom Du Bois spoke in his graduation speech at Fisk), Bismarck in Germany (on whom he spoke in a valedictory address at Harvard), or the black nationalist leaders of Africa who began their rise to power in the early twentieth-century independence movements. Joel Williamson has suggested that Du Bois's thought was Hegelian in that it epitomized the view that consciousness is achieved not individually but through a people's rising to awareness of its collective spirit or soul. Appropriating theories of race nationalism available to him as a student at Fisk, Harvard, and Berlin, Du Bois thus struggled to institutionalize the world-spirit of Africa and made himself, in Williamson's curious but apt phrase, "the Christ of the soul movement."[9]

The messianic dimensions of Du Bois's intellectual efforts and public leadership would not be fully evident for a number of years. Yet one can find the prophecy of that achievement in *The Souls of Black Folk,* not simply because generations of black readers would remember their encounter with it as a stunning experience (James Weldon Johnson, for example, maintained that it "had a greater effect upon and within the Negro race in America than any other single book published in this country since *Uncle Tom's Cabin,*" while Claude McKay recalled that "the book shook me like an earthquake. Dr. DuBois [*sic*] stands on a pedestal illuminated in my mind. And the light that shines there comes from my first reading of *The Souls of Black Folk*"),[10] but rather because the book is so completely saturated with the simultaneously bardic and polemical spirit of the great documents of nationalist consciousness. To what degree Du Bois, at different points in his career, may be considered a "nationalist" is, of course, worth careful scrutiny. It is possible, indeed, to locate Du Bois entirely outside of a black nationalist tradition and to place him, for example, in the tradition of American pragmatism.[11] I want to argue, however, that because the concept of African American "nationalism," like the concept of race itself, was utterly fluid for Du Bois—was, in effect, a kind of matrix against which he could measure fluctuating images of what it meant to be a black American as well as a race leader—it must be taken as instrumental to his transformation of the role of priest and the "text" of the spirituals into the defining elements of modern African American leadership.* The racial consciousness that is a cornerstone of Du Bois's philosophy was most of all a means for him to harness those national "powers of body and mind" that have "in the past been strangely wasted, dispersed, or forgotten" and fashion them toward the purpose of the African American's historical "striving: to be a co-worker in the kingdom of culture, to escape both death and isolation, to husband and use his best powers and his latent genius."[12]

To the extent that *The Souls of Black Folk* advanced what would today be recognized as a moderate Afrocentric argument—that African social and historical customs, however fragmentary, and to some degree the spiritual framework of African belief systems are retained in African American culture—it is logically succeeded by *Darkwater*. The latter, a post–World War I messianic text that culminated the first long stage of Du Bois's evolution of Pan-African philosophy, tied the labor and language of the black American South, in slave culture and after, to that of Africa and the greater colonial world abroad. From the very beginning of his career, however, nationalist tendencies were poised to become paradigms for Pan-Africanism, and Du Bois, as one of the first Third World writers,

---

* I have in mind a definition of nationalism as glossed by Clifford Geertz: "The images, metaphors, and rhetorical turns from which nationalist ideologies are built are essentially devices, cultural devices designed to render one or another aspect of the broad process of collective self-redefinition explicit, to cast essentialist pride or epochalist hope into specific symbolic forms, where more than dimly felt, they can be described, developed, celebrated, and used. To formulate an ideological doctrine is to make (or to try to make—there are more failures than successes) what was a generalized mood into a practical force." See Clifford Geertz, *The Interpretation of Cultures: Selected Essays* (New York: Basic Books, 1973), p. 252.

must always be judged with such an imaginative horizon in view. If that fact makes Du Bois seem a less "American" writer, however, it is only because our definitions of American modernism (not to say American authorship) have been inadequate. My two chapters on Du Bois, organized respectively around *The Souls of Black Folk* and *Darkwater,* create something of an artificial division within roughly two decades of his career, in part because the former text so stands out in its general argument and, as I will contend, in its particular use of the spirituals, and in part because a proper interpretation of the latter has to be constructed from diverse sources. It will be nonetheless clear, I hope, to what an extent Du Bois's thought and literary efforts were driven by a consistent, evolving philosophy of racial consciousness from the very outset.

Du Bois's celebration of the folk world represented by the spirituals tempered his own commitment to a progressivist ideal that was too easily identified with elite European American culture and with his own proclaimed belief in the elevating leadership of a black talented tenth whose achievements, he argued throughout his early career, would raise up the masses below them. Indeed, because Du Bois refused to accept as necessary the contradiction between elite and folk culture, his use of the spirituals was itself an example of this belief in action. When he put the spirituals at the center of *The Souls of Black Folk* and identified their slave creators as the foundational voice of black culture, Du Bois responded on the one hand to the white cultural critics and ethnographers who misconstrued, or at the least dominated the interpretations of, the value of African American culture, and on the other to what he took to be the inadequate assertiveness of black cultural leadership. In addition, his radical positioning of the black spirituals offered him a further way to subvert the authority of Booker T. Washington, the man whom he made his foremost antagonist in the early years of his career and the notorious centerpiece of his critique of African American leadership in *The Souls of Black Folk.* Washington had paid tribute to the spirituals as a coded language of liberation in *Up from Slavery,* where he noted that with the coming of the Civil War the slaves "gradually threw off the mask, and were not afraid to let it be known that the 'freedom' in their songs meant freedom of the body in this world." Moreover, in 1905, perhaps under the influence of Du Bois, Washington's preface to Samuel Coleridge-Taylor's *Twenty-Four Negro Melodies Transcribed for the Piano* (a work by a British black composer who answered contemporary calls for a classical treatment of the spirituals) announced that the black spiritual "reminds the race of the 'rock whence it was hewn,' it fosters race pride, and in the days of slavery it furnished an outlet for the anguish of smitten hearts."[13] For the most part, however, Washington's Franklinesque programs of domestic and industrial education had little place for reminders of slavery or celebrations of race consciousness. What would become Du Bois's best-known chapter in *The Souls of Black Folk* was devoted to his attack on Washington, and other chapters, most notably "Of the Wings of Atalanta," were also extended rebuttals of Washington's accommodationist policies. Not just the music he chose to associate with Washington—"A Great Camp-Meeting in the Promised Land," which heads the Washington chapter, turns out to be a most ambiguous salute to Washington's career—but the infusion of music itself into his text was a mode of resistance launched upon Washington's more familiar ground. Whereas Washington was a son of the South, born in slavery and resolutely tied to black southerners, Du Bois was a folk parvenu, as it were. His years at Fisk University and his summer of teaching in rural Tennessee constituted no more than an apprenticeship (in this he was an avatar of Jean Toomer's character Ralph Kabnis in *Cane*), and yet in one great rhetorical gesture he destroyed Washington's ascendancy. His superior intellectual training and taking of the higher moral ground might alone have been enough to defeat Washington on the issues of education, suffrage, and civil rights. But it was his seizure and celebration of indigenous African American culture that allowed Du Bois rebelliously to sweep away Washington's populist advantage, replacing his philosophy of the toothbrush with a philosophy of black soul and transfiguring the narrow conception of labor and nation building in Washington's program into a broad, exhilarating call for the labor necessary to construct a black American wing in the "kingdom of culture."[14]

Although his two signal decisions about the published form of the essay collection are related, the addition of the chapters on life within the Veil (that is, the last five chapters of *The Souls of Black Folk,* only one of which, "Of the Faith of Our Fathers," had been previously published) was not so provocative a cultural act as was the featuring of the spirituals at the head of each chapter. This act was itself complex in ways that have scarcely been examined. Previous readers have studied the role of the chapter devoted to the sorrow songs in the overall structure of *The Souls of Black Folk* or have commented generally on the contribution made by the musical epigraphs to Du Bois's notion of double consciousness. But there has been little attempt to chart the significance of the individual selections or to develop a theory of the music's function within the larger text. In his concluding chapter Du Bois identifies most but not all of the spirituals he has employed in the text, but he does not match the titles to the chapters in all cases; at best his documentation is haphazard, although I will suggest that it is of a piece with the central epistemological challenge posed by the spirituals themselves. For their part, critics and editors of *The Souls of Black Folk* have seldom used Du Bois's own clues to much purpose, let alone adduced the lyrics of the relevant spirituals or identified those musical epigraphs not named by him. In doing so, I leave somewhat open to question the exact nature of Du Bois's intentions in choosing the individual sorrow songs. The meaning of his choices must arise from inference and implication in the case of individual chapters and their epigraphic bars of music; while in the case of the text as a whole that meaning resides in its unique choral construction. First I offer a preliminary sketch of these issues before turning to a chapter-by-chapter interpretation of the spirituals and, finally, to a more speculative theory of the function of the songs in African American culture as Du Bois constructs it in *The Souls of Black Folk*.

"This Wonderful Music of Bondage"

All that was left were a few names of what they called nations which they could no longer even pronounce properly, the fragments of a dozen or so songs, the shadowy forms of long-ago dances and rum kegs for drums. The bares bones. The burnt-out ends. And they clung to them with a tenacity she suddenly loved in them and longed for in herself. . . .

Hands flashing, he spurred the drumming on. Yet every so often in the midst of the joyousness and speed he would pause, and placing his left elbow on the drumhead he would draw his right thumb across the top. . . .

And the single, dark, plangent note this produced, like that from the deep bowing of a cello, sounded like the distillation of a thousand sorrow songs. For an instant the power of it brought the singing and the dancing to a halt—or so it appeared. The theme of separation and loss the note embodied, the unacknowledged longing it conveyed summed up feelings that were beyond words, feelings and a host of subliminal memories that over the years had proven more durable and trustworthy than the history with its trauma and its pain out of which they had come. After centuries of forgetfulness and even denial, they refused to go away. The note was a lamentation that could hardly have come from the rum keg of a drum.

Its source had to be the heart, the bruised still-bleeding innermost chamber of the collective heart.

For a fraction of a second the note hung in the yard, knifing through the revelry to speak to everyone there. To remind them of the true and solemn business of the fete. Then it was gone.

Paule Marshall, *Praisesong for the Widow*

To begin with, the spirituals allowed Du Bois to offer commentary on all the essays, for the texts and titles that are deleted but nonetheless silently accompany each strand of music can be read as quite deliberate editorial selections. The musical bars thus function, as I have already implied, as epigraphs of a sort, and yet these "African" songs remain functionally at odds with the "Western" belletristic epigraphs with which each is matched, coiled in a kind of anarchic symbiosis until the sorrow songs finally prevail in the last chapter. Without question, Du Bois sought an ideal of culture beyond the color line, where, "wed with Truth," he could "dwell above the Veil," where he could "sit with Shakespeare . . . move arm in arm with Balzac and Dumas," and "summon Aristotle and Aurelius and what soul I will," all to meet him "graciously with no scorn or condescension."[15] His well-known passage defined a world in which the alternating epigraphs would be in communion, not in conflict, in which the Western and African traditions might harmoniously coexist. To the extent that *The Souls of Black Folk* achieves such a communion, however, it does so only hypothetically. Writing at a historical moment of bleak social and political prospects for African Americans, Du Bois marked the gulf between black and white America in many ways, not least in the blunt dialectical challenge of his epigraphs. At the interpretive level the paired epigraphs most often act as a joint dialectical commentary on the individual chapters; in this respect they might (to cite Boas again) be styled "alternating sounds" in the simple sense that they provide a double gloss on Du Bois's various essays in sociological and cultural analysis. Yet such a dialectic is clear only after the music has been recognized and the lyrics "transcribed"—only, one could say, after the musical epigraphs have been coded in a discourse that corresponds more closely to the poetic epigraphs.

Du Bois, of course, meant to gain for the spirituals (and black art generally) recognition as part of world culture; but to do so he risked the paradox that their "language" would remain alien or be dismissed by white (or black) readers, and he pursued the recuperation of a culture seemingly at odds with his own elite education and erudite tastes. The spirituals are thus one measure among others of the way in which the revisions Du Bois made when he gathered his essays into a book extended his identification with, and his commitment to, black American culture and to its nebulous African roots. By incorporating the spirituals into the fabric of his text, Du Bois turned sociological commentary into a sensate, vocalized text—radically crossing generic boundaries, employing the languages of silence and implication to carry significant communicative burdens, and dwelling in the most profound autobiographical way in the spiritual resources of his texts. William Ferris would later complain in *The African Abroad* that Du Bois wrote too much as an individual, "crying out in righteous indignation and piteous wail" rather than speaking in "a prophetic voice, freighted with a message of the eternal."* In fact, however, the personal and the prophetic were embedded within each other for Du Bois, as the remainder of his career would prove time and again. The subtitle of his third book that could be called an autobiography, *Dusk of Dawn: The Autobiography of a Race Concept* (1940), reflected this peculiar conjunction of the subjective and the transhistorical in more stark terms than had *Darkwater* in 1920 or *The Souls of Black Folk* before it. In a 1904 review of his own book, moreover, Du Bois spoke of the style of *The Souls of Black Folk* as "tropical—African," and explained the "intimate tone of self-revelation" that runs through the book, in contrast to a more traditional impersonality and judiciousness, as a function of the fact that "the blood of my fathers spoke through me and cast off the English restraint of my training and surroundings."[16] Such a self-conceptualization, yoked to his prefatory assertion that the folk spirituals of slavery were "of me and mine" and his appropriation of their prophetic structure, is the clearest evidence that Du Bois identified early on with a "race concept" (as he would conceive himself according to the subtitle of *Dusk of Dawn*) that was partly

* Ferris's rather self-serving remarks chided Du Bois for not having written a book (more like his own) that swept dramatically through history to prove that the entirety of Western religious and political thought could be marshaled against the injustices of American racism. By the same token, however, Ferris recognized that the personal element and what he considered Du Bois's thorough pessimism were perhaps necessary to rouse the American conscience and had made *The Souls of Black Folk* what it appeared by 1913 to have become—"the political Bible of the Negro race," with Du Bois "the long-looked-for political Messiah, the Moses that will lead them out of the Egypt of peonage, across the Red Sea of Jim Crow legislation, through the wilderness of disfranchisement and restricted opportunity and into the promised land of liberty of opportunity and equality of rights." See William H. Ferris, *The African Abroad, Or His Evolution in Western Civilization*, 2 vols. (New Haven: Tuttle, Morehouse, and Taylor, 1913), I, 274–76.

willed into being, adopted like a messianic mantle, and partly delivered from spiritual resources within.

The musical epigraphs are therefore "alternating sounds" in the other sense that I have outlined already in the example of Chesnutt—an example of a cultural "language" (in this case black) that cannot be properly interpreted, or even "heard" at all, since it fails to correspond to the customary mapping of sounds and signs that make up the languages of the dominant (in this case white) culture. The spirituals represented Du Bois's pointed assertion that African American culture could be codified, that it was worthy of preservation, and, whatever the degree of its assimilation by the dominant European American culture, that it spoke identifiably in a language of its own. But it was also a language at the very least open to misconstruction, and more likely to remain opaque to the dominant culture, a fact scarcely less true today than when Du Bois wrote. To the uninformed reader the musical texts are but printed notes; whereas to the initiated listener not only do they constitute the language of song, but the unarticulated text (the unprinted words) is heard as well. The bars of music posed a pointed challenge to their contemporary audience, for they demanded a familiarity with a cultural language that most whites did not have and that an increasing number of middle-class blacks renounced as an unhealthy reminder of slavery (in 1909, for example, black students at Howard University refused to sing spirituals, though similar resistance had arisen ever since the conclusion of the Civil War).[17] And they did so, I will suggest as well, by incorporating and rearticulating the trope of silence—one of the central tropes, as we have seen in the case of Chesnutt's folktales, of African American cultural expression. Hidden within the veil of black life, the music and words of the sorrow songs form a hidden, coded language in *The Souls of Black Folk,* one that recapitulates the original cultural function of the spirituals themselves. In a more comprehensive sense, therefore, the music functions antiphonally with respect to Du Bois's written text, such that one must "hear" sounds that are not on the page.

Du Bois's text in this way amplified the traditional remarks by folk music collectors that no common annotations were adequate to capture the slides, blue notes, and shouts of black song. A full discussion of the theoretical dimensions of this issue can be postponed for the moment, but the long-standing recognition that black spirituals defied accurate transcription bears directly on Du Bois's act of cultural preservation. Of paramount importance here are the remarks by James Miller McKim and his daughter Lucy (who together transcribed and published a group of songs by blacks in Port Royal, South Carolina, in 1862), by William Allen in *Slave Songs of the United States* (1867), by Theodore Seward, the musical arranger for J. B. T. Marsh's *Story of the Jubilee Singers with Their Songs* (1872), and by Thomas Fenner in his contribution of arrangements and commentary to *Hampton and Its Students* (1874), all of whom it appears Du Bois read. In addition to Du Bois's firsthand experience in northern and southern churches, he also had before him the repeated comments of these song collectors and numerous ethnographers that black music was difficult to annotate according to European standards. Three representative remarks may be excerpted. William Allen felt that "the best that we can do . . . with paper and types, or even with voices, will convey but a faint shadow of the original. The voices of the colored people have a peculiar quality that nothing can imitate; and the intonations and delicate variations of even one singer cannot be reproduced on paper. And I despair of conveying any notion of the effect of a number singing together, especially in a complicated shout." Lucy McKim offered a poetic description that would often be quoted: "It is difficult to express the entire character of these negro ballads by mere musical notes and signs. The odd turns made in the throat; and that curious rhythmic effect produced by single voices chiming in at different irregular intervals, seem almost as impossible to place on score, as the singing of birds, or the tones of an Aeolian Harp." Writing in the *Journal of American Folklore* in 1903, the year *The Souls of Black Folk* was published, Charles Peabody gave the example of a black Mississippi man's work song periodically "intoned" as he plowed behind a mule for fifteen hours a day, a song that "melted into strains of apparently genuine African music, sometimes with words, sometimes without. Long phrases there were without apparent measured rhythms, singularly hard to copy in notes." Likewise, Peabody found a black woman's lullaby "quite impossible to copy, weird in interval and strange in rhythm; peculiarly beautiful."[18]

As I noted when citing Peabody's fieldwork in the discussion of dialect in chapter 4, the difficulty of transcription was common in the case of music and oral narrative alike, and was frequently noted by white folklorists in the 1890s. The same could be said for some other folk songs or tales in ethnic dialect, of course, but African Americans presented the greater complexity of generations of isolating enslavement and a cultural inheritance in which the tonal semantics of oral African culture were pronounced. The more common interpretation even among schooled theoreticians of socialization, as one can note in the case of Robert Park, was that blacks brought very little culture with them from Africa, losing what they did in the vicissitudes of slavery, and produced seemingly incomprehensible or fragmentary songs solely because of their inadequate grasp of the English language.[19] As Boas might have argued on the basis of the thesis brought forward in "On Alternating Sounds," however, the white American (European) ear simply did not "hear" black sound and had but imperfect instruments to transcribe and preserve it. A comparable problem faces the reader of Du Bois's text. His theory of black culture, imparted indirectly and embedded in conventionally transcribed texts that replicated these very problems, must be deduced from a context, as well as a text, filled with barriers to common European American epistemological models. In its very structure and modality, however, Du Bois located *The Souls of Black Folk* on a critical dividing line between two worlds schematically epitomized by the distinction between word and music, organically vocalizing his text at a moment of political and cultural crisis in the African American world.

One sign of the crisis lay in the fact that black spiritual music was under siege. True, spirituals were being collected and published in great quantities by the turn of the century (a fact from which Du Bois benefited since the transcriptions he used were not his own). This was accompanied, however, by an overwhelming sense that black music was about to be lost as the older generations died and the middle class sought to distance itself from all reminders of slavery. Older African Americans, particularly those who had known the spirituals under the regime of southern slavery, frequently remarked that "new" versions of the songs, performed or collected in volumes, were but pale imitations of the "originals." As on the black musical stage in its evolution out of minstrelsy in the late nineteenth century, so in modern choral presentation of the spirituals the issues of originality and authenticity were unavoidably complex. In the arts as in social and political life, cultural preservation and memory itself, the very roots of a people's being, were set in contest with demanding notions of progress and assimilation to white cultural models.

Toward the end of the century, an elderly Kentucky woman delivered a superb description of the folk view of the "origin" of the spirituals as well as a vivid jeremiad against the declension of black faith in the younger generations. Recalling the form of worship and the relationship between the preacher's scripture and the evolution of African American music under slavery, she said:

And, honey, de Lord would come a-shinin' thoo dem pages and revive dis ole nigger's heart, and I'd jump up dar and den and holler and shout and sing and pat, and dey would all cotch de words and I'd sing it to some ole shout song I'd heard 'em sing from Africa, and dey'd all take it up and keep at it, and keep a-addin' to it, and den it would be a spiritual. Dese spirituals am de best moanin' music in de world, case dey is de whole Bible sung out and out. Notes is good enough for you people, but us likes a mixtery. Dese young heads ain't wuth killin', fur dey don't keer bout de Bible nor de ole hymns. Dey's completely spiled wid too much white blood in 'em, and de big organ and de eddication has done took all de Holy Spirit out en 'em, till dey ain't no better wid der dances and cuttin' up dan de white folks.

Or, as Sterling Brown would later write in "Children's Children":

> When they hear
> These songs, born of the travail of their sires,
> Diamonds of song, deep buried beneath the weight
> Of dark and heavy years;
> They laugh. . . .
>
> They have forgotten, they have never known
> Long days beneath the torrid Dixie sun,
> In miasma'd rice swamps;
> The chopping of dried grass, on the third go round
> In strangling cotton;
> Wintry nights in mud-daubed makeshift huts,
> With these songs, sole comfort. . . . [20]

However metaphorically the Kentucky woman intended her remark about the infusion of "white blood" to be taken, it summed up the generational change from "Old" to "New" Negro that Du Bois would dramatize most effectively in "Of the Coming of John" and illustrated an essential component of the paradox of double consciousness. Such a declension of ancestral traditions, a vexing issue in black cultural and intellectual history from the Civil War on through the early decades of the twentieth century, had stringent political implications insofar as plantation mythology required a perpetuation of the Christian submissiveness associated with the faith of "old-time darkies." But to remember and honor slave culture, even to continue its central communal traditions, was not, Du Bois and others set out to prove, necessarily at odds with the New Negro's fight for justice and rights. Indeed, the remembrance of the slave past was continuous with social struggle, as the important place of the freedom songs within the civil rights movement a half century later would prove. Du Bois could easily have taken to heart the remarks of Howard Odum and Guy Johnson in their 1925 study *The Negro and His Songs,* a book he was to review favorably: "Posterity has often judged peoples without having so much as a passing knowledge of their inner life, while treasures of folklore and song, the psychic, religious, and social expression of the race, have been permitted to remain in complete obscurity."[21]

In the particular case of the spirituals there was the additional question of how best to preserve them. As Du Bois argued, numerous more or less authentic groups seeking to emulate the famous Fisk Jubilee Singers "filled the air with debased melodies which vulgar ears scarce know from the real." What constituted a "real" spiritual, however, was a serious question. Well before the end of the century the difficulty of properly transcribing and annotating the spirituals was compounded by the obverse difficulty introduced by concert and published versions that inevitably simplified the songs, forcing them into a regularized tempo and the more rigid mold of the European tempered scale. In the view of Thomas Fenner, musical director at Hampton Institute and arranger of one of the two collections from which Du Bois evidently drew most of his sorrow songs, so little of the spirit that created black music—"the overpowering chorus . . . the swaying of the body; the rhythmical stamping of the feet; and all the wild enthusiasm of the negro campmeeting"—could be "transported to the boards of a public performance" that it became a fine point whether or not one could "develop" the music (that is, transcribe and arrange it for choral presentation) "without destroying its original characteristics." Writing in the *Southern Workman,* F. G. Rathbun reiterated Fenner's arguments in claiming that education itself was causing the decay of the original music at Hampton: "Corrected punctuation and singing make the difference. It is very difficult to teach an educated colored youth to render these songs in the old time way. White people, however well trained musically, make absolute failures of them. How to sing them cannot be explained in words. Study all the rules you please and then go listen to a native." Within one or two more generations the problem was more acute. In his new edition of the Hampton spirituals, published in 1927, Nathaniel Dett (who was African American) apparently attempted to elide the differences between the slave generations and the early twentieth century when he remarked that "the harmonizations and tunes in this book are as they are sung at Hampton Institute where the singing of these songs has been traditional since 1868." But in an appendix which included several of the spirituals that were most radically different from their earlier published forms, Dett admitted that a comparison of his new edition of the Hampton songs with previous editions would "show that the way many of the Negro folk-songs are sung at present is quite different from that recorded nearly a half-century ago." (Among those included so that "nothing may be lost" is Dett's most notable example of "Roll, Jordan, Roll," in which the blue tonality characteristic of much African American performance is transcribed although it is missing from the modern, concertized version.) At extremity, any theory of the spirituals would have to confront directly Zora Neale Hurston's claim, to which I will return, that no "real" spirituals had ever been recorded or transcribed since to do so entailed a necessary violation of the essential improvisatory freedom of African American song. Whether or not one agrees with Hurston, it is beyond doubt that concert performances modified the spirituals to make them more acceptable to a wide (and often white) audience in the North and in Europe, and that their publication typically in standardized English and regularized musical transcriptions exacerbated the process of simplification and debasement.[22]

In his revised commentary Dett indicated further consequences of publication that bear on Du Bois's cultural history. Although he deplored the musical deracination of the spirituals on the minstrel stage and in much modern concert performance, Dett himself always referred to the songs as "hymns" and grouped them under various headings ("Hymns of Consolation," "Hymns of Deliverance," "Hymns of Judgment," and so on), deliberately subordinating their unique musical and ideological character to a prescribed conformity to white Protestant practice. "While it is true that the songs of themselves offer much that is novel in the way of poetry, melody, harmony, and rhythm," he noted, "fundamentally it will be discovered that they correspond in sentiment with all the basic ideas of orthodox religious dogma." Dett's judgment here is correct in outline, of course, but it entirely obscures the multiple political-cultural meanings— of escape from slavery, of resistance to the regime's brutality, of both actual and spiritual journeys to the North or to the motherland of Africa—that had become semantically encoded in the language of the sorrow songs. Whatever the motive for Dett's editorial procedure (one is inclined to think he was driven by the necessity of patronage for Hampton Institute), he concluded his preface with an admission that "the younger Negro student of today is not quite the slave of yesterday," that contemporary spirituals and their singers have suffered not just by their distance from antebellum slavery but more particularly from "the influence of the white man's education, of the concert-hall, the phonograph, and the radio." The best that can be hoped for is a slight recovery of "the depth, sincerity, and pathos which marked [the singing] of the other days." In this losing battle Dett's admonition was itself but a dim echo of the argument already made by his predecessor, Fenner, more than a generation earlier and well in advance of *The Souls of Black Folk*. As Fenner recognized, publication of the spirituals, whatever its cost to "originality," was imperative if the songs were to be saved: "The freedmen have an unfortunate inclination to despise [the music], as a vestige of slavery; those who learned it in the old time, when it was the natural outpouring of their sorrows and longings, are dying off, and if efforts are not made for its preservation, the country will soon have lost this wonderful music of bondage."[23]

Fenner's arresting last phrase (like most of Hampton's early staff, he was white) captures the ratio between oppression and cultural creativity that would remain a hallmark of black music long after slavery. The rhetorical meaning of the "lost" music varied between plantation mythology for many whites and something akin to conscious cultural nationalism for some blacks. It is inevitably one of the pointed ironies of the African American cultural record that many of the more than one hundred collections of spirituals published in various formats by 1930, the majority by whites, were wrapped in the memorial shroud of plantation mythology or perpetuated offensive stereotypes. The burlesque of the spirituals by blackface minstrelsy was only an overt sign of the pervasively racist evaluation that African American music would continually face in a Jim Crow culture.[24] In their sympathy for the fading world of the Old South, historiography and memoirs dominated by neo-Confederate nostalgia could, in fact, blithely reinscribe racist norms within the crucial work of cultural preservation. A fairly late text by a southern woman, Lily Young Cohen's *Lost Spirituals,* was one of many written overtly in the tradition of Uncle Remus. Cohen touchingly recalled the love of her family's faithful post–Civil War servants, especially her mammy, but she also interspersed her maudlin memories with valuable transcriptions of lullabies, work songs, spirituals, and shouts. As her publisher pointed out in an introductory note: "Here the Negro himself is treated as a spiritual; so is his prose; so is his verse. And all are *lost*." The spirituals, of course, were no more about submission to bondage and acceptance of racial hierarchy (even if those elements were present in the language) than were the folktales that formed the basis for the work of Harris and Chesnutt. A number were straightforward testaments of faith in Christian salvation, and in this they corresponded to the assertion of Henry Burleigh in the preface to his popular arrangement of spirituals for solo voice—that they were "spontaneous outbursts of intense religious fervor" that bespoke a deep "faith in the ultimate justice and brotherhood of man." But the majority were also infused with the coded language of protest, escape, and liberation. As Sterling Brown would later write, echoing Du Bois, Douglass, and others, the spirituals' allegories of freedom spoke with finality *against* the legend of the contented slave—"this world was not their home," Brown remarks—but too few white listeners were ready by the turn of the century to hear more than reanimated strains of the Old South.[25] The enervating influence of plantation mythology throughout American culture made it difficult for blacks or whites to write sincerely about the legitimate value of black music, let alone deploy it as an instrument of racial consciousness for a skeptical (black) or hostile (white) audience.

The collective record of white and black America's joint preservation of the spirituals therefore makes for a unique, complex case of ethnography in which *The Souls of Black Folk* has a central role. The relationship of the spirituals to prevailing notions of "progress" was marked by continual tension. In an article appearing in *Century Magazine* in 1899, for example, Marion Haskell transcribed a number of spirituals in careful dialect. Noting in conclusion the increasing aversion of black colleges to the singing of spirituals, however, he relegated their social message and artistic value to a receding historical moment. "While rejoicing in the progress of the race," he added, "one cannot but feel that these quaint old spirituals, with their peculiar melodies, having served their time with effectiveness, deserve a better fate than to sink into oblivion as unvalued and unrecorded examples of a bygone civilization." The turn-of-the-century view of the spirituals as "quaint" (Du Bois himself used the word) drained them of immediacy and power while reflecting the common assumption that the spirituals not only represented a passing stage in black American "thought" but occupied a distinctly lower rung on the evolutionary ladder of culture. For example, the black essayist Kelly Miller, writing soon after Du Bois, reiterated the widespread argument that the sorrow songs were the spontaneous "folk-genius" of the race, a "blind, half-conscious poetry" that rose from the "imprisoned soul" of slaves and could now be seen to have served as a kind of cultural prelude to more advanced forms of thought: "Music is the easiest outlet of the soul. The pent-up energy within breaks through the aperture of sound while the slower and more accurate deliberations of the intellect are yet in the process of formulation." Miller's provocative metaphor of the aperture of sound, a most useful figure for the release into the flow of historical expression of African American music, nearly occludes his troubling reliance on a developmental schema that subordinates the "childlike" phase of oral folk culture to the "maturity" of intellect and writing. Unmediated by "cumbersome intellectual machinery," the spirituals were a plaintive "cry," in Miller's definition a beautiful, compelling, but necessarily primitive articulation of black aspirations.[26]

In this view Miller and others echoed the standard interpretation of professional musicologists. In the opinion of Richard Wallaschek, the spirituals, at best imitations of European compositions as he saw it, were "not musical songs at all, but merely simple poems." And in the same year, 1893, Frederick Root's address to the International Folk-Lore Congress at the World's Columbian Exposition asserted that "the utterances of the savage peoples" could be omitted from a concert of folk songs and national music because they were "hardly developed to the point at which they might be called music." Foreshadowing Dvořák's famous call for a national music founded upon the "primitive" melodies of black and American Indian music, Thomas Fenner two decades earlier had hoped, somewhat more charitably, that "this people which has developed such a wonderful musical sense in its degradation will, in its maturity, produce a composer who could bring a music of the future out of this music of the past." The fact that James Weldon Johnson would say much the same thing half a century later in *The Book of American Negro Spirituals* (1925) is a measure of the compelling ideology of progressivism and the stifling cultural climate with which black vernacular art in particular had to contend. In 1934 V. F. Calverton's provocative view that blacks had created in their spirituals and folktales "a form of expression, a mood, a literary *genre*, a folk-tradition, that are distinctly and undeniably American," while whites had been satisfied to continue their inferior imitation of European culture, was certainly a minority opinion and was destined to remain so for years to come.[27]

At the heart of the doubts voiced by whites and blacks alike about the value of the original spirituals lay the prevailing conceptions of African history, and hence of African cultural inheritances, as primitive and debased, a belief that in turn substantially informed contemporary ethnographic contentions, in the case of the spirituals as well as that of folktales, over the joint questions of African retentions and African American creativity. Du Bois would not begin to argue vigorously for the African roots of black American culture for another ten years. Nonetheless, he put himself decisively on the Africanist side in the debate over retentions; more important, he discovered a formal means by which he could foreground the creation of an original culture, whatever its exact borrowings, by black Americans in slavery and after.

The best known of the spirituals tended to be ones that had no demonstrable white models, while even those that did were greatly transmuted. From the 1890s forward, as I indicated in my earlier discussion of Harris and Chesnutt, a minority of folklorists who were simply misinformed or who resisted the notion that blacks could have been responsible for creating such a great body of musical work either denied that there were any African elements in the spirituals or, by focusing on the Protestant origins of the spirituals, belittled the creation that took place in the crucible of black enslavement. This was less true of early commentators but became more frequently the case as analysis was undertaken after the turn of the century by professional folklorists, a group, it is fair to say, that was not always immune to the racism of the day. In this case, too, the problem of transcription contributed to, rather than revealed, forms of cultural blindness. Because transcriptions could not get very close to the hearts of the people and, as published, constituted a rather small body of the available material, they were also responsible for misleading opponents of the African retentions theory into believing that virtually all black spirituals were simply crude derivations from white hymns. There is little question that, although black slaves (or free persons) in some cases borrowed generously from Protestant hymns or other Anglo-American materials (as did black preachers), and that some of the elements characteristic of black musical tonality and rhythm can also be found in other ethnic folksongs, the spirituals were an African American creation in which syncretism played a strong role but in which the foremost voice was that of the heterogeneous African peoples carried into slavery and there fused into one diverse but recognizable "nation." Even Newman White, who argued vigorously in favor of the theory that the spirituals were derived almost exclusively from white Protestant models, nonetheless allowed that they had been "thoroughly naturalized as vehicles of the Negro imagination," and he bluntly pointed out that "the white man would be both stupid and prejudiced if he failed to see that the Negro has long since made [the spirituals] his own." White's theories of origins are demonstrably problematic, yet whatever the degree of syncretism, borrowed Anglo-American materials appearing in the spirituals tended to be thoroughly "reassembled"—to use the term put forward by John Work, a scholar at Fisk University whose studies Du Bois would later praise—almost always given a more powerful tonality and a more intricate rhythm in which the scalar and rhythmic roots in African music are often strong. Most important, the message of the spirituals—deliverance from bondage, the return to a lost homeland, reward for extreme persecution and suffering—added an ideological dimension to the music that was seldom present in any white models.[28]

On the face of it, *The Souls of Black Folk* belongs only in limited ways to the debate over African retentions, Du Bois's contribution appearing to be occasionally insightful but relatively minor. Indeed, he writes at times with a quizzical detachment. Of the "characteristics of Negro religious life," for example, he says: "Numerous are the attractive lines of inquiry that here group themselves. What did slavery mean to the African savage? What was his attitude toward the World and Life? What seemed to him good and evil,—God and Devil? Whither went his longings and his strivings, and wherefore were his heart-burnings and disappointments? Answers to such questions can come only from a study of Negro religion as a development, through its gradual changes from the heathenism of the Gold Coast to the institutional Negro church of Chicago." Du Bois goes on to offer an extremely truncated analysis of the transformation of the "heathen rites" of African "Voodooism" into the Negro Christian church; and although it is far from insignificant that he posits a followable line of development from West Africa to urban America, he adds little to existing ethnographic arguments. Even his more forthright claims about the sources of black spirituals are sometimes marked by borrowed generalizations: "The Music of Negro religion is that plaintive rhythmic melody, with its touching minor cadences, which, despite caricature and defilement, still remains the most original and beautiful expression of human life and longing yet born on American soil. Sprung from the African forests, where its counterpart can still be heard, it was adapted, changed, and intensified by the tragic soul-life of the slave, until, under the stress of law and whip, it became the one true expression of a people's sorrow, despair, and hope." Du Bois's location of the source of the spirituals in the "African forests" coincided with his argument that the slave preacher derived his leadership from the central role of the African priest (a view he would repeat and extend in his 1903 study *The Negro Church*), and together these claims made up a substantial early argument in favor of African retentions. Still, Du Bois's characterization of the spirituals' melodic line echoes a number of earlier commentators, and from the point of view of content this is a far less rigorous analysis than that found, for instance, in Jeanette Robinson Murphy's 1899 article in *Popular Science Monthly*, one of the first to make a strong case for African sources of the spirituals and one of the first to detail ably some of the technical features of African American vocalization. Employing recognizably archetypal terms of civilization and savagism (just one index of her own rather reactionary views on southern race issues), Murphy argued that "the stock is African, the ideas are African, the patting and dancing are African. The veneer of civilization and religious fervor and Bible truth is entirely superficial. The African is under it all, and those who study him and his weird music at short range have no difficulty in recalling the savage conditions that gave it birth."[29] Although the degree of their belief in African retentions might vary, a growing number of folklorists and commentators in the 1890s had begun to reach similar conclusions. In that context Du Bois's elegantly concise description of the American transmutation—or "tragic intensification," as he puts it—of original African song into black American sorrow song was a description in small of *The Souls of Black Folk* itself, an act of cultural transfiguration that melded African and white American traditions into a distinctly African American cultural form, as had the spirituals themselves.

Du Bois admitted that he did not write from a technical standpoint; he knew only that "these songs are the articulate message of the slave to the world," that although the songs "came out of the South unknown to me, one by one . . . yet at once I knew them as of me and mine."[30] He wrote, that is to say, not as a musicologist (not even as an ethnographer in any particular sense) but rather as a cultural historian and racial advocate. Even though he made significant local additions to the analytic literature on spirituals (his remarks on the relative absence of the themes of fatherhood, of successful love, courtship, or wedding, and of home were striking), Du Bois's most telling contribution was conceptual. His commitment to a cultural ideal of double consciousness kept him from outright racial chauvinism, and he argued, for instance, that the pathos of "Poor Rosy" (a black folk song that he probably took either from the 1862 studies of James Miller McKim or from William Allen's collection) was comparable to that of a familiar German folk song. From the perspective of scholarship, his chapters on black religion and the sorrow songs extended a tradition of commentary initiated among black writers by Frederick Douglass in his remarks on slave music. At the same time, Du Bois did so with an eye to the fact that the explication of black music had been largely taken over in the post–Civil War years by sympathetic white commentators such as Allen, Higginson, McKim, Barton, and Murphy. Without question, he relied on the work done by these writers; but *The Souls of Black Folk,* which William Stanley Braithwaite would later call "a book of tortured dreams woven into the fabric of the sociologist's document," constructed for the spirituals and the eviscerating experience of slavery on which they were based a rich impressionistic history from "within the Veil" of blackness that no white critic could entirely inhabit. In stark contrast to the untenable claim by Newman White that New Negro pride in the spirituals was taught *to* blacks by the many whites who published collections in the early twentieth century—revealingly, White does not mention Du Bois—*The Souls of Black Folk* was the most vital essay in African American historical and artistic reconstruction.[31] Du Bois's own critical act was thus one of reappropriation, a critically syncretic gesture that mimicked the history of the spirituals as Du Bois simultaneously put black music at the center of black history; preserved it from loss in an age devoted to extreme racism on the one hand and blithe dismissals of the Negro past on the other; and retrieved it from the cultural stewardship of white ethnographers and cultural critics, insisting that the memory of African dispossession and life under slavery belonged first of all to those still living out its legacy.

In designating the African American preacher the "most unique personality developed by the Negro on American soil," at once "a leader, a politician, an orator, a 'boss,' an intriguer, [and] an idealist," Du Bois was therefore very close to painting his ideal self-portrait in *The Souls of Black Folk*. Foremost among the duties of the black minister, he said in an essay of 1905, was to raise "life to a plane above pay and mere pleasure" in order to generate "the sort of spiritual rebirth which the black millions of America are consciously or unconsciously looking for." More telling in his assessment of such spiritual leadership, perhaps, was James Weldon Johnson, who wrote of the preacher in *God's Trombones* (1927) that "it was through him that the people of diverse languages and customs who were brought here from diverse parts of Africa and thrown into slavery were given their first sense of unity and solidarity," a point that might be debated but that corresponds to Du Bois's own view and is not a bad characterization of Du Bois's intentions in *The Souls of Black Folk*. Du Bois's provisional identification with the preacher was even more pronounced in one aspect of the role that he drew directly from the "Priest or Medicine-man" (conjurer) of Africa, namely, his capacity as "the interpreter of the Unknown, the comforter of the sorrowing, the supernatural avenger of wrong, and the one who rudely but picturesquely expressed the longing, the disappointment, and resentment of a stolen and oppressed people." Du Bois could take on the conjurer's roles of judge and physician only in figurative terms, yet he was preeminently a "bard," perhaps the most revealing name that he used to describe the black preacher and one that accorded with the function of the itinerant minister, often also a fine singer, who traveled among plantations in the role of a bard.[32] Indeed, it is perhaps the bardic function that most distinguishes *The Souls of Black Folk* from the narrower genres of autobiography, political history, or social essay. All of those elements are present, to be sure; but the addition of the sorrow songs and Du Bois's self-conscious identification with the preacher as a kind of cultural priest, fused here to the bardic function of epic and Romantic poetry which Du Bois borrowed equally from a Western cultural tradition, are the key elements that make the book the first properly theoretical document of African American culture.

Within a few years Johnson would celebrate the anonymous collective composers of the slave spirituals in his famous poem "O Black and Unknown Bards" (which first appeared in *Century Magazine* in 1908). Likewise, in his portrait of "Singing Johnson," a traveling black singer from Johnson's childhood, he found the means to fix metonymically the unknown bards—preachers, collective worshippers, laboring men and women in slave cabins and cotton or cane fields—who together created the primary reservoir of African American vocal culture. Singing Johnson was remembered by his namesake as a man of great vocal and improvisatory skill, but also a man "with a delicate sense of when to come to the preacher's support after the climax in the sermon had been reached by breaking in with a line or two of a song that expressed a certain sentiment, often just a single line." The singer appeared barely fictionalized in *The Autobiography of an Ex-Coloured Man* (begun in 1905 but not published until 1912) and again in *The Book of American Negro Spirituals,* and he provided the reservoir of experience on which Johnson drew directly for his own contribution to the literary stylization of black folk culture, *God's Trombones,* where he outlined his conception of the proper mode of "intoning" the sung sermonic verse. The black bards epitomized by Singing Johnson were "makers of songs and leaders of singing. They had to possess certain qualifications: a gift of melody, a talent for poetry, a strong voice, and a good memory."[33] The communal singer's role was antiphonal; his music answered or extended the preacher's text—a text that, in the predominant African American form, was already highly vocalized, largely improvised, and filled with the sonoral features that characterize much black (and some white) folk preaching—and thus existed in the liminal modality between word and music that defined the essence of spirituals as they shaded into shouts and sermons. Like the freely improvised spiritual, the black sermonic performance moves between song and chant. In its recourse to polyrhythmic structure and the inflections of blue tonality, the folk preacher's style moves in and out of the domain of the spiritual— to such an extent, as Winthrop Sargeant remarked in his classic study of the origins of jazz and blues, that "just where the song begins and speech leaves off . . . is a difficult point to establish." Metrical patterns and dramatic tension created out of the possibilities of sound itself shape the semantic content of the black sermonic style, and the audience participates through its own cries and shouts in the narrative creation of a lived scriptural story that has sources in the African chants of tribal law, historical narrative, and folk story.[34]

Needless to say, there is no literal equivalent for such a folk performance in *The Souls of Black Folk*. Whatever his experiments in genre and composition, Du Bois for the most part hewed to a formal, academic style of writing. Even so, his role as bard continually pressed him toward such theorizing, most notably in the concluding chapter of the volume, where the problem of "anonymity" laid bare in each of the musical epigraphs— the problem, in effect, of basing a cultural theory on a set of ceaselessly shifting texts composed, singly or communally, by "unknown bards" and preserved in widely disparate and insufficient transcriptions—is most fully set forth and the relationship between music and language revealed to be rife with hidden messages. Like James Weldon Johnson (or, for that matter, like Singing Johnson), Du Bois had before him no less a task than the creation of a black national culture—or rather, not so much its creation as the proof of its existence. The bardic function of his task went beyond the elucidation of American slave culture or its origins as a conglomeration of many distinct languages and traditions during the middle passage. It entailed developing Frederick Douglass's central insight: "I have sometimes thought, that the mere hearing of those songs would do more to impress truly spiritual-minded men and women with the soul-crushing and death-dealing character of slavery, than the reading of whole volumes of its mere physical cruelties." As James Miller McKim remarked in one of the first interpretations of the spirituals: "They tell the whole story of these people's life and character. There is no need after hearing them, to inquire into the history of the slave's treatment."[35] But more than that, the task demanded the location of an African ground, even one that remained mythic in scope; and it entailed, therefore, tying the prophetic dimension of the spirituals to an African past. The establishment of an African American cultural poetics had to demonstrate the continued presence in America of an African culture where speech and song more closely approached each other on the continuum of cultural sound, where the vocalized "talk" of drums and rhythmic instruments was paramount, and where *nommo,* the power of the word in its oral dimension, governed human interaction to a far greater degree than in the Western tradition. Du Bois sought not to erase the Western, European American tradition but to balance it through a black ethnography capable of establishing the lyrical code lying within African American culture.[36]

It is this dimension of "double-consciousness"—one allied to his more open-ended remarks about the conflict between "American" and "Negro"—that Du Bois most brilliantly exploited in composing *The Souls of Black Folk.* A brief look at the changes Du Bois made in his description of double consciousness—the most famous idea advanced by Du Bois, perhaps the most famous advanced by any African American—will clarify this point. As Robert Stepto has shown, all of the revisions Du Bois made in his already published essays when he prepared them for inclusion in *The Souls of Black Folk* showed a pronounced philosophical and poetic deepening of his analytic vision. Among them was one revision concerning his theory of double consciousness that can be said to have shaped his thought for the remainder of his long life. The passage reads: "One ever feels his twoness,—an American, a Negro; two souls, two thoughts, two unreconciled strivings; two warring ideals in one dark body." In its most basic sense the passage is a definition of the social, psychological, and spiritual effects of America's harsh segregation, which yields the African American "no true self-consciousness, but only lets him see himself through the revelation of the other world." More, however, is at stake. The passage goes on to proclaim Du Bois's desire to derive from this double self one that transcends such strife, a "better and truer self" according to which he would neither "Africanize America, for America has too much to teach the world and Africa," nor "bleach his Negro soul in a flood of Americanism, for he knows that Negro blood has a message for the world." The last phrase is a revision of "for he believes—foolishly, perhaps, but fervently—that Negro blood has yet a message for the world." Du Bois thus turns his theory much more decidedly in the direction of the racial essentialism he had announced a few years earlier in "The Conservation of Races." Wanting to avoid the imputation of biological racialism, and yet uncomfortable with the environmentalist reduction of race to "culture," Du Bois had placed his emphasis on the quasi-mystical notion of "strivings," which now recurs with new weight in the title of the chapter, "Of Our Spiritual Strivings," in which the theory of double consciousness appears. The message of "Negro blood" is further underlined by a more significant addition to the ensuing passage. Elaborating on his view that the racist denial of opportunity to blacks in America has allowed the "powers of body and mind" to be "wasted and dispersed," Du Bois now adds the crucial verb "forgotten" and immediately inserts a telling idea: "The shadow of a mighty Negro past flits through the tale of Ethiopia the Shadowy and of Egypt the Sphinx. Throughout history, the powers of single black men flash here and there like falling stars, and die sometimes before the world has rightly gauged their brightness." This focus on what has been forgotten, on a great African–African American past and great heroes (evoked in the beautiful metaphor of the falling stars as souls, itself possibly derived from African belief, which would reappear in the spirituals, for instance in "Stars in the Elements") would become ever more important to Du Bois.* Yet even at this point he recognizes its

---

* Like "My Lord, What a Mourning," Du Bois's musical epigraph to chapter 2 of *The Souls of Black Folk*, "Stars in the Elements," which he later quotes in "The Sorrow Songs," is one of several spirituals with comparable symbolism in the narrative line:

> Oh, the stars in the elements are falling,
> And the moon drips away into blood,
> And the ransomed of the Lord are returning unto God.
> Blessed be the name of the Lord.

Other versions read "returning home to God." As Du Bois notes, "Stars in the Elements" is a spiritual of "the Last Judgment," but "with some traces of outside influence." To extend the decidedly less Christianized, more African resonance of Du Bois's passage in a cosmological direction, one might also suggest that he sought to revitalize an African notion that had been easily submerged in the analogous teachings of Christianity, namely, the belief in the true self as a "little man" or soul within that was waiting not so much to be reborn, as in the Christian cosmos, as to be discovered as always existing and already engaged, during life, in its journey

strong implications for him as an artist and for the founding of an African American cultural theory: "The innate love of harmony and beauty that set the ruder souls of his people a-dancing and a-singing raised but confusion and doubt in the soul of the black artist; for the beauty revealed to him was the soul-beauty of a race which his larger audience despised, and he could not articulate the message of another people."[37]

Such a war of "two unreconciled ideals," a stock subject in African American writing from Phillis Wheatley and Frederick Douglass on through the Harlem Renaissance (most notably in James Weldon Johnson's 1928 essay "The Dilemma of the Negro Author") and beyond, seems hardly surprising now, so completely has Du Bois's observation entered our thinking. Although the theory of double consciousness, as I will note in chapter 6, had already been elaborated by William James and others as a psychological theory of personality, with which Du Bois was likely familiar, few had seen so clearly as he its special application to race, most of all the degree to which the core of African American identity not only had been shaped but likely would remain shaped for years to come by a series of paradoxical doublings at once painful and empowering. Few had seen so clearly, as Thomas Holt writes, that "alienation—raised to a conscious level, cultivated, and directed—has revolutionary potential." Even so, it is the less obvious aspect of double consciousness that is worth more attention. As Du Bois's revisions of his famous passage indicate, the doubling at issue is not simply that of "Negro" and "American"—that is, black American versus a universalized, colorless American—but rather African versus American. The second doubling is contained within the first (doubles it, as it were) and bears directly upon the artist, for example, who would display the beauty of black song and dance to an audience who despises it—a white audience in the first place, but also that portion of the black middle-class audience that sought to deny its heritage, to "bleach [its] Negro soul in a flood of Americanism." The question of double consciousness seen within this set of terms is open to a variety of constructions, including Arnold Rampersad's suggestion that it be understood as a contest in African American consciousness between "memory" and "amnesia" about the slave past and Africa, and Sterling Stuckey's argument that Du Bois had to call forth a theory of Africanity from behind

---

back to the world of spirit. See W. E. B. Du Bois, *The Souls of Black Folk* (New York: Viking Penguin, 1989), p. 213; Mechal Sobel, *Trabelin' On: The Slave Journey to an Afro-Baptist Faith* (1979; rpt. Princeton: Princeton University Press, 1988), pp. 14, 71, 109–16.

the veil of his own initial skepticism that it could be traced through the chronology of the diaspora. Those things that are "hidden" and "buried," which Du Bois in his "Forethought" to the volume sets out to recover, would therefore have to include the amorphous elements of black consciousness derived concretely or figuratively from an African heritage that would eventually mature into a Pan-African philosophy.[38]

Over the course of Du Bois's literary work, the recurrent notion of "soul-beauty" becomes more and more charged with political, separatist significance, but even in the revisions of *The Souls of Black Folk* the African dimension is clearly marked, as his first major foray into African history and culture, *The Negro* (1915), would prove. "Negro" is thus not equivalent to "black American" but is already a term of the diaspora for Du Bois, pointing to a "nation," or, as the earlier text has it, a "folk," whose double consciousness is grounded in the soil of slavery but may ultimately be traced to an African home. He was already driving toward the recognition that would come in 1923 when the Christmas singing he heard in Monrovia, a transfiguration of mission revival hymns in an "unknown tongue— liquid and sonorous . . . tricked out and expounded with cadence and rhythm," seemed to Du Bois the "same rhythm I heard first in Tennessee forty years ago: the air is raised and carried by men's strong voices, while floating above in obbligato, come the high mellow voices of women—it is the ancient African art of part singing, so curiously and insistently different."[39] The germ of *The Negro* and its fundamental cultural premise lay in *The Souls of Black Folk.* Du Bois had the voice but not yet the historical knowledge to tell his Pan-African story; the two would finally join forces in *Darkwater.*

These revisions to what would come to be the most dramatic and often-cited passage of *The Souls of Black Folk,* which point to a crucial intensification in Du Bois's consciousness of African culture as a source of black soul, also bear closely on the theory of the sorrow songs adumbrated in the book's last chapter. Important though the discovery and preservation of identifiable retentions might be, the incorporation of African elements into black American literary art—in a process that might both pay tribute to and augment the example of black music—was equally important. Whereas Chesnutt did so in his folktales and Johnson, Hurston, Brown and others in their poetry and fiction, Du Bois initially connected himself to Africa through the role of the bard, or *griot,* as a communal singer and historian. The spirituals themselves constitute a profound panoramic chronicle of early black America—one of grand epic scope, as commentators such as Hiram Moderwell and Alain Locke argued, for which the best historical analogy is the spiritual account of the Jews' deliverance from bondage and the best analogue the scripture and psalms devoted to it.[40] In his fusion of them with his own text, Du Bois accentuated his role as the epic singer of the New Negro nation—and of a nation, the United States itself, that was Negro in critical ways. Along with Chesnutt, Twain, Harris, Johnson, and coming writers of the New Negro Renaissance and the Southern Renaissance alike, he redirected American culture into a channel that was decidedly southern, decidedly black.

At the same time, the interaction between music and prose argument in *The Souls of Black Folk* carried forward into an American setting a role whose origins lay in African communal life. In West African traditions that had already been detailed by eighteenth- and nineteenth-century travelers, the *griot* performed on a number of ritual occasions—during preparations for hunting or war, for example, at religious services or rites of birth, marriage, and death, or in praise of individuals, where such songs were on occasion infused with satire or the spirit of subversive signifying. The archetypal ancestors of Singing Johnson, the African *griots* were communal genealogists and historians who sang of their people's historical events and their kings and rulers in a repertoire of song that was constantly subject to innovation. Singly or in groups, sometimes employing the accompaniment of drums and other instruments, such bards preserved the national memory—if one may use "national" in the loose sense of peoples unified by culture, custom, and "race" that Du Bois seemed to prefer. As Maurice Delafosse wrote of African oral culture in the early twentieth century: "It is curious to note that peoples reputed to be ignorant and barbarous have found a means to take the place of libraries by supporting amongst themselves successive generations of living books, each one of which adds to the heritage it has received from the precedent. These so-called savages have at their call, historical compendiums and codes just as we have, only it is in the cerebral convolutions of their traditionalist griots, and not on paper, that their annals and theirs laws are imprinted."[41] The figure of the "living book" contains within it a classic erasure of the line between oral and written; of more concentrated significance, the figure contains an erasure of the line between language (speech) and music that defines much African expressivity. The praise songs of *griots* in traditional as well as contemporary African practice dwell within the assumption that sound is tangible, that it has epistemological "force" that is carried in the aural dimension. The performance of the bard elides the distinction be-

tween word and music, sermon and song, and their reciprocal relationship—what Ben Sidran refers to as the "galvanization of meaning and
pitch into a single vocalization"—constitutes the foundation of African
American artistic culture.[42]

Du Bois's style itself could not achieve such a unification of force; but
his deliberate merger of poetic and sociological discourses, of the musicological and the historiographic, was itself a radical acquisition of power
that was simultaneously political and performative. Simply the formal
relationship between music and language in *The Souls of Black Folk* alerts
us to the fact that Du Bois, as Houston Baker has remarked, was composing a "singing book" (in constrast to Washington's "speaking manual,"
Up from Slavery). His representations of musical language were a means
to conflate African and American selves and "invoke ancestral spirits and
ancient formulas that move toward an act of cultural triumph," building,
like the Fisk Jubilee Singers, a new edifice of culture out of "melodies of
ancient spiritual song." Du Bois's "singing book" was an extension of the
"living book" of the African bard. Indeed, a closer examination of the
spirituals that Du Bois chose, of his evocation of important African survivals, whether deliberate or accidental, and of the remarkable vocalizations
that his revision and extension of published material entailed substantiates
the fact that the musico-cultural and historical functions of Du Bois's text
were inseparably fused into a single vocalized unit. If one follows out the
logic of Sidran's claim that blue tonality and vocalization were "a means
of bringing out the individualism in an otherwise destroyed personality"—
destroyed, that is, by slavery's ravaging of an African consciousness—
Du Bois opened to view the theoretical underpinnings of a cultural
poetics capable of both recovering and magnifying the language of African
America.[43]

Bright Sparkles: Music and Text

Sidran's claim is metaphoric. Countertheories both early and late notwithstanding, African consciousness—or, indeed, African "personality," to borrow a term popularized by Edward Blyden that would become important
for Du Bois—was not destroyed by slavery. Without question, it was
radically transmuted into a distinctive national consciousness that was and
was not American, was and was not Christian. The spirituals were both a
record of that transmutation and an assertion of the survival of African
consciousness in idea and in form. Before we go further with a theory of

The Souls of Black Folk as a text of African-American cultural ideology, the role played by individual spirituals in Du Bois's antiphonal composition must be considered. My claim is not that every spiritual that functions as an epigraph headnote (or "head," if one may appropriately adopt a term from jazz) can be explicated in intricate detail as part of the text. Although most of them can to a striking degree, Du Bois's choices will withstand only a certain amount of interpretive pressure. Some choices seem perfectly strategic, others perhaps fortuitous or applicable across the range of the text rather than illuminating a single chapter.

One of the most common means by which the spirituals were transmitted in early black worship, where hymnals were scarce, where improvisation was typical, and where, in any case, only a handful of the songs were borrowed directly from white tradition, was by "lining out" or "deaconing." The preacher or another strong vocalist such as Singing Johnson would sing or chant a few lines, and his congregation would follow in response. The black church style joined lining out as it was practiced in white churches to the African traditional form of call and response, which characterized much musical practice, whether instrumental (drum) performance or chanted work music.[44] Recalling sanctified worship in backwoods Tennessee when he wrote the chapters "within the Veil," Du Bois may well have had in mind something like lining out when he set the brief measures of music at the outset of his chapters. In this respect the chapters may be seen to improvise upon and extend the ideas laid out in the spiritual epigraphs.

The spirituals that Du Bois chose to head his chapters and to mention by name in his last chapter were, with a few exceptions, widely known by the turn of the century. Because of their familiarity, some songs could have been taken from any of numerous sources, whether song sheets, essays with commentary, or published collections, and they continued to appear in popular editions well into the twentieth century. (For example, many of the spirituals Du Bois used can also be found in James Weldon Johnson's two *Books of American Negro Spirituals,* in Rosamond Johnson's arrangements.) But it would appear that Du Bois's bars of music, with a few minor variations, were most likely taken from the versions published either in *Hampton and Its Students* or *The Story of the Jubilee Singers,* both of which had appeared in several editions by the turn of the century. One can cite fairly clear evidence for Du Bois's use of these volumes as well as other common sources, such as his repeating of the Hampton volume's anecdote about a brigadier general's address to the black inhabitants of the confiscated Sea Islands in the Civil War. (When the gathered mass, led by an elderly woman, began singing "Nobody Knows the Trouble I've Seen," the general himself was said to be moved to tears.) Likewise, "Wrestling Jacob" and "Lay This Body Down," which provide the two epigraphs for his concluding chapter on the sorrow songs (the first in its music, the second in its lyrics), appear side by side in Thomas Wentworth Higginson's famous essay on the spirituals.[45] For the sake of reference, a list of the spirituals employed as musical epigraphs follows, with an indication of which version Du Bois followed (some appear identically in both volumes, others in variations that are usually slight but in several cases pronounced):

"Of Our Spiritual Strivings"—"Nobody Knows the Trouble I've Seen" (*Hampton*)

"Of the Dawn of Freedom"—"My Lord, What a Mourning" (*Hampton*)

"Of Mr. Booker T. Washington and Others"—"A Great Camp-Meeting in the Promised Land" (*Hampton;* same in *Jubilee*)

"Of the Meaning of Progress"—"My Way's Cloudy" (*Jubilee*)

"Of the Wings of Atalanta"—"The Rocks and the Mountains" (*Jubilee*)

"Of the Training of Black Men"—"March On" (*Jubilee*)

"Of the Black Belt"—"Bright Sparkles in the Churchyard" (*Hampton;* same in *Jubilee*)

"Of the Quest of the Golden Fleece"—"Children, You'll Be Called On" (*Jubilee*)

"Of the Sons of Master and Man"—"I'm A Rolling" (*Jubilee*)

"Of the Faith of the Fathers"—"Steal Away" (*Jubilee*)

"Of the Passing of the First-Born"—"I Hope My Mother Will Be There" (*Hampton*)

"Of Alexander Crummell"—"Swing Low, Sweet Chariot" (*Jubilee*)

"Of the Coming of John"—"I'll Hear the Trumpet Sound" (or "You May Bury Me in the East") (*Jubilee*)

"The Sorrow Songs"—"Wrestling Jacob" (*Jubilee*)

The structure of *The Souls of Black Folk* offers a means to organize any commentary about the spirituals, for the book is presented in broad thematic sections: chapters 1–3, an overview of freedom and the issue of black leadership; chapters 4–6, an extension of the question of leadership into that of education; chapters 7–9, the economy and geography of the postwar South; chapters 10–14, life "within the Veil" and the meaning of black culture. My intention is not to offer an exhaustive commentary on the relationship between the spirituals and Du Bois's text. Rather, I want to focus on three things: on the spirituals' most overt implications; on the means by which they serve to anchor the text in an implied African past and the Negro world of the diaspora; and ultimately on the theory of the text that can be drawn from the implied antiphonal sound of *The Souls of Black Folk*. My analysis relies, paradoxically, on evidence that is not in Du Bois's text at all. That is, the dialectical relation between the epigraphic bars of music and the chapters they head appears first of all in the hidden language of the spirituals, in their lyrics, which Du Bois does not reproduce. I will return to the theoretical complications posed by this fact but begin with the assumption that what is *heard* by knowledgeable readers of *The Souls of Black Folk,* and what sets in motion the dialectical commentary, is first of all the familiar, if invisible, words of the spirituals. Because Du Bois seems to have used the versions in the Hampton and Jubilee volumes, I have followed them for citations of lyrics. Like the music, the lyrics as published are found in variant forms or with additional verses, since the improvisation of verses and borrowing from other songs was common vocal practice.* I have also italicized that portion of the song's text that corresponds exactly to the bars of music reproduced by Du Bois. My contention, however, is that the epigraphic bars are often metonymic, that they encapsulate the extended message of the spiritual and therefore must be understood to invoke, if not literally to cite, the song as a whole, and my analysis of the relationship between the spirituals' texts and Du Bois's own chapter-length arguments draws on the message of each spiritual as a whole.

"Nobody Knows the Trouble I've Seen," which opens the first chapter,

---

* Except in the case of titles, I have also reproduced black dialect—although one might note that to some degree it is simply a *southern* dialect—when it appears in the lyrics of the published versions. Dialect, as the example of Chesnutt proves, presents theoretical problems allied to those evident in the tonal elision of words and music in some black song, a problem I will mention in a few examples that follow and return to in the section on the theory of the sorrow songs. The published texts of the spirituals were varied and often random in their reproduction of black dialect. Conceivably, Du Bois deleted the lyrics so as not to place the dialect of slave culture before his readers. Such an interpretation, however, seems entirely at odds with his attempt otherwise to lay claim to the intellectual dignity and historical importance of ancestral African and slave life (and in any event versions in standard English might have been used). The deletion of the words seems instead, as I will argue, to belong to Du Bois's more complex theorizing about the very sources of African American cultural traditions.

is one of the best-known and most variously adapted spirituals. Samuel Coleridge-Taylor incorporated it into his *Song of Hiawatha* (1899); Bert Williams may well have secularized its combined statement of alienation and faith in his classic minstrel performance of "Nobody"; and there have been countless arrangements of its two distinctive original (or rather its preserved) versions, at least one of which has been provisionally (perhaps apocryphally) traced to a slave giving vent to his torment after his wife and children were sold away from him.[46] Although it may be construed as a hymn of salvation at the Judgment Day, its chorus refers more immediately to salvation received on earth through the acceptance of Jesus, the only one able to mediate the suffering of slaves in a world where "nobody" outside their world cared for their troubles:

> [Chor.] *Oh, nobody knows de trouble I've seen,*
> Nobody knows but Jesus,
> Nobody knows de trouble I've seen,
> Glory Hallelujah.

The first verse speaks of trials that nearly break the body and the spirit ("Sometimes I'm up, sometimes I'm down / Sometimes I'm almost to the groun'"), but the subsequent verses are notable for their bearing on Du Bois's ideas in "Of Our Spiritual Strivings":

> One day when I was walkin' along, Oh yes, Lord—
> De element opened, an' de Love came down, Oh yes, Lord.
>
> I never shall forget that day, Oh yes, Lord—
> When Jesus washed my sins away, Oh yes, Lord. . . .[47]

Du Bois's opening chapter, with its famous theory of double consciousness and its resolute assertion that black emancipation must be intellectual as well as physical, that freedom must be found in the "kingdom of culture," transfigures the message of the spiritual into secular terms. The delivery into the Promised Land that forms the allegorical substructure of the whole of *The Souls of Black Folk* is here internalized. Strivings become educational and "national," while the veil that yields black men and women "no true self-consciousness," but allows them to see themselves only "through the revelation of the other world," is given its initial definition as a figure of oppression rather than sin. Invoking the trope of the journey along the mountain path to Canaan, a constant in the spirituals, Du Bois restructures the message of "Nobody Knows the Trouble I've Seen" into his own terms:

> To the tired climbers, the horizon was ever dark, the mists were often cold, the Canaan was always dim and far away. If, however, the vistas disclosed as yet no goal, no resting-place, little but flattery and criticism, the journey at least gave leisure for reflection and self-examination; it changed the child of Emancipation to the youth of dawning self-consciousness, self-realization, self-respect. In those sombre forests of his striving his own soul rose before him, and he saw himself,— darkly as through a veil; and yet he saw in himself some faint revelation of his power, his mission. He began to have a dim feeling that, to attain his place in the world, he must be himself, and not another.[48]

This rich passage includes Du Bois's own spiritual autobiography, a statement of his own mission. But its broader application to the race, in contrast to the vision of Washington, is more significant. Du Bois counters the common racist assertion that the Negro is still a "child" in need of white supervision, and he offers the remarkable opinion that the descent into the nadir—the burden of ignorance, poverty, and illegitimacy that the passage goes on to depict as the legacy of race slavery and "two centuries of legal defilement of Negro women"—has been a time for reflection and spiritual growth toward consciousness of a racial soul.

Du Bois would reject out of hand various arguments made by Washington, Henry Turner, and other black leaders (leave aside white apologists) that slavery had been a providential means to bring African Americans into the light of Christian civilization. In his secular adaptation of the spirituals' message of faith, however, he rewrote Providence in liberal cultural terms. Whereas "Nobody Knows the Trouble I've Seen" portrays salvation coming from heaven ("De element opened, an' de Love came down"), Du Bois finds it to issue from within: the veil opens, and the soul of a person free to constitute himself anew appears as a "revelation." His opening chapter argues that individual dreams of physical freedom, political power, and manual and mental training must be melded into one "unifying ideal of Race." Such an ideal will not contest those of white America but will redeem them, for just as there is "no true American music but the wild sweet melodies of the Negro slave," so there are "no truer exponents of the pure human spirit of the Declaration of Independence than the American Negroes." This merger of American and African principles, one of Du Bois's strongest extensions of the intellectual heritage of Frederick Douglass, is no simple invocation of the trope of revolutionary independence but instead a protest that for African Americans the United States is "the land of their fathers' fathers" as well, a combined geographical and spiritual domain Du Bois develops in more detail, as the volume unfolds, into the historic "ground" of African American soul.[49]

The succeeding chapters of the opening section of *The Souls of Black Folk,* "Of the Dawn of Freedom" and "Of Mr. Booker T. Washington and Others," examine two aspects of postwar striving for the "unifying ideal of Race." The critique of Washington is by now a thoroughly familiar one. Attacking his stands on suffrage, education, and civil rights, Du Bois portrays Washington as the false inheritor of the revolutionary mantle. The chapter begins with two forceful literary epigraphs on liberation from Byron's "Childe Harold's Pilgrimage." The first ridicules the impotence of Washington's programs and vision: "From birth till death enslaved; in word, in deed, unmanned!" The second ("Hereditary bondsmen! Know ye not / Who would be free themselves must strike the blow?") was a well-known rhetorical trope also employed in, among other places in nineteenth-century African American letters, Martin Delany's nationalist revolutionary novel *Blake* and Douglass's recent revision of his autobiography, the *Life and Times of Frederick Douglass,* and it serves as the opening frame of a chapter that ends with a passage from the Declaration of Independence. Du Bois's opinion that "deep regret, sorrow, and apprehension" should greet Washington's ascendancy among "educated and thoughtful" blacks also finds particularized support in the spiritual that functions as a terse counterpoint to the Byron epigraphs. "A Great Camp-Meeting in the Promised Land" is a song of hope with a moving melodic line and lyrics that promote comradeship. At the same time, however, its message, like Washington's, is easily construed as accommodationist:

> Oh walk togedder, childron,
> Dont yer get weary,
> Walk togedder, childron,
> Dont yer get weary,
> Dere's a great camp-meetin' in de Promised Land.
>
> [Chor.] *Gwine to mourn an' nebber tire,*
> *Mourn an' nebber tire,*

Mourn an' nebber tire,
Dere's a great camp-meetin' in de Promised Land.[50]

Following verses ("Gwine to hab it in heben," "Dere's a better day comin'") enforce the aura of patient acceptance that could be interpreted as a sign of strength (as would be the case when it was adopted as a song of civil rights protest in the 1960s). Although Du Bois did not shrink from paying tribute to Washington's hard work and the dignity of his effort, such an interpretation must also be counted in contrast to the chapter's unambiguous message and the counterpointed epigraphs. That Du Bois chose for reproduction the portion of the spiritual that accents most harshly a quality of conjoined perseverance and mourning also suggests that the tribute paid to Washington was tinged with irony.* In slave culture and beyond, the camp meeting might be the occasion for the transmission not just of religious beliefs but also of political ideals, plans for escape and revolt, or at the least the creation of a spiritual consciousness of racial solidarity through transmitted survivals of African life such as the ring-shout. Such possibilities are minimized in this spiritual, and the Promised Land is here literalized as a future beyond this life—the future, according to Du Bois, for which Washington and his policies were condemned simply to wait, still "from birth till death enslaved."

Something of the same ambiguity, but put to a different purpose, appears in "My Lord, What a Mourning," which heads the chapter on the Freedman's Bureau, "Of the Dawn of Freedom." The double meaning latent in the title is bound up in the fact that it is variously spelled as

---

* The Hampton volume, the apparent source of Du Bois's epigraph, includes an explanatory note from the song's collector, J. B. Towe, that is of interest both for its account of the possible origins of the spiritual and for the light it may have cast upon Washington: "This hymn was made by a company of slaves, who were not allowed to sing or pray anywhere the old master could hear them; and when he died their old mistress looked on them with pity, and granted them the privilege of singing and praying in the cabins at night. Then they sang this hymn, and shouted for joy, and gave God the honor and praise." Although this passage records a measured achievement of freedom to worship, it is dominated by the sort of dependence on white masters for the least reward that Du Bois might well have found replicated in Washington's contemporary subservience to white authority. See M. F. Armstrong and Helen W. Ludlow, *Hampton and Its Students, with Fifty Cabin and Plantation Songs,* arranged by Thomas P. Fenner (New York: Putnam's, 1874), p. 222. (In addition, the fact that the lyrics in the Hampton version, as my extract indicates, were recorded in a pronounced black dialect may perhaps be construed as the sign of a further satiric thrust at Washington's accommodationism on the issue of higher education.)

"mourning" and "morning." Even though the music of his epigraph is closest to the version in *Hampton and Its Students,* where the spelling is "morning," Du Bois refers to the song in his later commentary as "the song of the End and the Beginning" and adopts the spelling "mourning." In the spiritual the allegorical construction is clear in either case:

> [Chor.] *My Lord, what a mourning,*
> *My Lord, what a mourning,*
> *My Lord, what a mourning,*
> *When the* stars begin to fall.
>
> You'll hear the trumpet sound
> To wake the nations underground,
> Looking to my God's right hand
> When the stars begin to fall. . . . [51]

The hymn of resurrection can contain both "morning" and "mourning"— the first signifying the dawn of the new millennial day, when the dead are raised (or the enslaved are emancipated); the second signifying a transfigurative power in the act of mourning, the conversion of the song of grief into a song of joyful deliverance. As it is applied to "Of the Dawn of Freedom," however, the ambiguity is particularly purposeful. Reconstruction has turned out to be a false dawn; instead, the song of joy has been transformed into a song of grieving once again, as the new slavery of racism and economic oppression, the marks of the emancipated black world Du Bois would go on to describe in successive chapters of *The Souls of Black Folk,* have undermined the hoped-for resurrection. The double message of the spiritual as Du Bois employs it might be suggested, too, in the fact that it was sung by the Hampton Singers in 1874 at the grave of Charles Sumner, famed abolitionist and black political rights advocate, who, as Du Bois's chapter mentions, had been a prime architect of the Freedman's Bureau. On that occasion one of the singers spoke eloquently of Sumner—"this Union Star of America"—and remembered his valiant fight for the civil rights bill that was to pass Congress the next year. What Du Bois would remember, however, was that Sumner's bill was overturned in a landmark Supreme Court case in 1883 that cleared the way for segregation and might arguably be interpreted as the single gravest attack on African American economic and political rights in the wake of Reconstruction. Like this possible veiled allusion to Sumner, James Russell Lowell's

1844 poem "The Present Crisis," the source of the textual epigraph, reinforces the contemporary replication of antebellum struggle. In the combat between "old systems and the Word," between neo-slavery and freedom, it seems that truth is once more "on the scaffold / Wrong forever on the throne." The legacy of work not done is the "heavy heritage of this generation," the "nations" to be wakened now perhaps less the reposing dead than the living, whether the recalcitrant whites or the unknowing blacks.[52]

The metaphor of the falling stars that announces the coming of Judgment Day also has two echoes—one in Du Bois's image of the northern campfires that "shone like vast unsteady stars" to fugitive slaves during the war, and, more important, perhaps, in the pellucid metaphor, cited earlier, of the lives of great black men who "flash here and there like falling stars, and die sometimes before the world has rightly gauged their brightness." The possible African meaning of the figure (in Kongo lore falling stars have been interpreted as spirits flashing across the sky) is no doubt subordinate to its Christian significance as a revelation of the Kingdom, but the semantic overlay of the traditions is considerable and supports Du Bois's intention to refashion the notion of "soul" into an idea capable of evoking race unity as well as resurrection from the bondage of race slavery.[53] The failure of Reconstruction and the rise of a more virulent, and often legally sanctioned, racism must now be answered by an awakening of the many "nations" of Africa. The spirits of the ancestors, in the homeland as well as in the diaspora, need to be fused with those present generations who continue to lead an oppressed "underground" existence. Those who have gone before thus sustain and raise up those who live still on the soil of American slavery, the vertical (spiritual) figure of death and resurrection coinciding with the horizontal (secular) figure of memory and progress. The line between "morning" and "mourning" is therefore just as thin as the more famous "line" that frames the chapter in repeated sentences is stark: "The problem of the twentieth century is the problem of the color-line." It is not a problem, the following chapter on Washington tells us, that his tentative, submissive programs are prepared to solve.

Chapters 4–6 function as a unit and constitute an extension of the argument against Washington. All are concerned with the value of education and show the development of Du Bois's theories, from his experience as a rural schoolteacher during his years at Fisk to his advocacy of higher education to produce a "talented tenth" of black leaders who would orchestrate the uplift of the race.

The implication of the spiritual in the first of the triad, "My Way's Cloudy," is fairly straightforward. Du Bois calls it a "song of groping," and, as in most other instances, the lines are taken from the opening chorus:

> [Chor.] Oh! breth-er-en, my way, my way's cloud-y, my way,
> Go send them angels down,
> *Oh! breth-er-en, my way, my way's cloud-y, my way,*
> Go send them angels down.[54]

The song is one of jubilee which typically conflates freedom and salvation (the fourth verse is the clearest: "This is the year of Jubilee, / Send them angels down, / The Lord has come to set us free, / O send them angels down"). But the ambiguity of the freedom attained, a distinct element of the spirituals in antebellum years that took on a more pronounced significance during Reconstruction and after, is contained in the central metaphor of the "cloudy way," which stands in contrast to the clear sky, the starlit heaven, or the falling stars of salvation. The song's bearing on Du Bois's chapter is not hard to find. "Of the Meaning of Progress" is structured as a comparison. On the one hand is Du Bois's immersion in the poor but dignified backwoods life of Tennessee, where he finds a "dull and humdrum" world of black "common consciousness," born of shared hardship and governed by a "dark fatalism" that takes refuge in the will of God. On the other hand is Du Bois's prospect on the scene when he returns for a visit ten years later. Josie, the young girl who first told him of the place where he might get a teaching job, is dead, dragged down by a life of poor health and little opportunity; some have achieved a meager success, but others have moved away or fled criminal prosecution. The log schoolhouse that Du Bois taught in has been replaced by a board structure that represents "Progress," which, as Du Bois remarks, is "necessarily ugly."[55]

Progress, however, is precisely what is at issue in this chapter, which represents Du Bois's first true descent into life within the Veil. It is conceivable that he intends to portray himself here, with a certain self-conscious irony, as one of the angels come down to lead southern blacks to educated freedom, part of that line of northern educators who came south beginning in Reconstruction that he had already written about in chapter 2. Be that as it may, "My Way's Cloudy" registers the grim reality of the rural South, where a people are waiting for an overdue deliverance, and the younger generation, lacking the forlorn faith of their fathers and mothers, have begun to split away or have descended into despair and anger. It is not the rural black South's way alone that is cloudy, however, but also Du Bois's. At the conclusion of the chapter, sadly musing upon the impoverishments of the new slavery, he rides to Nashville in the Jim Crow car.

"Of the Wings of Atalanta" and "Of the Training of Black Men" constitute a single essay on the necessity of higher education and the risk of sacrificing humane learning for material gain. Both chapters extend Du Bois's critique of Washington, constrasting Atlanta University to Tuskegee, and striving to reanimate the ideals that were once embodied in "the Preacher and the Teacher" (and not, evidently, in Washington)—"the strife for another and a juster world, the vague dream of righteousness, the mystery of knowing," ideals of "simple beauty and weird inspiration" that today are in danger of sinking to "a question of cash and a lust for gold." Black Atlanta, like "Atalanta" in the myth of the golden apple which Du Bois invokes, is in danger of succumbing to the deceitful lure, the "lawless lust," of Hippomenes, and allowing "the fair flower of Freedom . . . sprung from our fathers' blood" to degenerate into a new slavery of material satisfaction. As subsequent chapters demonstrate, material gain for the underclass is a cruel hoax; sharecropping is the new bondage. But for the middle class, at least, knowledge and culture ought to be the key to African American progress. Invoking lines from *Faust* that he would many years later apply to African nations struggling with the alluring prospects unleashed by independence from colonial rule, Du Bois intones, "Entbehren sollst du, sollst entbehren" (You must forebear, forebear you must). Only higher education—the development of Fisk, Atlanta, and Howard as well as Tulane, Vanderbilt, and Georgia—can bring the black world within sight of the Promised Land and allow it to "dwell above the Veil."[56]

It is not insignificant that Du Bois, although he does not name it for his readers, identifies the spiritual that opens "Of the Wings of Atalanta" as a common song of the escaped slave. Once again the double meaning of the spiritual, self-evident now but still open to dispute by those of Du Bois's day who lamented "the slow, steady disappearance of a certain type of Negro,—the faithful, courteous slave of other days, with his incorruptible honesty and dignified humility,"[57] is important:

[Chor.] Oh, the rocks and the mountains shall all flee a-way,
And you shall have a new hid-ing place that day.[58]

The hiding place is heavenly, of course, but it is also of this earth. In the new context created by Du Bois—in Atlanta, the City of a Hundred Hills, and within Atlanta University's Stone Hall—it is the hiding, nurturing place of education and culture, the true delivery from bondage.* The verses ask a series of petitioners ("seeker," "mourner," "sinner," "sister," and so on) to "give up your heart to God, / And you shall have a new hiding place that day," thus accentuating the chapter's focus on the spiritual in place of the material. As a gloss on Du Bois's own argument, moreover, the very language of "The Rocks and the Mountains" shows his strong dissent from Washington's materialist solutions. In spiritual cadences comparable to his own mythological cadences, the song demonstrates the continuity between the inherent wisdom of the slave generations—the wisdom passed down by black and unknown bards—and the necessity of higher education for their children.

In the case of "March On," which opens "Of the Training of Black Men," Du Bois quotes music that corresponds to the first verse:

Way o-ver in the E-gypt land,
You shall gain the vic-to-ry,
Way o-ver in the E-gypt land,
You shall gain the day.

But the chorus, a martial chant ("March on, and you shall gain the vic-to-ry, / March on, and you shall gain the day") gives perhaps a stronger sense of the spirit of demand that animates Du Bois's chapter.[59] The Egypt of the South, which figures in the next section of *The Souls of Black Folk* as a land of ruin and desolation, is here the site of challenge, confrontation,

---

* George Pullen Jackson asserted that "The Rocks and the Mountains" was derived from a standard Protestant hymn (the chorus quoted in my text, he argued, was an imitation of "Ah, poor sinner, you run from the rock. . . . / To hide yourself on the mountain top / To hide yourself from God"). As John Lovell has pointed out, if this attenuated evidence holds any lesson, it is that the "composer" of the black song was a far greater poet than the author of the white version. See George Pullen Jackson, *White Spirituals in the Southern Uplands* (Chapel Hill: University of North Carolina Press, 1933), p. 281, and John Lovell, Jr., *Black Song: The Forge and the Flame: The Story of How the Afro-American Spiritual Was Hammered Out* (New York: Macmillan, 1972), p. 97.

and struggle. For the slave, "March On" was a song of hope, even of controlled militancy; for the free men and women of the post-Reconstruction South, it was adamantly a song of demand and of resistance to the lures of simple materialism and, by the same token, the Washingtonian philosophy of manual training. The adjoining epigraph from Omar Khayyam ("were't not a Shame for him [the Soul] / In this clay carcase crippled to abide?") enforces the correspondence between mind, soul, and culture on the one hand and body, wealth, and labor on the other, the reiterated dualism that Du Bois examines throughout his book—not to sustain but rather fruitfully to collapse it—and which comes to a critical point in the next three chapters on labor in the black South.

Chapter 7, "Of the Black Belt," is to a great degree the spiritual center of *The Souls of Black Folk*, for although the book builds to a concluding rhetorical climax in "The Sorrow Songs," Du Bois's immersion in life behind the Veil finds its rich spiritual ground in the chapters on black peonage in the now fallen, desolate garden of the plantation South. Du Bois's journey recapitulates two earlier models: it reenacts the narrative of travel through the cotton South popularized by figures such as Fanny Kemble and Frederick Law Olmstead; and it reverses the seminal journey north of nineteenth-century black literature in order to recover the ground of black consciousness that underlies the extended community and culture of the African American world. His journey thus incorporates as well the frequent image of the sacred journey or "travel" that appears repeatedly in the spirituals. That journey syncretically joins two vectors. It is a sign of ultimate salvation through faith, but it also borrows from an inherited African conception of life as a journey in which one is guided by the inner spirit of the doubled self, a figure particularly germane to Du Bois's conception of double consciousness as enabling spiritual force.[60] Descending into the South in the Jim Crow car at the outset of "Of the Black Belt," he repeats the journey of the previous chapters and once again, with a sharper ideological edge to his descriptive powers, enters a ritualized geography, a "historic ground" that is not just the "geographical focus" of the black population but "the centre of the Negro problem,—the centre of those nine million men [and women] who are America's dark heritage from slavery and the slave-trade." The essence of the three chapters that follow lies in the simple formula of Black Belt neo-slavery: "Only by the slavery of debt can the Negro be kept at work."[61]

The reversal of the journey north has several dimensions. To begin with, it reminds us that freedom is—or should be—without a specific geography, and that the coded language of escape and rebellion that identifed the North as the Promised Land in slave talk and music can now be generalized. The obvious point of Du Bois's chapters, however, as of the transformed significance of the spirituals in the postwar years, is that freedom is far from realized, North or South; the journey is far from over, and the spirituals still speak with as much authority and as much painful necessity as they did during slavery. For Du Bois the northerner and the would-be challenger to the leadership of Washington on his home ground, moreover, the journey into the South represents a necessary invocation of the southern ancestry that forms part of that "shadow of a mighty Negro past." Because "Of the Black Belt" offers the most striking articulation of Du Bois's ritual descent, as it does the most provocative antiphonal relationship with its spiritual, "Bright Sparkles in the Churchyard," let us first look briefly at the following two chapters before returning to "Of the Black Belt."

Like "March On," "Children, You'll be Called On" evokes a military spirit appropriate to the economic warfare that makes up the reality of post-Reconstruction black life as it is detailed in "Of the Quest for the Golden Fleece":

> *Children, you'll be called on*
> *To march in the field of bat-tle,*
> *When this war-fare'll be end-ed,*
> *Hal-le-lu.*
>
> [Chor.] When this war-fare'll be end-ed,
> I'm a sol-dier of the ju-bi-lee,
> This warfare'll be ended,
> I'm a sol-dier of the cross.

William Vaughn Moody's poem "The Brute," from which the poetic epigraph is drawn, gives a fitting account of the brutality of the sharecropping system against which the spirit of "March On" must be judged. Along with the warning in chapter 6 of the danger of turning the black South into a disfranchised and angry proletariat, there are here the seeds of Du Bois's eventual transfiguration of the trope of the Black Christ, the suffering redeemer, into economic man. At the moment when Du Bois published his volume, peonage was receiving dramatic news coverage because of Justice Department investigations that had uncovered the most grotesque kinds of abuse in a number of southern locations. As in other cases governed by reunion politics, however, the prosecution by southern courts of what amounted to a new version of chattel slavery was less than adequate. The battle that Du Bois alludes to is thus economic, political, and judicial, and "Children, You'll Be Called," far from being a relic of plantation days, functions as a propagandistic call to action.[62]

Although it is less martial in cadence, the head to the following chapter, "I'm A Rolling," is no less appropriate. The dominant message in "Of the Sons of Master and Man" is the need for the kind of guidance of the black population that had been tested and then tragically renounced in Reconstruction. Land and vote fraud, increasing black crime, intellectual degradation, extreme physical, economic, and social segregation—all of these elements of turn-of-the-century life within the Black Belt call forth the message of the sorrow song:

> [Chor.] I'm a rolling, I'm a rolling,
> I'm a rolling through an unfriendly world. . . .
>
> O brothers, wont you help me to pray?
> O brothers, wont you help me,
> *Wont you help me in the service of the Lord?*[63]

"I'm A Rolling" refers to service on behalf of God, yet even in this case the spiritual's note of passivity is undergirded by a plea for brotherhood that may perhaps be cross-racial but in any case ranges the Lord's cause against that of American injustice, during slavery and after. For Du Bois, too, such service always represents an acute spiritual intervention into secular work. As he writes in this chapter, it must be the "strife of all honorable men of the twentieth century to see that in the future competition of races the survival of the fittest shall mean the triumph of the good, the beautiful, and the true."[64] Like "Children, You'll Be Called On," then, "I'm A Rolling" carries an organizing anthem of racial solidarity from the antebellum world into the era of neo-slavery in order to address the racism and economic servitude that have not disappeared but, if anything, have been augmented in the era of segregation.

"Of the Quest of the Golden Fleece" and "Of the Sons of Master and Man" elaborate the political and social dimensions of the systematic peonage that is outlined in "Of the Black Belt" with far starker, far more haunting force. Alluding to the dispossession of lands once held by Cherokee and Creek Indians, and subsequently turned into a vast plantation by slave labor, Du Bois portrays a landscape of human victimage and ruin. It may be that the king is dead, but

> the parks and palaces of the Cotton Kingdom have not wholly dis-appeared. We plunge even now into great groves of oak and towering pine, with an undergrowth of myrtle and shrubbery. This was the "home-house" of the Thompsons,—slave-barons who drove their coach and four in the merry past. All is silence now, and ashes, and tangled weeds. . . . The Big House stands in half ruin, its great front door staring blankly at the street, and the back part grotesquely restored for its black tenant. A shabby, well-built Negro he is, unlucky and irresolute. He digs hard to pay rent to the white girl who owns the remnant of the place. She married a policeman and lives in Savannah.

The South of the nadir is fully portrayed in the minimalist lines of Du Bois's tableau. What was once the "Egypt of the Confederacy" is now studded with dilapidated big houses, riddled by military defeat, debt, and corruption; the natural world itself, once the "richest slave kingdom the modern world ever knew," is a terrain of tangled, moss-covered trees, brackish, burning swamps, and immense shadows, "until all is one mass of tangled semi-tropical foliage, marvellous in its weird savage splendor." The trope of exotic jungle entanglement surrounding the Thompson big house and the forsaken Waters-Loring plantation leads Du Bois to assert, after he has already turned back toward Albany, that "the spell still lay upon us." It is no coincidence, perhaps, that his more famous use of the same phrase would come more than two decades later when he first visited Africa and ventured an apparently similar romantic description of the landscape: "The spell of Africa is upon me. The ancient witchery of her medicine is burning my drowsy, dreamy blood. This is not a country, it is a world . . . a great black bosom where the Spirit longs to die."[65] It might seem implausible to claim that Du Bois's passage in "Of the Black Belt" proleptically anticipates his later characterization of Africa in the pages of *Crisis*. In fact, however, the political resonance of the passage was to be clarified within several years in the opening of Du Bois's biography of John Brown, at the outset of a chapter entitled "Africa and America": "The mystic spell of Africa is and ever was over all America. It has guided her hardest work, inspired her finest literature, and sung her sweetest songs. Her greatest destiny—unsensed and despised though it be,—is to give back to the first of continents the gifts which Africa of old gave to America's fathers' fathers."⁶⁶

The exact nature of these gifts, presumably moral ones, is rather obscure in Du Bois's formulation; but the prophetic context of the passage— Brown, as we shall see in the case of Du Bois's Pan-Africanism, is portrayed as a kind of revolutionary black Christ—demonstrates that the spell of Africa and the spell of the South are already yoked in Du Bois's mind into a single transgeographical mode of consciousness, one eventually articulated as a diasporic nationalism. In *The Souls of Black Folk*, then, the savage exoticism that suggests an African landscape transplanted to the Egypt of the South is no mistaken literary strategy. As the spirituals figured it, Egypt signified the condition of bondage that was to be escaped. But more than that, as "March On" suggests, it was the ground of struggle and the site of potential victory. As in the amended passage on double consciousness of which I took note earlier, Egypt, along with Ethiopia, was also nearly a generic designation for Africa as a homeland or a moment of prophetic historicity. (Du Bois chose Matthew 2:15 as his scriptural epigraph to the opening chapter of the Brown biography: "That it might be fulfilled which was spoken of the Lord by the prophet saying, Out of Egypt have I called My son.") Allegorically mapping them onto the ruined world of the southern Confederacy, Du Bois gave Egypt and the "spell of Africa" a complex figuration that combined past and future, the passage into bondage and the deliverance from it.

Two different registers of meaning therefore coincide in Du Bois's trope. On the one hand, the Egypt of the Confederacy is historical: it is the ruined landscape of slavery from which blacks have been incompletely delivered, as well as the land of indebted peonage to which they are still enslaved. On the other hand, Egypt is spiritual: it is the site of salvation, as in "O It's Goin' to Be a Mighty Day" ("As I went down into Egypt, I camped down on the groun', / At the soundin' of the trumpet, the Holy Ghost came down"), or a return to ancestral roots. One of Du Bois's purposes in the chapter is to merge the slave trade and the establishment of "the corner-stone of the Cotton Kingdom" with present history, dragging from the national memory and from the hidden life of the contemporary South a "strange land of shadows, at which even slaves paled in the past, and whence come now only faint and half-intelligible murmurs to the world beyond." (By 1934, in *Black Reconstruction*, Du Bois would make the black labor of the Cotton Kingdom "the foundation stone not only of the Southern social structure, but of Northern manufacture and commerce, of the English factory system, of European commerce, of buying and selling on a world-wide scale." In fact, however, such a view is implicit in some of his essays dating from the early years of the century.) The South is a land inhabited by white ghosts of the Confederacy but also the living ghosts of African American slavery, those "black, sturdy, uncouth country folk" who are trapped in a timeless world beyond the bounds of civilization and seemingly beyond the bounds of hope for the promised improvements of progress, let alone the ideals of cultural refinement to which Du Bois's program of education aspires.[67]

At this point we come to the most peculiar and unsettling antiphonal construct of spiritual and text in *The Souls of Black Folk*. Other better-known spirituals are more easily explicated in their relationship to the subsequent chapters of the book, but none is as adventurous as "Bright Sparkles in the Churchyard," which heads the chapter "Of the Black Belt." Here, Du Bois's imagination arced across a dark sky, creating one of the most profound tropological arguments for African survivals in early modern African American culture. Du Bois rightly remarks in his commentary that "Bright Sparkles" is a mazelike medley belonging to a group of songs that seem "a step removed from the more primitive types," by which he means those closer to African music. The spiritual as published is a melange of duos, trios, quartets, and choral segments, with the section reproduced by Du Bois appearing in a number of variations upon the same melody and words:

> May the Lord, He will be glad of me,
> May the Lord, He will be glad of me,
> May the Lord, He will be glad of me,
> In the heaven He'll rejoice. . . .
>
> Bright spar-kles in the churchyard
> Give light un-to the tomb,
> Bright summer, Spring's o-ver,
> Sweet flow-ers in their bloom.
> Bright spar-kles in the churchyard
> Give light un-to the tomb. . . .
>
> Mother, rock me in the cra-dle all day,
> Mother, rock me in the cra-dle all day . . .
> All the day, all the day,
> Oh, rock me in the cra-dle all the day. . . .

Oh, mother, don't you love your darling child,
Oh, rock me in the cra-dle all the day.
Mother, rock me in the cra-dle,
Mother, rock me in the cra-dle,
Mother, rock me in the cra-dle all the day. . . .[68]

Characteristically, the harmonic structure of "Bright Sparkles" as published is simple; only in performance would one begin to find the characteristic blue tonalities of the black spiritual. The text, however, is more complex. It speaks of resurrection—through entrance into the Lord's heaven; through being raised from the dead (as flowers in summer bloom); and through the comfort of a mother that could be variously understood as the church (as in Mother Zion, an African Methodist Episcopal Zion church), as the slave mother from whom children may be torn away, or as a figure for an African homeland (the more famous "Sometimes I Feel Like a Motherless Child," for example, combines the last two senses).

Resurrection from the new slavery of peonage is a dominant trope in the chapters of *The Souls of Black Folk* devoted to the post-Reconstruction South. The mood of combined desolation and faith in "Bright Sparkles" corresponds to that in "Of the Black Belt," where Du Bois's focus is on the continued bondage to poverty suffered by the new generations. "Bright Sparkles," like many spirituals, was also a black work song, popular in this case, according to Fenner, among tobacco factory hands in Danville, Virginia. Its relatively overt call-and-response structure underlines the fact that the spirituals were in many instances adaptations of Christian texts to the heavily African format of the work song.[69] "Bright Sparkles," then, vocalizes the long tradition of black labor on which the South was built and the backbreaking and illegal peonage through which the rural black population was still held in virtual slavery.

What, however, of the title itself and its central image, "Bright sparkles in the churchyard / Give light unto the tomb"? It is here, strikingly, that Du Bois appears to show his most stringent comprehension of the African elements of southern Black Belt culture. The Egypt of the South that he describes is a graveyard: the vast ruined landscape littered with desolate big houses is the graveyard of the Confederate dream. But more important, it is the graveyard of countless black men and women fallen under servitude. Again calling forth a remembered landscape at odds with that of Booker T. Washington and borrowing the firsthand account of a contemporary sharecropper who had also been a slave, Du Bois is at pains to show that the massive facade of southern wealth, "all this show and tinsel [was] built upon a groan. 'This land was a little Hell,' said a ragged, brown, and grave-faced man to me. We were seated near a roadside blacksmith-shop, and behind was the bare ruin of some master's home. 'I've seen niggers drop dead in the furrow, but they were kicked aside, and the plough never stopped. And down in the guard-house, there's where the blood ran.'"[70] The Black Belt, in other words, is "historic ground" less for its rotted grandeur and reminders of the Confederate past than for its being the blood-soaked "ground," the spiritual foundation of African American life, a soil of painful labor and cultural resilience. Ground and grave merge in this haunted landscape, a landscape of suffering in this life but also of resurrection into a better life beyond.

The most compelling message of "Bright Sparkles," however, has a distinctly African resonance. For although the title might be construed (as in the verse just quoted) as referring to the flowers of resurrection, it also seems likely that the African American significance lies in reference to the custom, a survival of African practice, of decorating graves with broken glass, china, shells, pottery, bric-a-brac, and sundry household items. Such decorations function in different ways: to signify the breaking of the chain of life, to keep the dead from returning, or to prevent evil spirits from harming the grave. Grave decorations are one element among other aspects of African American funeral customs, particularly in the nineteenth-century South, that indicate some survival of strong African beliefs in the continued presence and communion with generations of ancestors, and they may be said to constitute, as John Vlach argues, "a visual environment which in the Afro-American tradition is seen as the world of the spirits, often the spirits of the ancestors. Graveyard goods," he continues, "are a statement of homage; their function is to keep a tempestuous soul at rest." More particularly, bits of broken glass, mirrors, or other reflective or sparkling objects have a spiritual function. They represent what Robert Farris Thompson calls the "flash of the spirit," the glint or spark of the soul that is released in death on its journey to the home world of the ancestors.[71] Like African American grave decorations, the spiritual's "bright sparkles" thus "give light unto the tomb" by creating a pathway between the material and spiritual worlds, keeping spiritually present, spiritually alive, the killing ground of slavery in the graveyard of the South. The message of the song, like the message of "Of the Black Belt," allows Du Bois himself to have communion with those generations who have passed but who remain vitally alive on the new African ground of America.

This dimension of the spirituals is even stronger in the last chapters of *The Souls of Black Folk* devoted to life within the Veil, which represent a compelling conjunction of autobiography, social analysis, and creativity, all grounded in an African American ethos and consciousness of race that was unlike anything written in America to date—anything, that is, but the spirituals from which Du Bois drew his inspiration. Both his commitment to recovering ancestral African roots and his willingness to see slavery's legacy without illusion come to the fore here; and the choice of spirituals demonstrates exceptional care on Du Bois's part to underscore his contention that the black church "is the social centre of Negro life in the United States, and the most characteristic expression of African character." The last group of chapters also codifies his compelling adoption of the roles of bard, preacher, and cultural prophet. Du Bois's black church includes, but is hardly limited to, organized religious bodies (as he notes, enrollment and attendance are inadequate signs of belonging to a black church). Instead, his main object of concern is "the inner ethical life of the people who compose" the church and its "historical foundations." His aim, in other words, is to offer proof that the church *is* African American and that the social history of black Americans began in the clan life of Africa, was transfigured aboard the slave ships of the middle passage, and revolutionized on the plantations of the Americas.[72] Both "Of the Faith of the Fathers," the fullest evocation of black spirit in the volume, and "Of Alexander Crummell," a praise song for a towering spiritual ancestor who has gone before—one of those stars that flashed across the sky without sufficient notice from the world—show Du Bois's bardic functions and his incipient Pan-African aesthetic at their highest pitch to date. It is no mistake that the two sorrow songs that head these chapters, "Steal Away" and "Swing Low, Sweet Chariot," are among the most powerful that have survived and that both embody African and slave culture in the fullest measure.

"Steal Away," as countless former slaves recalled the phrase, was a thinly coded song used to announce secret religious service or secular celebration; it could also act as a profession of rebellion, a call used by Nat Turner and Harriet Tubman, among others, to organize slave resistance and plans of escape. In Turner's case, Miles Fisher has argued, many of the words of the spiritual were nearly literalized in his prophetic call to lead a slave conspiracy—so much so that Fisher, rather implausibly, identifies Turner as the author of the song. Whether or not it can be argued that secret meetings epitomized by Turner's rebellion constituted the transplantation of African cults to American soil, the lyrics of "Steal Away" do represent an angry God who is without question a projection of the slave's ardent will to freedom:

> [Chor.] *Steal away, steal away, steal away to Jesus!*
> Steal away, steal away home,
> I hain't got long to stay here.
>
> My Lord calls me,
> He calls me by the thunder;
> The trumpet sounds it in my soul;
> I hain't got long to stay here.[73]

Subsequent verses ("Tombstones are bursting, / Poor sinners are trembling") accentuate the dramatic resurrection that is the core of the song; but the extraordinary martial spirit gives credence to the view that Turner's prophecy (whether or not he was the song's composer) represented a seizure of power in the tradition of radical nationalism.

Du Bois's focus in "Of the Faith of Our Fathers" is not on the radical tradition personified in Nat Turner but rather on the instability of the black church as a political instrument. Nevertheless, the resources of black religion as Du Bois depicts them are decidedly the product of belief that is at once supernatural and ideological, even though Du Bois's account of African spiritualism is framed in nationalist terms that partially undermine the legitimacy of ancestral belief patterns and social practice, and consequently censure African American folk belief as uneducated "superstition." The transplanted African, Du Bois writes, lived "in world animate with gods and devils, elves and witches," and therefore interpreted slavery as the striving of "all the hateful powers of the Under-world" against him. When the "spirit of revenge and revolt filled his heart," he called witchcraft, orgies, and mystic conjuration to his aid, putting the witch and conjurer at the center of his worship and deepening the superstitions that governed "the unlettered Negro" even in the early twentieth century. The power of slave masters, however, finally triumphed, Du Bois argues, and by the mid-eighteenth century

> the black had sunk, with hushed murmurs, to his place at the bottom of a new economic system, and was unconsciously ripe for a new philosophy of life. Nothing suited his condition then better than the doctrines of passive submission embodied in the newly learned

Christianity. . . . The long system of repression and degradation of the Negro tended to emphasize the elements in his character which made him a valuable chattel: courtesy became humility, moral strength degenerated into submission, and the exquisite native appreciation of the beautiful became an infinite capacity for dumb suffering. The Negro, losing the joy of this world, eagerly seized upon the offered conceptions of the next; the avenging spirit of the Lord enjoining patience in this world, under sorrow and tribulation until the Great Day when He should lead His dark children home,—this became his comforting dream.

Although it rather grates against our own moral sensibilities, Du Bois's account of the course of black faith was not exceptional in his time, no more so than his following argument that one of the most vexing aspects of the Negro's double consciousness was the contemporary temptation of the great masses of the faithful, faced with increasing racism, to drift into the polar camps of cursing, anarchy, and revolt on the one hand, and meekness, hypocrisy, and cowardice on the other. Du Bois separates these "hardly reconcilable streams of thought and ethical striving" geographically, allying the side of resistance with the black North (something akin to his own side) and that of submission with the South (the camp of Washington). What is striking in his passage about the creation of Christian submissiveness over the course of African American history, however, is Du Bois's attempt to locate the *African* virtues (courtesy, moral strength, aesthetic sensibility) that were converted into *American* vices. In doing so he countered the racialist theories of black docility and nonviolence first popularized in antebellum years by abolitionists and proslavery advocates alike, and in Du Bois's own day often given cruder racist connotations; and he opened a space for the recovery of a lost national consciousness grounded in the faith of the fathers. Both the general argument of the last five chapters of *The Souls of Black Folk* and specific celebrations of leaders such as Crummell, institutions such as the Fisk Jubilee Singers, and the inheritance of the spirituals themselves allow Du Bois prophetically to engage "the deep religious feeling of the real Negro heart, the stirring, unguided might of powerful human souls who have lost the guiding star of the past and are seeking in the great night a new religious ideal."[74]

Du Bois acknowledges in his chapter that the deaths of Denmark Vesey and Nat Turner long ago proved the futility of mass physical rebellion. Nevertheless, by his invocation of their names and acts of radical resistance

Du Bois, like Frederick Douglass and other nineteenth-century black leaders, places the slave rebels in the pantheon of spiritual ancestors who provide guiding examples in the contemporary struggle for black economic and political rights. In this way Du Bois also adds a further refutation of the prevailing strategy of the Washingtonians, the hypocritical "defence of deception and flattery, of cajoling and lying." The spirit of Turner embodied in "Steal Away" is indeed a stronger counter than Du Bois's own chapter, which dwells on the double consciousness that has nearly immobilized the African American nation and threatened to reduce its ancient will of resistance to bitter fatalism and hypocrisy in which "the price of culture is a Lie."[75] In contrast, both the spiritual and the legacy of Turner in the militant perspective represented by Du Bois demonstrate the possibility of awakening a black Christian tradition—the "nations underground," as "My Lord, What a Mourning" puts it—that is neither subservient nor vindictive.

It would seem that Du Bois's tribute to Alexander Crummell in the following chapter arises principally from his sense that Crummell, a man whose ministerial career stretched across half a century and whose long years in Africa gave him a particular claim on black attention, was barely known to Americans, that his name "comes to fifty million ears laden with no incense of memory or emulation." Even though he was not known to the general public, however, Crummell was certainly known to black churchmen and to anyone familiar with the American Negro academy. One of his own recent papers presented before the academy, "Civilization the Primal Need of the Race" (1898), was a significant presentation of the civilizationist argument for the spiritual and material advancement of black culture, with which Du Bois would largely have agreed. If Du Bois's tribute is sincere, though, his motives for choosing Crummell may have been complicated. It is likely that he picked Crummell as a symbolic father for *The Souls of Black Folk*—a father his epigraphic citation from Tennyson's poem "The Passing of Arthur" asks us to liken to "a king returning from his wars"—in order to deflect attention from the more imposing figure, Frederick Douglass, who had died in 1895, and to undercut yet again Washington's eminence. Du Bois, as I will suggest in chapter 6, was probably intellectually as indebted to Edward Blyden and Henry Turner, for all his differences from them, as to Crummell; but in honoring Crummell he chose a figure whose Pan-African credentials seemed to have a concrete American application. Despite the fact that Crummell's ardent Christianity and his Pan-African views set him apart from Washington, the self-made man, the two shared the view, as Du Bois decidedly did not, that civil rights activism was secondary to the acquisition of the tools of civilization. Crummell had argued, as recently as 1885, that black political agitation was "a useless expenditure of forces," that for a long time "the political ambitions of colored men are sure to end in emptiness."[76] This single regressive position aside, Crummell can be shown to be the source of a number of Du Bois's fundamental views, beginning with "The Conservation of Races" and running through *Darkwater* twenty years later. His major works would obviously have been known to Du Bois, primarily, perhaps, the collection of essays entitled *Africa and America,* which had appeared in 1891.

One address in particular, entitled "Right-Mindedness," presented to students at Lincoln University in the 1880s, focused on the problem of leadership in the black community, and it offers an instructive means to see how Du Bois positioned Crummell against Washington (and also against himself) as a model race leader. Speaking of the aesthetic sensibilities of blacks, Crummell averred that "the mind of our people seems to be a hot-bed of rich, precocious, gorgeous and withal genuine plants:— and, if I mistake not, I discover in it all, that permanent *tropical* element which characterizes all the peoples whose ancestral homes were in the southern latitudes." Such tendencies, suggested Crummell—accepting, as did Du Bois, a distinctive part of the racialist apparatus of nineteenth-century thought—were "natural outgrowths from the soil of our African nature," part of the abiding and persistent "race peculiarities" in which he believed. At the same time, Crummell warned that black Americans spent too much time on the aesthetic and too little on studies that would "furnish that hardy muscle and strong fibre which men need in the stern battle of life," the tenacity and endurance that are "the special need of a new people, running a race which they have never before entered upon; and undertaking civilizing achievements, from which their powers and capacities have been separate for long centuries." Up to this point there is little with which Du Bois would quarrel in Crummell's early statement of New Negro philosophy, and his own argument in "The Conservation of Races" on behalf of "the first fruits of this new [African American] nation, the harbinger of that black to-morrow which is yet destined to soften the whiteness of the Teutonic to-day," similarly adopts a philosophy of ameliorative racialism to forecast the contributions of American Negroes, "members of a vast historic race . . . but half awakening in the dark forests of its African fatherland," to the uplift of both the race and America. Du

Bois's elevation of the aesthetic would be more pronounced than that of Crummell, but his language in *The Souls of Black Folk* seems to borrow directly from his mentor (the "transplanted African," he argued in the passage devoted to the declension of black resistance in "Of the Faith of the Fathers," was "endowed with a rich tropical imagination and a keen, delicate appreciation of Nature"). Du Bois would have been attracted, moreover, to the fact that Crummell proposes something decidedly different from the manual arts programs of Washington. The muscle and moral fiber that Crummell calls for are mental as well as physical; rigorous study and spiritual betterment are the prime tools with which black Americans can answer racism in the fields of "domestic, civil, political, religious and educational" endeavor. Nonetheless, this early invocation of the concept of the "new people" by Crummell is followed by an argument that must have had a mixed message for Du Bois. Even more emphatically than Washington, Crummell swept away recent African American history, claiming that "everything in this work [before us] is new." "The past," he said, "is forever gone; and it has no teachings either for the present or the future. Nowhere in our *American* history can you light upon any instructive antecedents. What was supposed to [be] fit and suitable to our Race under a past regime, we know now was but chaff and sawdust!"⁷⁷

Here was the point at which Du Bois would swerve most sharply from Crummell's intellectual path. Without question, Du Bois was struck by this and other instances of Crummell's salute to African culture as a model for American efforts, a clear alternative to Washington's view, and that of many other black leaders, that African society was simply "heathen." But Crummell's dismissal of slave culture was too extreme. One need not argue, as did Henry Turner, that slavery had been a providential gift that brought black people into the modern world. Yet in arguing just the opposite—that slavery had been a thoroughly degrading experience that stripped away the vigor of an African heritage, leaving its victims morally corrupt—Crummell slighted the concrete cultural preservations and strengths of character developed in African American life, just those things that Du Bois was most determined to locate. As Wilson Moses has pointed out, Crummell's leap back to an African past as the source of racial pride was founded on his view that the "barbarian" African had a strength of character and moral purity that had been annihilated by slavery; this view, in turn, had a basis in the fact that Crummell had been born in the North, outside of slavery, the son of an African man who had escaped slavery and later become an abolitionist, and who instilled in his son a luxuriant pride in his undiluted African heritage. In this respect Crummell offered a model clearly differentiated from that of Washington, who underscored the travail of his birth in slavery in order to augment his regime of self-help and uplift. Even so, Du Bois had to modify Crummell's view of slavery as a formative institution in order to reach his own ideology. Like Crummell, he believed that races are "families," the "organisms and ordinances of God; and [that] race feeling, like the family feeling, is of divine origin." To extinguish race feeling by political oppression or by amalgamation, Crummell contended, was a virtual impossibility. Because race signifies a "compact, homogenous population of one blood, ancestry, and lineage" settled in a geographical home, as he had argued in 1888, only the "haziest imagination can anticipate the future dissolution of [the Negro] race and its final loss," after "generations and generations," through a long process of physical and social amalgamation. For Du Bois, however, the logic of Crummell's position entailed a belief in the continuity, not the extinction, of African "race life" through African American history.[78]

The full effect of Crummell upon Du Bois would be evident only in the development of his Pan-African thought over the next twenty years. His tribute to Crummell in *The Souls of Black Folk,* moreover, remains a partial curiosity because it has little to say about Crummell's thought as such, and even the sketch of his career is thin. Instead, the chapter functions as a paean to Crummell the symbol. One of Crummell's early addresses in Monrovia, devoted to the creation of a generation of leaders of a republican Liberia, had been entitled "The Responsibility of the First Fathers of a Country for Its Future Life and Character" (1863). For Du Bois, Crummell functioned symbolically as such a father, although one can deduce that his purpose was in fact one of psychological transference in which Crummell became the mechanism for Du Bois's own ascendancy to the position of founding father of modern African American thought, thus eliding the alternative challengers Douglass and Washington. Du Bois's portrait of Crummell is dominated by the latter's constant fight against the despair induced by racist roadblocks in his career as a minister. But the intellectual essence of the chapter is hard to find, so effusive and opaque is Du Bois's prose. The mood of the piece affords Crummell a mystic connection to the oppression of American slavery that suggests more of what Du Bois wanted to find in Crummell (or in himself) than what Crummell claimed to be his own inspiration. Of Crummell as a young boy, for example, Du Bois writes: "The black-faced lad that paused over his mud and marbles seventy years ago saw puzzling vistas as he looked down the world. The slave-ship still groaned across the Atlantic, faint cries burdened the Southern breeze, and the great black father whispered mad tales of cruelty into those young ears. From the low doorway the mother silently watched her boy at play, and at nightfall sought him eagerly lest the shadows bear him away to the land of slaves." Or, consider Du Bois's account of Crummell's Oneida school days:

> Yonder, behind the forests, he heard strange sounds; then glinting through the trees he saw, far, far away, the bronzed hosts of a nation calling,—calling faintly, calling loudly. He heard the fateful clank of their chains, he felt them cringe and grovel, and there rose within him a protest and a prophecy. And he girded himself to walk down the world.
>
> A voice and vision called him to be a priest,—a seer to lead the uncalled out of the house of bondage.

Du Bois's highly romanticized picture of Crummell's calling to the priesthood takes the latter's known abolitionist views, inculcated by his father's antislavery activities, and makes of them a spiritual parable that ties Crummell more unreservedly to the history of enslaved African Americans. As Ethiopia was stretching forth her hands to God—in the passage from Psalms 68:31 cited repeatedly by Pan-Africanists from the early nineteenth century forward—so Crummell "stretched forth his hands eagerly" to embrace his prophetic calling, only to be rebuffed again and again by the racism of the church and the world of which it was a part.[79]

Du Bois's idealization of Crummell's prophetic calling was a means of giving new scope to the imaginative, spiritual tendencies in his own thought which had been held in check by the methods of historical and sociological writing in which he had been trained. This "history of a human heart,—the tale of a black boy who many years ago began to struggle with life that he might know the world and himself," was Crummell's to a degree, but it was also his own. In this respect, the spiritual that heads the chapter, "Swing Low, Sweet Chariot," represented an especially cunning selection:

> [Chor.] *Swing low, sweet chariot,*
> *Coming for to carry me home,*
> *Swing low, sweet chariot,*
> Coming for to carry me home.

I looked over Jordan, and what did I see,
Coming for to carry me home?
A band of angels coming after me,
Coming for to carry me home.

Of the several spirituals incorporated into Dvořák's 1893 symphonic tribute to American folk art, *From the New World,* "Swing Low, Sweet Chariot" was among the most beautiful and was probably the most famous of those that had become known to a wide public by the time Du Bois was writing. It has been transcribed in many melodic variations (the version that appeared in the Hampton collection, for instance, has a very different melodic line from the Jubilee version used by Du Bois) and is remarkably open to tonal improvisation. As "the cradle-song of death which all men know," the song functions as a funereal tribute to Crummell, who reached the Promised Land in 1898 (the second verse, beginning "If you get there before I do . . . / Tell all my friends I'm coming too," accentuates this fact), and it is an appropriate measure of Du Bois's respect for his achievements. More important, however, the subtext of the chapter, Crummell's role as a father figure whose service in Africa represents both a cultural link and an alternative model of spiritual leadership, is underscored by the African dimensions of the song.[80]

Like "Steal Away" and other spirituals, "Swing Low, Sweet Chariot" was transparently available to being coded with the ideology of resistance to and escape from slavery—the slave carried home to freedom in the North, where others had gone before him. Home, heaven, and political freedom were synonymous. A more radical interpretation would insist that the home was the motherland of Africa, the true destination of at least some slaves (or colonizationists) and the spiritual world to which some assumed they would return after death.[81] All of these dimensions are present in Du Bois's tribute to Crummell. Crummell himself would not have accepted any but a Christian interpretation of the afterlife promised in the hymn, but his devotion to an African cultural past gave special point to the constellation of nationalist meanings that Du Bois introduced in "Swing Low, Sweet Chariot." What Du Bois may or may not have known, but what reinforces the semantic effect of the spiritual as an epigraph to the Crummell chapter, is that it is one of the few songs that has been traced with any precision, in message as well as melody, to an African origin. The simplest explanation available is that the song was a transformation of an African boat song adapted as a work song by black

American rivermen. But an account more steeped in mythical significance is also possible. In his 1926 collection of spirituals, William Arms Fisher recorded the testimony of an Anglican missionary who had heard the same song in Rhodesia, where it was sung by a group of natives near the Victoria Falls:

> When one of their chiefs, in the old days, was about to die, he was placed in a great canoe together with the trappings that marked his rank, and food for his journey. The canoe was set afloat in midstream headed toward the great Falls and the vast column of mist that rises from them. Meanwhile the tribe on the shore would sing its chants of farewell. The legend is that on one occasion the king was seen to rise in his canoe at the very brink of the Falls and enter a chariot that, descending from the mists, bore him aloft. This incident gave rise to the words "Swing Low, Sweet Chariot," and the song, brought to America by African slaves long ago, became anglicized and modified by their Christian faith.

In a separate essay appearing the following year in Charles S. Johnson's collection *Ebony and Topaz,* Dorothy Scarborough reported that she had information from a missionary in the Belgian Congo who had heard "Swing Low," with the same melody, and had been told by the Africans that it was a funeral dirge "as old as our tribe."[82] It is most unlikely, of course, that the more elaborate legend was known to Du Bois, and it is anecdotal evidence in any case. But the corroborating evidence that "Swing Low" derives from a funeral song bears it out as a remarkable instance of the survival of African cultural expression in transmuted American form.*

---

* Opponents of such a strict argument about African retentions might counter that, if the stories are not apocryphal, they were nevertheless based on the fact that Africans could themselves have learned the spiritual from American missionaries, black or white, and incorporated it into their historical memory and ancestral legends. Although I find this view less plausible than the other, what seems most important is that the claim of an African origin was being made at all. In either case, "Swing Low" was a *black* creation, not an obvious derivation from white Protestantism. Maud Cuney-Hare, for instance, relates the story that the song arose from the sale of a Mississippi slave woman: "Rather than be separated from her child, she was about to drown herself and [her] little one in the Cumberland River, when she was prevented by an old Negro woman, who exclaimed, 'Wait, let de Chariot of de Lord swing low and let me take de Lord's scroll and read it to you.' The heart-broken mother became consoled and was reconciled to the parting. The song became known with the passing of the story, which seems more legendary than real." See Maud Cuney-Hare, *Negro Musicians and Their Music* (Washington, D.C.: Associated Publishers, 1936), p. 69.

The possible source of "Swing Low, Sweet Chariot" in African song thus gives the Crummell chapter a powerful resonance; as one of those spirituals closest to African music, it provided a tonal screen through which Crummell's message could be articulated and appropriated to Du Bois's own cultural nationalism.

Chapters 11 and 13 of *The Souls of Black Folk* are Du Bois's most personal, the one a lyrical account of the death of his son, the other a short story that strangely unites the opposing cultural tendencies of his own psyche. The two chapters—not least because they are mediated by the Crummell chapter and its tribute to one who has passed into the world of spirits— are joined together as well by their shared concern with death and transfiguration. Possibly because of its intense personal nature, "Of the Passing of the First-Born" figures as a concentrated commentary on Du Bois's conception of race. His son is born "within the Veil," though its "shadow," as it falls across the baby, takes the peculiar inverted form not of the "blood of Africa [that is] moulded into his features" but of the ominous gold of his hair and blue of his eyes. In a small but potent way, Du Bois thus reverses the archetypes of racial identity. Moreover, as in the case of Crummell, he endows his son with a lineage that reflects his own aspirations, writing that he envisioned "the strength of my own arm stretched onward through the ages through the newer strength of his own; saw the dream of my black fathers stagger a step onward in the wild phantasm of the world; heard in his baby voice the voice of the Prophet that was to rise within the Veil." Du Bois would recapitulate the birth of such a prophet figure in both *Darkwater* and *Dark Princess;* here he imagines his son to live in a world of "souls alone, uncolored and unclothed"—an innocent world soon to be blasted by the fact that he is "a Negro and a Negro's son" and only to be transcended in death, where he now sleeps "above the Veil."[83]

The text of the epigraphic spiritual ("I hope my mother will be there, / In that beautiful world on high") needs no explanation as a gloss on the chapter.[84] Unlike most of the other spirituals Du Bois chooses, it has a less pronounced secondary level of allegory pointing to slave resistance or escape. The same cannot be said for "I'll Hear the Trumpet Sound" (also known as "You May Bury Me in the East"), which heads "Of the Coming of John." The plot of the story itself is a perfect incarnation of double consciousness encoded in the intertwined fates of the doubled black and white figures. Of more pressing interest, however, is the mechanism of transfiguration with which Du Bois concludes his powerful, moving story.

As John is pursued by the lynching party after having killed his white double, his childhood companion now raised above him by class and color, he enters a kind of dream vision that merges the allegorical meaning of his escape with the cultural sign of his denied aspirations. "I'm going— North," he tells his mother, signifying, by the pause in his remark, that the allegorical import has been reversed: now North means death, not death means North, as is often the case in the spirituals. As the galloping horses approach, he hums not "I'll Hear the Trumpet Sound" but the "Song of the Bride" from *Lohengrin*. Du Bois's fascination with Wagner, a product of his studies in Germany, would not reach its maturity until the 1920s, but even here it adumbrates the flexibility and complications of his notion of racial nationalism. (Wagner's racism, as we will see, made him a peculiar source for some of Du Bois's later sentiments of cultural nationalism. Leaving aside Nazi Germany's appropriation of Wagnerian nationalism, Wagner's music could be put to uses rather different from those evident in Du Bois's short story. When he adapted Thomas Dixon's Ku Klux Klan saga as *Birth of a Nation*, for example, D. W. Griffith would propel the famous galloping rescue by the Klan with Wagner's "Ride of the Valkyrie.") In the short story, the strains of music are a reminder of John's humiliation at a New York concert when his white double forces him out of the theater; more broadly, it is a reminder, as it was for Du Bois, that his intellect and his aspirations, no matter their power, would be judged not fit for European American high culture simply because of his color. The visionary moment of transcendence that precedes John's lynching—or his suicide, as the case may be—thus has the potential for deep irony, and yet Du Bois deliberately holds the two cultural moments in taut suspension. The spiritual projects an image of resurrection at the Judgment Day:

> *You may bury me in the East,*
> *You may bury me in the West,*
> *But I'll hear that trumpet sound*
> *In that morning.*

> [Chor.] In that morning, my Lord,
> How I long to go,
> For to hear that trumpet sound,
> In that morning.

Successive verses offer a further clue to Du Bois's meaning:

> Father Gabriel in that day,
> He'll take wings and fly away. . . .
>
> Good old Christians in that day,
> They'll take wings and fly away. . . . [85]

In addition to alluding to a central legend of African tradition that survived in the slaves' folk belief that they might one day fly home to Africa, the spiritual offers an African American version of the act of transcendence that Du Bois borrows from the figure of the swan, translating martial power into Romantic idealism, at the conclusion of Wagner's opera. In this story of cultural doublings, the sounding trumpet of resurrection in the spiritual is appropriately doubled in the Wagnerian brass that accompanies the climax of *Lohengrin*. The two pieces of music therefore stand in a relationship that is not unlike that of the two Johns—the one black, the other white—whose contrasting lives are shown in the story to be the products of racist society.

But doubling here is not simply mirroring. In *Lohengrin*, as in Du Bois's story, a brother acts as saving hero for his sister's honor. Nonetheless, the corresponding nationalist foundations of culture that would emerge in Du Bois's work over the next twenty years, culminating in *Darkwater*, cannot be found in the climax of the short story, at least not directly. John goes to his death humming the song that, one might say, represents the shadow of doom under which he has lived as a black man ever since birth. Moreover, Wagner's music is both a measure of his rightful aspirations and a sign of his distance from his own home community. When John returns after his long years away, he appears sullen and conceited. His welcome at the Baptist church is ruined by his brusque manner and by his dismissal, during his short speech on education, of the African American church as an antiquated institution. His rebuke by a church elder is a powerful sketch of the quality of faith that Du Bois located in the slave generation:

> Then at last a low suppressed snarl came from the Amen corner, and an old bent man arose, walked over the seats, and climbed straight up into the pulpit. He was wrinkled and black, with scant gray and tufted hair; his voice and hands shook as with palsy; but on his face lay the intense rapt look of the religious fanatic. He seized the Bible

with his rough, huge hands; twice he raised it inarticulate, and then fairly burst into words, with rude and awful eloquence. He quivered swayed and bent; then rose aloft in perfect majesty, till the people moaned and wept, wailed and shouted, and a wild shrieking arose from the corners where all the pent-up feeling of the hour gathered itself and rushed into the air. John never knew clearly what the old man said; he only felt himself held up to scorn and scathing denunciation for trampling on the true Religion, and he realized with amazement that all unknowingly he had put rough, rude hands on something this little world held sacred.

Du Bois's brilliant portrait of the lay preacher (frequently the pastor was not the only, or even the best, preacher in the congregation) draws a stark line between generations, disclosing the problem of double consciousness with greater refinement and more comprehensive allegorical significance. John's obliviousness to what is sacred in his tradition is underscored by his humming of Wagner at the point of death. The grim visage of the "haggard white-haired man" that bears down on him with the "coiled twisted rope" is first of all the symbolically entitled Judge, white John's father, out to avenge his son's murder; but he may also contain something of the judgment passed by the grim black elder who accuses John of betraying his people's faith.[86] The two old men, then, are also doubles, the generations of slaveholding and slavery arrayed against each other like white John and black John.

The vise in which John is caught, of course, is nothing less than the vise of divided identity in which Du Bois himself was caught: how to balance the acquisition of white, European cultural forms against the preserved beliefs and cultural patterns of black America that had originated in slavery. John is denounced by the embodiment of the preacher as Du Bois defined him in "Of the Faith of the Fathers," a combined tyrant, judge, and seer. His "sermon," if one may call it that, takes John as its text, and with the passion, frenzy, and extraordinary vocality characteristic of the fundamentalist black preacher, denounces all that John stands for, his educational and social aspirations forged at once of assimilation and alienation. In this chapter, as in *The Souls of Black Folk* as a whole, Du Bois stood in the yawning cultural gap between two worlds, his double consciousness embodied in seemingly irreconcilable extremes that were not so much ironic as contradictory, despite his efforts to collapse them into one cultural discourse. The chapters on the death of his son, on

Alexander Crummell, and on the sacrificial death of the fictive but semi-autobiographical John are bound together by their representation of death as the moment of final salvation—what had always been represented in the spirituals as the movement into freedom but which, in the realm of Du Bois's secular prophecy, remains inevitably provisional, as much a dark trope of potential cultural declension and loss as of ultimate spiritual triumph.

Black and Unknown Bards: A Theory of the Sorrow Songs

> Anybody should ask you who made up this song,
> Tell 'em Jack the Rabbit, he's been here and gone.
>
> African American folk song

> Who first from midst his bonds lifted his eyes?
> Who first from out the still watch, lone and long,
> Feeling the ancient faith of prophets rise
> Within his dark-kept soul, burst into song? . . .
> How did it catch that subtle undertone,
> That note in music not heard with the ears?
>
> James Weldon Johnson,
> "O Black and Unknown Bards"

The last chapter of *The Souls of Black Folk* brings text and music into their greatest antiphonal proximity. At the outset of "The Sorrow Songs" the alternating epigraph from the European tradition of "high" literature has been replaced by the lyrics of a sorrow song, "Lay This Body Down," which does not just stand in juxtaposition to but virtually merges with the musical bars from "Wrestling Jacob." Jacob's wrestling with the angel (or the Lord, as it may be) in Genesis 32 signifies both the triumph and reconciliation that make him a patriarch of Israel:

> *Wrestling Jacob, Jacob, day is a-breaking,*
> *Wrestling Jacob, Jacob, I will not let thee go. . . .*
> I will not let thee go,
> Until thou bless me.

Thomas Wentworth Higginson considered the song "one of the wildest and most striking" of those he collected, and he rightly pointed out that its "mystical effect and passionate striving" were captured less in the words than in the music. Like "Lay This Body Down," with its great lines also commended by Higginson, "Wrestling Jacob" points to a conversion that is in addition a salvation. It underlines the fact that the "sorrow" of the songs referred not just to an emotion generated by the pains of slavery among a people whose epic story could be likened to that of the Hebrews but also, as Edward Blyden and others had already argued, to the imposition of the religion of Jesus, the "Man of Sorrows," upon African American slaves, affording them "consolation in their deep disasters" and putting "new songs in their mouths." The significance, however, is more than Christian. The haunting lines of "Lay This Body Down" ("I walk through the churchyard . . . / I'll lie in the grave and stretch out my arms") recall the central trope of "Bright Sparkles in the Churchyard" and remind us that the African American interpretation of crossing the "separatin' line" could include a more concrete belief in the ritual journey and the reunification with ancestors in a lost homeland. Likewise, "Wrestling Jacob" tells us to look very carefully at the opening of Du Bois's chapter, where the patriarchs—more accurately the ancestral generations, men and women alike—of black America are celebrated:

> They that walked in darkness sang songs in the olden days—Sorrow Songs—for they were weary at heart. And so before each thought that I have written in this book I have set a phrase, a haunting echo of these weird old songs in which the soul of the black slave spoke to men. Ever since I was a child these songs have stirred me strangely. They came out of the South unknown to me, one by one, and yet at once I knew them as of me and mine. Then in after years when I came to Nashville I saw the great temple builded of these songs towering over the pale city. To me Jubilee Hall seemed ever made of the songs themselves, and its bricks were red with the blood and dust of toil. Out of them rose for me morning, noon, and night, bursts of wonderful melody, full of the voices of my brothers and sisters, full of the voices of the past.

Significantly, the opening rhetorical question of Du Bois's preface has now become a stirring declaration that the songs are "of me and mine." Jubilee Hall, built of the labors of George L. White and the Fisk Jubilee Singers, whose initial seven-year tour "brought back one hundred and fifty thousand dollars to found Fisk University," is a structure that embodies the spirit Du Bois seeks to emulate in his own labors.[87] The souls with which Du Bois has ritually joined himself over the course of *The Souls of Black Folk* are in great part the souls of the black South, the souls of slavery, those who have gone before and yet speak still in the bequeathed voices of the sorrow songs, to which Du Bois was tied through the educational mediation of Fisk. Du Bois's remark that the sorrow songs came out of the South "unknown to me" recalls the painful cultural separation he fictionalized in "Of the Coming of John," both instances suggesting that his intellectual separation from the tradition of the folk required that he "wrestle" with it, seeking his own salvation, by ancestral blessing, in the crucible of black culture.[88]

I have already touched on a number of Du Bois's remarks in "The Sorrow Songs"; his own explications of the texts of various spirituals constitute an important contribution to the literature on African American folk culture and African retentions that grew up at the turn of the century and do not need repetition.* In gathering together his identification of most, but not all, of the musical epigraphs and his own brief interpretation of the songs, "The Sorrow Songs" displays the means of Du Bois's deliberate immersion in the world of the ancestors, his mastery of a language capable of creating a pathway to Africa and establishing the coherence of African American culture as a set of values and expressions that were not annihilated by slavery but rather nurtured and sustained by it. Rather than reiterate Du Bois's own commentary here, I would like instead to look more closely at the tropological meaning of the final chapter and of the songs within the text of *The Souls of Black Folk* as a whole.

Du Bois's concluding tribute to the sorrow songs and their singers— whether the performers at Fisk, Hampton, and other schools, or more

---

* Most of the spirituals that Du Bois discusses or alludes to in "The Sorrow Songs" and other chapters can also be found in the *The Story of the Jubilee Singers* or *Hampton and Its Students,* as well as in early collections such as William Allen's *Slave Songs in the United States* (1867). See, for example, "Dust and Ashes" *(Hampton),* "Zion, Weep a Low" *(Hampton),* "Keep Me From Sinkin' Down" *(Hampton),* "Roll, Jordan, Roll" *(Jubilee),* "Been A-Listening" *(Jubilee),* and "Children We Shall All Be Free" *(Jubilee).* Allen includes "Lay This Body Down," "Michael Row the Boat Ashore," and "Poor Rosy." Others, such as "Oh, Freedom" and "Sometimes I Feel Like a Motherless Child," appeared in subsequent Hampton and Jubilee editions or in other collections of the day which Du Bois may have consulted. Most all of the spirituals cited or mentioned in *The Souls of Black Folk* continued to appear in popular collections in the next generation, most notably in James Weldon Johnson and Rosamond Johnson's two volumes of the *Book of American Negro Spirituals* (1925, 1926).

generally those unknown bards and common folk who composed and sustained the sounds of black culture—is saturated in their words, if not their melodies. And yet, as the musical epigraphs demonstrate, the words are in some sense secondary. The music, Du Bois notes, "is far more ancient than the words," but more than that it is inevitably a translation, as it were. Du Bois's deepest immersion into the songs of his fathers and mothers appears in his reproduction of the African song first sung in his family, he says, by his grandfather's grandmother, who was stolen from Africa by a Dutch trader. Her song ("Do bana coba gene me, gene me . . .") has traveled down the generations for two hundred years, "and we sing it to our children, knowing as little as our fathers what its words may mean, but knowing well the meaning of its music." (In fact, the words of the song as Du Bois transliterates them appear to be neither in any language of the Bantu group nor in any other known African language.)[89] The music, then, signifies slavery and the inheritance of ancestral strength as well as ancestral hardship; the words' lack of meaning, though, is significant in several senses. To begin with, it is the utmost sign of the loss of ancestral language (or, in a more accurate sense, of its fragmentary survival in the words and phrases that have entered American English), remaining a secret language that cannot be correctly translated even by those who remember and repeat it. The African words of "Do bana coba" may also be said to represent a signifying critique of the English words of the spirituals, a reminder that English is a borrowed language, one put to marvelous inventive use but nonetheless an alien tongue for the first generations of African Americans. The fact that "Do bana coba" is meaningless—a kind of *nonsense,* to recall the tonal semantic register so important in several of Chesnutt's stories—accentuates the decimation of African culture under slavery while at the same time pointing to the ordeal of its recovery and preservation in now fragmentary forms. Both the music and words of "Do bana coba" stand in the liminal region beyond the African American spirituals, the crucial but only partly decipherable world of an African past situated on the horizon of myth—and of memory for the slave generations who were passing.

But African in what way? In its amorphous claim to an ancestral inheritance, Du Bois's anecdote partially resolves the racialist leanings evident in "The Conservation of Races" into an account of political-cultural, not racial, genealogy. At the same time, the spirituals stood at the divide of culture in ways that were, and remain, difficult not to racialize. Increasingly in the early twentieth century, it was claimed that whites were not musically (or spiritually) competent to perform black music. Kelly Miller, for example, argued that because black music's "racial quality is stamped on every note," a white man "attempting a plantation melody" is a "racial anomaly." "The requisite melodic, pathetic quality of voice," Miller contended, "is a natural coefficient which is as inalienable as any other physical characteristic." In a later critique of Henry Burleigh's arrangements, which he rightly found mechanical, Carl Van Vechten maintained that white singers were incapable of rendering the spirituals correctly (he also lamented that many black singers, on the basis of published arrangements such as Burleigh's, were avoiding all dialect and any "natural Negro inflections" in the music). W. C. Handy said simply that "no other people can sing [the spirituals] with complete success, not even Negroes other than those born in the United States."[90] It is doubtful that Du Bois would have accepted the implications of such a blunt racialization of black musical "soul," although his theory of racial "gifts" or "strivings" that are neither purely biological nor purely societal could be said to be borne out in *The Souls of Black Folk.* By the same token, however, it is obvious that a poor vocal student need not be white; indeed, Du Bois's own black character in "Of the Coming of John" displays a similar loss of familiarity with black folk language; and John, as I have already suggested, is without question a model for Du Bois's own anxiety that he too may have become similarly divorced from the roots of slave culture.

The story of his great-great-grandmother reappears throughout Du Bois's autobiographical writings, and there are questions to be raised about its accuracy. In "The Sorrow Songs," however, it anchors his theory of the songs—indeed, the entirety of his bardic history of black American life—in a symbolic, if not a demonstrably actual, African ground. The story and the song are an African equivalent of "Sometimes I Feel Like a Motherless Child" or, from "Bright Sparkles," the line "Mother, rock me in de cradle all de day," both of which can be construed as recalling the ancestral origin of a people as well as the familial origin of an individual. Precisely because it cannot be translated, the Bantu song, as he styles it, reduces language to *sound* and in doing so enters onto the most revealing theoretical plane of his argument. The antiphonal relationship between word and music that structures the unfolding argument of *The Souls of Black Folk,* to expand an earlier point, is an elaboration of the concept of vocalization—the alliance of speech and music at the base of the African American artistic tradition. "Do bana coba" literalizes that vocalization as an unknown language beyond words, a cry out of the territory of sound that is transgeographical and Pan-African in the most elemental sense. It offers an ancestral equivalent for the cries and shouts, the laboring hollers, typically long, wavering single- or double-line calls, that were the basis for the black work song and consequently for some forms of the spiritual.[91] And it locates in ancestral cultural gifts never to be fully recovered the sign of difference that was routinely designated a "problem" by white commentators.

As his later pageant "The Star of Ethiopia" would indicate, Du Bois was enamored of theatrical presentations of history. Like *Darkwater* after it, *The Souls of Black Folk* must be seen as a narrative experiment with dramatic form. The volume cannot be performed, in so many words, but neither can it be understood apart from the concept of performance. Yet the most significant difficulty, and one that goes to the heart of African American vocalization and the creation of the spirituals, lies in the fact that the musical bars are themselves an inadequate sign of the sound within them. Nothing is more characteristic of black religious music as it issues into the blues and jazz than the wavers, glissandi, blue tonality, and improvisation—what Ernest Borneman suggestively refers to as the communicative timbre that is "veiled" by vibrato, tremolo, and overtones in the tradition of African music—that would be heard in numerous renditions of the spirituals but are inevitably regularized in the transcriptions in *The Story of the Jubilee Singers* and *Hampton and Its Students,* from which Du Bois drew most of his examples.* I have already taken note of several observations about the difficulty of transcribing the spirituals in a conventional scalar and rhythmic format, but the remarks of Jeanette Robinson Murphy in her landmark essay are worth quoting at length for the light they cast on Du Bois's own spiritual "quotations":

> We may find many of the genuine negro melodies in Jubilee and Hampton Song Books, but for the uninitiated student of the future

---

* It is not necessary to claim that blue tonality itself or the pentatonic scale with which it is often allied are exclusively African in origin in order to assert that, along with creative rhythmic irregularity, variations on the blues scale are characteristically African and/or African American ("Negroid," to use Winthrop Sargeant's old terminology) and the most significant source of difficulties in transcription. As my examples suggest, it is not the conventional blues scale (flatted thirds and fifths) that is most at issue but rather the bent notes, stretched by rhythmic variation, which together may be said to constitute the elements of "black" sound. For the most careful account, see Winthrop Sargeant, *Jazz: Hot and Hybrid,* 3rd ed. (New York: Da Capo, 1975), pp. 148, 188, 196. Cf. Gunther Schuller, *Early Jazz: Its Roots and Musical Development* (New York: Oxford University Press, 1968), pp. 43–57.

there is little or no instruction given, and the white singer in attempting to learn them will make poor work at their mastery; for how is he, poor fellow, to know that it is bad form not to break every law of musical phrasing and notation? What is there to show him that he must make his voice exceedingly nasal and undulating; that around every prominent note he must place a variety of small notes, called "trimmings," and he must sing tones not found in our scale; that he must on no account leave one note until he has the next one well under control? He might be tempted, in the *ignorance* of his twentieth-century education, to take breath whenever he comes to the end of a line or verse! But this he should never do. By some mysterious power, to be learned only from the negro, he should carry over his breath from line to line and from verse to verse, even at the risk of bursting a blood-vessel. . . . He must also intersperse his singing with peculiar humming sounds—"hum-m-m-m."

Murphy's partly tongue-in-cheek analysis of the "intonations and tortuous quavers of this beautiful music" offers a serious judgment in favor of African American vocalization, one that would be elaborated in twentieth-century recognitions, as we have already seen, that a key feature of the roots of black American music was vocal tonality—the talk-singing of black sermonic style and the humming or moaning that extends both the spiritual and the sermon into a musically iterative drone, the domain of sheer sound: "hhhhhhmmmmmmm."[92] Because it *cannot* be translated, the sound of the field holler or the moan of the preacher, like Du Bois's "Do bana coba," inhabits the secret domain of silence that the folktales of talking skull and talking bones projected as the extremity of African American cultural expression, the domain where the cry fades into an articulacy reaching beyond European American apprehension. Moreover, although he clearly expected his readers to hear the lyrics as well as the music in his epigraphic bars, the fact that Du Bois reproduces only the music of the spirituals gives greater weight to his contention that the music is "ancient," that is, an African inheritance.

The difficulty of annotating the spirituals recounted by Murphy, William Allen, and others is therefore a sign of a much larger web of cultural problems: that there were any number of melodic and textual versions of some spirituals; that the spirituals did not have identifiable composers or authors but arose from a shifting communal act of creation, preservation, and transmission; that their creators sang them differently on different occasions and ruthlessly transferred phrases or verses from one song to another; and that, even leaving aside the local question of blue tonality, transcription of the most diligent kind could not fix musical texts whose essence was improvisatory freedom. As Rudi Blesh put it: "A title by no means indicates a certain piece of music but is merely a text to which a spiritual has been improvised."[93]

One can see an example of this in W. C. Handy and Abbe Niles's 1926 collection *Blues: An Anthology*. In his account of "lining out" (which I have suggested may be read as a feature of Du Bois's construction of *The Souls of Black Folk*) Niles remarks that once the preacher had lined out in his own wail or shout, typically full of blue notes (a source of Handy's early composition, he said), the congregation would adapt the example to their own purposes: "From every note each singer would start on a vocal journey of his own, wandering in strange pentatonic figures, but returning together at the proper moment to the next note of the melody." Handy offers a sample transcription of "On Jordan's Stormy Banks" as written and as sung (Figure 1).[94] Or take as a further instance the difference between the version of "Swing Low, Sweet Chariot" that Du Bois reproduces at the outset of his Crummell chapter—first in the transcription as it appears in *The Story of the Jubilee Singers,* with the lyrics (Figure 2), then as it appears in *The Souls of Black Folk,* with the lyrics deleted and the quotation from Tennyson that Du Bois cites (Figure 3)—and the version sung by Roosevelt May of Halifax County, North Carolina, in the late 1970s (Figure 4).[95] May's rhythmic and tonal manipulations make a mockery out of the comparatively concertized version Du Bois employed—and which he recognized to be an inadequate representation of the singing he heard in Tennessee churches and at Fisk. May's improvisation is not just a variation on "Swing Low." Rather, the very mutability that his version represents *is* "Swing Low," while the concertized, frozen text of the published version is the variant, as it were, the hollow core of the song that remains once it is stripped of vocalization.

It is perhaps ironic that the "caricature" and "debasement" that Du Bois complains had spoiled some contemporary performance is necessarily incorporated to a significant degree in the epigraphic music that he reproduces from the Hampton and Jubilee collections. More to the point, however, is the fact that any reproduction would be inadequate, for, as he argues, "the true Negro folk-song still lives in the hearts of those who have heard them truly sung and in the hearts of the Negro people." What, though, were the "true" songs? In her landmark essay "Spirituals and Neo-

Spirituals" Zora Neale Hurston offers the challenging theory that "there never has been a presentation of genuine Negro spirituals to any audience anywhere." The concert performance, the "neo-spiritual," inevitably destroys the irregular and dissonant harmonic structures and improvisatory freedom of the true music. "Each singing of the piece is a new creation," Hurston argues, a series of "unceasing variations around a theme" in which the "liquefying of words" is a natural product of the combined "harmony and disharmony, the shifting keys and broken time that make up the spiritual." The full implications of Hurston's remarks about vocalization in both spiritual and sermonic style take us beyond Du Bois. Yet her argument that spirituals are not confined to the inherited canon of slave songs (with characteristic brusqueness she takes a shot at Du Bois and dismisses the notion that the whole body of spirituals are "sorrow songs" as "ridiculous") but rather "are being made and forgotten every day" is much to the point.[96] Transcription, even if one did not take the radical view of Hurston, was at best a frail representation of the "genuine" music. What Du Bois had indelibly fixed as a theoretical problem with which Johnson, Hurston, Langston Hughes, and Sterling Brown would struggle in their own creative work was the vocalism of African American expression and the multiple ironies of representing it in print.

It is such vocalization and its improvisatory qualities that one must hear in contemplating the musical epigraphs to Du Bois's chapters, all of which, if heard in performance, would move beyond the rather rigidly conceptualized arrangements of the Jubilee and Hampton volumes and need to be "rewritten" in the reader's mind in order to capture their significance. Du Bois's reader must therefore work through two superimposed interpretive problems. The words of the spirituals are not present; like any other complex set of allusions or quotations, they must be known in advance or learned. The music must likewise be known or played; it is not present in the text except as it is "heard" by the reader. The interpretable text of the sorrows songs as Du Bois uses them in *The Souls of Black Folk* thus turns on the most unstable, quasi-material modes of representation, in which the fluent iteration of the underlying lyric code of African America can only be implied until the text is vocalized within the theater of actual or imagined performance.

The code of black America, although Du Bois was loath to reduce it to a separatist philosophy, was latent in those elements of the spirituals that had not been appropriated by the dominant culture. Without arguing that Du Bois himself had in mind any such musicological characterization, I

Figure 1. W. C. Handy, "On Jordan's Stormy Banks"

Figure 2. "Swing Low, Sweet Chariot," from *The Story of the Jubilee Singers*

Then from the Dawn it seemed there came, but faint
As from beyond the limit of the world,
Like the last echo born of a great cry,
Sounds, as if some fair city were one voice
Around a king returning from his wars.

TENNYSON

Figure 3. "Swing Low, Sweet Chariot," from *The Souls of Black Folk*

Figure 4. "Swing Low, Sweet Chariot," as sung by Roosevelt May

would suggest that the notoriously difficult concept of "swing" defines the code of slave culture as it survived in turn-of-the-century African American culture. Like Fenner, Barton, and others, Theodore Seward takes special note of the swaying of the body and patting of hands and feet that accompanied black spirituals, arguing that it provided a hidden temporal line, so that "however broken and seemingly irregular the movement of the music," those irregularities "invariably conform to the 'higher law' of the perfect rhythmic flow." The most comprehensive and useful account of such combined phenomena of rhythm and intonation was to appear in James Weldon Johnson's superior discussion of "swing" in the preface to his first book of spirituals, where he linked together Afro-Christian worship, African rhythms and nonscalar tonality, and the performed physical incorporation of song and vocal expression into the labor of servitude. Johnson drew a distinction between the kinds of swing characteristic in the song forms of the spiritual and the work song:

> The "swing" of the Spirituals is an altogether subtle and elusive thing. It is subtle and elusive because it is in perfect union with the religious ecstasy that manifests itself in the swaying bodies of a whole congregation, swaying as if responding to the baton of some extremely sensitive conductor. . . . The swaying of the body marks the regular beat or, better, surge, for it is something stronger than a beat, and is more or less, not precisely, strict in time; but the Negro loves nothing better in his music than to play with the fundamental time beat. . . . In listening to Negroes sing their own music it is often tantalizing and even exciting to watch a minute fraction of a beat balancing for a slight instant on the bar between two measures, and, when it seems almost too late, drop back into its proper compartment. There is a close similarity between this singing and the beating of the big drum and the little drums by the African natives. In addition, there are the curious turns and twists and quavers and the intentional striking of certain notes just a shade off key, with which the Negro loves to embellish his songs. These tendencies constitute a handicap that has baffled many of the recorders of this music. I doubt that it is possible with our present system of notation to make a fixed transcription of these peculiarities that would be absolutely true; for in their very nature they are not susceptible to fixation. Many of the transcriptions that have been made are far from the true manner and spirit of singing the Spirituals.

He observed further that the swing of African American work songs was governed less by internal musicological choices than by "rhythmic motions made by a gang of men at labor":

> All the men sing and move together as they swing their picks or rock-breaking hammers. They move like a ballet; not a ballet of cavorting legs and pirouetting feet, but a ballet of bending backs and quivering muscles. It is all in rhythm but a rhythm impossible to set down. There is always a leader and he sets the pace. A phrase is sung while the shining hammers are being lifted. It is cut off suddenly as the hammers begin to descend and gives place to a prolonged grunt which becomes explosive at the impact of the blow. Each phrase of the song is independent, apparently obeying no law of time. After each impact the hammers lie still and there is silence. As they begin to rise again the next phrase of the song is sung; and so on. . . . There are variations that violate the obvious laws of rhythm, but over it all can be discerned a superior rhythmic law.[97]

Johnson's argument, one of the most penetrating definitions of the phenomenon of swing, correctly fuses the rhythmic and harmonic into a single plane. His distinction between the swing of the spirituals and that of the work songs is technically instructive; and yet his own descriptions make evident the comparable rhythmic and tonal features that ally the two song forms in African American tradition. In explicating the fact that the spirituals can be seen to develop some of the central features of black work songs—the use of call and response, rhythmic repetition, the limitless improvisation of verses—Johnson gathered the problems of transcription and tonality cited by others into a comprehensive cultural statement of black poetics while extending African American labor back into the customary work patterns and artistic resources of Africa.

One might say that Johnson spelled out, with the ear and eye of a trained musician, discoveries that were implicit in Du Bois's own theorizing. The cultural code of the black spirituals themselves suggests the operation of comparable superior rhythmic laws, comparable historical strata of expression, within *The Souls of Black Folk* itself. The labor of slavery that built much of white America, in this view, is one with the labor of cultural striving and nation building that created African America and preserved it, for example, in the work of the Fisk Jubilee Singers. Du Bois did not incorporate swing into his style, as would Brown, Hurston, and Hughes, but he structured his volume on the basis of a culturally

coded, almost subliminal language that challenged the ability of his audience, whether white or black, to comprehend his book. As it enacts his
theory of double consciousness, the code of the spirituals epitomizes the
paradox upon which Du Bois founded his career—that cultures could be
learned, shared, and made universal, but that the hierarchy of racism left
the dominant culture ignorant of the singular spiritual heritage that the
institution of slavery had embedded within its own nation: "Our song,
our toil, our cheer, and warning have been given to this nation in blood-
brotherhood. Are not these gifts worth the giving? Is not this work and
striving? Would America have been America without her Negro people?"[98]

The concluding song of *The Souls of Black Folk,* the only one (excepting
"Do bana coba") in which music and text coexist, is "Let Us Cheer the
Weary Traveller." It brings the metaphor of the journey to a conclusion
and functions as an envoy for the book as well as Du Bois's message to
the modern world. Weariness encapsulates not just a physical state of
exhaustion but a spiritual enervation that is the inheritance of generations:
they who walked in darkness were "weary at heart," as Du Bois says of
the ancestral generations at the outset of the chapter. Uniting the spiritual
and the physical, weariness is a trope constantly invoked in black song. In
"A Great Camp-Meeting in the Promised Land," the spiritual that heads
the Washington chapter, the gathered are commanded to walk, talk, and
sing together, but "dont yer get weary"; in the 1920s both Langston
Hughes and Louis Armstrong would adopt the common blues phrase
"weary blues" as the title of two of their most important respective works.
As in these works, weariness signifies in the conclusion of *The Souls of
Black Folk* not just the work that Du Bois himself has done but also the
source of inspiration to which he turns in his own anxiety and weariness.
He reproduces the chorus only of "Let Us Cheer the Weary Traveller,"
but the first verse (in the version of the song published by Handy and
Niles) is an explicit commentary on his work: "Sometimes I feel discour-
aged, / I think my work in vain, / And then the Holy Spirit revives my
soul again."[99]

The crucial function of music as an accompaniment to work in African
society and later in African American adaptations of the practice can thus
be employed to illuminate the function of song in Du Bois's text, where
Du Bois's work as cultural critic, extending the new nation building begun
at Fisk University and elsewhere, draws inspiration from and extends the
work of the spirituals. If African work songs have the effect of drawing
forth the latent forces of nature into a dialectic with labor such that work

and song assist each other—even to the degree that work may be said to propel song, rather than the reverse—Du Bois's labor of writing and his vocalizing of the tradition of the black spirituals may be said likewise to constitute a single act. His book hid within it and at the same time explicated the expressive power comprehensively signified in Hurston's figure of "High John de Conquer," who came from Africa to America "walking on the waves of sound," incarnate in the "black bodies down there in the middle passage." "It is no accident that High John de Conquer has evaded the ears of white people," Hurston adds. "They were not supposed to know. . . . They could not understand because they had nothing to hear things like that with." Mediating between the double worlds of his own consciousness, which were nothing less than the double worlds of America itself, however, Du Bois spoke to both a black world and a white, demanding recognition that African Americans, in both their labor and their song, had "woven [themselves] with the very warp and woof of this nation."[100] His own intellectual labor links his cultural work, not in comparison but in tribute, to the cruel toil of the slave generations of the middle passage and of the Old South and, even more important, to those who still labor in peonage in the Black Belt of the New South and whose lives constitute the central chapters of *The Souls of Black Folk*. In doing so he recovers, preserves, and celebrates both the killing labor in cotton and rice fields and the creative labor of song making. Du Bois's own spiritual autobiography becomes empowered by and joined to the anonymous lives of those who have "been here and gone," as the folk song quoted at the outset of this section puts it, those unknown bards and common folk from whose toil have sprung the present generations and the foundations of African American culture. It is in this way that Du Bois records what may be his most compelling modulation in the trope of double consciousness. While writing his own book and placing it within the canonical tradition of Western individual authorship—making himself first among the "co-workers in the kingdom of culture"—he at the same time wove into its most essential structure the communal creation of African America, the cultural work not of "unknown bards" alone but of a whole people whose words and song continued to be recorded and transformed in the constant evolution of the spirituals. Joining his own labors to the labor of those "who walk in darkness," Du Bois composed a musical book whose bardic role was commensurate with his own.

· 6 ·

The Spell of Africa

The short story entitled "The Comet" occupies much the same position in *Darkwater: Voices from within the Veil* (1920) as does "Of the Coming of John" in *The Souls of Black Folk*. Because the political and sociological commentary of the later volume is more thoroughly infused with poetic thought than the first, as Du Bois pressed exposition and trope, editorial and lyric closer and closer, it thus represents his increasing reliance on visionary language as a means of articulating his most profound insights into the meaning of race consciousness for African Americans. Even so, "The Comet" stands out among the book's various parables and its messianic sketches of the Black Christ for its coherent statement of a theory of racial difference. When a comet (one that follows in the wake of the actual Halley's comet of 1910) destroys New York City, a black man and a white woman, who assume the entire world has been devastated, appear to be the only persons left alive. But the moment of mystic communion that they share, to which I will return in more detail, is swept away by the realization that others have survived and that the hero is therefore still a "nigger" in the white man's world.[1] Du Bois's apocalyptic fiction, here as elsewhere, remained locked within the category of allegory, its eschatology pointing to the end of white global dominance that he, in his more optimistic moments following the crisis of the First World War, expected to crumble under anti-imperialist pressures. With increasing bitterness over the course of the twentieth century, Du Bois discovered that the rigid racial hierarchy supporting colonialism abroad and segregation at home would be dismantled only with great difficulty. As in "The Comet," moreover, his allegorical scenarios could not easily translate philosophical consciousness into revolutionary political actuality but more often ended in irony.

540

Here as elsewhere throughout his extraordinarily varied intellectual life, however, the significant but circumscribed power of Du Bois's literary work is best clarified by a contextualization comparable in spirit to his own intentions. In at least one African instance the appearance of Halley's comet was interpreted as a literal harbinger of the end of white rule. The prophecy was made by Enoch Mgijima, a convert to the Church of God and Saints of Christ, founded in South Africa in 1909 by John Msikinya, who had been dismissed from his Methodist ministerial position and traveled to America for study before returning to found an African post of the black American church. Upon the appearance of Halley's comet, Mgijima preached that God was commanding Africans to renounce the New Testament as a fiction and return to their own ancient religion, on the model of the Israelite patriarchs who had once been liberated from their enslavers. Following Msikinya's death in 1918, Mgijima was ejected by the American parent church; he then founded his own sect, known as the Israelites. In 1920, after a celebration of the Passover, they settled at Buelhoek commonage, armed with swords and spears, to await the end of the world according to his prophecy. After they had refused to leave for over a year, there ensued a bloody battle against South African police and military units, armed with machine guns and rifles, which left 163 of Mgijima's followers dead.[2]

The slaughter of the Israelites as they awaited millennial deliverance from imperial rule and the proportionately ironic conclusion to the millennial action of "The Comet" are perhaps less analogous than coincidental. Yet the underlying structures of intention, as the complete text of *Darkwater* makes evident, are informed by the same motives—the casting off of racial dominance; the return to an integrity of black (African or African American) belief, even if it retains the formal guise of biblical eschatology; and a belief that blacks in Africa and the diaspora are linked in a common destiny. Enoch Mgijima's prophecy and the fate of the Israelites were part of a much greater constellation of radical black Christian uprisings in Africa in the early twentieth century—the most significant spurred by the crisis of the world war and its seeming promise to dismantle imperial rule—which have gone under the heading of Ethiopianism, a term that refers both to the biblical passage (Psalms 68:31) that was widely interpreted to forecast the rise of African nationalism or Pan-African unity, and to the specific splinter churches, such as Mgijima's, that arose in the colonial setting, typically invoking the millennial redemption of a Black Christ and calling for black separatism, if not the overthrow of white rule.

Several such uprisings and their leaders were influenced directly by American churches or religious movements. From the perspective of intellectual and literary history, however, what is of more significance is the web of ideas concerning the crisis in prevailing assumptions about racial hierarchy that may be elicited from both African and African American sources during the same period and the context they provide for understanding Du Bois's creation of a Pan-African political aesthetic. What is more, because African American invocations of Ethiopianism as a political philosophy date from the early nineteenth century, Du Bois's own turn in this direction gathers up strands of black thought that had surfaced in the earlier radicalism of David Walker, Nat Turner, Frederick Douglass, and Martin Delany, for example, and demonstrates that their transnational, syncretic philosophies of hemispheric slave resistance were applicable as well to the new age of colonialism.

Although his critical, historical, and creative work over the first decades of the century provides a superior if diffuse basis for studying the rise of a Pan-African literary ideology, Du Bois's contribution to that ideology, as to the tradition of American black nationalism, remains elusive. In speaking of Du Bois and Pan-Africanism, I have in mind here not the entire scope of his career, which from the 1930s forward was identified increasingly with the development of a socialist theory of American and African life and which concluded with his settlement in Ghana, when he ironically took the step back to Africa that he had earlier rejected in his quarrels with Marcus Garvey and other emigrationists. An appreciation of the complete trajectory of Du Bois's life would require an analysis of the Marxism he espoused as he rewrote his autobiographies and histories of Pan-Negro life during the 1940s and 1950s, just as it would require one to measure his revised understanding of American black social and economic life since the Civil War, for example in the classic 1935 volume *Black Reconstruction in America,* in which he codified his long-evolving characterization of slaves and ex-slaves as an industrial proleteriat whose surplus labor was the cornerstone of global capitalism. Much of his later thought, however, has clear roots in his first essays, and I want to concentrate instead on the early part of his career, from the 1890s through the 1920s, before his conversion to a more dogged Marxism that was to issue at last in a largely uncritical embrace of Stalin and Mao and a romantic faith in world communism that far surpassed his early ardor for Bismarck or his mature commitment to Pan-African nationalism. The years leading up to *Darkwater* constitute both his greatest influence, as editor of *Crisis* and a leader of the NAACP, and his most inventive period as a literary figure. Despite the fact that a younger generation of black intellectuals and writers associated with the Harlem Renaissance sometimes perceived Du Bois as the embodiment of a reactionary, Victorian cultural ethos, he remained at the center of thought and action about issues of racial justice and the realization of a black aesthetic throughout the 1920s, and no one came close to equaling, let alone surpassing, *The Souls of Black Folk* as a comprehensive cultural and historical statement about African America.

Du Bois was hardly alone in recognizing that the First World War was crucial to both African and African American aspirations to freedom. In practical terms, its concentrated horror summed up for him and other blacks the crisis over civil rights at home in Jim Crow America and the final collapse of the purportedly civilized ideals of European colonialism abroad. On a more theoretical level, it crystallized his view of race as a category defined less by color or by nationality than by inclusion in the African diaspora. The rise of black political consciousness that accompanied the New Negro movement—spurred on in the United States by reaction to the role played by Africa in the war and the failure of black American veterans to win any significant civil rights at home through their sacrifices abroad; by the great migratory influx into the urban North, with its resulting labor problems and violence in the early decades of the twentieth century; and by the ascendancy of white supremacist thought over the same period—had its counterpart in the growth of African independence movements and a worldwide Pan-African philosophy to which Du Bois made a significant contribution. Historical studies have paired the comparable rises of race conflict and segregated social structures in the United States and South Africa,[3] and cultural interpretations of the concepts of negritude and Africanity have touched on the relationships between African American literature and Pan-African thought.[4] But with the exception of Tony Martin's studies of Marcus Garvey's literary circle and those of Wilson Moses on Du Bois and Crummell, there have been few attempts to draw out explicit links between the two historical spheres of action at the heart of Du Bois's thought and aesthetics. There is no doubt that Du Bois's political theories suffered from abstraction and that— at least until his more explicit avowal of Marxism—his radicalism was always tempered by elitism. Nonetheless, it is not entirely correct to claim, as one historian has, that Du Bois ignored black mass culture, defusing its threatening aspects by aestheticization.[5] As *The Souls of Black Folk* demonstrated, aesthetics and politics—or spirituality and ideology—were implicitly one for Du Bois well before his public embrace of that view in the mid-1920s.

Without question, Marcus Garvey was the black American (technically, black West Indian) most widely known in Africa. Even though he blamed Garvey and his failed emigration plans for the decline of African American interest in Pan-Africanism by the mid-1920s, Du Bois did not have as strong an influence on incipient African independence movements as did Garvey, whose importance would later be cited by Kwame Nkrumah, Jomo Kenyatta, and other leaders, and whose newspaper, *Negro World,* was circulated widely enough in Africa in the 1920s to be held responsible for several nationalist uprisings. Nor would it be correct to claim that Du Bois's literary theory of negritude had a prominence or philosophical sophistication comparable to those brought forward by French and West Indian intellectuals of the 1930s. Nevertheless, it was Du Bois who conceptualized an early form of negritude and whose writing and thinking most closely paralleled the widening course of Ethiopianist uprisings. At times vacillating between integrationism and separatism, or between a nonracial aestheticism and the advocacy of propagandistic art, Du Bois nonetheless kept race pride at the forefront of his thought, courting but at the same time avoiding the debilitation of confusing cultural inheritance with outright racial mysticism.[6] In spite of his apparent slighting of African leaders who made contact with him or whose writings were sent him, Du Bois himself, perhaps more comprehensively than any other figure of his time, even Marcus Garvey, embodied in transhistorical terms the idea of "African Personality" first popularized in the 1880s by Edward Blyden; and his work, in fact, constantly belies the separation between art and propaganda that he tried to maintain until his visit to the Soviet Union in 1926.

Darkwater, a landmark text in the cross-currents between America and Africa, as well as the literature of the Black Christ, consolidated that union of forces in Du Bois's mature thought. It is a text, I will argue, that bears careful examination in its own right; but just as important are its representative qualities. *Darkwater* is not so accomplished, so fully passionate, so thoughtful, or so influential as *The Souls of Black Folk;* and although the book's experimental combination of fiction, lyric, and essay is quite compelling, it is not formally as well crafted as Jean Toomer's *Cane* (1923), the most comparable African American literary work of the day. Still, in the essays of which the volume is composed, Du Bois carries foward the Africanist elements of his American cultural analysis into an international setting, and he enunciates a black "nationalist" philosophy—rather, a vision, with all the messianic overtones implicit in a story such as "The Comet"—that has both European and African intellectual roots and is specifically diasporic in its effects. *Darkwater* therefore acts as both text and context, a point of intersection for Du Bois's own writings over more than a twenty-year period and analogous writing or argument by other African American and African intellectuals. Not least because it is a far less appreciated part of the flowering of black literature that came to be known as the Harlem Renaissance, Du Bois's Pan-African work deserves our attention. But a demanding corollary of that argument is that Du Bois, more so than any other writer of his day—and his day was a very long one—made the entire African diaspora, not the United States alone, his arena. Just as *The Souls of Black Folk* looked backward, summarizing the history of African America, *Darkwater* and allied works looked forward, anticipating as well as instigating modern Pan-African philosophy and literature. And any comparison of the two works in the evolution of Du Bois's career shows how completely their animating ideas interpenetrate and coalesce.

This chapter sometimes ranges outside of an American, or strictly African American, tradition as well as outside of Du Bois's own writings. My argument takes its lead from Du Bois, however, in assuming that his Pan-Africanism, though its point of departure was always the problem of American racism, was inevitably diasporic in its horizons. Moreover, the unusual character of *Darkwater* and Du Bois's other Pan-African writings of the period makes necessary some attention to topics as different as German nationalism and African anticolonialism; to contemporary black leaders such as Marcus Garvey, Edward Blyden, Henry Turner, and J. E. Casely Hayford; and to Du Bois's rather remarkable—and uniquely creative—analysis of the role of black women in the political economy, and hence in his literary critique, of slavery and segregration in the United States and colonial rule in Africa. Although *Darkwater* is quite unlike Nat Turner's "Confessions," the text with which I began, it is equally unorthodox as a work of literature, requiring unusual methods of interpretation but in the process extending our notion of literary history and the textual artifact. Both the "Confessions" and *Darkwater* are avowedly polemical, the one continuing the work of slave revolt in the domain of documentary terror, as it were, the other joining black American and black African traditions of resistance into a single ideology. Like the hemispheric accounts of slave revolt rendered by Martin Delany and Herman Melville, moreover, Du Bois's Pan-African argument was increasingly both global and national. It was American argument; but Du Bois's America was indisputably *African* America.

The Color Line Belts the World

Du Bois's role in the Pan-African conferences of 1900, 1919, 1921, 1923, and 1945 has been analyzed often, as has his classic essay "The African Roots of the War," which appeared in 1915 and was later incorporated into *Darkwater*. The Pan-African conferences put him in touch with a number of European and African intellectuals, even though their views frequently conflicted. Generally rather moderate in their anticolonial platforms, the conferences produced little in the way of concrete analysis and were not notable for their results, issuing mainly in stirring oratory and declarations against forced labor, loss of land-holdings, and exploitation by foreign capital. (Over the next several decades, moreover, Du Bois remained bluntly, and characteristically, egotistical both in his appraisal of his own leadership and in his implausible estimation that the League of Nations Mandate Commission, which oversaw former German colonial holdings, was a direct result of his own plan.) Yet the Pan-African meetings clearly acted as a lightning rod for Du Bois's intellect and imagination. His sustained efforts to keep alive the ideals of the Pan-African Congress, Arnold Rampersad has argued, had consequences best measured in his own work and in the ultimate arising of African independence movements: "Having identified disunity as an instrument of colonial subjugation, Du Bois brought Africa together in a symbolic but unprecedented way." The 1900 conference produced Du Bois's famous dictum "The problem of the twentieth century is the problem of the color line," and his central critique of colonial rule and the world war that he argued had come from it lay in his simple insistence, articulated in the conference manifestos and his numerous writings on the war, that Africa must be ruled by Africans and its resources not harvested for foreign profit without the participation of Africans themselves, by which he generally meant, as in the theory of the black talented tenth he advanced in the United States, an educated class acting in the best interests of the masses.[7]

Du Bois sometimes was blind to African exploitation of other Africans or ignored tangible benefits that accrued from colonial improvement; and he was on just as shaky economic ground as Lenin in claiming that colonialism was driven by the investment of surplus wealth.[8] Nonetheless, his few questionable assumptions did not invalidate his claims about the destructive social and political consequences of colonial rule. Moreover, his sustained attack on colonialism from 1900 through the end of his life was most impressive in the links he drew between colonialism abroad and racism at home. Even before *The Souls of Black Folk* gave wide currency to his aphorism, Du Bois had made clear that the "problem of the color line" was international in scope. In "The Present Outlook for the Dark Races of Mankind" (1900), he directed his audience at the third annual meeting of the American Negro Academy to consider the "marvelous drama" being played out in the colonial struggle of Africa, "the centre of the greater Negro problem," before he surveyed race conflicts over the whole of the globe. As the third millennium dawns, Du Bois asserted, it is evident that "the color line belts the world and that the social problem of the twentieth century is to be the relation of the civilized world to the darker races of mankind." Both the millennial project and the metaphor of the world belt of color and color segregation would remain constants in Du Bois's work for the next two decades. The "color line," elaborated beyond a simple boundary of segregation into a figure for worldwide labor exploitation, is the primary structuring device for his examination of the postwar colonial world in the 1925 essay "Worlds of Color." By the time of the publication of *Black Folk Then and Now* in 1939, his Marxist reconceptualization of the color line into a vertical rather than horizontal marking would be complete: "The proletariat of the world consists . . . overwhelmingly of the dark workers of Asia, Africa, the islands of the sea, and South and Central America. These are the ones who support a superstructure of wealth, luxury, and extravagance. . . . The problem of the twentieth century is the problem of the color line."[9] The color line, that is to say, was a fluid metaphor, less a theoretical or legal barrier in Du Bois's mind than a figure with temporal and geographical dimensionality, a figure that both segregates and grounds at the same time. In his weighty political novel *Dark Princess,* the Black Belt of the South, the ritual ground of *The Souls of Black Folk,* is linked geographically to a world-encompassing latitudinal belt of colored labor exploitation and colored messianism. Such a Pan-African perspective is implied in *The Souls of Black Folk,* but it remains noticeably subordinated to the history and sociology of American slavery and segregation. However powerfully, Africa exists in the earlier text for the most part in the register of cultural retentions. Within the next two decades, however, Du Bois more and more tied American slavery and European imperialism together in a net of exploitation that brought into sharp relief the meaning of Pan-African spirituality and the early modern political poetics of the diaspora.

Participation in the Pan-African conferences also sparked Du Bois's interest in Africa as a historical subject as well as a contemporary problem, a conjunction of interests that was further stimulated, he recalled, by Franz Boas's lecture at Atlanta University in 1906, which helped fix Du Bois's attention upon ancient African history. Although Boas denied that there were significant survivals of African life in America, his arguments about the "early and energetic development of African culture" and achievements such as the smelting of iron or bronze casting were consonant with those of Du Bois. The title of his Atlanta address, "The Outlook for the American Negro," indicates the historical continuum that Boas told his audience they must cultivate while at the same time, like Jews in the diaspora, seeking fruitful cooperation with the dominant ethnic groups of America. As *The Souls of Black Folk* had shown, and as future work would demonstrate, Du Bois tended to view African retentions, such as those he found evident in the African American church and the spirituals, to be as much a set of theoretical ideals as a set of concrete practices that had left their stamp on post–Civil War black culture. The study of black history therefore became an act of recovery that could itself rekindle latent African sources of spiritual belief in African America. Du Bois would have concurred with Boas's statement to his black audience: "You not only have to recover what has been lost in transplanting the Negro race from its native soil to this continent, but you must reach higher levels than your ancestors ever attained." (By 1921, however, Boas, who always reserved some slight judgment about the possibility of innate black inferiority, had become so pessimistic about American prejudice that he advocated race mixing, arguing that the race problem would not disappear "until the negro blood has been so much diluted that it will no longer be recognized just as anti-Semitism will not disappear until the last vestige of the Jew as Jew has disappeared." Although this represented a position Du Bois would never have espoused, his own assimilationist tendencies and his equal pessimism about racism by the 1920s might have made him sympathetic to Boas's view.)[10]

Africa gradually came in Du Bois's thought to play a fundamental, if sometimes sketchy, role in his racial theories. The sociological studies published during his early years at Atlanta University demonstrated a growing, sometimes rather ephemeral perception of the links between Africa and black American culture. In *Horizon*, which he edited from 1907 until 1910, when he joined the NAACP and launched *Crisis*, Du Bois printed both brief accounts of contemporary African events and early versions of some of the lyric assaults on racism and colonialism that would ultimately be incorporated into *Darkwater*. During his tenure as editor, *Crisis*, like most other African American journals and newspapers, carried a fair amount of both historical and contemporary African material, and it is evident that Du Bois was inspired by the primary research sparked by the founding of the Negro Society for Historical Research by John E. Bruce and Arthur Schomburg in 1911 and the Association for the Study of Negro Life and History by Carter Woodson in 1915. In the decade before the war Du Bois immersed himself in the study of Africa and produced in *The Negro* one of the most important surveys of African (and African American) history in the early twentieth century. The "Bible of Pan-Africanism," as Rampersad has called it, *The Negro* was widely read and, alongside his contemporaneous essay "The African Roots of the War," spawned a number of derivative studies such as Benjamin Brawley's *Africa and the War* (1918) and A. Philip Randolph and Chandler Owen's *Terms of Peace and the Darker Races* (1917).[11] Like Du Bois's subsequent volumes that revised its central material, *The Gift of Black Folk* (1924) and *Black Folk Then and Now*, the first volume mixed history, ethnology, and cultural study, tracing a transgeographical Negro history from ancient Africa through contemporary black worlds of the Caribbean and the United States.

Despite his detailed study of Africa, however, Du Bois was often primarily interested in its impact on black American life, and it is hard to assess accurately just what he knew or responded to at a given time about events in contemporary Africa. The record of his reviews, columns, and correspondence shows that he was widely informed about recent African history and the advent of independence movements and independence writings in a number of African countries. (Indeed, in his first noteworthy position as a very young writer, from 1883 to 1885, he contributed local Massachusetts news to Thomas Fortune's *New York Globe*, a newspaper that included much material on Africa and editorial commentary on early Pan-Africanism.) On occasion, though, there are unexpected omissions in his work. For example, in the section of *The Negro* that recapitulates the history of South Africa, although he alludes to the separatist church movements that began in the 1890s (what he calls the "curiously significant 'Ethiopianist' movement"), Du Bois concludes his account at the Zulu and Boer wars, ignoring such issues as the Native Land Act of 1913 and the Bambata Rebellion of 1906, a poll and hut tax revolt with nativist origins, which at the time was blamed on the subversive influence of

Ethiopianist ideas, even on ideas imported from black America.[12] Neither his advocacy for Africa nor his reference to contemporary events was constant, and his literary work requires an exigent distillation of ideas if one is to find the workings of African history in his thought. Even so, the diaspora poetics of *Darkwater* and allied writings constitutes not just a supplement to Du Bois's work in the Pan-African conferences or his several volumes of African and African American history, but perhaps his strongest brief for Pan-Africanism.

Du Bois's imagination was tropological and messianic, and his egotism only increased his capacity to project through the resonance of his own experience and strident opinions an aura of prophetic intensity. Those who have placed Du Bois in the black messianic tradition[13] have typically done so on the basis of his leadership as an educator, scholar, and writer; as a founder of the NAACP and the editor of its famous magazine, *Crisis;* and as a prophet of Third World triumph over white colonial and, as Du Bois saw it, capitalist exploitation. What is missing from these individually compelling accounts is a more precise look at the problem of leadership as it converges with the role of the messiah, in America and Africa alike, particularly the significance of the Black Christ as an organizing figure for a Pan-African political aesthetic. It is in his two major literary works of the postwar period, *Darkwater* and *Dark Princess,* that this abstract trans-geographical world receives its most compelling American elucidation. Each work displays some egregious stylistic flaws, but together they con-stitute a remarkable correlate of the foundation for modern African Amer-ican culture that Du Bois had begun in *The Souls of Black Folk* and a strong articulation of his nationalist aesthetic, which exists in no one simple formulation but must be put together like a collage from his various writings of the period. The evident similarities in structure and cultural meaning between the first text and *Darkwater* can be explored in more detail; what the two later texts complete is Du Bois's search for the spiritual source of African American life and his own messianic vision of the "souls"—the double European American and African soul—of black folk. The tonal dimension of *The Souls of Black Folk* that is added by his treatment of the sorrow songs as a extension of the text, through which Du Bois's voice was united with a vast mystic pool of ancestral voices harrowed by slavery, remains the prime instance of his incorporation of prophecy. But the more far-reaching instances, present but not yet com-pletely developed in the function of the spirituals in *The Souls of Black Folk,* lay in his increasing attempt in the Pan-African writings to make his double consciousness a double vision—that is, to write as an American but always to see as an African American, a "Negro" in the transhistorical and transgeographical sense adumbrated early in his career but only reaching full flower during the years of the war.

To say that Du Bois wrote often as an ideologue does nothing to discredit his philosophy. He wrote at the high noon of racialist theory and white supremacy, when the advocates of Teutonic, Aryan, and Anglo-Saxon superiority had combined romantic historicism with pseudoscientific quantification to eliminate the "darker races" from the scheme of civilization.[14] Du Bois's own romanticism about Africa was a product of his times, a necessary instrument of idealization, and a means to combat the extension of the world's political and economic color line. His role as a Pan-African leader must therefore be seen outside the narrow conception of his involvement in organizing and writing declarations of African rights for the Pan-African conferences, or his stewardship of the NAACP beween 1910 and 1934, where he focused the greatest part of his energy on racial injustice within the United States. It is in the confluence of his historical work on Africa and his allegorical fragments on the global color line—which as often took the form of lyric poems or short stories as they did editorials and essays—that Du Bois's Pan-African strategy is to be found. Perhaps the key framework in which to locate Du Bois's intellectual and literary contribution to Pan-African thought and in which to trace his contribution to modern diaspora literature lies in the complex set of political and aesthetic issues that go under the ethereal heading of Ethiopianism.

"Ethiopia Shall Stretch Forth Her Hands": Toward Pan-Africanism

> So long,
> So far away
> Is Africa.
> Not even memories alive
> Save those that history books create,
> Save those that songs
> Beat back into the blood— . . .
>
> Langston Hughes,
> "Afro-American Fragment"

Although it has received relatively little attention in interpretations of early modern African American literature and culture, Ethiopianism is of great importance to any interpretation of Pan-African culture, offering as it does an alternative perspective on the reductively imagistic representations of Africa common in the works of both the Harlem Renaissance and primitivist modernism, and yoking modern black thought to century-old African American expressions of a nationalist philosophy. George Shepperson has rightly remarked that Ethiopianism, though it had become by the mid-twentieth century little more than "a sentimental, nebulous symbol" that could no longer inspire nationalist dissent, once constituted a crucial factor in the rise of African independence movements as well as "a significant, if overlooked, section of the 'glory road' of American Negro history."[15] In the case of Du Bois, Ethiopianism has been understood for the most part strictly as a vague philosophical and poetic element in his thought, perhaps a clumsy key to the mysticism of *Darkwater* and other texts based on potent echoes of Edward Blyden or borrowings from contemporary work on ancient African history. But the narrower historical meaning of Ethiopianism associated with the rise of black independent churches in Africa has an equal place in any reconstruction of Du Bois's intellectual career, even though that relationship is oblique and its key elements scattered throughout diverse writings. Despite the fact that he is known to have corresponded or met with several African nationalists, discussed African revolts with Joseph Booth, a dissident American missionary whose protégé, John Chilembwe, would lead an abortive uprising in Nyasaland in 1915, and was obviously aware of similar stirrings of rebellion in other parts of Africa, Du Bois did not often introduce such events directly into his writing about Pan-Africanism. Moreover, he appears to have absorbed a good deal from others without leaving the fullest account of his tutelage. Du Bois's seemingly egotistical reluctance to give complete credit for the origins of some of his own ideas to early American Pan-Africanists such as Alexander Crummell, Edward Blyden, and Henry Turner obscures the fact that his secular nationalism remains rooted in Christian millennial concepts that have their strongest echo not in the African American church structure, which he largely ignored, except as a source of cultural and political stewardship in *The Souls of Black Folk* and in his Philadelphia and Atlanta sociological studies, but in the separatist African church movements and periodic messianic revolts against colonial rule that frequently depended on American philosophical or institutional connections.

Du Bois's intellectual development during the main phase of his writing career, beginning in the 1890s and reaching a crest in the early 1920s, was inspired by much the same ideology of protest and evinced the same messianic dimensions as the church-inspired independence movements in Africa. Just as the First World War was at the historical center of Ethiopianism, so for Du Bois it crystallized his view of race as a category defined, in the case of blacks, not by color or nationality but by the African diaspora and his apprehension of the parallels between the problem of liberating leadership in America and messianic independence movements in Africa. That Du Bois's protest took place in the secular theater of ideas and the columns of magazines, whereas Mgijima, John Chilembwe, Simon Kimbangu, and others who led African millennial revolts engaged in actual violence and based their rebellions on a specific dissenting reading of church doctrine, does not minimize what is to be gained by a consideration of the parallels, which both advance our understanding of Du Bois and enlarge our sense of how best to read American (not just African American) culture in the volatile post–World War I period. The prevalence of the Black Christ in the essays and poems that Du Bois wrote during and immediately after the war—a number of which went into *Darkwater* in 1920—suggests an internalization of the messianic vision and a psychological diversion of energy devoted to the struggle for equal rights, which he felt was achieving too little in the public arena. One can look to the rise of Ethiopianist ideas for a key to Du Bois's thought, then, not because direct models or influences are always readily available but instead because they provide a critical dimension to his prophetic self-conception, at a specific moment in American history, and a better context for reading his relationship with rival African American leaders.

The meaning of Ethiopianism is notoriously protean, but it may generally be regarded as a set of beliefs, derived in the classical instance from a reading of Psalms 68:31, "Princes shall come out of Egypt, [and] Ethiopia shall soon stretch forth her hands to God," that portrayed colonized Africa or enslaved Africans in the diaspora as prepared for providential delivery from bondage. In a more radical interpretation the scripture could be seen to prophesy a black millennium, a violent seizure of freedom through acts of revolt sanctioned by God and led, literally or figuratively, by a black redeemer from within Africa or, in some interpretations, from America. Although it is obscure and capable of withstanding many diverse interpretations, the psalm, as a triumphal song of David apparently referring to Israel's political situation, lodged between the great powers of Egypt and Assyria, rightly acquired a combined spiritual and political significance that was repeatedly summoned up by African and African American leaders from the 1890s through the 1920s. The magic of Ethiopia as a symbolic homeland (usually the portion of the scripture pertaining to Egypt was dropped) derived principally at the turn of the century from the idealized history of Ethiopia itself, a Christian state that had retained its sovereignty during the African scramble and achieved a surprising military victory over Italy in 1896. As Menelik, the emperor of Ethiopia, had put it in his 1889 rejection of Italian treaty claims, he was decended from an imperial dynasty that was three thousand years old, one that had never required outside assistance for its defense: "Ethiopia has never been conquered and she never shall be. . . . Ethiopia will stretch out her hand only to God." Ethiopia's exceptionalist history thus gave it the figurative status of an African Zion, which took on special significance in contemporary debates over the origins of world civilization and Ethiopia's legacy to Egypt and the Middle Eastern world. Based on the use of the term in the King James Bible, Ethiopianism referred generally to all Africans as "Ethiopian," or "black-skinned," as well as to the whole of sub-Saharan Africa as "Ethiopia." Additionally, the term was sometimes applied by non-Africans to blacks in the diaspora, whom Garvey, for example, regularly referred to as Ethiopians displaced or scattered from their homeland of Africa, even though most African Americans had no literal basis for tracing their ancestry to Ethiopia.[16] Likewise, one of the first American black nationalists, Robert Alexander Young, had entitled his quasi-mystical 1829 jeremiad against slavery and the denial of black rights "The Ethiopian Manifesto," and had addressed himself to the "whole of the Ethiopian people," a "most persecuted people" to whom God had promised, "I will stretch forth mine hand and gather them to the palm, that they become unto me a people." Throughout the nineteenth century, the text of the psalm was casually invoked by Douglass, Delany, and others; and it became a cornerstone of emigrationist thought and black historical writing about Egypt and Ethiopia, which African Americans then as later were determined to prove had been not just the founding civilizations of Western culture but had been *black* civilizations. Contemporary works such as Paul Laurence Dunbar's "Ode to Ethiopia" (1892) and Charles Henry Holmes's utopian novel *Ethiopia, the Land of Promise* (1917) addressed African Americans but envisioned a race pride defined by the diaspora and an ancient genealogy. As Rufus Perry asserted in *The Cushite, or the Descendants of Ham* (1893), contemporary blacks could take pride in the ancient Ethiopians and Egyptians and "cherish the hope of racial celebrity, when in the light of a Christian civilization, Ethiopia shall stretch out her hands unto God."[17]

Young's text indicates the strength of an ideal of African unity that lies within the concept of Ethiopianism, whether that strength took the form of calls for an actual emigration to Africa or an advocacy of Pan-African political solidarity among black peoples of different nationalities. Like Young, Alexander Crummell took Psalms 68:13 as his text in his 1853 sermon "Hope for Africa," but for Crummell, as for later ecclesiasticals, the message of the scripture was more complex. More than half a century before Garvey, he addressed himself to blacks "scattered through the world, as well as dwelling in their homes in Africa," but his sermon sought not just a proto–Pan-African consciousness but more specifically the missionary regeneration of Africa, "the benighted fatherland." As elsewhere in his thought, however, Crummell's intent here was to forecast, through the Christian salvation of Africa and the diaspora, a multination black rise to prominence as the next great civilization of the world. In such a teaching, an important forerunner to the Christian radicalism of early African independence movements, the seemingly submissive character of the scripture veered in a more militant direction.[18]

It is true that Alexander Crummell might, on the basis of his role in *The Souls of Black Folk*, be considered the "spiritual father" of Du Bois; but the influence of two other figures, Edward Blyden and Henry Turner, played a prominent role in his conception of Pan-African philosophy and an African American ideological aesthetic. Of any of them he might have said, as he did of Turner upon his death in 1915 (the same year Washington died and a year of signal importance in the development of Du Bois's thought), he was "the last of his clan: mighty men, physically and mentally, men who started at the bottom and hammered their way to the top by sheer brute strength." At the same time that he virtually refuses to name them, the ideas of Turner and Blyden appear throughout Du Bois's work, giving some secondary support to the charge later leveled by William Ferris and other Garveyites that Du Bois had borrowed—"plagiarized," they said—much of his knowledge of African and Afro–New World history from George Washington Williams and other black scholars of the late nineteenth century.[19] Perhaps it would be correct to say that Du Bois himself repressed a cluster of interrelated beliefs and events—the Ethiopianist roots of Pan-Africanism; the emigrationist-evangelist writings of Turner, Blyden, and Crummell; and the messianic nature of black leadership itself—while allowing them to appear in his most imaginative moments of literary creation. Du Bois's evident romanticism could then be understood to represent not so much a certain naiveté about Africa as, in a more positive formulation, an expression of his racialist aesthetic—that is, the preeminence of black "soul" as a property that he often defined in characteristic nineteenth-century racialist terms. More than that, however, Du Bois's romanticism would represent his subtle appropriation of the very essence of the separatist black nationalism that he appears intimately to have valued but was reluctant to accept forthrightly in his public life and scholarly writing. In this line of argument, Africa represented a source of spiritual and cultural value that could be used to counter both European colonialism and American racism, and Du Bois's relationship to the leading proponents of Ethiopianism, hardly common knowledge, is worth attention for the light it casts on his work and on the late nineteenth-century resurgence of interest in Afrocentric culture.

In its most powerful forms, like that enunciated by Edward Blyden, Ethiopian thought was a vehicle not so much for the revision of Western thought as its reversal. A West Indian Presbyterian missionary, who had once been denied admission to Rutgers Theological College because he was black, before being educated in Liberia under the auspices of the American Colonization Society, Blyden was a brilliant and prolific scholar who used his classical erudition to argue from the 1850s forward that African civilizations had once been great at a time when Europe was composed of barbarous tribes. This argument, repeated and extended by black historians and writers throughout the years leading up to Du Bois's own writings, laid the groundwork for his insistence that the Europeanization of Africa was a catastrophe. Blyden and others inverted the traditional reading of Genesis 9—the curse, said to be marked by his black skin, purportedly placed upon Ham by his father, Noah, which proslavery theologians had used to justify the enslavement of Africans—by arguing that the diaspora was an opportunity for the regeneration of Africa. In "Ethiopia Stretching Out Her Hands unto God; or, Africa's Service to the World," a discourse first delivered in the United States in 1880, Blyden interpreted the scripture in the first instance to refer to Africa's piety, kindness, and fidelity, and to its people's vast economic service to the world, like that of the Hebrews. But the passage also entailed, in this fact, that Africa had become an important "spiritual conservatory" against the materialism of the civilized world and that Africans throughout the diaspora had an inherited title to Africa. In America, Blyden argued, the black man is forced to "surrender his race integrity," whereas in Africa "his wings develop, and he soars into an atmosphere of exhaustless truth for him." Anticipating Du Bois's argument in "The Conservation of Races,"

Blyden too believed that each race had a unique "soul" embodied in its physiology and its institutions. Yoking together the primary symbol of African mystery—one that Du Bois would repeat in numerous variable contexts—and the primary nationalist slogan ("Africa for the Africans," apparently derived from Martin Delany's initial use of it in *Blake*), Blyden asserted that "the Sphinx must solve her own riddle at last. The opening up of Africa is to be the work of Africans."[20]

Advocating pride in "African Personality," a phrase he originated in 1893, Blyden had absorbed prevailing notions of physiological race distinctions while condemning the evolutionary hierarchy on which they were based, and moved toward a notion of racial integrity that was equivalent to racial purity. "Love of race," he argued, must overwhelm the spirit of integration with which the American Negro has been burdened; it "must be the central fire to heat all his energies" and drive "the great idea of a genuine race development." Blyden asserted that Islam and Christianity need not be antagonistic forces in the redemption of Africa, but he had also insisted in "Christianity and the Negro Race" (1876) that acceptance of Christianity did not require that the black man remain the white man's "ape," "imitator," and "parasite." Like Du Bois, Blyden admired Bismarck for his successful embodiment of the militant spirit of race pride. Like Garvey, however, and like the era's Anglo-Saxon race purists, whose opposing theories both men reacted against, he also conceived of racial integrity as a mode of resistance to the "suicide" of race mixing: "The great mass of the Race has not, thank God, been tampered with. . . . The contamination has affected only a few millions in the western hemisphere and a few thousands along the margin of the continent." In Blyden's conception, "African Personality" entailed a condemnation of both biological and cultural absorption of blacks by the dominant white race. It was just this strain in Blyden's thought that J. E. Casely Hayford featured in *Ethiopia Unbound* (1911) when he set Blyden's Africanist ideas against what he argued was the parochial and degrading assimilationist mentality of Du Bois: "The average Afro-American citizen of the United States has lost absolute touch with the past of his race, and is helplessly and hopelessly groping in the dark for affinities that are not natural, and for effects for which there are neither national nor natural causes. That being so, the African in America is in a worse plight than the Hebrew in Egypt. The one preserved his language, his manners and customs, his religion and household gods; the other has committed national suicide, and at present it seems as if the dry bones of the vision have no life in them." Blyden had counseled fellow Africans that reliance upon Europeans would "expose our institutions to the dangers and decay of mongrelism." Yet his notion that only blacks of pure blood (predominantly those of the southern Black Belt in the case of America, as he argued) could lead the regeneration of Africa was, in fact, largely contradicted by his call for African American emigration to the homeland.[21] His theory of racial purity would have found little sympathy in Du Bois's racial liberalism. Nevertheless, Du Bois may well have borrowed elements of his fluctuating concept of black "soul" from Blyden; and it seems more likely than not, I will contend, that the stinging critique administered by Casely Hayford, as well as the experimental literary form of *Ethiopia Unbound*—part novel, part documentary, and part polemic—had a noteworthy impact on the course of Du Bois's Pan-African theories in the years leading up to *Darkwater* and *Dark Princess*.

Blyden's thought, one might say, bifurcated between Du Bois and Garvey. So did Henry Turner's, but for a different reason. According to Turner, before Garvey the most fervent advocate of emigration, missionary work was a means both to redeem Africa and to cultivate a fatherland independent of white control. Turner had served as a chaplain during the Civil War and had briefly entered Georgia politics afterward before joining the African Methodist Episcopal (AME) church in 1880. Disillusioned by the failure of Reconstruction and the reactionary civil rights decisions of the Supreme Court, Turner underwent a shift toward a philosophy of Africanism that might be said to parallel, one generation earlier, Du Bois's own shift toward Pan-African socialism in the next century. After traveling to Africa for the first time in 1891, Turner became a strong advocate of emigration and in 1893 founded a journal, *Voice of Missions,* that provided a platform for his views on missionary and commercial involvement in Africa and plans for settlement there.[22] What is perhaps his most important address, "The American Negro and His Fatherland," was delivered at the missionary conference held at Gammon Theological Seminary in Atlanta in 1895. The Gammon conference brought together a number of distinguished African and American churchmen of various views, but most were united by a variously explicit belief in the nationalist doctrine of "Africa for the Africans." The entire conference, like Turner's own contribution, was especially significant for its critical reflection on Booker T. Washington's famous Atlanta Compromise address of two months earlier. Turner had been openly hostile to Washington's speech at the time, but at the Gammon conference he went much further, arguing that "there is no manhood future in the United States for the Negro," that mulattoes who passed for white were "unracing" themselves, and that enslavement and the diaspora constituted a providential opportunity for Africans to learn the gifts of white civilization. He countered this unsettling aspect of his argument (which was shared to a degree, at least rhetorically, by Washington) with a celebration of blackness and a plea for emigration to the African fatherland, where the black man, in his words, could "build up a nation of his own, and create a language in keeping with his color."[23]

Turner's Atlanta address, which anticipated Garvey's theory of "African Fundamentalism" by two decades, is one of many texts of the period that underline the relationship between Jewish Zionism and what was often referred to as Black or African Zionism. Not only was Garvey's emigrationist philosophy very much in the mold of Turner's, but his Ethiopianist argument was at times similarly providential, as in his invocation of Scripture in a speech reprinted in the *Negro World* that began: "We are going to build up in Africa a government of our own, big enough and strong enough to protect Africa and Negroes everywhere." Africa is our true homeland, Garvey argued here; although our forefathers brought to America as slaves did not know "what the consequences would be," God already "had his plan when he inspired the Psalmist to write: 'Princes shall come out of Egypt, and Ethiopia shall stretch forth her hand unto God.'"[24] In fact, arguments over America versus Africa as the rightful home of those blacks descended from slavery paralleled contemporary arguments among American Jews about whether America or Palestine should be the new Zion of Slavic and European immigrants. Extending a central analogy of antislavery rhetoric—the slaves' delivery from pharaonic bondage—Du Bois would write in 1919, for example, that "the African movement means to us what the Zionist movement must mean to the Jews, the centralization of the race effort and the recognition of a racial fount."[25]

Turner's and Garvey's Zionism, at least in principle, meant a return to the homeland, whereas for Du Bois the term was more a synonym for Pan-Africanism, a spiritual rather than a geographical idea—a "nation" that consisted primarily of a transhistorical consciousness outside of property or the literal black body. Constructing his own life as the autobiography of a "race concept," as he put it in the subtitle of *Dusk of Dawn,* Du Bois made the philosophy of Ethiopianism more powerful than the repatriation to a homeland espoused by Turner or Garvey. For him, "Ethiopia" was to become an uncolonized territory of the spirit, the black soul that had not been extinguished by slavery or colonial rule and that could never be fully assimilated to European American culture. In order to rebuild a shattered cultural memory and advance a claim to diasporic nationhood, Du Bois lived with the paradox that racialism—the claim for an essentially black "soul," "genius," or "gift"—was inevitably one foundation of political racism. His attempt to extend the notion of race unity to embrace the collective colored races of the world became increasingly problematic for theoretical as well as practical reasons, but the ambiguous concept of a racial fount captures well his idea of the role played by the diaspora in constructing the double consciousness of blacks in the New World.

Of equal importance in Turner's thought was his radical suggestion, one that again looked forward to Garvey as well as to later formulations by Malcolm X and the Nation of Islam, that blacks would forever be degraded in their faith so long as they worshipped a white God. "We have as much right biblically and otherwise to believe that God is a Negro," he wrote, "as you buckra, or white, people have to believe that God is a fine, symmetrical and ornamented white man." Turner's public assertion that God was black was mocked in the mainstream press of the United States churches and considered dangerous in South Africa, but he defended his point by combining historical and linguistic evidence with spiritual intention in arguing that "black was here before white" and that in his "personality" God was a Negro.[26] Henry Turner's importance, however, lay not simply in his formulation of a doctrine of emigration or an early philosophy of negritude but also in the instrumental role he played in the practical exchange of African and American ideas about Pan-Africanism. The alliance that he helped to establish between the AME church and the Ethiopian church of South Africa was for him a natural step in the process of emigration and reunification of black peoples that he envisioned. His condemnation of black American prospects and his insistence that God was black flowed together in his contribution to a theory of Ethiopianism broadly conceived; but his work in Africa offers a fine lens on the strand of Ethiopianism that became a political force in African anticolonialism. And it is here that one finds a peculiar but pressing confirmation of Du Bois's own messianic construction of an African American cultural-political foundation.

In its narrower historical sense Ethiopianism describes the independent church movement within South Africa that originated as early as the 1870s but took institutional form in the establishment of a separatist Tembu Nationalist church by the Wesleyan Nehemiah Tile in 1884 and more particularly the founding of the Ethiopian church by Mangena Mokone in 1892. Disconcerted by racial segregation within the Wesleyan church, Mokone established a dissenting church that derived its name from Psalms 68:31 and forecast the evangelization of Africa by African leaders. The mechanism for Mokone's eventual alliance with Turner is of special note. In the aftermath of an 1890 tour in South Africa by the Virginia Jubilee Singers, an African choir was organized to visit the United States. When the choir was stranded by financial misfortune in Ohio in 1895, several of its members, including Charlotte Mayne, were helped to enroll in Wilberforce University, the AME school where Du Bois taught in his first professional position, from August 1894 through spring 1896. Wilberforce was dominated by Turner's evangelization spirit, as Du Bois quickly discovered, and it was Charlotte Mayne, who, by means of a letter to her family in South Africa, provided the initiative for the affiliation between Mokone's Ethiopian church and the AME church.* Mokone's church sought formal ties with the American church through the visit of James Dwane to the United States in 1896, a union achieved in 1898 during Turner's visit to South Africa. Within the next twenty years an array of separatist churches, many of them loosely tied to American denominations or leaders, was established in South Africa.[27]

Because most such connections were tenuous, it is difficult to trace causal relations between American church groups and African independence movements. Nor were the visionary plans of a Henry Turner shared by all black African churchmen, many of whom feared yet another brand of colonial interference, or by all black Americans. Booker T. Washington, though he never visited Africa, promoted his philosophy through various educational and agricultural institutions in Togo, Sudan, South Africa, and the Congo Free State, all of them working in cooperation with colonial authorities and taking their direction from Washington's denun-

---

* Du Bois's autobiographies offer only the merest sketch of his year at Wilberforce; the focus is on his courtship of Nina Gormer and his distaste for the religious atmosphere and insider church politics of the campus (and a later short essay on Wilberforce in *Crisis* focuses on the problems of the school's finances). In 1930, however, Du Bois contributed an introduction to a biographical study of Charlotte Mayne, in which he noted her friendship with Nina Gormer and praised her as a race leader. This seems but one indication that Du Bois was more than superficially affected by the well-publicized relationship between the churches and by writings about Ethiopianism appearing in Turner's organ, *The Voice of Missions*. See Du Bois, foreword to Alfred Xuma, *Charlotte Mayne: "What an Educated African Girl Can Do"* (n.p.: Women's Parent Mite Missionary Society of the AME Church, 1930).

ciation of missionary subversion of colonial rule. (Despite what seem his characteristically conservative views, Washington engaged in a friendly correspondence with various African nationalist leaders, and several of them spoke warmly of his leadership and influence.)[28] In its own right American evangelization of black Africa, needless to say, was somewhat paradoxical. Assumptions that Africa was savage and heathen, given to devil worship and barbarous rites, were widespread among both black and white Americans, as well as westernized Africans. Charlotte Mayne, for instance, wrote in a Wilberforce essay that she wished more Africans might study at the school and then return to "teach our people so that our home may soon lose that awful name, 'the Dark Continent,' and be properly called the continent of light." Even when their participants were split over the theological meaning of color or the necessity of nationalist churches in Africa, and even though they produced a scattering of documents critical of colonial domination, events such as the Gammon Theological Conference, where Turner made his famous speech in 1895, the Congress on Africa at the Columbian Exposition of 1893, or the Ecumenical Conference on Foreign Missions in New York in 1900 were generally united in their view of African depravity and thus inevitably cast Christian missions in a peculiar ideological role.[29] With a most slippery logic, the black American Baptist missionary Charles Morris, a counterpart to Turner who facilitated the union of the African Native church with the National Baptist Convention, argued in 1900 that God had planned the evangelization of Africa by submitting the "naked savages" of Africa to American slavery—whereby they were "redeemed, regenerated, [and] disenthralled"—and then calling them "to go with the [Christian] message to South Africa and to the rest of Africa and vindicate American slavery as far as it can be vindicated by taking across the ocean the stream of life." Americans, moreover, might well be disillusioned by African realities, whether native or colonial. For example, although it created a formal bond between the AME church and the Ethiopian church and accelerated educational exchange between blacks on the two continents, Turner's visit to South Africa convinced him that white control was so well established that black nationalists would have to seek their own state in Liberia or Central Africa.[30]

Even so, such black "manifest destiny," as Shepperson calls it, cannot be discounted. Some Africans entirely misconceived the state of race relations in the United States, assuming that blacks were the great majority of the population and idealizing the kind of education open to blacks in America. Both this stereotype and those held by Americans, who often believed Africans to be unredeemed savages, were put to rest by the missionary ties. Colonial and institutional (white) church reaction also was often exaggerated—but for just that reason it is a good barometer of what the Ethiopian churches symbolically represented and how their programs might provide the basis for a legitimate diasporic political philosophy. As an article in *Missionary Review of the World* pointed out in 1904, the antiwhite character of the Ethiopianist movement would only be stimulated by "the appearance of the American negro [fresh] from the bitter scenes enacted in the Southern States," for the "native possessed of this genius [for intrigue] and already estranged from the European in religion, is but a step removed from organized resistance in matters social and political."[31] Not only did Henry Turner and Charles Morris envision the founding of a Pan-African *black* church, but the increasingly strong elements of "nationalist"—that is, native or tribal—resistance to white rule gave the Ethiopian churches and similar radical offshoots of mission activity a direction that had little in common with ruling imperial institutions, even when they had themselves been nurtured in such institutions.

As an overarching nationalist philosophy and as a product of the anticolonial dissent of black African churches and their radical leaders, to whom I will return, Ethiopianism therefore forms the critical bond between America and Africa in the decades around the turn of the century. Its fragmentary, widely diffused historical sources are reflected in the equally diffuse literary structures in which Du Bois chose to work. Before we return to a more detailed consideration of Du Bois's response to black church independence movements and their Ethiopianist politics, however, it is important to examine other origins of the race theory that lay at the heart of his Pan-African philosophy.

Africa: The Hidden Self and the Pageant of Nationalism

The figurative portraits of Ethiopia the Shadowy and Egypt the Sphinx that Du Bois added to his revised discussion of double consciousness in *The Souls of Black Folk* represented a deeper dimension of life within the Veil that would soon exfoliate in his work. As the Black Belt of the United States became more and more comprehensively linked to the Black Belt of the world in Du Bois's mind, race became an increasingly mobile concept. The concept of racial "gifts" and "strivings" that had preserved his tenuous hold on an essentialist theory of race was placed under growing stress and yet at times paradoxically became more pronounced. From one perspective it would be accurate to say that Du Bois's definitions of race hardly changed from the 1890s through the end of his life; race was simply more and more subordinated to economics. Yet two features of his thought, the African diaspora and an increased focus on a wider "colored" world, moved him toward a specifically cultural or historical definition of race at the same time that he clung in some of his work to an ever more mystic racialism. By the time he published *The Negro* in 1915, Du Bois could say more forthrightly that race was "dynamic" and that races were "continually changing and developing, amalgamating and differentiating." His concern, therefore, was with what he could only refer to as "the darker part of the human family, which is separated from the rest of mankind by no absolute physical line and no definite mental characteristics, but which nevertheless forms, as a mass, a series of social groups more or less distinct in history, appearance, and in cultural gift and accomplishment." Because the concept of the Negro itself was far from stable, Africa, as a continent but also as a geosocial entity that had produced the "family" to which Du Bois belonged, was defined by him as "the Land of the Blacks"—his capitalizations representing the kind of allegorical domain into which his thinking about race was continually pushed.[32]

The problem of where race was to be located, as much as the rise of invidious sciences of race, led to Du Bois's volksgeistian definitions of race as spiritually differentiated families or "folks" infused with a common purpose or idea, to cite the German formulation he had clearly appropriated. What mattered was not a satisfactory definition of race (Du Bois seemed comfortable with the uncertainty) but rather a language with which to articulate this particular and more difficult "double consciousness," namely, the fact that "Negro" meant nothing that could be measured yet represented a clearly definable historical experience. The Universal Races Congress held in London in 1911 gave a very broad account of the collective view, as Du Bois summarized it in *Crisis,* that "so far at least as intellectual and moral aptitudes are concerned, we ought to speak of civilizations where we now speak of races," and that even differing physical characteristics are signs predominantly of environment.[33] The papers of the congress actually showed a wider range of opinions than Du Bois's essay (or his more detailed later summary) suggests. Yet by 1911 Du Bois himself had come close to reading race only as civilization or culture, and he increasingly transfigured his central tropes, the soul and the veil, into expressions of labor, artisanship, geography, or sociopolitical life. As Du Bois's thought evolved, the mystic import of the concepts of veil and soul did not diminish but, like race itself, acquired a more vital Pan-African shape. For Du Bois, one could say, race both constituted a veil and remained hidden behind one.

A common figure throughout African American writing, the important metaphor of the veil has a variety of meanings in Du Bois's work, all of them comprehended by his repeated phrase "within the Veil." In *The Souls of Black Folk* alone it is used as a marker separating whites and blacks, a sign of legal and social segregation; as a figure for the obscurity or ignorance on the part of whites behind which the majority of blacks live, as in the case of the southern Black Belt explored at length by Du Bois; and as the symbol of mystic vision—the Negro as "a seventh son, born with a veil, and gifted with second-sight in this American world." Like the concept of race itself, the figure of the veil floats in Du Bois's work, but its supernatural dimensions are directly connected to the issue of messianic leadership. For the prophetic element in his poetry of the veil includes not just the spirit or soul so dramatically expressed in the sorrow songs, the promise of deliverance from bondage, but also the promise of reunion with an African ancestral spirit that could be achieved by a "modern lifting of the veil" that has long covered Africa.[34]

To uncover that ancestral spirit and to make the achievements of African civilization known would do more than augment race pride. It would also counter the white racist view exemplified by William B. Smith in *The Color Line: A Brief for the Unborn* that because civilization is "the slow and toilsome growth of centuries, an unfolding of the people's spirit itself," blacks could put it on "only as an outer garment; it can never become truly theirs, the efflorescence of their own souls." Unlike Garvey, who courted racist doctrine in order to generate belief in his version of black separatism, the pluralist Du Bois flatly rejected such a view. His uninhibited biculturalism did not, however, prevent him from arguing that Africans and African Americans, quite apart from their necessary internalization of different aspects of European culture, had unfolded their own transhistorical civilization, their own efflorescence of soul. For Garvey, who echoed the theories of "mongrelization" advanced by Blyden, Du Bois's status as a "mulatto" would become symbolic of his treason against "pure" black civilization.[35] For Du Bois, on the contrary, race mixing no more destroyed black soul than did enslavement or colonial rule. Both physiology and politics were fluid states that bore on a people's culture and self-definition, perhaps limiting their freedom and keeping them in a condition of perpetual resistance; but neither blood nor hegemony constituted civilization, and Du Bois's appeal to Africa everywhere countered the two modes of racism he considered destructive of true African American recognition.

Black revisionist writing in Du Bois's era worked on several fronts at once. It had to counter middle-class black reluctance to value anything associated with Africa, an extension of the corresponding post-Reconstruction desire to forget the history of enslavement. In addition, it had to counter two aspects of racist historiography. Du Bois's book *The Negro* joined a number of others that refuted the argument that whatever greatness had been achieved in African civilization came from outside influences or the infusion of non-Negro blood. From the perspective of American race relations, moreover, the restoration of the significance of African civilizations was a necessary counter to the racism and stereotypes of plantation mythology, to ethnological doubts about the value (or the very existence) of African cultural retentions, and to influential social theory, especially prevalent in academic writing about slavery and Reconstruction, which predicted not the advance but the regression of African American culture. At the same time, however, no univocal argument for or against African retentions could be advanced on moral or political grounds alone. Not just the popular press but the majority of academic historians depicted slavery as a benign, if not beneficent, institution that had rescued blacks from superstition and savagery; and they agreed with Ulrich Phillips's statement that black Americans were thus "as completely broken from their tribal stems as if they had been brought from the planet Mars." Others, such as Philip Bruce and Paul Barringer, argued conversely that the original "race spirit" of the Africans had *not* been modified by transplantation to America, and that the result was cowardice, sexual dissipation, criminality, superstition, and a lack of rational control among blacks; or, like Joseph Tillinghast, asserted that the strain of competing with white civilization drove blacks to seek their own separate society (race violence and segregation laws did not much enter into Tillinghast's theory) and slowly to revert to African "barbarism." Although he was quite critical of Tillinghast's central thesis and his command of relevant research, and although he remained lukewarm toward the theory of "tribal" influences, Du Bois in a review of *The Negro in Africa and America* complimented Tillinghast for at least understanding that black life in America had to be studied in connection to its African origins. Of *The Color Line* by William Smith, Du Bois concluded straightforwardly that it was "a naked, un-

ashamed shriek for the survival of the white race by means of the annihilation of all other races."[36]

The black refutation of racist theory required restructuring prevailing
beliefs about African civilization and providing a more credible theory
than Henry Turner's view that slavery was a providential step in the
regeneration of Africa. Such efforts, however, were hardly new at the turn
of the century. Arguments about the priority of black African civilizations
dated in the United States from the first colonizationist movement in the
early nineteenth century, and over the subsequent decades Henry Highland
Garnet, James W. C. Pennington, Frederick Douglass, and Martin Delany
among others appealed to the writings of Homer, Herodotus, and other
classical writers to argue that Egypt and Ethiopia had been great and
progressive civilizations—and that they had been Negro. A number of the
significant black historical and sociological works on Africa and African
America in the late nineteenth and early twentieth centuries—among them
George Washington Williams's *History of the Negro Race in America* (1883),
William T. Alexander's *History of the Colored Race in America* (1887),
C. T. Walker's *Appeal to Caesar* (1900), Pauline Hopkins's *Primer of Facts
Pertaining to the Early Greatness of the African Race* (1905), Booker T.
Washington's *Story of the Negro* (1909), William Ferris's *African Abroad*
(1911), and Du Bois's own *The Negro* (1915)—eloquently refuted the regnant
white argument, summarized by John T. Morgan, that Africans "have not
contributed a thought, or a labor, except by compulsion, to aid the progress of civilization." The tradition of black history writing that stood
behind Du Bois's Pan-African work was occasionally grandiloquent or
mistaken in its claims, but it provided its audience three things: a strong
counterargument to the more insidious racist assumptions of evolutionary
theory and neo-Confederate historiography; a source of communal pride
at a moment when African American rights were under the greatest assault
since slavery; and a reservoir of ideas to spur new conceptualizations of
race consciousness.[37]

African American history writing drew on the mostly unexamined social
and political life of Africa and in turn gave inspiration to some Ethiopianist
and nationalist movements in Africa itself. More important than the minor
alarm of colonial authorities over the intrusion of American ideas were
the analogies to be found in both African and African American expressions of nationalist consciousness. The achievement of freedom in both
instances entailed the (re)creation of a separate but not segregated culture,

and a revival of the capacity to throw off demeaning beliefs and imprisoning models of behavior. As nationalists such as the West African Attoh Ahuma argued, the *imperium in imperio* of colonial rule stripped black Africans of their "consciousness" and left them "clever imitator[s] of everything the Whiteman thinks." Black America's position within the "empire" of white rule was different in geographical respects, but in this case, too, it could be said, Western thought and racial prejudice had left African American "national life" and "mental machinery" enervated and paralyzed. Invoking Emerson, as Du Bois might also have done, Ahuma remarked: *"Thinking is the most difficult thing in life. . . .* As a people, we have ceased to be a THINKING NATION."[38] Like the chapters of *The Souls of Black Folk* devoted to the necessary role of higher education in African American liberation, Du Bois's Pan-African advocacy entailed not a renunciation of Western thought in its own right but a casting off of its fetters.

To become thinking nations, Africans had to overthrow colonial rule, even if, as in the case of the Ethiopianist churches, they employed the instruments of white culture to do so. Because participation in American life was denied them on so many fronts, African Americans had also to recover a sense of African national life in order to be a "thinking nation." Or, as Garvey would write in 1934: "If I had the power of a Divine Magician, I would reach into the mind of every Negro and stir him to individual and collective action: yes, I would set him to restore the Empire of the glorious Ethiopians." The rise of interest in back-to-Africa movements, which flourished briefly around Henry Turner and others well in advance of Garvey's more magnetic appeal, was less a sign of black capitulation to racism than of black discovery of African worth and the desire for political power. Like the populist repatriation movements, the advent of Africa as a historical subject coincided with the decline of black civil rights and the acceleration of segregation in the 1890s, but it had the further consequence of creating a stronger imaginative space for consciousness of Africa in America. From this perspective Du Bois's central contribution was not his historical research on Africa, which was based on secondary sources, including George Washington Williams and William Ferris, as well as standard nineteenth-century accounts by colonial explorers and administrators.[39] Instead, his principal breakthrough lay in the argument, advanced in *The Negro* and elaborated more impressively in his creative work, that Africa was literally at the center of the triumph of a modern industrial economy. The crisis of the world war gave Du Bois the great hook on which to hang his thesis that the world's color line problem was epitomized by Africa, which as the result of the imperial scramble of the nineteenth century had now become, in his view, the turning point for world conflagration and the inevitable collapse of colonial rule and its racial assumptions. Returning to Africa or participating in its political liberation depended first upon *thinking* clearly about Africa's centrality to the Western world order and recovering a belief in the value of black nationhood, the legitimacy of "African Personality."

The back-to-Africa movements that grew up in the 1890s were spurred in part by increased calls for colonization by southern racist ideologues and in part by the alienation felt by the black generations born outside of slavery and living increasingly in urban areas where social and economic problems were most acute. Although they remained practically ineffective (and of no interest to Du Bois), back-to-Africa schemes, especially when motivated by the clearly articulated philosophy of a Turner or a Garvey, remained of special rhetorical importance as a means to channel resistance and leap over the painful history of enslavement.[40] They also provided a vehicle for some of the most compelling revivals of the Africanist roots of black American life. For example, in Pauline Hopkins's remarkable magazine novel *Of One Blood* (1903), which appeared in the same year as *The Souls of Black Folk* and looks forward to certain elements of Du Bois's mystic historicism in *Darkwater* and *Dark Princess,* contemporary interest in the mystical dimensions of the mind is fused with a supernatural return to African ancestral life by means of voodoo and actual emigration. In Hopkins's syncretic conception, the race leader—her hero is not unlike Du Bois himself, who had already appeared in vague fictional form in Hopkins's major novel, *Contending Forces* (1900)—is distinctly assimilated and bourgeois (and "white"). At the same time, he is infused with the racial survivals of ancient Africa, and his career leads him back into a mystical transhistorical dimension where he can assume his rightful place in the lineage of deified Ethiopian kings. To go "back to Africa" in Hopkins's patently escapist fiction meant to flee the brutality and racism of American history in favor of a lost history of great wealth, material achievement, and intellectual superiority. Like the prizewinning oration given at Columbia University by the Zulu student P. Ka Isaka Seme in 1906, which linked the "regeneration of Africa" to the modern world's recognition of the brilliance of its ancient past, Hopkins's novel lifts or rends the obfuscating veil that covers Africa in contemporary opinion in order to take her readers spiritually back to Africa.[41] The relevance of her allegory of recovered Pan-African nationhood to the transgeographical, transhistorical notion of black soul that Du Bois was to develop is especially striking.

Hopkins's novel is an awkward but beautiful compression of popular metaphysics, black history (much of it borrowed from sources such as William Wells Brown's 1874 volume *The Rising Son; Or, the Antecedents and Advancement of the Colored Race*), and contemporary psychology. Its plot, a signifying inversion of the colonial adventure story widely popular in the work of H. Rider Haggard and others, is the merest occasion for an incisive critique of white racial theory and American ignorance of African history. What her protagonist, Reuel Briggs, finds in his journey back to Africa is not so much a geographic locale and a material history as a spiritual dimension of contemporary life, an African temporal frame that, like the glorious Ethiopian city of Meroe he rediscovers, is at once buried deep in history and at the same time coexistent with the melodrama of his current life in Jim Crow America. The novel thus functions as a combined critique of plantation mythology and treatise on African repatriation philosophy. A physician specializing in mesmeric states of suspension and theories of double consciousness, Briggs is a concatenation of Pan-African philosophical vectors. In his realization that he is the descendant of the great Ethiopian kings (and truly named Ergamenes), Briggs exhumes what he at one point refers to as "the undiscovered country within ourselves—the hidden self lying quiescent in every human soul." Such a "country" is both a figurative region—an unconscious reservoir of ideas, as the novel elaborates it—and the actual territory of Africa, which in turn is conflated by Hopkins into a "self" hidden from present consciousness. Because the "hidden self" of Africa is both known and unknown to those whose mental lives are fed by its ancestry, the action of Hopkins's novel must tear away the veil of slave genealogy to reveal an African genealogy worthy of pride and study.[42]

Hopkins borrowed the notion of the "hidden self" (as well as the title of, and passages from, the book, *The Unclassified Residuum,* that Briggs is reading at the outset of the novel) from William James's essay "The Hidden Self," which first appeared in *Scribner's Magazine* in 1890 and was incorporated into "What Psychological Research Has Accomplished" for inclusion in *The Will to Believe* in 1897. James's essay was in good part a summary of theories of double and multiple consciousness recently advanced by Alfred Binet, the French author of *On Double Consciousness* and other works on multiple personality translated by the late 1890s, who is mentioned by Hopkins and whose central theory posited an unconscious portion of the mental self, a "hidden personality," that was unknown but nonetheless watchfully participating in mental life. Likewise, James's pre-Freudian essay speculates about the influence of a "buried" or subconscious self, which he associates with the feminine mystical mind evidenced in case studies of hysterics. Just as hypnosis might bring forth the "fully conscious" double self in the hysteric, James hypothesizes that every consciousness might contain such layers of selves, each with an extensive set of memories unavailable to the other (or others) but nonetheless influencing the behavior of the antagonistic or double self.[43] For James as well as for Binet, the existence of double or multiple selves opened the possibility that hypnotic or mesmeric states could function as a means of telepathic communication into the "other" world of the hidden self and its experiences; because one body "may be the home of many consciousnesses," as James put it in another essay, "the margins and outskirts of what we take to be our personality extend into unknown regions." Given that James was one of Du Bois's most influential teachers at Harvard—Du Bois later recalled him as a "friend and guide to clear thinking"—it can hardly be doubted that James's theories of psychology, so amenable to Du Bois's own complex notion of double consciousness, were as important to the young scholar as his views on moral philosophy. For both Hopkins and Du Bois, James provided the key to a theory of diasporic consciousness that was capable of yoking together the conception of a split-off, perhaps hidden but in any case cuturally oppositional "personality" and the conceptions of race nationalism comprised by the ideological watchword "African Personality."[44]

The remembrance or reinvention of the "shadow of a mighty Negro past" that Du Bois made central to his own theory of double consciousness in *The Souls of Black Folk* provides for Hopkins's protagonist a way out of the bondage not just of racism but of blood itself. *Of One Blood* is a novel of passing and miscegenation as well as a novel of African return; its deliberately paradoxical title allows Hopkins first to invoke a monogenetic argument (because all races are descended from a common ancestry, all are equal) but at the same time to trace the black strand of Briggs's mixed blood to Ethiopian royalty.* Hopkins's deployment of black blood is thus

---

* The more common interpretation of the scriptural passage from which Hopkins drew her title (Acts 17:26) would be adopted by Du Bois in the opening of his 1904 "Credo," a homiletic statement later reprinted as the opening of *Darkwater* that became so popular as to be reprinted on posters that hung in a number of black American homes. But his second paragraph also

a counter to prevailing racist physiology and an inversion of one-drop legal ideology. Her proto-Faulknerian miscegenation plot allows Briggs's fiancée, Dianthe, a beautiful Fisk Jubilee Singer who turns out to be his half-sister, to be replaced by a more appropriate mate, the virgin queen Candace (a "Venus in bronze," as Hopkins calls her, in what may be a less than nationalistic description), one of the historical line of great Ethiopian queens who periodically ruled Meroe during its ascendancy. Sheared away in his return to African kingship, Briggs's white blood and skin, associated with slavery, incest, cruelty, and betrayal, are subordinated to his black lineage. In Africa, perhaps, he will escape the "mongrelization" that Blyden thought destructive of African purity in the United States. At the same time, the suggestion that Dianthe and Candace are part of the same "personality" or "soul" that lives beyond the confines of the physical body and its death empties consanguity of any threat in the novel. The white rape of black women, which Hopkins here and elsewhere makes the historical primal scene of slavery's moral catastrophe, generates not regression and racial decay but nationalist triumph. The melodramatic story of intrigue, a wooden incest and miscegenation plot in which the love of Reuel and Dianthe is doomed by the machinations of the villain who also turns out to be their brother, has always running within it the Africanist plot signified by her entranced state and the clairvoyant power of her voice when she sings "Go Down, Moses" and other spirituals. Dr. Briggs's revival of Dianthe from a seeming state of death early in the novel is simply a prefiguration of the reanimation that he (and perhaps Dianthe, if we are to take her "reincarnation" as Candace seriously) undergoes in the novel's Ethiopianist transfiguration.[45]

In her state of suspended animation, Dianthe exists "behind the Veil," as Hopkins writes, and her haunted singing voice is also "veiled"; likewise,

---

implied the validity of the racialist interpretation, a double consciousness of blood genesis in keeping with his ambivalence in "The Conservation of Races": "I believe in God who made of one blood all races that dwell on earth. I believe that all men, black and brown and white, are brothers, varying through Time and Opportunity, in form and gift and feature, but differing in no essential particular, and alike in soul and in the possibility of infinite development. Especially do I believe in the Negro Race: in the beauty of its genius, the sweetness of its soul and its strength in that meekness which shall yet inherit this turbulent earth." Du Bois, of course, could not claim any kind of blood purity but identified himself in *Darkwater* as the issue of "a flood of Negro blood, a strain of French, a bit of Dutch, but, thank God! no 'Anglo-Saxon.'" W. E. B. Du Bois, *Darkwater: Voices from within the Veil* (1920; rpt. New York: Schocken Books, 1969), pp. 3, 9; see also Du Bois, *Writings by W. E. B. Du Bois in Periodicals Edited by Others,* ed. Herbert Aptheker, 3 vols. (Millwood, N.Y.: Kraus-Thomson, 1982), I, 229.

Reuel's researches into the psychic unknown are attempts to "rend the veil" that covers the unknown territory of the hidden self.[46] If there are elements in the novel that link its plot to literal back-to-Africa movements (in his guise of Ergamenes, Briggs, following Henry Turner, announces that he intends to teach redemptive belief in Jesus Christ), it is the conception of Africanity that is most important in the book. Whether or not Hopkins borrowed her mystic idea of "personality" from the psychological tradition of James or from the Pan-African ideology of Blyden, it represented an amalgam of the two forces. Reuel's Ethiopian teacher, Ai, invokes Psalms 68:31 to forecast a tide of African American repatriation. But Hopkins, who could not have expected any such return on a significant scale, instead made the Ethiopian scripture a figure for the discovery of hidden territory within the black American psyche. Dianthe's spirituals, as well as her ultimate return to the cabin of her grandmother, Aunt Hannah, an old woman of the slave generation skilled in voodoo, are conduits to that hidden part of the self (in this detail and others Hopkins's novel looks ahead to Du Bois's *Dark Princess*). Mystified by occultism and paranormal psychological states, the hidden African self literalized in the melodramatic plot of the novel is buried all around us, Hopkins argues, latent in the rich ancestral retentions of African American culture. *The Colored American Magazine*, where *Of One Blood* was serialized beginning in 1902, also ran a concurrent set of articles on "Contemporary Ethiopians"—that is, black Americans who had achieved significant success in various fields—and one can be certain that Hopkins's intent was less to promote back-to-Africa philosophy than to draw from it a popularized basis for pride in black history and, more important, a theoretically complex way to understand African American double consciousness. Africanity, according to *Of One Blood,* can be awakened in the individual psyche, just as it can be awakened in the political dimension of national consciousness: it exists "behind the Veil" of racist historiography and evolutionary social theory, but also behind the veil of ignorance about their African past, in some cases even their slave past, that has fallen on the present generation. Hopkins placed in one concentrated allegorical form a virtual catalogue of the Pan-African ideas that Du Bois would develop as he extrapolated, from the foundation set down in *The Souls of Black Folk,* a theory of Africa's psychological and cultural importance to black America's life behind, and within, the veil of color.

For Du Bois no less than Hopkins, the veil is alternately a simple and intricate trope. He may have alluded obliquely to Thomas Jefferson's well-known reference in *Notes on the State of Virginia* to "that immovable veil of blackness which covers all the emotions of the [black] race,"[47] but his usage was of course far more in keeping with the veil's complexity in *Of One Blood*. Like the "color line," which was finally less a linear than a spatial trope for Du Bois, the veil was a metaphor with different degrees of temporal and spatial dimensionality. At once a sign of segregation and a vehicle of spirituality, the veil designated a liminal domain—a historical imaginative space in which the state of "middle passage" between worlds, as from the shores of Africa to the New World, was continual and in which African American culture came into being and flourished. Within the veil the double actions of recovery and prophecy together formed the messianic "gift" of second sight that Du Bois claimed as his own. The prophetic element in Du Bois's figure of the veil includes both the spirit or soul exemplified in the sorrow songs, the promise of deliverance, and the promise of reunion with an African ancestral spirit or "personality." Coincident with his greater prophetic voice, Du Bois's conception of Africa, even as it acted as a pivot in his materialist analysis of the world economic order, paradoxically functioned more and more transcendentally, becoming the eschatological icon for a liberating consciousness still waiting to be awakened.

As this description of the trope of the veil indicates, nationalism and spiritualism converge in Du Bois's aesthetic, much as they did in that of William Butler Yeats at about the same time; and strong parallels may be found between Du Bois's thought and both Zionism and Irish nationalism, from both of which he, like many other African and African American intellectuals, frequently drew political analogies. From the American perspective, in fact, Pan-African philosophy unified the two comparable but dissimilar nationalist drives—to recover a lost homeland and to win freedom from political oppression. As I have already indicated, the longstanding identification in the African American imagination between the pharaonic bondage of the Israelites and American slavery made Zionism a continual reference point in the black American tradition from the beginnings of bondage, but one that took on greater urgency with the rise of agitation for a Jewish homeland in Palestine at the end of the nineteenth century. Beginning with Blyden, who wrote admiringly of Theodore Herzl's landmark work *Der Judenstaat* (1896) and its implications for the African diaspora, numerous modern black writers identified the Pan-African cause with Jewish nationalism. Without adopting the repatriation schemes and more radical racialist philosophy of Garvey's Negro Zionism or Black Zionism, as it was variously called, Du Bois found in Zionism a philosophy compatible with his own double consciousness.[48] Like the best-known American Zionist, Louis Brandeis, who saw no contradiction between American patriotism and Jewish political Zionism (and who, like Du Bois, espoused a belief in ideological uplift by the cultured elite), Du Bois at this point in his career considered Africa a homeland for Africans and for those African Americans who might choose to settle there; but Pan-Africa itself he identified with the diaspora.[49] Just as Herzl had stressed that the Jewish question was carried with Jews everywhere and that Zionism exceeded any geographical stricture, so for Du Bois Pan-Africanism demanded allegiance to the political philosophy of Africa for Africans, but it transcended the particularity of African nations.

Even though he would later denounce Garvey by comparing his Universal Negro Improvement Association (UNIA) strategies to those of the Irish radical group Sinn Fein, Du Bois (like Garvey) wrote in support of the Irish Republican uprising of 1916. Du Bois did not go as far as Casely Hayford, who advocated the formation in the United States of "Ethiopian Leagues," comparable to the Gaelic League in Ireland, for promoting the study of Fanti, Yoruba, Hausa, and other African languages for American use, but his recourse to Irish nationalism is nonetheless instructive on several levels. Not only are there various parallels to be found in their work, but Du Bois and Yeats might be said to occupy similar respective positions within the Irish and the New Negro renaissances, both of which depended in part on the construction of national mythologies based on ancient sources and on the identification of models of heroic leadership. For both, the revolutionary potential of a militant Christ or an Easter political rising would be used to exemplify the rebirth of a nationalist culture and its release from "colonial" oppression. Garvey's invocation of parallels between his movement and that of the Irish Republicans was more overt (for instance, the UNIA's Liberty Hall in Harlem echoed Dublin's Liberty Hall, the seat of the Irish revolution), but Du Bois's writings and his advocacy of an African culture make him, like Yeats, the central figure.[50] More than a decade before Alain Locke in *The New Negro* and Claude McKay in *Banjo* invoked Irish nationalism as a model for the African American nationalism of the New Negro, Du Bois had written poetry close in figuration and in spirit, if not in execution, to that of Yeats, and he had constructed the most important statements of nationalist theory to date—without himself being a thoroughgoing nationalist at all. Because a full portrait of his thesis has to be assembled piecemeal, it is appropriate that its most coherent version appeared in the strange generic mélange *Darkwater,* a work that, like *The Souls of Black Folk* before it, gathered together several previously published essays and joined them to other new work, driving the whole through a furnace of Pan-African oratory and mystic cultural poetics. Subtitled *Voices from within the Veil,* the book appeared in 1920, at the height of Garvey's early influence and public attention, and it may be that Du Bois's more militant tone was both a culmination of his own thought and a response to Garvey's rise.

Darkwater is a compelling instance of political art, similar in scope and intention to *Ethiopia Unbound,* as I will suggest, and to Yeats's nationalist mythology. Like Yeats, Du Bois merged the ideological and the spiritual in the trope of the veil. In addition, Du Bois owed a significant debt to Germanic thought, from which he took not just his appreciation for the philosophy of history but also a good deal of scholarly interest in Africa and the history of world civilizations. But it was also a debt that left his historical analysis, more so than Yeats's, acutely vulnerable to the latent fascism of race mysticism and politicized race theory. Although Du Bois's inclination toward nationalistic leadership may have been spurred on by the romantic nationalism espoused by his Berlin professor Heinrich von Treischke (the "fire-eating Pan-German," as Du Bois later called him, downplaying von Treischke's pronounced anti-Semitism), it was present from the outset of his intellectual life. His commencement speeches on Bismarck, given at Fisk, and on Jefferson Davis, given at Harvard, had identified national leadership with the embodiment of racial spirit. (The characteristics that Du Bois assigned to Bismarck were to some degree, in fact, an idealized version of his own personality: "The man of Iron, one of the strongest personalities the world has ever seen; brilliant, stubborn;—reckless, careful, a patriot, a despot: the Man of One Idea." Later, in *Dusk of Dawn,* Du Bois took a less sanguine view of the results of European nationalism, but he recalled that Bismarck's example "foreshadowed in my mind the kind of thing that American Negroes must do, marching forth with strength and determination under trained leadership.")[51] It is possible, moreover, that Du Bois, like Yeats, borrowed his metaphor of the veil not just from the Bible and folk tradition but also from the ideas of theosophy associated with figures such as Madame Blavatsky and her 1877 manifesto *Isis Unveiled,* perhaps the most influential spiritualist text of the late nineteenth century. For Blavatsky, the lifting of the veil would reunite man with his spiritual, or astral, self in a harmonious universe and was thus a means to reveal a hidden, ancient race soul. Her occultist version of multiple consciousness partook of the same psychological interpretation of personality that lay behind Hopkins's *Of One Blood* and therefore could be utilized to promote a positive rediscovery of the lost ancestral self. As a reaction against positivist philosophy, her theories reconciled occultism and imperialist adventure, lending credence to the discovery of a racial unconscious in the quest romances of Haggard and others. In Germany, most prominently, the lifting of the veil could be transfigured into a revelation of the Aryan soul invoked by racial biologists and social theorists that prepared the way for the Third Reich.[52] Thus, the idea of a racial soul hidden behind a mystic veil in nationalist thought *could* flower into racism, but it could also lead to a release from bondage or oppression, as in Pan-African thought. Whether or not Du Bois borrowed anything directly from Blavatskian occultism, he had clearly absorbed a good deal of its echoes through Germanic philosophy.

It is no surprise, additionally, that Du Bois was an avid Wagnerian. He shared in the Wagner craze of his day, as he immersed himself in German nationalist thought, without foreseeing the ends to which both could be put. It is worth noting that his most extensive remarks on Wagner appeared in the *Pittsburgh Courrier* in 1936, a late date in the anti-Semitic appropriation of Wagnerism; but Du Bois himself, while he had expressed guarded admiration for some achievements of the Third Reich, was nevertheless openly critical of Hitler's race policies by this time. What is of interest here, however, is Du Bois's understanding of Wagner in relation to his own race nationalism. Of *The Ring* he writes: "It is as though someone of us chose out of the wealth of African folklore a body of poetic material and, with music, scene and action, re-told for mankind the suffering and triumphs and defeats of a people."[53] One could argue that Du Bois's entire body of work, especially through the 1920s, does just that— indeed, that the model of opera, already implicit in the structure of text, music, and dramatic development in *The Souls of Black Folk,* is central to his aesthetic, not least because both Du Bois and Wagner were engaged in the creation of national heroic art. As we have seen, Du Bois's invocation of *Lohengrin*—which he would later call Wagner's glorious "hymn of Faith"—in the one fictional episode in *Souls,* "Of the Coming of John," is not the sign of a dilettante, as many of his contemporaries thought, but a carefully chosen analogy for the story's action. Rich with tormenting reflections on subservience and revolt in the age of Jim Crow, the story concludes with John's mystic transfiguration into a world beyond, humming the "Song of the Bride" as he awaits his certain lynching or takes his own life. Further exact parallels to *Lohengrin* are tenuous, but it appears that Du Bois intended some rudimentary conception of John as a black knight of the Holy Grail, though with what irony it is difficult to say. In German national thought the Grail legend was eventually used to depict the Aryan race as the sole guardians of Christian purity, the knights of a Christ figure entirely detached from Judaism and subsumed into a trans-historical racial mystique. It is evident in the Wagner festivals of the late nineteenth century that race nationalism was a central element in this myth, and it is certain that Du Bois responded not as a racist but as a race nationalist to the power of Wagnerism—to its conjunction of aesthetics, prehistorical myth, and national identity—for a black world in search of a similar determining force.[54]

For all his claims that Garvey was a militant buffoon commanding a "comic opera," Du Bois himself was enamored of pageantry. The form of the opera appealed to him precisely because it offered a potentially ener-gizing union of aesthetics and politics—or art and propaganda, to use his preferred terms. Du Bois's unequivocal commitment to an art of overt ideology was finally announced in 1926, following his first trip to Africa and his increasing admiration for the Soviet Union, when he delivered an address, "Criteria of Negro Art," in which he claimed, against the "wailing of the purists," that "all Art is propaganda and ever must be."[55] Never-theless, just as his socialist critique of the world color line is implicit from the beginning of his writings, so Du Bois's art was political from the beginning, a fact that perhaps accounts for a good deal of his experimen-tation with different genres and for the inability of modern critical thought to deal effectively with his work. Like Martin Delany, Du Bois saw fiction and the polemical essay as extensions of each other; and, like Hopkins, he found the panoramic allegory—at once melodramatic, historically revisionist, and psychologically acute—to offer the most comprehensive vehicle of spiritual nationalism.

One of the most important instances of Du Bois's search for a suitable formal union of art and politics, now difficult to reconstruct accurately, was "The Star of Ethiopia," a dramatic pageant that presented the history of Africa and African America in episodic, masquelike form illustrating the gifts of black people to the world from ancient Egypt to modern America. The intent of "The Star of Ethiopia," as Du Bois summarized it, was to realize the Negro's essential dramatic qualities and demonstrate that "his greatest gift to the world has been and will be a gift of art." In the words of the pageant's herald, the audience is commanded to *"learn the ancient Glory of Ethiopia, All-Mother of men, whose wonders men forgot. See how beneath the Mountains of the Moon, alike in the Valley of Father Nile and in ancient Negro-land and Atlantis the Black Race ruled and strove and fought and sought the Star of Faith and Freedom, even as other races did and do. Fathers of Men and Sires of Children golden, black and brown, keep silence and hear this mighty word."* First produced at the Emancipation Exposition in New York City in 1913, the pageant was revived by Du Bois with some success in 1915 for performances in Washington, Philadelphia, and Los Angeles. In its final form, with musical direction by J. Rosamond Johnson, "The Star of Ethiopia" had five central scenes: "The Gift of Iron"; "The Relation of Mulatto Egypt to Black Africa"; "The Culmination of African Civilization" (A.D. 200–1500); "The Valley of Humiliation" (slavery); and "The Triumph of the Negro over the Ghosts of Slavery," which ended with the building of the Tower of Light. The Washington performance included over fifty musical selections performed by a chorus of two hundred and required a cast of some twelve hundred people. A precursor to the interest in national theater that would soon result in increased use of American folk materials, the pageant was a short-lived but enormously popular form in the early part of the century; and for African Americans it was a particularly useful pedagogical tool in black education. School plays such as Edward McCoo's "Ethiopia at the Bar of Justice" (1924), the work of an AME minister that became quite popular as a feature during early celebrations of Negro History Week, and Dorothy Guinn's chronicle pageant "Out of the Dark" (1924) were among many such works that blacks employed to give theatrical form to an Afrocentric philosophy.[56]

The last scene of Guinn's pageant, in which the curtain draws back to reveal a tableau based on Meta Fuller's sculpture *Ethiopia Awakening,* while the assembled cast sings James Weldon Johnson and Rosamond Johnson's "Lift Every Voice," demonstrates how completely bound together were the theatricality of the black history pageant and the lifting of the veil that covered the African past. Like the nationalist opera, the historical pageant was a form that raised the curtain on history, revealing in this case the hidden shadow of Ethiopia within the African or African American self and pointing to the contemporary promise of freedom. In the visual arts one can find an equivalent in works such as Lois Mailou Jones's *Ascent of Ethiopia* (1932) and the paintings and murals of Aaron Douglass, particularly his series *Aspects of Negro Life* (1934), which employs translucence and layered geometric shapes to give the effect of a set of veils shrouding and revealing successive scenes in a panoramic depiction of African–African American life. Even though they sometimes contained similar scenes, such African American pageants and artworks of the postwar years were refutations of the plantation mythology that had stocked minstrel historical extravaganzas such as *Black America* in the nineteeth century and that still appeared in stage burlesque and in some black musicals, notably the "back-to-Africa" farces such as *In Dahomey* (1903) and *Abyssinia* (1906).* Despite their obvious differences, what the historical pageant and the black musical stage had in common was an inheritance, from Africa in some part and certainly from slave culture, of syncretic modes of performance in which dance, lyrics, and visual tableaux were combined into an art that was public, to be sure, but also intensely communal in the sense of belonging to a particular people.

The drama was hardly Du Bois's chosen arena, but he experimented with the form often, and he helped establish a small theater company, the Krigwa Players, in 1925. Just as important, his multigenred creative writings, such as *The Souls of Black Folk* and *Darkwater,* were dramas in which the veil was lifted, like a stage curtain, to reveal various episodes and dimensions of diaspora history. The main interpretive difficulty presented by these two volumes, easily Du Bois's best creative work, lies in their unorthodox formal properties. *The Souls of Black Folk,* as I have argued, is a trenchant experiment in the twin African American vocalism of song and language. The text operates equally in the musical register of the

---

* The back-to-Africa musicals were mostly vaudeville routines transferred to a cardboard Africa, with virtually nothing African about them except the claim by Bert Williams and George Walker, as noted in chapter 4, that they had studied the native Dahomean performers at the San Francisco midwinter fair of 1893. *In Dahomey*'s "On Emancipation Day," with lyrics by Paul Laurence Dunbar, was a standard coon song, and "On Broadway in Dahomey Bye and Bye" was musical farce indistinguishable from popular stereotypes:

> If we went to Dahomey, suppose the king would say,
> We want a Broadway built for us, we want it right away. . . .
> We'd sell big Georgia possums—some watermelons too—
> To git the coin for the other things we'd like to do. . . .
> We'd git some large Gorillas and we'd use them for police,
> Then git a Hippopotamus for Justice of the Peace. . . .

In Dahomey: A Negro Musical Comedy music by Will Marion Cook, book by Jesse A. Shipp, lyrics by Paul Laurence Dunbar et al. (London: Keith, Prowse, n.d.), pp. 43–50. See also Allen Woll, *Black Musical Theater: From Coontown to Dreamgirls* (Baton Rouge: Louisiana State Unversity Press, 1989), pp. 36–46, and Thomas L. Riis, *Just before Jazz: Black Musical Theater in New York, 1890–1915* (Washington, D.C.: Smithsonian Institute Press, 1989), pp. 91–117.

spirituals, which must be brought into performative action, as it were, like a cultural "hidden self" awakened and brought forth from a concealed racial-cultural past so as to be heard as part of the volume's living argument. Arranged in a series of alternating essays and poems or vignettes, *Darkwater* partakes of the same bardic intentions as the first work, formally uniting the two main forms of discourse, allegory and polemic, that Du Bois used in his editorial writings for *Crisis*. A number of structural and thematic parallels can be found: whereas the Civil War is the historical watershed in *The Souls of Black Folk*, the First World War performs a similar function in *Darkwater*; the labor and education of African Americans in the Black Belt is now examined across the spectrum of the world's colored population; the model life of Alexander Crummell is repeated in that of Samuel Taylor-Coleridge; the prophecy-tinged short story "Of the Coming of John" is echoed in "The Comet"; the elements of classical and German mythology alluded to in the first book are transformed now into Du Bois's own ornate mythology of Pan-African deities, fairies, princesses, and the like; and the eschatology of the sorrow songs reappears in the constant reference to black redeemers and a revolutionary end of secular time. In its more overt collapse of generic and aesthetic boundaries, however, *Darkwater* also moves in the direction of the pageantlike theatricality of "The Star of Ethiopia." If the counterpoint of music and text in *The Souls of Black Folk* created a harmonic relationship in the tonality of Du Bois's "preaching" voice, the alternating lyric and analytic sections of *Darkwater* make for a nearly complete fluidity between the aesthetic and political spaces of the text. The book's subtitle, *Voices from within the Veil*, is calculated to recompose Du Bois's central racial metaphor, suggesting a three-dimensional space, as of a stage—not just a color bar or line of separation but a transhistorical and transgeographical extended space of black soul, African America's hidden self, within which the volume's voices will be found coming to consciousness.

The Burden of Black Women

> Sometimes I feel like a motherless child,
> Sometimes I feel like a motherless child,
> Sometimes I feel like a motherless child,
> A long ways from home;
> A long ways from home.
>
> African American spiritual

> . . . wherefore a woman has many fathers,
> i keep dreaming of my birth
> of two hands moving against chills
> tilting the flesh till it flaked.
> i became the mother of sun. moon. star children.
> and the hour of after birth when i turned
> into my breath you came and i proclaimed
> you without sound.
>
> you. you. Black Man. standing straight
> as a sentry. staring at monotony.
> LOOK. a savior moves in these breasts,
> i who have waltzed the sea hear my
> seed running toward your seasons.
> you. you. Black redeemer star.
> sweeten your points.
> i need old silver for my veins.
>
> Sonia Sanchez, "Rebirth"

The combined lyric and analytic structure of *Darkwater* powerfully represents the illusion of dimensional racial space. One can take as a primary example the strategy by which "The Riddle of the Sphinx," a poem originally entitled "The Burden of Black Women" and published in *Horizon* in 1907, is placed before "The Hands of Ethiopia," a revised version of Du Bois's landmark 1915 essay in the *Atlantic Monthly,* "The African Roots of War." The revised essay places less emphasis on colonial economic statistics and on Du Bois's dubious anticipation of Lenin's thesis about the colonial investment of surplus capital. Instead, "The Hands of Ethiopia" more strongly articulates a philosophy of "Africa for Africans" and argues that Ethiopia's hands are "hard, gnarled, and muscled for the world's real work; they are the hands of fellowship for the half-submerged masses of a distempered world." The concluding paragraph of the essay, identical in both forms, speaks of black Africa as "prostrated, raped, and shamed," figuring her as an impoverished black woman "weeping and waiting, with her sons on her breast." What is an incidental element in "The African Roots of the War," however, becomes by the juxtaposition of the essay with "The Riddle of the Sphinx" the commanding figure for the colonial devastation of the "body" of the African continent:

Dark daughter of the lotus leaves that watch the Southern Sea!
Wan spirit of a prisoned soul a-panting to be free! . . .

The will of the world is a whistling wind, sweeping a cloud-swept sky,
And not from the East and not from the West knelled that
    soul-waking cry,
      But out of the South,—the sad, black South—it screamed from
        the top of the sky,
      Crying: "Awake, O ancient race!" Wailing, "O woman arise!"
And crying and sighing and crying again as a voice in the
    midnight cries,—
But the burden of white men bore her back and the white world
    stifled her sighs.[57]

Du Bois's command of verse is by no means spectacular, and the poem as it develops out of these opening stanzas depends for its powers on what one might style its action in the theater of propaganda. Still, it is a remarkable precursor to the best poetry of the Harlem Renaissance. I will return to the figure of the Black Christ that is called forth in the remarkable conclusion of the poem, where the implication that the act of colonial rape is productive of messianic deliverance or apocalypse is more evident. Like other parts of *Darkwater*, though, "The Riddle of the Sphinx" functions pivotally to connect surrounding texts by a kind of impressionistic logic. "The Souls of White Folk," the well-known 1910 essay that is reprinted as the preceding chapter, is both a fierce denunciation of colonial exploitation in Africa, Asia, the American South, and other parts of the world's black "belt" of colonies, and an adumbration of Du Bois's 1915 thesis that colonialism lay at the root of the war: "What is the black man but America's Belgium?" Unlike the souls of black folk, purified in the crucible of racial suffering, the souls of white folk are decaying and diseased, unleashing an "avalanche of filth and immorality" over the "Hell" they have created. In an unnerving Whitmanesque moment, Du Bois announces that he sees "these souls undressed and from the back and side. I see the working of their entrails . . . crouching as they clutch at rags of facts and fancies to hide their nakedness." The outbursts of excoriation that punctuate the more prosaic colonial critique in this essay are rendered more starkly and effectively in "The Riddle of the Sphinx." What follows the initial invocation of the raped colonial body in the poem is an incanted chronicle of the debaucheries of colonial rule and exploitation ("the white world's vermin and filth") that are inflicted upon the ravished continent. The lines in question serve to set up not just the remainder of the poem but also the subsequent essay, "The Hands of Ethiopia," tying it back to "The Souls of White Folk." In the figure of the raped woman borne back by her multiple attackers who stifle her sighs (an interesting anticipation of Yeats's "Leda and the Swan," made more pointed by Du Bois's further allusion, as the poem develops, to a militant Black Christ born in an Easter uprising), the violation of Africa is extended both temporally and geographically, as Du Bois offers his most significant delineation to date of the soil of Africa as a complement of the Black Belt of America. The "South" of the poem is both African and American, and the raped woman calls forth an awakening Pan-African consciousness that encompasses both the African nations of the continent under colonial rule and the states of the American South, which have imprisoned African Americans in the new slavery of sharecropping peonage. Slavery and colonial rule are coterminous in Du Bois's imagination, both of them productive of "shameless breeders of bastards, / Drunk with the greed of gold," who bait their "blood-stained hooks" with Christian "cant for the souls of the simple."[58]

The "rape" of Africa first by the slave trade (what Du Bois in *The Negro* called "the Rape of Ethiopia—a sordid, pitiful, cruel tale") and second by imperial rule was a common figure in critiques of colonialism. But Du Bois, in a far-reaching and powerful trope, made more pronounced than any previous writer the feminist dimensions of anticolonial ideology. In doing so he extended into two more encompassing claims about the black political economy Anna Julia Cooper's argument in *A Voice from the South* (1892) that "these bodies of ours [women] often come to us mortgaged to their full value by the extravagance, self-indulgence, sensuality of some ancestor."[59] Following the lead of Hopkins and Crummell, Du Bois bound together the physical violation of African women and the slave trader's destruction of the African family structure with the expropriation of Africa's wealth. Like Hopkins, he argued that the rape of black women in the American South was an extension of the same imperial rule, that it was the body of Pan-Africa, as it were, a simultaneously geographical and physiological body, that was being violated. In countering the contemporary archetype of the Negro as licentious or race-mixing "beast," both Hopkins and Du Bois sought to restore in the image of the black family the moral integrity that had been undermined by the social effects of slavery and by racist theory. A pivotal chapter in *Darkwater* is therefore "The Damnation of Women," which first appeared as an essay, "On Being

Black," in the *New Republic* in 1920. In arguing that "the uplift of women is, next to the problem of the color line and the peace movement, our greatest modern cause," Du Bois mounts a remarkable argument on behalf of women's freedom to work and bear children:

> The world today wants healthy babies and intelligent workers. Today we refuse to allow the combination and force thousands of intelligent workers to go childless at a horrible expenditure of moral force, or we damn them if they break our idiotic conventions. Only at the sacrifice of intelligence and the chance to do their best work can the majority of modern women bear children. This is the damnation of women.
>
> All womanhood is hampered today because the world on [*sic*] which it is emerging is a world that tries to worship both virgins and mothers and in the end depises motherhood and despoils virgins.
>
> The future woman must have a life work and economic independence. She must have knowledge. She must have the right of motherhood at her own discretion. The present mincing horror at free womanhood must pass if we are ever to be rid of the bestiality of free manhood; not by guarding the weak in weakness do we gain strength, but by making weakness free and strong.
>
> The world must choose the free woman or the white wraith of the prostitute. Today it wavers between the prostitute and the nun.

Du Bois's fascination with the twin principles of motherhood and virginity, which do not stand in opposition but together define female freedom and reproductive integrity, reaches beyond a prescription of contemporary socialist ideals to his more embracing vision of Africa as the "primal black All-Mother of men," a race idea that he finds radiating throughout the diaspora. In his earlier work on black social life Du Bois had questioned the direct links between Africa and black America. For example, in *The Negro American Family* (1909), one of his Atlanta University studies, he found it "exceedingly difficult to know just where to find the broken thread of African and American social history," though he argued nonetheless that "there is a distinct nexus" associated with African matriarchy and linking the two worlds that could not be neglected. By the time of *Darkwater* that nexus was unquestionably the black woman herself, more specifically the black mother.[60]

Du Bois, of course, had no substantiation for his view that "the great black race in passing up the steps of human culture" was alone responsible for giving the world the "mother-idea"; and his mythic recollection of African womanhood ("as I remember through memories of others, backward among my own family, it is the mother I ever recall,—the little, far-off mother of my grandmothers, who sobbed her life away in song, longing for her lost palm-trees and scented waters") is patently sentimental.[61] The mythic dimension of African motherhood, however, is crucial to Du Bois's expansion of the figure in two incongruous but allied directions—the problem of the modern black family and the redemptive power of the Black Christ. By combining Du Bois's blistering editorial condemnations of lynching and his advocacy not just of political rights but also of social equality—a form of freedom, racists rightly understood, that permitted racial mixing and intermarriage—*Darkwater* distilled his fundamental beliefs into a single attack in which economic *production* and biological *reproduction* were inseparable. Only a militant philosophy and a revolutionary savior capable of redeeming the literal bodies of black women *and* the geographical body of the African diaspora could give true meaning to the cause of freedom.

In its plea for the restitution of the family through the elevation of the black woman, "The Damnation of Women" also draws on previous work by Alexander Crummell and Anna Julia Cooper. (Du Bois quotes extensively from Crummell's 1883 essay "The Black Woman of the South"; and without naming her as the author, he cites a now famous passage from Cooper's *Voice from the South:* "Only the black woman can say 'when and where I enter, in the quiet, undisputed dignity of my womanhood, without violence and without suing or special patronage, then and there the whole Negro race enters with me.'") Notably, Du Bois shared with Crummell and other black leaders of the day, all of them influenced by pervasive middle-class family norms and Victorian sensibilities about sexuality, a devotion to chastity that caused him to spurn modernist depictions of sexual freedom and occasionally to idealize the African family. He later condemned the casual immorality portrayed in Claude McKay's *Home to Harlem,* for example, and he asserted in a notorious pronouncement that during two months in West Africa, when he routinely saw "children quite naked and women usually naked to the waist," he witnessed "less of sex dalliance and appeal than I see daily on Fifth Avenue."[62] Yet his own sometimes prudish views, commonplace enough for the day, were hardly unbending, as we shall see. Rather, they were frequently strategic and in any event must be judged in the context of his reaction to white racist attacks on African American sexuality and family morality.

The peculiar strain of Victorianism in racist theory in America had important implications for, and created certain contradictions in, Du Bois's aesthetic. He recognized as well as anyone that the sexual suppression of women went hand in hand with racial suppression, locking white women and blacks, especially black men, into opposite mythological postures that served both the political and psychological needs of many white men. Of the white rape complex and lynching frenzy in post-Reconstruction years, Joel Williamson writes: "Never before had white men in the South elevated white women so high on the pedestal as did this first generation of boys born to Victorian mothers, and never before had they punished any men, white or black, as horrendously as they punished some black men in those years." The African American response to white racial violence needed only to cite the large mixed-race population and the legacy of rape during slave trading and slavery; but such counterarguments weighed little in the balance against racist denunciations of the black "beast" and purported black sexual degeneracy. Although Du Bois's response to racist mythology and to lynching was unswerving, his own views of the "pathology" of the black family were somewhat equivocal. At times he minimized familial separations and sexual immorality, while on other occasions he highlighted domestic fragmentation in order to attack their sources in discrimination and economic injustice. Racial bondage, Du Bois argued on numerous occasions from 1900 forward, had destroyed the "ancient African chastity" of the black family, as he described it in a resonant phrase from *The Souls of Black Folk,* and left promiscuity, concubinage, rape, and a loss of the nuclear familial ideal in its wake. At the same time, Du Bois also asserted iconoclastically in *Darkwater* that the paradigm of the male breadwinner and female "nurse and homemaker" harked back to a notion of the home as a "sheltered harem," with the inevitable contemporary results, given the number of working black women, of broken families. In this respect, he claimed, the breakdown of the family was caused not by racial problems but by economic ones. The result, however, *was* a racial problem, and Du Bois directly anticipated the work of E. Franklin Frazier and others in his prediction that the increased economic independence of black women would lead to a slower decrease in illegitimacy and the proliferating "mighty dilemma" of "the unhusbanded mother and the childless wife."[63]

Du Bois's unwillingness in *Darkwater* to separate racial from economic causes for such breakdowns in the black family results in something of a disequilibrium in his argument, but one in which the central trope of his volume, the black messiah, is securely anchored. In "The Damnation of

Women" and *Darkwater* generally, the "blasphemy" of white rape of southern black women is not so much a cause as an analogue for black familial fragmentation. The figure that runs between white rape on the one hand and the breakdown of the black family on the other is illegitimacy. In fact, the birth and growth of the black individual, as of the black nation, is the governing preoccupation of *Darkwater*, just as the training of black minds was in *The Souls of Black Folk*. In both instances illegitimacy is a negative blockage that must be defeated or transfigured if the racial soul is to survive and prosper. Although the New Negro (or Harlem) Renaissance had not yet reached critical mass, Du Bois may be said to have joined cultural legitimacy to moral legitimacy in *Darkwater*. The "rebirth" of American Negro culture, in his conception, had to be accompanied by a purification of soul that restored "African chastity," not as a repressive restriction on sexual freedom but as the focal point of familial cohesion and, consequently, the redemption of independent African American nationhood. Here as elsewhere, however, Du Bois may have identified his own life with that of the black nation, and it would not be unreasonable to contend that his preoccupation with illegitimacy had autobiographical roots. As Allison Davis has argued, Du Bois was very sensitive about the circumstances of his own parentage and birth. Although it is not clear that his birth was legally illegitimate, his father apparently deserted the family when Du Bois was a few months old (in *Dusk of Dawn* he reports that his father died while he was was an infant, but there seems to be no conclusive basis for either view). Only in later accounts of his ancestry would Du Bois admit that he had no clear evidence to back up the rather grandiose and detailed genealogy that he gives himself in the autobiographical opening of *Darkwater*, and the exaggerated belief in his essential Africanity is based on assertion rather than any persuasive account of his close familial ties.[64] Rather than see Du Bois's claims as evidence of an archetypal Freudian family romance, the fabrication of great ancestral lineage to mask personal anxieties or deficiencies, however, one may take his family portrait in the first chapter of *Darkwater* as a rhetorical strategy that underwrites the book's messianic statements and prophetic dimension.

That Du Bois to some degree invented his Africanity—for instance, in his recurrent focus on his great-great-grandmother's "Bantu" song, "Do bana coba," passed down in the family tradition as his single direct link to the All-Mother of Africa—should be neither a surprise nor a means of discrediting the sincerity of his Pan-African philosophy. For one thing, Du Bois's view of Africa, despite his command of recent historiography and his incisive theoretical understanding of the colonial problem (he was less precise when it came to local detail), was overwhelmingly romantic. But it was also romance with a decided and identifiable purpose. His notorious report after his visit in 1923, for instance, contains the germ of his later utopian view of African socialism. "The spell of Africa is upon me," Du Bois announced in a passage worthy of Joseph Conrad or André Gide:

> The ancient witchery of her medicine is burning my drowsy, dreamy blood. This is not a country, it is world—a universe of itself and for itself, a thing Different, Immense, Menacing, Alluring. It is a great black bosom where the spirit longs to die. It is life so burning, so fire encircled that one bursts with terrible soul inflaming life. One longs to leap against the sun and then calls, like some great hand of fate, the slow, silent crushing power of almighty sleep—of Silence, of immovable Power beyond, within, around. Then comes the calm. The dreamless beat of midday stillness at dusk, at dawn, at noon, always. Things move—black shiny bodies, perfect bodies, bodies of sleek unearthly poise and beauty. . . . Life slows down and as it slows it deepens; it rises and descends to immense and secret places.

In its resemblance to the white imperial imagination sinking into the unconscious domain of the black Other, languid if not erotic, this re-markable passage reminds us that Du Bois, too, despite his color and his race consciousness, was something of a colonial intruder into Africa. But its incantatory quality recalls Du Bois's earliest poems of Pan-African negritude, "The Song of the Smoke" (1907) and "A Day in Africa" (1908); and the near disintegration of semantic control also suggests a throwing off of the bonds of definition, an attempt to capture a quality of existence beyond available written constraints by penetrating to a hidden self within the veil of African blackness. That this was a psychological projection goes without saying, but that does not discount the purpose served by the passage in providing the grounds for Du Bois's conclusion—namely, that Africa, as "the Spiritual Frontier of human kind," offers a model of primitive socialism. A day will come, Du Bois intones, when "there will spring in Africa a civilization without coal, without noise, where machin-ery will sing and never rush and roar, and where men will sleep and think and dance and lie prone before the rising sons [sic], and women will be happy."[65]

Such incandescent naiveté is not uncommon in Du Bois at his most

intense rhetorical moments. His primitivism was different from that characteristic of the Harlem Renaissance, though, in that it was always driven
by anticolonial resistance and aspired to a theory of communistic society,
however eccentric or implausible its point of view might become.* More
important, it also allows us to understand the function of similar passages
in *Darkwater,* where rigorous economic logic and pungent analysis can
suddenly give way to a lyric moment that is nearly incomprehensible. For
example, following "The Hands of Ethiopia" and preceding "Of Work
and Wealth," a powerful quasi-socialist critique of the Jim Crow economics
that resulted in the bloody East St. Louis riots of 1917, one finds "The
Princess of the Hither Isles," an opaque allegorical dialogue in which an
unidentified princess spurns a colonial king's offer of the "golden entrails"
of Africa's spoil, choosing instead to tear open her breast and offer her
"bleeding heart" to a "nigger," a black beggar. Disgusted, the king, no
doubt on the model of King Leopold's horrendous policy of punitive
amputation in the Congo, cuts off her hand with its offered bleeding
heart. Identified with "babe-raped mothers" of the colonial world, the
princess, in something of a reversal of Thomas Dixon's (and D. W. Griffith's) most famous scene of suicide, leaps into an abyss.[66] Like other such
moments in Du Bois's lyric imagination, this vignette can be explicated,
after a fashion, but it functions primarily as a kind of iconographic condensation of the analytic essays that surround it. Like an intense moment
of melodrama within the larger historical pageant of the volume, the

---

* In "What Is Civilization? Africa's Answer" (1925), for example, Du Bois launched another
attack on the "soulless Leviathan" of the modern city. Here he idealized the African "village
unit," which he considered "a perfect human thing" that was burdened by "no monopoly, no
poverty, no prostitution" but that had "disintegrated before the white invader, before machine
goods and imperial compulsion." In *Dusk of Dawn,* a work certainly governed in conception and
execution by the materialist philosophy of history to which Du Bois's Marxism had led him by
the end of the 1930s, he would often lament his youthful inability to see clearly the grand design
of imperial rule. Nevertheless, one could say that his romanticization of Africa simply took a new
turn, so willing was he, for example, to excuse modern slavery in Liberia (a point on which
George Schuyler took him much to task) and to blame every conceivable political and social evil
on capitalism and its handmaiden, colonial rule. See "What Is Civilization? Africa's Answer," in
W. E. B. Du Bois: A Reader, ed. Meyer Weinberg (New York: Harper and Row, 1970), pp. 377–
78. In his later admiration for Stalin, Mao, and other totalitarian masters of dehumanized state
planning, he carried this romantic materialism to its unfortunate conclusion. On Du Bois's later
faith in communism and its implication for his political aesthetic, see Arnold Rampersad, *The
Art and Imagination of W. E. B. Du Bois* (Cambridge, Mass.: Harvard University Press, 1976),
pp. 245–93, and William Cain, "W. E. B. Du Bois's Autobiography and the Politics of Literature,"
Black American Literature Forum 24 (Summer 1990), 299–313.

dialogue presses one's vision to the limits of representation, crystallizing historical forces into a tragic figuring of the world conflict Du Bois saw being acted out through the agencies of labor and race. "The Princess of the Hither Isles" is thus a further means of lifting the veil on Africa's history, a theatricalized scene whose enigmatic figures raise Du Bois's own invention of modern Africa to a different intellectual plane.

Darkwater is throughout a work of such theatrical invention in the sense that in it Du Bois intended to create, across a full spectrum of topics, a foundation for black America's Pan-African cultural mythos, repeating the strategy of *The Souls of Black Folk* now on a global scale. Published when he was fifty years of age—because he lived to be ninety-four, it is easy to lose track of the shape of Du Bois's career—*Darkwater* might well have turned out to be a late work and in any event must be seen as a commandingly mature work, a summary view of the world crisis of race and labor as Du Bois saw it and an articulation of his own messianic intentions. Du Bois did not proclaim himself a kind of Christ, as did Garvey; instead, his secularized appeal to the messianic myth was a means to organize his overall discovery and promotion of Pan-African culture. Like Douglass's *Narrative* and Washington's *Up from Slavery* before it, *Darkwater* begins in the autobiographical mode of the reconstructed slave narrative ("I was born . . ."), but Du Bois's recounting of his life, despite its flattering mythic dimensions, quickly gives way to a series of essays and creative works that are far more important than his autobiography. His genealogy therefore functions less as a cover for his personal anxiety about his father's desertion or his ancestors' lack of greatness than as a key to his construction of belief in the African dimension of African American life—the belief in racial soul. Like his mythologizing of the African family and African labor, Du Bois's mythologizing of his family allowed him not simply to penetrate "behind" the veil of race prejudice or ignorance but to place himself "within" the veil of life throughout the diaspora—as his epigraphic allusion to "My Lord, What a Mourning" in *The Souls of Black Folk* had put it, "to wake the nations underground."

For this reason, illegitimacy is a trope that reaches beyond Du Bois's autobiography and also beyond the statistical problem of broken families (in *The Souls of Black Folk* Du Bois had rebuked sociologists who "gleefully count [the Negro's] bastards and his prostitutes")[67] to include the legitimation of African American life through a recovery of its historical sources, its ancestry, and a mythologized celebration of its triumphs over racism. As for Yeats, such mythology was for Du Bois not fictive but ultrahistorical, standing outside the linear confines of human temporality and the age's nearly undebatable doctrine of teleological progress. Illegitimacy is redeemed in *Darkwater* through one particular agency—the birth of the Black Christ. The debauchery and bastardy left in the wake of slavery and colonialism, which Du Bois took to be the most damning evidence of their moral evil, are submerged in his compelling representation in *Darkwater* and allied texts of the delivering redeemer as the incarnation of the diasporic nation. Figured in a variety of ways, the Black Christ, as Du Bois radically imagines him, is often the offspring of the violated black woman, the illegitimate heir of the world's racial crisis. The Black Christ appears in a number of *Darkwater*'s sections, including, as I have intimated, "The Riddle of the Sphinx," the poem that Du Bois made into a prolegomena to his landmark essay on Africa and the war. Similarly, "The Damnation of Women" is surrounded on one side by "The Call," an annunciation fragment in which a black Mary-like figure is summoned before God and discovers him to be black also, and on the other by the obscure "Children of the Moon," a strange allegorical account of freedom as it is configured in the "blazing blackness" of God's "one veiled face." The product no longer of rape or illegitimacy but of immaculate conception in these instances, the Black Christ allows Du Bois the most profound embodiment of his own secular vision, the theological value of the trope less significant than its ideological value. The Black Christ represents a climax of Du Bois's own messianic thinking as it pervades *Darkwater;* and it is no mistake that the volume is framed by two liturgical works, "A Prayer at Atlanta," Du Bois's Mosaic prayer for deliverance written in the aftermath of the 1906 Atlanta riot, and "A Hymn to the Peoples," a Pan-African poem composed for the Universal Races Congress in 1911. But more than that, the Black Christ sums up the contradictions and paralyzed hovering on the brink of nationalist consciousness that Du Bois found to characterize the state of African American life by 1920.

The Black Christ and Other Prophets

> sing a get up time to nationfy
> singaa miracle fire light
> sing a airplane invisibility for the jesus niggers come from the grave
> for the jesus niggers dead in the cave, rose up, passt jewjuice
> on the shadow world
> raise up christ nigger

Christ was black
krishna was black shango was black
        black jesus nigger come out and strike
                come out and strike boom boom . . .
niggers come out, brothers are we
    with you and your sons your daughters are ours
    and we are the same, all the blackness from one black allah
        when the world is clear you'll be with us
                come out niggers come out
                come out niggers come out
It's nation time eye ime
        It's nation ti eye ime
                chant with bells and drum
                it's nation time . . .

> Amiri Baraka, "It's Nation Time"

By the time Countee Cullen wrote his long narrative poem "The Black
Christ" in 1929, the concept of a black messiah, as his flaccid poem proves,
had nearly been drained of literary effectiveness. The hero's race pride and
religious skepticism are an adequate summary of Cullen's own significant
poetic achievement, and one can find in the poem a working out of his
idealist aesthetic; but "The Black Christ" otherwise adds little to an over-
worked trope. By 1932, in "Goodbye, Christ," Langston Hughes would
dismiss Christ as an object of black faith and a model of black emulation:

> Listen, Christ,
> You did alright in your day, I reckon—
> But that day's gone now.
> They ghosted you up a swell story, too,
> Called it Bible—
> But it's dead now. . . .

Before this end game had been reached, the Christ figure—more specifically the Black Christ—had been a trope of significant force in the New
Negro movement, as indeed it would be revived once more several generations later in the civil rights and black arts movements. Cullen, Hughes,
Claude McKay, Jean Toomer, and lesser writers had composed lyrics on
the black redeemer or his black cross-bearer Simon; in his popular stage

play *Simon the Cyrenian* (1917) the white dramatist Ridgely Torrence, finding in Simon's story "a fact that holds a certain suggestion bearing upon a phase of modern society," had depicted him as an antislavery insurrectionist who intends to free Christ but is converted to nonviolence; throughout the 1920s Garvey had made the Black Christ and Black Madonna important elements in the liturgy of his civil religion; and the lynched Christ had appeared often in the illustrations and cover art of African American and left-wing journals. Just a year before his renunciation of Christ as a potent figure in the modern world, Hughes employed the Crucifixion to protest the Scottsboro case in "Christ in Alabama":

> Christ is a Nigger,
> Beaten and black—
> *O, bare your back.*
>
> Mary is His Mother—
> *Mammy of the South,*
> *Silence your mouth.*
>
> God's His Father—
> *White Master above,*
> *Grant us your love.*
>
> Most holy bastard
> Of the bleeding mouth:
> *Nigger Christ*
> *On the cross of the South.*

Hughes's brilliant lyric, which succinctly encapsulated the violence of African American slavery, Reconstruction, and Jim Crow, brought to a culmination the deployment of Christ as a figure of protest against lynching and racism. Poems such as "Christ in Alabama" or Frank Marshall Davis's "Christ Was a Dixie Nigger" were militant extensions of the radical strain in New Negro intellectual history and its new Christology; but the implied trope of immaculate conception in the form of the white master's rape of the black woman was one that Du Bois had already explored in some detail.[68]

This sudden saturation of figures of the Black Christ in the early twentieth century constituted an intellectual rejection of the archetype of Negro submissiveness central to plantation mythology and promulgated in different fashion by the evangelical theory, advanced variously by Turner, Blyden, and Crummell, that slavery itself was a providential vehicle for the redemption of the black race. Contrary to Jean Wagner's assertion that Cullen's 1922 sonnet "Christ Recrucified" represents the first instance of the crucified Christ to symbolize the lynched Negro, Du Bois had made the connection many years earlier and, indeed, had elaborated it in more than a dozen provocative variations that spelled out all the implications—particularly the immaculate conception issuing from the white master's rape of the black woman—condensed so strikingly into Hughes's "Christ in Alabama." Beyond that, of course, the Christ figure had been easily adapted to the longtime labor and suffering of African Americans, as in Dunbar's representation, in "Ode to Ethiopia," of the "Mother Race" in the diaspora as a kind of collective Christ:

> Thou hast the right to noble pride,
> Whose spotless robes were purified
>   By blood's severe baptism.
> Upon thy brow the cross was laid,
> And labour's painful sweat-beads made
>   A consecrating chrism. . . .

One could trace the roots of the figure in popular American literature at least to *Uncle Tom's Cabin,* and the crucified Christ, if not specifically black, was for good reason a prevalent theme in some abolitionist rhetoric and in slave spirituals such as "He Never Said a Mumblin' Word."* Even in

---

* James Weldon Johnson noted in the preface to his second *Book of American Negro Spirituals* the unusual fact that spirituals based on the *birth* of Christ were rare: "The crucifixion and the resurrection have been treated over and over by the creators of the Spirituals, but apparently the birth of Christ made very little appeal to them, and there are practically no 'Christmas Spirituals.' . . . It would seem that the lowly birth of Jesus, from which more than one analogy could have been drawn, would have furnished the makers of the Spirituals with an inspiring theme. . . . It may be that the old-time plantation preacher, nonplussed by the Immaculate Conception, touched upon the birth of Christ only lightly or not at all, and, therefore, that part of the story of his life was not deeply impressed upon the bards." See James Weldon Johnson and J. Rosamond Johnson, *The Books of American Negro Spirituals,* 2 vols. in 1 (1925, 1926; rpt. New York: Da Capo, 1969), II, 14. This analysis seems somewhat naive, given Johnson's otherwise incisive interpretations. (Even less plausibly he points to the minimal importance given Christmas as a holiday in the slave regime; Christmas and Easter were in fact the primary holidays on most plantations.) In any case, Johnson does not speculate upon the psychological drama of punishment and salvation contained in Christ's Passion, the central feature of the Black Christ in both African and African

its more radical forms, the Black Christ predates the Harlem Renaissance, appearing in the early years of New Negro thought. As S. P. Fullinwider has comprehensively demonstrated, at the end of the nineteenth century a number of black historians and ministers, writing often in the AME *Church Review,* began to turn against the consensus reading of Christ as the model for black forbearance in order to promote a more militant resistance to oppression.[69] For Du Bois as for other writers of the First World War period, the suffering Christ was even more overtly radical, an inspiring symbol in the fight against segregation and colonialism. Lynching, poverty, and discrimination were his crucifixion, and resistance, not docility, was the message of his new parables, even if it remained shrouded in the same sort of scriptural allusiveness that marked the spirituals. But whereas the best Harlem Renaissance figurations of the Black Christ tended to be occasional poems or, as in the case of some of the lyrics in Toomer's *Cane,* subordinate elements of New Negro historical consciousness, those of Du Bois were messianic signs of his Pan-African interpretation of the diaspora.

Du Bois's different experiments with the trope coalesce in *Darkwater,* where the Black Christ is not just a militant leader but the harbinger of a new age of global revolution among the world's people of color. In this respect the volume provides a fitting site of analysis and closure for this study, which began with Nat Turner's "Confessions." Both the formal and authorial differences between the texts are obvious; yet *Darkwater* too is a fragmented text held together by the complex set of allusions that serve to create its historical textuality and by a prophetic voice that is at once American and African. Turner himself was the Black Christ in his narrative, whereas Du Bois only borrows on the messianic power offered in the trope. For both, however, the crucifixion of the black savior, which was the crucifixion of all black peoples in the history of slavery and colonial rule, contained redemption within a surprising militancy. As in the spirituals, the message of Christianity set resistance alongside salvation, the advent of racial consciousness derived from African spiritualism alongside the white man's Jesus. Out of the language and central myth of the masters came a signifying inversion in which spirit, politics, and culture were one for Du Bois as for Nat Turner a century before him.

American settings. As Du Bois's borrowing of this theme of the spirituals indicates, resurrection and birth could be fused in the trope of Christ's Second Coming and the Immaculate Conception harnessed to the politics and sociology of segregation.

Any description of Du Bois's radicalization over the course of the war and the 1920s runs into the fact that the seeds of his strongest dissent can be found much earlier. His interest in the figure of the messianic leader, for instance, can be located in his comments in *The Souls of Black Folk* on the survival of the African priest's role in the African American community—a role that Du Bois had clearly already begun in that volume to appropriate to himself. An even stronger dimension of radical leadership is indicated in his biography of John Brown published in 1909. Du Bois had initially been approached in 1903 to do a biography of Frederick Douglass for the series Beacon Biographies of Eminent Americans, but a confusion on the publisher's part had resulted in the Douglass volume's being offered to Booker T. Washington. After Du Bois had suggested Nat Turner to the skeptical editors, he compromised on John Brown. The step from Turner to Brown in his intentions was not a large one, however, for the Brown biography is dominated by a comparable aura of prophetic fulfillment and represents a perfect amalgamation of Du Bois's sense of his own twin American revolutionary and African heritages now put in service of an incipient socialist critique of the world's racial and economic hierarchy. The analogy of Brown's leadership was in fact already present in Du Bois's invocation of him in one of his early civil rights speeches, his address to the Niagara Movement when it convened at Harper's Ferry in 1906. There he assailed segregation and discrimination, and called for a realization of the rights of political and social equality guaranteed to "all true Americans." Brown's role as a prophet was even more explicit in an essay entitled "John Brown and Christmas," which Du Bois prepared for *Horizon*'s December 1909 issue. Calling up Brown's "crucifixion" at Harper's Ferry fifty years earlier, Du Bois asked that his audience let Brown "rise from the dead in every Negro-American home. Jesus came not to bring peace but a sword. So did John Brown."[70]

Drawing largely from widely available published material, Du Bois recomposed his life of Brown into a parable of puritanic righteousness called forth in condemnation and destruction of slavery. Du Bois wrote according to the influential model of Hippolyte Taine, making John Brown both a great individual, a maker of history, and a sum of the transcendent factors of race, milieu, and moment. Du Bois's perspective was not, however, limited to America and to Brown's role in antislavery provincially understood. And it is not simple coincidence that the chapter devoted to the significance of Brown's leadership for abolitionism and later postwar civil rights efforts was also entitled "The Riddle of the

Sphinx," the title Du Bois would reassign to *Darkwater*'s most compelling Pan-African poem. Brown, as Du Bois portrays him, was both a prophet and "fit to be named with Jesus Christ." The riddle is this: confronted with the "clear white logic" of Brown's raid, which led the South to "crucify a clean and pure soul," how can subsequent generations discover a similar compelling righteousness in their own day? Nor is it incidental that Brown is presented at the outset as a Christlike martyr born during Toussaint's "shudder of Haiti" and defined according to the unorthodox opening of Du Bois's book: "The mystic spell of Africa is and ever was over all America." Even at this relatively early moment in his career, Du Bois was willing to represent the animated collective of the world's enslaved masses as the force that drove Brown and, eventually, Du Bois himself. Harper's Ferry, he argued, was a natural entrance to the "Great Black Way," the territory of black American slavery that was but one segment of the global Black Belt already in the 1850s, as Du Bois imagined it, in the throes of anticolonial revolt: "The vision of the damned was stirring the western world and stirring black men as well as white. Something was forcing the issue—call it what you will, the Spirit of God or the spell of Africa. It came like some great grinding ground swell,—vast, indefinite, immeasurable but mighty, like the dark low whispering of some infinite disembodied voice—a riddle of the Sphinx."[71]

This passage puts Du Bois's later, seemingly romantic effusions about the "spell of Africa" in a rather more demanding context. The key for Du Bois lay not in the fact that John Brown was a white abolitionist but in the power of worldwide revolt that spoke through him. In *The Negro* Du Bois would speak of Toussaint as "the greatest of American Negroes." Likewise, Brown's significance reaches beyond the geography of United States slavery; he is an "inspiration that America owes to Africa"—a *white* Black Christ, as it were.[72] In an addendum published in the 1957 edition of *John Brown,* Du Bois attempted to claim Brown for Marxist utopianism. If this step was dubious, it nevertheless highlights the seamless transformation of the messianic figure over the history of Du Bois's imagination. "Slavery" expanded in his argument beyond the bounds of black American chattel slavery to include global exploitation, but the Pan-African meaning of the messianic leader was already well articulated in Du Bois's framing conception of John Brown, one that more and more reflected his own self-conception as a black leader, which in turn was energized by analogous appeals to the sacrificial figure of Christ by white supremacists, Marcus Garvey, and African anticolonialist prophets alike.

Du Bois's embrace of Brown as a messianic leader and his increasing recourse to Christian parables to delineate resistance to Jim Crow violence has to be seen explicitly to answer the reigning racial orthodoxy of white extremists, who continued the old tradition of biblical proslavery argument in different forms. For this reason as well one might say that Du Bois modernized the message of Nat Turner. The post-Reconstruction southern appeal to the mystique of Christian knighthood, a core element not just of radical race hate groups such as the Klan but also of less virulent neo-Confederate mythology, provided one of the strongest incorporations of the semantics of martyrdom. In the New South's self-lacerating jeremiads, Robert E. Lee and Jefferson Davis were examples of manly Christianity, even figures of the Passion, whose holy war was reborn in the white struggle with the "Negro problem." Promoted through a number of racially prejudicial political strategies that I have examined in previous chapters and against which Du Bois's efforts in the Niagara Movement and the NAACP were ranged, sectional reunion was also supported by appeals to Christian doctrine. The underlying message of reunion depended on acceptance of the plantation mythology of Old Negro contentment and Christian meekness. (Among other southern tributes to loyal blacks, something of a commonplace at the turn of the century, was a monument to those blacks who had refused to join John Brown, planned by the United Daughters of the Confederacy just after the turn of the century in Harper's Ferry but not completed until 1937.) The plantation stereotype became less and less serviceable during the heyday of Jim Crow, however, and the ascendancy of white supremacist race doctrine during the first decades of the century, though it was less sincere and widespread than in Germany, brought forth more explicit invocations of the Christian justification of racial superiority, ones that dehumanized blacks and transferred Christian virtue to Anglo-Saxons and Teutons. Were Jesus alive today, it was claimed by Alfred Wiggam, a best-selling science author of the early 1920s, he would have been "president of the First Eugenics Conference" and a supporter of the differential improvement of the more advanced white race. The Klan, both as it was portrayed in the artistic renderings of Thomas Dixon (himself an ordained minister) and D. W. Griffith, and as it was represented in regalia and propaganda at the grass-roots level, afforded the most ostentatious appropriation of militant race Christianity. As one anonymous minister wrote in a Klan magazine: "I joined the Knights of the Ku Klux Klan because: I believed in Jesus Christ and His church; I believed in a militant Christianity; I believed in the

Cross—a symbol of service and sacrifice for the right. . . . If there isn't enough in that to challenge a real red-blooded, virile minister to a sense of duty, he has lost his vision."[73]

The Black Christ was therefore a figure born of the African American tradition of resistance latent in black religious orthodoxy, and now reborn in the New Negro movement as an assertion of black masculinity against the propaganda of white racism and the castrating threat of the lynch mob. Whereas the "Uncle Tom" Jesus had been constructed in the pose of "feminine" submission, the new black Jesus evoked a mirroring manliness in reply to white supremacy's appeal to Christian militancy. It was this insistence on accepting Christ for their own purposes that Garvey had in mind when he told black audiences that "Jesus Christ was the greatest radical that the world ever saw," and that "the black man has a greater claim to the Cross than all other men." Garvey's Christmas and Easter sermons were governed by conventional theological doctrine; and despite the UNIA's ritual portraiture of a black redeemer and a black Madonna, his claim that God is black followed Henry Turner and was limited to the eminently democratic proposition that each race should see God as its own reflection: "We shall worship him through the spectacles of Ethiopia." From this perspective, Garvey's argument was more conservative than that of W. L. Hunter's popular pamphlet *Jesus Christ Had Negro Blood in His Veins* (first published in 1901 and reprinted many times) or James Morris Webb's *A Black Man Will Be the Coming Universal King* (1918), two of many ephemeral texts that recapitulated the Ethiopianist argument in black theology.[74]

Despite his conservatism, Garvey's advocacy of racial purity (especially after his temporary exclusion from the United States in 1921), the separatist platform of the UNIA and the editorial stance of *Negro World,* and much of the literary effort identified with Garvey's circle all ran counter to the predominantly integrationist vision of Du Bois and the NAACP, exerting a powerful influence in the tense, racially inflamed postwar atmosphere. Garvey himself clearly had a pronounced messianic attraction that Du Bois could not equal in terms of popularity. As E. Franklin Frazier wrote in 1926, Garvey's "black klan of America" had a mass appeal not unlike that of its white racist counterparts (a fact that Garvey exploited in courting the support of white supremacists), and his masterly use of Christian liturgy allowed him to make Christmas and Easter the symbols of "the resurrection of an oppressed and crucified race." Like Bruce Barton and other 1920s promoters of self-fashioning success through the cult of personality, that is to say, Garvey made Christ an instrument of organizational marketing. In the liberal social gospel of New Thought, part of the larger cultural fascination with occultism and psychic phenomena that inspired Hopkins's *Of One Blood,* Christ was an inspiration to self-worth and material success, two central tenets of Garvey's own secular theology. Although they came too late to influence his business ventures, the writings that accompanied Garvey's imprisonment and deportation only augmented his own "Passion" and his messianic nationalist appeal. The UNIA's anthems, catechism, and prayers, the *Negro World's* explicit missionary tones (it was referred as the "testament of the UNIA"), and the proselytizing of various churchmen on Garvey's behalf all combined with his magnetic appeal to make the movement one of the most notable instances of civil religion in American history.[75]

Whatever the influence of the NAACP and *Crisis,* which declined over the course of the 1920s, Du Bois could hardly lay claim to a similar popularity. In 1920 he thought Garvey "an honest and sincere man with a tremendous vision" but a poor businessman with little capacity to realize his dreams of repatriation; by 1924 he had decided, after Garvey's overtures to the Klan, that Garvey was "either a lunatic or a traitor" who should be "locked up or sent home" to Jamaica. Given his growing hostility, it is not surprising that Du Bois would caricature Garvey in *Dark Princess,* his messianic alternative to what he took to be the bombast and fraud of Garvey's redemptive schemes.[76] Had *Darkwater* appeared even a year or two later, one might argue with certainty that competition with Garvey had galvanized Du Bois's imagination in that volume as well; in the event, the precise literary effect of his reaction to Garvey remains in this case a matter of speculation.

Despite the fact that the two would grow to be bitter enemies, divided by tactics, by colorism, and by equally egotistical personalities, Garvey and Du Bois had some common aims and relied on a similar Pan-African Christian world view that has useful points of contact, more perhaps than Du Bois would have admitted. Both seized the eschatological significance of black Christianity and put it to political uses that the churches had not envisioned; and both conceived of the plight of black America in Pan-African terms. Although Du Bois articulated the more imaginative and philosophically profound Pan-African vision, Garvey—at least according to the contemporaries who cited him—had the greater immediate impact on African independence and negritude movements. In order to further his separatist goals, however, Garvey sought a notorious rapprochement

with the Ku Klux Klan and southern racists, among them Senator Theodore Bilbo of Mississippi and Earnest Cox, author of white supremacist
tracts such as *White America* (1923), a brief for colonization arguing that,
because "hybridization" with colored races had led to the downfall of all
the world's great civilizations, America could be saved from the "bounte-
ously fecund" black race only by eliminating the threat of miscegenation.
Garvey not only invited Cox to speak at Liberty Hall but advertised *White
America* at the conclusion of his second volume of *Philosophy and Opinions*
in a full-page ad that faced a reproduction of his own creed, "African
Fundamentalism: A Racial Hierarchy and Empire for Negroes."[77] In stark
contrast, of course, Du Bois remained a firm integrationist throughout
the 1920s, taking seriously the model of radical egalitarian protest he had
located in John Brown and sought to realize in the NAACP. What must
be stressed, moreover, is that despite the fact that Du Bois organized no
civil religion comparable to Garvey's and had, according to wide testimony, little of Garvey's magnetic personal appeal, his messianic vision was
well fixed, and with far greater philosophical and literary rigor, in the
decade before Garvey began stumping in Harlem. That vision may have
been drawn from a Hegelian philosophy of history in which freedom
would be achieved through the rising to consciousness of the Pan-African
people, and it was certainly molded, as has already been shown, by his
Germanic conception of the historical *Volksgeist*.[78] Yet his sacralization of
black soul was born in the American situation and fueled by the more
elemental dialectic of racism; it had far greater historical depth than Garvey's and certainly relied on a more sweeping command of the cultural
resources of Africans in the United States and the diaspora.

Du Bois's messianic personality, then, combined autobiographical inclination with the exigency of competition with American racists on the one
hand and black rivals such as Garvey on the other. As *Darkwater* and *Dark
Princess* suggest, both of these factors are nevertheless subordinate to his
commitment to constructing a well-grounded Pan-African critique of
American racism and European colonialism, the double governing force
of the diaspora. *Darkwater* appeared at a point of culmination in millenarian anticolonial agitation, and like René Maran's *Batouala*, also published
in 1921, it can be taken as a turning point in the development of a literary
protest against colonialism in the broadest global sense.[79] Before looking
more closely at the range of Du Bois's constructions of a black redeemer
and following out that figure's place in *Darkwater*, however, I will return
to the context of African Ethiopianism, in which the notion of a Black

Christ had far more pragmatic significance than it did for most American writers and in which one may find moments of prophetic leadership that have never been given due consideration as potential influences upon Du Bois or, more significantly, as analogues to his own leadership.

As the examples of Henry Turner and Marcus Garvey indicate, the Black Christ had a profound appeal for black followers of American religious movements (the UNIA, of course, was not a church, but Garvey's appeal and the paraphernalia of his meetings were overtly Afro-Christian). Nonetheless, with the isolated exception of Nat Turner and perhaps the less traceable effects of scriptural militancy in other slave preaching and in the spirituals, the notion of a black redeemer was almost purely metaphorical in the African American tradition. Scripture and spirituals were open to radical interpretation, but their efficacy remained an underground current, only rising into a mass political movement with the mid-twentieth-century civil rights activism. Even though churchmen such as Alexander Crummell and Henry Turner were influential figures in their African American (and African) communities, the most politically effective black leaders up through the early twentieth century—Douglass, Delany, Washington, Wells, and Du Bois, for example—had only tangential ties to organized churches. The same was not true in early African independence movements, which, although they scarcely constitute the whole of African leadership, do provide signal instances of anticolonial activity parallel to secular New Negro militancy in the United States and constitute versions of what would today be designated "liberation theology." Ethiopianism was rightly regarded by colonial authorities as a subversive, often American-inspired force, and black African political leadership often came directly out of separatist church movements, a phenomenon that would not find a comparable analogy in the United States until later in the twentieth century with the rise of the Southern Christian Leadership Conference. In looking to the African Ethiopianist movement for a further means to understand Du Bois's thought, one cannot claim that he was immersed in its activities, of course. Rather, he found inspiration for his own leadership, and it is possible to discern there the outlines in reality of the Pan-African revolution he argued in theory.

In South Africa the aftermath of the Boer War (1899–1902) and the Zulu Rebellion (1906) saw a marked rise in colonial preoccupation with the "Ethiopian Problem," which was to be repeated in various locales over the next decades. As forerunners to more overtly political organizations such as the South African Native Congress, which was founded in 1912 and became the African National Congress in the 1920s, the Ethiopian separatist churches were credibly feared to form an underground movement whose purpose was to overthrow colonial rule. At the least it was feared that the Ethiopian churches founded by Mangena Mokone and others were poised to establish their own national church that would subvert the evangelization of the Bantu by colonial churches. But more overt radicalism was also in evidence. Seditious preaching appears to have been widespread during the Zulu Rebellion, and Ethiopianist ministers of various denominations in South Africa and elsewhere foretold the coming of a day when the colonial racial hierarchy would be reversed. The churches have sometimes been distinguished in stricter denominations such as Ethiopian, Zionist, Millenarian, and so forth; but contemporary African authorities tended to group all the secessionist churches under the heading of Ethiopian and regard them as constituting a broad subversive conspiracy against white rule, one in which black Americans played a prominent part. For example, in the case of the 1906 Bambata Rebellion in South Africa, a poll and hut tax revolt given extensive coverage by Thomas Fortune's black newspaper *New York Age* and during which four thousand Africans were killed, black American subversion was held partly responsible. As a local correspondent wrote in an article on the Ethiopian movement: "An evil star rose in the American firmament and sent its satellites to preach sedition in Natal." Likewise, John L. Dube, the black principal of the Zulu Christian Industrial School, criticized American black missionaries for preaching sedition and creating race hatred in South Africa.[80] That such subversion does not in restrospect appear to have played so great a part in the Bambata Rebellion itself does not lessen the power it was felt to have at the time. Whether the seeds of sedition came from within or without, the churches tended to follow a prophetic pattern: a leader arose within the colonial Christian church; his dissent from racist or unacceptable doctrine, perhaps inspired by dreams or visions, would lead to the founding of a separatist church, worship of a Black (or non-white) Christ by the elect, and the prophecy of an end to white rule; and ultimately, resistance to colonial suppression would result in violence and the subsequent creation of martyrs. Ethiopianist movements flourished where European influence (and hence domination) was strong and the Western-educated class of Africans larger. Because they drew together a triangle of black intellectual and political ferment—African, American, and West Indian—the Ethiopianist churches were often inherently "Pan-African" in a broad if unparticularized sense.[81]

Without affording him the opportunity to lead a literal revolt, the confluence of civil rights activism and anticolonial thought in the war years gave Du Bois the means of turning the eschatological tropology of the spirituals, the foundation of African American culture, in a distinctly messianic direction. His career in this way internalized and transfigured the parallel model of messianic African nationalism. Any assessment of the role played by white or black Christianity in the colonial oppression of Africa has to take account of the fact that the church of a Black Christ was no more univocal an agent of repression in Africa than it had been in the America that produced the messianic leadership of John Brown and those postwar African American church movements increasingly inclined toward militancy. In both instances, even though the policies of the black church or its missions were accommodationist, they were still capable of fomenting rebellion or, at the least, advancing the subversive transfiguration of doctrine and Scripture. A number of figures would be important in such an analysis, but two, John Chilembwe and Simon Kimbangu, might be chosen for attention.

As ill-starred as Nat Turner's revolt and like it in some details, Chilembwe's short-lived rising took place in the context of native millennial prophecies about the First World War as the apocalyptic conclusion of colonial rule, and the shape of his career is relevant to an understanding of Du Bois's complex radicalization by the war. Chilembwe was a protégé of the British Baptist missionary Joseph Booth, whose radical missionary work in South Africa and Nyasaland (British Central Africa, now Malawi) spread subversion of colonial authority on a number of fronts (he was eventually deported after 1902). Booth was also the author of a book on African self-determination entitled *Africa for the African,* published by Morgan College in Baltimore in 1897, which popularized the multivalent phrase derived from Delany and Blyden that became a watchword of African nationalism. After Booth took him to the United States on one of several trips he made to gather support for his missions, Chilembwe was educated at the Virginia Theological Seminary in Lynchburg before returning to Nyasaland as a missionary of the National Baptist Convention. His studies and his continued ties to the United States thus brought the National Baptist Convention into a Pan-African role in British Central Africa similar to the role of the AME church in South Africa. Like Booth, Chilembwe maintained correspondence with activists in America and was strongly influenced by the fundamentalist eschatology of the Seventh-Day Adventists and the Watch Tower Bible Society (later the Jehovah's Witnesses), which had a significant following among Christian black Africans and had forecast the emergence of the Christian Millennium in 1914 or 1915. One vaguely prophetic movement against colonial taxation and political control, led by Elliott Kamwana, had already been subjugated when Chilembwe rose to prominence in about 1912. By that time he led the largest mission in Nyasaland, situated on the edge of the prestigious A. L. Bruce estates, the locale of acute labor problems and a focus of native dissent.

With the outbreak of the world war, Chilembwe's radicalization reached a pitch. Although some of his followers conceived of the war as a realization of the Watch Tower prophecy, Chilembwe's motives appear to have been overtly secular. Comparable to Du Bois in his frustration with the war's results for black people, Chilembwe wrote a public letter of protest that excoriated the British government for failing to honor the patriotic contribution of black Africans and asking their service on behalf of a government that kept them oppressed: "The poor Africans who have nothing to own in this world, who in death leave only a long line of widows and orphans in utter want and dire distress are invited to die for a cause which is not theirs." Chilembwe's actual rebellion was brief, if bloody. It began with an attack on William Livingstone, manager of the Bruce estates, and his family. Although it is not clear whether Chilembwe was present, what is clear is that Livingstone was decapitated and his head stuck on a pole, which was the next day exhibited to the congregation as Chilembwe preached his usual Sunday sermon. Terror, not force of arms, was Chilembwe's principal instrument of resistance. Few others were killed in the rising; Chilembwe himself was killed after a brief period of pursuit; and the revolt, like that of Nat Turner, was set down as an isolated instance of radical madness. Precisely because it had no chance of wider success, Chilembwe's revolt must be understood as a ritual blow at colonialism. The display of Livingstone's head was a grotesque moment of charismatic leadership and a dramatic inversion of the Christian colonialism nurtured by his great ancestral figure David Livingstone in the previous century. Unlike Nat Turner, Chilembwe was not a millennial figure called to his rebellion by visions, dreams, or admonitions of apocalypse; but his acts of political violence took place within a context far more charged with millenarian expectancy than was 1830s Virginia.[82]

A second important manifestation of messianic leadership may be found in the movement fostered by Simon Kimbangu in the Congo. There is some evidence that Kimbangu's messianic cult, if not his own rise, was influenced by Garvey's *Negro World,* which was circulated in Leopoldville by 1921, the year of Kimbangu's arrest on charges of anticolonial sedition; and it is more certain that the anticolonial strands of his thought were prompted in some degree by the war. Of equal interest, however, are the elements of Christian millennialism that surrounded Kimbangu. Originally a catechist of the English Baptist Mission who failed his exams for the ministry, he came forth in a Congo tradition that had witnessed the appearance in the early eighteenth century of Kimpa Vita, a Congolese girl baptized Donna Beatrice, who was burned at the stake by Portuguese authorities for subversively prophesying the coming of a Black Christ and the restoration of the ancient kingdom of the Kongo. Kimbangu's teaching, which began in 1918, was somewhat less dramatic, but his purported visions and miracles, along with the militancy ironically associated by colonial rulers with the sect's embrace of allusive Ethiopianist scripture and hymns such as "Onward, Christian Soldiers," sparked a deification of Kimbangu that mixed anticolonial politics with Pentecostal faith in his founding of a New Jerusalem at the town of Nkamba. One hymn of the Kimbanguists (originally in French) was straightforward in its radicalization of doctrine:

> Jesus, Savior of the Chosen and Savior of us all,
> We shall be the victors, sent by your call.
> The kingdom is ours. We have it for sure.
> As for the whites, they have it no more.[83]

Kimbangu's arrest on largely fabricated charges that he preached the replacement of colonial government by an African national church, his sentencing to death (which was commuted), and his final exile to life imprisonment at Elizabethsville completed his own enactment of what his followers considered the Passion of a new Black Christ and what a later historian termed a classic messianic eruption of "libération psychologique."[84] In his case, too, rumors of a militant deliverance by black Americans circulated in the wake of his trial, and his punishment was followed by a rise in anticolonial resistance to European materialism, education, and political control.*

* At extremity in the anticolonial imagination, Americans would be perceived as divine liberating agents. When the Gold Coast African James Aggrey, after twenty years of studying and teaching in America, returned to South Africa and Nyasaland as a member of the Phelps-

Because there were no comparable modern figures of liberation in black America—only continued celebrations of the revolutionary lives of Toussaint L'Ouverture, Nat Turner, John Brown, and less militant abolitionists such as Frederick Douglass and Harriet Tubman—the examples of Chilembwe and Kimbangu provide stronger analogies for Du Bois's messianic thought and the acceleration of images of the Black Christ in his anticolonial, anti–Jim Crow writings during and after the war than any contemporary figures in America. The Black Christ transcended the regressive role of the church itself, standing instead for the messianic political leadership Du Bois sought to convey in *Darkwater* and *Dark Princess,* and which was best to be seen at that moment not in the martyrs of the lynchings and frequent race riots of the postwar United States, and not even in Garvey, but in the prophetic leaders arising in Africa. The African leaders were realizations of liberation theology as it has been described by Cornel West and others. Du Bois and Garvey in their different ways were secular instances that proved such theology functionally impractical but spiritually of great moment to black thought at the zenith of white supremacist ideology.[85]

It is evident that Garvey and others were familiar with the movements associated with both Kimbangu and Chilembwe, as well as the "Africa for

---

Stokes Commission on African Education in 1921, he was taken by some to be the herald of an invasion by black Americans. In the same year, which also witnessed the suppression of the Israelite revolt led by Enoch Mgijima, the South African Wellington Butelezi posed as an American and told his followers that all Americans were Negroes who were coming to South Africa in airplanes to rescue the Bantu from European rule. The form in which Butelezi's fantasy was cast—the rescue or apocalyptic deliverance of a more "primitive" population by means of advanced technology, what Bryan Wilson refers to as "commodity millennialism"—is common to various cargo cults. See Edward Roux, *Time Longer Than Rope: A History of the Black Man's Struggle for Freedom in South Africa* (London: Victor Gollancz, 1949), pp. 148–49; George Shepperson, "Nyasaland and the Millennium," in Sylvia L. Thrupp, ed., *Millennial Dreams in Action* (The Hague: Mouton, 1962), pp. 144–45, 152–53; and Bryan R. Wilson, *Magic and the Millennium: A Sociological Study of Religious Movements of Protest among Tribal and Third-World Peoples* (New York: Harper and Row, 1973), pp. 309–47. If his prophecy of the arrival of airplanes marked the outer reaches of the Pan-African imagination, however, it showed with a particular urgency the myth of black American influence. (In addition it offered a considerable critique of the West's postwar fascination with "primitivist" philosophies as antidotes to modern materialism, a fascination that dominated a number of Harlem Renaissance documents and, as we have seen, underlay some of Du Bois's own representations of African tribal life as a socialist alternative to industrial capitalism.) Yet if deliverance was more likely to come from Africans themselves than from millennial agents from the technological world, the presence of Americans was not insignificant, as their roles in the inspiration of various anticolonial risings makes clear.

Africans" philosophy that Booth and Chilembwe promulgated; and it is known that Du Bois not only was a friend of Lewis Garnett Jordan, the National Baptist Convention foreign mission secretary who oversaw Chilembwe's work in Africa, but also discussed black revolts in South and Central Africa with Joseph Booth during one of Booth's trips to America in about 1912. In addition, Du Bois took note in *Crisis* of inaccurate accounts of Chilembwe's revolt that had appeared in the British press.[86] Given Du Bois's willingness to style John Brown a revolutionary leader in the Pan-African cause, it is unlikely that the radical Christian revolts failed to make an impression on his theory of black consciousness. Du Bois's adoption of Africanist elements in his thinking may also be said to parallel that of Kimbangu, Chilembwe, and other messianic African leaders in a further way, namely, his self-definition as a leader whose ideology is marked by a syncretic blending or incorporation of traditions. Kimbangu's leadership featured a conjunction of elements from African fetishism and Christian orthodoxy. Like many African nationalists born of the missionary situation, he assimilated white cultural elements to African spiritual patterns in order to forge an eschatological vision that promised not so much the end of time as an end to the misery and oppression associated with colonial rule.

Du Bois may be approached from the opposite direction—that is, not as an emigrationist or missionary carrying the salvation of Western technology or texts to Africa, but one for whom the incorporation of African survivals and Pan-African ideology into an American framework produced a similarly syncretic vision of liberation. The meaning of "Africa for the Africans" or of the "African Personality" lay for Du Bois not in the evangelization of Africa or, in truth, in the subordinate assimilation of black American life to a colorless integration, as critics such as Garvey charged. Pan-African "double consciousness" remained real for Du Bois, empowering rather than debilitating. (Sarah Simons's contemporary view of assimilation as a process of "denationalization" in which racial distinctions were far less important than cultural ones was close to Du Bois's view.)[87] Yet as long as segregation and racism lasted, neither social integration nor cultural assimilation of the kind the often Eurocentric Du Bois championed by the example of his work entailed a loss of "nationality." Rather, black soul, largely equivalent for Du Bois to black nationhood, transcended geographical and political structures, as well as specific cultural survivals, even though it was expressed syncretically through them. The intellectual efforts and scattered texts gathered together in *Darkwater* enact that syncretism, as Du Bois reconstructed and preserved in cultural memory the African race spirit in the diaspora—that ambiguous "nation" where the act of sustained resistance, as if rising from the colonial unconscious, defined consciousness, nationhood, and, in fact, race itself.

Mixing poetry, vision, and political critique, *Darkwater* constructs a pageant of scenes lifting the veil on Pan-African struggle. The volume is a perfect instance of J. Saunders Redding's point that Du Bois, not unlike Thomas Carlyle, excelled in "a combination of scholarship and emotional power woven into bolts of symbolism." And yet William Ferris, repeating the claim he had made about Du Bois in *The African Abroad,* asserted that *Darkwater* proved Du Bois to be a Jeremiah rather than a prophet with a message of hope or a Moses leading the way to a Promised Land. Not only that, Ferris excitedly argued, but the book is "an amazing revelation of the soul of a cultured, refined Negro of mixed blood . . . writhing and twisting and turning in the cage in which the Anglo-Saxon has confined it."[88] Part of the repetitious Garveyite critique of Du Bois as a mulatto and integrationist, Ferris's review makes a useful distinction between jeremiad and prophecy (although the two are hardly mutually exclusive), but it also loses track of Du Bois's public life—the countless editorials, columns, and essays that Du Bois, now at the height of his powers, was writing—in which he did act the part of Moses. *Darkwater* was not intended as a practical guide to Pan-African political action but as a kind of philosophical scripture, a militant cry from within the veil that fused the forms of the jeremiad and the visionary lyric.

I have already indicated that the form of *Darkwater* (as well as *Dark Princess*) may owe something to Casely Hayford's *Ethiopia Unbound,* whose subtitle, *Studies in Race Emancipation,* Du Bois might have taken for his own. Du Bois mentions *Ethiopia Unbound* in his bibliography to *The Negro,* and in one of his own 1908 columns in *Horizon* he had quoted extensively from a pungent public letter by Casely Hayford: "The crux of the educational question, as it affects the African, is that Western methods denationalized him. He becomes a slave to foreign ways of life and thought." Posing a question of much interest to Du Bois—"How may the West African be trained so as to preserve his national identity and race instincts?"—Casely Hayford answered himself in a way also likely to provoke Du Bois's admiration: "A Tuskegee Institute is very useful in its way, but where would you get the teachers unless you drew them from the ranks of the University-trained men?" In *Ethiopia Unbound,* however, Casely Hayford described *both* Washington's and Du Bois's programs as provincial in comparison to the more Africanist vision of Blyden. Specifically, he nearly ridicules Du Bois's opening query in *The Souls of Black Folk* ("How does it feel to be a problem?") and his theory of double consciousness. Although he excuses Du Bois for the debility of writing from an American standpoint, he drives straight to the point by arguing: "To be a puzzle unto others is not be a puzzle unto one's self. The sphinx in the Temple of the Sphinx in ancient Egypt is a recumbent figure with the head of a lion, but with the features of King Chephron, the Master of Egypt, somewhere about 3960 B.C. Now, fancy Candace, Queen of Ethiopia, or Chephron, the Master of Egypt, being troubled with a double consciousness. Watch that symbolic, reposeful figure yonder, and you can see one soul, one ideal, one striving, one line of natural, rational progress. Look again, and you must agree that the idea of a double consciousness is absurd with these representative types."[89]

Casely Hayford's penetrating criticism does not seem to have prevented Du Bois from drawing inspiration either from *Ethiopia Unbound*'s unique experimental form or from its advocacy of Pan-Colored unity. One is inclined to speculate, rather, that the West African's admonitions were in part responsible for Du Bois's increasing turn toward a legitimate Pan-African philosophy that transcended the local history of African American slavery and racism. Without renouncing those elements of political and social training available through a Western education, Casely Hayford speculated that Christ had been born to an Ethiopian woman; elevated native African songs above the Christian hymns imposed by colonial religion; defended West African polygamy; and inveighed against the mere imitation of Western governmental institutions. Like Du Bois and others, he also applauded Japan's military superiority and saw the "Yellow Peril" as a cause for African pride. By tracing the growth to maturity of the anticolonial nationalist philosophy of a West African student, Kwamankra, trained at Hampton Institute and London University, *Ethiopia Unbound* mixes a prophetic fictional narrative with astute commentary on contemporary colonial politics, American race relations, and Ethiopianist ideology. Perhaps stung by Casely Hayford's criticisms, or at the least motivated by them, Du Bois surpassed *Ethiopia Unbound* in subtlety and scope in *Darkwater*. Like Casely Hayford, he too converted the black man's "impotent cry" at the "dawn of the twentieth century" into a more organized cultural expression: "For there has never lived a people worth writing about who have not shaped out a destiny for themselves, or carved out their own opportunity."[90]

Both Casely Hayford and Du Bois understood that, whatever role might be played by militant revolutionaries, liberation from colonial rule required also sustained intellectual argument, which could be powerfully driven by poetry and pageant, and made vital in the black messiah. The thesis of *Darkwater,* to return now to an argument advanced earlier, is best summed up in the poem "The Riddle of the Sphinx," a short but pageantlike work of remarkable imagery that fuses in the sphinx the body of Africa and the body of the southern or African black woman, both violated and crying out for vengeance. The "Rape of Ethiopia," as Du Bois had termed it in *The Negro,* referring neither to that country nor to Africa alone but to Pan-Africa, is the grand scene of modern industrial struggle, and his condemnation of colonialism acts as a prelude to the colored masses dragging down their enemies:

> Till the devil's strength be shorn,
> Till some dim, darker David, a-hoeing of his corn,
> And married maiden, mother of God,
> Bid the black Christ be born!
> Then shall our burden be manhood,
> Be it yellow or black or white;
> And poverty or justice or sorrow,
> The humble and simple and strong
> Shall sing with the sons of the morning
> And daughters of even-song:
>> Black mother of the iron hills that ward the blazing sea,
>> Wild spirit of a storm-swept soul, a-struggling to be free,
>> Where 'neath the bloody finger-marks thy riven bosom quakes,
>> Thicken the thunders of God's Voice and lo! a world awakes![91]

In compressing the rape of the woman-continent into the act of child-bearing deliverance by a Black Christ, Du Bois accomplished a remarkable fusion: he joined together the two senses of "labor" that his attacks on industrial exploitation and the "damnation of women" had spoken to; and at the same time he transfigured the woman-continent's rape ("the burden of white men bore her back and the white world stifled her sighs," and "where 'neath the bloody finger-marks thy riven bosom quakes") into a moment to be redeemed by some "darker David" and "mother of God," a moment capable of generating its own salvation.

It is not accidental that his heterodox vision of this Black Christ's conception (in imagery that might be said also to unite Yeats's poems "The Second Coming" and "Leda and the Swan") comes close to fusing the acts of rape and of redemptive generation. In other portraits of the Black Christ Du Bois makes this simultaneity even more telling, replacing the Immaculate Conception with sexual violation not in order blasphemously to revel in it but rather to redeem it. The conception of the black redeemer forcibly enacted in the colonial master's rape is "immaculate" in that the woman, like Africa, preserves her true chastity. She cannot be despoiled by an act of brutality that she cannot prevent; rather, her violation is transfigured into the means of resistance to racism and enslavement. The frequent appearance of the Black Christ in Du Bois's creative writings of the decade preceding *Darkwater* and soon after offers a rich array of variations on this trope. The vignette "Easter" published in *Crisis* in 1911 is a parable of sectional reunion. A giant black laborer, his feet chained, his neck yoked, and his body scarred, inspires such fear in the southern brothers that they lynch him and bury the body in a "cavernous grave" of "Oppression." When the northern brothers, "oily tongued, unctuous and rich," come to call, they all find that the body has risen from the tomb, "risen to a dawning determination to be free; risen to a newer and greater ideal of Humanity than the world has known." In "The Gospel According to Mary Brown" (1919) and "Pontius Pilate" (1920), the Black Christ is lynched for preaching the gospel of "social equality," and in "The Sermon in the Cradle" (1921) he is born in colonial Nigeria, a potential Chilembwe or Kimbangu. The mulatto Black Christ will not save the life of the black convict in "Jesus Christ in Georgia" (1911, revised as "Jesus Christ in Texas" in *Darkwater*) but offers instead eternal life, transforming himself into a giant flaming cross that functions as a tableau for the convict's lynching. The mother who bears the illegitimate Black Christ in "The Second Coming" (1917), also included in *Darkwater*, is herself the offspring of a white man's rape of a black woman; and in the most remarkable variation of all, the late story "The Son of God" (1933), Mary is black, her husband, Joe, is white, but the child she bears is an illegitimate son that she can identify, much to Joe's initial outrage, only as "the son of God." In a symbolic narrative that has some elements in common with Faulkner's *Light in August* and Hughes's "Christ in Alabama" (both appearing in 1932), the boy, Joshua, grows up in the pattern of young Jesus, and when he is presently lynched for the vague crimes of worshipping a new God, living with white women, and fomenting a revolution, his sacrifice throws across the world a sign of salvation in the form of "the black shadow of a noosed and hanging rope."[92]

All of these instances of Du Bois's fascination with Christ's illegitimacy and revolutionary character may have autobiographical sources in his own anxiety about illegitimacy, but they appear here in the service of a grand ideological argument. The effect of the group taken together is to compress Christmas and Easter into a single conceptual moment, not in its own right an eccentric theological argument but one that takes added power from the way in which Du Bois fashions from it a striking narrative of the intersection of race and sexuality. That Christmas and Easter were the primary holidays of plantation slavery underlines Du Bois's argument that the "damnation" of black women—that is, their sexual exploitation—was born of slavery and represents the hidden truth behind the white racist caricature of the black man as a rapist and the black woman as immoral. By comparison, Garvey's similar Christmas and Easter sermons were quite conventional, with virtually no hint of the imaginative richness found in Du Bois's doubling of the Christmas and Easter messages. Superimposing the act of childbearing (Christmas) on the act of lynching (Easter), Du Bois wrote the symbolic equation of American racism in parabolic form. The Immaculate Conception, as Du Bois figured it, had little to do with theology but was instead a sociomythic phenomenon. The history of white rape of black women and the legacy of broken familes left in the wake of slavery, Du Bois asserts, are *not* signs of African American immorality. The southern rape complex and an unforgiving Victorian ethos of sexuality and motherhood conspired to provide a shield behind which theories of racial degeneracy could hide. The Black Christ, at once forgiving and militant, was born of the double "colonial" situation, which fed upon the labor of blacks in two senses—exploiting its toil for the production of wealth and exploiting its bodies for sexual pleasure, in both cases leaving its families broken by racial and economic injustice.

The trope of conception is not always transcendental in *Darkwater*, however, for Du Bois, as we have seen, intended to write seriously about the position of women, especially black women, in American society and the effect of that "damnation" on child development, a primary concern of his Atlanta and Philadelphia sociological studies that now assumed the form of a parable. In "The Immortal Child," for example, the career of Samuel Taylor-Coleridge, the gifted British black composer, is only the ostensible subject. As in the Crummell chapter of *The Souls of Black Folk*, the model life is a key to a larger issue, the fact that American race prejudice is destructive of potential genius. By means of racism and inadequate educational programs (the chapter furthers Du Bois's attack on Washington), "we know in America how to discourage, choke, and murder ability when it so far forgets itself as to choose a dark skin." Repeating an earlier pattern, "The Immortal Child" is tied back to the preceding prose piece, "The Damnation of Women," by means of the intervening poem, "Children of the Moon." "The Damnation of Women" ends with a lament for the "hell of force and temptation which once engulfed and still surrounds black women in America," and "The Immortal Child" portrays the near impossibility of bringing forth the black genius that is born and crushed every day. Between the two essays stands an elliptical poem, spoken by a dead woman, who tells of the act, somewhere in "Time's weird contradiction," through which "I brought to Children of the Moon / Freedom and vast salvation." As Wilson Moses has demonstrated, the poem is a compendium of Western and Ethiopianist mythological elements; the narrator is a black Isis, a moon goddess who both gives birth to and is deity to the "children" of Africa. (*The Moon* was also the title of one of Du Bois's first editing ventures, a weekly publication brought out at Atlanta University which looked forward to *Crisis* in styling itself "a record of the darker races" and reporting news items about the United States, the Caribbean, Africa, and the Middle East.) The figure of the folding and unfolding wings, described at once as a Promethean vulture and a radiant divinity, is drawn from an Ethiopian reference in the Book of Isaiah and makes the God upon whose face the narrator looks ("the blazing blackness / of one veiled face") an incarnation of the Ethiopianist argument for a Black God and Christ. But the winged figure may also, as in the proleptic allusion of "The Riddle of the Sphinx," point to the rape of Leda by Zeus, which Yeats would make paradigmatic of mythological nationalist consciousness.[93]

"Children of the Moon" is nearly impenetrable at moments. Yet its significance in the larger scheme of DuBois's Ethiopianist thought is illuminated by the fact that it originally appeared, in almost the same form, as an Easter poem in the 1913 *Crisis,* there entitled "Easter-Emancipation, 1863–1913." Not only is there a further coincidental anticipation of Yeats here, but the poem may be more certainly associated with other writings in celebration of the half-century anniversary of emancipation, such as James Weldon Johnson's narrative poem "Fifty Years." The freedom envisioned in Du Bois's poem, however, is conspicuously Pan-African. Its mythology is predominantly African and classical, yet the inclusion of America is implied in the legion of the black underclass (the "dumb, dark, and dusky things" confined to an "underground," to "great black caves of utter night") and is suggested more overtly by the inclusion of a huddled group of black men "moaning in mournful monotone" a classic African American spiritual that Du Bois had already included in the chapter "Of the Faith of the Fathers" in *The Souls of Black Folk:*

> O Freedom, O Freedom,
> O Freedom over me;
> Before I'll be a slave,
> I'll be buried in my grave,
> And go home to my God,
>   And be free.

Fusing resurrection and emancipation, the poem is spoken not so much by the mother of a Black Christ as by an ephemeral savior figure that is both Christian and Ethiopian, both masculine and feminine. By incorporating the spiritual from *The Souls of Black Folk,* moreover, Du Bois augmented his masterpiece, thrusting the foundation of black American culture into a wider Pan-African context, once again dramatically enlarging the geography of the "nations underground" and linking the spirituals' own Africanity back to the motherland. The woman narrator's own ascension into heaven, where she is united with the veiled black figure, replaces childbearing as the mechanism of salvation; and yet that union is also a kind of consummation that binds together freedom with her death, partaking of Christian belief and the promised release from earthly bondage articulated again and again in the sorrow songs.[94] "Children of the Moon" therefore links the preceding essay on women's oppression and the stigma of illegitimacy to the following essay on the birth and nurturing of black artistic genius by means of a concentrated, if opaque, meditation on redemption, one that crystallizes the several vectors of Du Bois's thought and his mystic conception of his own Pan-African leadership.

Both *Dark Princess* and the culminating story of *Darkwater,* "The Comet," offer clearer instances of sexual union that promise resurrection and rebirth—not so much of a black nation as of a world that is beyond the confines of race categorization. "The Comet" combines the melancholy prophetic qualities of "Of the Coming of John" and "Of the Sorrow

Songs" in *The Souls of Black Folk*. I commented earlier on the coincidental relationship between Du Bois's use of the comet and the prophetic (and tragic) interpretation of deliverance in the wake of Halley's comet among the South African Israelites at about the same time. Meditations on Halley's comet led Ferris, one of many who contemplated the possibility that the earth might be destroyed "by collision with a great sun," to draw out an analogy between the laws of astronomy and those of civilization. Just as solar systems are constantly being destroyed and reborn, Ferris surmised, nations and great leaders rise and fall, passing "off the stage of existence" but living on "in the ideas they have bequeathed to civilization. . . . So our striving is not in vain. It ultimately becomes a part of the structure of civilization." Du Bois made much the same point about the cycle of civilizations and the coming rise of the Pan-African world on a number of occasions, for example in his essay "The Future of the Negro Race in America" (1904).[95] But Halley's comet also provided him a more striking trope for his parables of deliverance.

In his annual Christmas writing for *Crisis* in 1913, Du Bois had begun a sketch of "The Three Wise Men" in search of Christ with the portrayal of a comet blazing across the sky. And yet when Du Bois returned to the figure of the comet in the concluding story of *Darkwater,* it was to function in a decidedly antiprophetic mode. After the destruction of New York City by the comet, the black man and white woman think they are the only people left alive in the world. In this state of new grace, shorn of their inherited prejudices and charged with the recreation of the world by a mystical "Angel of Annunciation," they become divine, she the "primal woman; mighty mother of all men to come and Bride of Life," and he "her Brother Humanity incarnate, Son of God and great All-Father of the race to be." A visionary moment of propagation, not unlike the transhistorical return to the ur-moment of mankind's African beginnings that Hopkins imagines in *Of One Blood,* displays a simultaneous sexual and ideological ecstasy, a lifting of both the bridal veil and the veil of race:

Suddenly, as though gathered back in some vast hand, the great cloud-curtain fell away. Low on the horizon lay a long, white star—mystic, wonderful! And from it fled upward to the pole, like some wan bridal veil, a pale, wide sheet of flame that lighted all the world and dimmed the stars.

In fascinated silence the man gazed at the heavens and dropped his rockets [signal flares] to the floor. Memories of memories stirred to life in the dead recesses of his mind. The shackles seemed to rattle and fall from his soul. Up from the crass and crushing and cringing of his caste leaped the lone majesty of kings long dead. He arose within the shadows, tall, straight, and stern, with power in his eyes and ghostly scepters hovering to his grasp. It was as though some mighty Pharaoh lived again, or curled Assyrian lord. He turned and looked upon the lady, and found her gazing straight at him.

Silently, immovably, they saw each other face to face—eye to eye. Their souls lay naked to the night. It was not lust; it was not love— it was some vaster, mightier thing that needed neither touch of body nor thrill of soul. It was a thought divine, splendid.[96]

This climax, at once figuratively sexual and spiritual in the most comprehensive Hegelian sense, shows the endpoint of Du Bois's conceptualization of the Black Christ, one that would be repeated on a more elaborate scale in *Dark Princess*. In the new world beyond the veil, interracial union and Pan-African idealism are not contradictory. In Du Bois's thinking, though consciousness of the "race" might hinge on the recognition of a shared heritage of "striving," it never required allegiance to unalloyed blackness. The act of procreation that will bring forth a new world population will begin as an act of miscegenation—one in which the mixing of races is not a threat but a salvation, and in which the newborn Christ, like the idealized son portrayed in "Of the Passing of the First-Born" in *The Souls of Black Folk,* will be a child born beyond the artificial boundaries of race.

But of course it is fantasy: just as they are about to embrace and consummate the divine union, the couple is interrupted by rescuers from the outside world, which has not been destroyed after all. Julia is reunited with her father, and Jim with his wife and his dead child. Not only is the mystic couple separated, but the black hero—now a "nigger" again—is momentarily threatened with lynching for daring to be with a white woman. Except for the framing Pan-African poem, "A Hymn to the Peoples," which partially restores the visionary "human rainbow of the world," the antiprophetic turn of the story is the volume's last word. It brings the hyperactive Pan-African rhetoric, which surges forth in waves throughout the volume, to a numbing halt. Only in *Dark Princess* would Du Bois finally drive through to an ending in keeping with his messianic vision. Although *Darkwater* provoked a certain number of anxious reviews in the white press, which worried that Du Bois was promulgating a race war,[97] the volume exists so completely in the conjoined realms of lyric and rhetoric that it is never likely, nor does it deserve, to receive the attention that belongs to *The Souls of Black Folk*. It is hard to imagine *Darkwater* having anything like the impact that Casely Hayford's *Ethiopia Unbound* had in West Africa, despite the fact that it is the more powerful and coherent literary statement of Pan-African philosophy. It remains one of the most unusual and provocative documents in African American intellectual and literary history, and a work that can hardly be ignored in any evaluation of race conflict and race consciousness in American culture. Even so, the text of *Darkwater* remains perplexing and challenging, and one can argue with good reason that it was not truly finished until the apppearance of *Dark Princess,* a decidedly less successful work, which completes the paradigm haltingly set in motion over and over in *Darkwater.*

Brought together first in the symbolism and political jeremiad of "The Riddle of the Sphinx" and given free expression in *Dark Princess,* the various converging forces of the Black Christ demonstrate Du Bois's by then certain belief that the liberation of Africa and the destruction of American Jim Crow were indivisible. Characterized by Du Bois in a letter to his publisher as a "romance with a message," *Dark Princess* has sources as far back as his 1906 *Colliers* essay "The Color Line Belts the World" and his labor romance of cotton production, *The Quest of the Silver Fleece* (1911), but it borrows from other traditions—the fiction of political terrorism and messianic allegory—in order to prophecy the arrival of not simply a Black Christ but a Pan-African, Pan-Asian colored messiah. It is difficult to make any plausible claims for the artistic craft of *Dark Princess.* But Du Bois would perhaps have been the first to admit that it was above all an instance of art as propaganda, and that is primarily where its interest as an early example of Third World anticolonial fiction lies. Appropriately, the novel's Ethiopianist plot also provoked some suspicious reviews in the white press, while black reviewers found it alternately visionary and garbled. George Schuyler was not entirely alone in thinking it "a masterful piece of work" and a great "portrayal of the soul of our people"—a fact that may help explain Schuyler's own 1936–1938 publication in the *Pittsburgh Courier,* under the pen name Samuel I. Brooks, of two utopian novels of black liberation, *The Black Internationale* and *Black Empire.*[98] As most readers have noted, however, *Dark Princess* is split between a sturdy realistic plot and a framing allegory given over to the birth of the Pan-African messiah that is only marginally interwoven into the political drama. Although the novel's serial stories of black urban politics, labor organizing, and Third

World salvation are at best awkwardly unified, its incorporation of prophetism into a nationalistic novel is compelling. There is no doubt that the novel is laced with incongruous oratorical devices and stilted dramatization; but it is worth keeping in mind that the realistic features of the plot—the hero Matthew Towns's involvement with the radical black nationalist group run by a Garvey-like figure named Perigua and his subsequent involvement in black Chicago politics—function with respect to the high allegory in much the same way as the more prosaic essays in *Darkwater,* in order to provide an anchor for Du Bois's visionary critique.

The novel's protagonist, a medical student forced to leave school by race prejudice, was modeled on a contemporary Philadelphia student but also recalls Martin Delany, who faced similar discrimination in medical school at Harvard and whose own novel of radical race prophecy, *Blake,* may have provided a vague model for *Dark Princess.* (It is also conceivable that Delany's 1859 article on comets for the *Anglo-African Magazine,* where *Blake* was also serialized, had some influence on Du Bois's own "The Comet.") More important, Towns resembles Du Bois in his subsequent studies at Berlin, where he becomes involved in a cabal of Third World intellectuals who await the messianic moment that Towns himself will eventually provide by fathering an illegitimate son with the dark princess, the Indian Kautilya. The plot's flirtation with terrorism—Towns is nearly embroiled in the dynamiting of a train full of Ku Klux Klansmen—provides a somewhat cumbersome opportunity for Du Bois to ridicule Garvey, who is caricatured in the unattractive leader of the radicals but whose flirtation with the Klan provoked Du Bois's outrage. (There are also some equally strong resemblances between Perigua's organization and the African Blood Brotherhood, one of the earliest black communist groups in the United States and decided opponents of Garvey.)[99] Yet it may also be ironic in the sense that the messianic plot line demands that Du Bois, however canny his writing about black radicalism and about machine politics in Chicago, veer away from the discussion of plausible—or even revolutionary—political solutions. The doubts expressed by the Pan-African cabal—actually "Pan-Asian" cabal would be more accurate, since black Africans have virtually no role in the book, despite Du Bois's several attempts to characterize all people of color as "black"—that black Americans were ready to participate in world revolution is answered by Towns's organizing of a political cohort in America.

Despite the novel's constant romanticization of labor and the world underclass, however, *Dark Princess* is a novel that stops short of the more extreme claims, already implicit as early as the John Brown biography, that Du Bois would make for the power of the proletariat in *Black Reconstruction* in 1935. Instead, it celebrates deliverance by the talented tenth. When Matthew sings "Go Down, Moses" in the midst of a discussion of high European culture, a scene that echoes Dianthe's rendition of the famous spiritual in *Of One Blood,* a mystic intervention is created. The aristocratic cabal and the royal Indian princess accept his "prophecy" and recognize in him "a method of discovering real aristocracy." Although many Africans considered his views naive, Du Bois on more than one occasion asserted that black American thought would become the instrument for initiating a revolution that would have its greatest impact not in America itself but elsewhere. As the princess tells Matthew: "America is not the center of the world's evil. That center today is Asia and Africa. In America is Power. Yonder is Culture, but Culture gone to seed, disintegrated, debased. Yet its re-birth is imminent. America and Europe must not prevent it. Only Asia and Africa, in Asia and Africa, can break the power of America and Europe to throttle the world. . . . In America your feet are further within the secret circle of that power that half-consciously rules the world. That is the advantage of America. . . . [Your people] are standing here in this technical triumph of human power and can use it as a fulcrum to lift earth and seas and stars."[100] This speech puts the best face on Casely Hayford's criticisms of African American parochialism, but such characteristically cloudy philosophy finds a more able analogy in the relationship between Matthew and the princess. In choosing marriage to Matthew and insemination by the spirit of black America, nurtured in slavery, the princess gives birth to a messiah who in blood and ideals alike embodies yet another version of the double consciousness that Du Bois, because he could not escape it, continually idealized.

The conception and birth of the messiah are represented in terms that would have been appropriate to the envisioned repopulation of the world by the divine mixed couple in "The Comet." Their relationship, one of adultery since Matthew is still married to Sara, a corrupt political opportunist, is depicted with rather daring eroticism by Du Bois (who otherwise scorned Harlem Renaissance novelists for what he considered their lewdness); and the Madonna and Child are sensually drawn, a wealth of jewels and a sleeping child alike at Kautilya's naked golden breasts when Matthew first sees his son.* Born illegitimately in the Virginia cabin of Matthew's

---

* The Princess Kautilya may have sources in the Ranee of Sarawak, who gave a reception for Du Bois at the Universal Races Congress in 1911, or in the ancient Indian political philosopher

mother, herself a survivor of slavery and a visionary prophetess identified by the princess as "Kali, the Black One; wife of Siva, Mother of the World," the colored messiah is sanctified by a marriage ceremony conducted by an elderly black preacher and Matthew's mother. He will serve the greater dark world described in the princess's Pan-African geography: "The black belt of the Congo, the Nile, and the Ganges reaches by way of Guiana, Haiti, and Jamaica, like a red arrow, up into the heart of white America."[101] In extending the Black Belt around the colonial world, as he had begun to do even as he was composing *The Souls of Black Folk,* Du Bois entered the ongoing debate about race and global geographic zones from an oblique angle. Charles Pearson, Earnest Cox, and other white supremacists argued variously that because whites could not survive outside the temperate zones, they would slowly be extinguished by growing pressure from tropical populations, or that the world Black Belt promoted hybridization and therefore the destruction of white civilization.[102] Du Bois's counterargument about the Black Belt was twofold. Because he was sometimes oblivious to exploitation of Africans by Africans or Asians by Asians, the Black Belt represented a sometimes simplistic region of white colonial exploitation of black, or colored, labor that ringed the world; but the Black Belt also represented, as it had more obviously in *The Souls of*

---

of the same name. See Wilson J. Moses, *The Golden Age of Black Nationalism* (1978; rpt. New York: Oxford University Press, 1988), p. 291 n.28, and Rampersad, *The Art and Imagination of W. E. B. Du Bois,* p. 210. But it is also likely that the image of the "dark princess" was inspired by Langston Hughes's 1926 story "Luani of the Jungles." The storyteller in Hughes's intriguing Conradian tale, a white Englishman who has fallen in love with a wealthy and beautiful Nigerian woman in England and then followed her back to her native village under a romantic illusion of the life they will lead, is left existentially torn when his lover insists on being polygamous, taking a Nigerian lover as well as her English one. Although it is this "dark princess who saved me from the corrupt tangle of white civilization," the Englishman remarks, he is left disoriented, perpetually stranded on the dock in Lagos and unable to leave Africa or return to endure Luani's "humiliation" of him. See Langston Hughes, "Luani of the Jungles," in Nathan Irvin Huggins, ed., *Voices from the Harlem Renaissance* (New York: Oxford University Press, 1976), p. 150. Du Bois's novel does not have a great deal in common with Hughes's parable of cultural relativism, but the figure of the beautiful colored princess who will lift the hero out of the corrupt tangle of white civilization (in Matthew's case the corrupt tangle of Chicago politics; though the players here are black, the power in American politics remains white) may owe something to Hughes's story. Likewise, Du Bois's conception of the colored savior in a radical tradition may owe something to the Japanese communist revolutionary Sen Katayama, who was active in radical American politics during the war years before traveling to Moscow in the 1920s. See Hyman Kublan, *Asian Revolutionary: The Life of Sen Katayama* (Princeton: Princeton University Press, 1964), pp. 235–315.

Black Folk, the geography, the very soil of racial soul. The romantic portrait of labor in *Dark Princess* (Matthew's work on the Chicago subway has an explicitly symbolic ideological cast: "The bowels of the great crude earth must be pierced and plumbed and explored if we would wrest its secrets from it") is less a socialist vision than a return to the vision of labor in the black spirituals and work songs as the source of racial strength and the conduit of cultural memory.[103]

The final effect of Du Bois's new messiah upon the world remains undramatized in *Dark Princess,* but his birth within a black American context, which Du Bois constructs as though it were continuous with the colonial world, suggests for this Christ-Buddha child the role of Ethiopianist prophet—but one whose roots lie in the experiences of both New World slavery and the colonial situation. Whatever his role, he is certainly the child of Du Bois, a vital sign of the complex persona of the black messiah that was now spread throughout his work, an embodiment—or better, an incarnation—of the mysterious idea of race-nationhood transcending geography and time that Du Bois's Pan-African aesthetic could achieve only in the fictive moment of prophecy. *Dark Princess* is at odds with the predominantly apolitical, often primitivist aesthetic of the Harlem Renaissance, and Moses is correct to say that the Wagnerian extravagance of its staged speeches, songs, and melodrama make it an "opera in prose," though one that can perhaps bear sustained comparison to the nationalist dimensions of Wagnerism.[104] *Dark Princess* brought to a culmination the first stage of Du Bois's search for a messianic solution to the world's race crisis. His public avowal of Marxism, the hints of which had been present in his work for many years, would necessitate a diminishing of divinity in favor of prophecy based on more bluntly material analysis, and race nationalism would increasingly give way in his developing thought to socialism and class advocacy.

Dark Princess is a marginal work, a rudimentary example of political literature that is less engaging, for example, than *Blake* and far less so than *The Marrow of Tradition.* Du Bois would return to polemical fiction late in his career in a historical trilogy entitled *The Black Flame,* but by then his best writing was far behind him. It seems unlikely in any case that he could ever have equaled his own achievement in *The Souls of Black Folk.* In *Darkwater* in particular, however, he constructed one of the most compelling literary documents of modern racial consciousness and diasporic nationalism. Extending the foundation of African American spiritual unity, recovered from slave culture and preserved from the onslaught of post-Reconstruction racism in *The Souls of Black Folk,* Du Bois's Pan-African writings in the first decades of the twentieth century constituted an incisive addition to anticolonial literature and a landmark of Pan-African theory. Whereas *The Souls of Black Folk* broke down generational barriers in order to codify African American cultural memory as an essential element of protest politics, *Darkwater* and *Dark Princess* crossed geographic boundaries in order to link African Americans to Africans throughout the diaspora. Du Bois wrote a world literature grounded in a particularly American experience and sensibility, and it is only the failings of literary history that have obscured his valuable legacy. His career recapitulated both the history of race politics and the history of African American literature since slavery; he kept alive the memory of antebellum black struggle while opening the way to Pan-African modernity; and he never ceased to press the formal powers of literature in new directions and advocate cultural ideals antithetical to the provincial mainstream.

In the scope of his vision and the inventiveness of his messianic imagination, but most of all in his profound recreation of the origins of African American culture and the depth of his argument for racial justice, Du Bois stood astride the color line, one of the major writers of his generation, one of America's major writers. He would have been the first to appreciate the fact that sea changes in cultural history, as in political history, may bring an intellectual figure to prominence long after his most important work. It required about half a century for Melville to be seen clearly; by comparison Du Bois has perhaps enjoyed a better reception, despite the ignorance that still attends some compilations of great works. Although this is an age of criticism in which judgments of importance and worth are not much in favor, except typically by censure, I have, by dwelling on a rather small group of writers at length and by venturing in some cases to analyze unusual texts from unconventional perspectives, made such judgments. Even within the boundaries of criticism devoted to the problem of race, needless to say, other constructions of cultural importance and literary worth are possible and welcome. I have attempted to reconfigure the geography of the American literary imagination during the defining period of what is arguably the nation's defining event—slavery and its aftermath. In doing so I have also tried to reexamine the capacity of literature to transmute the narrative of history and our inherited strategies of reading. This relative handful of writers, black and white, southern and northern, affords us the means to see with greater clarity and conscience the limitations of past judgments and, one hopes, pathways to better, more just ones. "To the extent that American literature is both an art of discovery and an artistic agency for creating a consciousness of cultural identity," Ralph Ellison has written, "it is of such crucial importance as to demand of the artist not only an eclectic resourcefulness of skill, but an act of democratic faith."[105] The same might just as well be demanded of the critic and the reader.

Notes

Introduction

1. Ralph Ellison, "Blues People," in *Shadow and Act* (1964; rpt. New York: Vintage, 1972), p. 253; Toni Morrison, "Unspeakable Things Unspoken: The Afro-American Presence in American Literature," *Michigan Quarterly Review* 28 (Winter 1989), 18. See also Morrison, *Playing in the Dark: Whiteness and the Literary Imagination* (Cambridge, Mass.: Harvard University Press, 1992).
2. W. E. B. Du Bois, *The Souls of Black Folk* (1903; rpt. New York: Penguin, 1989), pp. 214–15.
3. Franz Boas, "On Alternating Sounds," *American Anthropologist* 2 (January 1889), 47–53; also rpt. in *A Franz Boas Reader,* ed. George W. Stocking (Chicago: University of Chicago Press, 1974), pp. 72–77.
4. Zora Neale Hurston, "Characteristics of Negro Expression," in Nancy Cunard, ed., *Negro: An Anthology* (1934; rpt., abridged ed. Hugh Ford, New York: Frederick Ungar, 1970), p. 28.
5. The many sources from which I have benefited are cited throughout these notes, but among recent studies I would call attention to Wilson J. Moses, *The Golden Age of Black Nationalism, 1850–1925* (1978; rpt. New York: Oxford University Press, 1988); Sterling Stuckey, *Slave Culture: Nationalist Theory and the Foundations of Black America* (New York: Oxford University Press, 1987); Houston A. Baker, Jr., *Modernism and the Harlem Renaissance* (Chicago: University of Chicago Press, 1987); Henry Louis Gates, Jr., *The Signifying Monkey: A Theory of Afro-American Literary Criticism* (New York: Oxford University Press, 1988); and Charles P. Henry, *Culture and African American Politics* (Bloomington: Indiana University Press, 1990). Although it barely touches on literature as such, and perhaps for that reason remains strangely unappreciated by most literary critics, one of the landmark books of the last (or any) generation, and one to which I owe a great deal, is Lawrence W. Levine's *Black Culture and Black Consciousness: Afro-American Folk Thought from Slavery to Freedom* (New York: Oxford University Press, 1977). Some of my own further thoughts on the appearance of folk culture, or vernacular culture, in the early twentieth century,

627

focusing on selected works by James Weldon Johnson, Zora Neale Hurston, and Arna Bontemps, have been published in *The Hammers of Creation: Folk Culture in Modern African-American Fiction* (Athens: University of Georgia Press, 1993).

6. Arnold Rampersad, *The Art and Imagination of W. E. B. Du Bois* (1976; rpt. New York: Schocken Books, 1990), p. vi.

7. Du Bois, *The Souls of Black Folk*, p. 5.

8. Patricia Williams, *The Alchemy of Race and Rights* (Cambridge, Mass.: Harvard University Press, 1991), p. 121.

9. Arna Bontemps, "Why I Returned," in *The Old South* (New York: Dodd, Mead, 1973), pp. 11–12.

1. Signs of Power

1. Herman Melville, *Benito Cereno: Great Short Works of Herman Melville*, ed. Warner Berthoff (New York: Harper and Row, 1969), pp. 294–95; Frederick Merk, *Manifest Destiny and American Mission in American History* (1963; rpt. New York: Vintage Books, 1966), p. 214.

2. Zora Neale Hurston, "Characteristics of Negro Expression," in Nancy Cunard, ed., *Negro: An Anthology* (1934; rpt., abridged ed. Hugh Ford, New York: Frederick Ungar, 1970), p. 28.

3. Frederick Douglass, *My Bondage and My Freedom*, ed. William L. Andrews (Urbana: University of Illinois Press, 1987), p. 151.

4. Theodore Parker, "A Letter on Slavery" (1847), in *The Slave Power*, ed. James K. Hosmer (New York: Arno Press, 1969), p. 50.

5. W. E. B. Du Bois, *The Suppression of the African Slave-Trade to the United States of America, 1638–1870* (1896; rpt. Baton Rouge: Louisiana State University Press, 1969), p. 70; Spenser St. John, *Hayti, or the Black Republic* (London: Smith, Elder, 1884), p. x; David Brion Davis, *The Problem of Slavery in the Age of Revolution, 1770–1823* (Ithaca, N.Y.: Cornell University Press, 1975), pp. 329–30; Alfred N. Hunt, *Haiti's Influence on Antebellum America: Slumbering Volcano in the Caribbean* (Baton Rouge: Louisiana State University Press, 1988), pp. 37–83; C. L. R. James, *The Black Jacobins: Toussaint L'Ouverture and the San Domingo Revolution*, rev. ed. (New York: Vintage Books, 1963), p. 127; Clement Eaton, *The Freedom-of-Thought Struggle in the Old South*, rev. ed. (New York: Harper and Row, 1964), pp. 89–90; David Brion Davis, *The Slave Power Conspiracy and the Paranoid Style* (Baton Rouge: Louisiana State University Press, 1969), p. 35; Julius S. Scott III, "The Common Wind: Currents of Afro-American Communication in the Era of the Haitian Revolution" (Ph.D. diss., Duke University, 1986), passim.

6. William Lloyd Garrison, *The Liberator*, 7 January 1832, rpt. in *William Lloyd Garrison*, ed. George Fredrickson (Englewood Cliffs, N.J.: Prentice-Hall, 1968), pp. 27–30; Angelina Emily Grimké, *Appeal to the Christian Women of the South*

(1835; rpt. New York: Arno Press, 1969), pp. 34–35; Catharine Beecher, *An Essay on Slavery and Abolitionism* (Philadelphia: Henry Perkins, 1837), pp. 88–95.

7. Bryan Edwards, *An Historical Survey of the Island of Saint Domingo* (London: John Stockdale, 1801), p. 226; James T. Holly, "A Vindication of the Capacity of the Negro Race for Self-Government and Civilized Progress, as Demonstrated by the Events of the Haitian Revolution" (1857), in Howard H. Bell, ed., *Black Separatism and the Caribbean, 1860* (Ann Arbor: University of Michigan Press, 1970), p. 63; Edwin C. Holland, quoted in Robert S. Starobin, ed., *Denmark Vesey: The Slave Conspiracy of 1822* (Englewood Cliffs, N.J.: Prentice-Hall, 1970), p. 137; Whitemarsh Seabrook, quoted in Hunt, *Haiti's Influence on Antebellum America*, p. 114.

8. See Hunt, *Haiti's Influence on Antebellum America*, pp. 84–101; William Wells Brown, *St. Domingo: Its Revolutions and Its Patriots* (Boston: Bela Marsh, 1855), pp. 23, 36–38.

9. Thomas R. Dew, "Abolition of Negro Slavery," in Drew Gilpin Faust, ed., *The Ideology of Slavery: Proslavery Thought in the Antebellum South, 1830–1860* (Baton Rouge: Louisiana State University Press, 1981), pp. 56–59; Douglass, *My Bondage and My Freedom*, p. 165.

10. George B. Forgie, *Patricide in the House Divided: A Psychological Interpretation of Lincoln and His Age* (New York: W. W. Norton, 1979), pp. 13–53, 89–122; Gary B. Nash, *Race and Revolution* (Madison, Wisc.: Madison House, 1990), pp. 3–50 passim. Cf. Bernard Bailyn, *The Ideological Origins of the American Revolution* (Cambridge, Mass.: Harvard University Press, 1967), pp. 232–46, and Duncan J. MacLeod, *Slavery, Race, and the American Revolution* (New York: Cambridge University Press, 1974).

11. Thomas Wentworth Higginson, "Nat Turner's Insurrection," in *Travellers and Outlaws: Episodes in American History* (Boston: Lee and Shepard, 1889), pp. 322–25. Cf. Eugene D. Genovese, *From Rebellion to Revolution: Afro-American Slave Revolts in the Making of the New World* (New York: Random House, 1979), pp. 116–17, and Herbert Aptheker, *American Negro Slave Revolts* (New York: International Publishers, 1952), pp. 293–324.

12. Winthrop D. Jordan, *White Over Black: American Attitudes toward the Negro, 1550–1812* (New York: Norton), p. 375.

13. For accounts of the relationship between Turner and the Styron controversy, see Henry Irving Tragle, *The Southampton Slave Revolt of 1831: A Compilation of Source Material* (Amherst: University of Massachusetts Press, 1971), pp. 397–414; Seymour L. Gross and Eileen Bender, "History, Politics, and Literature: The Myth of Nat Turner," *American Quarterly* 23, no. 4 (October 1971), 487–518; and Albert E. Stone, *The Return of Nat Turner: History, Literature, and Cultural Politics in Sixties America* (Athens: University of Georgia Press, 1992). Other essays on Styron's novel and materials on Gray's text and Turner can be found in John B. Duff and Peter M. Mitchell, eds., *The Nat Turner Rebellion: The Historical Event and the Modern Controversy* (New York: Harper and Row, 1971); John Hendrick Clarke, ed., *William Styron's Nat Turner: Ten Black Writers Respond* (Boston:

Beacon, 1968); and Eric Foner, ed., *Nat Turner* (Englewood Cliffs, N.J.: Prentice-Hall, 1971).

14. William L. Andrews, *To Tell a Free Story: The First Century of Afro-American Autobiography, 1760–1865* (Urbana: University of Illinois Press, 1986), pp. 72–77; Thomas C. Parramore, *Southampton County, Virginia* (Charlottesville: University Press of Virginia, 1978), p. 121.

15. Tragle, *The Southampton Slave Revolt of 1831,* pp. 21–22.

16. G. W. F. Hegel, *The Phenomenology of Mind,* trans. J. B. Baille (1910; rpt. New York: Harper and Row, 1967), pp. 234–37; Davis, *The Problem of Slavery in the Age of Revolution,* pp. 557–64.

17. Edmund S. Morgan, "Slavery and Freedom: The American Paradox," in *The Challenge of the American Revolution* (New York: W. W. Norton, 1976), pp. 171–72; Theodore Parker, "The Nebraska Question," in *Additional Speeches, Addresses, and Occasional Sermons,* 2 vols. (Boston: Little, Brown, 1855), I, 362–63; Genovese, *From Rebellion to Revolution,* p. 49.

18. On the panic and abiding fear of slave revolts after Turner, see Aptheker, *American Negro Slave Revolts,* pp. 293–324; Harvey Wish, "American Slave Insurrections before 1861," *Journal of Negro History* 22 (July 1937), 299–320; Stephen B. Oates, *The Fires of Jubilee: Nat Turner's Fierce Rebellion* (New York: Harper, 1975), pp. 105–13; Higginson, *Travellers and Outlaws,* pp. 308–12; Kenneth Stampp, *The Peculiar Institution: Slavery in the Ante-Bellum South* (New York: Random House, 1956), pp. 132–40; and Eaton, *The Freedom-of-Thought Struggle in the Old South,* pp. 94–99.

19. Fanny Kemble, *Journal of a Residence on a Georgia Plantation in 1838–1839,* ed. John A. Scott (1863; rpt. New York: Alfred A. Knopf, 1961), p. 39; Turner folk song quoted in Albert Murray, *The Omni-Americans: Black Experience and American Culture* (New York: Da Capo, 1970), p. 136.

20. Tragle, *The Southampton Slave Revolt of 1831,* p. 173.

21. Thomas R. Gray, "The Confessions of Nat Turner," reprinted in Herbert Aptheker, *Nat Turner's Slave Rebellion* (New York: Humanities Press, 1966), pp. 128–32; Tragle, *The Southampton Slave Revolt of 1831,* pp. 402–3.

22. On authentication in slave narratives, see Robert B. Stepto, *From Behind the Veil: A Study of Afro-American Narrative* (Urbana: University of Illinois Press, 1979), pp. 3–31.

23. Gray, "Confessions of Nat Turner," pp. 128–32.

24. Ibid., pp. 128–31.

25. Ibid., pp. 131, 147.

26. *Richmond Enquirer,* 25 November 1831, in Tragle, *The Southampton Slave Revolt of 1831,* p. 143. For other readings that generally accept the authenticity of Turner's own language, see Oates, *The Fires of Jubilee,* p. 123, and Mechel Sobel, *Trabelin' On: The Slave Journey to an Afro-Baptist Faith* (1979; rpt. Princeton: Princeton University Press, 1988), pp. 161–62.

27. Gray, "Confessions of Nat Turner," p. 135. See, for example, George P. Rawick, *From Sundown to Sunup: The Making of the Black Community* (Westport, Conn.:

Greenwood, 1972), pp. 97–105; Robert D. Pelton, *The Trickster in West Africa: A Study of Mythic Irony and Sacred Delight* (Berkeley: University of California Press, 1980), pp. 259–61; and Lawrence W. Levine, *Black Culture and Black Consciousness: Afro-American Folk Thought from Slavery to Freedom* (New York: Oxford University Press, 1977), pp. 121–33.

28. Gray, "Confessions of Nat Turner," pp. 128–29. See also chapter 2 for Melville's characterization of Babo and chapter 4 for a further discussion of the Master-John tales and African American folklore in literature.

29. Gray, "Confessions of Nat Turner," pp. 147–48, 134.

30. Dew, "Abolition of Negro Slavery," pp. 57, 67–68. See also Alison Goodyear Freehling, *Drift toward Dissolution: The Virginia Slavery Debates of 1831–32* (Baton Rouge: Louisiana University Press, 1982), and Hunt, *Haiti's Influence on Antebellum America,* pp. 119–36.

31. *The Liberator,* 3 September 1831 and 10 March 1832, quoted in Robert H. Abzug, "The Influence of Garrisonian Abolitionists' Fear of Slave Violence on the Antislavery Argument, 1829–40," *Journal of Negro History* 55 (January 1970), 15–28. See also John Demos, "The Antislavery Movement and the Problem of Violent 'Means,'" *New England Quarterly* 37 (December 1964), 501–26.

32. Rawick, *From Sundown to Sunup,* pp. 95–96.

33. John W. Blassingame, *The Slave Community: Plantation Life in the Antebellum South,* rev. ed. (New York: Oxford University Press, 1979), pp. 230–33. See also Stanley Elkins, *Slavery: A Problem in American Institutional and Intellectual Life* (1959; rev. ed. Chicago: University of Chicago Press, 1976), and Ann J. Lane, ed., *The Debate over Slavery: Stanley Elkins and His Critics* (Urbana: University of Illinois Press, 1971).

34. Gray, "Confessions of Nat Turner," pp. 130, 138, 150; Gerald W. Mullin, *Flight and Rebellion: Slave Resistance in Eighteenth-Century Virginia* (New York: Oxford University Press, 1972), pp. 141, 156–57; Starobin, "Introduction," in *Denmark Vesey,* pp. 3–4; Higginson, *Travellers and Outlaws,* p. 248.

35. Gray, "Confessions of Nat Turner," p. 131.

36. Harriet Jacobs, *Incidents in the Life of a Slave Girl,* ed. Jean Fagan Yellin (Cambridge, Mass.: Harvard University Press, 1987), pp. 67–68.

37. Samuel Warner, "Authentic and Impartial Narrative," in Tragle, *The Southampton Slave Revolt of 1831,* p. 280; Albert Raboteau, *Slave Religion: The "Invisible Institution" in the Antebellum South* (New York: Oxford University Press, 1978), pp. 152–210; Eugene D. Genovese, *Roll, Jordan, Roll: The World the Slaves Made* (New York: Random House, 1974), pp. 183–93; Blassingame, *The Slave Community,* pp. 80–95; Margaret Washington Creel, *"A Peculiar People": Slave Religion and Community Culture among the Gullahs* (New York: New York University Press, 1988), pp. 167–302 passim; Blake Touchstone, "Planters and Slave Religion in the Deep South," in John B. Boles, ed., *Masters and Slaves in the House of the Lord: Race and Religion in the American South, 1740–1870* (Lexington: University of Kentucky Press, 1988), pp. 99–126; blues fragment quoted in Paul Oliver, *The Story of the Blues* (Philadelphia: Chilton Books, 1969), p. 10.

38. Orlando Patterson, *Slavery and Social Death: A Comparative Study* (Cambridge, Mass.: Harvard University Press, 1982), pp. 71–76; John Lovell, Jr., *Black Song: The Forge and the Flame* (New York: Macmillan, 1972), pp. 223–29; Miles Mark Fisher, *Negro Slaves Songs in the United States* (1953; rpt. Secaucus, N.J.: Citadel Press, 1978), pp. 66–67; Raboteau, *Slave Religion*, pp. 305–11; Melvin Dixon, "Singing Swords: The Literary Legacy of Slavery," in *The Slave's Narrative*, ed. Charles T. Davis and Henry Louis Gates, Jr. (New York: Oxford University Press, 1985), pp. 298–317.

39. Gray, "Confessions of Nat Turner," p. 135; William S. Drewry, *The Southampton Insurrection* (Washington, D.C.: The Neale Company, 1900), p. 114; Levine, *Black Culture and Black Consciousness*, pp. 30–55; Gayraud S. Wilmore, *Black Religion and Black Radicalism: An Interpretation of the Religious History of Afro-American People*, rev. ed. (Maryknoll, N.Y.: Orbis Books, 1983), pp. 44–73, quote at p. 50.

40. Mullin, *Flight and Rebellion*, pp. 149, 159–60; Starobin, *Denmark Vesey*, pp. 21–22, 34–35, 56, 96–98, 112, 133–34; William W. Freehling, *Prelude to Civil War: The Nullification Controversy in South Carolina, 1816–1836* (New York: Harper and Row, 1966), p. 55.

41. Gray, "Confessions of Nat Turner," p. 136; *Norfolk Herald*, 4 November 1831, in Tragle, *The Southampton Slave Revolt of 1831*, pp. 134–35, and see 31–157 passim, 455–62 for more detail. On slave religion and suppression, see also Aptheker, *American Slave Revolts*, pp. 209–358 passim; Leslie Howard Owens, *This Species of Property: Slave Life and Culture in the Old South* (New York: Oxford University Press, 1976), pp. 200–205; Genovese, *From Rebellion to Revolution*, pp. 7–8; and Raboteau, *Slave Religion*, pp. 163–80.

42. Tragle, *The Southampton Slave Revolt of 1831*, pp. 134–40.

43. Gray, "Confessions of Nat Turner," pp. 133, 149. I thank Ernest Tuveson for the point about "enthusias."

44. Rawick, *From Sundown to Sunup*, pp. 33–44; Fisher, *Negro Slave Songs in the United States*, pp. 66–110; Owens, *This Species of Property*, pp. 155–57; Sterling Stuckey, *Slave Culture: Nationalist Theory and the Foundations of Black America* (New York: Oxford University Press, 1987), pp. 35–40; Raboteau, *Slave Religion*, pp. 215–16, 360n.7.

45. Gray, "Confessions of Nat Turner," p. 136; W. E. B. Du Bois, *The Souls of Black Folk* (New York: Viking Penguin, 1989), pp. 159–60; Melville J. Herskovits, *The Myth of the Negro Past* (1941; rpt. Boston: Beacon, 1958), p. 138. On Vesey's use of conjure and Africanisms generally, see Stuckey, *Slave Culture*, pp. 43–53, and Creel, *"A Peculiar People,"* pp. 150–66.

46. Oates, *The Fires of Jubilee*, pp. 10–12; John W. Cromwell, "The Aftermath of Nat Turner's Insurrection," *Journal of Negro History* 5 (1920), rpt. in Tragle, *The Southampton Slave Revolt of 1831*, p. 388; Gray, "Confessions of Nat Turner," p. 133; Sobel, *Trabelin' On*, pp. 161–66. See also Molefi Kete Asante, *The Afrocentric Idea* (Philadelphia: Temple University Press, 1987), pp. 128–39.

47. Robert Hayden, *Collected Poems,* ed. Frederick Glaysher (New York: Liveright, 1985), pp. 56–57.

48. Genovese, *Roll, Jordan, Roll,* pp. 272–76.

49. Robert Alexander Young, "The Ethiopian Manifesto," in Sterling Stuckey, ed., *The Ideological Origins of Black Nationalism* (Boston: Beacon Press, 1972), pp. 36–37; David Brion Davis, *The Problem of Slavery in Western Culture* (Ithaca: Cornell University Press, 1966), pp. 294–96. On African American use of the jeremiad tradition, see especially Wilson Jeremiah Moses, *Black Messiahs and Uncle Toms: Social and Literary Manipulations of a Religious Myth* (University Park: Pennsylvania State University Press, 1982), pp. 30–48.

50. Aptheker, *American Negro Slave Revolts,* pp. 283–85, quote at p. 284n.57.

51. Douglass, *My Bondage and My Freedom,* p. 156; Sacvan Bercovitch, *The American Jeremiad* (Madison: University of Wisconsin Press), pp. 141–48; Genovese, *From Rebellion to Revolution,* pp. 126, 129–32; Eaton, *The Freedom-of-Thought Struggle in the Old South,* pp. 96–97.

52. Garnet, "Address to the Slaves of the United States," in Stuckey, *The Ideological Origins of Black Nationalism,* pp. 171–73.

53. Hayden, *Collected Poems,* p. 56; Gross and Bender, "History, Myth, and Literature," p. 515; David Walker, *Appeal to the Coloured Citizens of the World* (1829), in Stuckey, *The Ideological Origins of Black Nationalism,* p. 63–64, 68; Oates, *The Fires of Jubilee,* p. 48. On Walker, see Stuckey, *Slave Culture,* pp. 98–137, and Vincent Harding, *There Is a River: The Black Struggle for Freedom in America* (New York: Random House, 1981), pp. 81–94.

54. Gray, "Confessions of Nat Turner," pp. 134, 138.

55. Aptheker, *American Negro Slave Revolts,* pp. 303–12; Oates, *The Fires of Jubilee,* pp. 68–69. The second epigraph to this section, from Sun Tzu, *The Art of War,* follows the translation by Thomas Cleary (Boston: Shambhala, 1988), p. 113.

56. Gray, "Confessions of Nat Turner," pp. 129, 144; F. Roy Johnson, *The Nat Turner Slave Insurrection* (Murfreesboro, N.C.: Johnson, 1966), pp. 150–59.

57. Richmond *Constitutional Whig,* 3 September 1831 and 26 September 1831, in Tragle, *The Southampton Slave Revolt of 1831,* pp. 70, 95. On the Turner countermyth, see Gross and Bender, "History, Politics, and Literature," pp. 502–5.

58. Drewry, *The Southampton Insurrection,* pp. 37, 51; Stephen Beauregard Weeks, "The Slave Insurrection in Virginia, 1831," rpt. in Duff and Mitchell, *The Nat Turner Rebellion,* p. 71.

59. Gross and Bender, "History, Myth, and Literature," pp. 496–98; Gray, "Confessions of Nat Turner," pp. 142–44.

60. Johnson, *The Nat Turner Slave Insurrection,* p. 176; Harding, *There Is a River,* p. 99.

61. I am summarizing here the principles set forth in B. H. Liddell Hart's classic study *Strategy,* 2d rev. ed. (1967; rpt. New York: Signet, 1974), pp. 365–67.

62. Cf. Oates, *The Fires of Jubilee,* pp. 68–69.

63. Gray, "Confessions of Nat Turner," p. 135.

64. Ibid., pp. 137–38.

65. Ibid., p. 135.

66. Ira Berlin, "After Nat Turner: A Letter from the North," *Journal of Negro History* 55 (April 1970), 144–51. In the context of Turner's use of Scripture, the signature "Nero" is notable also for its possible allusion to the "beast," or Antichrist, of Revelation (13:1–18), which has been interpreted by scholars to mean the emperor Nero. Dead some time when John composed the account of his revelation, Nero was the subject of a growing cult that believed he would return to Rome with an avenging army. As either the tyrannical emperor himself, the Antichrist, or the reborn leader of a vengeful military force, the antislavery "Nero" was to be feared.

67. Tragle, *The Southampton Slave Revolt of 1831*, p. 433. A dime novel account of a slave conspiracy purportedly organized by an outlaw named John A. Murrell (*History of the Detection, Conviction, Life and Designs of John A. Murel*) was published by Virgil Stewart, under the pseudonym "A. Q. Walton," in 1835; the book had a brief vogue in the lower South before being recognized as fiction. See Eaton, *The Freedom-of-Thought Struggle in the Old South*, p. 96.

68. Quoted in Harding, *There Is a River*, p. 95; Gray, "Confessions of Nat Turner," p. 139.

69. Guenter Lewy, *Religion and Revolution* (New York: Oxford University Press, 1974), pp. 237–74; Genovese, *From Rebellion to Revolution*, pp. 122–23.

70. Bercovitch, *The American Jeremiad*, pp. 132–34. Cf. Davis, *The Problem of Slavery in the Age of Revolution, 1770–1823*, pp. 307–8.

71. Gray, "Confessions of Nat Turner," pp. 136–38; Andrews, *To Tell a Free Story*, p. 75.

72. *The Life and Writings of Abraham Lincoln*, ed. Philip Van Doren Stern (New York: Modern Library, 1940), pp. 841–42; Ernest Lee Tuveson, *Redeemer Nation: The Idea of America's Millennial Role* (1968; rpt. Chicago: University of Chicago Press, 1980), pp. 187–214; Timothy L. Smith, *Revivalism and Social Reform: American Protestantism on the Eve of the Civil War* (1957; rpt. New York: Harper and Row, 1965), pp. 230–33.

73. James Baldwin, "Everybody's Protest Novel," in *Notes of a Native Son* (1955; rpt. New York: Bantam Books, 1979), p. 13.

74. Letter of 26 September 1831, *Constitutional Whig*, quoted in Tragle, *The Southampton Revolt of 1831*, pp. 91–92.

75. Lewy, *Religion and Revolution*, pp. 583–84.

76. Gray, "Confessions of Nat Turner," p. 133.

77. Gross and Bender, "History, Myth, and Literature," pp. 490, 498; Tragle, *The Southampton Revolt of 1831*, p. 156; Wood, "Nat Turner," pp. 22–23.

78. Douglass, *My Bondage and My Freedom*, pp. 164, 104, 124, 170–71.

79. Ibid., pp. 173, 165.

80. Ibid., p. 23; Rayford Logan, "Introduction," in *Life and Times of Frederick Douglass* (New York: Collier Books, 1962), p. 15.

81. Blassingame, *The Slave Community*, pp. 223–322. See also Bertram Wyatt-Brown,

"The Mask of Obedience: Male Slave Psychology in the Old South," *American Historical Review* 93 (December 1988), 1228–52.

82. On Douglass and northern abolitionists, see, for example, Leon Litwack, "The Emancipation of the Negro Abolitionist," in *The Antislavery Vanguard: New Essays on the Abolitionists,* ed. Martin Duberman (Princeton: Princeton University Press, 1965), pp. 137–55; Harding, *There Is a River,* pp. 140–71; Lawrence J. Friedman, *Gregarious Saints: Self and Community in American Abolitionism, 1830–1870* (Cambridge: Cambridge University Press, 1982); Jane H. Pease and William H. Pease, *They Who Would Be Free: Blacks' Search for Freedom* (New York: Atheneum, 1974); and Andrews, *To Tell a Free Story,* pp. 216–19, 234–36.

83. Douglass, *Narrative of the Life of Frederick Douglass, An American Slave,* ed. Houston A. Baker, Jr. (New York: Penguin, 1982), p. 151; Douglass, *My Bondage and My Freedom,* p. 220.

84. William S. McFeely, *Frederick Douglass* (New York: Norton, 1991), p. 116. For representative arguments in favor of the *Narrative* over *My Bondage and My Freedom,* see, for example, James Matlack, "The Autobiographies of Frederick Douglass," *Phylon* 40 (March 1979), 15–28; Michael Meyer, "Introduction," in *Frederick Douglass: The Narrative and Selected Writings* (New York: Modern Library, 1984), pp. xxvi–xxx; and Albert E. Stone, "Identity and Art in Frederick Douglass's Narrative," *CLA Journal* 17 (December 1973), 212–13. For counterstatements that agree with my view, see Andrews, *To Tell a Free Story,* pp. 214–67 passim, and also Stephen Butterfield, *Black Autobiography in America* (Amherst: University of Massachusetts Press, 1974), p. 88.

85. Cf. Houston A. Baker, Jr., *The Journey Back: Issues in Black Literature and Criticism* (Chicago: University of Chicago Press, 1980), p. 43.

86. Douglass, *My Bondage and My Freedom,* p. 43.

87. Ibid., pp. 65–66, 304–5.

88. Douglass, *The North Star,* 14 July 1848, in *Life and Writings of Frederick Douglass,* ed. Philip S. Foner, 5 vols. (New York: International Publishers, 1950–75), I, 317; Peter F. Walker, *Moral Choices: Memory, Desire, and Imagination in Nineteenth-Century American Abolition* (Baton Rouge: Louisiana State University Press, 1978), pp. 209–61; Allison Davis, *Leadership, Love, and Aggression* (New York: Harcourt Brace Jovanovitch, 1983), pp. 17–101.

89. Douglass, *My Bondage and My Freedom,* p. 43. On slave kinship ties, see Herbert G. Gutman, *The Black Family in Slavery and Freedom, 1750–1925* (New York: Random House, 1976).

90. Douglass, speech of 24 September 1847, in Foner, *Life and Writings,* I, 271; Douglass, *The North Star,* 9 February 1849, in Foner, *Life and Writings,* I, 357–58; George Fitzhugh, *Cannibals All! Or, Slaves without Masters* (1857; rpt. Cambridge, Mass.: Harvard University Press, 1960), pp. 205–6. See also Eugene D. Genovese, *The World the Slaveholders Made: Two Essays in Interpretation* (New York: Random House, 1969), pp. 118–244.

91. Biographical information here and elsewhere is taken from McFeely, *Frederick Douglass;* Dickson J. Preston, *Young Frederick Douglass: The Maryland Years*

(Baltimore: Johns Hopkins University Press, 1980); Foner, *Life and Writings;* Waldo E. Martin, Jr., *The Mind of Frederick Douglass* (Chapel Hill: University of North Carolina Press, 1984); Nathan Irvin Huggins, *Slave and Citizen: The Life of Frederick Douglass* (Boston: Little, Brown, 1980); and Benjamin Quarles, *Frederick Douglass* (New York: Associated Publishers, 1948).

92. Douglass, *My Bondage and My Freedom,* pp. 270–71.

93. Douglass, *Life and Times,* p. 443; Douglass, *My Bondage and My Freedom,* p. 267; Preston, *Young Frederick Douglass,* p. 168.

94. Douglass, speech of 30 March 1847, in Foner, *Life and Writings,* I, 224–25.

95. McFeely, *Frederick Douglass,* pp. 23–24, 29, 41–45, 56–57, 198.

96. Douglass, *My Bondage and My Freedom,* pp. 269–70. Cf. McFeely, *Frederick Douglass,* pp. 158–60, and Preston, *Young Frederick Douglass,* pp. 166–69.

97. See, for example, Ronald G. Walters, *The Antislavery Appeal: American Abolitionism after 1830* (Baltimore: Johns Hopkins University Press, 1976), pp. 70–110, and Karen Sanchez-Eppler, "Bodily Bonds: The Intersecting Rhetorics of Feminism and Abolition," *Representations* 24 (Fall 1988), 28–59.

98. For an account of the whipping scene as it bears on the gender dynamics of Douglass's narratives, see Jenny Franchot, "The Punishment of Esther: Frederick Douglass and the Construction of the Feminine," in Eric J. Sundquist, ed., *Frederick Douglass: New Literary and Historical Essays* (New York: Cambridge University Press, 1990), pp. 141–65.

99. Douglass, *My Bondage and My Freedom,* p. 38; Andrews, *To Tell a Free Story,* pp. 281–91.

100. Douglass, *Narrative,* p. 48; Douglass, *My Bondage and My Freedom,* pp. 29, 41–43. On the impact of *Uncle Tom's Cabin,* see Eric J. Sundquist, ed. *New Essays on Uncle Tom's Cabin* (New York: Cambridge University Press, 1986); J. C. Furnas, *Goodbye to Uncle Tom* (New York: William Sloane, 1956); Jane Tompkins, *Sensational Designs: The Cultural Work of American Fiction, 1790–1860* (New York: Oxford University Press, 1985), pp. 122–46; Joel Porte, *In Respect to Egotism: Studies in American Romantic Writing* (New York: Cambridge University Press, 1991), pp. 213–28; and Robert S. Levine, "*Uncle Tom's Cabin* in *Frederick Douglass' Paper:* An Analysis of Reception," *American Literature* 64 (March 1992), 71–93.

101. Douglass, *My Bondage and My Freedom,* p. 243; *The Rising Sun,* quoted in Foner, "Introduction," in *Life and Writings,* I, 93; Douglass, *Life and Times,* p. 264; Douglass, "Address," *The North Star,* 29 September 1848, in Foner, *Life and Writings,* I, 332. See also Shelley Fisher Fishkin and Carla L. Peterson, "'We Hold These Truths to Be Self-Evident': The Rhetoric of Frederick Douglass's Journalism," in Sundquist, *Frederick Douglass,* pp. 189–204.

102. Douglass, *My Bondage and My Freedom,* p. 100.

103. See Frantz Fanon, *Black Skin, White Masks,* trans. Charles Lam Markman (New York: Grove Press, 1967), p. 18: "Every colonized people—in other words, every people in whose soul an inferiority complex has been created by the death and burial of its local cultural originality—finds itself face to face with the language

of the civilizing nation; that is, with the culture of the mother country. The colonized is elevated above his jungle status in proportion to his adoption of the mother country's cultural standards. He becomes whiter as he renounces his blackness, his jungle." Fanon's important remarks, which have had great resonance in recent minority culture studies, are suggestive but only marginally applicable to African Americans, let alone Frederick Douglass.

104. Douglass, *My Bondage and My Freedom*, p. 53; Alexander Crummell, *The English Language in Liberia* (1861), extracted in J. Ayodele Langley, ed., *Ideologies of Black Liberation, 1856–1970* (London: Rex Collings, 1979), pp. 359, 361.

105. Eugene D. Genovese, *Roll, Jordan, Roll*, pp. 561–66; Albert Taylor Bledsoe, *Liberty and Slavery*, in E. N. Elliott, ed., *Cotton Is King, and Pro-Slavery Arguments* (Augusta, Ga.: Pritchard, Abbott, and Loomis, 1860), p. 289; Douglass, *My Bondage and My Freedom*, p. 31.

106. Douglass, *Narrative*, p. 78; Douglass, *My Bondage and My Freedom*, pp. 92–93, 30, 185, 84, 46.

107. Douglass, *Narrative*, p. 84; Douglass, *My Bondage and My Freedom*, pp. 100–101.

108. Douglass, speech of 2 May 1846 (England), in Foner, *Life and Writings*, I, 57–58.

109. See Philip Fisher, *Hard Facts: Setting and Form in the American Novel* (New York: Oxford University Press, 1985), pp. 95–105. On the gothic in antislavery rhetoric, see Karen Halttunen, "Gothic Imagination and Social Reform: The Haunted Houses of Lyman Beecher, Henry Ward Beecher, and Harriet Beecher Stowe," in Sundquist, *New Essays on Uncle Tom's Cabin*, pp. 107–34, and Davis, *The Problem of Slavery in Western Culture*, pp. 358–59. The role of sentiment in the law of slavery is examined by Mark V. Tushnet, *The American Law of Slavery, 1810–1860: Considerations of Humanity and Interest* (Princeton: Princeton University Press, 1981), pp. 18–27.

110. Fitzhugh, *Cannibals All!*, p. 205.

111. Harriet Beecher Stowe, *Uncle Tom's Cabin; or, Life among the Lowly* (New York: Penguin, 1981), p. 392; Douglass, *My Bondage and My Freedom*, p. 63.

112. Douglass, *My Bondage and My Freedom*, pp. 68, 74, 57–59, 125, 83, 49–50.

113. Ibid., p. 152.

114. On slavery and total institutions, see Elkins, *Slavery*; Blassingame, *The Slave Community*, pp. 223–331; and Lane, *The Debate over Slavery*.

115. Douglass, *My Bondage and My Freedom*, pp. 46–47; Douglass, *Narrative*, p. 49.

116. Genovese, *Roll, Jordan, Roll*, pp. 88–89. On paternalism, see also James Oakes, *The Ruling Race: A History of the American Slaveholders* (New York: Random House, 1982), pp. 192–224, and Clarence E. Walker, *Deromanticizing Black History: Critical Essays and Reappraisals* (Knoxville: University of Tennessee Press, 1991), pp. 56–72.

117. Douglass, *Frederick Douglass' Paper*, 2 June 1854, in Foner, *Life and Writings*, II, 284–89.

118. Daniel Webster, *The Works of Daniel Webster*, 5 vols. (Boston: Little, Brown,

1851), I, 59–60, 72–73, 77–78, 81, 89–90; Theodore Parker, "Reply to Webster," speech of 25 March 1853, in Hosmer, *The Slave Power*, pp. 246–47; Ralph Waldo Emerson, "The Fugitive Slave Law" (3 May 1851), in *The Complete Writings of Ralph Waldo Emerson* (New York: William H. Wise, 1929), pp. 1155–56; *The Collected Works of Abraham Lincoln*, ed. Roy P. Basler, 8 vols. (New Brunswick, N.J.: Rutgers University Press, 1953), I, 109, 111.

119. See Forgie, *Patricide in the House Divided;* R. A. Yoder, "The First Romantics and the Last Revolution," *Studies in Romanticism* 15 (Fall 1976), 493–529; and Kenneth M. Stampp, *The Imperiled Union: Essays on the Background of the Civil War* (New York: Oxford University Press, 1980), pp. 3–36.

120. Douglass, speech of 31 May 1849, in Foner, *Life and Writings,* I, 398–99; Douglass, broadside of 21 March 1863, ibid., III, 319; Dew, "Abolition of Negro Slavery," p. 59.

121. Douglass, speech of 23 April 1849, in Foner, *Life and Writings,* V, 117; Douglass, speech of 4 August 1857, ibid., II, 438–39.

122. Douglass, "The Heroic Slave," rpt. in Ronald Takaki, ed., *Violence in the Black Imagination: Essays and Documents* (New York: Putnam's, 1972), pp. 71, 76–77.

123. Howard Jones, "The Peculiar Institution and National Honor: The Case of the *Creole* Slave Revolt," *Civil War History* 21 (March 1975), 28–50; Robert M. Cover, *Justice Accused: Antislavery and the Judicial Process* (New Haven: Yale University Press, 1975), pp. 109–14; William Jay, *The Creole Case and Mr. Webster's Dispatch* (New York, 1842), pp. 20–21, 29–30.

124. Jones, "The Peculiar Institution and National Honor," p. 38.

125. Robert B. Stepto, "Storytelling in Early Afro-American Fiction: Frederick Douglass' 'The Heroic Slave,'" *Georgia Review* 36 (Summer 1982), 363n.8; Douglass, "The Heroic Slave," pp. 64, 38; Jones, "The Peculiar Institution and National Honor," p. 30; Richard Yarborough, "Race, Violence, and Manhood: The Masculine Ideal in Frederick Douglass's 'The Heroic Slave,'" in Sundquist, *Frederick Douglass,* pp. 166–80. On Douglass and "heroism," see also Martin, *The Mind of Frederick Douglass,* pp. 253–78; and for a further consideration of Douglass's fictionalizing of Washington's story, see William L. Andrews, "The Novelization of Voice in Early African American Narrative," *PMLA* 105 (January 1990), 23–30.

126. M. H. Abrams, *Natural Supernaturalism: Tradition and Revolution in Romantic Literature* (New York: Norton, 1971), pp. 327–72; Douglass, "The Heroic Slave," pp. 39–41, 75.

127. Stepto, "Storytelling in Early Afro-American Fiction," p. 356; Douglass, *My Bondage and My Freedom,* p. 241; *Concord* (New Hampshire) *Herald of Freedom,* quoted in Foner, "Introduction," in Douglass, *Life and Writings,* I, 58.

128. Andrews, *To Tell a Free Story,* p. 187; Yarborough, "Race, Violence, and Manhood," p. 180; Douglass, "The Heroic Slave," p. 75.

129. Gray, "The Confessions of Nat Turner," p. 138.

130. Douglass, *My Bondage and My Freedom,* pp. 119, 152. Among the many readings of this episode in Douglass's autobiographies, see especially Andrews, *To Tell*

a Free Story, pp. 280–91; David Van Leer, "Reading Slavery: The Anxiety of Ethnicity in Douglass's *Narrative,*" in Sundquist, *Frederick Douglass,* pp. 118–26; David Leverenz, *Manhood and the American Renaissance* (Ithaca: Cornell University Press, 1989), pp. 108–34; and Donald B. Gibson, "Reconciling Public and Private in Frederick Douglass' *Narrative,*" *American Literature* 57 (December 1985), 549–69.

131. Patterson, *Slavery and Social Death,* pp. 97–101, quote at p. 98; Douglass, *My Bondage and My Freedom,* p. 151.

132. Douglass, *My Bondage and My Freedom,* p. 148; Gray, "The Confessions of Nat Turner," p. 138.

133. Douglass, *My Bondage and My Freedom,* p. 167.

134. David Walker, *Appeal to the Colored Citizens,* in Stuckey, *Ideological Origins of Black Nationalism,* p. 114; Douglass, speech of 5 July 1852, in Foner, *Life and Writings,* II, 182–88.

135. Genovese, *From Rebellion to Revolution,* pp. 126, 129, 132, 134.

136. Douglass, *My Bondage and My Freedom,* pp. 155–56. See also Genovese, *Roll, Jordan, Roll,* pp. 566–84; Oakes, *The Ruling Race,* pp. 142–43; Eileen Southern, *The Music of Black Americans: A History* (New York: Norton, 1971), p. 67; Blassingame, *The Slave Community,* p. 107; and Katrina Hazzard-Gordon, *Jookin': The Rise of Social Dance Formations in African-American Culture* (Philadelphia: Temple University Press, 1990), pp. 22, 32, 34.

137. Douglass, *My Bondage and My Freedom,* p. 155; Sterling Stuckey, "'Ironic Tenacity': Frederick Douglass's Seizure of the Dialectic,'" in Sundquist, *Frederick Douglass,* pp. 23–46. See also Berndt Ostendorf, *Black Literature in White America* (Totowa, N.J.: Barnes and Noble, 1982), pp. 35–36.

138. A. M. Chirgwin, "The Vogue of the Negro Spiritual," *Edinburgh Review* 247 (January 1928), 62. For collections of plantation advice literature that include statements about the use of music and dance as elements of disciplnary control, see Paul E. Paskoff and Daniel J. Wilson, eds., *The Cause of the South: Selections from De Bow's Review, 1846–1867* (Baton Rouge: Louisiana State University Press, 1982), and James O. Breeden, ed., *Advice among Masters: The Ideal in Slave Management in the Old South* (Westport, Conn.: Greenwood, 1980).

139. Among the many accounts of juba in studies of African American culture, see Dena J. Epstein, *Sinful Tunes and Spirituals: Black Folk Music to the Civil War* (Urbana: University of Illinois Press, 1977), pp. 141–44; Southern, *The Music of Black Americans,* pp. 169, 184; and Bessie Jones and Bess Lomax Hawes, *Step It Down: Games, Plays, Songs, and Stories from the Afro-American Heritage* (Athens: University of Georgia Press, 1972), pp. 37–40.

140. Douglass, *My Bondage and My Freedom,* pp. 171, 164–65.

141. Ibid., p. 247; Andrews, *To Tell a Free Story,* pp. 230, 238–39. Cf. McFeely, *Frederick Douglass,* pp. 51–55.

142. Douglass, *My Bondage and My Freedom,* pp. 165, 168, 179–80.

143. Ibid., p. 187.

144. Abraham Lincoln, *Collected Works,* V, 10; Douglass, speech of 4 July 1862, in Foner, *Life and Writings,* III, 242–46.

145. Douglass, *Douglass' Monthly* (December 1860); in Foner, *Life and Writings,* II, 532; Douglass, speech of 14 April 1876, ibid., IV, 312–17.

146. Quarles, *Frederick Douglass,* p. 277. On Douglass and the legacy of the Civil War, see also David W. Blight, *Frederick Douglass' Civil War* (Baton Rouge: Louisiana State University Press, 1989). The Ball monument is reproduced in Hugh Honour, *The Image of the Black in Western Art: From the American Revolution to World War I,* vol. 4 (Cambridge, Mass.: Harvard University Press, 1988), pt. 1, p. 265.

2. Melville, Delany, and New World Slavery

1. Amasa Delano, *Narrative of Voyages and Travels in the Northern and Southern Hemispheres* (Boston: E. G. House, 1817), p. 336; see also Harold H. Scudder, "Melville's *Benito Cereno* and Captain Delano's Voyages," *PMLA* 43 (1928), 502–32; Melville, *Benito Cereno: Great Short Works of Herman Melville,* ed. Warner Berhoff (New York: Harper and Row, 1969), p. 310.

2. John Edwin Fagg, *Cuba, Haiti, and the Dominican Republic* (Englewood Cliffs, N.J.: Prentice-Hall, 1965), pp. 114–15; Jonathan Brown, *The History and Present Condition of St. Domingo,* 2 vols. (Philadelphia: William Marshall, 1836), I, 22–33; Samuel Eliot Morison, *Admiral of the Ocean: A Life of Christopher Columbus* (Boston: Little, Brown, 1942), pp. 297–313, 423–38; Daniel P. Mannix and Malcolm Cowley, *Black Cargoes: A History of the Atlantic Slave Trade, 1518–1865* (1962; rpt. New York: Viking, 1965), pp. viii, 1–5. On Melville's use of Columbus, see also Mary Y. Hallab, "Victims of 'Malign Machinations': Irving's *Christopher Colombus* and Melville's 'Benito Cereno,'" *Journal of Narrative Technique* 9 (1979), 199–206.

3. Antonio de Herrera, quoted in Brown, *History and Present Condition of St. Domingo,* I, 36–37; Henry Highland Garnett, *The Past and Present Condition and Destiny of the Colored Race* (1848; rpt. Miami: Mnemosyne Publishing, 1969), pp. 12–13.

4. Melville, *Benito Cereno,* pp. 246, 240; H. Bruce Franklin, *The Wake of the Gods: Melville's Mythology* (Stanford: Stanford University Press, 1963), pp. 136–50; David Brion Davis, *Slavery and Human Progress* (New York: Oxford University Press, 1984), p. 40; George Bancroft, *History of the United States of America,* 10 vols. (New York: Appleton and Co., 1885), I, 121–25; Melville, *Benito Cereno,* pp. 294–95.

5. Charles MacKenzie, *Notes on Haiti, Made during a Residence in That Republic,* 2 vols. (London: Colburn and Bentley, 1830), I, 263–66; Melville, *Benito Cereno,* p. 241. On Melville's composition of Benito Cereno, see Leon Howard, *Herman Melville: A Biography* (Berkeley: University of California Press, 1951), pp. 218–22.

6. C. L. R. James, *Mariners, Renegades, and Castaways: The Story of Herman Melville and the World We Live In* (London: Allison and Busby, 1985), p. 119; Robert C.

Toll, *Blacking Up: The Minstrel Show in Nineteenth-Century America* (New York: Oxford University Press, 1974), p. 83.

7. Jefferson, letter of 1797, quoted in Winthrop D. Jordan, *White over Black: American Attitudes toward the Negro, 1550–1812* (1968; rpt. New York: Norton, 1977), p. 387; David Brion Davis, *The Problem of Slavery in the Age of Revolution, 1770–1823* (Ithaca, N.Y.: Cornell University Press, 1975), pp. 329–30; Alfred N. Hunt, *Haiti's Influence on Antebellum America: Slumbering Volcano in the Caribbean* (Baton Rouge: Louisiana State University Press, 1988), pp. 37–83; C. L. R. James, *The Black Jacobins: Toussaint L'Ouverture and the San Domingo Revolution,* rev. ed. (New York: Vintage Books, 1963), p. 127; Clement Eaton, *The Freedom-of-Thought Struggle in the Old South,* rev. ed. (New York: Harper and Row, 1964), pp. 89–90; William Faulkner, *Absalom, Absalom!* (1936; rpt. New York: Vintage, 1972), pp. 250–51; Eugene D. Genovese, *From Rebellion to Revolution: Afro-American Slave Revolts in the Making of the New World* (1979; rpt. New York: Vintage Books, 1981), pp. 35–37, 94–96; Jordan, *White over Black,* pp. 375–402.

8. Ludwell Lee Montague, *Haiti and the United States, 1714–1938* (Durham: Duke University Press, 1940), pp. 35–46; Rayford W. Logan, *The Diplomatic Relations of the United States with Haiti, 1776–1891* (Chapel Hill: University of North Carolina Press, 1941), pp. 112–51; Henry Adams, *History of the United States during the Administrations of Jefferson and Madison,* quoted in Logan, *Diplomatic Relations,* p. 142; Genovese, *From Rebellion to Revolution,* p. 85.

9. Genovese, *From Rebellion to Revolution,* pp. 119–21; C. Duncan Rice, *The Rise and Fall of Black Slavery* (1975; rpt. Baton Rouge: Louisiana State University Press, 1976), pp. 262–63; Miranda quoted in Salvador de Madariaga, *The Fall of the Spanish American Empire* (London: Hollis, Carter, 1947), pp. 322–23; James Bennett, quoted in Frederick Merk, *Manifest Destiny and American Mission in American History* (1963; rpt. New York: Vintage Books, 1966), p. 46. See also Allan Moore Emery, "'Benito Cereno' and Manifest Destiny," *Nineteenth-Century Fiction* 39 (June 1984), 48–68.

10. Herbert Aptheker, *American Negro Slave Revolts* (New York: International Publishers, 1952), p. 33; Genovese, *From Rebellion to Revolution,* p. 15.

11. Richard Chase, *Herman Melville: A Critical Study* (New York: Macmillan, 1949); p. 156; Melville, *Benito Cereno,* pp. 156, 250, 292, 261.

12. Benjamin C. Clark, *A Geographical Sketch of St. Domingo, Cuba, and Nicaragua* (Boston: Eastburn's Press, 1850), p. 7; "About Niggers," *Putnam's Monthly* 6 (December 1855), 608–12.

13. William Wells Brown, *St. Domingo: Its Revolutions and Its Patriots* (Boston: Bela Marsh, 1855), pp. 32–33; James, *Black Jacobins,* pp. 360–74; MacKenzie, *Notes on Haiti,* II, 61. See also Brown, *History and Present Condition of St. Domingo,* II, 152–54, 147–48.

14. Mark B. Bird, *The Black Man; Or, Haytian Independence* (New York: American News Co., 1869), pp. 60–61; Mary Hassal, *Secret History; or, The Horrors of St. Domingo* (Philadelphia: Bradford and Inskeep, 1808), pp. 151–53.

15. "Hayti and the Haytiens," *De Bow's Review* 16 (January 1854), 35; David Brion Davis, *The Slave Power Conspiracy and the Paranoid Style* (Baton Rouge: Louisiana State University Press, 1969), pp. 72–78; Lyman Beecher, *A Plea for the West* (Cincinnati: Truman and Smith, 1835), pp. 37, 109, 144.

16. Theodore Parker, "The Nebraska Question," in *Additional Speeches, Addresses, and Occasional Sermons,* 2 vols. (Boston: Little, Brown, 1855), I, 301–3, 352, 367, 378.

17. Melville, *Benito Cereno,* pp. 276, 245, 250–51, 258, 241, 239, 283. Cf. Carolyn Karcher, *Shadow over the Promised Land: Slavery, Race, and Violence in Melville's America* (Baton Rouge: Louisiana State University Press, 1980), pp. 136–39.

18. Jean Fagan Yellin, *The Intricate Knot: Black Figures in American Literature, 1776–1863* (New York: New York University Press, 1972), pp. 215–27; Melville, *Benito Cereno,* pp. 283, 314. See also James H. Kavanagh, "That Hive of Subtlety: 'Benito Cereno' and the Liberal Hero," in Sacvan Bercovitch and Myra Jehlen, eds., *Ideology and Classic American Literature* (New York: Cambridge University Press, 1986), pp. 352–83.

19. Melville, *Benito Cereno,* pp. 279, 314; Daniel Webster, *The Writings and Speeches of Daniel Webster,* 18 vols. (Boston: Little, Brown, 1903), XIII, 405–7. Cf. Michael Paul Rogin, *Subversive Genealogy: The Politics and Art of Herman Melville* (New York: Alfred A. Knopf, 1983), pp. 142–46.

20. Melville, *Benito Cereno,* pp. 269, 267.

21. Ibid., pp. 276, 242; Delano, *Narrative of Voyages,* p. 326.

22. Melville, *Benito Cereno,* pp. 307, 293.

23. Delano, *Narrative of Voyages,* pp. 337, 323, 73. On Delano's claim of salvage rights and further court documents related to the revolt, see Sterling Stuckey and Joshua Leslie, "Aftermath: Captain Delano's Claim against Benito Cereno," *Modern Philology* 85 (February 1988), 265–87.

24. David Brion Davis, *The Problem of Slavery in Western Culture* (Ithaca: Cornell University Press, 1966), pp. 333–90; Melville, *Benito Cereno,* pp. 278–79; William Ellery Channing, *Slavery* (Boston: James Munroe, 1835), p. 103.

25. [Y. S. Nathanson], "Negro Minstrelsy—Ancient and Modern," *Putnam's Monthly* 5 (January 1855), 74. For other relevant perspectives on romantic racialism, see George Fredrickson, *The Black Image in the White Mind: The Debate on Afro-American Character and Destiny, 1817–1914* (New York: Harper and Row, 1971), pp. 97–129, and Allan Moore Emery, "The Topicality of Depravity in 'Benito Cereno,'" *American Literature* 55 (October 1983), 316–31.

26. Saidiya Hartman, "'Innocent Amusements': The Stage of Sufferance," in "Performing Blackness" (unpublished manuscript); Gary D. Engle, *This Grotesque Essence: Plays from the American Minstrel Stage* (Baton Rouge: Louisiana State University Press, 1978), pp. xxvi–xxviii; Alexander Saxton, "Blackface Minstrelsy and Jacksonian Ideology," *American Quarterly* 27 (March 1975), 3–28; Robert C. Toll, *Blacking Up: The Minstrel Show in Nineteenth-Century America* (New York: Oxford University Press, 1974), pp. 73–88; Eric Lott, "'The Seeming Counter-

feit': Racial Politics and Early Blackface Minstrelsy," *American Quarterly* 43 (June 1991), 223–54. For another view of the sources of Babo's masquerade in mummery, see Gerald Early, *Tuxedo Junction: Essays on American Culture* (New York: Ecco Press, 1989), pp. 215–30.

27. Melville, *Benito Cereno*, p. 283.

28. Melville, *Pierre; Or, the Ambiguities,* ed. Harrison Hayford et al. (Evanston: Northwestern University Press, 1971), p. 227.

29. Melville, *Benito Cereno*, pp. 289, 263, 266, 270–71. Cf. Robert S. Levine, *Conspiracy and Romance: Studies in Brockden Brown, Cooper, Hawthorne, and Melville* (New York: Cambridge University Press, 1989), pp. 223–24.

30. Melville, *Benito Cereno*, pp. 268, 271–73, 263, 258.

31. Ibid., pp. 277–83; all quotations in the discussion that follows are drawn from these pages.

32. Higginson quoted in Tilden G. Edelstein, *Strange Enthusiasm: A Life of Thomas Wentworth Higginson* (New Haven: Yale University Press, 1968), p. 211.

33. John W. Blassingame, *The Slave Community: Plantation Life in the Antebellum South,* rev. ed. (New York: Oxford University Press, 1979), pp. 192–248; Thomas Wentworth Higginson, "Nat Turner's Insurrection," in *Travellers and Outlaws: Episodes in American History* (Boston: Lee and Shepard, 1889), pp. 322–25.

34. George Fitzhugh, *Cannibals All! or, Slaves without Masters,* ed. C. Vann Woodward (Cambridge, Mass.: Harvard University Press, 1960), pp. 204–5; Rogin, *Subversive Genealogy,* p. 215; Melville, *Benito Cereno,* pp. 283, 285; Ira Berlin, "After Nat Turner: A Letter from the North," *Journal of Negro History* 55 (April 1970), 145.

35. Philip Fisher, "Democratic Social Space: Whitman, Melville, and the Promise of American Transparency," *Representations* 24 (Fall 1988), 96–97; Melville, *Benito Cereno,* p. 277.

36. Delano, *Narrative of Voyages,* p. 550; Melville, *Benito Cereno,* pp. 295, 299; *Richmond Enquirer,* 30 August 1831, quoted in Henry Irving Tragle, *The Southampton Slave Revolt of 1831: A Compilation of Source Materials* (Amherst: University of Massachusetts Press, 1971), p. 44.

37. Melville, *Benito Cereno,* p. 243.

38. Ibid., p. 278; Sterling Stuckey, *Slave Culture: Nationalist Theory and the Foundations of Black America* (New York: Oxford University Press, 1987), p. 19; Harold Courlander, *The Drum and the Hoe: Life and Lore of the Haitian People* (Berkeley: University of California Press, 1960), pp. 189–202.

39. Dena J. Epstein, *Sinful Tunes and Spirituals: Black Folk Music to the Civil War* (Urbana: University of Illinois Press, 1977), pp. 45–60; Blassingame, *The Slave Community,* pp. 35–36; James Pope-Hennessy, *Sins of the Fathers: A Study of the Atlantic Slave Traders, 1441–1807* (London: Weidenfeld and Nicolson, 1967), 140–43; Hunt, *Haiti's Influence on Antebellum America,* pp. 77–80; Eileen Southern, *The Music of Black Americans: A History* (New York: Norton, 1971), p. 67.

40. See Gloria Horsley-Meacham, "The Monastic Slaver: Images and Meaning in *Benito Cereno*," *New England Quarterley* 55 (June 1983), 261–66; Genovese, *From Rebellion to Revolution,* pp. 28–32.

41. R. S. Rattray, *Religion and Art in Ashanti* (London: Oxford University Press, 1927), pp. 115–16, 139–43; Sterling Stuckey, "'Follow Your Leader': The Theme of Cannibalism in Melville's *Benito Cereno*" (unpublished paper). Stuckey notes also that the impression given that Aranda's body has been shaved clean of its flesh may have been derived from the wounds to the blacks, made by the white crew's sharp lances, that were observed by the actual Delano ("some with half their backs and thighs shaved off," *Narrative of Voyages,* p. 328), and in turn changed by Melville into his remark about the wounds ("mostly inflicted by the long-edged sealing-spears, resembling those shaven ones of the English at Preston Pans, made by the poled scythes of the Highlanders," *Benito Cereno,* p. 299).

42. Geoffrey Sanborn, "Cannibalism and Skepticism in Melville's *Benito Cereno*" (unpublished paper).

43. R. S. Rattray, *Ashanti* (1923; rpt. New York: Negro Universities Press, 1969), pp. 77–85, 241–86; George P. Rawick, *From Sundown to Sunup: The Making of the Black Community* (Westport, Conn.: Greenwood, 1972), pp. 27–28; Genovese, *From Rebellion to Revolution,* p. 100; John Beecham, *Ashanti and the Gold Coast* (1841; rpt. London: Dawsons, 1968), pp. 241–43; Henry Edward Krehbiel, *Afro-American Folksongs: A Study in Racial and National Music* (1913; rpt. New York: Frederick Ungar, 1962), p. 65; Melville, *Benito Cereno,* pp. 268, 310; Joshua Leslie and Sterling Stuckey, "The Death of Benito Cereno: A Reading of Herman Melville on Slavery," *Journal of Negro History* 67 (Winter 1982), 289–90.

44. Melville, *Benito Cereno,* pp. 250–53, 261–62.

45. Hunt, *Haiti's Influence on Antebellum America,* p. 2; Webster quoted in Mary Cable, *Black Odyssey: The Case of the Slave Ship Amistad* (1971; rpt. New York: Penguin, 1977), p. 152.

46. Robert I. Rotberg, *Haiti: The Politics of Squalor* (Boston: Houghton Mifflin, 1971), pp. 76–90; Bird, *The Black Man,* pp. 288–306; Spenser St. John, *Hayti, or the Black Republic* (London: Smith, Elder, 1884); pp. 90–99; "On the Rumored Occupation of San Domingo by the Emperor of France," *United States Democratic Review* 32 (February 1853), 181–83.

47. Dexter Perkins, *The Monroe Doctrine, 1826–1867* (Baltimore: Johns Hopkins University Press, 1933), pp. 253–317; Charles Callan Tansill, *The United States and Santo Domingo, 1798–1873: A Chapter in Caribbean Diplomacy* (Baltimore: Johns Hopkins University Press, 1938), pp. 137–212; Logan, *Diplomatic Relations,* pp. 238–92; Basil Rauch, *American Interest in Cuba, 1848–1855* (New York: Columbia University Press, 1948), pp. 280–94; David M. Potter, *The Impending Crisis, 1848–1861* (New York: Harper and Row, 1976), pp. 177–98, quote at p. 198; Robert E. May, *The Southern Dream of a Caribbean Empire, 1854–1861* (Baton Rouge: Louisiana State University Press, 1973), pp. 21–75; "The Kansas Question," *Putnam's Monthly* 6 (October 1855), 425–33; John Bigelow, quoted in Logan, *Diplomatic Relations,* p. 281.

48. Delano, *Narrative of Voyages,* pp. 146–47, 347; Joshua Leslie and Sterling Stuckey, "Avoiding the Tragedy of Benito Cereno: The Official Response to Babo's Revolt," *Criminal Justice History,* 3 (1982), 125–32; Aptheker, *American Negro Slave Revolts,* pp. 300–310; James, *Black Jacobins,* pp. 95–96; Genovese, *From Rebellion to Revolution,* pp. 43, 106; Vincent Harding, *There Is a River: The Black Struggle for Freedom in America* (New York: Random House, 1981), pp. 34–35, 99; Melville, *Benito Cereno,* p. 315.

49. See Brook Thomas, *Cross-Examinations of Law and Literature: Cooper, Hawthorne, Stowe, and Melville* (New York: Cambridge University Press, 1987), pp. 94–105.

50. Melville, *Benito Cereno,* pp. 241, 295; Frederick Douglass quoted in Jane H. Pease and William H. Pease, *They Who Would Be Free: Blacks' Search for Freedom, 1830–1861* (New York: Atheneum, 1974), pp. 236–37; *New London Gazette,* 26 August 1839, quoted in John W. Barber, *A History of the Amistad Captives* (New Haven: E. L. and J. W. Barber, 1840), p. 4.

51. John Quincy Adams, *Argument in the Case of the United States vs. Cinque* (1841; rpt. New York: Arno Press, 1969), p. 9. See also Cable, *Black Odyssey,* pp. 76–108; Sidney Kaplan, "Herman Melville and the American National Sin," *Journal of Negro History* 41 (October 1956), 311–38; Rogin, *Subversive Genealogy,* pp. 211–12; and Howard Jones, *Mutiny on the Amistad: The Saga of a Slave Revolt and Its Impact on American Abolition, Law, and Diplomacy* (New York: Oxford University Press, 1987), pp. 175–82.

52. Robert M. Cover, *Justice Accused: Antislavery and the Judicial Process* (New Haven: Yale University Press, 1975), pp. 111–16, quote at p. 111; Jones, *Mutiny on the Amistad,* pp. 130–31, 146–47, 189–93.

53. Melville, *Benito Cereno,* pp. 268, 310; Delano, *Narrative of Voyages,* p. 341; James, *Black Jacobins,* p. 117; Franklin, *Present State of Hayti,* p. 62. On the appeal to "nature" in the antebellum discourse of racism, see, for example, William R. Stanton, *The Leopard's Spots: Scientific Attitudes toward Race in America, 1815–59* (Chicago: University of Chicago Press, 1966), and Reginald Horsman, *Race and Manifest Destiny: The Origins of American Racial Anglo-Saxonism* (Cambridge, Mass.: Harvard University Press, 1981), pp. 116–57.

54. Newton Arvin echoes the misguided sentiments of some early readers and reviewers when he calls the tale an "artistic miscarriage" and notes that "the scene of the actual mutiny on the San Dominick, which might have been transformed into an episode of great and frightful power, Melville was too tired to rewrite at all, and except for a few trifling details, he leaves it all as he found it, in the drearily prosaic prose of a judicial deposition." See *Herman Melville* (New York: William Sloane, 1950), pp. 238–39.

55. Melville, *Benito Cereno,* pp. 299–300.

56. Ibid., pp. 307, 313.

57. Ibid., pp. 313, 315.

58. Ibid., pp. 260, 313, 269, 314.

59. Ibid., p. 315; Barber, *A History of the Amistad Captives,* p. 4; Robert S. Starobin,

ed., *Denmark Vesey: The Slave Conspiracy of 1822* (Englewood Cliffs, N.J.: Prentice-Hall, 1970), p. 112; John R. Beard, *The Life of Toussaint L'Ouverture: The Negro Patriot of Hayti* (1853; rpt. Westport, Conn.: Negro Universities Press, 1970), p. 256. Cf. James, *Black Jacobins,* pp. 361–62, and Genovese, *From Rebellion to Revolution,* p. 108.

60. Melville, *Benito Cereno,* pp. 281, 260, 274, 246, 257, 276.

61. Rauch, *American Interest in Cuba,* pp. 275–77; Philip S. Foner, *A History of Cuba and Its Relations with the United States,* 2 vols. (New York: International, 1963), II, 75–85; Charles W. Davis quoted in Foner, *History of Cuba,* II, 81–82; "Ostend Manifesto," *Documents of American History,* 2 vols. in 1, ed. Henry Steele Commager (New York: F. S. Croft, 1934), I, 333–35.

62. Martin R. Delany, *Blake; or the Huts of America* (Boston: Beacon Press, 1970), pp. 19–20, 84–85, 112–13, 251; *Anglo-African Magazine* 1 (January 1859), 20; Allan D. Austin, "The Significance of Martin Robison Delany's *Blake; or the Huts of America*" (Ph.D. diss., University of Massachusetts, 1975), pp. 14–17, 25–26, 52–53.

63. C. Duncan Rice, *The Rise and Fall of Black Slavery* (Baton Rouge: Louisiana State University Press, 1975), pp. 278–79; A. Curtis Wilgus, "Official Expression of Manifest Destiny Sentiment Concerning Hispanic America, 1848–1871," *Louisiana Historical Quarterly* 15 (July 1932), 486–506; Edward A. Pollard, *Black Diamonds Gathered in the Darkey Homes of the South* (New York: Pudney and Russell, 1859), pp. 106–15; William Walker, *The War in Nicaragua* (Mobile: S. H. Goetzel, 1860), pp. 251–80.

64. C. Stanley Urban, "The Ideology of Southern Imperialism: New Orleans and the Caribbean, 1845–1860," *Louisiana Historical Quarterly* 39 (January 1956), 48–73; "The Cuban Debate," *United States Magazine and Democratic Review* 31 (November–December 1852), 433–56; Donald S. Spencer, *Louis Kossuth and Young America: A Study of Sectionalism and Foreign Policy, 1848–1852* (Columbia: University of Missouri Press, 1977), pp. 166–69.

65. "Destiny of the Slave States," *De Bow's Review* 17 (September 1854), 280–84. Cf. Eugene Genovese, *The Political Economy of Slavery: Studies in the Economy and Society of the Slave South* (New York: Vintage Books, 1967), pp. 243–74.

66. May, *Southern Dream,* pp. 148–50; Mannix and Cowley, *Black Cargoes,* pp. 266–74; J. Dennis Harris, "A Summer on the Borders of the Caribbean Sea" (1860), reprinted in Howard H. Bell, *Black Separatism and the Caribbean, 1860* (Ann Arbor: University of Michigan Press, 1970), p. 172; James T. Holly, "A Vindication of the Capacity of the Negro Race Demonstrated by Historical Events of the Haytian Revolution," in Bell, *Black Separatism,* p. 64.

67. Martin Delany, "The Political Destiny of the Colored Race," in Sterling Stuckey, ed., *The Ideology of Black Nationalism* (Boston: Beacon, 1972), pp. 196–97, 201–3; Victor Ullman, *Martin R. Delany: The Beginnings of Black Nationalism* (Boston: Beacon, 1971), p. 50; Delany, *Official Report of the Niger Valley Exploring Party,* in Howard H. Bell, ed., *Search for a Place: Black Separatism and Africa,*

1860 (Ann Arbor: University of Michigan Press, 1971), pp. 110, 121–22. See also Ullman, *Martin R. Delany*, pp. 141–71, 211–46; Floyd J. Miller, *The Search for a Black Nationality: Black Emigration and Colonization, 1787–1863* (Urbana: University of Illinois Press), pp. 93–231 passim; Stuckey, *Slave Culture*, pp. 228–31; and Harding, *There Is a River*, pp. 186–90.

68. Harding, *There Is a River*, p. 208. See also Wilson Jeremiah Moses, *The Golden Age of Black Nationalism, 1850–1925* (1978; rpt. New York: Oxford University Press, 1988), pp. 149–55, and Ronald T. Takaki, *Violence in the Black Imagination: Essays and Documents* (New York: Putnam's, 1972), pp. 79–101.

69. Ronald T. Takaki, *A Pro-Slavery Crusade: The Agitation to Reopen the African Slave Trade* (New York: Free Press, 1971), pp. 1–68 passim; Davis, *Slavery and Human Progress*, pp. 238–43; W. E. B. Du Bois, *The Suppression of the African Slave Trade to the United States of America, 1638–1870* (1896; rpt. Baton Rouge: Louisiana State University Press, 1969), pp. 164–76, Jefferson Davis quoted at p. 176.

70. Delany, *Blake*, pp. 19–20; Ullman, *Martin R. Delany*, pp. 183–201; Pease and Pease, *They Who Would Be Free*, pp. 246–50.

71. Ullman, *Martin R. Delany*, pp. 38–40; Dorothy Sterling, *The Making of an Afro-American: Martin Robison Delany, 1812–1885* (Garden City, N.Y.: Doubleday, 1971), pp. 62–74; Delany, *Blake*, p. 85; Austin, "The Significance of Martin Robison Delany's *Blake*," pp. 110–39.

72. Delany, *Blake*, pp. 109, 38–41.

73. Ibid., pp. 91, 73, 127; (for Blake as prophet figure, see also pp. 89, 117, 121); Ira Berlin, "After Nat Turner: A Letter from the North," *Journal of Negro History* 55 (April 1970), 145.

74. Delany, *Blake*, 112–14, 124. Among other scientific essays, Delany also contributed an article, "Comets," to the *Anglo-African Magazine* in February 1859, while *Blake* was being serialized. See also Ullman, *Martin R. Delany*, pp. 209–10.

75. See Victor Turner, *The Ritual Process: Structure and Anti-Structure* (Ithaca, N.Y.: Cornell University Press, 1969), p. 128.

76. Herbert Aptheker, "Maroons within the Present Limits of the United States," in Richard Price, ed., *Maroon Societies: Rebel Slave Communities in the Americas*, 2nd ed. (Baltimore: Johns Hopkins Press, 1979), pp. 151–67; Blassingame, *The Slave Community*, pp. 208–14; Genovese, *From Rebellion to Revolution*, pp. 68–70.

77. Eaton, *The Freedom-of-Thought Struggle in the Old South*, pp. 99–102, John Pierce quote at pp. 101–2; Aptheker, *American Negro Slave Revolts*, pp. 345–49; Harvey Wish, "The Slave Insurrection Panic of 1856," *Journal of Negro History* 5 (May 1939), 206–22, *Richmond Enquirer* quoted at pp. 220–21.

78. Sterling, *The Making of an Afro-American*, p. 185.

79. Delany, *Blake*, p. 192.

80. Leslie B. Rout, *The African Experience in Spanish America, 1502 to the Present Day* (New York: Cambridge University Press, 1976), pp. 289–92; Franklin W. Knight, *Slave Society in Cuba during the Nineteenth Century* (Madison: Univer-

sity of Wisconsin Press, 1970), pp. 47–58; Arthur F. Corwin, *Spain and the Abolition of Slavery in Cuba, 1817–1886* (Austin: University of Texas Press, 1967), pp. 47–67; Mannix and Cowley, *Black Cargoes,* pp. 205–15; Davis, *Slavery and Human Progress,* pp. 285–86; Du Bois, *The Suppression of the African Slave Trade,* p. 162. A contemporary account of antislave trade cruisers is Andrew H. Foote, *Africa and the American Flag* (New York: D. Appleton, 1854).

81. Hugh Thomas, *Cuba: The Pursuit of Freedom* (New York: Harper and Row, 1971), p. 159; Mannix and Cowley, *Black Cargoes,* pp. 232–33.

82. Delany, *Blake,* pp. 215–20.

83. Corwin, *Spain and the Abolition of Slavery in Cuba,* pp. 56–59; Eugene D. Genovese, *The World the Slaveholders Made: Two Essays in Interpretation* (New York: Random House, 1969), p. 69; Herbert S. Klein, *Slavery in the Americas: A Comparative Study of Virginia and Cuba* (1967; rpt. Chicago: Elephant Reprints, 1989), pp. 194–214; Gwendolyn Midlo Hall, *Social Control in Slave Plantation Societies: A Comparison of St. Domingue and Cuba* (Baltimore: Johns Hopkins University Press, 1971), pp. 16–23; Rice, *The Rise and Fall of Black Slavery,* pp. 280–86; Robert L. Paquette, *Sugar Is Made with Blood: The Conspiracy of La Escalera and the Conflict between Empires over Slavery in Cuba* (Middletown, Conn.: Wesleyan University Press, 1988), pp. 51–80, quote at p. 56.

84. Delany, *Blake,* pp. 259–60. On Cuban and other Latin American maroons, see also Herbert S. Klein, *African Slavery in Latin America and the Caribbean* (New York: Oxford University Press, 1986), pp. 189–215; Genovese, *From Rebellion to Revolution,* pp. 40, 51–54, 77–78; and in particular the essays by Philalethes, Riva, and Franco in Price, *Maroon Societies.*

85. Delany, *Blake,* pp. 261, 285.

86. Ibid., p. 291.

87. Anonymous review of Kimball, *Cuba and the Cubans, North American Review* 79 (July 1854), 130. On La Escalera, see Thomas, *Cuba,* pp. 205–6; Corwin, *Spain and the Abolition of Slavery in Cuba,* pp. 74–82; Foner, *History of Cuba,* I, 214–18; Klein, *Slavery in the Americas,* pp. 219–21; and especially Paquette, *Sugar Is Made with Blood,* pp. 209–66.

88. Delany, *Blake,* p. 184; J. G. F. Wurdemann, *Notes on Cuba* (Boston: James Munroe, 1844), pp. 357–58.

89. Frederick S. Stimson, *Cuba's Romantic Poet: The Story of Placido* (Chapel Hill: University of North Carolina Press, 1964); [William Henry Hurlbert], "The Poetry of Spanish America," *North American Review* 68 (January 1849), 129–60; Austin, "The Significance of Martin Robison Delany's *Blake,*" pp. 145–54; Paquette, *Sugar Is Made with Blood,* pp. 117–18, 256–62.

90. Renato Rosaldo, *Culture and Truth: The Remaking of Social Analysis* (Boston: Beacon Press, 1989), p. 17.

91. Janheinz Jahn, *Muntu: An Outline of Neo-African Culture,* trans. Marjorie Grene (London: Faber and Faber, 1961), pp. 69–70; E. J. Hobsbawm, *Primitive Rebels: Studies in Archaic Forms of Social Movement in the Nineteenth and Twentieth Centuries* (New York: Norton, 1965), pp. 162–74.

92. Paquette, *Sugar Is Made with Blood,* pp. 108–9, 127–28; Klein, *Slavery in the Americas,* pp. 100–103; Thomas, *Cuba,* pp. 517–19; Hubert S. Aimes, "African Institutions in America," *Journal of American Folklore* 18 (January–March 1905), 15–32.

93. Paquette, *Sugar Is Made with Blood,* pp. 109, 72.

94. Delany, *Blake,* pp. 245, 266.

95. Wurdemann, *Notes on Cuba,* pp. 83–84; Delany, *Blake,* p. 301. I have not discovered the passage in likely sources such as *Putnam's Monthly, DeBow's Review, Southern Quarterly Review,* or *North American Review.*

96. Thomas, *Cuba,* p. 147; Jahn, *Muntu,* pp. 78–79; M. M. Bakhtin, *Rabelais and His World,* trans. Hélène Iswolsky (Bloomington: Indiana University Press, 1984).

97. Delany, *Blake,* pp. 297–98.

98. Foner, *History of Cuba,* II, 66–85; C. Stanley Urban, "The Africanization of Cuba Scare," *Hispanic American Historical Review* 37 (February 1957), 29–45; "The Invasion of Cuba," *Southern Quarterly Review* 21 (January 1852), 4; "Cuba," *Putnam's Monthly* 1 (January 1853), 16; Richard Burleigh Kimball, *Cuba and the Cubans* (New York: Samuel Hueston, 1850), pp. 191–93.

99. Delany, *Blake,* p. 302.

100. Corwin, *Spain and the Abolition of Slavery in Cuba,* pp. 93–106, Roncali quoted at p. 101; Thomas, *Cuba,* p. 214; Delany, *Blake,* p. 305.

101. Delany, *Blake,* pp. 313, 305.

3. Mark Twain and Homer Plessy

1. Mark Twain, *Pudd'nhead Wilson and "Those Extraordinary Twins,"* ed. Sidney E. Berger (New York: Norton, 1980), pp. 8–9.

2. See Hershel Parker, *Flawed Texts and Verbals Icons: Literary Authority in American Fiction* (Evanston: Northwestern University Press, 1984), pp. 115–45.

3. Twain, *Pudd'nhead Wilson,* p. 35; George W. Walker, "The Real 'Coon' on the American Stage," *Theatre Magazine* 6 (August 1906), 224–26. Cf. Nathan Huggins, *Harlem Renaissance* (New York: Oxford University Press, 1971) p. 282.

4. Mark Twain, "Which Was It?," in *Which Was the Dream and Other Symbolic Writings of the Late Years,* ed. John S. Tuckey (Berkeley: University of California Press, 1968), p. 320.

5. On the cultural reunion of North and South, see, for example, C. Vann Woodward, *Origins of the New South, 1877–1913* (Baton Rouge: Louisiana State University Press, 1951), pp. 142–74; Paul H. Buck, *The Road to Reunion, 1865–1900* (Boston: Little, Brown, 1937), pp. 209–35; Francis Pendleton Gaines, *The Southern Plantation: A Study in the Development and the Accuracy of a Tradition* (New York: Columbia University Press, 1925), pp. 62–94, 209–36; Rayford W. Logan, *The Betrayal of the Negro: From Rutherford B. Hayes to Woodrow Wilson* (1954; rev. ed. New York: Collier, 1965), pp. 242–75; Joyce Appleby, "Reconciliation and the Northern Novelist, 1865–1880," *Civil War History* 10 (June 1964), 117–

29; Rollin G. Osterweis, *The Myth of the Lost Cause, 1865–1900* (Hamden, Conn.: Archon, 1973), pp. 3–65, 92–117, 143–52; Paul M. Gaston, *The New South Creed: A Study in Southern Mythmaking* (New York: Alfred A. Knopf, 1970); Gaines M. Foster, *Ghosts of the Confederacy: Defeat, the Lost Cause, and the Emergence of the New South, 1865 to 1913* (New York: Oxford University Press, 1987); and Wayne Mixon, *Southern Writers and the New South Movement, 1865–1913* (Chapel Hill: University of North Carolina Press, 1980); Albion Tourgée, "The South as a Field for Fiction," quoted in Woodward, *Origins of the New South*, p. 165.

6. Twain, *Pudd'nhead Wilson*, p. 119. See, for example, Justin Kaplan, *Mr. Clemens and Mark Twain* (New York: Simon and Schuster, 1966), pp. 341–47; Arthur G. Pettit, *Mark Twain and the South* (Lexington: University Press of Kentucky, 1974), pp. 141–72; Evan Carton, "*Pudd'nhead Wilson* and the Fiction of Law and Custom," in *American Realism: New Essays,* ed. Eric J. Sundquist (Baltimore: Johns Hopkins University Press, 1982), pp. 82–94; and Susan K. Gillman, *Dark Twins: Imposture and Identity in Mark Twain's America* (Chicago: University of Chicago Press, 1989), pp. 53–95.

7. Mark Twain, *Adventures of Huckleberry Finn,* ed. Sculley Bradley et al. (New York: Norton, 1977), p. 215. See especially Laurence B. Holland, "A 'Raft of Trouble': Word and Deed in *Huckleberry Finn,*" in Sundquist, *American Realism: New Essays,* pp. 66–81; Forrest G. Robinson, *In Bad Faith: The Dynamics of Deception in Mark Twain's America* (Cambridge, Mass.: Harvard University Press, 1986), pp. 211–41; and Kenneth S. Lynn, *Mark Twain and Southwestern Humor* (Boston: Little, Brown, 1959), pp. 236–45.

8. Twain, *Pudd'nhead Wilson*, pp. 169–70; Charles Chesnutt, *The Marrow of Tradition* (1901; rpt. Ann Arbor: University of Michigan Press, 1969), p. 57. For an excellent alternative reading of Twain's novel in the context of *Plessy* (with particular attention to Tourgée) which has modified my own views, see Brook Thomas, "Tragedies of Race, Training, Birth, and Communities of Competent Pudd'nheads," *American Literary History* 1 (Winter 1989), 754–85. A further reading of *Pudd'nhead Wilson* in the context of legal theory is available in Richard Posner, *Law and Literature: A Misunderstood Relation* (Cambridge, Mass.: Harvard University Press, 1988), pp. 82–86.

9. My account of *Plessy v. Ferguson* and its background relies primarily on these sources: Otto H. Olsen, *The Thin Disguise: Plessy v. Ferguson, A Documentary Presentation* (New York: Humanities Press, 1967); Olsen, *The Carpetbagger's Crusade: A Life of Albion Winegar Tourgée* (Baltimore: Johns Hopkins University Press, 1965), pp. 312–31; C. Vann Woodward, "The National Decision against Equality," in *American Counterpoint: Slavery and Racism in the North-South Dialogue* (Boston: Little, Brown, 1971), pp. 212–33; Richard Kluger, *Simple Justice: The History of Brown v. Board of Education and Black America's Struggle for Equality* (New York: Random House, 1975), pp. 51–83; Robert J. Harris, *The Quest for Equality: The Constitution, Congress, and the Supreme Court* (Baton Rouge: Louisiana State University Press, 1960), pp. 82–108; Loren Miller, *The Petitioners: The Story of the Supreme Court of the United States and the Negro*

(New York: Random House, 1966), pp. 99–160; Leonard W. Levy and Harlan B. Phillips, "The *Roberts* Case: Source of the 'Separate but Equal' Doctrine," *American Historical Review* 56 (April 1951), 510–18; Barton J. Bernstein, "Case Law in *Plessy* v. *Ferguson,*" *Journal of Negro History* 47 (July 1962), 192–98; Paul Oberst, "The Strange Career of *Plessy* v. *Ferguson,*" *Arizona Law Review* 15 (1973), 389ff.; and Charles Lofgren, *The Plessy Case: A Legal-Historical Interpretation* (New York: Oxford University Press, 1987).

10. Charles Fenner, *Ex parte Homer A. Plessy,* 45 La. Ann. 80 (1893), reprinted in Olsen, *The Thin Disguise,* pp. 71–74; Fenner cites the Pennsylvania State Supreme Court in *Westchester R.R. Co.* v. *Miles,* 55 Penn. St. 209 (1867), and Shaw, *Roberts* v. *City of Boston,* 5 Cush. 198. For Shaw's decision in the Sims case, see *Thomas Sims's Case,* 61 Mass. 285 (1851).

11. Fenner, *Ex parte Homer A. Plessy,* in Olsen, *The Thin Disguise,* p. 73; Lofgren, *The Plessy Case,* pp. 52–53; Gregg Crane, "Mark Twain and John Marshall Harlan: Two Paradigms of Justice" (unpublished paper); Woodward, "The National Decision against Equality," p. 229; Brown, *Plessy* v. *Ferguson,* 163 U. S. 537, in Olsen, *The Thin Disguise,* pp. 108–12.

12. *Dred Scott* v. *Sandford,* 60 U.S. (19 Howard) 393 (1857); Kenneth Karst, *Belonging to America: Equal Citizenship and the Constitution* (New Haven: Yale University Press, 1989), pp. 43–46; Kluger, *Simple Justice,* pp. 39–40; Don Fehrenbacher, *The Dred Scott Case: Its Significance in American Law and Politics* (New York: Oxford University Press, 1978).

13. Lofgren, *The Plessy Case,* 174–91, quote at p. 179; Eric Foner, *Reconstruction: America's Unfinished Revolution, 1863–1877* (New York: Harper and Row, 1988), pp. 256–59.

14. Harris, *The Quest for Equality,* p. 101; Miller, *The Petitioners,* p. 106; Lofgren, *The Plessy Case,* pp. 61–78; Foner, *Reconstruction,* pp. 529–34. On the role of dual citizenship in the Civil War amendment debates, see also Herman Belz, *Emancipation and Equal Rights: Politics and Constitutionalism in the Civil War Era* (New York: Norton, 1978), pp. 119–40.

15. Frederick Douglass quoted in Miller, *The Petitioners,* p. 114.

16. Charles Sumner quoted in Harris, *The Quest for Equality,* pp. 50–51. On the legislation and its reversal, see also James M. McPherson, *The Abolitionist Legacy: From Reconstruction to the NAACP* (Princeton: Princeton University Press, 1975), pp. 13–23, and Karst, *Belonging to America,* pp. 46–61.

17. Bradley and Harlan, *Civil Rights Cases* 109 U.S. 3, quoted in Harris, *The Quest for Equality,* pp. 87–91; Miller, *The Petitioners,* pp. 138–44; Kluger, *Simple Justice,* pp. 65–66; Lofgren, *The Plessy Case,* pp. 74–76; Crane, "Mark Twain and John Marshall Harlan."

18. Fenner, *Ex parte Homer A. Plessy,* in Olsen, *The Thin Disguise,* p. 73; Waite, *United States* v. *Cruikshank,* 92 U.S. 554, quoted in Harris, *The Quest for Equality,* p. 85; Brown, *Plessy* v. *Ferguson,* in Olsen, *The Thin Disguise,* pp. 108–9.

19. Lofgren, *The Plessy Case,* pp. 196–99; Logan, *The Betrayal of the Negro,* pp. 211–12; Emma Lou Thornbrough quoted in C. Vann Woodward, *The Strange*

Career of Jim Crow, 2d rev. ed. (New York: Oxford University Press, 1966), p. 72.

20. Harlan, *Plessy* v. *Ferguson,* in Olsen, *The Thin Disguise,* p. 113–21; Lofgren, *The Plessy Case,* pp. 191–95. Harlan's position reverted toward that of Lemuel Shaw in 1899, however, when he wrote the majority opinion in *Cumming* v. *Richmond County Board of Education,* 175 U.S. 528, which upheld separate but equal schools. Both an advocate of black rights, in most cases, and a conservative defender of property rights, Harlan betrayed an unusual mix of attitudes. As a former slaveholder converted to the cause of civil rights, as Kluger points out, Harlan's evolution, not entirely unlike Twain's response to childhood memories of slave-holding and to postwar violence, might be "traceable to the brutalities he saw inflicted upon Negroes in his native Kentucky during the post–Civil War years—beatings, lynchings, terror tactics beyond any conceivable justification." See Kluger, *Simple Justice,* p. 81.

21. Tourgée, *Brief for Homer A. Plessy,* in Olsen, *The Thin Disguise,* pp. 80–103; Frederick Douglass, *Life and Writings of Frederick Douglass,* ed. Philip S. Foner, 5 vols. (New York: International, 1952–75), III, 292; Sumner, *Roberts* v. *City of Boston,* reprinted as "Equality before the Law," in *Complete Works* (1900; rpt. New York: Negro Universities Press, 1969), III, 81.

22. Twain, *Pudd'nhead Wilson,* p. 44.

23. Stanley P. Hirshson, *Farewell to the Bloody Shirt: Northern Republicans and the Southern Negro, 1877–1893* (Bloomington: Indiana University Press, 1962), pp. 78–258 passim.

24. Bertram Wyatt-Brown, *Southern Honor: Ethics and Behavior in the Old South* (New York: Oxford University Press, 1982), pp. 362–401; Crane, "Mark Twain and John Marshall Harlan."

25. C. Vann Woodward, *The Origins of the New South, 1877–1913* (Baton Rouge: Louisiana State University Press, 1951), pp. 321–49; McKenna, *Williams* v. *Mississippi,* 170 U.S. 213, quoted in Kluger, *Simple Justice,* pp. 67–68.

26. James Weldon Johnson, *Negro Americans, What Now?* (1934), quoted in Thomas F. Gossett, *Race: The History of an Idea in America* (1963; rpt. New York: Schocken, 1965), pp. 266–67; Twain, *Adventures of Huckleberry Finn,* p. 27.

27. Twain, "The United States of Lyncherdom" (from *Europe and Elsewhere*), in *The Portable Mark Twain,* ed. Bernard DeVoto (New York : Viking, 1968), p. 586; Joel Williamson, *The Crucible of Race: Black-White Relations in the American South since Emancipation* (New York: Oxford University Press, 1984), pp. 318–19. See also George Fredrickson, *The Black Image in the White Mind: The Debate on Afro-American Character and Destiny, 1817–1914* (New York: Harper and Row, 1971), pp. 256–82.

28. *Washington Post,* quoted in Logan, *The Betrayal of the Negro,* p. 211; Albion Tourgée, *A Fool's Errand: A Novel of the South during Reconstruction* (New York: Harper and Row, 1966), pp. 5–6.

29. Tourgée, *Brief for Homer A. Plessy,* in Olsen, *The Thin Disguise,* p. 83.

30. Joel Williamson, *New People: Miscegenation and Mulattoes in the United States*

(New York: Free Press, 1980), pp. 61–109; Eva Saks, "Representing Miscegenation Law," *Raritan* 8 (June 1988), 39–70.

31. Tourgée, *Brief for Homer A. Plessy,* in Olsen, *The Thin Disguise,* pp. 97–98.

32. George Washington Cable, *The Negro Question: A Selection of Writings on Civil Rights in the South,* ed. Arlin Turner (New York: Doubleday, 1958), p. 92; Williamson, *The Crucible of Race,* p. 101; John Lauber, *The Inventions of Mark Twain* (New York: Hill and Wang, 1990), pp. 167–95; Pettit, *Mark Twain and the South,* pp. 131–32. See also Steven Mailloux, "Reading *Huckleberry Finn:* The Rhetoric of Performed Ideology," in Louis J. Budd, ed., *New Essays on Huckleberry Finn* (New York: Cambridge University Press, 1985), pp. 109–24, and *Satire or Evasion: Black Perspectives on Huckleberry Finn,* ed. James S. Leonard et al. (Durham, N. C.: Duke University Press, 1992).

33. Williamson, *New People,* pp. 101–3; Warner quoted in Olsen, *The Thin Disguise,* pp. 43–45.

34. Buck, *The Road to Reunion,* pp. 186–95; Robert W. Rydell, *All the World's a Fair: Visions of Empire at American International Expositions, 1876–1916* (Chicago: University of Chicago Press, 1984), pp. 72–104.

35. Logan, *The Betrayal of the Negro,* pp. 180–82; Osterweis, *The Myth of the Lost Cause,* pp. 127–42; Gaston, *The New South Creed,* pp. 87–150; Booker T. Washington, *Up from Slavery,* in *Three Negro Classics* (New York: Avon, 1965), p. 149.

36. Twain, *Pudd'nhead Wilson,* p. 52, 112; Gillman, *Dark Twins,* pp. 88–91; Anne P. Wigger, "The Source of Fingerprint Material in Mark Twain's *Pudd'nhead Wilson* and 'Those Extraodinary Twins,'" *American Literature* 28 (January 1957), 517–20; Michael Rogin, "Francis Galton and Mark Twain: The Natal Autograph in *Pudd'nhead Wilson,*" in Susan Gillman and Forest Robinson, eds., *Mark Twain's Pudd'nhead Wilson: Race, Conflict, and Culture* (Durham: Duke University Press, 1990), pp. 73–85. On Galton, see also John Higham, *Strangers in the Land: Patterns of American Nativism, 1860–1925* (1955; rpt. New York: Atheneum, 1963), pp. 150–52; Gossett, *Race,* pp. 155–58; and Daniel J. Keveles, *In the Name of Eugenics: Genetics and the Uses of Human Heredity* (Berkeley: University of California Press, 1985), passim.

37. Twain, *Pudd'nhead Wilson,* pp. 112, 103.

38. Ibid., pp. 5–6, 103.

39. Ibid., p. 19.

40. Gabriel Tarde, *The Laws of Imitation,* trans. Elsie Clews Parsons (1903; rpt. Gloucester, Mass.: Peter Smith, 1962), p. 77.

41. John S. Haller, Jr., *Outcasts from Evolution: Scientific Attitudes of Racial Inferiority, 1859–1900* (1971; rpt. New York: McGraw-Hill, 1975), pp. 142–44; Charles A. Ellwood, "The Theory of Imitation in Social Psychology," *American Journal of Sociology* 6 (May 1901), 721–41; Jerome Dowd, "The Racial Element in Social Assimilation," *American Journal of Sociology* 16 (March 1911), 633–35; Philip A. Bruce, *The Plantation Negro as a Freeman* (New York: Putnam's, 1889), pp. 134, 256. See also George W. Stocking, Jr., *Race, Culture, and Evolution: Essays in the History of Anthropology* (New York: Free Press, 1968), pp. 234–69, and Thomas,

"Tragedies of Race, Training, Birth, and Communities of Competent Pudd'n-heads," pp. 863–65.

42. Twain, *Pudd'nhead Wilson*, p. 45.

43. Ibid., pp. 191, 127. Cf. Thomas, "Tragedies of Race, Training, Birth, and Communities of Competent Pudd'nheads," pp. 761–69.

44. Twain, *Pudd'nhead Wilson*, pp. 119–20.

45. Ibid., p. 22; Carolyn Porter, "Roxanna's Plot," in Gillman and Robinson, *Mark Twain's Pudd'nhead Wilson*, p. 134.

46. *Mark Twain–Howells Letters,* ed. Henry Nash Smith and William M. Gibson, 2 vols. (Cambridge, Mass.: Harvard University Press, 1960), I, 10–11; Twain, *Pudd'nhead Wilson*, pp. 5, 125; Sigmund Freud, "The Uncanny," in *Standard Edition of the Complete Psychological Works,* trans. and ed. James Strachey et al. (London: Hogarth, 1953), XVII, 241.

47. Robert C. Toll, *Blacking Up: The Minstrel Show in Nineteenth-Century America* (New York: Oxford University Press, 1974), pp. 195–233 passim; James H. Dormon, "Shaping the Popular Image of Post-Reconstruction American Blacks: The 'Coon Song' Phenomenon of the Gilded Age," *American Quarterly* 40 (December 1988), 450–71.

48. Twain, *Pudd'nhead Wilson*, p. 127.

49. Toll, *Blacking Up,* pp. 136–44; Gossett, *Race,* pp. 378–82; Haller, *Outcasts from Evolution,* pp. 72–73; Stocking, *Race, Culture, and Evolution,* pp. 48–49; Twain, *Pudd'nhead Wilson*, pp. 28, 136–37.

50. René Girard, *Violence and the Sacred,* trans. Patrick Gregory (Baltimore: Johns Hopkins University Press, 1977), pp. 49–67, 159–68, quotes at pp. 63–64, 75.

51. Mark Twain, "Personal Habits of the Siamese Twins," in *Sketches, New and Old* (New York: Harper and Brothers, 1875), pp. 273–79. See also Leslie Fiedler, *Freaks: Myths and Images of the Second Self* (New York: Simon and Schuster, 1978), pp. 204–18; Gillman, *Dark Twins,* pp. 55–69; and Marc Shell, "Those Extraordinary Twins," *Arizona Quarterly* 47 (Summer 1991), 29–75.

52. John E. Coxe, "The New Orleans Mafia Incident," *Louisiana Historical Quarterly* 20 (October 1937), 1066-1110; Maldwyn Allen Jones, *American Immigration* (Chicago: University of Chicago Press, 1960), p. 266; Higham, *Strangers in the Land,* pp. 66, 90–92; Logan, *The Betrayal of the Negro,* pp. 85–86.

53. J. Alexander Karlin, "The Italo-American Incident of 1891 and the Road to Reunion," *Journal of Southern History* 8 (May 1942), 242–46.

54. Twain, *Pudd'nhead Wilson*, p. 2.

55. Ibid., pp. 149, 169.

56. Ibid., pp. 153–54.

57. Pettit, *Mark Twain and the South,* p. 17; Twain, *Pudd'nhead Wilson*, pp. 45, 93–94; James M. Cox, *Mark Twain: The Fate of Humor* (Princeton: Princeton University Press, 1966), p. 232. See also Henry Nash Smith, *Mark Twain: The Development of a Writer* (Cambridge, Mass.: Harvard University Press, 1962), p. 174: "From the standpoint of imaginative coherence Judge York Leicester Driscoll is the father of Tom just as clearly as Roxy is his mother. But Mark

Twain places the unmentionable fact of sexual intercourse between master and slave at two removes from the actual story—first by making Roxy, Tom's mother, the slave of the shadowy brother of Judge Driscoll at the time of Tom's birth; and then by the further precaution of creating an even more shadowy figure, Colonel Cecil Burleigh Essex, to be his father."

58. Twain, *Pudd'nhead Wilson,* pp. 24, 99.

59. Twain, "Which Was It?," pp. 415, 423. See also Pettit, *Mark Twain and the South,* pp. 159–73, and Shelley Fisher Fishkin, "False Starts, Fragments, and Fumbles: Mark Twain's Unpublished Writings on Race," *Essays in Arts and Societies* 20 (October 1991), 17–31.

60. Thomas Nelson Page, "The Negro Question," in *The Old South: Essays Social and Political* (New York: Scribner's Sons, 1892), p. 284; Twain, *Pudd'nhead Wilson,* p. 169.

4. Charles Chesnutt's Cakewalk

1. Charles Chesnutt, *The Marrow of Tradition* (Ann Arbor: University of Michigan Press, 1969), pp. 115–17.

2. Robert W. Rydell, *All the World's a Fair: Visions of Empire at American International Expositions, 1876–1916* (Chicago: University of Chicago Press, 1984), pp. 87–88.

3. See Paul Laurence Dunbar, "We Wear the Mask," in *The Complete Poems of Paul Laurence Dunbar* (New York: Dodd, Mead, 1913), p. 71, and Houston A. Baker, Jr., *Modernism and the Harlem Renaissance* (Chicago: University of Chicago Press, 1987), pp. 25–41.

4. Chesnutt, *The Marrow of Tradition,* p. 118.

5. William Dean Howells quoted in Helen M. Chesnutt, *Charles Waddell Chesnutt: Pioneer of the Color Line* (Chapel Hill: University of North Carolina Press, 1952), p. 177; Benjamin Brawley, *The Negro in Literature and Art,* rev. ed. (New York: Duffield, 1910), pp. 76–81; J. Saunders Redding, *To Make a Poet Black* (Chapel Hill: University of North Carolina Press, 1939), pp. 68–77.

6. Letter to Booker T. Washington, November 5, 1901, quoted in Sylvia Lyons Render, *Charles W. Chesnutt* (Boston: Twayne, 1980), p. 82.

7. Tom Fletcher, *One Hundred Years of the Negro in Show Business* (1954; rpt. New York: Da Capo, 1984), p. 103; Marshall Stearns and Jean Stearns, *Jazz Dance: The Story of American Vernacular Dance* (London: Macmillan, 1966), p. 123.

8. Shephard Edmonds quoted in Rudi Blesh and Harriet Janis, *They All Played Ragtime: The True Story of an American Music* (New York: Alfred A. Knopf, 1950), pp. 96–97; Stearns and Stearns, *Jazz Dance,* p. 22; Katrina Hazzard-Gordon, *Jookin': The Rise of Social Dance Formations in African-American Culture* (Philadelphia: Temple University Press, 1990), pp. 13–47.

9. Henry Edward Krehbiel, *Afro-American Folksongs: A Study in Racial and National Music* (1914; rpt. New York: Frederick Ungar, 1962), pp. 141–44; Melville Herskovits, *The Myth of the Negro Past* (1941; rpt. Boston: Beacon, 1958), p. 158;

Rudi Blesh, *Shining Trumpets: A History of Jazz,* rev. ed. (1958; rpt. New York: Da Capo, 1976), p. 133; Marshall W. Stearns, *The Story of Jazz* (New York: Oxford University Press, 1958), p. 11.

10. Krehbiel, *Afro-American Folksongs,* p. 33; Roscoe Lewis, *The Negro in Virginia* (New York: Hastings House, 1940), pp. 89–90; Stearns and Stearns, *Jazz Dance,* pp. 13–15, 28–31; Hazzard-Gordon, *Jookin',* p. 19; Sterling Stuckey, *Slave Culture: Nationalist Theory and the Foundations of Black America* (New York: Oxford University Press, 1987), p. 65.

11. Will Marion Cook, "Clorindy, the Origin of the Cakewalk," in Lindsay Patterson, ed., *Anthology of the Afro-American in the Theater* (Cornwall Heights, Pa.: Publishers Agency, 1978), p. 55. Information on the cakewalk throughout this section comes from Cook, "Clorindy, the Origin of the Cakewalk," pp. 51–55; James Weldon Johnson, *Black Manhattan* (1930; rpt. New York: Atheneum, 1972), pp. 95–107; Fletcher, *One Hundred Years of the Negro in Show Business,* pp. 103–16; Ann Charters, *Nobody: The Story of Bert Williams* (New York: Macmillan, 1970), pp. 34–40; Allen Woll, *Black Musical Theatre: From Coontown to Dreamgirls* (Baton Rouge: Louisiana State University Press, 1989), pp. 1–49; Nathan Huggins, *Harlem Renaissance* (New York: Oxford University Press, 1971), pp. 273–77; Eileen Southern, *The Music of Black Americans: A History* (New York: Norton, 1971), pp. 273–74; Stearns and Stearns, *Jazz Dance,* pp. 13–31, 118–24; and Edith J. R. Isaacs, *The Negro in American Theater* (New York: Theatre Arts, 1947), pp. 28–42.

12. Rayford W. Logan, *The Betrayal of the Negro: From Rutherford B. Hayes to Woodrow Wilson* (1954; rpt. New York: Collier Books, 1965), pp. 169–70, 242–75; Janette Faulkner et al., *Ethnic Notions: Black Images in the White Mind* (Berkeley: Berkeley Art Association, 1982).

13. Woll, *Black Musical Theatre,* p. 2; J. Stanley Lemons, "Black Stereotypes as Reflected in Popular Culture, 1880–1920," *American Quarterly* 29 (1977), 102–16; William J. Schafer and Johannes Riedel, *The Art of Ragtime: Form and Meaning of an Original Black American Art* (1973; rpt. New York: Da Capo, 1977), pp. 161–75; Joseph Boskin, *Sambo: The Rise and Demise of an American Jester* (New York: Oxford University Press, 1986), pp. 121–47; and James H. Dormon, "Shaping the Popular Image of Post-Reconstruction American Blacks: The 'Coon Song' Phenomenon of the Gilded Age," *American Quarterly* 40 (December 1988), 450–71; Ernest Hogan quoted in Fletcher, *One Hundred Years of the Negro in Show Business,* pp. 138–43, and in Stearns and Stearns, *Jazz Dance,* p. 120.

14. "Who Dat Say Chicken in Dis Crowd?" lyrics and Mrs. Cook quoted in Woll, *Black Musical Theatre,* p. 8; sheet-music illustration reproduced in Charters, *Nobody,* p. 39.

15. Robert C. Toll, *Blacking Up: The Minstrel Show in Nineteenth-Century America* (New York: Oxford University Press, 1974), pp. 238–45; Blesh and Janis, *They All Played Ragtime,* p. 85.

16. Cf. the notion of "imperialist nostalgia" advanced by Renato Rosaldo in *Culture*

and Truth: The Remaking of Social Analysis (Boston: Beacon Press, 1989), pp. 68–87.

17. Carl Wittke, *Tambo and Bones: A History of the American Minstrel Stage* (Durham: Duke University Press, 1930), pp. 153–54; Toll, *Blacking Up,* pp. 201–10.

18. Southern, *The Music of Black Americans,* pp. 274–75; Fletcher, *One Hundred Years of the Negro in Show Business,* pp. 94–97; Huggins, *Harlem Renaissance,* p. 278; Toll, *Blacking Up,* pp. 262–63.

19. Blesh and Janis, *They All Played Ragtime,* p. 100; Schafer and Riedel, *The Art of Ragtime,* pp. 8, 30–32, 112–15; Stearns and Stearns, *Jazz Dance,* p. 123.

20. Krehbiel, *Afro-American Folksongs,* pp. 92–93; *Musical Courier* quoted in Stearns and Stearns, *Jazz Dance,* p. 123.

21. *Boston Illustrated American* quoted in Marian Hannah Winter, "Juba and American Minstrelsy," in *Chronicles of the American Dance,* ed. Paul Magriel (1948; rpt. New York: Da Capo, 1978), pp. 61–62.

22. George W. Walker, "The Real 'Coon' on the American Stage," *Theatre Magazine* 6 (August 1906), 224–26; Charters, *Nobody,* pp. 69–70; *Frank Leslie's Popular Monthly* quoted in Rydell, *All the World's a Fair,* p. 66.

23. Johnson, *Black Manhatttan,* p. 105.

24. Huggins, *Harlem Renaissance,* pp. 270–74. Huggins observes that American high society was a society of performers in which the "newness and openness of society created its special anxieties. . . . All was a jumble of masks and costumes covering naked uncertainties. White men pretended to be black men of their fantasy, black men pretended to be the grotesques that white men had created, while other white men and women pretended to be aristocrats. . . . It was all theater of the absurd" (p. 274).

25. Courlander, cited in Stearns and Stearns, *Jazz Dance,* p. 13.

26. Ibid., pp. 15–31. Cf. Janheinz Jahn, *Muntu, An Outline of Neo-African Culture,* trans. Marjorie Grene (London: Faber and Faber, 1961), pp. 85–86.

27. Charles W. Chesnutt, "Superstitions and Folklore of the South," *Modern Culture* 13 (1901), 231–35; rpt. in Alan Dundes, ed., *Mother Wit from the Laughing Barrel: Readings in the Interpretation of Afro-American Folklore* (1973; rpt. New York: Garland, 1981), pp. 369–76.

28. Chesnutt, "Post-Bellum—Pre-Harlem," *Crisis* (1931), rpt. in *Breaking into Print,* ed. Elmer Adler (1937; rpt. Freeport, N.Y.: Books for Libraries, 1968), p. 50; Chesnutt, "Superstitions and Folklore of the South," p. 371.

29. Robert Hemenway, "The Functions of Folklore in Charles Chesnutt's *The Conjure Woman,*" *Journal of the Folklore Institute* 13 (1976), 283–309; Chesnutt, "Superstitions and Folklore of the South," p. 371.

30. Chesnutt, "Superstitions and Folklore of the South," p. 372.

31. Leroi Jones [Amiri Baraka], *Blues People: Negro Music in White America* (New York: William Morrow, 1963), pp. 58–59, 131–32.

32. Chesnutt, *The Wife of His Youth and Other Stories* (Ann Arbor: University of Michigan Press, 1968), pp. 8–10, 14.

33. Alice Walker, *In Search of Our Mother's Gardens* (New York: Harcourt Brace Jovanovich), p. 300; Chesnutt, *The Wife of His Youth,* pp. 7, 20.

34. Werner Sollors, *Beyond Ethnicity: Consent and Descent in American Culture* (New York: Oxford University Press, 1986), pp. 160–66; William L. Andrews, *The Literary Career of Charles W. Chesnutt* (Baton Rouge: Louisiana State University Press, 1980), pp. 39–73.

35. Anonymous essay in "Contributors' Club," *Atlantic Monthly* 67 (January 1891), 143–44; rpt. as "Word Shadows," in Bruce Jackson, ed., *The Negro and His Folklore in Nineteenth-Century Periodicals,* (Austin: University of Texas Press, 1967), pp. 254–56; Zora Neale Hurston, "Characteristics of Negro Expression," in Nancy Cunard, ed., *Negro: An Anthology,* abridged ed. Hugh Ford (1934; rpt. New York: Frederick Ungar, 1970), pp. 24–31.

36. William C. Elam, "Lingo in Literature," *Lippincott's Magazine* 55 (February 1895), 286–88; Toll, *Blacking Up,* p. 162; Howard W. Odum and Guy B. Johnson, *The Negro and His Songs: A Study of Typical Negro Songs in the South* (Chapel Hill: University of North Carolina Press, 1925), p. 10; L. W. Payne quoted in Ernest F. Dunn, "The Black-White Dialect Controversy: Who Did What to Whom?," in *Black English: A Seminar,* ed. Deborah Sears Harrison and Tom Trabasso (New York: John Wiley, 1976), pp. 114–15; Charles Chesnutt, *The House behind the Cedars* (New York: Collier Books, 1969), p. 10. On survivals of African language, see Lorenzo Dow Turner, *Africanisms in Gullah Dialect* (Chicago: University of Chicago Press, 1949); J. L. Dillard, *Black English: Its History and Usage in the United States* (New York: Random House, 1972), pp. 39–138, 186–228; and David Dalby, "The African Element in American English," in Thomas Kochman, ed., *Rappin' and Stylin' Out: Communication in Urban Black America* (Urbana: University of Illinois Press, 1972), pp. 170–86.

37. Dunbar, *Complete Poems,* p. 191; Alan Trachtenberg, *The Incorporation of America: Culture and Society in the Gilded Age* (New York: Hill and Wang, 1982), pp. 140–207 passim; Elsa Nettels, *Language, Race, and Social Class in Howells' America* (Lexington: University of Kentucky Press, 1988), pp. 72–86.

38. James Weldon Johnson, *The Book of American Negro Poetry* (1922; rpt. New York: Harcourt Brace, 1969), p. 41. Johnson makes the comparison between Dunbar and Burns and Synge in an unpublished paper quoted by Cary D. Wintz, *Black Culture and the Harlem Renaissance* (Houston: Rice University Press, 1988), p. 51, and he invokes Synge directly in his preface to the anthology. Cf. Dickson D. Bruce, Jr., *Black Writing from the Nadir: The Evolution of a Literary Tradition, 1877–1915* (Baton Rouge: Louisiana State University Press, 1989), pp. 102–16.

39. Charles S. Johnson, "The New Frontage on American Life," in Alain Locke, ed., *The New Negro* (1925; rpt. New York: Atheneum, 1974), p. 297.

40. Berndt Ostendorf, *Black Literature in White America* (Totowa, N.J.: Barnes and Noble, 1982), pp. 77–84; Newbell Niles Puckett, *Folk Beliefs of the Southern Negro* (1926; rpt. Montclair, N.J.: Patterson Smith, 1968), p. 28.

41. Roger D. Abrahams, ed., *Afro-American Folktales: Stories from Black Traditions in the New World* (New York: Pantheon, 1985), pp. xv–xvi; Joel Chandler Harris,

Nights with Uncle Remus: Myths and Legends of the Old Plantation (Boston: Houghton Mifflin, 1881), p. xxxii.

42. Annah Robinson Watson, "Comparative Afro-American Folk-Lore," in *The International Folk-Lore Congress of the World's Columbian Exposition* (Chicago: Charles H. Seigel, 1898), pp. 327–40; Henry Louis Gates, Jr., *Figures in Black: Words, Signs, and the "Racial" Self* (New York: Oxford University Press, 1987), pp. 172–79. Gates notes also: "With the passage of dialect [in literature] went, in the main, the potential for the expression of that which was hermetic and singular about the black in America. With the passage of dialect went a peculiar sensitivity to black speech as music, poetry, and a distinct means of artistic discourse on the printed page" (p. 181).

43. Watson, "Comparative Afro-American Folk-Lore," pp. 338–40.

44. Chesnutt, letter of May 20, 1898, quoted in Helen Chesnutt, *Charles Waddell Chesnutt*, pp. 94–95.

45. Thomas Fenner, preface to *Cabin and Plantation Songs as Sung by the Hampton Students* (1874; rpt. New York: Putnam's, 1881), unpaginated.

46. Janheinz Jahn, "Residual African Elements in the Blues," in Dundes, *Mother Wit from the Laughing Barrel*, pp. 99–100.

47. Houston A. Baker, Jr., *Modernism and the Harlem Renaissance* (Chicago: University of Chicago Press, 1987), pp. 43–47.

48. Franz Boas, "On Alternating Sounds," *American Anthropologist* 2 (January 1889), 47–53; rpt. in *A Franz Boas Reader*, ed. George W. Stocking (Chicago: University of Chicago Press, 1974). See also George W. Stocking, Jr., *Race, Culture, and Evolution: Essays in the History of Anthropology* (New York: Free Press, 1968), pp. 157–60. Stocking points out that Boas's new theory "sees cultural phenomena in terms of the imposition of conventional meaning on the flux of experience. It sees them as historically conditioned and transmitted by the learning process. It sees them as determinants of our very perceptions of the external world. And it sees them in relative rather than in absolute terms" (p. 159).

49. *The Short Fiction of Charles W. Chesnutt*, ed. Sylvia Lyons Render (Washington, D.C.: Howard University Press, 1981), pp. 98–99; cited hereafter as Chesnutt, *Short Fiction*.

50. Robert Farris Thompson, *Flash of the Spirit: African and Afro-American Art and Philosophy* (New York: Random House, 1983), p. 105.

51. Chesnutt, *Short Fiction*, pp. 98, 105.

52. Ibid., p. 104.

53. Ibid., pp. 97–98.

54. John Edgar Wideman, "Charles Chesnutt and the WPA Narratives: The Oral and Literate Roots of Afro-American Literature," in Charles T. Davis and Henry Louis Gates, Jr., eds., *The Slave's Narrative* (New York: Oxford University Press, 1985), p. 66.

55. Antonin Dvořák, "Music in America," in Jackson, *The Negro and His Folklore in Nineteenth-Century Periodicals*, pp. 263–73; Southern, *The Music of Black Americans*, pp. 282–85. See also Blesh, *Shining Trumpets*, pp. 15, 25, 382; Joel Williamson,

The Crucible of Race: Black-White Relations in the American South since Emancipation (New York: Oxford University Press, 1984), pp. 37–38; and Lawrence Levine, who argues in *Black Culture and Black Consciousness: Afro-American Folk Thought from Slavery to Freedom* (New York: Oxford University Press, 1977), that "it is not necessary for a people to originate or invent all or even most of the elements of their culture. It is necessary only that these components become their own, embedded in their traditions, expressive of their world view and life style" (p. 24).

56. Natalie Curtis, *Songs and Tales from the Dark Continent* (New York: G. Schirmer, 1920), p. 9; Charles S. Peabody, "Notes on Negro Music," *Journal of American Folklore* 16 (1903), 148–52.

57. William Francis Allen et al., *Slave Songs of the United States* (New York: A. Simpson, 1867), p. iv.

58. See Roger D. Abrahams, *Deep Down in the Jungle: Negro Narrative Folklore from the Streets of Philadelphia* (1963; rpt. New York: Aldine, 1970); Geneva Smitherman, *Talkin' and Testifyin': The Language of Black America* (Detroit: Wayne State University Press, 1986); Claudia Mitchell-Kernan, "Signifying, Loud-Talking, and Marking," in Kochman, *Rappin' and Stylin' Out,* pp. 315–35.

59. Smitherman, *Talkin' and Testifyin',* pp. 100, 134–40; Ben Sidran, *Black Talk* (1971; rpt. New York: Da Capo, 1981), pp. 6–14, quote at p. 13.

60. Sidran, *Black Talk,* p. 13.

61. Julia Collier Harris, *The Life and Letters of Joel Chandler Harris* (London: Constable, 1919), pp. 169–70; Harris, *Nights with Uncle Remus,* pp. xli–xlii.

62. Joel Chandler Harris, *Uncle Remus: His Songs and Sayings,* rev. ed. (New York: Appleton, 1896), pp. 212, 204–5.

63. Joel Chandler Harris, *The Complete Tales of Uncle Remus,* ed. Richard Chase (Boston: Houghton Mifflin, 1955), p. 115.

64. Letter of May 20, 1898, quoted in Helen Chesnutt, *Charles Waddell Chesnutt,* p. 94.

65. Charles W. Chesnutt, *The Conjure Woman* (Ann Arbor: University of Michigan Press, 1969), pp. 71–72, 76–77, 82–84, 91.

66. Ibid., pp. 75, 65.

67. Abrahams, *Afro-American Folktales,* pp. 291–92; Levine, *Black Culture and Black Consciousness,* p. 129; Richard M. Dorson, *American Negro Folktales* (New York: Fawcett, 1968), pp. 151–52; Zora Neale Hurston, *Mules and Men: Negro Folktales and Voodoo Practices in the South* (New York: Harper and Row, 1970), pp. 112–14.

68. Hurston, *Mules and Men,* pp. 65–68; Dorson, *American Negro Folktales,* p. 124; Levine, *Black Culture and Black Consciousness,* pp. 127–29; Dickson A. Bruce, Jr., "The 'John and Old Master' Stories and the World of Slavery: A Study in Folktales and History," *Phylon* 35 (December 1974), 418–29; John W. Roberts, *From Trickster to Badman: The Black Folk Hero in Slavery and Freedom* (Philadelphia: University of Pennsylvania Press, 1989), pp. 44–64; Charles Joyner,

Down by the Riverside: A South Carolina Slave Community (Urbana: University of Illinois Press, 1984), pp. 183–89.

69. Harry Oster, "Negro Humor: John and Old Master," in Dundes, *Mother Wit from the Laughing Barrel,* p. 560; Charles C. Jones, Jr., *Negro Myths from the Georgia Coast: Told in the Vernacular* (Boston: Houghton Mifflin, 1888), pp. 115–16.

70. Edward Marble, *The Minstrel Show, or Burnt Cork Comicalities* (New York: F. M. Lupton, 1893), pp. 39–41; Paul H. Buck, *The Road to Reunion, 1865–1900* (Boston: Little, Brown, 1937), pp. 196–235 passim; William L. Van Deburg, *Slavery and Race in American Popular Culture* (Madison: University of Wisconsin Press, 1984), pp. 115–19.

71. Chesnutt, *The Conjure Woman,* p. 99.

72. Ibid., pp. 95, 100.

73. Locke, *The New Negro,* pp. 3–4.

74. August Meier, *Negro Thought in America, 1880–1915: Racial Ideologies in the Age of Booker T. Washington* (Ann Arbor: University of Michigan Press, 1963), pp. 260–61; Logan, *The Betrayal of the Negro,* p. 341; Henry Louis Gates, Jr., "The Trope of a New Negro and the Reconstruction of the Image of the Black," *Representations* 24 (Fall 1988), 136–47; Wilson J. Moses, *The Golden Age of Black Nationalism, 1850–1925* (1978; rpt. New York: Oxford University Press, 1988), pp. 58–131 passim; Bruce, *Black Writing from the Nadir,* pp. 11–189 passim; Sutton Griggs, *Imperium in Imperio* (New York: Arno Press, 1969), p. 62; J. W. E. Bowen quoted in Gates, "The Trope of a New Negro," p. 136; Alexander Crummell, *Africa and America: Addresses and Discourses* (1891; rpt. Miami: Mnemosyne, 1969), p. 377.

75. Wilson J. Moses, "The Lost World of the New Negro, 1895–1919: Black Literary and Intellectual Life before the 'Renaissance,'" *Black American Literature Forum* 21 (Spring 1987), 71–72.

76. I. A. Newby, *Jim Crow's Defense: Anti-Negro Thought in America, 1900–1930* (Baton Rouge: Louisiana State University Press, 1965), pp. 124–26; Thomas Nelson Page, *The Negro: The Southerner's Problem* (New York: Scribner's, 1904), p. 163.

77. *Harper's Weekly* quoted in C. Vann Woodward, *The Origins of the New South, 1877–1913* (Baton Rouge: Louisiana State University Press, 1951), p. 354.

78. Harris, *Nights with Uncle Remus,* pp. xv–xvi; Julia Harris, *Life and Letters of Joel Chandler Harris,* pp. 384–86; Bernard Wolfe, "Uncle Remus and the Malevolent Rabbit," in Dundes, *Mother Wit from the Laughing Barrel,* pp. 524–40.

79. Harris, *Uncle Remus: His Songs and Sayings,* pp. 249, 256, 232.

80. Joel Chandler Harris, *Uncle Remus and His Friends* (Boston: Houghton Mifflin, 1892), pp. 340, 346, 350.

81. Joel Chandler Harris, "The Negro of Today," *Saturday Evening Post,* 30 January 1904, and "The Old Plantation," *Atlanta Constitution,* 9 December 1877, in Julia Collier Harris, ed., *Joel Chandler Harris: Editor and Essayist* (Chapel Hill: University of North Carolina Press, 1931), pp. 135, 91–92.

82. Darwin Turner, "Daddy Joel Harris and His Old-Time Darkies," in R. Bruce Bickley, ed., *Critical Essays on Joel Chandler Harris* (Boston: G. K. Hall, 1981), pp. 113–29; Wayne Mixon, "The Irrelevance of Race: Joel Chandler Harris and Uncle Remus in Their Time," *Southern Review* 56 (August 1990), 457–80.

83. Harris, *Complete Tales of Uncle Remus*, p. xxv; Florence Baer, *Sources and Analogues of the Uncle Remus Tales* (Helsinki: Folklore Fellows Communications, 1981).

84. W. S. Scarborough, "Negro Folk-Lore and Dialect," *Arena* 18 (January 1897), 188; Frantz Fanon, *Black Skin, White Masks*, trans. Charles Lam Markmann (New York: Grove Press, 1967), p. 174; Robert Bone, *Down Home: Origins of the Afro-American Short Story* (New York: Columbia University Press, 1975), p. 30.

85. Arthur H. Fauset, "American Negro Folk Literature," in Locke, *The New Negro*, pp. 238–44.

86. Howard Odum and Guy Johnson, *The Negro and His Songs: A Study of Typical Negro Songs in the South* (Chapel Hill: University of North Carolina Press, 1925), p. 166; Michael Flusche, "Joel Chandler Harris and the Folklore of Slavery," *Journal of American Sociology* 9 (December 1975), 347–63; Harris, *Complete Tales of Uncle Remus*, pp. xxvii, 114–15.

87. Harris, *Complete Tales of Uncle Remus*, p. 110; Abigail Christensen quoted in Levine, *Black Culture and Black Consciousness*, p. 113; Julia Harris, *Life and Letters of Joel Chandler Harris*, p. 156; Thomas Nelson Page quoted in Julia Harris, *Life and Letters of Joel Chandler Harris*, pp. 164–5; Harris, *Uncle Remus and His Friends*, p. x.

88. Harris, *Complete Tales of Uncle Remus*, p. 209; Lucinda Hardwick MacKethan, *The Dream of Arcady: Place and Time in Southern Literature* (Baton Rouge: Louisiana State University Press, 1980), p. 71.

89. Bone, *Down Home*, p. 81. See also John F. Callahan, *In the African-American Grain: Call-and-Response in Twentieth-Century Black Fiction*, 2nd ed. (Middletown, Conn.: Wesleyan University Press, 1989), pp. 25–61, and Craig Werner, "The Framing of Charles Chesnutt: Practical Deconstruction in the Afro-American Tradition," in Jefferson Humphries, ed., *Southern Literature and Literary Theory* (Athens: University of Georgia Press, 1990), pp. 339–65.

90. Chesnutt, "Superstitions and Folklore of the South," p. 370; William Wells Brown, *My Southern Home; Or, the South and Its People* (Upper Saddle River, N.J.: Gregg Press, 1968), pp. 68–79; Puckett, *Folk Beliefs of the Southern Negro*, p. 248; Albert J. Raboteau, *Slave Religion: The "Invisible Institution" in the Antebellum South* (New York: Oxford University Press, 1978), p. 278; Thompson, *Flash of the Spirit*, p. 105.

91. William Owens, "Folkore of the Southern Negro," *Lippincott's Magazine* 20 (December 1877), 748–51; rpt. in Jackson, *The Negro and His Folklore in Nineteenth-Century Periodicals*, pp. 144–56; T. F. Crane quoted in R. Bruce Bickley, Jr., *Joel Chandler Harris* (Athens: University of Georgia Press, 1987), pp. 66–67; A. Gerber, "Uncle Remus Traced to the Old World," *Journal of American Folklore*

6 (1893), 245–57. For other representative essays from the period and commentary on them, see those collected by Jackson and by Dundes in *Mother Wit from the Laughing Barrel;* and see also Levine, *Black Culture and Black Consciousness,* pp. 81–135; Mary F. Berry and John W. Blassingame, "Africa, Slavery, and the Roots of Contemporary Black Culture," *Massachusetts Review* 18 (Autumn 1977), 501–16; and Roberts, *From Trickster to Badman,* pp. 17–43.

92. Wolfe, "Uncle Remus and the Malevolent Rabbit," p. 532; Stocking, *Race, Culture, and Evolution,* pp. 120–24. On Harris and folklore, see also Stella Brewer Brookes, *Joel Chandler Harris, Folklorist* (Athens: University of Georgia Press, 1950); Kathleen Light, "Uncle Remus and the Folklorists," in Bickley, *Critical Essays on Joel Chandler Harris,* pp. 146–57; Eric L. Montenyohl, "Joel Chandler Harris and American Folklore," *Atlanta Historical Journal* 30 (Fall-Winter 1986–87), 79–88.

93. Harris, *Uncle Remus and His Friends,* p. vii; Julia Harris, *Life and Letters of Joel Chandler Harris,* p. 153.

94. Harris, *Complete Tales of Uncle Remus,* p. 590.

95. Harris, *Nights with Uncle Remus,* p. xlii; Harris, *Complete Tales of Uncle Remus,* p. 407.

96. Dorothy Scarborough, *On the Trail of Negro Folk-Songs* (Cambridge, Mass.: Harvard University Press, 1925), p. 159.

97. Julia Harris, *Joel Chandler Harris: Editor and Essayist,* pp. 114–29.

98. Ibid., p. 116; Harris, *Complete Tales of Uncle Remus,* p. 406.

99. Puckett, *Folk Beliefs of the Southern Negro,* pp. 31–32.

100. Harris, *Complete Tales of Uncle Remus,* pp. 98, 203, 434, 226, 339, 701, 590, 186. See also Mixon, "The Irrelevance of Race," pp. 472–73.

101. "Folk-Lore and Ethnology," *Southern Workman* (September 1895); this issue repeated the original call for material; rpt. in Jackson, *The Negro and His Folklore in Nineteenth-Century Periodicals,* p. 283; Harris, *Complete Tales of Uncle Remus,* p. 785.

102. Charles Chesnutt, letter of June 13, 1890, quoted in Frances Richardson Keller, *An American Crusade: The Life of Charles Waddell Chesnutt* (Provo, Utah: Brigham Young University Press, 1978), p. 122.

103. Chesnutt, "Post-Bellum—Pre-Harlem," *Crisis* (1931); rpt. in Adler, *Breaking into Print,* p. 49; Chesnutt, journal of August 13, 1875, quoted in Keller, *An American Crusade,* p. 54.

104. Chesnutt, letter of summer 1891, quoted in Helen Chesnutt, *Charles Waddell Chesnutt,* pp. 68–69; Keller, *An American Crusade,* p. 166.

105. Hemenway, "The Functions of Folklore in Charles Chesnutt's *The Conjure Woman,*" 297; Joyner, *Down by the Riverside,* p. 180.

106. Chesnutt, *The Conjure Woman,* p. 5; W. E. B. Du Bois, *The Souls of Black Folk* (New York: Viking Penquin, 1989), p. 100. For Chesnutt's comments on Tourgée, see Keller, *An American Crusade,* pp. 19–21, 192.

107. Richard Yarborough, "The First Flowering: Chesnutt and Dunbar" (unpublished essay); Wittke, *Tambo and Bones,* pp. 138–42; Henry Wehman, *Brudder*

Bones' 4-11-44 Joker (New York: Henry Wehman, 1897); Hemenway, "The Functions of Folklore in Charles Chesnutt's *The Conjure Woman*," p. 289; Chesnutt, *The Conjure Woman*, p. 6.

108. Chesnutt, *The Conjure Woman*, pp. 8, 31, 127, 4, 13; Ralph Ellison, *Invisible Man* (1952; rpt. New York: Vintage Books, 1982), p. 258.

109. Chesnutt, *The Conjure Woman*, pp. 12–13, 8–10.

110. Thaddeus Norris, "Negro Superstitions," *Lippincott's Magazine* 6 (July 1870), 90–95; Puckett, *Folk Beliefs of the Southern Negro*, p. 521.

111. Leonora Herron and Alice Bacon, "Conjuring and Conjure-Doctors," *Southern Workman* (1895), rpt. in Dundes, *Mother Wit from the Laughing Barrel*, p. 360; Puckett, *Folk Beliefs of the Southern Negro*, pp. 167–310; Raboteau, *Slave Religion*, pp. 275–88; Thompson, *Flash of the Spirit*, pp. 128–31; Mechal Sobel, *Trabelin' On: The Slave Journey to an Afro-Baptist Faith* (Westport, Conn.: Greenwood Press, 1979), pp. 39–48; Roberts, *From Trickster to Badman*, pp. 65–95; Berry and Blassingame, "Africa, Slavery, and the Roots of Contemporary Black Culture," p. 508.

112. Molefi Kete Asante, *The Afrocentric Idea* (Philadelphia: Temple University Press, 1987), pp. 59–70, 85–95; Roberts, *From Trickster to Badman*, pp. 77–78; Jahn, *Muntu*, pp. 121–40; Hurston, *Mules and Men*, p. 229; Paul Oliver, *Blues Fell This Morning: Meaning in the Blues* (London: Cambridge University Press, 1960), pp. 121–28.

113. Gladys-Marie Fry, *Night Riders in Black Folk History* (1975; rpt. Athens: University of Georgia Press, 1991), pp. 59–81; Julien Hall, "Negro Conjuring and Tricking," *Journal of American Folklore* 10 (1897), 241–43; Mary Alicia Owen, reprinted as *Ole Rabbit's Plantation Stories* (Philadelphia: George N. Jacobs, 1898), p. vi.

114. Eugene D. Genovese, *Roll, Jordan, Roll: The World the Slaves Made* (New York: Random House, 1974), pp. 222–23; Levine, *Black Culture and Black Consciousness*, pp. 73–74.

115. Chesnutt, *The Conjure Woman*, pp. 103–4, 108, 164, 127, 130; Bruce, *Black American Writing from the Nadir*, pp. 180–85; Henry Louis Gates, Jr., *The Signifying Monkey: A Theory of Afro-American Literary Criticism* (New York: Oxford University Press, 1988), pp. 59–61; Daniel Crowley quoted in Abrahams, *Afro-American Folktales*, p. 31. For other views of Julius as a trickster and conjure figure, see Melvin Dixon, "The Teller as Folk Trickster in Chesnutt's *The Conjure Woman*," *CLA Journal* 18 (December 1974), 186–97; Valerie Babb, "Subversion and Re-Patriation in *The Conjure Woman*," *Southern Quarterly* 25 (Winter 1987), 66–75; Lorne Fienberg, "Charles W. Chesnutt and Uncle Julius: Black Storyteller at the Crossroads," *Studies in American Fiction* 15 (Autumn 1987), 161–74; and H. Nigel Thomas, *From Folklore to Fiction: A Study of Folk Heroes and Rituals in the Black American Novel* (New York: Greenwood Press, 1988), pp. 83–88.

116. Baker, *Modernism and the Harlem Renaissance*, p. 44.

117. Abrahams, *Afro-American Folktales*, p. 6; Robert D. Pelton, *The Trickster in*

West Africa: A Study of Mythic Irony and Sacred Delight (Berkeley: University of California Press, 1980), pp. 31–36, 236–43, quote at p. 243.

118. Puckett, *Folk Beliefs of the Southern Negro*, pp. 167–95 passim; Louis Pendleton, "Notes on Negro Folk-Lore and Witchcraft in the South," *Journal of American Folklore* 3 (1890), 201–7.

119. Chesnutt, *The Conjure Woman*, pp. 130–31, 106; Joel Williamson, *New People: Miscegenation and Mulattoes in the United States* (New York: Free Press, 1980), pp. 94–96.

120. Chesnutt, *The Conjure Woman*, pp. 109, 111, 121, 127–28.

121. Ibid., p. 128; James Weldon Johnson, *The Autobiography of an Ex-Coloured Man* (New York: Hill and Wang, 1960), pp. 166–67.

122. Chesnutt, *The Conjure Woman*, pp. 42, 54–55.

123. Ibid., p. 60, 57–58; Herron and Bacon, "Conjuring and Conjure-Doctors," p. 365; Du Bois, *The Souls of Black Folk*, p. 163.

124. Chesnutt, *Short Fiction*, pp. 143–48; Hurston, *Mules and Men*, pp. 290–92.

125. Chesnutt, *Short Fiction*, pp. 136–41.

126. Keller, *An American Crusade*, p. 141; Helen Chesnutt, *Charles Waddell Chesnutt*, pp. 69, 101.

127. Chesnutt, *Short Fiction*, pp. 123, 125, 130–31; Newman I. White, *American Negro Folk-Songs* (Cambridge, Mass.: Harvard University Press, 1928), p. 242; Harris, *Uncle Remus and His Friends*, p. 323; Baker, *Modernism and the Harlem Renaissance*, pp. 27, 33–36.

128. Chesnutt, *Short Fiction*, pp. 132, 141.

129. Ibid., p. 133.

130. Philip M. Peek, "The Power of Words in African Verbal Arts," *Journal of American Folklore* 94 (1981), 19–43.

131. Chesnutt, *The Conjure Woman*, p. 40; Chesnutt, *Short Fiction*, p. 144.

132. William Bascom, "African Folktales in America: I. The Talking Skull Refuses to Talk," *Research in African Literatures* 8 (Fall 1977), 266–91. Bascom gives twenty-four versions of African tales in which a skull or animal refuses to speak, and eighteen from the United States, including instances featuring mules, snakes, turtles, and frogs, as well as skulls. Bascom's essay was the first in a series of essays he wrote in refutation of Dorson's view that the African contribution to African American folklore is negligible.

133. Abrahams, *Afro-American Folktales*, pp. 274–75.

134. Leo Frobenius and Douglas C. Fox, *African Genesis* (1937; rpt. New York: Benjamin Blom, 1966), pp. 161–62; Roger D. Abrahams, ed., *African Folktales: Traditional Stories of the Black World* (New York: Pantheon, 1983), pp. 1–2, 16, 22, 24.

135. Dorson, *American Negro Folktales*, pp. 147–51; Herskovits, *The Myth of the Negro Past*, pp. 156–58; Smitherman, *Talkin' and Testifyin'*, pp. 97–100; Joyner, *Down by the Riverside*, pp. 183–89; Gates, *The Signifying Monkey*, pp. 74–75.

136. Susan Stewart, *Nonsense: Aspects of Intertextuality in Folklore and Literature* (Baltimore: Johns Hopkins University Press, 1979), pp. 88–89.

137. William D. Pierson, "Puttin' Down Old Massa: African Satire in the New World," in Crowley, *African Folklore in the New World*, pp. 20–34. See also note 9.

138. Chesnutt, *Short Fiction*, p. 158.

139. Ibid., pp. 154–55, 162.

140. Ibid., p. 156–57; Robert B. Stepto, "'The Simple but Intensely Human Inner Life of Slavery': Storytelling, Fiction, and the Revision of History in Charles W. Chesnutt's Uncle Julius Stories," in Gunter H. Lenz, ed., *History and Tradition in Afro-American Culture* (Frankfurt: Campus Verlag, 1984), pp. 29–55; Chesnutt, letter to Tourgée, September 26, 1889, cited in Andrews, *The Literary Career of Charles W. Chesnutt*, p. 21.

141. Keller, *An American Crusade*, pp. 131–32; Chesnutt, "Superstitions and Folklore of the South," pp. 372–73; Ray Stannard Baker, *Following the Color Line: American Negro Citizenship in the Progressive Era* (1908; rpt. New York: Harper and Row, 1964), p. 164; Williamson, *New People*, p. 119; Chesnutt, journal of July 31, 1875, quoted in J. Noel Heermance, *Charles Waddell Chesnutt: America's First Great Black Novelist* (Hamden, Conn.: Archon, 1974), p. 68; Chesnutt, speech of July 3, 1928, quoted in Andrews, *The Literary Career of Charles W. Chesnutt*, p. 5.

142. Howard W. Odum, *Social and Mental Traits of the Negro* (New York: Columbia University Press, 1910), pp. 163–65; Philip A. Bruce, *The Plantation Negro as a Freeman* (New York: Putnam's, 1889), p. 9; Nathaniel Southgate Shaler, "The Permanence of Race Characteristics" (1890), in *The Development of Segregationist Thought*, ed. I. A. Newby (Homewood, Ill.: Dorsey Press, 1968), p. 61.

143. Williamson, *New People*, pp. 94–100. See also John S. Haller, Jr., *Outcasts from Evolution: Scientific Attitudes of Racial Inferiority, 1859–1900* (1971; rpt. New York: McGraw-Hill, 1975), pp. 40–45, 64–68, 117–19, 177–79; Newby, *Jim Crow's Defense*, pp. 122–40; and Claude H. Nolen, *The Negro's Image in the South: The Anatomy of White Supremacy* (Lexington: University of Kentucky Press, 1967), pp. 29–39.

144. William Hannibal Thomas, *The American Negro: What He Was, What He Is, What He May Become* (New York: Macmillan, 1901), pp. 180–82; Chesnutt, letters of April 20 and 26, 1901, quoted in Helen Chesnutt, *Charles Waddell Chesnutt*, pp. 161–62.

145. Keller, *An American Crusade*, pp. 25–35, 173–87; Andrews, *The Literary Career of Charles Chesnutt*, pp. 1–8.

146. Chesnutt, quoted in Andrews, *The Literary Career of Charles Chesnutt*, p. 76.

147. Chesnutt, *The House behind the Cedars*, pp. 154, 28, 69, 67, 61, 199–200.

148. Keller, *An American Crusade*, pp. 167–69, 236–38; Chesnutt, *The House behind the Cedars*, p. 77. See also Bruce, *Black American Writing from the Nadir*, pp. 173–74.

149. Chesnutt, *The Wife of His Youth*, pp. 51–55, 33.

150. Ibid., pp. 32, 59, 39, 40.

151. Chesnutt, *Short Fiction*, pp. 402, 398.

152. Ibid., p. 404.

153. Peter Brooks, *The Melodramatic Imagination: Balzac, Henry James, Melodrama, and the Mode of Excess* (New Haven: Yale University Press, 1976), pp. 72–73.

154. Chesnutt, *Short Fiction*, p. 112–14; Mary Douglas, *Purity and Danger: An Analysis of the Concepts of Pollution and Taboo* (1966; rpt. New York: Ark, 1985), pp. 160–61.

155. Keller, *An American Crusade*, pp. 70, 192; Chesnutt, *The Marrow of Tradition*, p. 329.

156. Chesnutt, *The Marrow of Tradition*, p. 228; Leon Prather, *We Have Taken a City: The Wilmington Racial Massacre and Coup of 1898* (Cranbury, N.J.: Associated University Press, 1984); Helen Edmonds, *The Negro and Fusion Politics in North Carolina, 1894–1901* (Chapel Hill: University of North Carolina Press, 1951), p. 171; Harry Hayden, *The Story of the Wilmington Rebellion* (Wilmington, N.C., 1936); David Bryant Fulton [Jack Thorne], *Hanover, Or the Persecution of the Lowly: A Story of the Wilmington Massacre* (New York: Arno Press, 1969); Chesnutt, letter of November 10, 1898, quoted in Helen Chesnutt, *Charles Waddell Chesnutt*, pp. 159, 104.

157. William B. Smith, *The Color Line: A Brief in Behalf of the Unborn* (New York: McClure, Phillips, 1906), pp. 7–8; Chesnutt, *The Marrow of Tradition*, pp. 269–70.

158. Thomas F. Gossett, *Race: The History of an Idea* (1963; rpt. New York: Schocken Books, 1965), pp. 158–60; Paul M. Gaston, *The New South Creed: A Study in Southern Mythmaking* (New York: Alfred Knopf, 1970), p. 136; *New York Times*, 21 February 1895, quoted in Logan, *The Betrayal of the Negro*, pp. 234–35.

159. Philip Bruce, *The Rise of the New South* (Philadelphia: George Barrie and Sons, 1905), pp. 438–39; Benjamin Tillman, congressional speech of 1906, quoted in Francis Butler Simkins, *Pitchfork Ben Tillman of South Carolina* (Baton Rouge: Louisiana State University Press, 1944), pp. 397–98; W. J. Cash, *The Mind of the South* (1941; New York: Vintage Books, 1960), pp. 117–20; Ida B. Wells, *On Lynchings* (1892; rpt. New York: Arno Press, 1969); Walter White, *Rope and Faggott: A Biography of Judge Lynch* (New York: Alfred Knopf, 1929), pp. 54–81; Page, *The Negro: The Southerner's Problem*, pp. 99–100, 112–13.

160. Thomas Jefferson, "Notes on the State of Virginia" (1787), in *The Portable Jefferson*, ed. Merrill D. Peterson, (New York: Viking, 1975), p. 187; Lester Ward, *Pure Sociology*, quoted in Gossett, *Race*, p. 166.

161. Chesnutt quoted in Andrews, *The Literary Career of Charles Chesnutt*, pp. 141–42.

162. Rebecca Latimer Felton quoted in Prather, *We Have Taken a City*, p. 71, and Richard Yarborough, "Violence, Manhood, and Black Heroism: The Wilmington Riot in Two Turn-of-the-Century Afro-American Novels" (unpublished paper); John E. Talmadge, *Rebecca Latimer Felton: Nine Stormy Decades* (Athens: University of Georgia Press, 1960), pp. 113–14. See also Williamson, *Crucible of Race*, pp. 124–30, 303.

163. Alexander Manly quoted in Prather, *We Have Taken a City*, pp. 71–73.

164. Ida B. Wells, quotations from *Southern Horrors: Lynch Law in All Its Phases* (1892) and *A Red Record* (1894), rpt. in Wells, *On Lynchings* (New York: Arno Press, 1969), pp. 1, 4, 11; Yarborough, "Violence, Manhood, and Black Heroism"; Bruce, *The Plantation Negro as a Freeman*, p. 55.

165. Prather, *We Have Taken a City*, pp. 155–57.

166. Ibid., pp. 22–23; Eric Anderson, *Race and Politics in North Carolina, 1872–1901: The Black Second* (Baton Rouge: Louisiana State University Press, 1981), p. 245.

167. Anderson, *Race and Politics in North Carolina, 1872–1901*, p. 255; Prather, *We Have Taken a City*, pp. 22–23, 49, 56–62.

168. Logan, *The Betrayal of the Negro*, pp. 220–26, 298–301; Edmonds, *The Negro and Fusion Politics in North Carolina, 1894–1901*, pp. 141–42; Prather, *We Have Taken a City*, pp. 55–58; Anderson, *Race and Politics in North Carolina, 1872–1901*, p. 264.

169. Prather, *We Have Taken a City*, pp. 68, 83–85; Edmonds, *The Negro and Fusion Politics in North Carolina, 1894–1901*, pp. 148–51; Williamson, *Crucible of Race*, pp. 130–39; Chesnutt, *The Marrow of Tradition*, p. 243.

170. Yarborough, "Violence, Manhood, and Black Heroism."

171. Fulton, *Hanover*, pp. 20–21; Prather, *We Have Taken a City*, pp. 89–90; Edmonds, *The Negro and Fusion Politics in North Carolina, 1894–1901*, p. 166; Williamson, *The Crucible of Race*, pp. 195–201.

172. Alfred M. Waddell, letter to Page, quoted in Thomas Cripps, "Introduction" to Fulton, *Hanover*, p. iv; Prather, *We Have Taken a City*, pp. 95, 108–9; Edmonds, *The Negro and Fusion Politics in North Carolina, 1894–1901*, p. 166.

173. Keller, *An American Crusade*, p. 134; Chesnutt, letter of November 13, 1889, quoted in Helen Chesnutt, *Charles Waddell Chesnutt*, p. 52.

174. Prather, *We Have Taken a City*, pp. 69–70; Baker, *Following the Color Line*, pp. 160–61.

175. Although there is no evidence that he bore her particular animosity, Chesnutt borrowed the name Ochiltree from that of his own stepmother (and young cousin), Mary Ochiltree, who married the widower Andrew Jackson Chesnutt in 1871. See Keller, *An American Crusade*, pp. 48, 57.

176. *Williams* v. *Mississippi* (170 U.S. 213); Logan, *The Betrayal of the Negro*, pp. 212–17; Gossett, *Race*, p. 266; John S. Bassett quoted in C. Vann Woodward, *Origins of the New South, 1877–1913* (Baton Rouge: Louisiana State University Press, 1951), p. 348.

177. Alfred M. Waddell quoted in Paul D. Escott, *Many Excellent People: Power and Privilege in North Carolina, 1850–1900* (Chapel Hill: University of North Carolina Press, 1985), pp. 259–60; Chesnutt, letter of March 22, 1899, quoted in Heermance, *Charles W. Chesnutt*, p. 126; Chesnutt, letter of August 11, 1903, quoted in Keller, *An American Crusade*, p. 220. See also Arlene Elder, "Chesnutt on Washington: An Essential Ambivalence," *Phylon* 38 (1977), 1–8.

178. Chesnutt, *The Marrow of Tradition*, pp. 31, 185, 233–34; Kelly Miller, "An Appeal to Reason on the Race Problem," in *Radicals and Conservatives and Other Essays*

on the Negro in America (original title: *Race Adjustment,* 1908), ed. Philip Rieff (New York: Schocken Books, 1968), pp. 81–83; Chesnutt, "A Deep Sleeper," in *Short Fiction,* p. 119.

179. Chesnutt, *The Marrow of Tradition,* p. 81.

180. Ibid., p. 242; William Toll, *The Resurgence of Race: Black Social Theory from Reconstruction to the Pan-African Conferences* (Philadelphia: Temple University Press, 1979), pp. 122–29; Penelope Bullock, *Afro-American Periodical Press, 1838–1909* (Baton Rouge: Louisiana University Press, 1981), pp. 118–25.

181. Woodward, *Origins of the New South,* pp. 154–58; Charles Reagan Wilson, *Baptized in Blood: The Religion of the Lost Cause, 1865–1920* (Athens: University of Georgia Press, 1980), pp. 18–57, 79-118; Gaines M. Foster, *Ghosts of the Confederacy: Defeat, The Lost Cause, and the Emergence of the New South, 1865 to 1913* (New York: Oxford University Press, 1987), pp. 36–144; Richard Gray, *Writing the South: Ideas of an American Region* (New York: Cambridge University Press, 1986), pp. 76–91; Anne Firor Scott, *The Southern Lady: From Pedestal to Politics, 1830–1930* (Chicago: University of Chicago Press, 1970).

182. Williamson, *New People,* pp. 89–91; Trudier Harris, *Exorcising Blackness: Historical and Literary Lynching and Burning Rituals* (Bloomington: Indiana University Press, 1984); Gaston, *The New South Creed,* pp. 177–85.

183. Thomas Dixon, *The Leopard's Spots* (New York: Doubleday, Page, 1902), p. 415; Helen Chesnutt, *Charles Waddell Chesnutt,* pp. 179–82.

184. See Carroll Smith-Rosenberg, *Disorderly Conduct: Visions of Gender in Victorian America* (New York: Oxford University Press, 1985), pp. 197–216.

185. Chesnutt, *The Marrow of Tradition,* pp. 263–73.

186. Faulkner, *Go Down Moses* (New York: Vintage Books, 1955), pp. 269–70; Chesnutt, *The Marrow of Tradition,* p. 270.

187. Williamson, *New People,* pp. 91ff.; Paul R. Spickard, *Mixed Blood: Intermarriage and Ethnic Identity in Twentieth-Century America* (Madison: University of Wisconsin Press, 1989), pp. 268–311 passim; Eva Saks, "Representing Miscegenation Law," *Raritan* 8 (Fall 1988), 51–53.

188. Chesnutt, *The Marrow of Tradition,* pp. 16, 165, 122, 25, 162.

189. Ibid., pp. 211–12.

190. Ibid., pp. 228, 235.

191. Ibid., pp. 238–39.

192. Ibid., pp. 119, 310; Nathaniel Shaler, "Race Prejudice," *Atlantic Monthly* 58 (October 1886), 512. See also Daniel Joseph Singal, *The War Within: From Victorian to Modernist Thought in the South, 1919–1945* (Chapel Hill: University of North Carolina Press, 1982), pp. 5–10.

193. Prather, *We Have Taken a City,* pp. 103–5, 109–14, quote at p. 111; Edmonds, *The Negro and Fusion Politics in North Carolina,* pp. 156–72.

194. Render, *Charles W. Chesnutt,* p. 110; Prather, *We Have Taken a City,* pp. 115–58 passim, quote at p. 128; Escott, *Many Excellent People,* p. 254.

195. Chesnutt, *The Marrow of Tradition,* p. 316; Charles Chesnutt, *Frederick Douglass* (Boston: Small, Maynard, 1899), p. 87. I am indebted to William Gleason, "Diverging Voices at the Turn of the Century: Charles W. Chesnutt and Jack Thorne" (unpublished essay), for this point.

196. On Robert Charles, see Williamson, *The Crucible of Race,* pp. 201–9, and William Ivy Hair, *Carnival of Fury: Robert Charles and the New Orleans Race Riot of 1900* (Baton Rouge: Louisiana State University Press, 1976).

197. See Robert B. Stepto, *From behind the Veil: A Study of Afro-American Narrative* (Urbana: University of Illinois Press, 1979), pp. 66–68, 78–82, 115–16.

198. Chesnutt, *The House behind the Cedars,* e.g., chap. 18; Chesnutt, *The Marrow of Tradition,* pp. 49, 60–61; Chesnutt, journal of 1879, quoted in Williamson, *Crucible of Race,* pp. 62–63.

199. Frank Clark, congressional speech of February 22, 1908, rpt. in Newby, *The Development of Segregationist Thought,* pp. 91–97.

200. Chesnutt, *The Marrow of Tradition,* p. 56. One might compare Chesnutt's scene to the protest against Jim Crow made by Thomas Fortune in the *New York Globe* in 1883. When an African Methodist Episcopal bishop who had purchased a first-class ticket on a southern railroad was forced to ride in the smoking car, Fortune attacked southern railroads for giving respectable Negroes accommodations "where the vilest of impudent white scum resort to swear, to exhale rotten smoke and to expectorate pools of stinking excrementation of tobacco." Fortune quoted in Meier, *Negro Thought in America, 1880–1915,* p. 71.

201. Chesnutt, *The Marrow of Tradition,* pp. 59–60.

202. Ibid., pp. 113–15.

203. Prather, *We Have Taken a City,* pp. 89, 94–96, 110, 141, 145–46; Edmonds, *The Negro and Fusion Politics in North Carolina,* p. 167.

204. Chesnutt, *The Marrow of Tradition,* p. 108.

205. Odum and Johnson, *The Negro and His Songs,* pp. 196–212; Norm Cohen, *Long Steel Rail: The Railroad in American Folksong* (Urbana: University of Illinois Press, 1981), pp. 122–31; Abrahams, *Deep Down in the Jungle,* pp. 129–42; Roberts, *From Trickster to Badman,* pp. 171–84; Levine, *Black Culture and Black Consciousness,* pp. 407–20; Thomas, *From Folklore to Fiction,* pp. 56–60, 71–80; H. C. Brearly, "Ba——ad Nigger," in Dundes, *Mother Wit from the Laughing Barrel,* pp. 578–85; Charles P. Henry, *Culture and African American Politics* (Bloomington: Indiana University Press, 1990), pp. 37–59.

206. Albert Murray, *Stomping the Blues* (New York: Da Capo, 1976), pp. 116–26; Houston A. Baker, Jr., *Blues, Ideology, and Afro-American Literature: A Vernacular Theory* (Chicago: University of Chicago Press, 1984), pp. 7–11; Odum and Johnson, *The Negro and His Songs,* p. 188. See also James A. McPherson, *Railroad: Trains and Train People in American Culture* (New York: Random House, 1976), pp. 6–9; Oliver, *Blues Fell This Morning,* pp. 53–68; and Southern, *The Music of Black Americans,* pp. 246–49.

207. Chesnutt, *The Marrow of Tradition,* pp. 277–84.

208. Asante, *The Afrocentric Idea,* pp. 106–9; Chesnutt, *The Marrow of Tradition,* pp. 62, 109.

209. Roberts, *From Trickster to Badman,* pp. 182–214; Chesnutt, *The Marrow of Tradition,* pp. 252–53.

210. See, for example, "The Jury Trial," in Marble, *The Minstrel, or Burnt Cork Comicalities,* pp. 37–38.

211. Chesnutt, *The Marrow of Tradition,* p. 316.

212. John Wideman, "Charles W. Chesnutt: The Marrow of Tradition," *American Scholar* 42 (1973), 133.

213. Meier, *Negro Thought in America,* p. 207; Thomas N. Page, *The Old South: Essays Social and Political* (New York: Charles Scribners' Sons, 1892), p. 338; Chesnutt, *The Marrow of Tradition,* pp. 252, 246.

214. H. F. Kletzing and W. H. Crogman, *Progress of a Race: Or, the Remarkable Advancement of the American Negro* (Atlanta: J. L. Nichols, 1897), pp. vi, 283; Haller, *Outcasts from Evolution,* pp. 203–10; Chesnutt, *The Marrow of Tradition,* p. 42.

215. Chesnutt, *Short Fiction,* pp. 409, 411.

216. Ibid., pp. 411–12.

5. Swing Low

1. William E. Barton, *Old Plantation Hymns* (Boston: Lamson, Wolffe, 1899), p. 20.

2. Arnold Rampersad, *The Art and Imagination of W. E. B. Du Bois* (Cambridge, Mass.: Harvard University Press, 1976), pp. 36–38, 76; Manning Marable, "The Black Faith of W. E. B. Du Bois: Sociocultural and Political Dimensions of Black Religion," *Southern Quarterly* 23 (Spring 1985), 15–33.

3. Rampersad, *The Art and Imagination of W. E. B. Du Bois,* p. 74.

4. W. E. B. Du Bois, *The Souls of Black Folk* (New York: Viking Penguin, 1989), pp. 13, 35, 205.

5. Ibid., p. 2.

6. W. E. B. Du Bois, "The Conservation of Races," in *W. E. B. Du Bois: Writings* (New York: Library of America, 1986), pp. 815–26; Anthony Appiah, "The Uncompleted Argument: Du Bois and the Illusion of Race," in Henry Louis Gates, Jr., *"Race," Writing, and Difference* (Chicago: University of Chicago Press, 1986), pp. 21–37.

7. W. E. B. Du Bois, *Dusk of Dawn: An Essay toward an Autobiography of a Race Concept* (New York: Schocken Books, 1968), p. 115.

8. Maurice S. Evans, *Black and White in the Southern States: A Study of the Race Problem in the United States from a South African Point of View* (New York: Longmans, 1915), pp. 13–15.

9. Du Bois, "The Conservation of Races," p. 817; Joel Williamson, *The Crucible of Race: Black-White Relations in the American South since Emancipation* (New York: Oxford University Press, 1984), p. 411.

10. James Weldon Johnson, *Along This Way: The Autobiography of James Weldon*

Johnson (1933; rpt. New York: Viking, 1968), p. 203; Claude McKay, *A Long Way from Home: An Autobiography* (1937; rpt. New York: Harcourt, Brace and World, 1970), p. 110.

11. See Cornel West, *The American Evasion of Philosophy: A Genealogy of Pragmatism* (Madison: University of Wisconsin Press, 1989), pp. 138–50.

12. Du Bois, *The Souls of Black Folk*, pp. 5–6.

13. Booker T. Washington, *Up from Slavery* (New York: Viking Penguin, 1986), p. 20; Samuel Coleridge-Taylor, *Twenty-Four Melodies Transcribed for the Piano* (Boston: Oliver Ditson, 1905), p. viii.

14. Du Bois, *The Souls of Black Folk*, p. 5. Cf. Arnold Rampersad, "Slavery and the Literary Imagination: Du Bois's *The Souls of Black Folk*," in Arnold Rampersad and Deborah McDowell, eds., *Slavery and the Literary Imagination* (Baltimore: Johns Hopkins University Press, 1989), pp. 104–24.

15. Du Bois, *The Souls of Black Folk*, p. 90.

16. William H. Ferris, *The African Abroad, Or His Evolution in Western Civilization*, 2 vols. (New Haven: Tuttle, Morehouse, and Taylor, 1913), I, 275. W. E. B. Du Bois, *Book Reviews of W. E. B. Du Bois*, ed. Herbert Aptheker (Millwood, N.Y.: Kraus-Thomson, 1977), p. 9.

17. Newman I. White, *American Negro Folk-Songs* (Cambridge, Mass.: Harvard University Press, 1928), p. 3.

18. William Francis Allen, Charles Pickard Ware, and Lucy McKim, *Slave Songs of the United States* (1867; rpt. New York: Arno Press, 1971), pp. iv–v; Lucy McKim, "Songs of the Port Royal Contrabands," *Dwight's Journal of Music* 21 (November 8, 1862); rpt. in Bruce Jackson, ed., *The Negro and His Folklore in Nineteenth-Century Periodicals* (Austin: University of Texas Press, 1967), p. 62; Charles S. Peabody, "Notes on Negro Music," *Journal of American Folklore* 16 (1903), 148–52.

19. Robert E. Park, *Race and Culture* (1918; rpt. Glencoe, Ill.: Free Press, 1950), pp. 267–79.

20. Anonymous woman quoted in Jeanette Robinson Murphy, "The Survival of African Music in America," *Popular Science Monthly* 55 (1899); rpt. in Jackson, *The Negro and His Folklore in Nineteenth-Century Periodicals*, pp. 328–29; Lawrence Levine, *Black Culture and Black Consciousness: Afro-American Folk Thought from Slavery to Freedom* (New York: Oxford University Press, 1977), pp. 163–64; Sterling Brown, *Collected Poems of Sterling A. Brown*, ed. Michael S. Harper (Chicago: Triquarterly Books, 1989), p. 104. See also Alain Locke, "Sterling Brown: The New Negro Folk Poet," in Nancy Cunard, ed. *Negro: An Anthology*, abridged ed. Hugh Ford (1934; rpt. New York: Frederick Ungar, 1970), pp. 88–92.

21. Howard W. Odum and Guy B. Johnson, *The Negro and His Songs: A Study of Typical Negro Songs in the South* (Chapel Hill: University of North Carolina Press, 1925), p. 8; Du Bois, *Book Reviews*, pp. 84–85. On the spirituals sung as freedom songs in the modern civil rights movement, see Pete Seeger and Bob Reiser, eds., *Everybody Says Freedom: A History of the Civil Rights Movement in*

Songs and Pictures (New York: Norton, 1989), and Guy Carawan and Candie Carawan, eds., *Sing for Freedom: The Story of the Civil Rights Movement through Its Songs* (Bethlehem, Penn.: Sing Out, 1990).

22. Du Bois, *The Souls of Black Folk*, p. 206; M. F. Armstrong and Helen W. Ludlow, *Hampton and Its Students, with Fifty Cabin and Plantation Songs*, arranged by Thomas P. Fenner (New York: Putnam's, 1874), p. 172; F. G. Rathbun, "The Negro Music of the South," *Southern Workman* 22 (November 1893), 174; R. Nathaniel Dett, ed., *Religious Folk-Songs of the Negro as Sung at Hampton Institute* (Hampton, Va.: Hampton Institute Press, 1927), preface p. xviii; appendix p. i. Because it is Fenner's commentary that I will cite in the case of the Hampton volume, subsequent notes will refer to Fenner as author rather than Armstrong and Ludlow.

23. Dett, *Religious Folk-Songs of the Negro*, pp. x, xviii; Fenner, *Hampton and Its Students*, p. 172.

24. Robert C. Toll, *Blacking Up: The Minstrel Show in Nineteenth-Century America* (New York: Oxford University Press, 1974), pp. 236–37.

25. Lily Young Cohen, *Lost Spirituals* (New York: Walter Neale, 1928), p. ix; H. T. Burleigh, *Negro Spirituals* (New York: G. Ricordi, 1917), unpaginated; Sterling Brown, "Negro Folk Expression: Spirituals, Seculars, Ballads and Work Songs," *Phylon* 14 (Winter 1953), 47–49. See also Levine, *Black Culture and Black Consciousness*, pp. 19–42; Albert J. Raboteau, *Slave Religion: The "Invisible Institution" in the Antebellum South* (New York: Oxford University Press, 1978), pp. 243–66; John W. Blassingame, *The Slave Community: Plantation Life in the Antebellum South*, rev. ed. (New York: Oxford University Press, 1979), pp. 137–48; Miles Mark Fisher, *Negro Slave Songs in the United States* (1953; rpt. Secaucus, N.J.: Citadel Press, 1978), pp. 66–146; James H. Cone, *The Spirituals and the Blues: An Interpretation* (New York: Seabury Press, 1972), pp. 34–57; and Wyatt Tee Walker, *"Somebody's Calling My Name": Black Sacred Music and Social Change* (Valley Forge, Pa.: Judson Press, 1979), pp. 15–96.

26. Marion Alexander Haskell, "Negro 'Spirituals,'" *Century Magazine* 36 (August 1899), 581; Kelly Miller, "The Artistic Gifts of the Negro," in *Radicals and Conservatives, and Other Essays on the Negro in America* (originally published as *Race Adjustment*, 1908; rpt. New York: Schocken Books, 1968), p. 248.

27. Richard Wallaschek, *Primitive Music* (London: Longmans, Green, 1893), p. 60; Frederick Root quoted in Levine, *Black Culture and Black Consciousness*, p. 20; Fenner, *Hampton and Its Students*, p. 172. See also Levine, *Black Culture and Black Consciousness*, pp. 166–69, and V. F. Calverton, "The Growth of Negro Literature," in Cunard, *Negro: An Anthology*, p. 79.

28. Dena Epstein, *Sinful Tunes and Spirituals: Black Folk Music to the Civil War* (Urbana: University of Illinois Press, 1977), p. 344; White, *American Negro Folk-Songs*, pp. 25, 57; John W. Work, *American Negro Songs and Spirituals* (New York: Bonanza Books, 1940), p. 8; W. E. B. Du Bois, "John Work: Martyr and Singer," *Crisis* 32 (May 1926), 32–34. The most extensive argument for the black borrowing from white models was made by George Pullen Jackson in *White*

Spirituals in the Southern Uplands (Chapel Hill: University of North Carolina Press, 1933), pp. 242–302, and *White and Negro Spirituals: Their Life Span and Kinship* (New York: J. J. Augustin, 1943), pp. 145–233, and White, *American Negro Folk-Songs,* passim. For countering views, see especially Marshall W. Stearns, *The Story of Jazz* (New York: Oxford University Press, 1956), pp. 79–89, 125–26; Rudi Blesh, *Shining Trumpets: A History of Jazz,* rev. ed. (1958; rpt. New York: Da Capo, 1976), pp. 25–148; John Lovell, Jr., *Black Song: The Forge and the Flame: The Story of How the Afro-American Spiritual Was Hammered Out* (New York: Macmillan, 1972), pp. 63–126; Gunther Schuller, *Early Jazz: Its Roots and Musical Development* (New York: Oxford University Press, 1968), pp. 3–62; and Portia K. Maultsby, "Africanisms in African-American Music," in *African-isms in American Culture,* ed. Joseph E. Holloway (Bloomington: Indiana University Press, 1990), pp. 185–210. Useful summaries of and commentary on the debate are available in D. K. Wilgus, "The Negro-White Spiritual," in Alan Dundes, *Mother Wit from the Laughing Barrel: Readings in the Interpretation of Afro-American Folklore* (1973; rpt. New York: Garland, 1981), pp. 81–94, and Paul Oliver, *Savannah Syncopators: African Retentions in the Blues* (New York: Stein and Day, 1970), passim.

29. Du Bois, *The Souls of Black Folk,* pp. 155–56; Murphy, "The Survival of African Music in America," p. 328. When it was included in her later collection *Southern Thoughts for Northern Thinkers* (New York: Bandanna Publishing, 1904), Murphy's important essay was further diminished by being surrounded by stereotypical portraits of southern mammies; defenses of southern handling of the "Negro problem"; black sermons in a minstrel mold; Murphy's own musical compositions (e.g., "Dat's What de Mammy Good For"); and indulgences in plantation mythology (e.g., "I have interviewed all of my life great numbers of ex-slaves, and I have yet to find one old slave who will say that he or she was cruelly treated" [p. 11]).

30. Du Bois, *The Souls of Black Folk,* pp. 206, 204, 212.

31. William Stanley Braithwaite, "The Negro in American Literature," in Alain Locke, ed., *The New Negro* (1925; rpt. New York: Atheneum, 1974), p. 40; White, *American Negro Folk-Songs,* p. 18.

32. Du Bois, *The Souls of Black Folk,* pp. 155, 159; W. E. B. Du Bois, "The Minister" (1906), in *Writings by W. E. B. Du Bois in Periodicals Edited by Others,* ed. Herbert Aptheker, 3 vols. (Millwood, N.Y.: Kraus-Thomson, 1982), I, 328; James Weldon Johnson, *God's Trombones: Seven Negro Sermons in Verse* (New York: Viking, 1927), p. 2. See also A. M. Chirgwin, "The Vogue of the Negro Spiritual," *Edinburgh Review* 247 (January 1928), 65, and Sterling Stuckey, *Slave Culture: Nationalist Theory and the Foundations of Black America* (New York: Oxford University Press, 1987), pp. 254–58.

33. James Weldon Johnson and J. Rosamond Johnson, *The Books of American Negro Spirituals,* 2 vols. in 1 (1925, 1926; rpt. New York: Da Capo, 1969), I, 21–23; Johnson, *God's Trombones,* pp. 5–10.

34. Winthrop Sargeant, *Jazz: Hot and Hybrid,* 3rd ed. (New York: Da Capo, 1975),

p. 185. See also Stearns, *The Story of Jazz*, pp. 130–33; Gerald L. Davis, *I Got the Word in Me and I Can Sing It You Know: A Study of the Performed African-American Sermon* (Philadelphia: University of Pennsylvania Press, 1985), pp. 24–66; Jon Michael Spencer, *Sacred Symphony: The Chanted Sermon of the Black Preacher* (New York: Greenwood Press, 1987), pp. 2–16; Bruce A. Rosenberg, *Can These Bones Live? The Art of the American Folk Preacher,* rev. ed. (1970; rpt. Urbana: University of Illinois Press, 1988), pp. 11–12, 50–54, 72–81; and C. Eric Lincoln and Lawrence H. Mamiya, *The Black Church in the African American Experience* (Durham, N.C.: Duke University Press, 1990), p. 349.

35. Frederick Douglass, *My Bondage and My Freedom,* ed. William L. Andrews (Urbana: University of Illinois Press, 1987), p. 65; James Miller McKim, "Negro Songs," *Dwight's Journal of Music* 19 (August 9, 1862), rpt. in Jackson, *The Negro and His Folklore in Nineteenth-Century Periodicals,* p. 59.

36. Janheinz Jahn, *Muntu: An Outline of Neo-African Culture,* trans. Marjorie Grene (London: Faber and Faber, 1961), pp. 132–40, 185–90; Molefi Kete Asante, *The Afrocentric Idea* (Philadelphia: Temple University Press, 1987), pp. 43–48, 85–93; Clyde Taylor, "'Salt Peanuts': Sound and Sense in African/American Oral/Musical Creativity," *Callaloo* 5 (October 1982), 3.

37. Du Bois, *The Souls of Black Folk,* pp. 5–6; Robert B. Stepto, *From behind the Veil: A Study of Afro-American Narrative* (Urbana: University of Illinois Press, 1979), pp. 54–55.

38. Thomas Holt, "The Political Uses of Alienation: W. E. B. Du Bois on Politics, Race, and Culture, 1903–1940," *American Quarterly* 42 (June 1990), 306; Du Bois, *The Souls of Black Folk,* p. 5; Rampersad, "Slavery and the Literary Imagination: Du Bois's *The Souls of Black Folk,*" p. 118; Stuckey, *Slave Culture,* pp. 258–73.

39. Du Bois, *Dusk of Dawn,* p. 119.

40. Hiram Kelly Moderwell, "The Epic of the Black Man," *New Republic* 12 (September 8, 1917), 154–55; Alain Locke, "The Negro Spirituals," in Locke, *The New Negro,* p. 200.

41. Eileen Southern, *The Music of Black Americans: A History* (New York: Norton, 1971), pp. 5–8, 14–15; Oliver, *Savannah Syncopators,* pp. 44–48; Maurice Delafosse, *The Negroes of Africa,* trans. F. Fligleman (c. 1931), quoted in Fisher, *Negro Slave Songs in the United States,* p. 2. The "living book," it might be added, is thus a trope related by inversion to that of the "talking book" (the slave, mystified by writing, assumes that the book speaks to its master), which Henry Louis Gates, Jr., has analyzed as the central trope by which black writers beginning in the eighteenth century confronted the problem of literacy, initiating "a motivated, and political, engagement with and condemnation of Europe's fundamental figure of domination, the Great Chain of Being." Refigured in the trope of the mastery of letters which constituted the essence of liberation in the slave narratives—the most exemplary case was that of Frederick Douglass—the talking book, according to Gates, became an ironic trap in which the registers of vocality and blackness were inevitably emptied of semantic power: "How can

the black subject posit a full and sufficient self in language in which blackness is a sign of absence?" See Henry Louis Gates, Jr., *The Signifying Monkey: A Theory of Afro-American Literary Criticism* (New York: Oxford University Press, 1988), pp. 167–69.

42. Paul Stoller, "Sound in Songhay Cultural Experience," *American Ethnologist* 3 (1984), 559–70; Ben Sidran, *Black Talk* (1971; rpt. New York: Da Capo, 1983), pp. 6–19, quote at p. 13. See also Blesh, *Shining Trumpets*, pp. 32–33, 42–46; Schuller, *Early Jazz*, pp. 5–6, 54–56; and Ernest Borneman, "The Roots of Jazz," in *Jazz: New Perspectives on the History of Jazz*, ed. Nat Hentoff and Albert J. McCarthy (1959; rpt. New York: Da Capo, n.d.), pp. 6, 14–16.

43. Houston A. Baker, Jr., *Modernism and the Harlem Renaissance* (Chicago: University of Chicago Press, 1987), pp. 58–68; Sidran, *Black Talk*, p. 13.

44. Stearns, *The Story of Jazz*, p. 129; Epstein, *Sinful Tunes and Spirituals*, p. 202; Leroi Jones [Amiri Baraka], *Blues People: Negro Music in White America* (New York: William Morrow, 1963), p. xi.

45. Du Bois, *The Souls of Black Folk*, p. 208; Fenner, *Hampton and Its Students*, p. 181; Thomas Wentworth Higginson, "Negro Spirituals," *Atlantic Monthly* 19 (June 1867); rpt. in Jackson, *The Negro and His Folklore in Nineteenth-Century Periodicals*, p. 92. In what follows I have used this edition of *Hampton and Its Students*, cited in note 22, and J. B. T. Marsh, *The Story of the Jubilee Singers with Their Songs* (1872; rev. ed. Boston: Houghton Mifflin, 1880). On the editions of Marsh and Fenner, see Henry Edward Krehbiel, *Afro-American Folksongs: A Study in Racial and National Music* (1914; rpt. New York: Frederick Ungar, 1962), p. 42.

46. Lovell, *Black Song*, pp. 122, 445. Cf. Ann Charters, *Nobody: The Story of Bert Williams* (New York: Macmillan, 1970), pp. 9–10. Du Bois follows the version in Fenner, *Hampton and Its Students;* a distinctly different melody appears in Marsh, *The Story of the Jubilee Singers*, p. 125.

47. Fenner, *Hampton and Its Students*, p. 181.

48. Du Bois, *The Souls of Black Folk*, pp. 5, 9.

49. Ibid., pp. 11–12.

50. Fenner, *Hampton and Its Students*, pp. 222–23; Seeger and Reiser, *Everybody Says Freedom*, p. 21.

51. Du Bois, *The Souls of Black Folk*, p. 208; Fenner, *Hampton and Its Students*, p. 176; Marsh, *The Story of the Jubilee Singers*, p. 199.

52. Lovell, *Black Song*, p. 409; Du Bois, *The Souls of Black Folk*, p. 34.

53. Du Bois, *The Souls of Black Folk*, pp. 14, 6; Robert Farris Thompson, *The Flash of the Spirit: African and Afro-American Art and Philosophy* (New York: Random House, 1983), p. 115.

54. Du Bois, *The Souls of Black Folk*, p. 208; Marsh, *The Story of the Jubilee Singers*, p. 167.

55. Du Bois, *The Souls of Black Folk*, pp. 51–62.

56. Ibid., pp. 67–68, 90. Du Bois would still be quoting the Goethe line in a 1958 address to the All-Africa People's Conference, in which he advised his audience:

"You can starve a while longer rather than sell your great heritage for a mess of western capitalist pottage." See W. E. B. Du Bois, *Pan-Africa, 1919–1958* (Accra, Ghana: Bureau of African Affairs, 1958), p. 6.

57. Du Bois, *The Souls of Black Folk*, pp. 208, 67.

58. Marsh, *The Story of the Jubilee Singers*, p. 141.

59. Ibid., p. 166.

60. Stepto, *From behind the Veil*, pp. 66–80; Mechel Sobel, *Trabelin' On: The Slave Journey to an Afro-Baptist Faith* (Westport, Conn.: Greenwood Press, 1979), pp. 118–26.

61. Du Bois, *The Souls of Black Folk*, pp. 91–92, 123.

62. Marsh, *The Story of the Jubilee Singers*, p. 140; James M. McPherson, *The Abolitionist Legacy: From Reconstruction to the NAACP* (Princeton: Princeton University Press, 1975), p. 369.

63. Marsh, *The Story of the Jubilee Singers*, p. 133.

64. Du Bois, *The Souls of Black Folk*, p. 134.

65. Ibid., pp. 97, 100–102; W. E. B. Du Bois, *Writings in Periodicals Edited by W. E. B. Du Bois: Selections from The Crisis*, ed. Herbert Aptheker, 2 vols. (Millwood, N.Y.: Kraus-Thomson, 1983), I, 392.

66. W. E. B. Du Bois, *John Brown* (New York: International Publishers, 1972), p. 15.

67. Lovell, *Black Song*, p. 258; Du Bois, *The Souls of Black Folk*, pp. 93–94; W. E. B. Du Bois, *Black Reconstruction in America* (Cleveland: Meridian Books, 1964), p. 5.

68. Du Bois, *The Souls of Black Folk*, p. 209; Fenner, *Hampton and Its Students*, pp. 200–205.

69. Fenner, *Hampton and Its Students*, p. 200. On the relationship between spirituals and work songs, see Krehbiel, *Afro-American Folksongs*, pp. 46–55; Stearns, *The Story of Jazz*, pp. 91–101; Blesh, *Shining Trumpets*, pp. 48–53; John Storm Roberts, *Black Music of Two Worlds* (New York: Praeger, 1972), pp. 139–94; Borneman, "The Roots of Jazz," pp. 11–14; Jones, *Blues People*, pp. 65ff.; and H. Bruce Franklin, *Prison Literature in America: The Victim as Criminal and Artist*, rev. ed. (1978; rpt. New York: Oxford University Press, 1989), pp. 73–123.

70. Du Bois, *The Souls of Black Folk*, p. 102.

71. John Michael Vlach, *The Afro-American Tradition in Decorative Arts* (Athens: University of Georgia Press, 1990), pp. 139–47, quote at p. 139; Melville Herskovits, *The Myth of the Negro Past* (1941; rpt. Boston: Beacon Press, 1967), pp. 197–206; Robert Farris Thompson, "African Influence on the Art of the United States," in *Afro-American Folk Art and Crafts* (Jackson: University of Mississippi Press, 1983), pp. 47–50; Robert Farris Thompson and Joseph Cornet, *The Four Moments of the Sun: Kongo Art in Two Worlds* (Washington, D.C.: National Gallery of Art, 1981), pp. 181–203; Thompson, *Flash of the Spirit*, pp. 118–42.

72. Du Bois, *The Souls of Black Folk*, pp. 157–61.

73. Lovell, *Black Song*, pp. 196, 379; Tom Fletcher, *One Hundred Years of the Negro*

in Show Business (1954; rpt. New York: Da Capo, 1984), pp. 15–18; Fisher, *Negro Slave Songs in the United States,* pp. 66–87; Marsh, *The Story of the Jubilee Singers,* p. 147.

74. Du Bois, *The Souls of Black Folk,* pp. 161–62, 165–68.

75. Ibid., pp. 165–66.

76. Ibid., pp. 184, 176; Alexander Crummell, "Civilization, the Primal Need of the Race," in *The American Negro Academy Occasional Papers, 1–22* (New York: Arno Press, 1969), pp. 3–7; Alexander Crummell, "The Need of New Ideas," in *Africa and America: Addresses and Discourses* (1891; rpt. Miami: Mnemosyne, 1969), p. 21. On the American Negro Academy, see Alfred A. Moss, *The American Negro Academy: Voices of the Talented Tenth* (Baton Rouge: Louisiana University Press, 1981).

77. Crummell, *Africa and America,* pp. 374–77; Du Bois, "The Conservation of Races," p. 822; Du Bois, *The Souls of Black Folk,* p. 161.

78. Wilson J. Moses, "Dark Forests and Barbarian Vigor: Paradox, Conflict, and Africanity in Black Writing before 1914," *American Literary History* I (Fall 1989), 643–45; Wilson J. Moses, *Alexander Crummell: A Study of Civilization and Discontent* (New York: Oxford University Press, 1989), pp. 11–16, 235–37; Crummell, *Africa and America,* pp. 46–49.

79. Du Bois, *The Souls of Black Folk,* pp. 177, 179.

80. Marsh, *The Story of the Jubilee Singers,* p. 126; Du Bois, *The Souls of Black Folk,* p. 176.

81. Lovell, *Black Song,* pp. 65, 196, 247; Fisher, *Negro Slave Songs in the United States,* p. 145.

82. Borneman, "The Roots of Jazz," p. 11; William Arms Fisher, *Seventy Negro Spirituals* (Boston: Oliver Ditson, 1926), p. xxx; Dorothy Scarborough, "New Light on an Old Song," in *Ebony and Topaz: A Collectanea,* ed. Charles S. Johnson (1927; rpt. Freeport, N.Y.: Books for Library Presses, 1971), p. 59.

83. Du Bois, *The Souls of Black Folk,* pp. 170–75.

84. Fenner, *Hampton and Its Students,* p. 218.

85. Marsh, *The Story of the Jubliee Singers,* p. 136.

86. Du Bois, *The Souls of Black Folk,* pp. 196–97, 203.

87. Edward Blyden, "Mohammedanism and the Negro Race," in *Christianity, Islam, and the Negro Race* (London: Whittingham, 1887), p. 15; Higginson, "Negro Spirituals," p. 92; Marsh, *The Story of the Jubilee Singers,* p. 180; Du Bois, *The Souls of Black Folk,* pp. 204–5.

88. For what it may be worth, Maud Cuney-Hare notes that "Wrestling Jacob" "had a special appeal to the Negro because Africans are very fond of stories of wrestling." See *Negro Musicians and Their Music* (Washington, D.C.: Associated Publishers, 1936), p. 413.

89. Du Bois, *The Souls of Black Folk,* p. 207. Personal communications from Morris Goodman, Northwestern University, and Mary Kolawole, Obafemi Awolowo University, Nigeria.

90. Miller, "The Artistic Gifts of the Negro," p. 251; Carl Van Vechten, "Folksongs

of the American Negro" (1925), in *"Keep A-Inching' Along": Selected Writings of Carl Van Vechten about Black Art and Letters,* ed. Bruce Kellner (Westport, Conn.: Greenwood Press, 1979), p. 38; W. C. Handy, *Father of the Blues* (New York: Macmillan, 1941), p. 163.

91. See, for example, Harold Courlander, *Negro Folk Music, U.S.A.* (New York: Columbia University Press, 1963), p. 25; Roberts, *Black Music of Two Worlds,* pp. 144–49; and Frederick Ramsey, Jr., *Been Here and Gone* (New Brunswick, N.J.: Rutgers University Press, 1960), pp. 31–36.

92. Borneman, "The Roots of Jazz," pp. 7, 17; Murphy, "The Survival of African Music in America," pp. 331–32, 328; Geneva Smitherman, *Talkin' and Testifyin': The Language of Black America* (Detroit: Wayne State University Press, 1986), pp. 100, 139–41.

93. Blesh, *Shining Trumpets,* p. 65.

94. W. C. Handy and Abbe Niles, *Blues: An Anthology* (1926; rpt. New York: Da Capo, 1990), pp. 31–32. Niles's introduction, from which the quotation and example arranged by Handy are taken, was revised in the later edition but contains the original 1926 material intact. In 1925 Du Bois wrote an essay entitled "The Black Man Brings His Gifts" that praised Handy, who in turn sent Du Bois a copy of *Blues: An Anthology* and praised his work as a race leader. See Marable, "The Black Faith of W. E. B. Du Bois," pp. 28, 31.

95. Marsh, *The Story of the Jubilee Singers,* p. 126; Du Bois, *The Souls of Black Folk,* p. 176; Roosevelt May, "Swing Low, Sweet Chariot," *Eight-Hand Sets and Holy Steps: Early Dance Tunes and Songs of Praise from North Carolina's Black Tradition,* Longleaf Records 001 (North Carolina Museum of History and North Carolina Art Council). Transcription of May by Eric J. Sundquist; some material elided.

96. Du Bois, *The Souls of Black Folk,* p. 206; Zora Neale Hurston, "Spirituals and Neo-Spirituals," in Cunard, *Negro: An Anthology,* pp. 223–24. Cf. Jahn, *Muntu,* who argues that the "purification" of the spirituals in concert performance destroyed their basic elements: "The definiteness prevents designation, Nommo cannot take shape or be given shape; in the concert hall Kuntu freezes into a dead form" (p. 220). For more on Hurston's theory and its implications for her fiction, see Eric J. Sundquist, *The Hammers of Creation: Folk Culture in Modern African American Fiction* (Athens: University of Georgia Press, 1993).

97. Theodore Seward, "Preface to the Music," in Marsh, *The Story of the Jubilee Singers,* p. 122; Johnson, *The Books of American Negro Spirituals,* I, 28–32. More recently Richard Waterman, from a different vantage point, has proposed a similar characterization of the implied linear structure underlying the complexity of African musical rhythms which he calls a "metronome sense." See Richard Waterman, "African Influence on the Music of the Americas," in Dundes, *Mother Wit from the Laughing Barrel,* pp. 86–87. The best technical discussions of "swing" are Schuller, *Early Jazz,* pp. 6–10, and André Hodeir, *Jazz: Its Evolution and Essence,* rev. ed., trans. David Noakes (1956; rpt. New York: Grove Press, 1980), pp. 198, 208–9.

98. Du Bois, *The Souls of Black Folk,* p. 215.

99. Handy and Niles, *Blues: An Anthology,* p. 49. The *Hampton* version, which reprints that of *Jubilee,* does not include this verse but instead expresses a comparable sentiment in the lines: "And if you meet with crosses, / And trials along the way, / Just keep your trust in Jesus, / And don't forget to pray" (p. 178). The lines transcribed by Handy and Niles appear in Dett's *Religious Folk-Songs of the Negro* as a verse of the different spiritual "There Is a Balm in Gilead" (p. 88).

100. See Jahn, *Muntu,* p. 224; Zora Neale Hurston, "High John de Conquer," in *The Sanctified Church: The Folklore Writing of Zora Neale Hurston* (Berkeley: Turtle Island, 1981), p. 70; Du Bois, *The Souls of Black Folk,* p. 215.

6. The Spell of Africa

1. W. E. B. Du Bois, *Darkwater: Voices from within the Veil* (New York: Schocken Books, 1969), pp. 253–73.

2. Edward Roux, *Time Longer Than Rope: A History of the Black Man's Struggle for Freedom in South Africa* (London: Victor Gollancz, 1949), pp. 143–45.

3. George Fredrickson, *White Supremacy: A Comparative Study of American and South African History* (New York: Oxford University Press, 1981); John W. Cell, *The Highest Stage of White Supremacy: The Origins of Segregation in South Africa and the American South* (Cambridge: Cambridge University Press, 1982).

4. See, for example, Janheinz Jahn, *Muntu: An Outline of Neo-African Culture,* trans. Marjorie Grene (London: Faber and Faber, 1961); Molefi Kete Asante, *The Afrocentric Idea* (Philadelphia: Temple University Press, 1987); and Henry Louis Gates, Jr., *The Signifying Monkey: A Theory of Afro-American Literary Criticism* (New York: Oxford University Press, 1988).

5. Tony Martin, *Race First: The Ideology and Organizational Struggles of Marcus Garvey and the Universal Negro Improvement Association* (Westport, Conn.: Greenwood Press, 1976), and *Literary Garveyism: Garvey, Black Arts, and the Harlem Renaissance* (Dover, Mass.: The Majority Press, 1983); Wilson J. Moses, *The Golden Age of Black Nationalism* (1978; rpt. New York: Oxford University Press, 1988), and *Alexander Crummell: A Study of Civilization and Discontent* (New York: Oxford University Press, 1989); Judith Stein, "Defining the Race, 1890–1930," in *Inventing Ethnicity,* ed. Werner Sollors (New York: Oxford University Press, 1989), p. 85.

6. Sterling Stuckey, *Slave Culture: Nationalist Theory and the Foundations of Black America* (New York: Oxford University Press, 1987), p. 274; Albert Murray, *The Omni-Americans: Black Experience and American Culture* (New York: Da Capo, 1970), p. 153.

7. Arnold Rampersad, *The Art and Imagination of W. E. B. Du Bois* (Cambridge, Mass.: Harvard University Press, 1976), p. 155. On Du Bois and the Pan-African conferences, including the context of the First World War, see especially Imanuel Geiss, *The Pan-African Movement: A History of Pan-Africanism in America, Eu-*

rope, and Africa, trans. Ann Keep (1968; rpt. New York: Africana Publishing, 1974), pp. 229–62; Elliott M. Rudwick, *W. E. B. Du Bois: Propagandist of the Negro Protest* (1960; rpt. New York: Atheneum, 1968), pp. 208–35; Moses, *The Golden Age of Black Nationalism*, pp. 197–250; J. Ayodele Langley, *Pan-Africanism and Nationalism in West Africa, 1900–1945: A Study in Ideology and Social Classes* (Oxford: Clarendon Press, 1973), pp. 60–90; and Clarence G. Contee, "W. E. B. Du Bois and African Nationalism, 1914–1945" (Ph.D. diss., American University, 1969), pp. 34–45.

8. "With the waning of the possibility of the Big Fortune, gathered by starvation wages and boundless exploitation of one's weaker and poorer fellows at home," Du Bois wrote two years before Lenin's *Imperialism: The Highest Stage of Capitalism*, "arise more magnificently the dreams of exploitation abroad." Like Lenin, Du Bois took for granted that colonial expansion was fueled by overripe capital that could not generate sufficient profit at home; but he too ignored the fact that the great bulk of European and American foreign investment was in other Western nations, that colonial investment involved enormous risk and often failed, and that it usually created wealth that, for all practical purposes, did not exist beforehand. See W. E. B. Du Bois, "The African Roots of the War," in *W. E. B. Du Bois: A Reader*, ed. Meyer Weinberg (New York: Harper and Row, 1970), p. 363, and also L. H. Gann and Peter Duignan, *Burden of Empire: An Appraisal of Western Colonialism in Africa South of the Sahara* (New York: Praeger, 1967), pp. 55–71.

9. W. E. B. Du Bois, *Writings by W. E. B. Du Bois in Periodicals Edited by Others*, ed. Herbert Aptheker, 3 vols. (Millwood, N.Y.: Kraus-Thomson, 1982), I, 73; ibid., II, 241ff.; Du Bois, *Black Folk Then and Now*, ed. Herbert Aptheker (Millwood, N.Y.: Kraus-Thomson, 1975), p. 383.

10. Franz Boas, "The Outlook for the American Negro," in *A Franz Boas Reader: The Shaping of American Anthropology, 1883–1911*, ed. George W. Stocking, Jr. (Chicago: University of Chicago Press, 1974), pp. 310–16; Boas, "The Problem of the American Negro," *Yale Review* 10 (1921), 395. On Boas in relation to Du Bois, see also Thomas F. Gossett, *Race: The History of an Idea in America* (1963; rpt. New York: Schocken Books, 1965), pp. 418–26; S. P. Fullinwider, *The Mind and Mood of Black America: Twentieth-Century Thought* (Homewood, Ill.: Dorsey Press, 1969), pp. 60–61; and Stuckey, *Slave Culture*, pp. 276–77.

11. Rampersad, *The Art and Imagination of W. E. B. Du Bois*, p. 234; William Toll, *The Resurgence of Race: Black Social Theory from Reconstruction to the Pan-African Conferences* (Philadelphia: Temple University Press, 1979), pp. 196–98.

12. Contee, "W. E. B. Du Bois and African Nationalism," pp. 14–15; W. E. B. Du Bois, *The Negro* (1915; rpt. New York: Oxford University Press, 1970), p. 78; George Shepperson, introduction to Du Bois, *The Negro*, pp. xviii–xxiii.

13. Notably, for example, Vincent Harding, "W. E. B. Du Bois and the Black Messianic Vision," *Freedomways* 9 (Winter 1969), 44–58, and Moses, *The Golden Age of Black Nationalism*, pp. 132–45.

14. See, for example, Gossett, *Race*, pp. 84–122; John Higham, *Strangers in the Land: Patterns of American Nativism, 1860–1925* (1955; rpt. New York: Atheneum, 1963), pp. 131–59; Moses, *The Golden Age of Black Nationalism*, pp. 251–71.

15. George Shepperson, "Ethiopianism and African Nationalism," *Phylon* 14 (Spring 1953), 17–18.

16. Emperor Menelik quoted in F. Nnabuenyi Ugonna, introduction to J. E. Casely Hayford, *Ethiopia Unbound: Studies in Race Emancipation* (1911; rpt. London: Frank Cass, 1969), p. xxv; Robert G. Weisbord, "Black America and the Italian-Ethiopian Crisis: An Episode in Pan-Negroism," *The Historian* 34 (February 1972), 230–35; Geiss, *The Pan-African Movement*, pp. 132–33; George Shepperson, "Ethiopianism: Past and Present," in C. G. Baeta, *Christianity in Tropical Africa* (London: Oxford University Press, 1968), pp. 249–51; Sylvia M. Jacobs, *The African Nexus: Black American Perspectives on the European Partitioning of Africa, 1880–1920* (Westport, Conn.: Greenwood Press, 1981), pp. 187–203.

17. Robert Alexander Young, "The Ethiopian Manifesto," in Sterling Stuckey, ed., *The Ideological Origins of Black Nationalism* (Boston: Beacon Press, 1972), pp. 33–35; Rufus L. Perry, *The Cushite, or the Descendants of Ham*, quoted in George Shepperson and Thomas Price, *Independent African: John Chilembwe and the Origins, Setting, and Significance of the Nyasaland Native Rising of 1915* (Edinburgh: Edinburgh University Press, 1958), p. 102.

18. Alexander Crummell, "Hope for Africa," quoted in Langley, *Pan-Africanism and Nationalism in West Africa, 1900–1945*, pp. 22–23; Moses, *Alexander Crummell*, pp. 78–79;

19. Manning Marable, *W. E. B. Du Bois: Black Radical Democrat* (Boston: Twayne, 1986), p. 34; Du Bois on Turner, *Crisis* (July 1915), quoted in Edwin S. Redkey, *Black Exodus: Black Nationalist and Back-to-Africa Movements, 1890–1910* (New Haven: Yale University Press, 1969), p. 287; Martin, *Race First*, pp. 291–92.

20. P. Olisanwuche Esedebe, *Pan-Africanism: The Idea and Movement, 1776–1963* (Washington, D.C.: Howard University Press, 1982), pp. 29–41; Gayraud S. Wilmore, *Black Religion and Black Radicalism: An Interpretation of the Religious History of Afro-American People*, rev. ed. (Maryknoll, N.Y.: Orbis Books, 1983), pp. 116–34; Edward W. Blyden, *Christianity, Islam, and the Negro Race* (London: Whittingham, 1887), pp. 130–49, quote at p. 147.

21. Edward Blyden, "Africa for the African," *African Repository* (1872), in Henry S. Wilson, ed., *Origins of West African Nationalism* (London: Macmillan, 1969), pp. 231–38; Blyden, "Christianity and the Negro Race," in *Christianity, Islam, and the Negro Race*, p. 44; Blyden, "Study and Race," *Sierre Leone Times* (1893), in Wilson, *Origins of West African Nationalism*, pp. 249–53; Casely Hayford, *Ethiopia Unbound*, pp. 172–73. See also Marion Berghahn, *Images of Africa in Black American Literature* (London: Macmillan, 1977), pp. 48–52, and Robert W. July, *The Origins of Modern African Thought* (London: Faber and Faber, 1968), pp. 208–33.

22. Redkey, *Black Exodus*, pp. 24–46, 99–194 passim; August Meier, *Negro Thought in America, 1880–1915: Racial Ideologies in the Age of Booker T. Washington* (Ann

Arbor: University of Michigan Press, 1963), pp. 65–68; Wilmore, *Black Religion and Black Radicalism*, pp. 122–25.

23. Henry M. Turner, "The American Negro and the Fatherland," in *Africa and the Negro: Addresses and Proceedings of the Congress on Africa* (Atlanta: Gammon Theological Seminary, 1896), pp. 195–98.

24. Marcus Garvey, *Negro World* (February 12, 1921), in Theodore G. Vincent, ed., *Voices of a Black Nation: Political Journalism in the Harlem Renaissance* (San Francisco: Ramparts Press, 1973), pp. 272–73.

25. W. E. B. Du Bois, *Writings in Periodicals Edited by W. E. B. Du Bois: Selections from The Crisis*, 2 vols., ed. Herbert Aptheker (Millwood, N.Y.: Kraus-Thomson, 1983), I, 169.

26. Henry M. Turner, "God Is a Negro," *Voice of Missions* (February 1898), in Edwin S. Redkey, ed., *Respect Black: The Writings and Speeches of Henry McNeal Turner* (New York: Arno Press, 1971), pp. 176–77.

27. Roux, *Time Longer Than Rope*, pp. 85–91; J. Mutero Chirenje, *Ethiopianism and Afro-Americans in Southern Africa, 1883–1916* (Baton Rouge: Louisiana State University Press, 1987), pp. 35–83; Bengt G. M. Sundkler, *Bantu Prophets in South Africa* (London: Lutterworth Press, 1948), pp. 39–43; Wilmore, *Black Religion and Black Nationalism*, pp. 126–29; Geiss, *The Pan-African Movement*, pp. 132–59.

28. Louis R. Harlan, "Booker T. Washington and the White Man's Burden," *American Historical Review* 71 (January 1966), 441–67; Manning Marable, "Booker T. Washington and African Nationalism," *Phylon* 35 (December 1974), 398–406.

29. Michael McCarthy, *Dark Continent: Africa as Seen by Americans* (Westport, Conn.: Greewood Press, 1983), pp. 59–119; Harold R. Isaacs, *The New World of Negro Americans* (London: Phoenix House, 1963), pp. 105–72; Walter L. Williams, *Black Americans and the Evangelization of Africa, 1877–1900* (Madison: University of Wisconsin Press, 1982), pp. 104–40; Charlotte Mayne, quoted in Chirenje, *Ethiopianism and Afro-Americans in Southern Africa*, p. 51.

30. Charles Morris, "What the Brethren in Black Are Doing in the Missions," quoted in Shepperson, "Ethiopianism and African Nationalism," p. 15; Williams, *Black Americans and the Evangelization of Africa*, pp. 70–72; Cell, *The Highest Stage of White Supremacy*, pp. 33–39.

31. "The Ethiopian Movement in South Africa," quoted in Moses, *The Golden Age of Black Nationalism*, p. 199.

32. Du Bois, *The Negro*, pp. 9, 6.

33. Du Bois, "Races," *Crisis* 2 (August 1911), in *Selections from The Crisis*, I, 14.

34. W. E. B. Du Bois, *The Souls of Black Folk* (New York: Viking Penguin, 1989), p. 5; Du Bois, *The Negro*, p. 10.

35. William B. Smith, *The Color Line: A Brief for the Unborn* (New York: McClure, Phillips, 1906), p. 260; Martin, *Race First*, pp. 299–300.

36. Ulrich B. Phillips, *Life and Labor in the Old South* (1929; rpt. Boston: Little, Brown, 1963), p. 160; Philip A. Bruce, *The Plantation Negro as a Freeman* (New York: Putnam's, 1889), pp. 126–34, 241–51; Joseph A. Tillinghast, *The Negro in*

Africa and America, in *Publications of the American Economic Association* 3 (May 1902), 225ff.; George Fredrickson, *The Black Image in the White Mind: The Debate on Afro-American Character and Destiny, 1817–1914* (New York: Harper and Row, 1971), pp. 253–55; W. E. B. Du Bois, *Book Reviews of W.E.B. Du Bois,* ed. Herbert Aptheker (Millwood, N.Y.: Kraus-Thomson, 1977), pp. 7–8, 12.

37. John T. Morgan, "The Race Question in the United States" (1890), in I. A. Newby, ed., *The Development of Segregationist Thought* (Homewood, Ill.: Dorsey Press, 1968), pp. 22–23. On black history, see, for example, Meier, *Negro Thought in America,* pp. 260–70; Dickson D. Bruce, Jr., "Ancient Africa and the Early Black American Historians, 1883–1915," *American Quarterly* 36 (Winter 1984), 684–99; Clarence E. Walker, *Deromanticizing Black History: Critical Essays and Reappraisals* (Knoxville: University of Tennessee Press, 1991), pp. 87–107; Toll, *The Resurgence of Race,* pp. 9–46; Gann and Duignan, *Burden of Empire,* pp. 129–32; Stuckey, *Slave Culture,* pp. 277–80; and Cary D. Wintz, *Black Culture and the Harlem Renaissance* (Houston: Rice University Press, 1988), pp. 30–47.

38. S. R. B. Attoh Ahuma, *The Gold Coast Nation and National Consciousness* (1911), excerpted in J. Ayodele Langley, ed., *Ideologies of Liberation in Black Africa, 1856–1970* (London: Rex Collings, 1979), pp. 163–70.

39. Marcus Garvey, *Black Man* (February 1934), quoted in Robert A. Hill, introduction to *The Marcus Garvey and Univeral Negro Improvement Association Papers,* 5 vols. to date (Berkeley: University of California Press, 1983), I, lxxxvi–lxxxvii; Toll, *The Resurgence of Race,* pp. 168–69.

40. See Redkey, *Black Exodus,* pp. 47ff.; David Jenkins, *Black Zion: The Return of Afro-Americans and West Indians to Africa* (London: Wildwood House, 1975), pp. 63–123; Robert Weisbord, *Ebony Kinship: Africa, Africans, and the Afro-American* (Westport, Conn.: Greenwood Press, 1973), pp. 12–50; and Asante, *The Afrocentric Idea,* pp. 148–56.

41. P. Ka Isaka Seme, "The Regeneration of Africa," in William H. Ferris, *The African Abroad, Or His Evolution in Western Civilization,* 2 vols. (New Haven: Tuttle, Morehouse, and Taylor, 1913), I, 436–38.

42. Pauline Hopkins, *Of One Blood,* in *The Magazine Novels of Pauline Hopkins* (New York: Oxford University Press, 1988), p. 448. See also Hazel Carby's introduction to this edition and her *Reconstructing Womanhood: The Emergence of the Afro-American Woman Novelist* (New York: Oxford University Press, 1987), pp. 155–61. For Du Bois's remarks on ancient Ethiopia, see *The Negro,* pp. 21–23; for a brief historical view of Meroe, see Basil Davidson, *Discovering Africa's Past* (London: Longman, 1978), pp. 20–25.

43. Alfred Binet, *On Double Consciousness* (1889; rpt. Chicago: Open Court, 1896), p. 45; William James, "The Hidden Self," in *Essays in Psychology* (Cambridge, Mass.: Harvard University Press, 1983), pp. 247–68. For Hopkins's use of James, I am much indebted to Thomas J. Otten, "Pauline Hopkins and the Hidden Self of Race," *ELH* 59 (1992), 227–56. On Binet, see also Gosset, *Race,* pp. 364–68.

44. William James, "Person and Personality," in *Essays in Psychology,* pp. 320–21;

W. E. B. Du Bois, *Dusk of Dawn: An Essay Toward An Autobiography of a Race Concept* (1940; rpt. New York, Schocken Books, 1968), p. 38. See also Francis L. Broderick, *W. E. B. Du Bois: Negro Leader in a Time of Crisis* (Stanford: Stanford University Press, 1959), pp. 30–31, and Rampersad, *The Art and Imagination of W. E. B. Du Bois,* pp. 25–26.

45. Hopkins, *Of One Blood,* pp. 561, 573, 585, 607.

46. Ibid., pp. 442, 475, 502.

47. Thomas Jefferson, *Notes on the State of Virginia,* in *The Portable Jefferson,* ed. Merrill D. Peterson (New York: Viking Press, 1975), p. 187.

48. Edward W. Blyden, "The Jewish Question," in *Black Spokesman: Selected Writings of Edward Wilmot Blyden,* ed. Hollis R. Lynch (London: Frank Cass, 1971), pp. 209–14; Robert G. Weisbord and Richard Kazarian, Jr., *Israel in the Black American Perspective* (Westport, Conn.: Greenwood Press, 1985), pp. 7–28; Du Bois, *Crisis* 17 (February 1919), in *Selections from The Crisis,* I, 169; Robert A. Hill, introduction to *Marcus Garvey: Life and Lessons* (Berkeley: University of California Press, 1987), pp. lii–liv.

49. In a well-known 1915 address, Brandeis had argued: "Let no American imagine that Zionism is inconsistent with Patriotism. Multiple loyalities are objectionable only if they are inconsistent. . . . Every Irish American who contributed towards advancing home rule was a better man and better American for the sacrifice he made. Every American Jew who aids in advancing the Jewish settlement in Palestine, though he feels that neither he nor his descendants will ever live there, will likewise be a better man and a better American for doing so. . . . Indeed, loyalty to America demands rather that each American Jew become a Zionist." In a penetrating observation about the relationship between nationalism and race, Du Bois noted as part of a critique of Thomas Dixon that Dixon was wrong to say "that the Jews are assimilated because of their beautiful daughters. His facts are mixed. The Jews are not assimilated, because they have the power to protect those same daughters. And when Negroes have in law and public opinion similar power to guard their families from lecherous whites, there will be far less amalgamation than to-day." Du Bois, of course, generally considered such aversion to racial mixing inimical to democracy. For his part, Brandeis, adopting a concept of racial separatism comparable to the threat of "race suicide" invoked by Marcus Garvey as well as Theodore Roosevelt, thought any thorough assimilation would amount to "national suicide" for the Jews. Louis Brandeis, "The Jewish Problem, How to Solve It," in *Brandeis on Zionism: A Collection of Addresses and Statements by Louis D. Brandeis* (Washington, D.C.: Zionist Organization of America, 1942), pp. 28–29; Du Bois, *Writings in Periodicals Edited by Others,* I, 266. See also Melvin I. Urofsky, *American Zionism from Herzl to the Holocaust* (New York: Anchor Press, 1975), pp. 118–24. Du Bois's perspective on the Jewish question and American Jews was anything but univocal. *The Souls of Black Folk* contains a number of disturbing references to corrupt Jews who had exploited poor blacks in the post–Civil War South. For a 1953 edition of the book Du Bois revised most of these

bigoted passages. See Herbert Aptheker, introduction to Du Bois, *The Souls of Black Folk* (Millwood, N.Y.: Kraus-Thomson, 1973), pp. 38–43.

50. Casely Hayford, *Ethiopia Unbound,* p. 175; Hill, introduction to *The Marcus Garvey and Universal Negro Improvement Association Papers,* I, lxx–lxxviii; Moses, *The Golden Age of Black Nationalism,* p. 225. On the relationship between the black, Irish, and Jewish renaissances, see also Abraham Chapman, "The Harlem Renaissance in Literary History," *CLA Journal* 11 (September 1967), 38–58.

51. Du Bois, *Dusk of Dawn,* p. 47; Du Bois, "Commencement Speech Delivered at Fisk University" (June 1888), quoted in Wilson J. Moses, "Dark Forests and Barbarian Vigor: Paradox, Conflict, and Africanity in Black Writing before 1914," *American Literary History* 1 (Fall 1989), p. 649; Du Bois, *Dusk of Dawn,* p. 32. Du Bois's own fullest account of his study in Germany and its effect on him appears in *The Autobiography of W. E. B. Du Bois* (New York: International Publishers, 1968), pp. 155–82. See also Rampersad, *The Art and Imagination of W. E. B. Du Bois,* pp. 41–46, and especially Moses, "Dark Forests and Barbarian Vigor," pp. 649–53.

52. Patrick Brantlinger, *Rule of Darkness: British Literature and Imperialism, 1830–1914* (Ithaca: Cornell Unversity Press, 1988), pp. 228–30; George L. Mosse, *Toward the Final Solution: A History of European Racism* (Madison: University of Wisconsin Press, 1985), pp. 94–112.

53. W. E. B. Du Bois, "Opera and the Negro Problem," in *Newspaper Columns,* ed. Herbert Aptheker, 2 vols. (White Plains, N.Y.: Kraus-Thomson, 1986), I, 130.

54. Wilson Moses, *Black Messiahs and Uncle Toms: Social and Religious Manipulations of a Religious Myth* (University Park: Pennsylvania State University Press, 1982), p. 144; Mosse, *Toward the Final Solution,* pp. 101–7, 130–49; Gossett, *Race,* pp. 346–53.

55. Du Bois, *Writings in Periodicals Edited by Others,* II, 173–82; Du Bois, *Selections from The Crisis,* II, 448.

56. Du Bois, "The Star of Ethiopia" and "The Drama among Black Folk," *Crisis* (December 1915 and August 1916), in *Selections from The Crisis,* I, 114–15, 121–23; Freda L. Scott, "*The Star of Ethiopia:* A Contribution toward the Development of Black Drama and Theater in the Harlem Renaissance," in *The Harlem Renaissance: Revaluations,* ed. Amritjit Singh, William S. Shriver, and Stanley Brodwin (New York: Garland, 1989), pp. 257–69; William L. Van Deburg, *Slavery and Race in American Popular Culture* (Madison: University of Wisconsin Press, 1984), pp. 120–21. The pageants by McCoo and Guinn are reproduced in Willis Richardson, ed., *Plays and Pageants from the Life of the Negro* (Washington, D.C.: Associated Publishers, 1930).

57. Du Bois, *Darkwater,* pp. 61, 74, 53.

58. Ibid., pp. 29–52, 53–54.

59. Du Bois, *The Negro,* p. 95; Anna Julia Cooper, *A Voice from the South* (New York: Oxford University Press, 1988), p. 237.

60. Du Bois, *Darkwater,* pp. 181, 164–65; W. E. B. Du Bois, *The Negro American Family,* in *W. E. B. Du Bois on Sociology and the Black Community,* ed. Dan S.

Green and Edwin D. Driver (Chicago: University of Chicago Press, 1978), p. 199.

61. Du Bois, *Darkwater,* pp. 165–68.

62. Ibid., pp. 171, 173; Alexander Crummell, "The Black Woman of the South," in *Africa and America: Addresses and Discourses* (1891; rpt. Miami: Mnemosyne, 1969), pp. 59–82; Cooper, *A Voice from the South,* p. 31; Du Bois, "The Primitive Black Man," *The Nation* (December 7, 1924), in *Writings in Periodicals Edited by Others,* II, 231.

63. Darwin Turner, "W. E. B. Du Bois and the Theory of a Black Aesthetic," in William L. Andrews, ed., *Critical Essays on W. E. B. Du Bois* (Boston: G. K. Hall, 1985), pp. 73–92; Joel Williamson, *The Crucible of Race: Black-White Relations in the American South since Emancipation* (New York: Oxford University Press, 1984), p. 308; Du Bois, *The Souls of Black Folk,* p. 9; Du Bois, *Darkwater,* pp. 180, 184. On Du Bois's middle-class morality as it was shared by Crummell, see also Moses, *Alexander Crummell,* pp. 217–19, 299–300.

64. Gregory Holmes Singleton, "Birth, Rebirth, and the 'New Negro' of the 1920s," *Phylon* 43 (March 1982), 29–45; Allison Davis, *Leadership, Love, and Aggression* (New York: Harcourt Brace Jovanovich, 1983), pp. 106–14; Berghahn, *Images of Africa in Black American Literature,* pp. 67–69.

65. W. E. B. Du Bois, "Little Portraits of Africa," *Crisis* (April 1924), in *Selections from The Crisis,* I, 392–93.

66. Du Bois, *Darkwater,* pp. 75–80.

67. Du Bois, *The Souls of Black Folk,* p. 9.

68. Langston Hughes, "Goodbye, Christ," *The Negro Worker* (November–December 1932); rpt. in Nancy Cunard, ed., *Negro: An Anthology* abridged ed. Hugh Ford (1934; rpt. New York: Frederick Ungar, 1970), p. 264; Ridgely Torrence, *Granny Maumee, The Rider of Dreams, Simon the Cyrenian: Plays for a Negro Theater* (New York: Macmillan, 1917), p. 78; Langston Hughes, "Christ in Alabama," quoted in Arnold Rampersad, *The Life of Langston Hughes,* 2 vols. (New York: Oxford University Press, 1986), I, 225. See also Walter C. Daniel, "Langston Hughes versus the Black Preachers in the *Pittsburgh Courier* in the 1930s," in Edward Mullen, ed., *Critical Essays on Langston Hughes* (Boston: G. K. Hall, 1986), pp. 129–35.

69. Jean Wagner, *Black Poets of the United States: From Paul Laurence Dunbar to Langston Hughes,* trans. Kenneth Douglass (Urbana: University of Illinois Press, 1973), p. 335; *The Complete Poems of Paul Laurence Dunbar* (New York: Dodd, Mead, 1913), pp. 15–16; Fullinwider, *The Mind and Mood of Black America,* pp. 26–46.

70. Marable, *W. E. B. Du Bois,* pp. 65–66; William E. Cain, "Violence, Revolution, and the Cost of Freedom: John Brown and W. E. B. Du Bois," *Boundary 2* 17 (Spring 1990), 305–30; W. E. B. Du Bois, "The Niagara Movement: Address to the Country," in *Pamphlets and Leaflets,* ed. Herbert Aptheker (White Plains, N.Y.: Kraus-Thomson, 1986), p. 63; W. E. B. Du Bois, "John Brown and Christmas," in *Writings in Periodicals Edited by W. E. B. Du Bois: Selections from*

The Horizon, ed. Herbert Aptheker (White Plains, N.Y.: Kraus-Thomson, 1985), p. 85.

71. Rampersad, *The Art and Imagination of W. E. B. DuBois,* pp. 109–15; W. E. B. Du Bois, *John Brown* (New York: International Publishers, 1972), pp. 254–56, 15, 204, 93.

72. Du Bois, *The Negro,* p. 103; Du Bois, *John Brown,* p. 15.

73. Charles Reagan Wilson, *Baptized in Blood: The Religion of the Lost Cause, 1865–1920* (Athens: University of Georgia Press, 1980), pp. 42–182, esp. p. 105; Gossett, *Race,* pp. 339–408; Wyn Craig Wade, *The Fiery Cross: The Ku Klux Klan in America* (New York: Touchstone, 1987), pp. 119–247, quote at p. 172.

74. Marcus Garvey, *Philosophy and Opinions of Marcus Garvey,* ed. Amy Jacques-Garvey, 2 vols. in 1 (1923, 1925; rpt. New York: Atheneum, 1971), I, 18; Garvey, *Life and Lessons,* p. 231; Garvey, *Philosophy and Opinions,* I, 44; Meier, *Negro Thought in America,* pp. 260–61.

75. E. Franklin Frazier, "Garvey: A Mass Leader," *The Nation* (August 18, 1926); rpt. in John Henrik Clarke, ed., *Marcus Garvey and the Vision of Africa* (New York: Vintage Books, 1974), pp. 236–41; Warren I. Susman, *Culture as History: The Transformation of American Society in the Twentieth Century* (New York: Pantheon, 1984), pp. 122–31; Richard Weiss, *The American Myth of Success: From Horatio Alger to Norman Vincent Peale* (1969; rpt. Urbana: University of Illinois Press, 1988), pp. 128–53, 195–223; Martin, *Race First,* pp. 67–80; Randall K. Burkett, *Garveyism as a Religious Movement: The Institutionalization of a Black Civil Religion* (Metuchen, N.J.: Scarecrow Press, 1978); Walker, *Deromanticizing Black History,* pp. 34–55.

76. Du Bois, *Selections from The Crisis,* I, 284, 394. On the relationship between Du Bois and Garvey, see especially Martin, *Race First,* pp. 273–343; Geiss, *The Pan-African Movement,* pp. 263–74; Marable, *W. E. B. Du Bois,* pp. 88–120; and Richard B. Moore, "The Critics and Opponents of Marcus Garvey," in Clarke, *Marcus Garvey and the Vision of Africa,* pp. 210–35. A selection of documents by Du Bois and Garvey on each other is available in Vincent, *Voices of a Black Nation,* pp. 93–113.

77. Edmund David Cronon, *Black Moses: The Story of Marcus Garvey and the Universal Negro Improvement Association* (Madison: University of Wisconsin Press, 1955), pp. 188–95; Martin, *Race First,* pp. 344–57; Earnest Sevier Cox, *White America* (Richmond, Va.: White America Society, 1923), p. 236; Garvey, *Philosophy and Opinions,* II.

78. Williamson, *The Crucible of Race,* pp. 402–13.

79. See Melvin Dixon, "Toward a World Black Literature and Community," in Michael S. Harper and Robert B. Stepto, eds., *Chant of Saints: A Gathering of Afro-American Literature, Art, and Scholarship* (Urbana: University of Illinois Press, 1979), pp. 175–94.

80. Anonymous report, quoted in Roux, *Time Longer Than Rope,* p. 105; Jacobs, *The African Nexus,* pp. 156–58. More tragic prophecy eventually appeared, as in the case of the Israelite followers of Enoch Mgijima's splinter church, noted at

the beginning of this chapter. Not only did Mgijima envision an apocalypse following the appearance of Halley's comet in 1909, but his ejection from the Church of God and Saints of Christ was also based on the fact that, like Nat Turner, he preached about visions in which baboons (black Africans) crushed two white governments (the Dutch and the English) in a battle. On the eve of the colonial military assault after the Israelites had taken their stand at Bullhoek, Mgijima told his followers that they were immune to the whites' bullets, which he declared would turn to water when fired. See Sundkler, *Bantu Prophets in South Africa,* pp. 72–73.

81. For general overviews of the Ethiopianist movements, including the involvement of Americans, see Thomas Hodgkin, *Nationalism in Colonial Africa* (New York: New York University Press, 1957), pp. 93–114; George Shepperson, "Notes on Negro American Influences on the Emergence of African Nationalism," *Journal of African History* 1 (1960), 299–312; Shepperson, "Ethiopianism: Past and Present," pp. 249–63; Shepperson, "Ethiopianism and African Nationalism," 9–18; Sundkler, *Bantu Prophets in South Africa,* pp. 19–79; Chirenje, *Ethiopianism and Afro-Americans in Southern Africa,* pp. 50–162 passim; Peter Duignan and L. H. Gann, *The United States and Africa: A History* (Cambridge: Cambridge University Press, 1984), pp. 226–78; Guenter Lewy, *Religion and Revolution* (New York: Oxford University Press, 1974), pp. 194–236; Michael Adas, *Prophets of Rebellion: Millenarian Protest Movements against the European Colonial Order* (Chapel Hill: University of North Carolina Press, 1979), passim; and Karen E. Fields, *Revival and Rebellion in Colonial Central Africa* (Princeton: Princeton University Press, 1985), pp. 14–21, 118–23.

82. Shepperson and Price, *Independent African,* pp. 127–319, quote at p. 235. See also George Shepperson, "The Politics of African Church Separatist Movements in British Central Africa, 1892–1916," *Africa* 24 (July 1954), 233–45; Shepperson, "Nyasaland and the Millennium," in Sylvia L. Thrupp, ed., *Millennial Dreams in Action* (The Hague: Mouton, 1962), pp. 144–59; and Bryan R. Wilson, *Magic and the Millennium: A Sociological Study of Religious Movements of Protest among Tribal and Third-World Peoples* (New York: Harper and Row, 1973), pp. 252–56.

83. Quoted in Mercer Cook and Stephen Henderson, *The Militant Black Writer in Africa and the United States* (Madison: University of Wisconsin Press, 1969), p. 10.

84. A. J. F. Kobben, "Prophetic Movements as an Example of Social Protest," *International Archives of Ethnography* 49 (1960), 117–64, quote at p. 137. See also Marie-Louise Martin, *Kimbangu: An African Prophet and His Church* (Oxford: Basil Blackwell, 1975); Efraim Andersson, *Messianic Popular Movements in the Lower Congo (Studia Ethnographica Upsaliensia* 14 [1958]) (Uppsala: Almquist and Wiksells, 1958); and Wilson, *Magic and the Millennium,* pp. 367–73.

85. On black liberation theology, see, for example, Cornel West, *Prophesy Deliverance! An African-American Revolutionary Christianity* (Philadelphia: Westminster Press, 1982); Albert Cleage, Jr., *The Black Messiah* (New York: Sheed and Ward, 1968); Nathaniel I. Ndiskwere, *Prophecy and Revolution: The Role of Prophets in the*

Independent African Churches and in Biblical Tradition (London: SPCK, 1981), pp. 28–52; and James H. Cone, "Black Theology as Liberation Theology," in Gayraud Wilmore, ed., *African American Religious Studies: An Interdisciplinary Anthology* (Durham: Duke Univerity Press, 1989), pp. 177–207.

86. Shepperson and Price, *Independent African*, pp. 117, 122, 184, 433–34, 454n; Herbert Aptheker, introduction to Du Bois, *Dark Princess: A Romance* (Millwood, N.Y.: Kraus-Thomson, 1974), pp. 8–9; Contee, "W. E. B. Du Bois and African Nationalism," p. 69.

87. Sarah E. Simons, "Social Assimilation," *American Journal of Sociology* 6 (May 1901), 790–822.

88. J. Saunders Redding, *To Make a Poet Black* (1939; rpt. College Park, Md.: McGrath, 1968), p. 80; William Ferris, "*Darkwater*," *African and Orient Review* (June 1920), in Vincent, *Voices of a Black Nation*, pp. 342–48.

89. Du Bois, *Selections from The Horizon*, pp. 63–64; Casely Hayford, *Ethiopia Unbound*, pp. 181–82.

90. Casely Hayford, *Ethiopia Unbound*, p. 1.

91. Du Bois, *Darkwater*, pp. 54–55.

92. W. E. B. Du Bois, *Creative Writings: A Pageant, Poems, Short Stories, and Playlets*, ed. Herbert Aptheker (White Plains, N.Y.: Kraus-Thomson, 1985), pp. 76–77, 107–8, 113–15, 118, 84, 101–2, 147–50.

93. Moses, *The Golden Age of Black Nationalism*, pp. 162–67; Rampersad, *The Art and Imagination of W. E. B. DuBois*, pp. 100–101; Du Bois, *Darkwater*, pp. 199, 187–92.

94. Du Bois, *Creative Writings*, pp. 28–32; Du Bois, *Darkwater*, p. 188; Du Bois *The Souls of Black Folk*, p. 163.

95. Ferris, *The African Abroad*, I, 9–10; W. E. B. Du Bois, "The Future of the Negro Race in America," in *Writings in Periodicals Edited by Others*, I, 191.

96. Du Bois, *Creative Writings*, p. 94; Du Bois, *Darkwater*, pp. 269–70.

97. Rudwick, *W. E. B. Du Bois*, p. 242.

98. W. E. B. Du Bois, letter of December 1927 to Harcourt, Brace quoted in Aptheker, introduction to *Dark Princess*, p. 19; George Schuyler, 1928 letter to Du Bois, quoted in Marable, *W. E. B. Du Bois*, p. 133; George Schuyler, *Black Empire*, ed. Robert A. Hill and R. Kent Rasmussen (Boston: Northeastern University Press, 1991).

99. Mark Naison, *Communists in Harlem during the Depression* (New York: Grove Press, 1983), pp. 4–16; Harold Cruse, *The Crisis of the Negro Intellectual: A Historical Analysis of the Failure of Black Leadership* (1967; rpt. New York: Quill, 1984), pp. 134–35.

100. Du Bois, *Dark Princess*, pp. 26, 225, 285–86. For more extended explications of *Dark Princess*, see Rampersad, *The Art and Imagination of W. E. B. Du Bois*, pp. 202–18; Berghahn, *Images of Africa in Black American Literature*, pp. 101–17; and Amritjit Singh, *The Novels of the Harlem Renaissance: Twelve Black Writers, 1923–1933* (University Park: Pennsylvania State University Press, 1976), pp. 120–27.

101. Du Bois, *Dark Princess,* p. 220, 286.
102. Richard Hofstadter, *Social Darwinism in American Thought* (1944; rpt. Boston: Beacon Press, 1955), pp. 185–86; Joel Williamson, *New People: Miscegenation and Mulattoes in the United States* (New York: Free Press, 1980), pp. 106–7.
103. Du Bois, *Dark Princess,* p. 264.
104. Moses, *Black Messiahs and Uncle Toms,* p. 154.
105. Ralph Ellison, "The Little Man at Chehaw Station," in *Going to the Territory* (New York: Random House, 1986), p. 9.

Acknowledgments

Many people have played a role in the writing of this book, no one more than my wife, Tania, to whom it is dedicated.

I am pleased to acknowledge the generous financial assistance provided by a National Endowment for the Humanities Fellowship, a University of California President's Research Fellowship in the Humanities, and the Committees on Research at the University of California at Berkeley and at Los Angeles. I have also benefited from the excellent work of three research assistants at UCLA, Alycee Lane, José Amaya and Mark Gruner.

Over the years a number of friends and colleagues have commented on various parts of the text. In particular I thank William L. Andrews, Martha Banta, Sacvan Bercovitch, Richard Bridgman, William E. Cain, Sharon Cameron, Eric Cheyfitz, Michael Colacurcio, Frederick Crews, Robert A. Ferguson, Shelley Fisher Fishkin, Winthrop Jordan, Robert Kaufman, Walter Benn Michaels, Wayne Mixon, Wilson J. Moses, Gary Nash, Robert Post, Valerie Smith, Ernest Tuveson, Ralph Watkins, C. Vann Woodward, and Richard Yarborough. For answers to various queries and for other useful instruction, I am indebted to Morris Goodman, Robert A. Hill, Mary Kolawole, William S. McFeely, Ross Posnock, Arnold Rampersad, William Simmons, Sterling Stuckey, Robert Farris Thompson, Clarence Walker, and Cornel West. All of these people will have to decide if I have made the right use of their good advice; the remaining errors and misinterpretations are my own.

My ideas have also been significantly shaped by responses I have received to papers presented at Cornell University, Northwestern University, Yale University, Georgetown University, Sonoma State University, Princeton University, Johns Hopkins University, the University of Washington, the University of Kansas, the University of California at Irvine, at Santa Cruz, and at Los Angeles, the University of Chicago, the Bread Loaf School of English, the American Studies Association, the Southern American Studies Association, the Modern Language Association, and the English Institute. Likewise, participants in two National Endowment for the Humanities Summer Seminars for College Teachers, as well as graduate seminar students at Berkeley and UCLA, have given me valuable guidance. For their superb assistance in the publication of the book, I thank Lindsay Waters, Alison Kent, Amanda Heller, and, for the illustrations, Johanna Baldwin.

Several portions of the book have been published in shorter form. I gratefully acknowledge permission to reprint material from: "Slavery, Revolution, and the American Renaissance," in *The American Renaissance Reconsidered*, ed. Walter Benn Michaels and Donald Pease (Baltimore: Johns Hopkins University Press, 1985), pp. 1–33; "*Benito Cereno* and New World Slavery," in *Reconstructing American Literary History*, ed. Sacvan Bercovitch (Cambridge, Mass.: Harvard University Press, 1986), pp. 93–122; "Frederick Douglass: Literacy and Paternalism," reprinted by permission from *Raritan: A Quarterly Review* 6, no. 2 (Fall 1986), copyright © 1986 by *Raritan,* 31 Mine St., New Brunswick, NJ, 08903, parts of which were incorporated in the introduction to *Frederick Douglass: New Literary and Historical Essays*, ed. Eric J. Sundquist (New York: Cambridge University Press, 1990), pp. 1–22; "Mark Twain and Homer Plessy," *Representations* 24 (Fall 1988), 102–28, © 1988 The Regents of the University of California, by permission; and "Conspiracy and Revolution in Martin Delany's *Blake*," in *Studies in American Literature: Essays in Honor of Enrique García Díez,* ed. Antonia Sánchez Macarro (Valencia: Universitat de Valencia, 1991), pp. 53–76. Parts of chapter 4 have also been adapted as an introduction to Charles W. Chesnutt, *The Marrow of Tradition* (New York: Viking Penguin, 1993).

In addition, I am grateful to the copyright holders for permission to reprint the following:

Robert Hayden: Lines from "The Ballad of Nat Turner" reprinted from *Collected Poems* of Robert Hayden, ed. Frederick Glaysher, by permission of Liveright Publishing Corp. Copyright © 1985 by Erma Hayden.

Langston Hughes: Excerpts from "Freedom's Plow" and "Afro-American Fragment" from *Selected Poems*. Copyright © 1959 by Langston Hughes. Reprinted by permission of Alfred A. Knopf, Inc. Excerpt from "Christ in Alabama" from *The Panther and the Lash*. Copyright 1932 by Langston Hughes. Reprinted by permission of Alfred A. Knopf, Inc., and Harold Ober Associates. "Goodbye, Christ" reprinted by permission of Harold Ober Associates Inc.; copyright 1932 by Langston Hughes.

Claude McKay: "Mulatto" from *The Passion of Claude McKay*, ed. Wayne Cooper (New York: Schoken Books, 1973).

Sterling Brown: "Children's Children" from *The Collected Works of Sterling A. Brown,* selected by Michael Harper. Copyright © 1980 by Brown. Reprinted by permission of HarperCollins Publishers.

Sonia Sanchez: "Rebirth" from *I've Been a Woman* (Chicago: Third World Press, 1990).

W. E. B. Du Bois: "The Riddle of the Sphinx" from *Darkwater: Voices from within the Veil*. New York: Harcourt, Brace, 1920. (Reprint: Millwood, NY: Kraus-Thomson Organization Limited, 1975.) Reproduced with permission of The Kraus Organization Limited.

Amiri Baraka (LeRoi Jones): "It's Nation Time" reprinted by permission of Sterling Lord Literistic, Inc. Copyright © 1970 by Amiri Baraka.

Index